Lecture Notes in Artificial Intelligence 4938

Edited by J. G. Carbonell and J. Siekmann

Subseries of Lecture Notes in Computer Science

Takenobu Tokunaga   Antonio Ortega (Eds.)

# Large-Scale Knowledge Resources

## Construction and Application

Third International Conference
on Large-Scale Knowledge Resources, LKR 2008
Tokyo, Japan, March 3-5, 2008
Proceedings

Series Editors

Jaime G. Carbonell, Carnegie Mellon University, Pittsburgh, PA, USA
Jörg Siekmann, University of Saarland, Saarbrücken, Germany

Volume Editors

Takenobu Tokunaga
Tokyo Institute of Technology
Department of Computer Science
Tokyo Meguro Oookayama 2-12-1
152-8552 Japan
E-mail: take@cl.cs.titech.ac.jp

Antonio Ortega
University of Southern California
Signal and Image Processing Institute
Department of Electrical Engineering
Los Angeles, CA 90089-2564, USA
E-mail: antonio.ortega@sipi.usc.edu

Library of Congress Control Number: 2008920448

CR Subject Classification (1998): I.2.7, I.2, I.4, I.5, H.3, H.5

LNCS Sublibrary: SL 7 – Artificial Intelligence

ISSN 0302-9743
ISBN-10 3-540-78158-7 Springer Berlin Heidelberg New York
ISBN-13 978-3-540-78158-5 Springer Berlin Heidelberg New York



Springer is a part of Springer Science+Business Media

springer.com


Printed in Germany

Typesetting: Camera-ready by author, data conversion by Scientific Publishing Services, Chennai, India
Printed on acid-free paper SPIN: 12227532 06/3180 5 4 3 2 1 0

# Preface

At the start of the 21st century, we are now well on the way towards a knowledge-intensive society, in which knowledge plays ever more important roles. Thus, research interest should inevitably shift from information to knowledge, with the problems of building, organizing, maintaining and utilizing knowledge becoming central issues in a wide variety of fields. The 21st Century COE program "Framework for Systematization and Application of Large-scale Knowledge Resources (COE-LKR)" conducted by the Tokyo Institute of Technology is one of several early attempts worldwide to address these important issues. Inspired by this project, LKR2008 aimed at bringing together diverse contributions in cognitive science, computer science, education and linguistics to explore design, construction, extension, maintenance, validation and application of knowledge.

Responding to our call for papers, we received 38 submission from a variety of research areas. Each paper was reviewed by three Program Committee members. Since we were aiming at an interdisciplinary conference covering a wide range of topics concerning large-scale knowledge resources (LKR), each paper was assigned a reviewer from a topic area outside the main thrust of the paper. This reviewer was asked to assess whether the authors described the motivation and importance of their work in a comprehensible manner even for readers in other research areas. Following a rigorous reviewing process, we accepted 14 regular papers and 12 poster papers.

While the technical program covered a broad range of application areas, papers can be roughly classified into four major areas. First, some authors reported on their experience building large-scale resources, with a particular emphasis on language resources and ontologies. Second, a major focus was in the extraction of knowledge from large sets of data, ranging from mining of text data to semantic analysis of content such as images and video. Third, some papers reported on experiences with operating actual LKR systems, including question and answer systems, inductive reasoning systems, etc. Finally, several papers focused on infrastructure problems to enable efficient LKR systems to be deployed.

We would like to thank the Program Committee members for their hard work. In addition to these technical papers, this volume includes six papers by the invited speakers. We hope the conference and this volume will contribute to opening up a new interdisciplinary research area on LKR.

March 2008

Antonio Ortega
Tokunaga Takenobu

# Organization

| | |
|---|---|
| Conference Chair | Furui, Sadaoki (Tokyo Institute of Technology) |
| Local Organizing Chair | Shinoda, Koichi (Tokyo Institute of Technology) |
| Program Co-chairs | Ortega, Antonio (University of Southern California) |
| | Tokunaga, Takenobu (Tokyo Institute of Technology) |
| Publicity Co-chairs | Yokota, Haruo (Tokyo Institute of Technology) |
| | Yonezaki, Naoki (Tokyo Institute of Technology) |

## Program Committee

Calzolari, Nicoletta (ILC-CNR, Italy)
Harman, Donna (NIST, USA)
Huang, Chu-Ren (Academia Sinica, Taiwan)
Ishizaki, Syun (Keio University, Japan)
Juang, Biing-Hwang (Georgia Institute of Technology, USA)
Kusumi, Takashi (Kyoto University, Japan)
Matsumoto, Yuji (Nara Institute of Science and Technology, Japan)
Nakazawa, Jin (Keio University, Japan)
Nilsson, Jorgen Fischer (Technical University of Denmark, Denmark)
Rigoll, Gerhard (Munich University of Technology, Germany)
Russell, Stuart (University of California, Berkeley, USA)
Sakamoto, Takashi (JAPET, Japan)
Sekine, Satoshi (New York University, USA)
Shibano, Koji (Tokyo University of Foreign Studies, Japan)
Sugiura, Masatoshi (Nagoya University, Japan)
Sugiyama, Shinya (Keio University, Japan)
Theeramaunkong, Thanuruk
(Sirindhorn International Institute of Technology, Thailand)
Thompson, Henry (University of Edinburgh, UK)
Tobe, Yoshito (Tokyo Denki University, Japan)
Tomimori, Nobuo (Tokyo University of Foreign Studies, Japan)
Washio, Takashi (Osaka University, Japan)
Yamada, Tuneo (National Institute of Multimedia Center, Japan)
Yano, Tamaki (Doshisha University, Japan)

# Table of Contents

## Keynote Talk



## Mining Knowledge



## Building Resources

## Image and Video

## Using Resources



## Infrastructure

# From Information to Intelligence: The Role of Relative Significance in Decision Making and Inference

Biing-Hwang Juang

Georgia Institute of Technology, Atlanta, GA 30332, USA
juang@gatech.edu

**Abstract.** The growth of the amount of information accessible to people is phenomenal in recent years. In one estimate, the amount of digital information created, captured, and replicated in 2006 was 161 exabytes, approximately three million times the information in all the books ever written [1]. The issue of finding or discovering intelligence from a sea of information thus becomes ever more important and challenging. Although computational algorithms have been developed to aid the user in search of information that may be deemed useful, automatic discovery of intelligence (ADI) beyond simple information matching is still beyond the reach of conventional search methods. In this paper, we address one important component, namely relative significance which is essential in forming the paradigm of intelligence beyond a simple recognition of pattern of information. We further formulate the concept of relative significance in the framework of Bayes decision theory so as to enable computational optimization and algorithmic development. We believe processing of true computational intelligence must include capabilities in dealing with non-uniform significance and cost issues.

**Keywords:** Intelligence, inference, decision theory, relative significance, non-uniform cost, pattern recognition, information extraction, knowledge discovery.

## 1 Introduction

The growth of the amount of information accessible to people is phenomenal in recent years. In one estimate, the amount of digital information created, captured, and replicated in 2006 was 161 exabytes, approximately three million times the information in all the books ever written [1]. And it is also estimated that this annual *addition* of information will increase at a compound annual growth rate of 57% to 988 exabytes in 2010. The issue of deriving the necessary knowledge or discovering the otherwise hidden intelligence from a sea of information thus becomes ever more important and challenging.

Deriving knowledge or discovering intelligence from a vast pool of information of course is related to human's desire in automating the process of finding relevant solutions to the problem at hand, be it to increase the yield of investment or to uncover unlawful conspiracies. Historically, automation mostly means mechanization,

T. Tokunaga and A. Ortega (Eds.): LKR 2008, LNAI 4938, pp. 1–12, 2008.

to replace manual labor with machinery, and may include the notion of robotization and programmed control of a physical process (perhaps in the form of a work flow as well). Today, computerization plays a dominant role in automation due to digitization of information which gives birth to informatics (use and processing of information) and which spawns the possibility of intelligence discovery. The driving force, aside from the availability of affordable and powerful computers, is obviously the need to customize or personalize the process of automation as the particular situation may call for. A simple example cited by Friedman in [2] is about the use of a GPS-coordinated data of the soil condition and the harvest of a farm at a resolution down to the level of individual acreage or finer; the individualized data or information facilitates local optimization of irrigation and the use of fertilizer to maximize the yield. As we continue to push the automation process further, the next frontier will be thus the automatic discovery of knowledge and intelligence that offers the user ever more immediate benefits. In our view, advances in information and communication technologies in the last couple of decades (e.g., the advent of Internet) may have made the fulfillment of this desire a lot closer to reality, but not without some major hurdles.

Computational algorithms have been developed to aid the user in search of information that may be deemed useful. Nevertheless, discovery of intelligence beyond simple information pattern matching is still beyond the reach of conventional search methods. As we contemplate on constructing large knowledge resources for effective use of the organized information through proper search and information retrieval methods, we may also ask the question: How can we satisfy the need for the discovery of relevant intelligence by and from the knowledge resources?

In this paper, as we make attempt on this rather broad question, we introduce and focus on one important component, namely relative significance, which is essential in forming the paradigm of intelligence beyond a simple pattern of information. We discuss the role of relative significance in intelligence and further formulate the concept of relative significance in the framework of Bayes decision theory so as to enable computational optimization and algorithmic development. We believe processing of true computational intelligence must include capabilities in dealing with non-uniform significance and cost issues.

## 2 Informatics and Intelligence

Informatics integrates the concept of information and automation. It is commonly accepted that it includes the science of information, the practice of information processing and the engineering of information systems. It in essence studies the structure, behavior, design and interactions of information as well as natural and artificial systems that store, process and communicate information.

Generally speaking, elements in informatics as being enunciated by most practitioners include: data acquisition (and conversion of data into information), processing of information, and optimization of decision (or optimization of objective in the use of information). Processing of information involves such tasks as information representation (digitization and coding), classification (or clustering) and indexing, recognition and identification, verification and authentication, search and association, query interface, and retrieval. In spite of the fact that most of these tasks touch on some aspects of intelligence as discussed below, they aim conventionally at processing of information (only) which is different from intelligence and inference as the latter often are left to the human user of the results from informatics tasks.

It may be necessary to bring the differentiation between information and intelligence to light in order to better articulate for the need of an extended paradigm for informatics. Intelligence is a property of mind that encompasses many related abilities such as the capability to plan, to reason, to think abstractly beyond physical existence, to understand and generalize ideas, to comprehend and use language, to learn, and to solve problems. Conventional informatics as a processing paradigm has not yet been extended to encapsulate the notion of intelligence, although the term "intelligent processing" has been widely (and liberally) used without rigorous justification.

A few philosophical definitions of intelligence found in on-line encyclopedia [3] entry page for "intelligence" may also be stimulating in the current context. According to Carolus Slovinec, intelligence is the *ability to recognize connections* [among individual events or pieces of evidence]. Jean Piaget: "Intelligence is what you use when you don't know what to do." A more detailed pronunciation of intelligence may be due to Howard Gardner: "To my mind, a human intellectual competence must entail a set of skills of *problem solving* … and must also entail the potential for finding or creating problems—and thereby laying the groundwork for the acquisition of new knowledge."

We can summarize the elementary manifests of intelligence as: the capability of handling informatics (i.e., conducting informatics tasks including use of references, context-dependent association, semantic generalization, etc.), the capability of constructing and testing hypothesis—"connecting dots" and verifying relationships—to solve problems, the capability of differentiating varying (non-uniform or relative) significance of events and pieces of evidence, and the capability of self-learning, self-critiquing, and self-evaluation (e.g., knowing where not to make mistakes or learning from fatal errors). Obviously, a thorough discussion of these capabilities is way beyond the scope of this paper. Here we focus on the element of differentiating significance, particularly in terms of the non-uniform cost or penalty in intelligent decision making, and discuss its role in intelligent informatics.

## 3 Non-uniform Significance in Intelligence

The idea of non-uniform significance has two somewhat different meanings. Intuitively it may be rather easy to envisage the existence of non-uniform relative significance with regard to a piece of information or evidence. For example, in deriving intelligence about the weather, the appearance of overcast cloud may be far more important than the wetness caused by sidewalk sprinklers. We consider a piece of information or evidence more significant if it, when compared to other information or evidence, is more likely to help us accomplish our objective or to reach the solution to the problem at hand. This is the conventional type of relative significance. The other type of relative significance has the following interpretation: if we do NOT use the particular piece of information, or if we MISUSE the particular piece of information, it will be more costly to us, the user of information, to reach our objective. This situation is often due to the uncertainty in the presented evidence. Since our discussion in the following will concentrate on the task of information recognition (a critical task of intelligent informatics), we use the example of automatic speech recognition to illustrate this type of non-uniform significance.

A spoken sentence containing the sequence of words "AT N.E.C. THE NEED FOR INTERNATIONAL MANAGERS WILL KEEP RISING" is recognized as the following sentences by two different recognizers:

S1: "AT ANY <del> SEE THE NEED FOR INTERNATIONAL MANAGERS WILL KEEP RISING"

S2: "AT N.E.C. <del> NEEDS FOR INTERNATIONAL MANAGER'S WILL KEEP RISING".

The acoustic evidence corresponding to the spoken portion of "N.E.C." obviously contains substantial amount of uncertainty which led to the possible misrepresentation (e.g., "ANY <del> SEE") and thus misuse of the evidence. However, for many purposes, S1 may be considered an inferior result to S2 because the particular entity, the name of a corporation, in the context is of critical importance, even though both sentences have the same amount of recognition errors according to a commonly accepted evaluation criterion. If one is to derive intelligence about the financial performance of a particular corporation (which is the objective of the problem at hand), missing the report in which the name is mentioned is likely to be rather costly. Most automatic speech recognition systems are designed with the assumption that all errors are equal, and only the amount of error counts. But can a recognizer be designed particularly to avoid certain errors that may be considered fatal or detrimental in the process of inferring intelligence?

The question may find answers from several different perspectives, which we'll not be able to thoroughly elaborate in the paper. Rather, we'll focus on the notion of non-uniform cost for making erroneous decisions. In other words, unlike traditional error counting in recognition tasks, we reflect the non-uniform significance of evidence in the cost of error—some errors are more costly than others—in hope of making fewer errors of significance. The following development has been extracted from [8].

### 3.1 The Rise of Non-uniform Cost

In the context of many pattern recognition problems, the rise of non-uniform cost manifests in at least two key scenarios. One relates to the observation of the so-called confusion matrix and the other involves composite or hierarchical modeling.

The performance of many conventional statistical pattern recognition systems can be tabulated in a confusion matrix, the element of which signifies the number of test tokens of class $i$ ($i$th row) recognized as class $j$ ($j$th column). These numbers may also be normalized by the total number of tokens (for each class) so that the entries are bounded in [0, 1]. From the confusion matrix, the performance of the system can be envisioned rather clearly in terms of its effectiveness towards any particular pair of classes. This confusion matrix is most likely non-uniform, displaying some class-pairs that are especially easy to be confused by the recognizer thus providing a diagnostic view for the system design. One can then contemplate on making the cost matrix non-uniform (i.e., not a 0-1 cost function), with heavier costs assigned to those confusing pairs or to those with particular significance, to "drive the errors away from them." (The relationship between the confusion matrix and the cost matrix is an interesting subject but few analytical results exist.) The assignment of non-uniform cost is obviously done in an ad hoc manner in this scenario.

The earlier example of misusing the spoken utterance of "N.E.C." in the search for financial intelligence about a corporation falls into the second category. In hierarchical modeling, the discriminant functions for the classes are built upon a layer of sub-class models or functions, which may be shared by a number of classes. One example again in the context of automatic speech recognition is the use of phone/phoneme modeling in automatic speech recognition with the word accuracy as the system objective. Many words in the recognition vocabulary may share some phonemes, each being represented by a model function. In this situation, mis-recognition of some phonemes (represented by the phone models) may cause more errors in word recognition than that of other phonemes. Therefore, as one uses labeled data to train these phone models, some carry more significance than others and this needs to be reflected in the training process for best results.

## 3.2 Incorporation of Non-uniform Cost in Statistical Pattern Recognition

The classical Bayes decision theory [4] is the foundation of statistical pattern recognition. Bayes' analysis of the pattern recognition problem is based upon the notion of an *expected* system performance. Consider a pattern recognition task involving $M$ classes of events or patterns. An unknown pattern, say $X$, is observed and recognized by a recognizer as one of the $M$ classes. Thus, a recognizer is a function $C$ that maps $X$ to a class identity denoted by $C_i$, where $i \in I_M = \{1, 2, \ldots, M\}$. We call this a decision function $C(X)$. Obviously, some decisions are likely to be correct while others wrong, and correct decisions are usually preferred over wrong decisions. Thus, every decision is associated with a cost which is defined as an entry $\varepsilon_{ij}$ in an $M \times M$ matrix where $i, j \in I_M$, signifying the cost of identifying a pattern of the $j^{\text{th}}$ class as one of the $i^{\text{th}}$ class. Suppose the knowledge of the a posteriori probabilities $P(C_i \mid X), \forall i \in I_M$ is available at our disposal. Then, following Bayes, given $X$, the conditional cost of making a decision of $C(X) = C_i$ can be defined as [4]

$$R(C_i \mid X) = \sum_{j=1}^{M} \varepsilon_{ij} P(C_j \mid X) \tag{1}$$

and the system performance in terms of the *expected* loss is

$$\mathfrak{L} = E\{R(C(X) \mid X\} = \int R(C(X) \mid X) p(X) dX \tag{2}$$

Traditionally, a simple error count is used as the cost of recognition decision with

$$\varepsilon_{ij} = \begin{cases} 1, & i \neq j \\ 0, & i = j \end{cases} \tag{3}$$

The cost of (3) is the most intuitive and prevalent performance measure in pattern recognition as it is related to the probability of error in simple terms. With the cost function of (3), (1) becomes

$$R(C_i \mid X) = \sum_{j \neq i}^{M} P(C_j \mid X) = 1 - P(C_i \mid X) \tag{4}$$

and if we institute the decision policy as

$$C(X) = \arg\min_i R(C_i \mid X) = \arg\min_i \{1 - P(C_i \mid X)\} = \arg\max_i P(C_i \mid X) \tag{5}$$

the expected cost of (2) will be minimized due to the fact that $p(X)$ is non-negative. This is the ubiquitous maximum a posteriori (MAP) decision that guarantees minimum system cost, or Bayes risk [4].

Note that the above Bayes decision theory requires that the a posteriori distribution be available to the system. In practice, the knowledge of a posteriori distribution needs to be "learned" from labeled data, so as to embed the knowledge of "ground truth" in the parameters for the recognition system to use. The result of (5) thus has led to the conventional paradigm of distribution estimation as a fundamental step towards the design of a working pattern recognition system. However, the *functional form* of the distribution is often prescribed and not necessarily consistent with the true distribution. As a result, true implementation of MAP usually cannot be achieved.

The cost function of (3) is not the only choice for evaluating a pattern recognition system. When the cost function is not uniform, the best decision policy may not be the one that achieves maximum a posteriori probability. For example, consider a 3-class case with the following cost matrix, a posteriori probability and conditional risk vectors:

$$[\varepsilon_{ij}] = \begin{bmatrix} 0 & 0.1 & 0.5 \\ 0.1 & 0 & 0.5 \\ 0.1 & 0.1 & 0 \end{bmatrix}, \quad [P(C_j \mid X)] = \begin{bmatrix} 0.35 \\ 0.4 \\ 0.25 \end{bmatrix}, \quad \text{and} \quad [R(C_i \mid X)] = \begin{bmatrix} 0.165 \\ 0.16 \\ 0.075 \end{bmatrix}.$$

The MAP rule would have resulted in $C(X) = C_2$, but

$$C_3 = \arg\min_{i=1,2,3} R(C_i \mid X) = \arg\min_{i=1,2,3} \sum_{j=1}^{M} \varepsilon_{ij} P(C_j \mid X).$$

Clearly, from the cost matrix, one can see that a mistake on a third-class pattern costs five times that of any other errors. That leads to the discrepancy between a MAP decision and a decision that attempts to minimize the non-uniform risk. This non-uniform or asymmetric error cost function is quite common in real world applications. For example, a handwritten digit 1 mistaken as a digit 7 may cause more concern than 7 as 1 in financial transactions. Thus, it is necessary to revisit the Bayes decision theory and discuss the validity of the conventional MAP policy when a non-uniform error criterion is employed.

The conditional risk of (1) and the expected loss of (2) are general expressions of the system performance without any particular conditions imposed on the error cost function, $\varepsilon_{ij}$. Again, since $p(X)$ is non-negative,

$$\min \mathfrak{L} = \min_C E\{R(C(X) \mid X\} = \int \min_C \{R(C(X) \mid X)\} p(X) dX \tag{6}$$

and to achieve the minimum risk, the recognizer function must implement the following policy,

$$C(X) = \arg\min_{C_i} R(C_i \mid X) = \arg\min_{C_i} \sum_{j=1}^{M} \varepsilon_{ij} P(C_j \mid X) \cdot \tag{7}$$

We called this the minimum risk (MR) or minimum cost (MC) rule. In practice, we generally require that $\varepsilon_{ij} = 0$ for $i = j$ and $\varepsilon_{ij} \geq 0$ for $i \neq j$.

The MR rule of (7) does not lead to the MAP policy of (5) even if the knowledge of the true distribution (a posteriori probabilities) is available to the recognizer. Implementation of the MR rule requires multiplication of the cost matrix and the posterior probability vector, a direct result of the non-uniformity of the cost function.

Note that the MR rule can be re-written as

$$C(X) = \arg\min_{C_i} \sum_{j=1}^{M} \varepsilon_{ij} P(C_j \mid X) = \arg\min_{C_i} \sum_{j=1}^{M} \varepsilon_{ij} P(X \mid C_j) P(C_j) \tag{8}$$

for ease in applying some empirical knowledge in choosing the form of distribution.

## 4 Machine Learning with Non-uniform Cost of Error

As discussed, when the error cost function is not uniform, the MAP policy no longer leads to optimal Bayes decision and the paradigm of distribution estimation as a fundamental system design methodology is no longer applicable. This is mainly because during system training, it is necessary not only to know which class a training token belongs to but also which class the token may be misrecognized as, in order to allow proper association of the error cost. The only framework that can be extended to handle non-uniform cost, to the best of our knowledge, is the method of Minimum Classification Error (MCE) [5], which optimizes the system parameters based on the evaluated error for each and every individual token in the training set.

### 4.1 The Minimum Classification Error Method

In this section we review the method of minimum classification error [5] as an alternative to the distribution estimation paradigm for pattern recognition system design. Machine learning algorithms based on MCE are then developed for pattern recognition system design. For more detailed development of the method, see [6, 7].

The method of Minimum Classification Error for pattern recognition system training [5] is built upon a fundamental concept in which the system's recognition decision on a given pattern/token is evaluated as part of the estimate of the overall system performance, which is defined as a smooth function of the system parameters that can be optimized.

Let $g_i(X;\Lambda) \geq 0$ be the discriminant function for the $i^{th}$ class, $i$=1, 2, …, $M$ where $\Lambda$ is the parameter set that defines the function. If the a posteriori probability (as a function of $X$) is available, $g_i(X;\Lambda)$ can be chosen as $P(C_i \mid X)$. Assume that the usual (uniform) error count of (3) is used as the cost function. The recognition decision is reached according to

$$C(X) = \arg\max_{C_i} g_i(X;\Lambda) \tag{9}$$

That is, the recognizer chooses the class that leads to the largest value among all discriminants evaluated on $X$. This decision rule has to be embedded in a performance function for parameter optimization over the given training set of data.

Suppose $X \in C_i$ and $C_j = \arg\max_{C_k, k \neq i} g_k(X;\Lambda)$; i.e., class $j$ is the most competitive class, given the training token $X$ with a label for class $i$. (Note that $C_i$ is used to denote the class label as well as the class set without ambiguity.) If $g_i(X;\Lambda) \geq g_j(X;\Lambda)$, no error is made; otherwise, an error has occurred. Define a misclassification measure for an $i^{th}$ class token:

$$d_i(X;\Lambda) = -g_i(X;\Lambda) + G_i(X;\Lambda) \tag{10}$$

where

$$G_i(X;\Lambda) = \left\{ \frac{1}{M-1} \sum_{j, j \neq i} \left[ g_j(X;\Lambda) \right]^{\eta} \right\}^{1/\eta} \tag{11}$$

represents a "smoothed" combination of the discriminants other than that of the label class ($i$). Note that when $\eta \to \infty$,

$$G_i(X;\Lambda) \to \max_{j, j \neq i} g_j(X;\Lambda) \,. \tag{12}$$

With this definition, $d_i(X;\Lambda) > 0$ implies a misclassification or misrecognition and $d_i(X;\Lambda) \leq 0$ means a correct decision. When the misclassification measure is cast in a sigmoid function, a token-based performance evaluation in the form of a smoothed error count is obtained:

$$l_i(X;\Lambda) = S(d_i(X;\Lambda)) \tag{13}$$

where the function $S$ may take the form of a smooth 0-1 function:

$$S(d) = (1 + e^{-\alpha(d+\beta)})^{-1} \tag{14}$$

with a smoothing parameter $\alpha$ and a threshold parameter $\beta$ properly chosen. Finally, the system performance is defined as the expected cost of error

$$\mathfrak{L} = E\{l(X;\Lambda)\} \tag{15}$$

which is estimated empirically as

$$\mathfrak{L} \leftarrow L = \frac{1}{N} \sum_{n=1}^{N} l(X^{(n)};\Lambda) \,. \tag{16}$$

In the above expression, $n$ denotes the token index in the training set, $\Omega = \{X^{(n)}\}_{n=1}^{N}$, and the identity label has been made implicit. The empirical loss $L$ is a smooth function in $\Lambda$ which can be optimized over the training set using the generalized probabilistic descent (GPD) algorithm or its variants [5]. This method has been used extensively, with good result, in automatic speech recognition applications where the data distribution is considered difficult to model.

It is important to note that the method of MCE/GPD directly evaluates the recognition system's decision on each presented token, while the conventional distribution estimation approach to pattern recognition attempts to learn the probability distribution function from the given data, without specifically knowing if a token will be misrecognized or not, not to mention which class the token may be incorrectly assigned to. Therefore, the conventional distribution estimation approach will find it impossible to incorporate a non-uniform class-dependent error cost in the design of a pattern recognition system. The MCE method nonetheless offers a possible solution to the problem of pattern recognizer design with non-uniform cost.

### 4.2 MCE with Non-uniform Error Cost

The incorporation of a class-dependent non-uniform error cost function incurs two factors that require careful consideration. First, the system needs to implement the MR rule defined in (7). Following the development of a smoothed error function in MCE, we need to embed this *decision rule* in a functional form so that optimization can be performed to obtain the values of the system parameter set. Second, as the overall system performance is defined over a non-uniform, weighted error cost, the particular decision for each of the training token becomes an integral part of the performance measure and has to be included in the objective function for optimization. The second factor is unique because once a decision is rendered by the recognizer, what matters is not only if the decision is right or wrong but how much error cost the decision actually incurs, a quantity that depends on the pattern of error. We shall see how these factors are taken into account in the proposed embedding schemes for non-uniform error cost minimization.

#### 4.2.1 Construction of Design Objectives with Non-uniform Error Cost

Recall that $\varepsilon_{ij}, i, j \in I_M$, signifies the cost or loss in identifying a $j^{\text{th}}$ class pattern as one of the $i^{\text{th}}$ class. Given a general set of cost $\varepsilon_{ij}$, we can explicitly write the optimal decision rule as (7) which leads to the optimal result of (6) which we continue to name the Bayes risk. Execution of (7) obviously requires the knowledge of the *a posteriori* probability $P(C_j \mid X), \forall j \in I_M$. As stated in [5], however, the true *a posteriori* probability is rarely available for a number of reasons. We approach the problem of constructing a system design objective with non-uniform cost in two steps, embedding of decision cost and prescription of the operating (discriminant) functions.

**a. Embedding of Decision Cost**

To overcome these difficulties in system training, the expected system loss of (2) needs to be expressed in terms of the empirical loss (yet to be defined) with the decision rule embedded in it. For clarity, let $i_X$ be the class identity index as decided by the recognizer and $j_X$ be the true identity index of *X*. A *single token* realized cost is defined as

$$l_{i_X}(X;\Lambda) = \varepsilon_{i_X j_X} \quad \text{for all } X \in \Omega. \tag{17}$$

Therefore if the empirical system loss is defined over the *realized* token-based costs (rather than the *expected* cost), an empirical non-uniform cost will result:

$$L = \sum_{X\in\Omega} \varepsilon_{i_X j_X} \quad \rightarrow \quad \int \varepsilon_{i_X j_X} p(X)dX. \tag{18}$$

Suppose each class is prescribed a discriminant function $g_j(X;\Lambda), \forall j$. Define the recognizer function as

$$C(X) = C_{i_X} = \arg\max_{C_i} g_i(X;\Lambda). \tag{19}$$

The empirical system loss of (18) based on $\Omega$ is then,

$$L = \sum_{X\in\Omega} \sum_{i\in I_M} \sum_{j\in I_M} \varepsilon_{ij} 1[j_X = j] 1\left\{ C_i = \arg\max_{C_k} g_k(X;\Lambda) \right\}. \tag{20}$$

Note that in the above the indicator function $1[j_X = j] = 1[X \in C_j]$.

### b. Prescription of Operating Functions

What is the proper choice of the operating or discriminant function for each class? Obviously, if the true a posteriori probability is available, a monotonically decreasing function of the conditional risk of (1) (to switch min into max operation) would be appropriate. For example,

$$g_i(X;\Lambda) = \exp\{-R(C_i \mid X)\} = \exp\left\{ - \sum_{j\in I_M} \varepsilon_{ij} P(C_j \mid X) \right\}. \tag{21}$$

In general, since $\{P(C_j \mid X)\}$ are not available, one would use $\tilde{P}(C_j \mid X) = \tilde{P}(X \mid C_j)\tilde{P}(C_j)/\tilde{P}(X)$ based on approximate and parameterized models in lieu of the true a posteriori distribution. This form of the discriminant function is appropriate in many simple pattern recognition tasks where good approximations to the conditional probabilities and the prior may be relatively easy to obtain. If one is confident about the approximation, the discriminant function of (21) will have the advantage of being closely (but inversely) related to the conditional risk.

When the above approximation of the a posteriori distribution cannot be ensured, it is not particularly advisable to insist on using the weighted summation form of (21) as the discriminant function. For other applications where the form of the a posteriori distribution (as a function of *X*) may be complex or hard to ascertain (such as those of speech signals), one may opt for other choices of the discriminant function based on some convention. One example is the use of hidden Markov models as the discriminant functions.

### c. Smoothing of the Empirical Cost for Parameter Optimization

The remaining challenge in designing a discriminative training algorithm with non-uniform error cost is to turn the objective functions, $L$ in (20) into an appropriate smooth function of the parameter so as to allow numeric optimization. Consider

$$L = \sum_{j \in I_M} L_j \; ; \tag{22}$$

$$L_j = \sum_{X \in \Omega} \left( \sum_{i \in I_M} \varepsilon_{ij} 1\left\{ C_i = \arg\max_{C_k} g_k(X;\Lambda) \right\} \right) 1[X \in C_j]. \tag{23}$$

That is, $L_j$ is the empirical error cost collected over all training tokens in $\Omega$ with $j_X = j$. The approximation then needs to be made to the summands. This can be accomplished by

$$\sum_{i \in I_M} \varepsilon_{ij} 1\left\{ C_i = \arg\max_{C_k} g_k(X;\Lambda) \right\} \approx \sum_{i \in I_M} \varepsilon_{ij} \frac{g_i^{\eta}(X;\Lambda)}{G(X;\Lambda)} \tag{24}$$

where

$$G(X;\Lambda) = \sum_{i \in I_M} g_i^{\eta}(X;\Lambda) \quad . \tag{25}$$

Note that as $\eta \rightarrow \infty$,

$$\frac{g_i^{\eta}(X;\Lambda)}{G(X;\Lambda)} \approx \begin{cases} 1, & g_i(X;\Lambda) = \max_k g_k(X;\Lambda) \\ 0, & \text{otherwise} \end{cases} \tag{26}$$

Finally, the smoothed empirical system cost becomes

$$L \approx \sum_{X \in \Omega} \sum_{j \in I_M} \left( \sum_{i \in I_M} \varepsilon_{ij} \frac{g_i^{\eta}(X;\Lambda)}{G(X;\Lambda)} \right) 1[X \in C_j] \tag{27}$$

which is a continuous function of the parameter set $\Lambda$. Similarly, the hyper-parameters can be chosen tradeoff between approximation and smoothness.

### d. Empirical Bayes Risk

Given a labeled training set $\Omega$, it is possible to compute the *empirical Bayes risk*:

$$L_B = \sum_{X \in \Omega} \sum_{j \in I_M} \varepsilon_{j_X j} P(C_j \mid X) \tag{28}$$

which is obtained when the correct labels are used to compute the conditional risk. The empirical Bayes risk is expected to be identical to the Bayes risk when $N$, the size of the training set, is infinite.

### e. Implementation

We have implemented the above methods for pattern recognition with non-uniform cost and demonstrated their validity. References [6-8] contain details of such implementations for pattern recognition and speech recognition.

## 5 Conclusion

We have pointed out an important factor in the construction of a framework for accomplishing the goal of automatic discovery of intelligence (ADI), namely the issue of non-uniform significance in recognition error (or contaminated evidence). The conventional decision theory of Bayes which led to the paradigm of probability distribution estimation as a fundamental methodology in pattern recognition was revised such that incorporation of non-uniform error costs becomes feasible. We propose an extension of the Minimum Classification Error (MCE) method for machine learning as the framework for pattern recognition system design that allows incorporation and optimization of the system over non-uniform error cost functions. We have implemented the method and related algorithms and demonstrated their effectiveness (published in separate articles). The issue of non-uniform significance of contaminated evidence and non-uniform error cost in the identification of information marks a unique departure from the conventional view of informatics, from simple information to intelligence.

## References

1. http://www.emc.com/about/destination/digital_universe/pdf/Expanding_Digital_Universe_Executive_Summary_022507.pdf
2. Friedman, T.: Lexus and the Olive Trees
3. http://en.wikipedia.org/wiki/Intelligence
4. Duda, R., Hart, P., Stork, D.: Pattern Classification, 2nd edn. John Wiley, New York (2001)
5. Juang, B.H., Katagiri, S.: Discriminative learning for minimum error classification. IEEE Trans. Signal Processing 40(12), 3043–3054 (1992)
6. Fu, Q., Mansjur, D., Juang, B.H.: Pattern recognition with non-uniform error criteria. IEEE Transaction on Pattern Analysis and Machine Intelligence (submitted, 2007)
7. Fu, Q., Juang, B.H.: An Investigation of Non-Uniform Error Cost Function Design in Automatic Speech Recognition. In: ICASSP-2008, September 2007 (submitted)

# Comparing LDA with pLSI as a Dimensionality Reduction Method in Document Clustering

Tomonari Masada, Senya Kiyasu, and Sueharu Miyahara

Nagasaki University, 1-14 Bunkyo-machi, Nagasaki 852-8521, Japan
{masada,kiyasu,miyahara}@cis.nagasaki-u.ac.jp

**Abstract.** In this paper, we compare latent Dirichlet allocation (LDA) with probabilistic latent semantic indexing (pLSI) as a dimensionality reduction method and investigate their effectiveness in document clustering by using real-world document sets. For clustering of documents, we use a method based on multinomial mixture, which is known as an efficient framework for text mining. Clustering results are evaluated by F-measure, i.e., harmonic mean of precision and recall. We use Japanese and Korean Web articles for evaluation and regard the category assigned to each Web article as the ground truth for the evaluation of clustering results. Our experiment shows that the dimensionality reduction via LDA and pLSI results in document clusters of almost the same quality as those obtained by using original feature vectors. Therefore, we can reduce the vector dimension without degrading cluster quality. Further, both LDA and pLSI are more effective than random projection, the baseline method in our experiment. However, our experiment provides no meaningful difference between LDA and pLSI. This result suggests that LDA does not replace pLSI at least for dimensionality reduction in document clustering.

## 1 Introduction

Document clustering is a classic problem of text mining. In recent years, clustering is proved to be effective in summarizing a search result or in distinguishing different topics latent in search results [29][7][5]. With respect to this type of application, clustering is expected to provide a result at query time. In contrast, enterprise documents stored in the intranet or the patent documents relating to a specific technical field form a document set which is not so small as a search result and, simultaneously, not so large as those targeted by open Web search services [12][15][18]. In this paper, we consider applications managing this type of document set, i.e., a document set of *middle-range* size and focus on *latent Dirichlet allocation (LDA)* [10] along with *probabilistic latent semantic indexing (pLSI)* [17], which are applicable to such document sets in realistic execution time. These two methods share the following special feature: topic multiplicity of each document is explicitly modeled. Therefore, we can consider topic mixture for each document. This feature makes LDA and pLSI differentiate from multinomial mixture model [24] and also from Dirichlet mixture model [21][19].

T. Tokunaga and A. Ortega (Eds.): LKR 2008, LNAI 4938, pp. 13–26, 2008.

However, LDA employes a Bayesian inference framework, which makes LDA more theoretically attractive than pLSI.

In this paper, we use LDA and pLSI for dimensionality reduction of feature vectors in document clustering and check if LDA can replace pLSI for this task. Our original feature vectors have frequencies of words as their entries and thus are of dimension equal to the number of vocabularies. Both LDA and pLSI reduce the dimension of document vectors to the number of topics, which is far less than the number of vocabularies. Roughly speaking, we can regard each entry of the vectors of reduced dimension as a topic frequency, i.e., the number of words relating to each topic. We investigate the effectiveness of dimensionality reduction by conducting a clustering on feature vectors of reduced dimension.

Our experiment uses four different sets of Japanese and Korean Web articles. Each article set consists of tens of thousands of documents, i.e., a document set of middle-range size. We use a clustering method based on multinomial mixture with EM algorithm for parameter estimation. Multinomial mixture is well-known as an effective framework for text mining applications, e.g. junk e-mail filtering [26]. While we have also tested $k$-means clustering method, this does not give clusters of satisfying quality in comparison with multinomial mixture. Therefore, we do not include those results in this paper. In evaluating cluster quality, we compare the quality before and after dimensionality reduction via LDA and pLSI. Further, we compare these two methods with random projection [9], which we regard as the baseline method in this paper. We use the category assigned to each article as the ground truth for evaluating cluster quality. Therefore, we try to recover document categories based on the topic frequencies obtained by the two multi-topic document models, LDA and pLSI. While the inference of the correct number of clusters is important, this is beyond our scope. We have used the true number of clusters as an input.

The rest of the paper is organized as follows. Section 2 gives previous work concerning applications of LDA to real-world data. Section 3 includes a short description of LDA. Since pLSI has already become more widely accepted than LDA, we omit the details about pLSI from this paper and refer to the original paper [17]. The results of evaluation experiment is presented in Section 4. Section 5 draws conclusions and gives future work.

## 2 Previous Work

Recently, many applications of LDA to real-world problems are proposed, e.g. multimodal information integration [8][20], topic-author relationship analysis [16], expert finding [22] and subject extraction from digital library books [23]. However, these researches do not compare LDA with other probabilistic model. Sadamitsu et al. [28] conduct intensive experiments comparing LDA with pLSI and Dirichlet mixture. While we can learn important things about the applicability of LDA and other document models, their work compares these document models not from a practical viewpoint, but from a theoretical one, because the authors use *perplexity* as a measure for evaluation. Perplexity tells how well a document model can generalize to test data, but does not tell how well a document model can solve text mining problems, e.g. information retrieval, document classification or document clustering.

In this paper, we employ LDA as a dimensionality reduction method in document clustering and evaluate its effectiveness by inspecting the quality of document clusters. Although Blei et al. [10] use LDA for dimensionality reduction, the authors compare LDA with no other methods. Further, their evaluation task is a binary classification of Reuters-21578 corpus, a slightly artificial task. Elango et al. [14] also use LDA to reduce the dimension of feature vectors. However, their feature vectors are obtained from image data, and LDA is not compared with any other methods. In this paper, we use LDA as a dimensionality reduction method to clarify its applicability to the document clustering task by comparing it with pLSI. Futher, we compare LDA and pLSI with random projection [9], the baseline method in our experiment. Since LDA is proposed as a sophistication of pLSI, it is worthwhile to check if LDA can provide better results than pLSI.

Recently, LDA has been extented to enable an automatic determination of the number of clusters. This method is based on a probabilistic model, called Dirichlet process mixture (DPM) [11]. With DPM, we do not need to conduct dimensionality reduction first and then execute a clustering, because DPM can provide a far smaller number of probability distributions over topics than the number of documents. Each of these topic distributions, in turn, can be regarded as the feature of a cluster. In contrast, LDA gives as many topic distributions as documents, where we can observe no clustering effects. If LDA do not give better results than pLSI in our evaluation, we can conclude that LDA is not a good choice at least for dimensionality reduction in document clustering, because we can use pLSI when the efficiency in execution time is required, or can use DPM when high computational cost is allowed.

## 3 Latent Dirichlet Allocation

### 3.1 Details of Model

Latent Dirichlet Allocation (LDA) [10] is a document model which explicitly models topic multiplicity of each document. This feature differenciates LDA from multinomial mixture [24] and also from Dirichlet mixture [21]. Probabilistic latent semantic indexing (pLSI) [17] shares the feature of topic multiplicity modeling with LDA. However, pLSI requires heuristic computations for obtaining the probability of unknown documents and is also likely to result in overlearning.

We denote a document set by $D = \{d_1, \ldots, d_I\}$, the set of vocabularies (i.e., word types) appearing in $D$ by $W = \{w_1, \ldots, w_J\}$ and the set of topics included in $D$ by $T = \{t_1, \ldots, t_K\}$. Formally speaking, topics are the values of hidden variables of a document model. With respect to each topic, we have a multinomial distribution defined over $W$. Namely, the topic difference is represented by the difference of word probabilities.

In LDA, with respect to each document, we select a multinomial distribution defined over $T$ according to the following Dirichlet distribution: $P(\theta;\alpha) = \frac{\Gamma(\sum_{k=1}^K \alpha_k)}{\prod_{k=1}^K \Gamma(\alpha_k)} \prod_{k=1}^K \theta_k^{\alpha_k}$. In generating documents, we regard each document $d_i$ as an empty array of length equal to the document length $n_i$. We fill this array as follows. First, we select a multinomial over $T$ from the Dirichlet distribution shown above. Second, we select a topic for each array element according to this multinomial over $T$. The topic assigned to the $l$th array element of document $d_i$ is denoted by $\mathbf{z}_{il}$. The entire topic sequence of $d_i$ is referred to by $\mathbf{z}_i$. Third, we select a word to fill this array element according to the multinomial over $W$ which corresponds to the topic $\mathbf{z}_{il}$. The word filling the $l$th array element of document $d_i$ is denoted by $\mathbf{x}_{il}$. The whole word sequence of $d_i$ is referred to by $\mathbf{x}_i$. As we repeatedly select a topic for each word, we can explicitly model the topic multiplicity within the same document. Let $\beta_{kj}$ be the probability of vocabulary $w_j$ in the multinomial distribution corresponding to topic $t_k$. Note that $\sum_j \beta_{kj} = 1$ holds for all $k$. The model parameters of LDA are $\alpha_k (k = 1, \ldots, K)$ and $\beta_{kj} (k = 1, \ldots, K, j = 1, \ldots, J)$. The total number of parameters is $K + KJ$. The probability of the word sequence $\mathbf{x}_i$ of document $d_i$ can be written as

$$P(\mathbf{x}_i; \alpha, \beta) = \int \sum_{\mathbf{z}_i} P(\theta;\alpha) P(\mathbf{z}_i|\theta) P(\mathbf{x}_i|\mathbf{z}_i, \beta) d\theta. \quad (1)$$

The probability of the word sequence of the whole document set $D$ is equal to $\prod_i P(\mathbf{x}_i; \alpha, \beta)$. By maximizing the log of this probability, i.e., $\log \prod_i P(\mathbf{x}_i; \alpha, \beta) = \sum_i \log P(\mathbf{x}_i; \alpha, \beta)$, we can determine model parameter values.

### 3.2 Variational Inference

In this paper, we employ variational inference method [10], where two probability distributions, $Q(\theta; \gamma_i)$ and $Q(\mathbf{z}_i; \phi_i)$, are introduced with respect to each document as follows:

$$\begin{aligned} &\log P(\mathbf{x}_i; \alpha, \beta) \\ &= \log \int \sum_{\mathbf{z}_i} P(\theta;\alpha) P(\mathbf{z}_i|\theta) P(\mathbf{x}_i|\mathbf{z}_i, \beta) d\theta \\ &= \log \int \sum_{\mathbf{z}_i} Q(\theta;\gamma_i) Q(\mathbf{z}_i;\phi_i) \frac{P(\theta;\alpha) P(\mathbf{z}_i|\theta) P(\mathbf{x}_i|\mathbf{z}_i, \beta)}{Q(\theta;\gamma_i) Q(\mathbf{z}_i;\phi_i)} d\theta \\ &\geq \int \sum_{\mathbf{z}_i} Q(\theta;\gamma_i) Q(\mathbf{z}_i;\phi_i) \log \frac{P(\theta;\alpha) P(\mathbf{z}_i|\theta) P(\mathbf{x}_i|\mathbf{z}_i, \beta)}{Q(\theta;\gamma_i) Q(\mathbf{z}_i;\phi_i)} d\theta \end{aligned} \quad (2)$$

We can move from the third line to the fourth by applying Jensen's inequality and obtain a lower bound of $\log P(\mathbf{x}_i; \alpha, \beta)$ for each $d_i$. In variational inference, we maximize this lower bound in place of $\log P(\mathbf{x}_i; \alpha, \beta)$. $Q(\mathbf{z}_i; \phi_i)$ is equal to $\prod_{l=1}^{n_i} Q(\mathbf{z}_{il}; \phi_{il})$ where $\phi_{ilk}$is the probability of the assignment of topic $t_k$ to the $l$th word of $d_i$. $\sum_{k=1}^K \phi_{ilk} = 1$ holds for all $i$ and $l$. Further, $Q(\theta; \gamma_i)$ is a

Dirichlet distribution defined over topic multinomials. While $Q(\theta;\gamma_i)$ plays a role similar to $P(\theta;\alpha)$, $Q(\theta;\gamma_i)$ is introduced separately for each document. The details of variational inference for LDA is described in [10]. Here we only present the resulting update formulas.

$$\phi_{ilk} \propto \beta_{kj_{il}} \exp\{\Psi(\gamma_{ik}) - \Psi(\sum_{k'} \gamma_{ik'})\} \tag{3}$$

$$\gamma_{ik} = \alpha_k + \sum_l \phi_{ilk} \tag{4}$$

$$\beta_{kj} \propto \sum_i \sum_l \delta_{ilj} \phi_{ilk} \tag{5}$$

$$\alpha_k = \hat{\alpha}_k + f_k(\hat{\alpha}) + \sum_{k'} f_{k'}(\hat{\alpha}) \Big/ \Big\{ \frac{\Psi_1(\hat{\alpha}_k)}{\Psi_1(\sum_{k'} \hat{\alpha}_{k'})} - \sum_{k'} \frac{\Psi_1(\hat{\alpha}_k)}{\Psi_1(\hat{\alpha}_{k'})} \Big\}$$

where

$$f_k(\alpha) = \frac{\Psi(\sum_{k'} \alpha_{k'})}{\Psi_1(\alpha_k)} - \frac{\Psi(\alpha_k)}{\Psi_1(\alpha_k)} + \frac{\sum_i \{\Psi(\gamma_{ik}) - \Psi(\sum_{k'} \gamma_{ik'})\}}{N\Psi_1(\alpha_k)} \tag{6}$$

In Eq. 3, $j_{il}$ is the index of the $l$th word of document $d_i$. Thus, the $l$th word of document $d_i$ is $w_{j_{il}} \in W$. In Eq. 5, $\delta_{ilj}$ is equal to 1 if the $l$th word of $d_i$ is $w_j$ (i.e., $j_{il} = j$), and 0 otherwise. In Eq. 6, $\hat{\alpha}_k$ is a value for $\alpha_k$ obtained in the previous iteration. $\Psi$ and $\Psi_1$ stand for digamma and trigamma functions, respectively. As Eq. 6 is an update formula only for $\alpha_k$, we repeatedly use this formula until convergence. Our implementation in C language for this paper terminates this update iteration when $\sum_k \alpha_k$ changes by less than 0.000001 of the previous value. After executing Eq. 3, 4 and 5, we use Eq. 6 repeatedly and then return to Eq. 3. Our implementation terminates the entire iteration ranging from Eq. 3 to Eq. 6 when $\sum_k \alpha_k$ changes by less than 0.005 of the previous value.

In this paper, we regard $\gamma_{ik}$ as a "pseudo-frequency" of topic $t_k$ in document $d_i$. Roughly speaking, $\gamma_{ik}$ is the "number" of words relating to topic $t_k$ in document $d_i$. We have called $\gamma_{ik}$ "pseudo-frequency," because this is not necessarily an integer. We use a $K$-dimensional vector $(\gamma_{i1}, \ldots, \gamma_{iK})$ as a feature vector of $d_i$ after dimensionality reduction via LDA. This vector can be used as a feature vector by the following reason. By taking the sum of the both sides of Eq. 4 for all $k$, we have $\sum_k \gamma_{ik} = \sum_k \alpha_k + \sum_k \sum_{l=1}^{n_i} \phi_{ilk}$. Further, $\sum_k \sum_l \phi_{ilk}$ is equal to $n_i$, the document length of $d_i$, because $\sum_{k=1}^{K} \phi_{ilk} = 1$. Consequently, $\sum_k \gamma_{ik}$ is of the same order with document lengths.

In estimating parameters of LDA, we have also tried a collapsed variational Bayesian inference [27] only for one of the four datasets in the evaluation experiment. As for the details, please refer to the original paper. This inference gives a probability that a topic is assigned to a vocabulary appearing in a document for all $K \times J \times I$ combinations of topics, vocabularies and documents. Therefore, by taking a summation of these probabilities over the vocabularies appearing in a document with respect to a fixed topic, we can have a value of the same meaning as $\gamma_{ik}$ shown above, i.e., a "pseudo-frequency" of a topic in each document.

# 4 Evaluation Experiment

## 4.1 Document Sets

In the evaluation experiment, we use one document set of Japanese Web news articles, one document set of questions from a Japanese Q&A Web site and two sets of Korean Web news articles.

The first set consists of news articles published at Japan.internet.com [1] from 2001 to 2006. Every article is uniquely labeled by one of the following six categories: mobile phone, Web business, e-commerce, Web finance, Web technology and Web marketing. We use MeCab morphological analyzer [3] to split every document into a sequence of word tokens. Then we count the frequencies of all vocabularies and eliminate the vocabularies of low frequency and those of high frequency. The resulting document set, denoted by JIC, includes 28,329 articles. The sum of the lengths of all documents in JIC amounts to 4,108,245. The number of vocabularies is 12,376. As the number of categories is six, we subdivide this set into six disjoint subsets by clustering. The number of documents and the document length sum for each category are included in Table 1.

The second set includes the queries submitted to a Japanese Q & A Web site, called "OKWave" [4]. In this experiment, we have not used the answers to each query, because we think that some of them explicitly introduce noisy information for document clustering. Every question is uniquely labeled by one of the following 11 categories: information for computer engineers, regional information, entertainment, digital life, business and career, money, daily life, education, society, hobbies, health and beauty. Here we also use MeCab morphological analyzer and eliminate the vocabularies of low frequency and those of high frequency. This document set, denoted by OKWAVE, includes 70,555 articles. The sum of the lengths of all documents is 2,511,221, and the number of vocabularies is 13,341. We split this set into 11 disjoint subsets by clustering. Note that the average document length of this document set is far shorter than the other three sets. Table 2 provides the number of documents and the document length sum for each category. We have used a collapsed variational Bayesian inference only for this set, because this inference method shows an advantage in computational cost when the number of documents is large.

**Table 1.** JIC dataset

| category | # of docs | sum of doc lengths |
|---|---|---|
| mobile phone | 3,049 | 499,368 |
| Web business | 9,059 | 1,214,335 |
| e-commerce | 2,522 | 327,264 |
| Web finance | 2,994 | 398,995 |
| Web technology | 6,109 | 922,164 |
| Web marketing | 4,596 | 746,119 |
| total | 28,329 | 4,108,245 |

**Table 2.** OKWAVE dataset

| category | # of docs | sum of doc lengths |
|---|---|---|
| info. for comput. engineers | 7,055 | 333,624 |
| regional info. | 4,103 | 128,800 |
| entertainment | 8,241 | 206,832 |
| digital life | 11,909 | 410,648 |
| business and career | 5,985 | 236,157 |
| money | 4,150 | 180,271 |
| daily life | 7,672 | 342,287 |
| education | 7,149 | 232,377 |
| society | 4,589 | 170,617 |
| hobbies | 6,725 | 159,666 |
| health and beauty | 3,030 | 109,942 |
| total | 70,555 | 2,511,221 |

**Table 3.** S2005 dataset

| category | # of docs | sum of doc lengths |
|---|---|---|
| economy | 6,172 | 461,592 |
| international | 3,048 | 216,462 |
| politics | 3,608 | 286,375 |
| society | 9,221 | 590,190 |
| total | 22,049 | 1,554,619 |

**Table 4.** S2006 dataset

| category | # of docs | sum of doc lengths |
|---|---|---|
| administration | 1,503 | 124,657 |
| culture | 4,870 | 347,438 |
| economy | 6,745 | 549,081 |
| entertainment | 1,710 | 125,787 |
| international | 2,498 | 186,753 |
| policitics | 3,806 | 324,076 |
| region | 3,923 | 280,676 |
| society | 8,946 | 607,158 |
| sport | 3,016 | 185,054 |
| total | 37,017 | 2,730,680 |

Two Korean document sets are obtained by gathering articles published at Seoul newspaper Web site [6] from 2005 to 2006. One set consists of the articles published in 2005. The articles of this set belong to one of the following four categories: economy, international, politics and society. Another set includes the articles published in 2006. The articles of this set belong to one of the following nine categories: administration, culture, economy, entertainment, international, politics, region, society and sports. We use KLT version 2.10b [2] for Korean morphological analysis. For each of the two sets, we eliminate the vocabularies of low frequency and those of high frequency. We denote the resulting document sets S2005 and S2006, respectively. S2005 includes 22,049 articles and 14,563 vocabularies. The sum of the lengths of all documents in S2005 amounts to 1,554,619. We conduct a clustering on this set and obtain four disjoint clusters, because the number of categories is four. S2006 includes 37,017 documents and 25,584 vocabularies. The document length sum is 2,730,680. We split this set into nine disjoint subsets by clustering. The number of documents and the document length sum for each category are given in Table 3 and Table 4 for S2005 and S2006, respectively.

### 4.2 Clustering Method

To obtain document clusters, we use a clustering based on multinomial mixture, an effective framework for text mining [26][24]. While we have also tested $k$-means method, no better results are obtained. Therefore, we do not include those results in this paper. In conducting a clustering with multinomial mixture, we randomly initialize model parameter values and execute EM algorithm [13] 20 times for each document set. We also use a smoothing techinque [24] and an annealing technique [25]. In applying a smoothing, we linearly mix the background word probability (i.e., the word probability in the entire document set) to the cluster-wise word probability. We test the following four mixture ratios for smoothing: 0.0, 0.01, 0.1 and 0.3. The ratio of 0.0 corresponds to the case where we have no smoothing effect. When the ratio is 0.3, for example, we use $(1-0.3)\times$(cluster-wise word probability)$+0.3\times$(background word probability) in place of the cluster-wise word probability when updating parameter values in EM algorithm. Only for OKWAVE dataset, which includes many short articles, we use the mixture ratio 0.5 instead of 0.01 and consequently use the following four mixture ratios: 0.0, 0.1, 0.3 and 0.5. This is because large smoothing is likely to give clusters of good quality for a set of short documents.

### 4.3 Evaluation of Cluster Quality

We evaluate the quality of clusters by F-measure, the harmonic mean of precision and recall. Precision and recall are computed as follows. We call the category assigned to the largest number of articles in a given cluster *dominating category* of the cluster. The precision of a cluster is defined to be the ratio of the number of the articles of dominating category to the size of the cluster. The recall of a cluster is the ratio of the number of the articles of dominating category to the number of articles of that category from the entire document set.

To obtain a precison and recall for each clustering result, we compute the sum of the numerators and the sum of the denominators used for computing precisions and recalls for different clusters included in the clustering result, and divide the former sum by the latter sum. Consequently, we have two evaluation measures called *microaveraged precision* and *microaveraged recall*. For example, when we

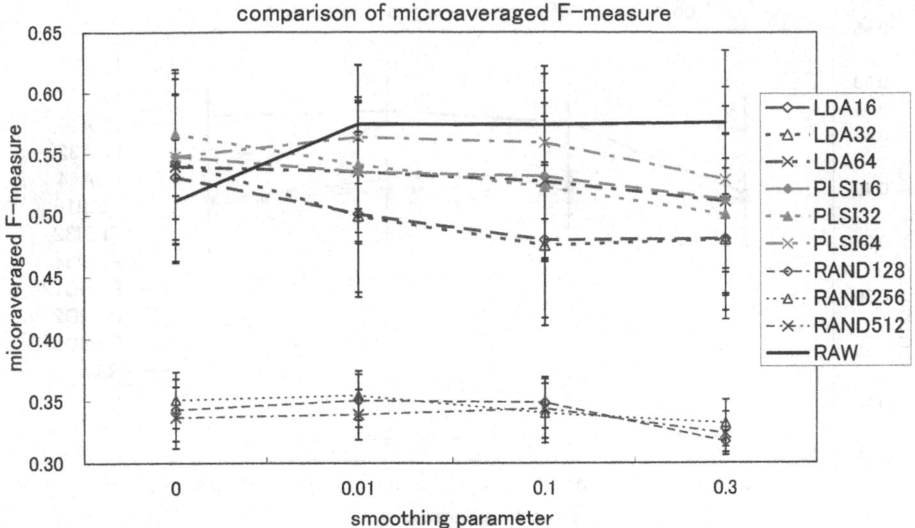


**Fig. 1.** Comparison of microaveraged F-measure for S2005 dataset

have a clustering result consisting of three clusters whose precisions are 2/3, 5/8 and 4/7, microaveraged precision of this clustering result is (2+5+4)/(3+8+7). Microaveraged recall is also computed in the same manner. From definition, when there are at least one categories which do not dominate any clusters, microaveraged precision can be different from microaveraged recall. Therefore, we use the harmonic mean of microaveraged precision and microaveraged recall as an integrated evaluation for a clustering result. In this paper, we simply call this harmonic mean *F-measure* in the rest of the paper.

In our experiment, we run a clustering algorithm 20 times on a document set from randomly initialized parameter values. Consequently, we obtain 20 F-measures for each document set. We use the average and the standard deviation of these 20 F-measures for evaluating the performances of different dimensionality reduction methods. Since we use four mixture ratios (i.e., 0.0, 0.01, 0.1 and 0.3, or, 0.0, 0.1, 0.3 and 0.5 only for OKWAVE set) for smoothing as is described in Section 4.2, we have four evaluation results for each document set with respect to each dimentionality reduction method.

### 4.4 Evaluation Results

The evaluation results for S2005 and S2006 are provided in Fig. 1 and Fig. 2, respectively. For JIC, we obtain the results shown in Fig. 3. Finally, Fig. 4 shows the results for OKWAVE dataset. The horizontal axis represents mixture ratio of smoothing. The vertical axis represents F-measure. Each graph shows the average of 20 F-measures obtained from 20 executions of clustering. The width of each marker indicates plus/minus one standard deviation of the 20 microaveraged F-measures. In all figures, the graph labeled with RAW shows the

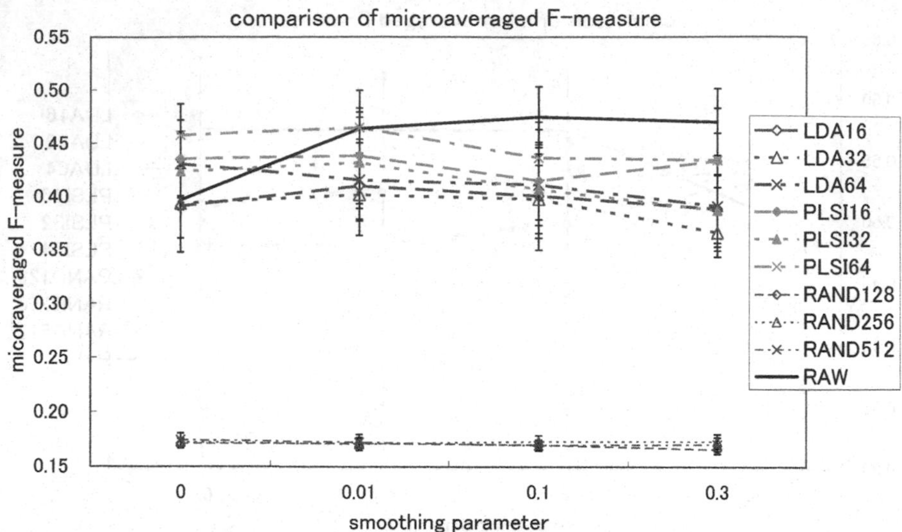


**Fig. 2.** Comparison of microaveraged F-measure for S2006 dataset

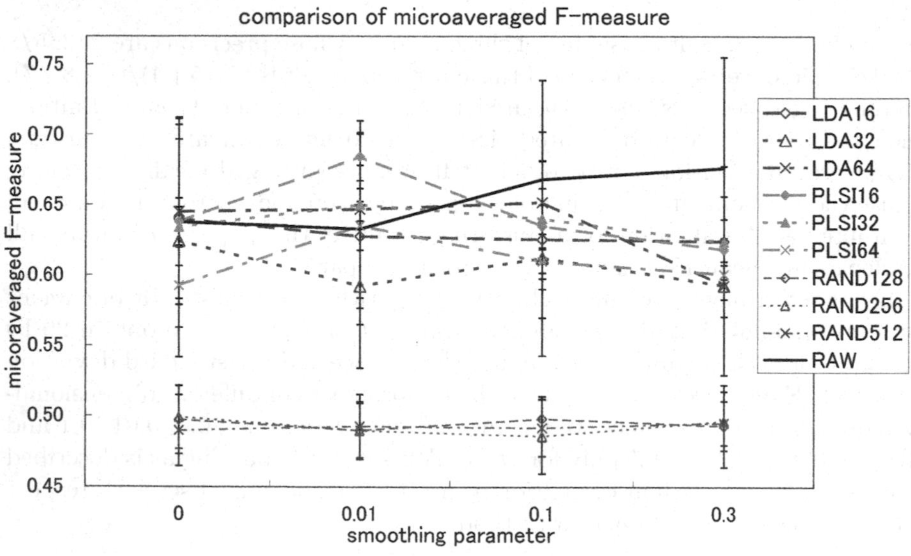


**Fig. 3.** Comparison of microaveraged F-measure for JIC dataset

average of 20 F-measures when we use no dimensionality reduction. Without dimensionality reduction, the quality of clusters gets better when we apply smoothing by choosing a non-zero value for mixture ratio.

The graphs labeled with LDA16, LDA32 and LDA64 present the averages of 20 microaveraged F-measures obtained when we reduce the vector dimension to 16, 32 and 64 via LDA, respectively. For any of these three cases, smoothing does not

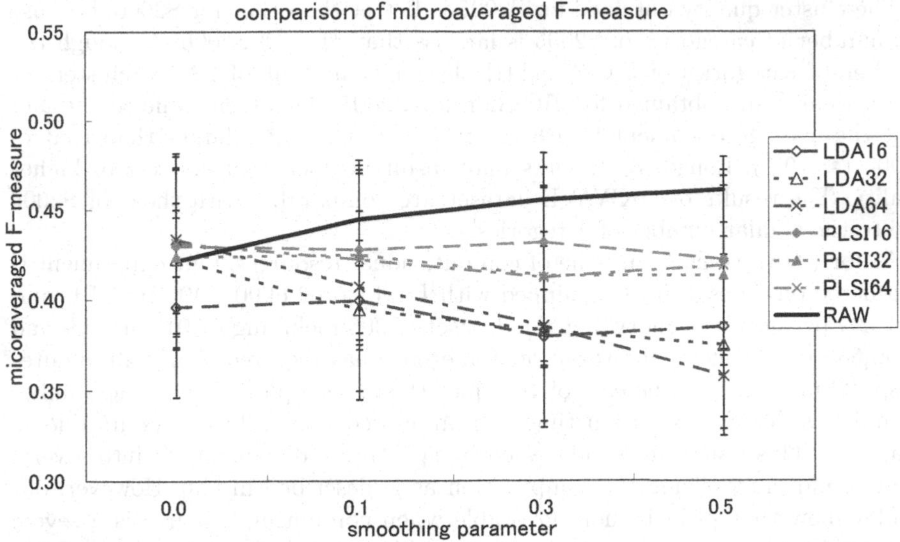


**Fig. 4.** Comparison of microaveraged F-measure for OKWAVE dataset. We do not include the cluster quality for the case of random projection, because this case almost always gives heavily degenerated clustering results where all input vectors are put into one or two clusters.

improve the quality of clusters. This seems because the dimensionality reduction implies a smoothing effect. Further, LDA provides F-measures comparable with RAW. We can say that LDA can reduce the dimension of feature vectors without degrading the cluster quality.

The graphs labeled with PLSI16, PLSI32 and PLSI64 indicate the results when we use pLSI for dimensionality reduction by setting the number of topics 16, 32 and 64, respectively. The standard deviation markers for pLSI intersect with those of LDA. Namely, LDA is not superior to pLSI as a dimensionality reduction method in document clustering.

However, both LDA and pLSI provide clusters of far better quality than random projection. The graphs having labels RAND128, RAND256 and RAND512 give the averages of 20 F-measures obtained by conducting a clustering on the feature vectors of dimension 128, 256 and 512, respectively, where dimensionality reduction is realized by random projection. When we reduce the dimension to 16, 32 or 64 by random projection, the cluster quality gets disastrous. Hence, only for random projection, we provide the evaluation results of clustering by using the vectors of dimension 128, 256 and 512. Further, for OKWAVE dataset, the reduced vectors obtained by random projection always give quite small F-measures (0.1181~0.1331). Therefore, we do not include these results in Fig. 4. This fact suggests that random projection is not applicable to the feature vectors of short documents, i.e., document vectors with many zero entries.

The cluster quality obtained for S2005 is better than that for S2006, because the number of categories of S2005 is far less than that of S2006. Although the number of categories of JIC is a little larger than that of S2005, clusters of better quality are obtained for JIC than for S2005. This seems due to the fact that the average document length of JIC ($\approx$ 145.0) is far larger than that of S2005 ($\approx$ 70.5). Longer documents may result in document clusters of higher quality. The results of OKWAVE dataset are comparable with those of S2006 due to the similar number of categories.

As for LDA, we have an issue of computational resources. Our experiment is conducted on a desktop PC equipped with Intel Core2 6600 2.40GHz CPU and with 2G byte main memory. For the dataset S2006 including 37,017 articles and 2,730,680 word tokens, the variational inference has required nearly 40 minutes (resp. 90 minutes) for the case of 16 topics (resp. 32 topics). When the number of topics is 64, the execution time has amounted to nearly five hours due to swapping. This issue can be addressed by splitting a document set into several subsets and parallelizing the computation as is described in [23]. However, our results show that pLSI is more favorable when computing resource is a severe problem. Further, even when the resource problem is not severe, we can use DPM [11], a more sophisticated version of LDA, at least for document clustering.

## 5 Conclusion

This paper provides the results of an evaluation experiment concerning dimensionality reduction in document clustering. We use LDA and pLSI to reduce the dimension of document feature vectors which are originally of dimension equal to the number of vocabularies. We conduct a clustering based on multinomial mixture for the set of the feature vectors of original dimension and for the set of the vectors of reduced dimension. We also compare LDA and pLSI with random projection. The results show that LDA can reduce the dimension of document feature vectors without degrading the quality of document clusters. Further, LDA is far superior to random projection. However, our experiment tells no significant difference between LDA and pLSI. When we consider the issue of computational cost, we have no positive reason to promote LDA beside pLSI for dimensionality reduction in document clustering.

The variational inference for LDA, however, gives a wide variety of results. In this paper, we only use a part of the results, i.e., "pseudo-frequencies" of topics with respect to each document ($\gamma_{ik}$ in Eq. 4). In addition to this, we can obtain topic probabilities with respect to each word token ($\phi_{ilk}$ in Eq. 3), word probabilities with respect to each topic ($\beta_{kj}$ in Eq. 5) and $\alpha_k$ in Eq. 6 which can be regarded as an importance of each topic in the entire document set. These information cannot directly be obtained by Gibbs sampling, an alternative inference framework for LDA [16][22][23]. Our future work is to propose better applications of LDA to various text mining problems by utilizing the above parameters effectively.

## References


1. http://japan.internet.com/
2. http://nlp.kookmin.ac.kr/HAM/kor/
3. http://mecab.sourceforge.net/
4. http://okwave.jp/
5. http://www.quintura.com/
6. http://www.seoul.co.kr/
7. http://vivisimo.com/
8. Barnard, K., Duygulu, P., de Freitas, N., Forsyth, D., Blei, D., Jordan, M.: Matching Words and Pictures. Journal of Machine Learning Research 3, 1107–1135 (2003)
9. Bingham, E., Mannila, H.: Random Projection in Dimensionality Reduction: Applications to Image and Text Data. In: Proc. of KDD 2001, pp. 245–250 (2001)
10. Blei, D., Ng, A.Y., Jordan, M.I.: Latent Dirichlet Allocation. Journal of Machine Learning Research 3, 993–1022 (2003)
11. Blei, D., Jordan, M.I.: Variational Inference for Dirichlet Process Mixtures. Bayesian Analysis 1(1), 121–144 (2005)
12. Conrad, J.G., Al-Kofahi, K., Zhao, Y., Karypis, G.: Effective Document Clustering for Large Heterogeneous Law Firm Collections. In: Proc. of ICAIL 2005, pp. 177–187 (2005)
13. Dempster, A.P., Laird, N.M., Rubin, D.B.: Maximum Likelihood from Incomplete Data via the EM Algorithm. Journal of the Royal Statistical Society, Series B 39(1), 1–38 (1977)
14. Elango, P.K., Jayaraman, K.: Clustering Images Using the Latent Dirichlet Allocation Model (2005), available at http://www.cs.wisc.edu/~pradheep/
15. Fattori, M., Pedrazzi, G., Turra, R.: Text Mining Applied to Patent Mapping: a Practical Business Case. World Patent Information 25, 335–342 (2003)
16. Griffiths, T., Steyvers, M.: Finding Scientific Topics. Proc. of the National Academy of Sciences 101(suppl. 1), 5228–5235 (2004)
17. Hofmann, T.: Probabilistic Latent Semantic Indexing. In: Proc. of SIGIR 1999, pp. 50–57 (1999)
18. Hsu, F.-C., Trappey, A.J.C., Trappey, C.V., Hou, J.-L., Liu, S.-J.: Technology and Knowledge Document Cluster Analysis for Enterprise R&D Strategic Planning. International Journal of Technology Management 36(4), 336–353 (2006)
19. Madsen, R.E., Kauchak, D., Elkan, C.: Modeling Word Burstiness Using the Dirichlet Distribution. In: Proc. of ICML 2005, pp. 545–552 (2005)
20. Malisiewicz, T.J., Huang, J.C., Efros, A.A.: Detecting Objects via Multiple Segmentations and Latent Topic Models (2006), http://www.cs.cmu.edu/~tmalisie/
21. Minka, T.: Estimating a Dirichlet distribution (2000), http://research.microsoft.com/~minka/papers/
22. Mimno, D., McCallum, A.: Expertise Modeling for Matching Papers with Reviewers. In: Proc. of KDD 2007, pp. 500–509 (2007)
23. Mimno, D., McCallum, A.: Organizing the OCA: Learning Faceted Subjects from a library of digital books. In: Proc. of JCDL 2007, pp. 376–385 (2007)
24. Nigam, K., McCallum, A., Thrun, S., Mitchell, T.: Text Classification from Labeled and Unlabeled Documents Using EM. Machine Learning 39(2/3), 103–134 (2000)
25. Rose, K., Gurewitz, E., Fox, G.: A Deterministic Annealing Approach to Clustering. Pattern Recognition Letters 11, 589–594 (1990)

26. Sahami, M., Dumais, S., Heckerman, D., Horvitz, E.: A Bayesian Approach to Filtering Junk Email. AAAI Technical Report WS-98-05 (1998)
27. Teh, Y.W., Newman, D., Welling, M.: A Collapsed Variational Bayesian Inference Algorithm for Latent Dirichlet Allocation. In: Proc. of NIPS 2006, pp. 1353–1360 (2006)
28. Yamamoto, M., Sadamitsu, K.: Dirichlet Mixtures in Text Modeling. CS Technical report CS-TR-05-1, University of Tsukuba (2005)
29. Zeng, H.-J., He, Q.-C., Chen, Z., Ma, W.-Y., Ma, J.: Learning to Cluster Web Search Results. In: Proc. of SIGIR 2004, pp. 210–217 (2004)

# Identification of MCMC Samples for Clustering

Kenichi Kurihara, Tsuyoshi Murata, and Taisuke Sato

Tokyo Institute of Technology, Tokyo, Japan
kurihara@mi.cs.titech.ac.jp, murata@cs.titech.ac.jp,
sato@mi.cs.titech.ac.jp

**Abstract.** For clustering problems, many studies use just MAP assignments to show clustering results instead of using whole samples from a MCMC sampler. This is because it is not straightforward to recognize clusters based on whole samples. Thus, we proposed an identification algorithm which constructs groups of relevant clusters. The identification exploits spectral clustering to group clusters. Although a naive spectral clustering algorithm is intractable due to memory space and computational time, we developed a memory-and-time efficient spectral clustering for samples of a MCMC sampler. In experiments, we show our algorithm is tractable for real data while the naive algorithm is intractable. For search query log data, we also show representative vocabularies of clusters, which cannot be chosen by just MAP assignments.

## 1 Introduction

Clustering is one of the most widely used methods for data analysis. In recent years, non-parametric Bayesian approaches have received a great deal of attention especially for clustering. Unlike traditional clustering algorithms, non-parametric Bayesian approaches do not require the number of clusters as an input. Thus, they are very useful in practice especially when we do not have any information about the number of clusters a priori. More specifically, the Dirichlet process mixture models[1,2] have been used for machine learning and natural language processing[3,4].

The Markov chain Monte Carlo (MCMC) sampler, e.g. the Gibbs sampler, is typically utilized to estimate a posterior distribution[3,4,5] while deterministic inference algorithms have also been proposed[6,7]. Since the MCMC sampler is unbiased, we can estimate the true posterior distribution by collecting many samples from a sampler. Inference on test data is done using collected samples. However, when a task is clustering, many studies use just maximum a posteriori (MAP) assignments to show clustering results. This is because it is not straightforward to show clustering results with whole samples instead of just MAP assignments.

Figure 1 shows an example. The left figure shows MAP assignments by a Gibbs sampler of a Dirichlet process Gaussian mixture. The middle figure shows all of the collected samples by the sampler. It is easy to see each cluster and

T. Tokunaga and A. Ortega (Eds.): LKR 2008, LNAI 4938, pp. 27–37, 2008.

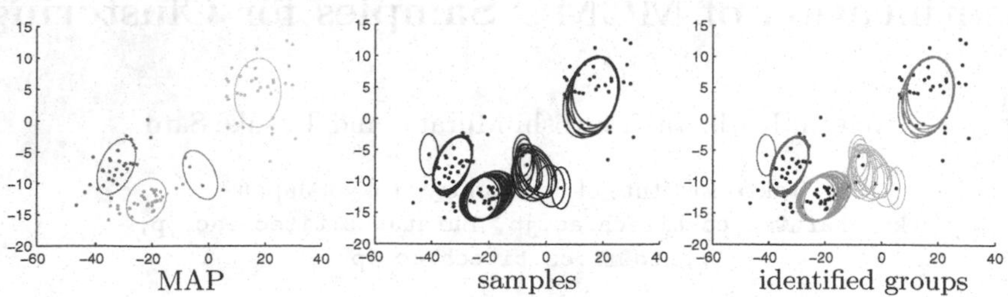


**Fig. 1.** MAP assignments (left), posterior samples from a MCMC sampler (middle) and identified groups of clusters (right)

the number of clusters, which is four, in the left figure. However, clusters overlap each other in the middle figure, hence it is not clear any more to distinguish clusters. Our goal of this study is to obtain the right figure from the middle one. This is done by identifying clusters from samples. In the right figure, each color represents one identified group consisting of clusters relevant to each other.

This identification is more informative for clustering than MAP assignments. For example, when a task is vocabulary clustering, we can estimate the probability of a vocabulary assigned to a group based on clusters in the group. This allows us to rank vocabularies in the group. On the other hand, such ranking is impossible only with MAP assignments.

In this paper, we propose an identification algorithm. To make it tractable, we also develop an efficient spectral clustering algorithm for samples. This paper is organized as follows. In Section 2 and 3, we briefly review the Dirichlet process mixture models[1,2] and the Gibbs sampler, which we use as a clustering algorithm. In Section 4, we propose an identification algorithm. Section 5 shows experimental results. We discuss and conclude this study in Section 6 and 7.

## 2 The Dirichlet Process Mixture Models

We briefly review the Dirichlet process mixture models[1,2] here. Finite mixture models consist of finite components, and the number of components is constant. On the other hand, the generative process of the Dirichlet process mixture models draws a new object from either one of existing components or a new component. Thus, the number of components may grow as the number of objects grows.

Let $Z$ be an $n$ by $K$ assignment matrix where $n$ is the number of objects and $K$ is the number of clusters. Note $K$ grows as $n$ grows, thus it is not constant. When object $i$ is assigned to cluster $c$, $Z_{i,c} = 1$ and $Z_{i,c'} = 0$ for $c' \neq c$. We denote the $i$-th row and the $j$-th column of $Z$ by $Z_i$ and $\zeta_j$, respectively. An example of assignments with notations, $Z$, $Z_i$ and $\zeta_j$, are presented in Figure 2.

matrix representation

$$Z = \begin{pmatrix} 10 \\ 10 \\ 01 \end{pmatrix} \Leftrightarrow \begin{matrix} Z_1 = (10) \\ Z_2 = (10) \\ Z_3 = (01) \end{matrix} \Leftrightarrow \zeta_1 = \begin{pmatrix} 1 \\ 1 \\ 0 \end{pmatrix}, \ \zeta_2 = \begin{pmatrix} 0 \\ 0 \\ 1 \end{pmatrix}$$

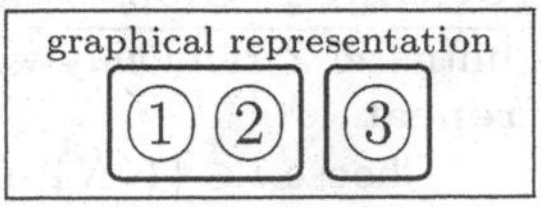

graphical representation

[① ②] [③]

**Fig. 2.** Matrix and graphical representations of assignments. Object 1 and 2 are clustered into one cluster, and 3 is clustered into another.

When $(Z_1, ..., Z_{i-1})$ is given, the $i$-th object would be assigned to the $c$-th component with probability,

$$p(Z_{i,c} = 1|Z_1, ..., Z_{i-1}) = \begin{cases} \frac{n_c^{\neg i}}{i-1+\alpha} & \text{if } n_c^{\neg i} > 0 \\ \frac{\alpha}{i-1+\alpha} & \text{otherwise} \end{cases} \tag{1}$$

where $n_c^{\neg i}$ is the number of objects currently assigned to component $c$, i.e. $n_c^{\neg i} = \sum_{j \neq i} Z_{j,c}$ and $\alpha$ is a hyperparameter. Every object can be assigned to a new component with probability $\frac{\alpha}{i-1+\alpha}$. Given $n$ objects, the probability of $Z$ is,

$$p(Z) = \frac{\Gamma(\alpha)}{\Gamma(n+\alpha)} \prod_{c=1}^{k} \alpha \Gamma(n_c) \tag{2}$$

where $n_c$ is the number of objects assigned to cluster $c$.

After $Z_i$ is drawn, when $Z_{i,c} = 1$, data point $\boldsymbol{x}_i$ is sampled as $\boldsymbol{x}_i \sim p(\boldsymbol{x}_i|\theta_c)$ where $\theta_c$ is the parameter of component $c$. Each $\theta_c$ is drawn from $G_0$ called base distribution. Thus, the joint probability of $X = (\boldsymbol{x}_1, ..., \boldsymbol{x}_n)$ and $Z$ is,

$$p(X, Z) = p(Z) \prod_{c=1}^{K} \int d\theta_c \, G_0(\theta_c) \prod_{i; Z_{i,c}=1} p(\boldsymbol{x}_i|\theta_c). \tag{3}$$

In the next section, we derive a Gibbs sampler for the Dirichlet process mixture models based on (3).

## 3 Gibbs Sampling for the Dirichlet Process Mixture Models

When a task is clustering, our goal is to infer $p(Z|X) = p(Z, X)/p(X)$. Although $p(X, Z)$ is given in (3), $p(X) = \sum_Z p(X, Z)$ is intractable due to $\sum_Z$ which requires exponential order computation. Instead of directly computing $p(Z|X)$, people use MCMC samplers including the Gibbs sampler, or variational algorithms. In the case of MCMC samplers, $Z$ is drawn from $p(Z|X)$ many times. The true posterior, $p(Z|X)$, is approximated by the collection of $Z$.

The Gibbs sampler for the Dirichlet process mixture updates one assignment, $Z_i$, in a step. Let $Z^{\neg i}$ be a matrix consisting of rows of $Z$ except for the $i$-th row,

**Algorithm 1.** Gibbs sampler for the Dirichlet process mixture models

```
1: Initialize Z randomly with K.
2: repeat
3:     Choose i ∈ {1..N} uniformly.
4:     Update Z_i based on probability given by (4).
5: until convergence
```

and $X_c^{\neg i}$ be $\{\boldsymbol{x}_j; Z_{j,c} = 1\}$. Since $p(Z_i|X, Z^{\neg i}) \propto p(X, Z)$ holds, $p(Z_i|X, Z^{\neg i})$ is derived from (3) as,

$$p(Z_{i,c} = 1|X, Z^{\neg i}) \propto p(Z_{i,c} = 1|Z^{\neg i})p(\boldsymbol{x}_i, X_c^{\neg i})/p(X_c^{\neg i})$$
$$= \begin{cases} n_c^{\neg i}\; p(\boldsymbol{x}_i, X_c^{\neg i})/p(X_c^{\neg i}) & \text{if } n_c^{\neg i} > 0 \\ \alpha\; p(\boldsymbol{x}_i, X_c^{\neg i})/p(X_c^{\neg i}) & \text{otherwise.} \end{cases} \tag{4}$$

Note that $p(\boldsymbol{x}_i, X_c^{\neg i})$ and $p(X_c^{\neg i})$ have closed forms when $G_0$ is a conjugate prior. We summarize this Gibbs sampler in Algorithm 1.

## 4 Identification of Samples

### 4.1 Preliminaries

Before we propose an identification algorithm, we introduce notations. We distinguish the following notations, *sample* $Z^{(i)}$, *collection of samples* $\mathbb{S} \equiv \{Z^{(1)}, ..., Z^{(S)}\}$, *cluster* $\zeta_i$, *collection of clusters* $\mathbb{C}(\mathbb{S})$ and *group of clusters* $G_j = \{\zeta_{j1}, \zeta_{j2}, ...\}$. Figure 3 shows an example of these notations. Note $\mathbb{C}(\mathbb{S})$ is a multiset.

$\mathbb{S}$ is collected by a MCMC sampler, i.e. $Z^{(i)} \sim p(Z|X)$. People typically use only MAP assignments, $Z^{\mathrm{MAP}}$, to show clustering results where $Z^{\mathrm{MAP}} = \mathrm{argmax}_{Z \in \mathbb{S}}\, p(Z|X)$. This is because it is very straightforward (see the left figure in Figure 1). Instead, we propose to use whole samples, $\mathbb{S}$, by identification (see the middle and right figures in Figure 1).

### 4.2 Identification by Clustering

Our task is to find groups $\{G_c\}_{c=1}^k$, s.t. $\bigcup_{c=1}^k G_c = \mathbb{C}(\mathbb{S})$[1]. Each group, $G_c$, consists of relevant clusters. To find such groups, we propose an identification algorithm, which group all clusters, $\mathbb{C}(\mathbb{S})$, i.e. clustering on clusters. The right figure in Figure 1 is an example of the identification. Clusters which have the same color are clustered into one group by the identification method.

The identification leads to better interpretation of clustering results. For example, when data is discrete, e.g. vocabularies, showing vocabularies contained by one cluster is a typical way to see clustering results. However, when we use

[1] Note $G_c$ and $\mathbb{C}(\mathbb{S})$ are multisets. Thus, regard $\bigcup$ as a union operator for multisets.

$$\mathbb{S} = \begin{pmatrix} Z^{(1)} = \boxed{\textcircled{1}\textcircled{2}}\boxed{\textcircled{3}} \\ Z^{(2)} = \boxed{\textcircled{1}\textcircled{3}}\boxed{\textcircled{2}} \\ Z^{(3)} = \boxed{\textcircled{1}}\boxed{\textcircled{2}}\boxed{\textcircled{3}} \\ \vdots \end{pmatrix} \Rightarrow \mathbb{C}(\mathbb{S}) = \left(\boxed{\textcircled{1}\textcircled{2}}\boxed{\textcircled{3}}\boxed{\textcircled{1}\textcircled{3}}\boxed{\textcircled{2}}\boxed{\textcircled{1}}\boxed{\textcircled{2}}\boxed{\textcircled{3}}\cdots\right)$$

$$\zeta_1 = \begin{pmatrix}1\\1\\0\end{pmatrix}, \zeta_2 = \begin{pmatrix}0\\0\\1\end{pmatrix}, \zeta_3 = \begin{pmatrix}1\\0\\1\end{pmatrix}, \zeta_4 = \begin{pmatrix}0\\1\\0\end{pmatrix}, \zeta_5 = \begin{pmatrix}1\\0\\0\end{pmatrix}, \zeta_6 = \begin{pmatrix}0\\1\\0\end{pmatrix}, \zeta_7 = \begin{pmatrix}0\\0\\1\end{pmatrix}$$

$$\overset{\text{identification}}{=} \underbrace{\left(\boxed{\textcircled{1}\textcircled{2}}\boxed{\textcircled{1}}\boxed{\textcircled{2}}\boxed{\textcircled{2}}\right)}_{G_1} \cup \underbrace{\left(\boxed{\textcircled{1}\textcircled{3}}\boxed{\textcircled{3}}\boxed{\textcircled{3}}\right)}_{G_2} \cup \cdots$$

**Fig. 3.** Collection of samples $\mathbb{S}$, collection of clusters $\mathbb{C}(\mathbb{S})$ and group of clusters $\{G_c\}_{c=1}^k$. Note that $G_c$ is a multiset.

only MAP assignments, $Z^{\text{MAP}}$, we cannot estimate the probability of a vocabulary assigned to a cluster.

We exploit spectral clustering[8] to find the groups of clusters, $\{G_c\}_{c=1}^k$. Many studies have shown that spectral clustering outperforms traditional clustering algorithms. When we apply spectral clustering to $\mathbb{C}(\mathbb{S})$, a problem is the number of clusters in $\mathbb{C}(\mathbb{S})$, i.e. $|\mathbb{C}(\mathbb{S})|$, can be very large. For example, when the number of samples, $S$, is 200, and the average of the number of clusters in each sample is 50, then $|\mathbb{C}(\mathbb{S})|$ is roughly 10,000. This is too large for spectral clustering. Spectral clustering can handle up to thousands objects on typical PCs. The computational time and memory space of spectral clustering is the order of $|\mathbb{C}(\mathbb{S})|^2$. This is because spectral clustering requires to solve eigenvectors of a $|\mathbb{C}(\mathbb{S})|$ by $|\mathbb{C}(\mathbb{S})|$ affinity matrix.

### 4.3 Unique Spectral Clustering

We ease the problem by using the fact that $\mathbb{C}(\mathbb{S})$ contains many identical clusters, but we can still solve the exact problem. For example, in the case of Figure 4, $\mathbb{C}(\mathbb{S})$ contains both of $\boxed{\textcircled{2}}$ and $\boxed{\textcircled{3}}$ twice. We denote unique clusters in $\mathbb{C}(\mathbb{S})$ by $\tilde{\mathbb{C}}(\mathbb{S})$. Let $n$ be $|\mathbb{C}(\mathbb{S})|$ and $\tilde{n}$ be $|\tilde{\mathbb{C}}(\mathbb{S})|$. We show that the eigenvalue problem in spectral clustering can be solved in $O(\tilde{n}^2 + n)$ time and memory instead of $O(n^2)$. In our experiments, we actually observe $\tilde{n} \equiv |\tilde{\mathbb{C}}(\mathbb{S})|$ becomes just 34.0% of $n \equiv |\mathbb{C}(\mathbb{S})|$.

Algorithm 2 is the pseudo code of spectral clustering with the normalized cut algorithm [8]. In step 3 of Algorithm 2, we need to solve an eigenvalue problem. This requires $O(kn^2)$ computational time and memory space in a naive way where $k$ is the number of eigenvectors. But, we can reduce it to $O(k(n + \tilde{n}^2))$ using the following theorem.

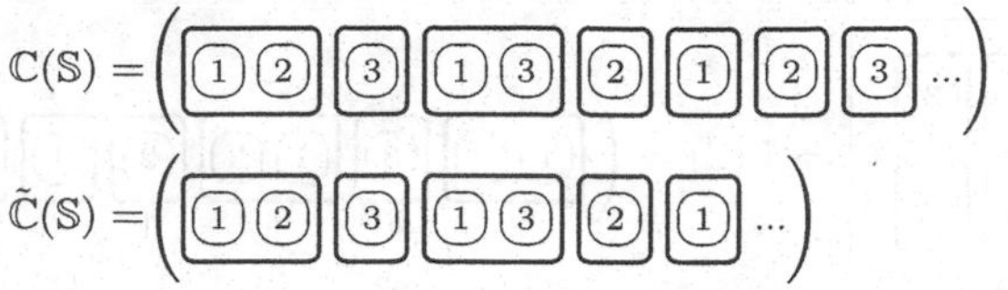

$\mathbb{C}(\mathbb{S}) = ( [1\,2]\ [3]\ [1\,3]\ [2]\ [1]\ [2]\ [3] \ldots )$

$\tilde{\mathbb{C}}(\mathbb{S}) = ( [1\,2]\ [3]\ [1\,3]\ [2]\ [1] \ldots )$

**Fig. 4.** Collection of all clusters $\mathbb{C}(\mathbb{S})$ and unique clusters $\tilde{\mathbb{C}}(\mathbb{S})$

---

**Algorithm 2.** Spectral Clustering with the Normalized Cut

1: Construct affinity matrix $W$, s.t. $W_{i,j}$ is the similarity of object $i$ and $j$, which takes a value between 0 and 1.
2: Calculate a normalized graph Laplacian, $L = I - D^{-\frac{1}{2}}WD^{-\frac{1}{2}}$ where $I$ is the identity matrix, and $D$ is a degree matrix which is diagonal with $D_{ii} = \sum_{j=1}^{n} W_{ij}$.
3: Obtain the $k$ smallest eigenvectors, $\{\boldsymbol{u}_1, ..., \boldsymbol{u}_k\}$ of $L$. Let $Y$ be a $k$ by $n$ matrix where $Y_{i,j} = \boldsymbol{u}_{i,j}/(\sum_{i'=1}^{k} \boldsymbol{u}_{i',j}^2)^{\frac{1}{2}}$.
4: Find assignments by k-means on $Y$ assuming each column of $Y$ is a mapped data point.

---

**Algorithm 3.** Proposed Algorithm

1: Collect samples $\mathbb{S}$ from a MCMC sampler.
2: Find unique clusters of $\mathbb{C}(\mathbb{S})$.
3: Construct $M$ and $\tilde{L}$.
4: Apply spectral clustering as if $M^T LM$ is a normalized graph Laplacian to find identified groups $\{G_c\}_{c=1}^{k}$ where $\bigcup_{c=1}^{k} G_c = \mathbb{C}(\mathbb{S})$.

---

**Theorem 1.** *Finding the k smallest eigenvectors of normalized graph Laplacian L requires $O(k(n+\tilde{n}^2))$ time and memory space where $n = |\mathbb{C}(\mathbb{S})|$ and $\tilde{n} = |\tilde{\mathbb{C}}(\mathbb{S})|$.*

*Proof.* $L$ is a $n$ by $n$ normalized graph Laplacian. $L$ has a $\tilde{n}$ by $\tilde{n}$ submatrix $\tilde{L}$ where $L = M^T\tilde{L}M$. $M$ is a sparse binary matrix s.t. $M_{i,j} = M_{i,j'} = 1$ if and only if $\zeta_j = \zeta_{j'}$ where $\zeta_j$ and $\zeta_{j'} \in \mathbb{C}(\mathbb{S})$. Thus, $L\boldsymbol{v} = M^T\tilde{L}M\boldsymbol{v}$ holds. This calculation requires $O(n+\tilde{n}^2)$. Typical algorithms for the eigenvector problem, e.g. the QR algorithm, just repeats the calculation. Clearly, memory space required the above computation is $O(k(n+\tilde{n}^2))$ as well. □

Directly from Theorem 1, the computational time of spectral clustering is also reduced to $O(k(n+\tilde{n}^2))$. We call the efficient spectral clustering *unique spectral clustering*. Again remember a solution given by the unique spectral clustering is the same as a solution given by a naive spectral clustering. In our experiments, in Section 5, we only use spectral clustering proposed by [8], but we can reduce computational complexity of other spectral clustering algorithms [9,10] as well.

Spectral clustering requires affinity matrix $W$ in step 1 of Algorithm 2. Thus, we need to define a similarity between cluster $\zeta_i$ and $\zeta_j$. Although we can use any similarities, we use *cosine* in this paper, i.e. $W_{i,j} = \cos(\zeta_i, \zeta_j) = \zeta_i^T\zeta_j/||\zeta_i||||\zeta_j||$.

Algorithm 3 summarizes the proposed algorithm.

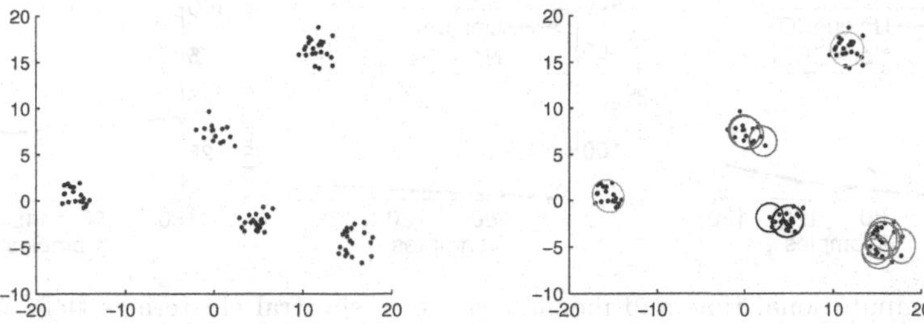

**Fig. 5.** A toy example of the proposed algorithm. The left figure shows input data, and the right is identified clusters, where ellipses that have the same color are assigned to one group. The identified groups are consistent with the five original crowds in the left plot.

# 5 Experiments

In this section, we show how the proposed identification works. We apply the proposed algorithm to two data sets, where one is synthetic and the other is real. We use the synthetic one for the evaluation of the proposed algorithm, and we show the tractability and identified groups by using the real one.

## 5.1 Quality of Identification

In general, it is not trivial to evaluate clustering results because data to be clustered does not typically have labels. It is also non-trivial to evaluate the proposed algorithm for the same reason. In this paper, we only use an ideal synthetic data set for which we easily evaluate the quality of identification done by the proposed algorithm. The data set is shown in the left plot of Figure 5, which consists of five crowds of points. Thus, the ideal grouping of clusters will find groups consistent with the five crowds.

We first collect samples with the Gibbs sampler for a Dirichlet process Gaussian mixture [3], then apply the identification algorithm to find groups of clusters of the sampler. In this experiment, we know the ideal number of groups is five. Thus, we use five as the input of the identification algorithm to identify five groups. Ellipses in the right plot in Figure 5 are clusters sampled by the sampler. Ellipses, i.e. clusters, that have the same color are assigned to one group. For example, the sampler drew many clusters, shown as ellipses, for the right-bottom crowd in the right plot in Figure 5. The algorithm grouped the clusters into one group, which is actually an ideal grouping.

As the right plot in Figure 5 shows, the discovered groups are completely consistent with the five crowds. From this experiment, it seems the proposed algorithm works well on an ideal case.

## 5.2 Tractability of the Identification Algorithm on Real Data

In this section, we apply the identification algorithm to a real data set. First of all, we show the proposed algorithm can handle much more samples than a

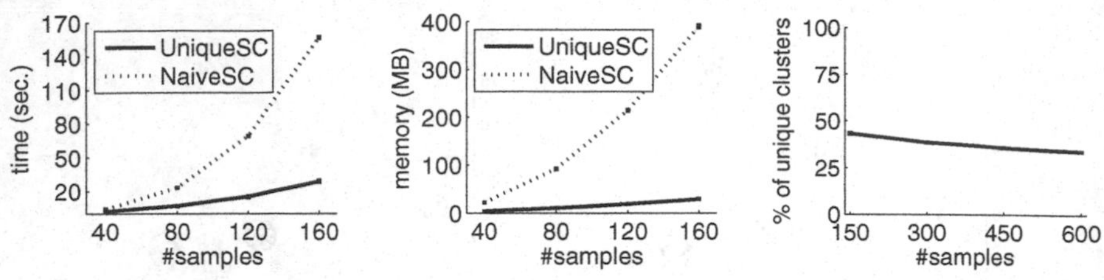


**Fig. 6.** Computational time and memory space of spectral clusterings (left and middle, respectively) and the percentage of unique clusters in $\mathbb{C}(\mathbb{S})$ (right). The standard deviations are shown on these figures although they are too small to be visible.

naive algorithm on a real data set. Next, we apply the identification algorithm to vocabulary clustering. We estimate the probability of a vocabulary assigned to an identified cluster, and show representatives of each cluster, which is impossible without identification.

The data we use is search query log data. The analysis of query data has become very important. It is clearly useful to improve search quality. Another example is the improvement of advertisement on the web. As the market of advertisement on the web grows, advertisers need to choose word on which they put advertisements, to maximize benefits from advertisements. In many cases, each query consists of couple words instead of a single word, e.g. "weather Tokyo". Thus, analysis of pairs of words in a single query is expected to discover informative structure of words.

We collected the data on SearchSpy `http://www.dogpile.com/info.dogpl/searchspy` from January 2007 to April 2007, In this period, we observed more than million vocabularies, but we omit vocabularies which are not used more than 1,600 times for our experiments. Finally, we use 4,058 vocabularies for clustering.

We apply a relational clustering to the data. We construct a binary matrix, $R$, where $R_{i,j} = 1$ if and only if vocabulary $i$ and vocabulary $j$ are used in the same query. We use the infinite relational model (IRM)[11,12] as a relational clustering algorithm, which utilizes the Dirichlet process. We run a Gibbs sampler for the IRM, which is described in Appendix A.2.

**Tractability.** We first compare the unique spectral clustering proposed in Section 4 with a naive spectral clustering because the tractability of spectral clustering leads to the tractability of the identification algorithm. The results are shown in Figure 6. We vary the number of samples, $|\mathbb{S}|$, from 40 to 160 in the left and middle figures, and from 150 to 600 in the right figure. For each $|\mathbb{S}|$, we run two spectral clustering algorithms 10 times. Figure 6 shows the average and the standard deviation of 10 trials. The left and middle figures in Figure 6 show the computational time and memory space of two spectral clustering algorithms. When the number of samples is 160, the unique spectral clustering is 5.5 times faster than the naive algorithm, and needs only less than 10% memory space of the naive one. The right figure in Figure 6 depicts the percentage of unique

**Table 1.** 10 representative vocabularies in identified clusters, $G_7$ and $G_{39}$. It seems $G_7$ consists of the names of places and something relating to places, and $G_{39}$ includes possible properties of $G_7$.

| | |
|---|---|
| $G_7$ | ca, atlanta, carolina, alabama, nc, kansas, nj, colorado, fort, pennsylvania, ... |
| $G_{39}$ | owner, lakes, lottery, avenue, zoo, landscape, camping, comfort, flights, hilton, ... |

samples in $\mathbb{C}(\mathbb{S})$. When the number of samples is 600, it is 34.0%. At this point, $n$ ($\equiv |\mathbb{C}(\mathbb{S})|$) reaches 24,000. Thus, the naive spectral clustering needs to solve the eigenvalue problem of a 24,000 by 24,000 matrix, which does not even fit into 4 GB memory even when the matrix is constructed in a sparse representation. On the other hand, unique SC only need to solve approximately 8,200 by 8,200 matrix, which is still tractable, i.e. $\tilde{n} \equiv |\tilde{\mathbb{C}}(\mathbb{S})| = 8200$. In this paper, we show the tractability only by experiments. Unfortunately, it does not seem very easy to show the reduction of $\tilde{n}$ from $n$ in theory.

**Identified Clusters.** We applied the proposed algorithm to 300 samples drawn from a Gibbs sampler to identify clusters. The gross number of clusters and the number of unique clusters in 300 samples are approximately 12,000 and 4,800, respectively. Since the average number of clusters in the 300 samples is 40, we identify 40 groups, i.e. 40 is the input parameter of the spectral clustering. Proposed unique spectral clustering takes two minutes for this data. As an example, we pick up $G_7$ and $G_{39}$. Their representative vocabularies are listed in Table 1. These vocabularies have probability one to be assigned to either of $G_7$ or $G_{39}$. The assignment probability can be estimated by the identification of a number of samples of $p(Z|X)$. In other words, the probability cannot be estimated only by $Z^{\text{MAP}}$.

The inference by the IRM tells that they likely to make co-occurrences, i.e. vocabularies in $G_7$ and $G_{39}$ are used in the same search query with relatively high probability. Actually, one can imagine situations to use these vocabularies simultaneously as a search query.

## 6 Discussion

We have proposed unique spectral clustering which is efficient for samples of a MCMC sampler. One may think we can also apply k-means, which has linear computational time and memory space. In this case, $\zeta_i$ is used as a feature vector of the $i$-th cluster. However, k-means does not necessarily fit to $\{\zeta_i\}_{i=1}^n$. This is because $\zeta_i$ is represented as a binary vector, while k-means is derived from a mixture of spherical multivariate Gaussians.

We have used *cosine* as a similarity measure for clusters. But, we can use other similarities as well. For example, similarity$(\zeta_i, \zeta_j) \equiv 1 - \text{HammingDist}(\zeta_i, \zeta_j)/d$ is also available where $d$ is the length of vector $\zeta_i$. We leave the study of other similarities as future work.

## 7 Conclusion

For clustering problems, we have pointed out many studies use just maximum a posteriori (MAP) assignments even when they use MCMC samplers. This is because it is not straightforward to recognize clusters with many samples from $p(Z|X)$. Thus, we have proposed an identification algorithm which constructs groups of clusters. Each group is recognized as the distribution of a cluster. We apply spectral clustering to group clusters. Although a naive spectral clustering algorithm is intractable due to memory space and computational time, we developed a memory-and-time efficient spectral clustering for samples of a MCMC sampler. In experiments, we have first applied the proposed algorithm to an ideal data set, and seen it works well. Next, we have shown the proposed algorithm is tractable for real data, search query log, although the naive algorithm is actually intractable. For the query log, we have also exhibited representative vocabularies of clusters, which cannot be chosen by just MAP assignments.

## References


1. Ferguson, T.: A bayesian analysis of some nonparametric problems. The Annals of Statistics 1, 209–230 (1973)
2. Antoniak, C.: Mixtures of Dirichlet processes with applications to bayesian nonparametric problems. The Annals of Statistics 2, 1152–1174 (1974)
3. Rasmussen, C.E.: The infinite gaussian mixture model. In: Solla, S.A., Leen, T.K., Muller, K.R. (eds.) Advances in Neural Information Processing Systems, vol. 12, pp. 554–560. MIT Press, Cambridge (2000)
4. Teh, Y.W., Jordan, M., Beal, M.J., Blei, D.M.: Hierarchical dirichlet processes. Journal of the American Statistical Association 101(476), 1566–1581 (2006)
5. Liang, P., Jordan, M.I., Taskar, B.: A permutation-augmented sampler for DP mixture models. In: Ghahramani, Z. (ed.) Proceedings of the 24th Annual International Conference on Machine Learning, pp. 545–552. Omnipress (2007)
6. Blei, D.M., Jordan, M.I.: Variational inference for dirichlet process mixtures. Bayesian Analysis 1(1), 121–144 (2005)
7. Kurihara, K., Welling, M., Vlassis, N.: Accelerated variational dirichlet process mixtures. Advances in Neural Information Processing Systems 19 (2007)
8. Ng, A.Y., Jordan, M.I., Weiss, Y.: On spectral clustering: Analysis and an algorithm. Advances in Neural Information Processing Systems 14 (2002)
9. Hagen, L., Kahng, A.B.: New spectral methods for ratio cut partitioning and clustering. IEEE Transactions on Computer-Aided Design of Integrated Circuits and Systems 11(9), 1074–1085 (1992)
10. Shi, J., Malik, J.: Normalized cuts and image segmentation. IEEE Transactions on Pattern Analysis and Machine Intelligence 22(8), 888–905 (2000)
11. Kemp, C., Tenenbaum, J.B., Griffiths, T.L., Yamada, T., Ueda, N.: Learning systems of concepts with an infinite relational model. In: AAAI, AAAI Press, Menlo Park (2006)
12. Xu, Z., Volker Tresp, K.Y., Kriegel, H.P.: Learning infinite hidden relational models. In: Proceedings of the 22nd International Conference on Uncertainty in Artificial Intelligence (2006)

# Appendix

## A Infinite Relational Models

Kemp et al. [11] and Xu et al. [12] independently proposed infinite relational models (IRMs). IRMs are a general model for clustering relational data. For example, when we have relational data consisting of people and relation "like", the IRM clusters people based on relation "like". People in one cluster share the same probability to "like" people in another cluster. In the following section, we describe a special case of the IRM, which we use in our experiments.

### A.1 Generative Model of the IRM

The generative model of the IRM is given in (5)–(7). It samples assignment $Z$ first of all. Next, $\eta$ is sampled from the beta distribution for $1 \le s \le t \le K$. Finally, $R$ is observed from the Bernoulli distribution with parameter $\eta$. $R(i,j) = 1$ means word i and word j are used in the same query, and $R(i,j) = 0$ means they are not used in the same query. This process is summarized as,

$$Z|\gamma \sim \mathrm{DP}(Z;\gamma) \tag{5}$$

$$\eta_{s,t}|\beta \sim \mathrm{Beta}(\eta_{s,t};\beta,\beta) \quad \text{for } 1 \le s \le t \le K \tag{6}$$

$$R(i,j)|z_i, z_j, \eta \sim \mathrm{Bern}(R(i,j);\eta(s,j)) \quad \text{for } 1 \le i \le j \le W. \tag{7}$$

Marginalizing out $\eta$, we obtain the marginal likelihood of the IRM as,

$$p(R,Z) = \prod_{1 \le s \le t \le K} \frac{B(m_{s,t}+\beta, N_s N_t - m_{s,t}+\beta)}{B(\beta,\beta)} DP(Z), \tag{8}$$

where $m_{s,t} = |\{(i,j)|R_{ij} = 1,\ Z_{i,s} = 1 \ \&\ Z_{j,t} = 1\}|$ and $N_s = \sum_i Z_{i,s}$.

### A.2 Inference for the IRM

Our task is clustering. Thus, what we want to do by the IRM is to infer $Z$ given $R$. We use the Gibbs sampler for the inference. To utilize the Gibbs sampler, we need a posterior distribution of $Z$ for each word, $p(Z_{i,u} = 1|Z^{\neg i}, R)$ where $Z^{\neg i}$ is assignments except for word $i$. We notice $p(Z_{i,u} = 1|Z^{\neg i}, R) \propto p(R,Z)$. Thus, we can use (8) for the Gibss sampler[2],

$$p(Z_{i,u} = 1|Z^{\neg i}, R) \propto \begin{cases} \prod_{1 \le s \le t \le K} B(m_{s,t}+\beta, N_s N_t - m_{s,t}+\beta)(N_u - 1) \\ \qquad \text{(if } u \text{ is an existing cluster)} \\ \prod_{1 \le s \le t \le K} B(m_{s,t}+\beta, N_s N_t - m_{s,t}+\beta)\gamma \\ \qquad \text{(if } u \text{ is a new cluster).} \end{cases} \tag{9}$$

[2] For efficiency, it should be better to simplify $p(Z_{i,u} = 1|Z^{\neg i}, R)$ than (9).

# TGC-Tree: An Online Algorithm Tracing Closed Itemset and Transaction Set Simultaneously

Junbo Chen and Bo Zhou

Department of Computer Science, ZheJiang University
Room 5035, Dorm 10, YuQuan Campus, Zhejiang University,
Hangzhou City, Zhejiang Province, China
chjb@zju.edu.cn
bzhou@cs.zju.edu.cn

**Abstract.** Finding Association Rules is a classical data mining task. The most critical part of Association Rules Mining is about finding the frequent itemsets in the database. Since the introduction of the famouse Apriori algorithm [14], many others have been proposed to find the frequent itemsets. Among all the algorithms, the approach of mining *closed itemsets* has arisen a lot of interests in data mining community, because the closed itemsets are the condensed representation of all the frequent itemsets. The algorithms taking this approach include TITANIC [8], CLOSET+ [6], DCI-Closed [4], FCI-Stream [3], GC-Tree [15], etc. While the above algorithms are trying to improve the performance of finding the *Intents* of *Formal Concepts* (in anther word, the closed *itemsets*), they missed another important information: the *Extents* of *Formal Concepts*. In this paper, we propose an online algorithm, TGC-Tree, which is adapted from the GC-Tree algorithm [15], that could be used to trace the closed itemsets(Intents) and the corresponding transaction sets(Extents) simultaneously in an incremental way.

## 1 Introduction

Frequent closed itemsets is a complete and condensed representation for all the frequent itemsets. It is an application of the *FCA(Formal Concept Analysis)* in data mining. The following gives the definitions of *Formal Context, Formal Concept, Closed Itemset, etc.*:

A triple $(G, M, I)$ is called a *Formal Context* if $G$ and $M$ are sets and $I \subseteq G \times M$ is a binary relation between G and M. We call the elements of $G$ *Objects*, those of $M$ *Attributes*, and $I$ the *Incidence* of the context $(G, M, I)$. For $A \subseteq G$, we define

$$f(A) = \{m \in M \mid (g, m) \in I, \forall g \in A\}$$

and dually, for $B \subseteq M$,

$$h(B) = \{g \in G \mid (g, m) \in I, \forall m \in B\}$$

A pair $(A, B)$ is called a *Formal Concept* if and only if

$$A \subseteq G, B \subseteq M, f(A) = B, h(B) = A$$

$A$ is called the *Extent* and $B$ is called the *Intent* of the concept $(A, B)$.

T. Tokunaga and A. Ortega (Eds.): LKR 2008, LNAI 4938, pp. 38–50, 2008.

In Data Mining, the elements of $G$ is termed *Transactions* and those of $M$ is termed *Items*. Each $A \subseteq G$ is called *Transaction Set*, each $B \subseteq M$ is called *Itemset*, and the support of an itemset $B$ is the number of transactions that contains $B$.

**Definition 1.** *An itemset $X$ is said to be closed if and only if $C(X) = f(h(X)) = f \circ h(X) = X$ where the composite function $C = f \circ h$ is called a Galois operator or a closure operator.*

We could see that the closed itemset is actually the *Intent* of a specific *Formal Concept*.

We consider the closed itemsets as a condensed representation of all the frequent itemsets because the closure operator $C$ defines a series equivalence classes in the search space, each of which contains many frequent itemsets, however, only one of of them, the "biggest" one, is *Closed Itemsets* and it contains all the information about the specific equivalence class. Extensive researches have been carried out in this area, in the following they are split to four categories :

Both A-Close [12] and TITANIC [8] exploit a level-wise process to discover closed itemsets through a breadth-first search strategy. In each iteration, they try to search for candidates of MGs (Minimum Generators) with the help of search space pruning technique, and then verify them. Finally the MGs are used to generate all the closed itesmsets . Usually these algorithms are required to scan the whole dataset many times.

For CLOSET [13] and CLOSET+ [6]. With the help of high compact data structure FP-Tree, they try to project the global extraction context to some smaller sub-contexts, and then apply FCI mining process recursively on these sub-context. Better performance can be achieved than the adoption of A-close and TITANIC algorithms.

CHARM [7] and DCI-Closed [4] exploit hybrid techniques which try to use the properties of both previous mentioned techniques. Due to a data structure called IT-Tree, CHARM simultaneously explores both the closed itemset space and transaction space, with the depth-first search strategy, and generates one candidate each time, then with tidset intersection and subsumption checking, it will see whether the candidate is closed. DCI-Closed could be considered as an improvement of CHARM.

FCI_Stream [3] and GC-Tree are online algorithms which performs the closure checking over a data stream sliding window. FCI_Stream uses a in memory data structure called DIU-tree to store all the Closed Itemsets discovered so far. With a specific search space pruning technique, it tries to perform the time consuming closure checking operation only when it's really needed. GC-Tree maintains a tree like structure in the memory. All closed itemset is represented as a node in the tree, and every path from the root to a node in the tree is an order preserving sequence, the definition of "order preserving" could be found in DCI-Closed [4], of closed itemsets.

All the above researches are focused on the *Intents* of the *Formal Concepts*. As far as we know, there's no algorithms paying attention to the *Extents* so far. So, in this paper, we propose an algorithm, TGC-Tree, that could trace the *Intents* and the *Extents* simultaneously and incrementally. This algorithm is potentially useful for many applications. For example, in addition to find association rules, it could answer another interesting question: to which users could these rules be applied? Another example is, this algorithm could be adapted to be a two-mode clustering algorithm.

The rest of this paper is organized as follows. Section 2 introduces the GC-Tree, which is the basic of TGC-Tree, and describes the notations to be used throughout the paper. Section 3 gives a simple example. Section 4 presents the proposed TGC-Tree algorithm. The performance evaluation is depicted in Section 5. Finally, section 6 gives the conclusion of this paper.

## 2 GC-Tree

GC-Tree is a tree like structure maintaining all the closed itemsets in the current sliding window as nodes. The idea of GC-Tree is based on the following theorem which is introduced by Claudio Lucchese *et al* [4]:

**Theorem 1.** *For each closed itemset* $Y \neq C(\emptyset)$*, there exists one and only one sequence of* $n(n \geq 1)$ *items* $i_0 \prec i_1 \prec \ldots \prec i_{n-1}$ *such that* $\{gen_0, gen_1, \ldots, gen_{n-1}\} = \{Y_0 \cup i_0, Y_1 \cup i_1, \ldots, Y_{n-1} \cup i_{n-1}\}$ *where the various* $gen_i$ *are order preserving generators, with* $Y_0 = C(\emptyset), Y_{j+1} = C(Y_j \cup i_j) \forall j \in [0, n-1]$ *and* $Y = Y_n$.

When we say a generator is order preserving, we mean:

**Definition 2.** *A generator* $X = Y \cup i$*, where* $Y$ *is a closed itemset and* $i \notin Y$ *, is said to be order preserving one iff* $i \prec (C(X) - X)$.

All through this paper, we'll use the concept "preset" and "posset" everywhere. The following is the definition:

**Definition 3.** *Let* $gen = Y \cup i$ *be a generator of a closed itemset where* $Y$ *is a closed itemset and* $i \notin Y$ *. preset(gen) is defined as* $\{j \prec i | j \notin gen\}$*. posset(gen) is defined as* $\{j \in \mathcal{I} | j \notin preset(gen)$ *and* $j \notin C(gen)\}$.

And the following rule is a shortcut used to check whether a generator is order preserving:

**Lemma 1.** *Let* $gen = Y \cup i$ *be a generator of a closed itemset where* $Y$ *is a closed itemset and* $i \notin Y$*. gen is not order preserving iff* $\exists j \in preset(gen)$*, such that* $h(gen) \subseteq h(j)$.

GC-Tree works under the data stream sliding window environment. This algorithm uses an in memory data structure called GC-Tree (Generator and frequent Closed itemsets Tree) to store all the frequent closed itemsets in the current sliding window. Each element in The GC-Tree has the following format: $< gen, eitem, clo >$[1]. Where $gen$ is the *closure generator*, $eitem$ is the extension item with which $gen$ used to extend another closed itemset[2], *clo* is the corresponding *closed itemset*[3].

GC-Tree is lexicographically ordered, for each closed itemset, there exists a path in GC-Tree from the root to the specific node which represents the closed itemset. All the elements in this path compose the order preserving generator sequence $\{gen_0, gen_1, \ldots, gen_{n-1}\}$ mentioned in Theorem 1.

---

[1] For the concision of representation, we omit the links between the parents and children, and the support of the closed itemsets.

[2] $eitem$ is the item $i$ in Definition 2.

[3] The GC-Tree Node may be written in the compact way in the rest of this paper: $< gen, clo >$.

GC-Tree also introduces a series of *Stopping Rules, Node Generation Rules and Node Pruning Rules* to avoid redundant computations, so that the tree could be maintained efficiently.

## 3 A Simple Example

In this section, we demonstrate a simple example, which based on a synthetic movie database that displayed in Table 1.

**Table 1.** Movie Database

| Customer Id | Die Hard | 007 | Indiana Johns | Matrix | Star War | A.I. | E.T. |
|---|---|---|---|---|---|---|---|
| 1 | 1 | 1 | 1 | 1 | 1 | | |
| 2 | 1 | 1 | 1 | 1 | 1 | | |
| 3 | 1 | 1 | 1 | 1 | 1 | | |
| 4 | | | | 1 | 1 | 1 | 1 |
| 5 | | | | 1 | 1 | 1 | 1 |
| 6 | | | | 1 | 1 | 1 | 1 |
| 7 | 1 | 1 | 1 | 1 | 1 | 1 | 1 |
| 8 | 1 | 1 | 1 | 1 | 1 | 1 | 1 |
| 9 | 1 | 1 | 1 | 1 | 1 | 1 | 1 |
| 10 | | | | 1 | 1 | | |
| 11 | | | | 1 | 1 | | |
| 12 | | | | 1 | 1 | | |

In this synthetic database, there're two types of movies: sci-fi and action. "Die Hard", "007" and "Indiana Johns" are assumed to be purely action movies, "A.I." and "E.T." are purely sci-fi movies, "Matrix" and "Star War" are action and sci-fi movies.

If we give id "1,2,3,4,5,6,7" to the movies "Die Hard, 007, Indiana Johns, Matrix, Star War, A.I., E.T." respectively. Then, by the definition of *Formal Concept*, there're 4 formal concepts in this movie database(See Table 2).

**Table 2.** Formal Concepts

| Formal Concept Comment | Extent | Intent |
|---|---|---|
| action movie | 1, 2, 3, 7, 8, 9 | 1, 2, 3, 4, 5 |
| sci-fi movie | 4, 5, 6, 7, 8, 9 | 4, 5, 6, 7 |
| action and sci-fi movie | 7, 8, 9 | 1, 2, 3, 4, 5, 6, 7 |
| action or sci-fi movie | 1, 2, 3, 4, 5, 6, 7, 8, 9, 10, 11, 12 | 4, 5 |

The Extents are customer id sets, and the Intents are movie id sets. Now, Let's take a look at the result of GC-Tree algorithm running on the synthetic movie database:

The first part of each node is the generator, and the second part is the closed itemset. Through Table 2 and Figure1, it's reasonable to make the assumption that each closed itemset is actually the intent of a formal concept. The dual assumption is each closed

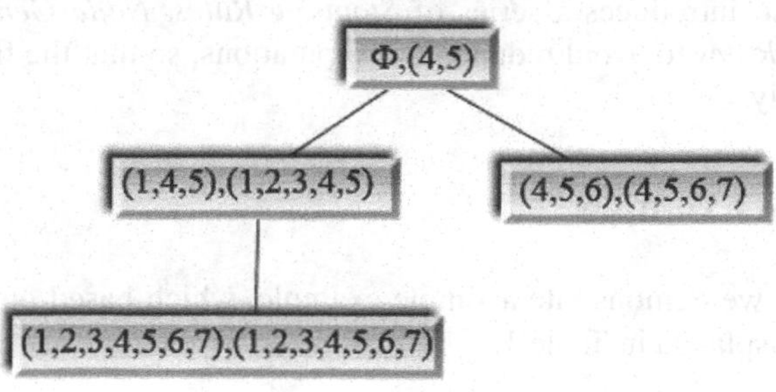


**Fig. 1.** GC-Tree

transaction set is the extent of a formal concept. In the following section of this paper, we will prove the assumptions, and give an algorithm to maintain both the intent and extent of the formal concept simultaneously.

# 4 The Tgc-Tree Algorithm

## 4.1 Algorithm Overview

In this section, we will first give the definition of the closed transaction sets, then prove that there exists a one-to-one mapping from the closed itemsets to the closed transaction sets.

**Definition 4.** *An transaction set A is said to be closed if and only if* $h(f(A)) = h \circ f(A) = A$.

**Theorem 2.** *There's a one to one mapping from Closed ItemSets to Closed Transaction Sets.*

*Proof:*

First, we proof there's a one to one map from closed itemsets to formal concepts:

For each closed itemset $B$, it satisfies $f(h(B)) = f \circ h(B) = B$. Let $A = h(B)$, we have: $h(B) = A$ and $f(A) = B$, that is, $(h(B), B)$ is a formal concept.

For each Formal Concept (A,B), we have, $f(A) = B$ and $h(B) = A$, that is $f(A) = f(h(B)) = B$, so the intent of the formal concept is the closed itemset.

This finishes the proof that there's a one to one map from closed itemsets to formal concepts.

Similarly, there's a one-to-one map from closed transaction set to formal concepts.

Finally, there's a one-to-one map from the closed itemsets to the closed transaction sets, the mapping function is actually the formal concepts (A,B), if we treat them as binary relations. The closed itemsets are the intents of the formal concepts while the closed transaction sets are the extents of them.

From the discussion above, we could find that there's a *dual tree* of *GC-Tree*, which is composed of closed transaction sets. For the example given in *Section 3*, the *dual tree* and the relation between the *dual tree* and the *origin tree* could be demonstrated in Figure 2.

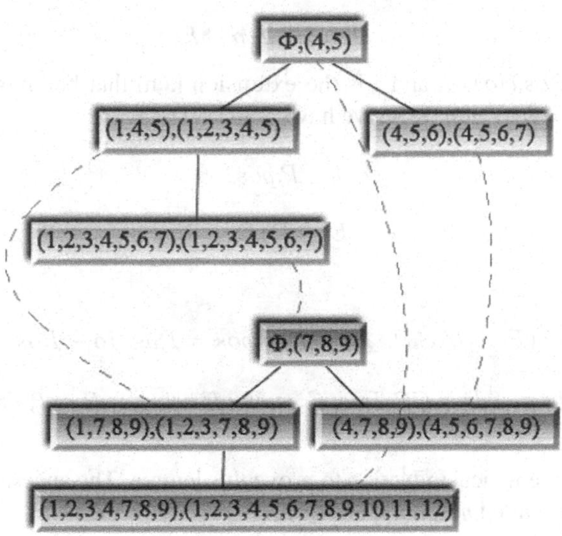


**Fig. 2.** TGC-Tree

The tree with blue nodes is the *GC-Tree of closed itemsets* and the one with red nodes is the *GC-Tree of closed transaction sets*. The red dashed lines connect the *Intents* and the *Extents* of the specific formal concepts.

**Definition 5.** *TGC-Tree is composed of three components: First, the GC-Tree of closed itemsets, which we called I-Tree. Second, the GC-Tree of closed transaction sets, which we called T-Tree. Third, a bidirectional mapping function(the formal concepts) connects nodes in both tree.*

The construction and maintenance of *I-Tree* is described in detail in [15]. In the following sections, we give the rules how to construct and maintain the *T-Tree* efficiently.

### 4.2 Add a Transaction to the Database

When a new transaction is added into the database, both *I-Tree* and *T-Tree* need to be updated. The rules about how to update *I-Tree* is introduced in [15]. In this paper, we focus on how to update the *T-Tree*.

When a new transaction is added, there're two kinds of changes will happen in *T-Tree*: One is adding new nodes into the tree which represent the new closed transaction sets; the Other is updating the existing nodes in the tree.

### 4.2.1 Add New Nodes

Following we give the rule of how to add a closed transaction set[4] to T-Tree.

**Lemma 2.** *Let P be a node in GC-Tree, C be an child node of P, then, C.clo - P.pos = P.clo*

*Proof:*

$$C.clo = C.gen \cup E$$

Here, $C.gen = Pos.clo \cup i$, and $i$ is the extension item that belongs to $P.pos$, $E = \{j \in P.pos | h(j) \supseteq h(C.gen)\}$. So we have

$$i \in P.pos$$

$$E \subset P.pos$$

Thus

$$C.clo - P.pos = (Pos.clo \cup i \cup E) - Pos.pos = Pos.clo - Pos.pos = Pos.clo$$

**Lemma 3.** *Let P be a node in GC-Tree, C be an offspring node of P, then, C.clo - P.pos = P.clo*

*Proof:* We use mathematical induction to prove this lemma. The ancestor of a node with $n$ midway nodes is called *n-depth ancestor*.

*The basic step*:

If $P$ is 0-depth ancestor of $C$, i.e. $P$ is the parent of $C$. For this situation, we have proved it in Lemma 2.

*The inductive step*:

Let $M$ be the m-depth ancestor of $C$, and the statement of Lemma 3 holds for $M$. Let $P$ be the (m+1)-depth ancestor of $C$, i.e. $P$ is the parent of $M$. Then, we have:

$$M.clo = C.clo - M.pos$$

$$P.clo = M.clo - P.pos$$

$$M.pos \subset P.pos$$

Thus

$$P.clo = (C.clo - M.pos) - P.pos = C.clo - P.pos$$

Proof Done.

**Lemma 4.** *Let clo_set be a closed set in the database, for any given node N in GC-Tree, there's at most one child of N, denoted C, satisfies C.clo = clo_set - C.pos*

*Proof:*

If there exist two children of $N$, denoted $C1$ and $C2$, let's say, $C1$ is a left sibling of $C2$, that satisfy the statement of Lemma 4, then we have:

[4] Actually, this rule is applicable for I-Tree as well.

$$C1.clo = clo\_set - C1.pos$$

$$C2.clo = clo\_set - C2.pos$$

Since $C1.eitem \in C1.clo$, thus

$$C1.eitem \in clo\_set$$

From the definition of *posset*, we have $C1.eitem \notin C2.pos$, thus

$$C1.eitem \in C2.clo$$

Because $C1$ is the left sibling of $C2$, so that $C1.eitem \in C2.pre$, thus, $C2.gen = N.clo \cup C2.eitem$ is not order preserving according to Lemma 1. But $C2$ is a node in GC-Tree, so that $C2.gen$ must be order preserving, this is a contradiction.

This finishes the proof.

According to Lemma 2,3 and 4, we have the following conclusion: Given a node $C$, if and only if a node $N$ is an ancestor of $C$, that it satisfies the condition $N.clo = C.clo - N.pos$. This observation leads to the following rule.

**Rule 1.** *Let clo_set be a new closed set, tree be the GC-Tree contains all the closed sets found so far. In order to add a new node into the tree for the clo_set, we identify all the ancestors of clo_set by the following rule*

$$N.clo = clo\_set - N.pos$$

*The test begins from the root of the tree, if the root passes, then test all its children, and so on. The last N passes the test is the parent of the new node, denoted P, and the attributes of the new node are*

$$NN.gen = P.clo \cup eitem(eitem = \min\{clo\_set - P.clo\})$$

$$NN.clo = clo\_set$$

$$NN.pre = \{i \in M | i \prec NN.eitem, i \notin clo\_set\}$$

$$NN.pos = \{i \in M | i \notin NN.pre, i \notin NN.clo\}$$

#### 4.2.2 Update Existing Nodes

Following we give the rule of how to update existing nodes in the T-Tree.

When a new transaction is added, if the transaction contains a specific *Intent* of a formal concept which is represented as a node in *I-Tree*, the corresponding node in the *T-Tree* represents the *Extent* should be expanded with the id of the new transaction.

**Lemma 5.** *Let $N$ be the node that is expanded with transaction id tid, then, if tid $\prec$ $N.eitem$, $N.gen$ remains order preserving.*

*Proof:*
The proof is obvious, since $tid \notin N.pre$

Lemma 5 leads to the following rule:

**Rule 2.** *When a new transaction is added to the database, the updating of the nodes in T-Tree begins from the root of the tree. If the new transaction contains the corresponding Intent of a given node* $N$*, then expand* $N.clo$ *with the id of the new transaction tid. If* $tid \prec N.eitem$*, then keep on looking its children, else, relocate* $N$ *to the tree according to Rule 1.*

According to Lemma 6, If $Y \nsubseteq t$, and $t \in T_1$ $Y$ will remain closed/un-closed in T2 as in T1. So, we simply omit this situation, too.

### 4.2.3 Pseudo Code

The pseudo code is composed of three parts, the first part in Table 3 is the code used to updating the existing nodes in the *T-Tree*, the second part in Table 4 is used to add new closed transaction sets to the tree, the third part in Table 5 is a utility function used by both part one and part two.

**Table 3.** T-Tree−Updating

```
1:  procedure update(t, curr)
2:     if(t ⊇ curr.intent.clo)
3:        curr.clo = curr.clo ∪ t.id;
4:        if(t.id ≺ curr.eitem)
5:           remove the subtree curr from T − Tree;
6:           expand all the nodes in the subtree with tid;
7:           relocateSubtree(curr);
8:           return;
9:        else
10:           curr.pos = curr.pos − t.id;
11:    for all (child of curr node)
12:       update(t,child);
```

The code in table 3 is a recursive function which is initially invoked as update(t,root), t is the added transaction and root is the root of *T-Tree*. The recursive invocation of this method is actually a pre-order iteration through the tree. When the iteration meet a node $curr$ that satisfies $t \supseteq curr.intent.clo$, $curr.intent$ is the corresponding node in the *I-Tree* which denotes the *Intent* of the specific *Formal Concept*, that means the *Extent* of the *Formal Concept* should include the new transaction. So, we call $curr.clo = curr.clo \cup t.id$ in line 3. After $tid$ is added to the $curr.clo$, if $tid \prec curr.eitem$, then, $curr.gen$ is no longer order preserving, so, we remove the subtree represented by $curr$, add $tid$ to every node of it, then try to relocate the subtree in the proper position in *T-Tree*. Else, $curr.gen$ is still order preserving, so $curr$ remains where it is.

The code in Table 4 is used to add a new node in the *T-Tree*. The 'clo_set' is the *extent* of the corresponding new node added to the *I-Tree*, e.g. whenever a new node added to *I-Tree* [5], *TGC-Tree* calculates the union of the *extents* of all the nodes in *I-Tree*

[5] [15] describes when and how to add new node to $I - Tree$.

**Table 4.** T-Tree–Add New Node

```
procedure add(clo_set)
   create empty node N
   N.clo ⟵ clo_set;
   relocateSubtree(N);
```

which satisfies $node.clo \supset newNode.clo$ and the id of the new transaction, the result is 'clo_set'. Then the procedure *add(clo_set)* is invoked to add the new *extent* to *T-Tree*.

**Table 5.** T-Tree–Relocation

```
1:  procedure relocateSubtree(subRoot)
2:     N ⟵ root;
3:     while(∃child of N, child.clo = subRoot.clo – child.clo)
4:        N ⟵ child;
5:     insert subRoot as a child of N;
6:     subRoot.eitem ⟵ min{subRoot.clo – N.clo};
7:     for all child of subRoot
8:        if(child.eitem ∉ subRoot.pos)
9:           remove child from tree
10:          relocateSubtree(child)
11:    for all child of N
12:       if(subRoot.clo = child.clo – subRoot.pos)
13:          remove child from tree
14:          relocateSubtree(child)
```

The code in Table 5 is used to relocate an updated node and all its offsprings in *T-Tree*. First, it finds the parent of the given node(line 2-4), insert it as a child(line 5). Second, it checks all the children of the given node, if any of them is not order preserving, relocate it(line 7-10). Third, it checks all the children of the parent node, if any of them could be a child of the given node, relocate it(line 11-14).

### 4.3 Delete a Transaction from the Database

Deleting a transaction from the database is a dual problem of Adding a transaction. We give the rules below, the proofs are similar with the ones for adding a transaction.

#### 4.3.1 Delete Nodes

**Rule 3.** *Whenever a node is deleted in* I-Tree, *the corresponding node in* T-Tree *is deleted, all the children of the deleted node need relocation.*

#### 4.3.2 Update Existing Nodes

**Rule 4.** *When an old transaction is deleted from the database, the updating of the nodes in T-Tree begins from the root of the tree. If the current node $N$ contains the id of the deleted transaction tid, then delete tid from N.clo. If $tid = N.eitem$, then relocate $N$ to the tree according to Rule 1.*

### 4.4 The Computational Complexity

Let $N$ be the number of nodes need to be added/deleted, $M$ be the number of nodes to be relocated, $H$ be the height of the tree, $S$ be the average number of children of each node. The computational complexity is $\mathcal{O}((N + M)HS)$, it's a pretty small number compared to the number of all the closed sets which is $\mathcal{O}(S^H)$.

## 5 Performance Evaluation

We compared our algorithm with GC-Tree[15] and CFI-Stream[3], the result shows that with a small extra effort, GC-Tree could be adapted to be TGC-Tree, which maintains both the *Intent* and *Extent* of *Formal Concepts*. A series of synthetic datasets are used. Each dataset is generated by the same method as described in [14], an example synthetic dataset is T10.I6.D100K, where the three numbers denote the average transaction size (T), the average maximal potential frequent itemset size (I) and the total number of transactions (D), respectively.

There are 7 datasets used in our experiments: T4.I3.D100K, T5.I4.D100K, T6.I4.D100K, T7.I4.D100K, T8.I6.D100K, T9.I6.D100K, T10.I6.D100K. The main difference between them are the average transaction size(T). Figure 3 shows the average processing time for GC-Tree and TGC-Tree over the 100 sliding windows under different average transaction size.

From Figure 3, we could conclude that with the increment of the average transaction size, the running time for TGC-Tree is increased linearly. Meanwhile, TGC-Tree is a little bit slower than GC-Tree, but much faster than FCI-Stream.

The lines represent GC-Tree and TGC-Tree in Figure 3 is too close to be distinguished from each other, so we represent the result in another view(Figure 4), in which y axis is a logarithmic scale.

Figure 5 shows the memory usage of TGC-Tree, GC-Tree and CFI-Stream according to the transaction size. TGC-Tree requires a little less memory than GC-Tree. It's

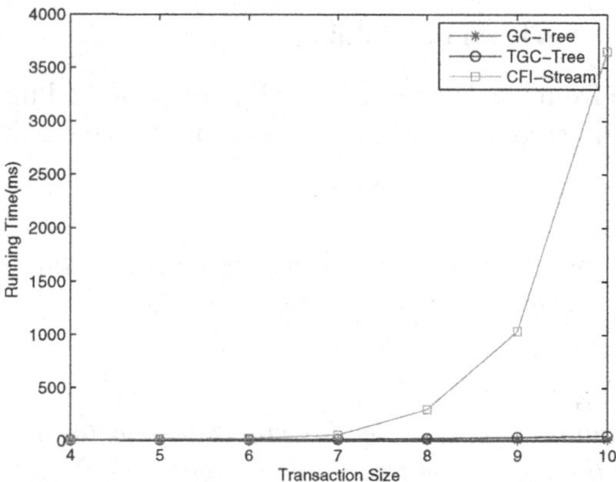


**Fig. 3.** Runtime Performance

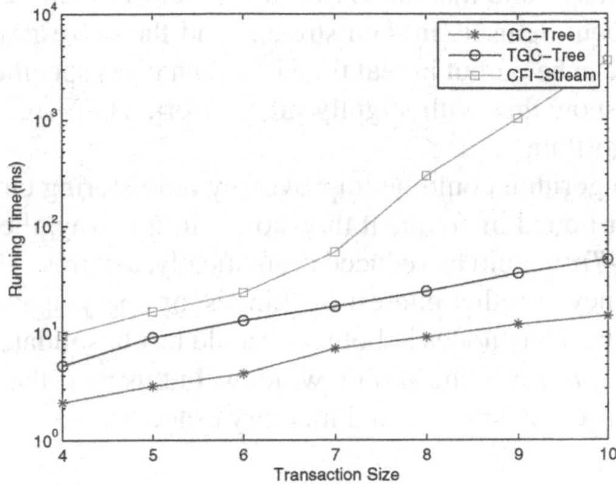


**Fig. 4.** Runtime Performance(log scale)

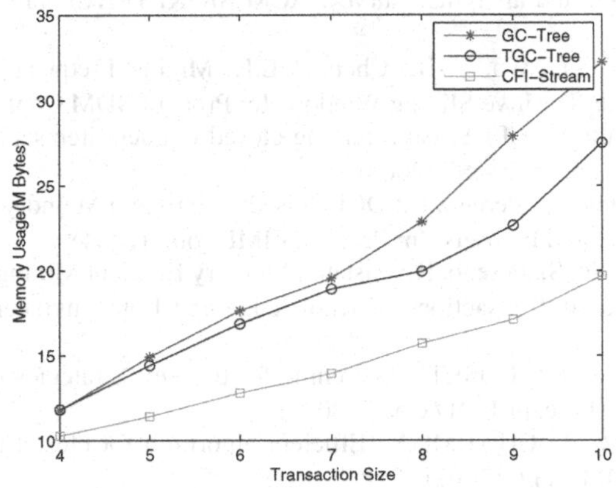


**Fig. 5.** Memory Usage

because GC-Tree caches all the transactions in the sliding window in memory, while TGC-Tree need not, since TGC-Tree keeps all the information about the transactions in the sliding window by *I-Tree* and *T-Tree*. Another interesting thing is CFI-Stream requires almost one third less memory than GC-Tree and TGC-Tree. It's because GC-Tree and TGC-Tree store all of the generators, the closed itemsets, the presets and the possets in the GC-Nodes, while CFI-Stream only cares about the closed itemsets.

From the above discussion, we could conclude that TGC-Tree could maintain both the *Intent* and *Extent* of *Formal Concepts*, meanwhile has similar performance as GC-Tree.

## 6 Conclusions and Future Work

In this paper we proposed a novel algorithm, TGC-Tree, to discover and maintain both *Intents* and *Extents* of all the *Formal Concepts* in the current data stream sliding window. The algorithm checks and maintains two closed set trees online in an incremental way. All closed frequent itemsets in data streams and the corresponding transactions which contains them can be output in real time based on users specified thresholds. Our performance studies show that with slightly more effort, TGC-Tree could be adapted from the GC-Tree algorithm.

In the future, the algorithm could be improved by only storing closed itemsets with a user specified lower bound of frequent thresholds. In this way, the number of nodes stored in *T-Tree* and *I-Tree* could be reduced dramatically, and this is beneficial for both time and space efficiency. Another interesting thing is, by applying the association rules find as soon as possible, many nodes in both tree could be consolidated to form a bigger but not strict *Formal Concept* in the sliding window. In this way, the trees could shrink quickly, so does the required cpu time and memory usage.

## References


1. Ben Yahia, S., Hamrouni, T., Mephu Nguifo, E.: Frequent closed itemset based algorithms: a thorough structural and analytical survey. ACM SIGKDD Explorations Newsletter 8(1), 93–104 (2006)
2. Lin, C.-H., Chiu, D.-Y., Wu, Y.-H., Chen, A.L.P.: Mining Frequent Itemsets from Data Streams with a Time-Sensitive Sliding Window. In: Proc. of SDM Conf. (2005)
3. Jiang, N., Gruenwald, L.: CFI-Stream: mining closed frequent itemsets in data streams. In: Proc. of KDD Conf., pp. 592–597 (2006)
4. Lucchese, C., Orlando, S., Perego, R.: DCI Closed: A Fast and Memory Efficient Algorithm to Mine Frequent Closed Itemsets. In: Proc. of FIMI Conf. (2004)
5. Lucchese, C., Orlando, S., Perego, R.: Fast and Memory Efficient Mining of Frequent Closed Itemsets. IEEE Journal Transactions of Knowledge and Data Engineering (TKDE) 18(1), 21–36 (2006)
6. Wang, J., Han, J., Pei, J.: CLOSET+: Searching for the Best Strategies for Mining Frequent Closed Itemsets. In: Proc. of KDD Conf. (2003)
7. Zaki, M.J., Hsiao, C.-J.: CHARM: An Efficient algorithm for closed itemsets mining. In: Proc. of SIAM ICDM Conf. (2002)
8. Stumme, G., Taouil, R., Bastide, Y., Pasquier, N., Lakhal, L.: Computing iceberg concept lattices with TITANIC. Journal of Knowledge and Data Engineering (KDE) 2(42), 189–222 (2002)
9. Zaki, M.J., Gouda, K.: Fast vertical mining using diffsets. Technical Report 01-1, Computer Science Dept., Rensselaer Polytechnic Institute (March 2001)
10. Lucchese, C., Orlando, S., Palmerini, P., Perego, R., Silvestri, F.: KDCI: a multistrategy algorithm for mining frequent sets. In: Proc. of ICDM Conf. (2003)
11. Orlando, S., Palmerini, P., Perego, R., Silvestri, F.: Adaptive and resource-aware mining of frequent sets. Proc. of ICDM Conf. (2002)
12. Pasquier, N., Bastide, Y., Taouil, R., Lakhal, L.: Discovering Frequent Closed Itemsets for Association Rules. In: Beeri, C., Bruneman, P. (eds.) ICDT 1999. LNCS, vol. 1540, pp. 398–416. Springer, Heidelberg (1998)
13. Pei, J., Han, J., Mao, R.: CLOSET: An efficient algorithm for mining frequent closed itemsets. In: Proc. of DMKD Conf. (May 2000)
14. Agrawal, R., Srikant, R.: Fast algorithms for mining association rules. In: Int'l Conf. on Very Large Databases (1994)
15. Chen, J., Li, S.: GC-Tree: A Fast Online Algorithm for Mining Frequent Closed Itemsets. In: Proc. of HPDMA, PAKDD Conf. (2007)

# Extracting Concepts from Religious Knowledge Resources and Constructing Classic Analysis Systems

Hajime Murai and Akifumi Tokosumi

Tokyo Institute of Technology, 12-1, Ohokayama-2, Meguro-ku, Tokyo, Japan
{h_murai,act}@valdes.titech.ac.jp

**Abstract.** Systematic thought has primarily been investigated using literature-based approaches. However, as systematic ideas and thought influence all areas of human activity and thinking, the application of NLP (Natural Language Processing) techniques and other information technologies may provide a more objective understanding of systematic thought. This paper focuses on documents of Christian teaching, and developed methods to extract characteristics of thoughts scientifically. These methods were implemented in the Classic Text Analysis System. This system has object-oriented design and will be applicable for other systematic thoughts written on some corpus.

**Keywords:** Religion, Semantic Analysis, Text Corpus, Digital Archive.

## 1 Introduction

### 1.1 Background

As an aspect of higher cognitive functions, systematic thought has primarily been investigated using literature-based approaches, with texts that are usually more abstract and subjective in nature than scientific papers. However, as systematic ideas and thought influence all areas of human activity and thinking, the application of NLP (Natural Language Processing) techniques and other information technologies may provide a more objective understanding of systematic thought. By utilizing these new scientific methods, we can (a) ensure the objectivity and replication of results, (b) handle large-scale data in a uniform manner.

We believe that it is possible to analyze the abstract thoughts and value systems embodied within a text corpus with such methods. In this paper, we construct and analyze a Christian text corpus. Traditional religions have exerted great influences on humanity throughout history. Most religions have at their core some canonical texts, with the hermeneutics, or interpretations, of the canon is also usually in text format. Thus, it is possible to represent key conceptualizations with the canonical texts through their objective analysis.

### 1.2 Goal of the Analysis

The goal of this paper is to develop a scientific analysis method for systematic thought. This paper utilized text that conveys systematic thoughts as data for analysis,

T. Tokunaga and A. Ortega (Eds.): LKR 2008, LNAI 4938, pp. 51–58, 2008.

and extracted main characteristics of thoughts numerically. Considering the process of constructing systematic thought, at first tradition was made from original thought, then A) traditions were edited and written on a paper, B) some written traditions were canonized, C) theologians interpret canon (Fig. 1). In this process, phase B) canonization and C) interpretation could be analyzed from objective text. B) canonization is examined in Section 2, and C) interpretation is in Section 3. Section 4 argues about the design and implementation of Classic Text Analysis System. The Classic Text Analysis System will be generally applicable to semantic analysis of classic text corpus.

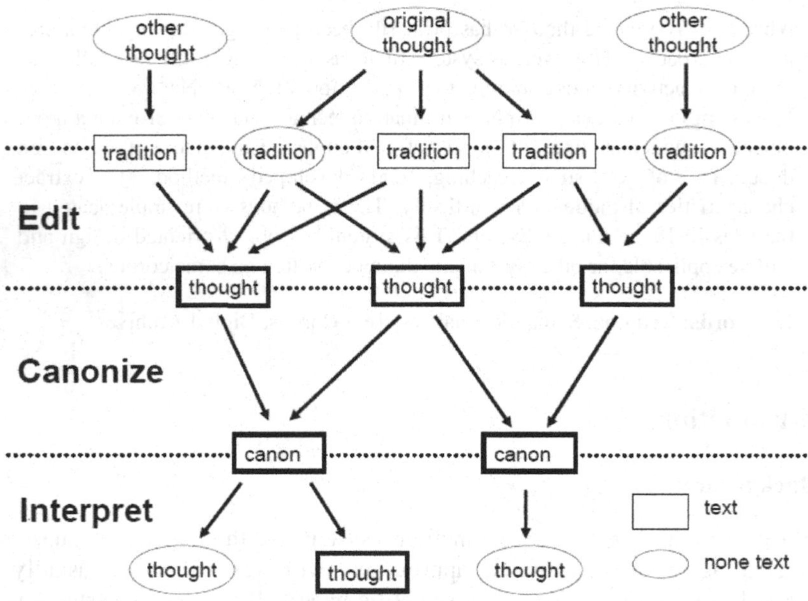


**Fig. 1.** Transition of Thought.

### 1.3 Data for the Analysis

It is necessary to make a text corpus for analyzing religious texts. The target of this paper is Christian teaching, so the corpus included Canon (the Bible), Catechism, Canon Law and Documents of the Second Vatican Council. These texts are arranged to XML form and added Dublin core [1]. In addition to those electrical texts, the Bible citation database of magnificent theologians was constructed.

## 2 Synoptic Analysis of Religious Texts

### 2.1 Background

There are undoubtedly many cases where a group of people have sought to spread their message and therefore developed a literature of "canonical documents," but where issues concerning the interpretations of the texts and the relationships between various individual documents have become problematic. This kind of situation exists not only within Christianity but within other religions and schools of political thinking. Such interpretative issues would seem to have direct influences on many matters in the modern world.

The central aim of this study is to develop a scientific information-technological method to analyze semantic differences that arise between multiple overlapping “canonical texts”. We believe that this method can be applied not just to the Bible but also to the interpretation of the systematic thinking embodied within collections of “canonical texts” in other spheres.

Specifically, the goal of this study is to develop a method that can analyze the way how the central messages emerge through the existence of multiple overlapping “canonical texts”. And, to apply this method to the four traditional Gospels included in the Bible and to compare with the Catechism of the Catholic Church and to discuss the results obtained. Through these aims, this study illustrates numerically which messages Christianity has sought to convey with the selection of the four traditional Gospels.

## 2.2 Making Network

The internal structures of the Gospels are divided into segments that are called pericopes. Pericope is an ancient Greek words meaning cut-out Each pericope corresponds to a small segment of a Biblical story that was transmitted orally.

In the Gospels, pericope units are numbered such as No. 235. However, a particular pericope in one Gospel may correspond to multiple pericopes in another Gospel.

This one-to-many relationship is due to the editing process, as each Gospel writer combined pericopes that he believed to be related. Thus, if one author saw a connection between one pericope to several others, that particular pericope unit would be repeated in a number of sections within the Gospel. Accordingly, there are many pericopes in the four Gospels that have the same verses, because they were taken and edited from the same source pericope.

As Fig.2 shows, pericopes containing verses in common with pericope No. 235 are Nos. 103, 290, 291, 296 and 302. This suggests that the writer of Matthew perceived some relationships between pericopes 235, 103, 290, 291 and 296. Similarly, the

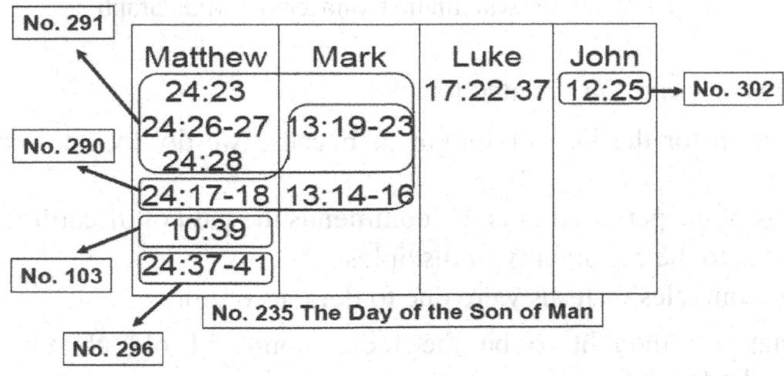


**Fig. 2.** Pericope Relation

writer of Mark imagined relationships to 290, 291, while the writer of John make a link between pericopes 235 and 302.

These pericopes relation could be converted to network, regarding pericopes as nodes and the relationships between pericopes as edges. This study uses the "Synopsis of the Four Gospels" as the data source of periscope relationships. This book based on Nestle Aland's "Greek New Testament" (version 26), [2] as this is believed to be the basis for various charts of pericopes relations that have been used as data source in defining pericopes and their relationships.

### 2.3 Clustering

In order to identify the internal structure, the maximum connected subgraph was clustered and the core element was extracted. 4 cores are extracted by combining node sharing cliques [3] (Fig. 3).

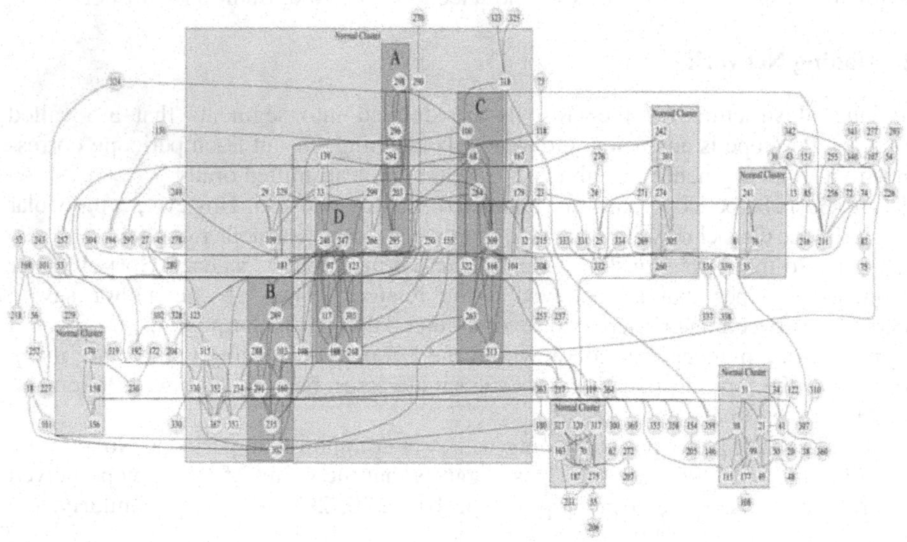


**Fig. 3.** Clustered Maximum Connected Partial Graph

The messages of 4 cores are related to

- A: Preparation for the Day of Judgment because we do not know when it will come
- B: Foretells of the persecution and recommends the path of discarding everything
- C: Teachings to the community of disciples
- D: Whether miracles of Jesus were due to demons or not

Those teachings are thought to be the focus points of old church fathers that canonized New Testament.

# 3 Co-citation Analysis of Religious Texts

## 3.1 Backgrounds

There are many differences in some specific religious group. As result of these differences, the interpretations of the Canon become different. If it is possible to extract these differences scientifically, the transition or mutual influence could be analyzed numerically.

Specifically, the goals of this study are to automatically extract the main elements of a number of key conceptualizations from a large-scale religious text corpus and analyze the cluster construction of them using an objective and replicable methodology. This, in turn, will provide an objective basis for the examination of systematic thought [4].

## 3.2 Making Network and Extracting Clusters

Here we focus on the writings of St. Augustine and St. Thomas Aquinas, two influential Church Fathers, as well as those of Jean Calvin, Karl Barth and Pope John Paul II to extract essential teachings of the Christian dogma through historical transition and to identify individual characteristics of hermeneutics. Based on the patterns of the Bible citations within their writings, we created networks for frequently cited sections of the Bible, and extracted the main elements and clusters of these, in order to compare a number of key conceptualizations. Cluster is extracted by

**Table 1.** Citations and Co-citations

| Author | Titles | Citation | Co-citation | Average Citation per verse |
|---|---|---|---|---|
| Augustine | 43 | 22674 | 215824 | 6.94 |
| Thomas Aquinas | 32 | 36015 | 800457 | 15.05 |
| Jean Calvin | 47 | 70324 | 2005864 | 13.51 |
| Karl Barth | 113 | 53288 | 2661090 | 23.67 |
| John Paul II | 1939 | 32166 | 643708 | 9.34 |

**Table 2.** Extracted Clusters

| Cluster \ Author | Augustine | Thomas Aquinas | Jean Calvin | Karl Barth | John Paul II |
|---|---|---|---|---|---|
| Incarnation | O | O | | O | O |
| Salvation from evil | O | | O | | |
| Spirit and Body | O | | | O | |
| Predestination | | | O | | |
| Commands | | | O | O | |
| Evangelization | | | | O | O |
| Sola Fidei | | | | O | |
| Suffering Servent | | | | O | |
| Creation | | | | | O |
| Judgement | | | | | O |

the threshold value of co-citation frequency. Table 1 depicts total citations and co-citations in each authors' writings.

The result clustered network of Augustine is shown in Fig.4. The nodes' alphabets and numbers are symbols that correspond to the Bible section. Dense parts are clusters. The differences of extracted clusters about authors are shown in Table2.

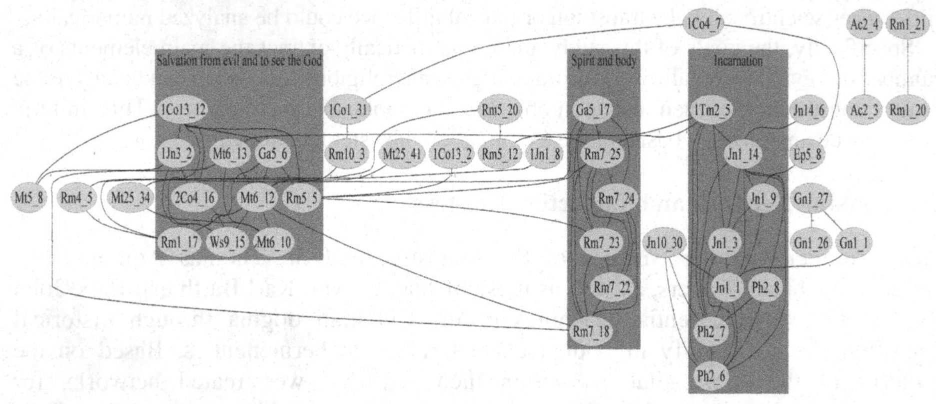


**Fig. 4.** Clustered Co-citation Network (Augustine)

These analyses were able to identify that the core element of Christian thought is Incarnation (Jn 1:14, Ph 2:6, Ph 2:7, Ph 2:8, Ga 4:4). as well as distinctions between the individual theologians in terms of their sect (Catholic or Protestant) and era (thinking about the necessity of spreading the Gospel).

## 4 Constructing Classic Text Analysis System

In section 2 and 3, this paper focuses on Christian teaching only, but there many other influential thoughts. If some general numerical text analysis system could be constructed, these analysis methods can be applicable to other text corpora. Moreover if users can add new analysis functions easily, the system become more general and useful.

To consider about applicable system design of general semantic analysis system, at first general text analysis methods and utilized information are arranged.

In semantic analysis, three type of information are utilized, intra textual information, inter textual information and linguistic information. Fig. 5 shows the relationships about those information and semantic analysis methods [5] [6].

In order to utilize all of these methods, object-oriented design is implemented to digital archive system. The types of objects are element, pair, list and network. In some analysis, objects are converted to some type of those objects and result objects also are applicable to other analysis method. The implemented methods and objects are illustrated in Fig. 6.

This design was implemented as a JAVA based server-client application[7].

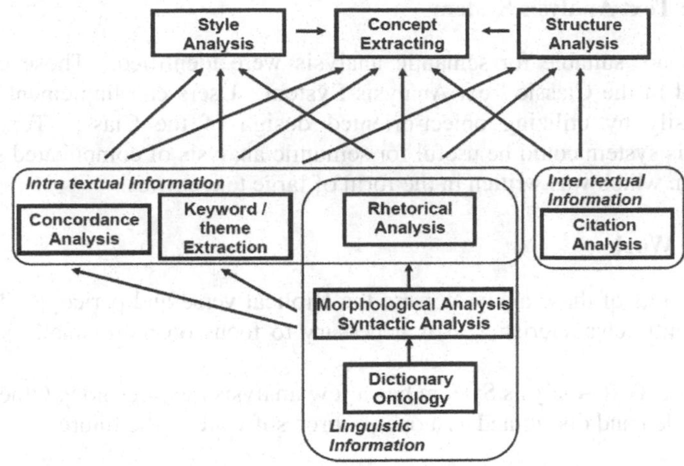


**Fig. 5.** Semantic Analysis Methods and Necessary Information

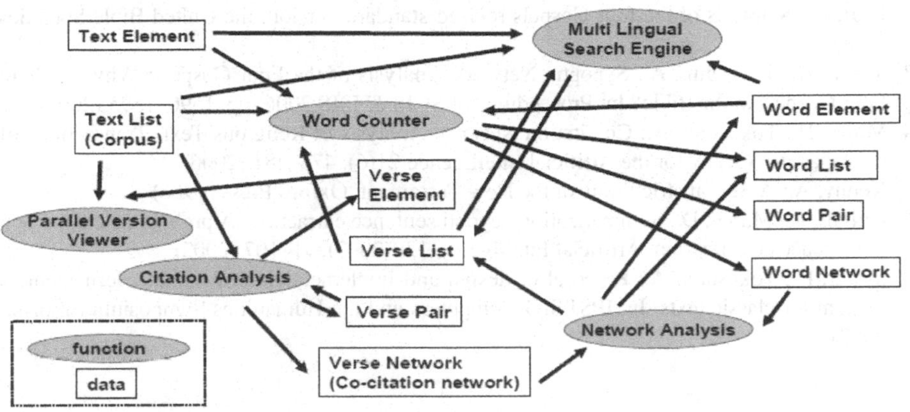


**Fig. 6.** Semantic Analysis Methods and Necessary Information

# 5 Conclusion and Future Works

## 5.1 Extracting Religious Thought Numerically

Teachings of old church fathers were extracted from the relationships of overlapping text contents in the Gospels. And core elements of the Bible interpretations of theologians were extracted and compared. Those operations are scientific and objective methods, and will be applicable to other type of thoughts such as Buddhism, Islamic and some type of political ideologies.

### 5.2 Classic Text Analysis System

Objects that are suitable for semantic analysis were identified. Those objects are implemented in the Classic Text Analysis System. Users can implement additional modules easily by utilizing object-oriented design of the Classic Text Analysis System. This system could be useful for semantic analysis of complicated systematic value system, which was written in the form of large text corpus.

### 5.3 Future Work

The textual units of these analyses were the Biblical verse and pericope. To analyze minute semantic characteristics, it is necessary to focus on more small level of text unit.

The Classic Text Analysis System has a few analysis modules now. Other modules should be added and distributed as a open source software in the future.

## References

1 Dublin Core Metadata Initiative (1995), `http://dublincore.org/index.shtml`
2 Kurt, A.: Synopsis of the four Gospels revised standard version, the United Bible Societies (1982)
3 Murai, H., Tokosumi, A.: Synoptic Network Analysis of the Four Gospels: Why are there Four Gospels in the Bible? In: Proceedings of SCIS & ISIS 2006, pp. 1590–1595 (2006)
4 Murai, H., Tokosumi, A.: Co-citation Network Analysis of Religious Text. Transactions of the Japanese Society for the Artificial Intelligence 21(6), 473–481 (2006)
5 Kenny, A.: A Stylometric Study of the New Testament. Oxford Press (1986)
6 Knight, K., Marcu, D.: Summarization beyond sentence extraction: A probabilistic approach to sentence compression. Artificial Intelligence 139(2002), 91–107 (2002)
7 Murai, H., Tokosumi, A.: Proposal of design and implementation of Digital Hermeneutics System for classic texts. In: IPSJ SIG Computers and the Humanities Symposium (in print, 2007)

# What Types of Translations Hide in Wikipedia?

Jonas Sjöbergh[1], Olof Sjöbergh[2], and Kenji Araki[1]

[1] Graduate School of Information Science and Technology
Hokkaido University
{js,araki}@media.eng.hokudai.ac.jp
[2] KTH CSC
olofsj@kth.se

**Abstract.** We extend an automatically generated bilingual Japanese-Swedish dictionary with new translations, automatically discovered from the multi-lingual online encyclopedia Wikipedia. Over 50,000 translations, most of which are not present in the original dictionary, are generated, with very high translation quality. We analyze what types of translations can be generated by this simple method. The majority of the words are proper nouns, and other types of (usually) uninteresting translations are also generated. Not counting the less interesting words, about 15,000 new translations are still found. Checking against logs of search queries from the old dictionary shows that the new translations would significantly reduce the number of searches with no matching translation.

## 1 Introduction

In the increasingly interconnected world, communication with people from different places all over the world is becoming more and more important. Since there are many languages being used in different parts of the world, tools that aid in communication between speakers of different languages, or in reading material produced in a language not one's own etc. can be very helpful. This is of course not a new problem, people have been dealing with the fact that it is often useful to communicate with people using other languages for a very long time, though the need is more prevalent in the modern globalized world. Many different tools have been developed, such as machine translation systems to automatically translate from one language to another, or computer programs that aid professional translators in their work.

One basic tool that has been used a lot is the bilingual dictionary. In its most basic form, a list of words in one language and their corresponding translations in another language. Such dictionaries can be useful in many situations, for instance as a reference for when not finding the appropriate word in conversation, as a support when reading in a foreign language, as one tool among many in a computer system for translation etc.

There are many ways to create bilingual lexicons. Traditionally they have been created by hand. A linguist assembles a set of words and their translations. This usually gives very high quality dictionaries, with high translation quality

T. Tokunaga and A. Ortega (Eds.): LKR 2008, LNAI 4938, pp. 59–66, 2008.

and containing the most important or useful words. It is however also very time consuming, and thus expensive.

Since bilingual dictionaries are so useful and manual creation is expensive, different ways to create them by automatic means have been devised. While automatic methods normally have drawbacks such as including erroneous translations or missing many important words, they are still useful because of their huge time saving potential. Automatic methods can also be used to generate a first rough draft of a dictionary, that is later cleaned up and extended by manual work.

One useful resource for creating bilingual dictionaries is large bilingual corpora, i.e. collections of text with the same text written in two languages. Depending on how detailed the information in the bilingual corpus is different methods to extract bilingual dictionaries can be used. The granularity could be which document corresponds to which document in the other language, or which sentence or even word. For good results, the bilingual corpus needs to be fairly large. Most large available parallel corpora are government texts, which gives a somewhat slanted dictionary. With a lack of appropriate parallel corpora, methods have also been developed that use "comparable corpora", i.e. texts that cover similar topics in different languages (such as international newspaper articles from roughly the same time in different countries), or even monolingual corpora for each language. An example where methods to create bilingual dictionaries from parallel corpora is compared to similar methods using only monolingual or comparable corpora can be found in [1].

Bilingual dictionaries have also been created by using other bilingual dictionaries. Given for instance a Swedish-English dictionary and a Japanese-English dictionary, a Japanese-Swedish dictionary can be generated by using the English translations as a pivot. Words with similar English translations have a high probability of having the same meaning. Ambiguous English words naturally cause problems, as does the fact that different English words can be used to describe essentially the same thing. Using English as a pivot language is common, since there are large dictionaries available between English and many other languages. If dictionaries are available with other possible pivot languages too, this can be used to achieve a higher quality result. The same ambiguity occurring in all pivot languages is unlikely, if the languages are not too closely related. For languages where large semantic lexicons, i.e. where the different meanings of the words and their relations to the meanings of other words are available, similar approaches can be used. For instance by mapping meanings from one such resource to meanings in another, or mapping translation candidates to semantic meaning representations to find words that mean the same in two different languages.

In this paper we extend a Japanese-Swedish dictionary created by using English as an interlingua and connecting two different bilingual dictionaries [2]. We extend it by using the online encyclopedia Wikipedia[1]. Wikipedia consists of articles written by volunteers, and many articles are available in many different languages. While not a parallel corpus it can at least give you comparable corpora in many languages. In our case we only use a very small set of Wikipedia

[1] http://www.wikipedia.org

that is easy to process when searching for translations. When an article on the same topic is available in another language this is indicated by a link in the source article. We automatically extract the article titles of articles available both in Japanese and Swedish. The title words used in the two languages can be assumed to be a good translation pair.

While this is a simple and useful method of extending the dictionary, the method is fairly trivial and not a very interesting research contribution. Indeed, for instance in [3] a bilingual dictionary is created in the same way, though the focus of the paper is on how to extract whole sentences that are similar in content but written in different languages (Dutch and English). Recently this method of finding translations has also been used in extending bilingual lexicons for information retrieval in multiple languages [4,5,6]. It has also been used in analyzing what people are currently interested in or concerned about, across different languages [7].

The main contribution of this paper is the evaluation of the generated translations. We examine what words are available to translation in this way, to see if the results are useful in our intended application.

## 2 Finding New Translations in Wikipedia

When extending the previously generated Japanese-Swedish dictionary we use Wikipedia, a multi-lingual freely available online encyclopedia. Wikipedia is a community project, created by volunteers from all over the world writing articles, editing other peoples writings or correcting mistakes etc. At the time of writing, there were about 2 million articles available in English (the largest language), and for Japanese and Swedish used in our experiments there were 403,000 and 245,000 articles respectively.

The new translation pairs for the dictionary were generated by checking each Swedish article in Wikipedia. If there was a link indicating that the same article was also available in Japanese, both these articles were fetched. The title was then extracted and the title words or expressions were considered as a new translation pair. We also did the same procedure using the Japanese articles, checking for links to Swedish translations. This gave essentially the same translation pairs, barring a few spelling variations.

This method is very simple, and more sophisticated methods that could find more translation pairs can be devised. Previously mentioned methods using comparable corpora are for instance applicable using the articles that are found to correspond to one another in the two languages. The method is of course also possible to use for other language pairs than Japanese and Swedish.

## 3 Evaluation

Using the method in the previous section, a list of 53,503 new translation pairs was generated. We evaluated the translations by manually going through a randomly selected subset of 3,000 of the translation pairs.

The first thing to be examined was the translation quality. The words were checked to see if the Japanese and Swedish expressions actually had the same meaning. This was grouped into three categories, good translations, erroneous translations and difference in scope. The last category was used for words where either the Japanese or Swedish expression had a much wider meaning than the suggested translation, but the suggested translation was a correct translation in some instances. All evaluators checking the translations were native speakers of Swedish and fairly fluent in Japanese.

The selected translation pairs were presented one pair at a time to an evaluator. The Wikipedia pages for the two translation candidates were also made available to use to determine if words the evaluator did not already know were good translations of each other. The evaluator then noted down the translation quality of the suggestion and some other information described below. The results are shown in Table 1.

**Table 1.** Translation quality of a sample of the generated translation pairs

| Good | Scope | Wrong |
|---|---|---|
| 99% | 1% | 0.2% |

As can be seen, the translation quality is very high. There were very few words that were not correctly translated. One example was the Swedish word "hage", which means roughly an enclosed pasture. The suggested Japanese translation was "Meadow" (i.e. written in English). This was caused by a link from the Swedish Wikipedia page that led to a Japanese page describing a software tool called Meadow, though it also explained that the word can also mean meadow in the sense of a field for cattle etc.

There are quite a few words that have a translation which sometimes overlap but has a wider meaning. Almost all such words are abbreviations.

Next, we examined what types of words are available for translation in this way, using the same randomly selected 3,000 translation pairs. Since they are taken from the title words of encyclopedia entries, one can expect mainly nouns and proper nouns. We also separated out dates and numbers, since there were many translations of the kind "1912"(Swedish)–"1912年"(Japanese), both meaning the year 1912. Such translations are generally uninteresting to include in a dictionary. The results are shown in Table 2.

As expected, most words are nouns or proper nouns. While there are many useless translations in the form of dates, they do not make up a very large part of the total set of words. Words that were neither nouns, dates, nor proper nouns were mostly short phrases or multi-word expressions. Examples include "Do not threaten to sue" (from a page of rules for behavior on Wikipedia) and "two of a kind". Since the majority of the words were proper names, we also examined what types of proper names occurred, see Table 3.

While translations of names are generally not what dictionaries are used for, there are applications where they are useful. While names of places, international

**Table 2.** Distribution (%) between word types

| Noun | Verb | Proper Noun | Date/Number | Other |
|---|---|---|---|---|
| 33 | 0.03 | 62 | 4 | 1 |

**Table 3.** Distribution (%) among proper names

| Person | Place | Group | Title | Product | Event | Other |
|---|---|---|---|---|---|---|
| 41 | 22 | 13 | 11 | 6 | 5 | 3 |

organizations and famous events are often similar in Japanese and Swedish, there are also many examples of such words were the words are wildly different in the two languages. One example from the generated translations is the "United Nations", "Förenta nationerna" (Swedish, literally "united nations") – "国際連合" (Japanese, literally "international union"). Translations of titles of books, movies, etc. are also often quite different, but perhaps less important.

Translations of personal names seem less useful, though it could be used to find the correct transliteration in the other language. This is not always trivial, since the writing systems are very different.

Names from the "other" category include such things as names of stars (astronomical) and names that can signify for instance both organizations and people.

We also checked if the words were predominantly made up of for instance specialized terminology from specific fields, slang, or other types of words not often encountered in "normal" texts. "Normal" was taken to mean words that also fairly frequently occur outside their specialized domain (if any). These categories were quite loosely specified, and are only meant to give an overview of the general trends. Proper names and dates were not included in this classification.

**Table 4.** Classification of translations (%) according to style

| "Normal" | Technology | Jargon | Species | Sports | Foreign Word |
|---|---|---|---|---|---|
| 41 | 15 | 15 | 9 | 1 | 19 |

As can be seen in Table 4, there are very many technical terms present. That an online encyclopedia written by interested volunteers contains many articles on for instance computer or network technology related subjects is perhaps not surprising.

Besides the technical jargon, there are also many words that are quite specific to a certain field. For instance there is medical jargon, chemistry jargon, architectural jargon etc. While there are many sports related words in Wikipedia, most of these are names of athletes, teams, or sports arenas. Sports related words that are not names are less common.

A large part of the generated translations are words that are foreign loan words in Japanese, generally coming from English. For a native speaker of Swedish, most of whom are fluent enough in English to know these loan words, such translations are not that helpful. It is useful to know when one can expect Japanese speakers to understand the English word, though, and to indicate such instances when the English word is used in Japanese with a meaning different from the original English word. It is of course also useful for speakers of Japanese who want to know the Swedish translations of such words.

Another related point is that in the Japanese Wikipedia names of flowers and animals are generally written with phonetic script in the title field. This is the usual way to write when specifying a certain species or so in a technical sense, but in a dictionary it would be more useful to have the normal (i.e. using a different alphabet) writing way. For example when writing about cherry trees in a non-technical sense, "桜" would normally be used instead of "サクラ" found in the generated translations, though they are both two written variants of the same word.

To see if the generated translations consisted mostly of new words or if there was a large overlap with the previously generated dictionary, we automatically checked what percentage of translations were found in the old list too.

**Table 5.** Availability of the new translations in the previously generated dictionary

| Availability | Words | Proportion |
|---|---|---|
| New Translations | 50,863 | 95% |
| Already Available | 2,640 | 5% |

As can be seen in Table 5, the majority of the words are new translations. This is natural since most of the translations are proper names, which the original dictionary did not contain to any large degree. However, most of the other translations are also new translations, with less than one in four of the new useful translations being available in the old dictionary.

The previously generated Japanese-Swedish dictionary is searchable on the Web[2], where it is also possible to add new translations or to correct errors. There is also an independently developed search field plug-in for some Web browsers that directly sends translation queries to that Web interface. In our final evaluation we checked the search logs for the Web interface. We examined whether the words searched for were present among the new translations, the old translations, or both. Each query is counted, so if the same word is searched for by several different users or by the same user many times, it will be counted many times. While the Web interface is not very heavily used, at least it gives an indication of what kinds of words are interesting to users of a Japanese-Swedish dictionary. About 380,000 queries were found in the logs. The results are shown in Table 6.

[2] http://www.japanska.se

**Table 6.** Distribution of search queries from the Web interface to the dictionary

| Type of Query | Words | Proportion |
|---|---|---|
| Available in Both | 96,558 | 26% |
| Only in Old Dictionary | 111,078 | 30% |
| Only in New Translations | 22,425 | 6% |
| Missing from Both | 142,566 | 38% |

Many words that users search for are not available in either set of translations. A very large part of these is made up from spelling mistakes and encoding problems, so they are not related to low coverage of the dictionary vocabulary. Searches using inflected forms are also common, and usually give no results. There are also (surprisingly) quite a lot of searches in English, Arabic and other languages, which naturally also fail to return results. It is clear that while the original dictionary covers more of the words users are interested in, the new translations also contribute with many sought after words that are missing.

## 4 Discussion

The previously generated dictionary that is used in the online search interface contains about 18,000 words. The newly generated translations numbered over 50,000, though many were not particularly useful. A rough estimate of how many new useful translations were generated can be calculated based on 33% of the new translations being interesting and about 5% of the translations already being in the old dictionary. Since the words that are in the original dictionary are almost exclusively interesting, this gives about 15,000 new interesting translations (28% of 53,000). Since the translation quality is very high and the method is very simple, this is a good method to almost double the size of the dictionary.

While many of the words searched for by users were already covered by the original dictionary, the new translations will significantly reduce the number of searched for but missing words. Reducing the failed searches from 44% to 38% is quite good, especially considering that many of the remaining failures are caused by spelling mistakes, inflected words, faulty character encodings etc. and are thus not related to lack of coverage of the dictionary.

For Japanese and Swedish, no really large electronic dictionaries are available as far as we know. There are dictionaries in printed form, with sizes ranging from 6,000 words to the order of 30,000 words. So a dictionary of the size generated can likely be quite useful, though naturally there are some important words missing, and some erroneous translations.

## 5 Conclusions

We generated over 50,000 new translation pairs between Japanese and Swedish from the online encyclopedia Wikipedia using a very simple method. Analyzing the generated translations we found that the translation quality is very high. Almost no actually erroneous translations were generated, though about 1% of the translations were not ideal.

There were many translations that seem fairly useless, such as translations of personal names. Even discarding all names, dates, and numbers, about 15,000 new translations were generated. Most of the generated translations were not available in the previously generated dictionary that we wanted to extend. Evaluating against the search logs from the interface to the old dictionary, a significant number of the searches that failed to return a match in the old dictionary would have resulted in a matching translation using the newly generated translations.

## References

1. Koehn, P., Knight, K.: Knowledge sources for word-level translation models. In: Proceedings of EMNLP 2001, Pittsburgh, USA (2001)
2. Sjöbergh, J.: Creating a free digital Japanese-Swedish lexicon. In: Proceedings of PACLING 2005, Tokyo, Japan, pp. 296–300 (2005)
3. Adafre, S.F., de Rijke, M.: Finding similar sentences across multiple languages in Wikipedia. In: EACL 2006 Workshop on New Text – Wikis and Blogs and Other Dynamic Text Sources, Trento, Italy (2006)
4. Wang, Y.C., et al.: IASL system for NTCIR-6 Korean-Chinese cross-language information retrieval. In: Proceedings of NTCIR-6 Workshop, Tokyo, Japan (2007)
5. Su, C.Y., Wu, S.H., Lin, T.C.: Using Wikipedia to translate OOV terms on MLIR. In: Proceedings of NTCIR-6 Workshop, Tokyo, Japan (2007)
6. Mori, T., Takahashi, K.: A method of cross-lingual question-answering based on machine translation and noun phrase translation using web documents. In: Proceedings of NTCIR-6 Workshop, Tokyo, Japan (2007)
7. Fukuhara, T., Murayama, T., Nishida, T.: Analyzing concerns of people from Weblog articles. AI & Society (in press, 2007)

# Initial Solution Set Improvement for a Genetic Algorithm in a Metadata Generation Support System for Landscape Photographs

Tetsuya Suzuki[1] and Takehiro Tokuda[2]

[1] Department of Electronic Information Systems
Shibaura Institute of Technology
Minuma, Saitama City, Saitama 337-8570, Japan
tetsuya@sic.shibaura-it.ac.jp
[2] Department of Computer Science
Tokyo Institute of Technology
Ohokayama, Meguro, Tokyo 152-8552, Japan
tokuda@cs.titech.ac.jp

**Abstract.** In our metadata generation support system for landscape photographs, we use a genetic algorithm to find locations of photographs. Given a set of randomly generated solutions, the genetic algorithm tends to redundantly explore the search space because it is often that many worse solutions are distributed globally and a few better solutions are distributed locally in the search spaces of our search problems. To avoid such redundant searches, we propose a heuristic method to relocate worse solutions near better solutions before we execute the genetic algorithm. We show that the relocated initial solutions contribute to finding better solutions than randomly generated solutions by an experiment.

## 1 Introduction

Geocoding of landscape photographs, which assigns their locations to them, is a kind of metadata generation for the photographs. Metadata generation techniques for such geocoding will be useful to construct not only contents for location oriented search systems but also photograph libraries such as "Japanese Old Photographs of the Bakumatsu-Meiji Periods" at the University of Nagasaki Library[2] where Japanese old photographs are provided with explanations of their locations.

We are interested in geocoding of landscape photographs already taken without recording their exact locations because there exist many such photographs in books, movies, television programs and so on.

As automatic geocoding for them is not easy, we have implemented a prototype system to support such geocoding[1]. Target photographs are landscape photographs such that terrain in the photographs is enough characteristic to specify the locations. Input to the system is a pair of a search problem definition and an initial solution set. The search problem definition includes features of

T. Tokunaga and A. Ortega (Eds.): LKR 2008, LNAI 4938, pp. 67–74, 2008.

landscape photographs and conditions of camera parameters. Each solution in the initial solution set represents the parameters. The system improves given solutions as follows. The system puts many virtual cameras into the world made by a digital elevation model(DEM) which represents terrain by altitudes. It then searches cameras which take photographs similar to a landscape photograph changing camera parameters. Output from the system is the improved solution set.

The system deals with a search problem as a maximum optimization problem. It constructs an objective function from a given search problem, and tries to find solutions which maximize the function using a real coded genetic algorithm. *Real coded genetic algorithms*(RCGAs) are genetic algorithms which use real number vectors as solutions. An RCGA maintains a set of solutions, which is called a *generation*, and iteratively improves the solution set by both a crossover operation and a generation alternation model. A *crossover operation* is a randomized operation which generates new solutions called *children* from some of existing solutions called *parents*. A set of children and parents is called a *family*. A *generation alternation model* updates a solution set by choosing parents, applying a crossover operation to the parents, and exchanging some solutions in the solution set with some solutions in the family. In randomly generated initial solutions for the system, the most of their objective function values are low. Such solution sets cause redundant searches.

To avoid such redundant searches, we propose a heuristic method to improve initial solutions for the RCGA in our system. The method relocates solutions with low objective function values near solutions with higher objective function values. It contributes to finding good solutions with higher probability.

The organization of this paper is as follows. We explain our metadata generation support process in section 2. In section 3, we point out the redundant searches in our system. In section 4, we explain our heuristic method for the problem. In section 5, we apply our method to a search problem, and evaluate the results. In section 6, we state our conclusions.

## 2 Geocoding Support Process of Landscape Photographs

To find the location of a landscape photograph by our system, we take the following four steps: (1) definition of a search problem, (2) generation of initial solution sets, (3) search of better solutions, and (4) check of the resulting solutions. We explain these steps in the following.

### 2.1 Definition of a Search Problem

In a search problem definition, we describe features of terrain in the photograph, camera parameters, and a search space declaratively. For example, we describe shapes of mountains which are boundaries between the earth and the sky, uneveness of the ground, and variables for camera parameters and their domains. Camera parameters are positions, directions, focus of cameras and so on.

Our system translates a defined problem to a corresponding maximum optimization problem such that:

$$\begin{aligned} \text{maximize}: \quad & f(x_1, \ldots, x_n) \\ \text{subject to}: & \ x_1 \in D, \ldots x_n \in D \end{aligned}$$

where $D$ is a closed interval $[0, 1]$. The objective function $f$ is a function from $D^n$ to $D$, which our system constructs from the defined problem. Evaluation of the function is a time consuming task because it involves ray tracing. The values strongly depend on terrain.

## 2.2 Generation of Initial Solution Sets

We generate initial solution sets for the constructed maximum optimization problem. A *solution* is a mapping from variables to their values. A generated solution set is used as start points of a search. Usually, we divide the whole search space into sub-search spaces, generate a solution set for each of the spaces, and start a search for each of the generated solution sets. Solutions distributed in a sub-search space contribute to local exploration of the sub-search space.

## 2.3 Search

We use as a search algorithm an RCGA which uses the unimodal normal distribution crossover (UNDX)-$m$ and the distance dependent alternation model (DDA) [3]. The UNDX-$m$ crossover operation uses $m$+2 solutions as parents. The RCGA with UNDX-$m$ and DDA preserves the diversity of solutions during searches [3]. Each resulting solution has a *score* which is its objective function value. The score 0 is the worst, and the score 1 is the best.

## 2.4 Check of the Resulting Solutions

We have to check if the resulting solutions with higher scores are what we expect. It is because they may not be expected ones if the problem is not defined well. For example, Fig. 1 is a landscape photograph taken at a place in the Nihon line.

**Fig. 1.** A photograph taken at a place in the Nihon line

(a) (b)

**Fig. 2.** The landscapes based on best solutions found as the location of Fig. 1

**Table 1.** The camera parameters of Fig.2(a)

| Parameter | Value |
|---|---|
| position | 35 deg 25 min 25.36 sec N,<br>137 deg 0 min 5.48 sec E |
| height from the earth | 1m |
| direction | 268 deg |
| elevation angle | -3 deg |
| bank angle | 1 deg |
| focus | 44mm |
| film size | 23.7mm x 15.7mm |

The Nihon line is a region along the Kisogawa river in Japan, and the length of it is about 12 kilometers. Fig. 2(a) and Fig. 2(b) show the landscapes rendered from the best solutions found in the region as the location of Fig. 1 by our system. Table 1 shows the camera parameters for Fig. 2(a), where the latitude and longitude are based on the WGS84 datum. We consider that Fig. 2(a) is more similar to Fig. 1 than Fig. 2(b) because of the shape of the mountain. Indeed, the distance between the locations of Fig. 1 and Fig. 2(a) is about 14 meters while the distance between the locations of Fig. 1 and Fig. 2(b) is about 4.8 kilometers.

## 3 Redundant Searches in Our System

We point out redundant searches in our system. It is often that the most of scores in a randomly generated solution set are 0. For example, Fig. 3(a) shows a distribution of randomly generated 1,000 solutions in a sub-search space of a maximum optimization problem with three variables, where 703 of the 1,000 solutions have zero score. Fig. 3(b) shows a distribution of solutions with non-zero scores among them, where they localize in the sub-search space. In other words, there exists area in the sub-search space which contains only solutions of Fig. 3(a) with zero score. Because the UNDX-$m$ crossover operation used in our

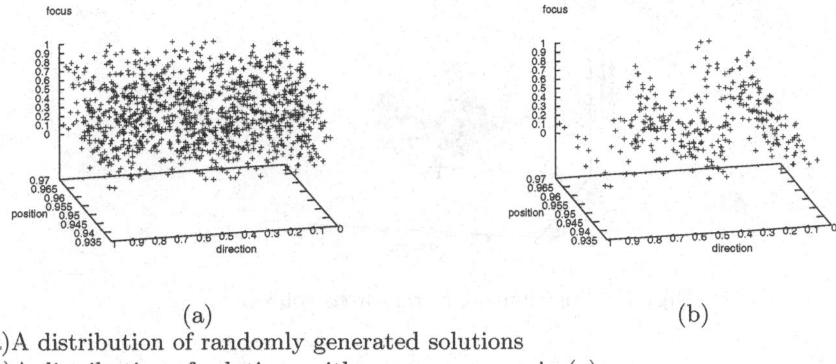


(a)A distribution of randomly generated solutions
(b)A distribution of solutions with non-zero scores in (a)

**Fig. 3.** Distributions of solutions in a sub-search space of a problem

system tends to generate children in interpolation area between their parents, children of parents with zero score also tend to have zero score in such situation. This causes redundant searches.

## 4 Our Relocation Method

To avoid the redundant searches, we relocate solutions with zero score near solutions with higher scores before we execute the genetic algorithm.

```
Procedure Relocate
Input:  A solution set X, where each solution is of the form (x_1, ..., x_d)
        A real number α, where 0 < α < 1
        An objective function f
Output: A solution set Y
begin
        W = {x ∈ X | f(x) > 0}
        if |W| ≥ 2 then
          Y ← W
          Z ← X − W
          while |Z| > 0 do
            Choose two different solutions x and y from W randomly.
            Choose d random numbers s_1, ..., s_d from an open interval (0, α).
            Y ← Y ∪ {((1 − s_1)x_1 + s_1 y_1, ..., (1 − s_d)x_d + s_d y_d)}
            Remove an element from Z
          enddo
        else
          Y ← X
        endif
end
```

**Fig. 4.** The relocation method Relocate

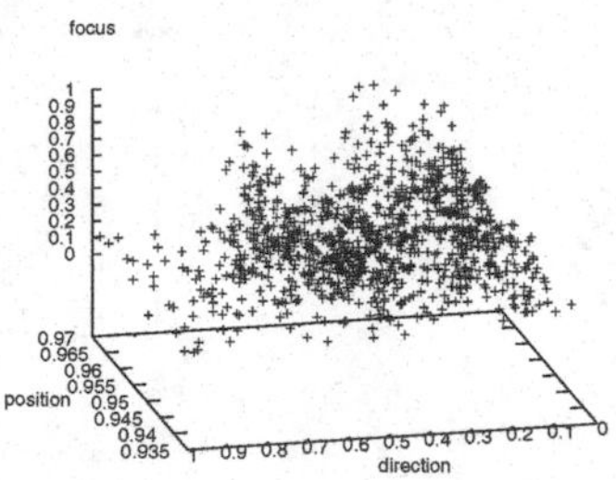


**Fig. 5.** A distribution of relocated solutions

Fig. 4 shows a pseudocode of the relocation method. Given a solution set $X$, for each solution $z$ with zero score in $X$, we randomly choose different two solutions $x$ and $y$ with non-zero scores from $X$. We then relocate $z$ to a randomly chosen position near $x$ within a hyper-rectangle whose diagonal is the line segment between the two solutions $x$ and $(1-\alpha)\ x + \alpha\ y$. The parameter $\alpha$ , which is a real number between 0 and 1, specifies the ratio of the diagonal length against the distance between $x$ and $y$.

Fig. 5 shows relocated solutions of Fig. 3(a) by our relocation method where $\alpha$ is 0.5. In Fig. 5 the solutions are distributed as the solutions with non-zero scores of Fig. 3(b).

## 5 Experiment

To confirm the effect of our relocation method, we compare searches with the relocation method and searches without it. We searched the location of the landscape photograph of Fig. 1 in the Nihon line as follows.

### 5.1 Initial Solution Sets

We generated 20 sets of initial solution sets as follows. First we divided the whole search space into 32 sub-search spaces $V_1$, ..., $V_{32}$. For each $i$ in $\{1, \ldots, 32\}$, we generated a solution set $S_{1,i}$ whose solutions were distributed in the sub-search space $V_i$. Each solution set contained 1,000 solutions. We call a set of solution sets $S_{1,1}$, ..., $S_{1,32}$ as $S_1$. For each $i$ in $\{1, \ldots, 32\}$, we applied our mthod to $S_{1,i}$, and obtained a relocated solution set $R_{1,i}$. We used 0.5 for the parameter $\alpha$ of the relocation method. We call a set of solution sets $R_{1,1}$, ..., $R_{1,32}$ as $R_1$. Similary, we generated sets of solution sets $S_2$, ..., $S_{10}$, and the corresponding sets $R_2$, ..., $R_{10}$. As a result, each of $S_i$ and $R_i$ totally contained 32,000 solutions.

### 5.2 Search

For each solution set $S_{1,i}$ in $S_1$, we applied the genetic algorithm and obtained the resulting solution set $S'_{1,i}$. We call a set of solution sets $S'_{1,1}$, ..., $S'_{1,32}$ as $S'_1$. Similary, we obtained solution sets $R'_{1,1}$, ..., $R'_{1,32}$ from $R_1$. We call a set of

**Table 2.** The results of the Nihon line problem

(a)

| $i$ | $S_i$ | $R_i$ |
|---|---|---|
| 1 | 31861 | 30018 |
| 2 | 31891 | 30270 |
| 3 | 31859 | 28089 |
| 4 | 31868 | 29115 |
| 5 | 31868 | 29259 |
| 6 | 31879 | 28991 |
| 7 | 31871 | 28512 |
| 8 | 31846 | 28603 |
| 9 | 31865 | 28806 |
| 10 | 31872 | 27946 |
| Avg. | 31868 | 28960.9 |

(b)

| $i$ | $S_i$ | $R_i$ | $S'_i$ | $R'_i$ |
|---|---|---|---|---|
| 1 | 0.619047619 | 0.714285714 | 0.857142857 | 0.904761905 |
| 2 | 0.476190476 | 0.761904762 | 0.80952381 | 0.857142857 |
| 3 | 0.80952381 | 0.857142857 | 0.857142857 | 0.904761905 |
| 4 | 0.533333333 | 0.80952381 | 0.619047619 | 0.904761905 |
| 5 | 0.428571429 | 0.80952381 | 0.80952381 | 0.952380952 |
| 6 | 0.571428571 | 0.904761905 | 0.761904762 | 0.904761905 |
| 7 | 0.4 | 0.904761905 | 0.952380952 | 0.952380952 |
| 8 | 0.542857143 | 0.952380952 | 0.80952381 | 1.0 |
| 9 | 0.444444444 | 0.666666667 | 0.857142857 | 1.0 |
| 10 | 0.571428571 | 0.80952381 | 0.761904762 | 0.952380952 |
| Avg. | 0.53968254 | 0.819047619 | 0.80952381 | 0.933333333 |
| Var. | 0.014015285 | 0.007961703 | 0.007558579 | 0.002116402 |

**(a)** The number of solutions with zero score in solution sets
**(b)** The best scores in solution sets

solution sets $R'_{1,1}, \ldots, R'_{1,32}$ as $R'_1$. Similary, we generated sets of solution sets $S'_2, \ldots, S'_{10}$, and the corresponding ones $R'_2, \ldots, R'_{10}$.

The RCGA generated 50 new solutions at one generation update, and computed at most 500 generations. We used 2 for the parameter $m$ of UNDX-$m$. When the algorithm found a solution with score 1.0, it stopped the search.

For one series of the three operations, which are generation, relocation and update, we limited the evaluation times of objective functions at most 26,000. Because one solution set contained 1,000 solutions, the number of evaluation times in generation was 1,000. The number of evaluation times in relocation depended on how many solutions with zero score the solution set included. For one execution of the RCGA, the number of evaluation times was at most 25,000. Once an objective function value for a solution was computed, it was recorded with the solution and re-evaluation of the value did not occur for the solution.

### 5.3 Results

Table 2(a) shows the number of solutions with zero score in $S_i$ and $R_i$. For each pair of $S_i$ and $R_i$ in the table, the number of solutions with zero score in $R_i$ is 88% to 95% of that in $S_i$. Table 2(b) shows the best scores in $S_i$, $R_i$, $S'_i$ and $R'_i$, their averages and their variances. In the table, $R_i$ and $R'_i$ are significantly larger than $S_i$ and $S'_i$ respectively.

### 5.4 Evaluation

Though our method did not reduce the number of solutions with zero score dramatically, relocated solutions contributed to finding better solutions than randomly generated solutions. in the experiment. It was because relocated solutions localized in their search spaces, and made the RCGA search more locally than randomly generated ones.

Our relocation method is similar to one update of the generation by an RCGA with the elite strategy and a crossover operation BLX-$\alpha$. The elite strategy chooses solutions with higher scores as parents. The BLX-$\alpha$[4] takes two parents and generates their children within an extended hyper-rectangle defined by the parents. The RCGA may generate children near vertices of the hyper-rectangle far from their parents while our method does not because our method generates children within a shrunk hyper-rectangle defined by their parents. So this result can be seen as that the combination of different two genetic algorithms worked better for the search problem.

## 6 Conclusion

An RCGA is used to find locations of photographs in our metadata generation support system for landscape photographs. To prevent the RCGA from searching redundantly, we proposed a heuristic method to relocate worse solutions in an initial solution set near better solutions in it before we executed the RCGA. We showed that the RCGA with relocated solutions often found better solutions than the RCGA with randomly generated solutions by an experiment.

## References

1. Suzuki, T., Tokuda, T.: A System for Landscape Photograph Localization. In: Proceedings of the Sixth International Conference Intelligent Systems Design and Applications(ISDA 2006), pp. 1080–1085 (2006)
2. The University of Nagasaki Library: Japanese Old Photographs of the Bakumatsu-Meiji Periods. `http://oldphoto.lb.nagasaki-u.ac.jp/`
3. Takahashi, O., Kita, H., Kobayashi, S.: A Real-Coded Genetic Algorithm using Distance Dependent Alternation Model for Complex Function Optimization. In: Proceedings of the Genetic and Evolutionary Computation Conference (GECCO 2000), pp. 219–226 (2000)
4. Eshelman, L., Schaffer, J.: Real-Coded Genetic Algorithms and Interval-Schemata. Foundations of Genetic Algorithms, vol. 2, pp. 187–202. Morgan Kaufmann Publishers, San Francisco (1993)

# Identifying Semantic Relations in Japanese Compound Nouns for Patent Documents Analysis

Kiyoko Uchiyama, Shunsuke Aihara, and Shun Ishizaki

Graduate School of Media and Governance, Keio University,
5322 Endo, Fujisawa-City, Kanagawa, 252-8520, Japan
{kiyoko,aihara,ishizaki}@sfc.keio.ac.jp

**Abstract.** The purpose of this study is to establish a method for identifying semantic relations in compound nouns in patent documents by using linguistic information. The information such as grammatical or semantic features plays a key role for analyzing semantic relations in compound nouns. We used the information about immediately succeeding case particles, adjective-forming suffixes and a verb *suru* "do" as grammatical features, concept classifications in EDR dictionary as semantic features. The performance of the fully automated statistical method was found to be good at 84% by using both grammatical and semantic features. This result shows advantage of our method.

**Keywords:** Compound nouns, semantic analysis, grammatical features, patent documents.

## 1 Introduction

The study proposes a semantic analysis method for identification of semantic relations in compound nouns. Japanese has diverse types of compound words and there are difficulties in processing them [2]. In order to extract various knowledge from texts, processing compound nouns and phrases has become more important. In technical domains such as a patent one, documents include a great number of compound words as technical terms. Such terms appear in various forms like noun phrase or verb phrase. For instance, a compound noun *keitaiso-kaiseki* "morphological analysis" can be described as follows:

- noun phrase
  - *keitaiso no kaiseki* "analysis of morpheme"
  - morpheme-**Gen**(genitive) analysis
- verb phrase
  - *keitaiso o kaiseki-suru* "analyze morpheme"
  - morpheme-**ACC**(accusative) analyze-do

The above examples show paraphrase patterns that a compound noun *keitaiso-kaiseki* can be expressed in a noun phrase *keitaiso no kaiseki* "analysis

T. Tokunaga and A. Ortega (Eds.): LKR 2008, LNAI 4938, pp. 75–81, 2008.

of morpheme" and a verb phrase *keitaiso o kaiseki-suru* "analyze morpheme". There are several paraphrase patterns of compound nouns in patent documents. It is difficult to search such patterns only by keyword retrieval in patent documents. To retrieve patent documents by using paraphrases of compound nouns makes it easy to obtain much of information. If each constituent of the compound noun can be tagged by semantic relations like "A is an object of B", we can paraphrase the compound noun in various forms. Therefore, the interpretation of compound nouns is required for patent retrieval to search similar and related patent documents effectively. In previous study, We constructed the analysis rules for analyzing semantic relations based on the grammatical features [13]. We carry out a fully automated method using the grammatical features in this study.

Our approach employs the following three steps; (1) to discuss grammatical features of constituent for analyzing semantic relations of compound nouns, (2) to extract compound nouns, (3) to evaluate our method by using a machine learning method.

The body of the paper is organized as follows: Section 2 mentions related work regarding the analysis methods of semantic relations in rule-based and statistical approaches. Section3 describes grammatical features of constituents in compound nouns in terms of grammatical categories. Section 4 defines semantic relations of compound nouns in this study. Section 5 evaluates our proposed method. The conclusion of our study and implication for future work are stated at the end.

## 2 Related Works

Analyzing methods of semantic relations in compound nouns have been discussed in natural language processing. In Japanese, there is no word segmentation and no clue for grammatical features in compound nouns. Miyazaki [7,8] proposed a dictionary construction method for machine translation supported by compound words retrieval. In this study, they made dependency patterns for verbal nouns and adjectival nouns in order to analyze semantic relations between constituents in compound nouns. The method is useful for compound nouns which consist of verbal nouns and adjectival nouns. It remains a difficult problem, however, to analyze compound nouns consisting only common nouns. Similarly, a method was proposed by using a case frame dictionary [10]. The study focused on verbal nouns in compound nouns and found their dependency patterns of noun with case particles.

A principled approach [11] was proposed for analyzing relations between constituent of compound nouns consisting verbal nouns based on the classification of verbal nouns by lexical conceptual structure (**LCS**). Both of them made hand-coded rules for analyzing compound nouns, therefore, the obtained accuracy were fairly good in their evaluation. On the other hand, it would take a lot of time and cost to construct rules for analyzing semantic relations.

Automatic interpretation of semantic relations of compound nouns has been conducted in a number of researches. Baker and Szpakowicz [3] proposed a semi-automatic method for compound nouns. Kim and Baldwin [5] proposed a method based on a predefined set of semantic relations. Their approach used the semantics of the seed verbs and grammatical roles of the head noun and modifier. The key of this study is to assign the actual verbs in sentences to suitable seed verbs and to use appropriate thesaurus. Our approach uses grammatical and semantic features of case particles, adjective-forming suffixes and a verb *suru* "do" in stead of using seed verbs.

## 3 Grammatical Features

It is crucial to examine useful grammatical features for analyzing semantic relations of compound nouns. The conventional grammatical categories for words in sentences are not sufficient for analyzing compounds.

It is expected to be useful to look into the grammatical features of general words for analyzing compound nouns. We started from examining nouns or nominal grammatical categories and tried to extract differences within nouns or nominal categories. Upon closer inspection of words in sentences, it became clear that what is commonly called nouns or nominal categories can be further classified as:

– Words can/cannot become a subject and a direct object in a sentence.
– Words are regarded as a verb, when words occur with the verb *suru*"do".
– Words can be used only in compound words or linked with adjective-forming suffix *-teki*, *-na*, and so on.
– Words have the same form as nouns and adjectives (adjectival nouns).

On the other hand, it is generally observed that relationship between constituent elements of compounds can be expressed by paraphrasing with case particles, i.e. transforming compounds into noun and verb phrases, where constituent of compound nouns can behave as words. Based on the basic observation of nominal words in sentences, we had recognized a few sub-types of distributions with respect to grammatical links and/or case particles and these sub-types help to identify the semantic interpretation of compound nouns based on the previous study [13,14].

We had tested several types of case particles and found that the most effective case particles are the nominative case *-ga* and accusative case *-o* to identify the semantic relations between constituent elements of compounds. We focused on the succeeding information with each constituent as follows [12]. The succeeding patterns are very simple, but make it easy to extract information out of a large corpus.

A. The nominative case *-ga* and/or accusative case *-o* normally indicate that the accompanying noun is the subject and/or the direct object of the sentence.
B. The verbal nouns with the verb *-suru* "do" is regarded as a verb. Many verbal nouns come from Sino-Japanese (Chinese character) compounds. These verbal nouns can be marked with case particles as nouns.
C. The suffix *-teki* can be compounded with a noun and an adjectival noun to modify a verb or to form a compound noun.
D. The adjective-forming suffix *-na* is added to an adjectival noun when it modifies the following noun.

## 4 Semantic Relations

To describe the semantic relations between constituent of compound nouns, we introduced **CDL** (Concept Description Language) relations [15]. **CDL** is a language that describes a wide variety of representation media and content, as well as conceptualization of their meaning, in a common format. The concept "relation" in **CDL** for Natural Languages uses for an analysis of semantic relations between constituent of compound nouns in this study. Basically, the **CDL** expresses the relation between each word in a sentence, however, we assume that it can be useful to analyze semantic relation between constituent of compound nouns. **CDL** can be applicable to not only Japanese but also multi-language following the common description specification.

Several studies on semantic relations between constituents have been discussed so far. In recent work, Baker and Szpakowicz [3] listed the noun modifier relations based on similar lists found in literature on the semantics of compound nouns. Their definition with paraphrases makes it easy to identify semantic relations. We would incorporate the definition into the **CDL**. Table 1 shows some examples of paraphrase by using case particles.

**Table 1.** Semantic relations and paraphrase

| relation | paraphrase & example |
|---|---|
| obj(affected thing) | A *o* B *suru*, A-Acc B |
| | *keitaiso-kaiseki* "morphological analysis" |
| pur(purpose or objective) | A *no-tame-no* B, B for A |
| | *tango-jisho* "word dictionary" |
| mod(modification) | A *teki-na* B, A adjective-forming suffix B |
| | *imi-kankei* "semantic relation" |

## 5 Data Collection

### 5.1 Extraction of Compound Nouns

We collected patent documents provided by Industrial Property Digital Library[1] in order to extract target compound nouns. We used a keyword-based retrieval method in a Patent Utility Model Search System and extracted 459 documents including a word *kikai-hon'yaku-souchi* "machine translation system". The documents were tagged by the morphological analysis system Sen[2] which is a Java implementation of Mecab[3] using IPA dictionary[4]. All compound nouns by combining two or more words are extracted from the tagged documents. From these, we excluded single words such as *jouki* "as mentioned above" and *tougai* "correspond to" so as to filter out terms frequently appeared in the patent documents. A total of 16890 compound nouns were contained in the final dataset.

[1] `http://www.ipdl.inpit.go.jp/homepg.ipdl`
[2] `http://ultimania.org/sen/`
[3] `http://mecab.sourceforge.net/`
[4] `http://chasen.naist.jp/stable/ipadic/`

### 5.2 Weighting Compound Nouns

There are several weighting methods for compound words [9]. Comparing with various weighting methods for compound nouns [1], we used tf-idf(term frequency-inverse document frequency) weight. The tf-idf weight is a weighting method often used in information retrieval. This statistical measure is used for evaluating the importance of a word/document in a collection or corpus. The importance increases frequency of a word in the document but decreases by the frequency of the word in the corpus. We sorted compound nouns by the weighting score and selected 2000 compound nouns from the top.

### 5.3 Assigning Grammatical and Semantic Features

The 448 types of compound nouns were found in the top 2000 compound nouns. We extracted compound nouns which consist of two nouns, and filtered out the constituents consisting of one Chinese character and suffixes. The total number of target compound noun was 224 including the 187 constituents for evaluation. We tagged semantic relations to each compound nouns, and selected mod, obj and pur semantic relations which were frequently used. Though it is difficult to collect a great amount of patent documents, the Mainichi newspaper articles [6] were used for counting the frequency of succeeding information of each constituent. The newspaper articles were tagged by the morphological analysis system Mecab.

All occurrence of target constituents with their immediately succeeding "noun-case particle", "noun-adjective suffix" and "noun-verb*suru*" were counted for frequency ratios. We used the frequency ratios of the each succeeding frequency and their total frequency as the grammatical features. Table 2 shows examples of distribution frequency ratio.

We focus on the grammatical features, however, semantic features is expected to be useful for analyzing semantic relations in compound nouns. Especially, a compound noun consisting of verbal noun needs semantic information [13].

**Table 2.** The distribution of frequency ratio

| constituent | A *ga/o* | B verb*suru* | C adjective suffix *-na* | D suffix *-teki* |
|---|---|---|---|---|
| *kikai* "machine" | 92% | 0% | 0% | 8% |
| *shori* "process" | 53% | 47% | 0% | 0% |
| *seikaku* "accuracy" | 2% | 0% | 98% | 0% |
| *fukanou* "impossibility" | 8% | 0% | 92% | 0% |

**Table 3.** Accuracy of our method

| | accuracy | base-line |
|---|---|---|
| grammatical features | 70% | 41% |
| grammatical &semantic features | 84% | 41% |

We introduce EDR concept classification as semantic features. The target constituents were assigned their semantic features by using EDR dictionary [4]. As EDR electronic dictionary is structured by a deep hierarchy of semantics, we mapped only the 4th semantic features from the top node to the constituent.

## 6 Evaluation

In order to evaluate our method, we performed statistical identification of semantic relations. The sense identification classifier was learned using the SVM support vector machine learner[5].

We prepared 180 training data (mod 90, obj 67 and pur 67) and 44 test data (mod 18, obj 13 and pur 13) for our evaluation. The polynominal kernel was found to be the optimal configuration for the given task employing a one-vs-rest method. We performed classification by using only grammatical features, and both grammatical and semantic ones. We also present a baseline accuracy, based on a majority class strategy (e.g. this corresponds to *mod* semantic relation). In evaluation, the obtained accuracy was 84% with both grammatical and semantic features, and 70% with only grammatical features.

Both of them are well above the baseline accuracy of 41%. This suggests that the fully automatic statistical method provides a powerful means of sense identification. The grammatical features play a key role to identify the semantic relations. There were 7 errors in the test data. We found that identification of the relation between pur and mod was the most difficult task. Especially, compound words, which consist of a verbal noun and a noun, have several relations. we need detailed analysis and information of succeeding patterns with other constituents in compound words.

## 7 Discussion and Future Work

We proposed an identifying method of semantic relations for compound nouns in patent documents, discussing grammatical features of constituent in compound nouns. We found that the performance of the fully automated statistical method was found to be good. The result shows the advantage of our method.

In future work, there are a number of additional grammatical features and the order of constituent in compound nouns. We are also very interested in applying the method proposed here to documents in the different domains or newspaper articles.

## Acknowledgements

This study is based upon work supported by the Strategic Information and Communications R&D Promotion Programme (SCOPe).

[5] `http://chasen.org/~taku/software/TinySVM/`

## References

1. Aihara, S., Uchiyama, K., Ishizaki, S.: Extraction of compound nouns for do-main specific ontology and definition of relation-ship between compound nouns in patent documents. In: Proceedings of the 11th annual meeting of the association for natural language processing, Shiga, Japan (2007)
2. Baldwin, T., Bond, F.: Multiword Expressions: Some Problems for Japanese NLP. In: Proceedings of the 8th annual meeting of the association for natural language processing (2002)
3. Barker, K., Szpakowicz, S.: Semi-automatic recognition of noun modifier relationships. In: Proceedings of COLING-ACL 1998, Canada, pp. 96–102 (1998)
4. Japan Electronic Dictionary Research Institute, Ltd.: EDR Electronic Dictionary Technical Guide, National Institute of Information and Communications Technology (1995)
5. Kim, S.N., Baldwin, T.: Interpreting semantic relations in noun compounds via verb semantics. In: Proceedings of COLING/ACL 2006, Sydney, Australia, pp. 491–498 (2006)
6. Mainichi Newspapers Co.: Mainichi Newspapers data collection. Mainichi Newspapers Co, Japan (1993, 1994, 1995, 2003, 2004)
7. Miyazaki, M.: Automatic segmentation method for compound words using semantic dependent between words. IPSJ Journal 25(6), 970–979 (1984)
8. Miyazaki, M., Ikehara, S., Yokoo, A.: Combined word retrieval for bilingual dictionary based on the analysis of compound words. IPSJ Journal 34(4), 743–753 (1993)
9. Nakagawa, H.: Term recognition based on statistics of compound nouns and their components. Terminology 9(2), 201–219 (2003)
10. Noguchi, S., Tokunaga, T.: Japanese compound noun analysis using case frame information. IPSJ SIG Techinical Report 179(12), 67–72 (2007)
11. Takeuchi, K., et al.: Analysis of Japanese deverbal compounds based on Lexical Conceptual Structure. IPSJ Journal 43(5), 1446–1456 (2002)
12. Tsujimura, N.: An Introduction to Japanese Linguistics. Blackwel Publishers, Cambridge (1996)
13. Uchiyama, K., et al.: A study of grammatical categories based on grammatical features for analysis of compound nouns in specialized field. Mathematical Linguistics 23(1), 1–24 (2001)
14. Uchiyama, K., Ishizaki, S.: Analysis of compound nouns in patent documents. In: Proceedings of the 9th Annual Meeting of Association for Natural Language Processing, Tokyo, Japan, pp. 1107–1110 (2006)
15. Institute of Semantic Computing.: Concept Description Language CDL.core Specifications, ISeC Technical Report:2007-1-29 (2007)

# Extracting Prehistories of Software Refactorings from Version Archives

Shinpei Hayashi and Motoshi Saeki

Department of Computer Science, Tokyo Institute of Technology
2–12–1 Ookayama, Meguro-ku, Tokyo 152–8552, Japan
{hayashi,saeki}@se.cs.titech.ac.jp

**Abstract.** This paper proposes an automated technique to extract prehistories of software refactorings from existing software version archives, which in turn a technique to discover knowledge for finding refactoring opportunities. We focus on two types of knowledge to extract: characteristic modification histories, and fluctuations of the values of complexity measures. First, we extract modified fragments of code by calculating the difference of the Abstract Syntax Trees in the programs picked up from an existing software repository. We also extract past cases of refactorings, and then we create traces of program elements by associating modified fragments with cases of refactorings for finding the structures that frequently occur. Extracted traces help us identify how and where to refactor programs, and it leads to improve the program design.

## 1 Introduction

From year to year, a great many software products are being developed, and furthermore many of them are large-scale and/or have highly complex structures. Maintaining large-scale and complex software products involves with keeping the software design of high quality. However, software is continuously modified in its lifetime, so that we have to recover the quality of the software design.

Software refactoring [1,2] is one of the promising techniques for improving program design by means of transformation with preserving behavior, and is widely taken into practice. It can be applied even to the program that has not been completed, so we can incrementally improve its quality while it is being developed.

Computer-aided refactoring techniques are useful. It is difficult for engineers to identify how and where to refactor programs because proper knowledge and skills are required of them. To automate refactoring activities, we can consider useful tools that automatically find refactoring opportunities. The tool free the programmers from troublesome activities that are manually performed in order to identify where and how to refactor a program.

From an empirical viewpoint, we can study where and how to refactor a program from existing software developing projects. In these days, many Free/Open Source Software (FOSS) are freely available, e.g. via SourceForge.net [3]. Their FOSS projects maintain a history of program modification stored in a version repository by using a version management system, such as CVS [4]. Our focus is that their repositories include many cases of refactorings and their cases are

T. Tokunaga and A. Ortega (Eds.): LKR 2008, LNAI 4938, pp. 82–89, 2008.

considered as knowledge for supporting refactoring activities. We then can analyze them for finding what kind of program modification lead to refactorings by performing a sort of historical analysis.

In this paper, we propose an automated technique to discover characteristic modification histories from its repository, which in turn a technique to find refactoring opportunities. Modified fragments of code and past cases of refactorings extracted from repositories help us create modification patterns for supporting refactoring activities. We indicate the effectiveness of our technique by applying it to an open-source software repository.

The rest of this paper is organized as follows. Section 2 shows some motivating examples of refactorings that illustrate typical situations we focused on. Section 3 includes proposed technique to find knowledge for supporting refactoring activities. Discussions about our case study are described in Sect. 4. Finally, Sect. 5 gives our conclusions and suggests future work.

## 2 Motivating Examples

In this section, we describe two examples which illustrate the typical situation of the cases of refactorings that we focused on [5].

### 2.1 Using the Information about Code Duplication

Code clone is defined as code fragments *similar to* an original code fragments, or *duplicated* code fragments. In order to decrease software management costs, code clones should be collected together into one occurrence, and this is realized by clone analysis. Some code clones occur when a developer duplicates a code fragment to several places in a program by using copy-and-paste editing operation. So we can suggest a refactoring to eliminate the occurrences of code clones by monitoring developer's duplication operations such as carrying out copy-and-paste command. Figure 1 shows an example of suggesting a refactoring which extracts a super class and forms Template Method pattern [6], in order to eliminate code clones of class $C$. A developer first duplicates a class $C$, and as a result, the program has the code clone $C_{dup}$ of $C$. After that, he/she modifies an internal method $M$ by adding a statement. In this case, we can observe the sequence of program modifications as: 1) Duplicate $C$ to $C_{dup}$, and 2) Add of a statement in $M$ (in $C_{dup}$). Since the program has an occurrence of a code clone of $C$, the refactoring to eliminate it can be recommended. More concretely, the refactoring operation called Form Template Method can be used to do it. We extract a super class $C_{super}$ and re-organize a template method $M$ and hook method $Mpo$, in order to represent the difference of the method $M$ in $C_{dup}$ from $C$.

### 2.2 Using the Changes of Complexity Measures

Some of software metrics such as WMC of C&K metrics [7] expresses the complexity of a component of the program, and it can be applied to decide when and where refactoring should be carried out. For example, suppose that a developer

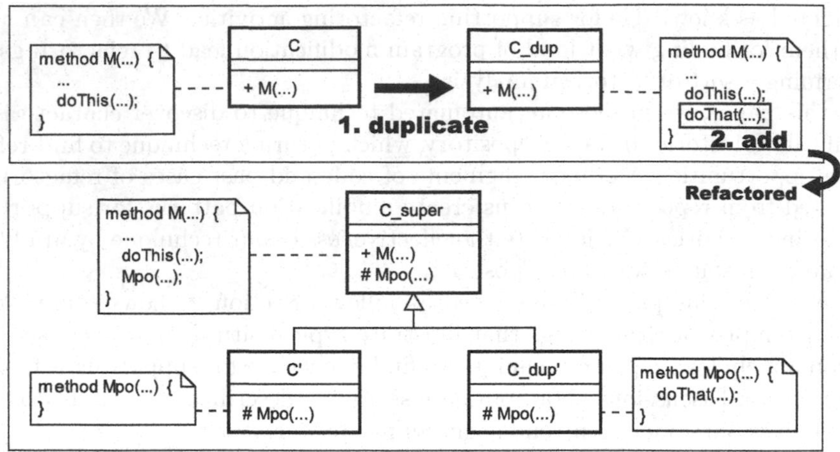


**Fig. 1.** Refactoring after the class duplication

finds that a class $A$ in the program is too large while a class $B$ is too small when he/she calculates the measures denoting the size of a code fragment. He/she can carry out the refactorings for decomposing $A$ into several smaller components and for inlining $B$ or the methods included in $B$. As shown above, by using the techniques of software metrics, especially complexity metrics, we can decide some refactorings to be carried out according to the value of metrics.

However, since the values of such measures represent a current snapshot of the program, they cannot reflect developer's intention on whether he/she will increase or decrease the complexity of the component. Obviously, just after starting coding a component, its complexity value is low but this fact does not necessary follow that inline refactoring should be carried out to it. That is to say, we may not suggest suitable refactoring based on a developer's intention, by using just a value of software metrics. It means that we should focus not on the value of software but on the changes of the metrics to extract the developer's intention. If he/she intends to build up a component in a program, he/she is adding some statements to the component and its complexity value is increasing. In this situation, when the complexity value comes near the threshold, i.e. the component comes to be too large, we can recommend the refactoring for decomposing it. On the other hand, if he/she performs consecutive deletions of statements in a component and its complexity value becomes too low, we can suggest inline refactoring operations. We can informally summarize this situation as follows: We should consider the fluctuation of the values of complexity measures in order to detect the refactorings for loosening the bias of complexities.

## 3 Proposed Technique

Above examples indicate a history of program modification gives suggestions to refactor the program. Cloning a code and editing the cloned one may be caused

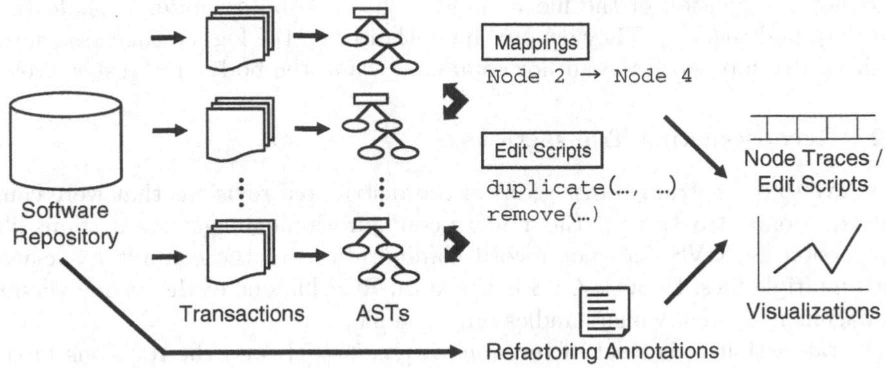


**Fig. 2.** An overview of the proposed system

by an intention to construct a similarly code. Consecutive modification indicates that a large amount of program editing may be going to be continued.

Detecting this kind of characteristic modification is valuable because they imply refactoring opportunities for improving the program which is being developed. Therefore, we should build a knowledge base of modification patterns to detect program modification leads to refactoring opportunities.

This section describes an automated technique to extract modification histories corresponding to refactorings for guidance to construct modification patterns. An overview of our technique is shown in Fig. 2. The procedure of proposed technique is following:

1. Preparing a software repository to be analyzed.
2. Reconstructing transactions from revisions.
3. Extracting traces of program elements by determining Edit Scripts.
4. Extracting the cases of refactorings from the repository.
5. Analyzing and/or visualizing the evolutions of program elements.

In the following subsections, we illustrate the descriptions of each procedure.

### 3.1 System Input: Preparing Software Repository

First, we should prepare a software repository as the target of analyses. The repository should contain 1) many revisions, and the contents of the repository should have structured syntax in order to extract traces of program elements, and 2) some additional information such as modification rationales, etc. in order to reconstruct the cases of refactorings. For example, some large-scale CVS [4] repositories that contain many of Java programs are suitable. We can find these repositories from websites for software clearing houses, e.g. SourceForge.net [3].

We formalize a repository as a set of versioned files: $R = \{F_1, F_2, \ldots, F_{|R|}\}$. $path(F_i)$ denotes the path name of the file $F_i$. $F_i$ also represents multiple versions of programs, and is formalized as the set of revisions: $F_i = \{r_1, r_2, \ldots, r_{|F_i|}\}$.

$r_i$ denotes a revision of the file $F_i$, and $r_i$ has attributes: $author(r_i)$, $log(r_i)$, $date(r_i)$, and $body(r_i)$. They denote the author of $r_i$, the log message associated with $r_i$, the date when the author commits $r_i$, and the body of $r_i$ respectively.

### 3.2 Reconstructing Transactions

We have to reconstruct transactions of the distributed revisions that were committed at once. Contrary to the modern configuration management systems like Subversion [8], CVS does not record configurations of the commit associated with multiple files. Because CVS is based on RCS [9], one of the legacy version management system which handles only one file.

A transaction $T_i$ is a set of revisions $\{r^i_1, \ldots, r^i_{|T_i|}\}$, and the revisions in the same transaction satisfy following conditions:

$$\forall j,k \quad author(r^i_j) = author(r^i_k) \ \wedge \ log(r^i_j) = log(r^i_k) \ \wedge$$
$$\forall j \neq 1 \quad |date(r^i_j) - date(r^i_{j-1})| < threshold.$$

The formula regard a transaction as a set of revisions committed by *almost* at once, and by the same developer with the same log message. A transaction $T_i = \{r^i_1, \ldots, r^i_{|T_i|}\}$ has also following attributes:

- $date(T_i) = \min_{r^i_j \in T_i} date(r^i_j)$,
- $log(T_i) = log(r^i_1)$: commit log of the $T_i$.

In order to reconstruct transactions, we use Zimmermann et al's approach with Sliding Time Window [10], that can extract the minimum set of transactions: $T = \{T_1, \ldots, T_{|T|}\}$ $s.t.$ $\forall i < j \ \ date(T_i) \leq date(T_j)$. We use 60 seconds as the size of the window, i.e. *threshold.*

### 3.3 Extracting Traces of Program Elements and Edit Scripts

To extract modification sequences as Edit Scripts, we first parse the input programs $body(r_i)$ to Abstract Syntax Trees (AST). In order to recover broken Java programs, e.g. including syntax errors, we use Eclipse JDT [11] as the parser because it can parse malformed programs. The attributes of the parsed program fragment $N$, i.e. a node of the AST, is represented as follows:

- $type(N)$: the type name of $N$,
- $property(N)$: mapping $Key \rightarrow String$,
- $children(N)$: mapping $Key \rightarrow a\ set\ of\ nodes.$

Next, we find the association between AST nodes in the older revisions and the new one, and then we extract program modifications as Edit Scripts. The nodes belonging to the transaction $T_i$ are compared with the nodes belonging to the transaction $T_{i+1}$, and mapped if two nodes are regarded as the same. In order to optimize the mapping, the hybrid top-down/bottom-up approach is used [12]. After the calculation of mapping between the nodes in $T_i$ and $T_{i+1}$,

Edit Scripts are generated. The nodes only in the $T_i$'s revision and the nodes only in the $T_{i+1}$'s revision are extracted as the removed and added nodes, respectively. Furthermore, similar nodes between transactions are associated with *duplication* relationship.

### 3.4 Refactoring Reconstruction

To extract the characteristic traces associated with refactoring activities, we use the cases of refactorings that are actually performed. We annotate the information about refactorings to transactions: $\mathit{refactor}(T_i, Op, Path, \ldots)$. The information indicates the refactoring operation $Op$ was performed in the transaction $T_i$, and the refactoring is associated with the node specified by *Path*. The annotator can refer the information to find the cases, e.g. refactoring candidates extracted from existing refactoring reconstruction techniques [13], or transactions that might be remarked as the refactoring activities, i.e. $\mathit{log}(T_i)$ includes the description about some refactorings.

### 3.5 Extracting and Analyzing Traces

Using the cases of refactorings and the above mappings, we obtain the following traces of nodes: $N_1 \to N_2 \to \ldots \to N_n$. $N_i$ associated with the revision $r_i$ and the transaction $T_i (\ni r_i)$ such that $N_i$ is a descendant of $\mathit{body}(r_i)$. We then get also the trace of transactions: $T_1 \to T_2 \to \ldots \to T_n$. Here, $\forall i < j \;\; \mathit{date}(T_i) \leq \mathit{date}(T_j)$.

If the transaction $T_n$ is annotated as the refactoring candidate, the trace should be analyzed to find the knowledge for finding refactoring. We consider the analysis of sequential pattern mining methods or visualizations by using some complexity measures like the size of node.

## 4 Case Study

We have developed an automated tool to extract traces of program elements and Edit Scripts, and have a plan to evaluate our technique. Our tool can extract a sequence of fine-grained program modification, traces of program elements, and cases of refactorings. Users can look up a sequence of modifications corresponding to a refactoring on which they focused.

A simple case study is shown as follows. We applied our technique to Apache Jakarta Commons [14] software repository. The size of the repository is shown in Table 1. Here, "# of revisions" denotes the total size of the revisions found in all the files in the repository, "# of transactions" denotes the size of transactions collected from all revisions. "# of refactorings" candidates denotes the size of transactions that might be remarked as the refactoring activities. The traces extracted from the repository should be analyzed.

From the repository, analyses indicate a relationship between duplication (code clone detection) to a Extracting Super Class refactoring. Figure 3 illustrates the relationship. The figure illustrates an evolution of two classes:

**Table 1.** The target repository of the analysis

| name | jakarta-commons-cvs |
|---|---|
| during | 20/3/2001 – 27/1/2005 |
| # of revisions | 64,054 |
| # of transactions | 13,718 |
| # of refactoring candidates | 161 |

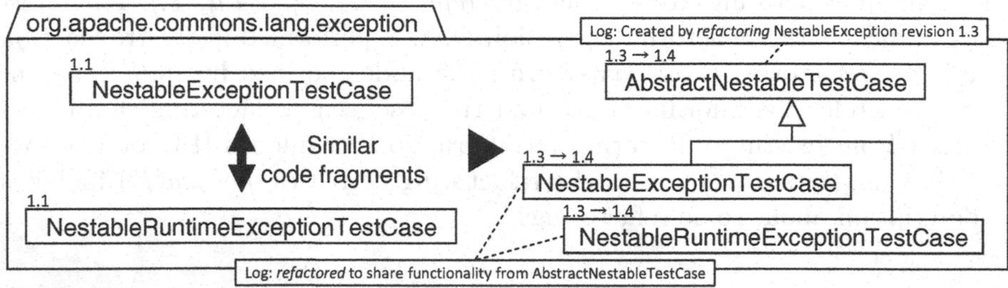


**Fig. 3.** The relationship between modification and refactoring

`NestableExceptionTestCase` and `NestableRuntimeExceptionTestCase`. In the revision from 1.3 to 1.4, a new class `AbstractNestableTestCase` is constructed and common functionalities of above two classes are pulled up to the new class by using Extracting Super Class refactoring. The evolution indicates code clones and code duplications are concerned with the refactoring, then it also suggests the effectiveness of modification analysis for supporting refactoring activities.

## 5 Conclusions

In this paper, we focused on the tracing of program elements. We then showed the technique for analyzing the evolutions of program elements as a prehistory of software refactoring in order to find undescribed refactoring opportunities.

We are considering following topics as future work:

- To discuss the suitable representation technique of modifications in terms of ease of our analysis. Now we regard modifications as a sequence of Edit Scripts, however, possibilities of other models, e.g. versioned tree structure, or graph structure, are considerable.
- To visualize past modifications. Modifications are collaborated with the other modifications and/or current programs, so it is desirable to show these relationships.
- To apply our technique to larger-scale software repositories.

## Acknowledgement

This work was supported by Japan Society for the Promotion of Science (The Grant-in-Aid for JSPS Fellows, #18·52403).

## References

1. Opdyke, W.F.: Refactoring Object-Oriented Frameworks. PhD thesis, University of Illinois at Urbana-Champaign (1992)
2. Fowler, M.: Refactoring: Improving the Design of Existing Code. Addison-Wesley, Reading (1999)
3. SourceForge, Inc.: SourceForge.net (2004), `http://sourceforge.net/`
4. Cederqvist, P.: Version management with CVS (2003), `http://ximbiot.com/cvs/manual/`
5. Hayashi, S., Saeki, M., Kurihara, M.: Supporting refactoring activities using histories of program modification. IEICE Trans. on Information and Systems E89-D(4), 1403–1412 (2006)
6. Gamma, E., et al.: Design Patterns: Elements of Reusable Object-Oriented Software. Addison-Wesley, Reading (1995)
7. Chidamber, S., Kemerer, C.: A metrics suite for object-oriented design. IEEE Trans. on Software Engineering 20(6), 476–493 (1994)
8. Behlendorf, B., et al.: Subversion (2003), `http://subversion.tigris.org/`
9. Tichy, W.F.: RCS, `http://www.cs.purdue.edu/homes/trinkle/rcs/`
10. Zimmermann, T., Weißgerber, P.: Preprocessing CVS data for fine-grained analysis. In: Proc. 1st Int'l Workshop on Mining Software Repositories, pp. 2–6 (2004)
11. The Eclipse Foundation: Eclipse Java Development Tools (JDT) Subproject. `http://www.eclipse.org/jdt/`
12. Lee, K.H., Choy, Y.C., Cho, S.B.: An efficient algorithm to compute differences between structured documents. IEEE Trans. on Knowledge and Data Engineering 16(8), 965–979 (2004)
13. Weißgerber, P., Diehl, S.: Identifying refactorings from source-code changes. In: Proc. 21st Int'l Conf. on Automated Software Engineering, pp. 231–240 (2006)
14. The Apache Software Foundation: Jakarta Commons (1999), `http://jakarta.apache.org/commons/`

# Initiatives, Tendencies and Driving Forces for a "Lexical Web" as Part of a "Language Infrastructure"

Nicoletta Calzolari

Istituto di Linguistica Computazionale del CNR,
56100 Pisa, Italy
glottolo@ilc.cnr.it

**Abstract.** While highlighting the infrastructural role of Language Resources (LR) I sketch my perception of the current situation in the LR field. I underline some of the priority areas of concern today with respect to implementing an open Language Infrastructure, and specifically what we could call a "Lexical Web". My objective is to show that it is imperative that there is an underlying global strategy behind the set of initiatives which are/can be launched in Europe and world-wide, and that a global vision and cooperation among different communities is necessary to achieve more coherent and useful results. I end up mentioning two new European initiatives that go on this direction and promise to be influential in shaping the future of the LR area.

**Keywords:** Language Resources, Language Infrastructure, Computational Lexicons, Standards, Language Technology.

## 1 Language Resources Today: Still a Virtual Infrastructure

After long years of disregard – if not contempt – for lexicons, corpora, and data in general, after the '80s the computational linguistics and natural language processing (NLP) community began to recognise not only the importance of language resources (LR) – as they started to be called in those years – but also their infrastructural role for Human Language Technologies (HLT). Infrastructural resources means that their value resides in enabling something else to work, i.e. NLP tools, systems, applications, evaluations, that depend on supporting resources which also strongly influence their quality. LRs thus indirectly generate value for producers and users.

### 1.1 Infrastructural Initiatives: Some Historical Notes

It was in the '90s that LRs started to be considered as the necessary common platform on which to base new technologies and applications, a recognition which is nowadays widely accepted for the development and takeoff of our field.

The following types of initiatives were considered, in the past two decades, the major building blocks of any action towards a LR infrastructure [1]:

- LR standardisation
- LR construction
- LR distribution.

T. Tokunaga and A. Ortega (Eds.): LKR 2008, LNAI 4938, pp. 90–105, 2008.

A number of projects or other initiatives were launched, often first in Europe then world-wide, in the three above mentioned areas. We mention here just a few:

i) Standards for LRs: the concept of reusability – directly related to the importance of "large scale" LRs within the increasingly dominant data-driven approach – has contributed significantly to the structure of many R&D efforts, such as EAGLES, ISLE, the recent LIRICS (e-Content) project aiming to provide ISO ratified standards for LRs & LT, and finally ISO itself with the many Working Groups in the ISO-TC37/SC4 committee.
ii) LR construction: with projects such as WordNet, PAROLE, SIMPLE, LC-Star, EuroWordNet, BalkaNet.
iii) LR Distribution: LDC (Linguistic Data Consortium) in US, ELRA (European Language Resources Association) in Europe.

To these three dimensions a fourth and a fifth were soon added as necessary complement, in particular to achieve the required robustness and data coverage and to assess results obtained with current methodologies and techniques, i.e.:

iv) Automatic acquisition of LRs or of linguistic information: projects such as ACQUILEX, SPARKLE, ECRAN.
v) Use of LRs for evaluation: evaluation campaigns such as MUC, TREC, CLEF, Senseval, ACE.

## 1.2 Relevance of Language Resources Today

LRs have plaid a critical role, as a horizontal technology, in different areas of the EC 6th Framework Programme, and have been recognized as a priority within national projects around Europe. The very large body of initiatives of the last two decades (see [2] for an overview) was decisive and instrumental for the formation of what we can call today a "LR community". This also gave rise to a set of other international initiatives of a more global nature, encompassing many various perspectives on LRs or dealing with policy and meta-level issues related to LRs, such as:

- The Thematic Network Enabler, grouping European National projects on LRs;
- The LREC Conference (about 900 participants in Lisbon-2004 and Genova-2006);
- The Asian Federation of Natural Language Processing (AFNLP);
- Bodies such as COCOSDA (International Committee for the Coordination and Standardisation of Speech Databases and Assessment Techniques) and WRITE (Written Resources Infrastructure, Technology and Evaluation);
- The new international journal *Language Resources and Evaluation* [3].

Not to mention the ever-increasing role of LRs in statistical and empirical methods, the growing industrial interest in using LRs and standards, specially for multilingual applications, and the availability of adequate LRs for as many languages as possible as a pre-requisite for the development of a truly multilingual Information Society.

This flourishing of international projects and activities contributed to substantially advance knowledge and capability of how to represent, create, acquire, access, tune, maintain, standardise, etc. large lexical and textual repositories. We can assert that there are today countless initiatives in the field of LRs, but we must also admit that they are somehow scattered, opportunistic, often unconnected, with no real ability to build on each other and to be seen as a unified space of LRs. We thus recognise that the LR infrastructure is still a virtual one. There is no real global coordination of efforts, and no body able to create the needed synergies among the various initiatives.

On the other side, the success itself of the field – as shown by LREC, but also by the pervasiveness of LR papers in all major HLT conferences – and its vitality and richness, coupled with the lack of coordination and of strategic thinking about future orientations, show that it is time to reflect again on the field as a whole, and ask ourselves which are/will be the major driving forces of today and of tomorrow to give to the field the necessary cohesion.

### 1.3 Need of a Change

The wealth of LRs, in comparison with few years ago, but coupled with the shortage, even now, of a) new types of LRs, b) multilingual LRs, c) LRs of much larger size, d) LRs with richer annotations, and so on, points towards the need to consider whether those mentioned above are still the basic/major driving forces. How have they changed and evolved? Which new building blocks do emerge today?

I believe that those dimensions are still relevant, even if with an obvious evolution. Consolidated or emerging pillars in current HLT are:

i) *Interoperability*, and even more *content interoperability*: language is recognised as key mediator to access content, knowledge, ontologies;
ii) *Collaborative creation and management of LRs*, even on the model of wiki initiatives;
iii) *Sharing of LRs*, as a new dimension of the distribution notion;
iv) *Dynamic LRs*, able to auto-enrich themselves; and finally the more comprehensive notion of:
v) *Distributed architectures and infrastructures for LRs*, encompassing and exploiting the realisation of the previous notions.

Could these notions be at the basis of a new paradigm for LRs and LT and influence the setting up of a "real" infrastructure? I will mention in the last section two new European initiatives where such notions will play a prominent role.

## 2 Some Tendencies and Driving Forces in the Lexical Domain

Mixing considerations on what is needed for a broad language infrastructure and for a "lexical web" – undoubtedly a key part of it –, I touch here issues linked to this view and relevant to establishing a lexical web. I do that by pointing at research activities carried out at ILC in Pisa[1] showing a variety of approaches to lexical resources, involving: i) procedures for linking, integrating and unifying existing lexical resources, ii) standardisation, iii) relation between lexical and terminological or ontological resources, iv) "ontologisation" of lexicons, v) architectures for managing, merging, integrating lexical resources.

[1] Many passages in this section are taken from various papers, listed in the References, of ILC colleagues.

### 2.1 Integration/Unification of Existing Lexicons

The market is increasingly calling for new types of lexical resources: lexicons that can be built rapidly – tailored to specific requirements – possibly by combining certain types of information from available lexicons while discarding others. Rather than building new lexical resources, this need could be satisfied exploiting the richness of existing lexicons, aiming at attaining their integration or virtual unification.

**ELRA Unified Lexicon.** An initiative in this direction has been carried out at ELRA by its Production Committee: the *Unified Lexicon* project [4]. This experiment consisted in linking the LC-Star and PAROLE lexicons to set up a methodology to connect Spoken and Written LRs, thus establishing new models of LR distribution. In the envisaged scenario the same lexicons may be made available to different types of users, who can select different portions of the same lexicon or combine information coming from different lexicons. This scenario calls for an environment where lexical resources can be shared, are reusable and openly customisable, instead of being static, closed, and locally managed repositories of lexical information.

**Linking ItalWordNet and SIMPLE Semantic Lexicons.** The two largest and extensively encoded Italian lexicons, ItalWordNet (IWN) and PAROLE-SIMPLE-CLIPS (PSC), although developed according to two different lexical models, present many compatible aspects. Linking – and eventually merging – these lexicons in a common representation framework means to offer the end-user a more exhaustive lexical information combining the potentialities and the outstanding features offered by the two lexical models [5]. Not only reciprocal enhancements are obtained, but also a validation of the two resources. Semantic integration of these lexicons is all the more desirable considering their multilingual vocation: IWN is linked to wordnets for many other languages, and PSC shares with eleven European lexicons the theoretical model, representation language, building methodology and a core of entries.

*Mapping the Ontologies and the Lexicons.* Due to a different organisational structure of the two ontology-based lexicons, the linking process involves elements having a different status, i.e. autonomous semantic units in PSC and synsets in IWN. Mapping is performed on a semantic type-driven basis: comparing their ontological framework and establishing correspondences between the conceptual classes of both ontologies, with a view to further matching their respective instances.

Notwithstanding the different approaches in their design and some diverse underlying principles, the two ontologies show a significant degree of overlapping. A tool devised to map the lexical units of both lexicons works in a semiautomatic way using ontological classifications, hyperonymic ('isa') relations and semantic features. Taking as starting point the lexical instances of a SIMPLE semantic type along with their PoS and 'isa' information, IWN is explored in search of linking candidates with identical string and PoS, whose ontological classification matches the correspondences established between the classes of both ontologies. The result of the first phase, devoted to linking concrete entities, sounds quite encouraging since 72.32% of the word-senses considered have been successfully linked.

The linking process makes it possible to enrich each resource by complementary information types peculiar to the other's theoretical model. In IWN, the richness of sense distinctions and the consistency of hierarchical links are remarkable. SIMPLE, on the other hand, focuses on richly describing the meaning and semantic context of a word and on linking its syntactic and semantic representation, which is crucial for most NLP applications. Moreover, the mapping lets inconsistencies that unavoidably exist in both lexicons emerge, allowing to amend them. To give but an example, consistency would require that, when a synset variant is linked to a SIMPLE sense (SemU), all the other variants from the same synset map to PSC entries sharing the same semantic type. Yet, especially for event denoting words, some SemUs corresponding to variants of the same synset do not share a common semantic type. The linking process implies a de facto reciprocal assessment of both coverage and accuracy, particularly relevant to hand-built lexicons.

Differences regarding the nature of linking units, the granularity of sense distinction and the ontological typing are complex issues that are also being addressed during the linking process.

## 2.2 Interoperability: Still at the Heart of the Field

We have made big steps forward with respect to interoperability. Work started in EAGLES and ISLE (http://www.ilc.cnr.it/EAGLES96/isle/) [6] is being consolidated in recent years in true international ISO standards.

**ISO.** The Working Group ISO TC37/SC4/WG4 dedicated to NLP lexicons[2] is in charge of defining lexical standards for NLP purposes. The result of the work is assembled in the so called LMF (*Lexical Markup Framework*) standard [7]. To cope with the challenge that actual lexicons differ very much both in complexity and in type of encoded information, a modular organization was adopted. As a consequence, the LMF specification is made up of a core model, a sort of simple skeleton, and various semi-independent packages of notions, used for the various linguistic layers that can make up a lexicon, attached to this core model. From the UML point of view, these specifications are UML packages, as shown in Figure 1.

Lexical specifications are split in separate object types: LMF defines the lexical structure and is kept simple, while the huge amount of attributes (e.g. Part-of-Speech) are recorded in a data category registry [8] where the peculiarities of languages and linguistic schools can be recorded. Also the text annotation standards for the various linguistic layers of annotation (see e.g. http://syntax.inist.fr/) refer to this registry, common to all TC37/SC4 standards[3], thus guaranteeing interoperability between lexicon and corpus annotation. This is summarized in the diagram in Figure 2. The ISO document defines also an XML DTD based on the UML modelling. Moreover an OWL format has been defined – as the representation of our knowledge about the words – that can be smoothly integrated into Semantic Web applications.

**NEDO.** While both EAGLES and ISLE dealt with European languages, the Japanese NEDO project [9], aiming at developing international standards for Semantic Web applications, is specifically geared to Asian languages: Chinese, Japanese, Thai. It applies and refines ISO standards so that they are adapted to Asian languages.

---

[2] With Nicoletta Calzolari as convenor and Gil Francopoulo and Monte George, respectively from France and US, as co-editors (or project leaders).

[3] The registry is common also to other standards outside SC4, e.g. to terminology.

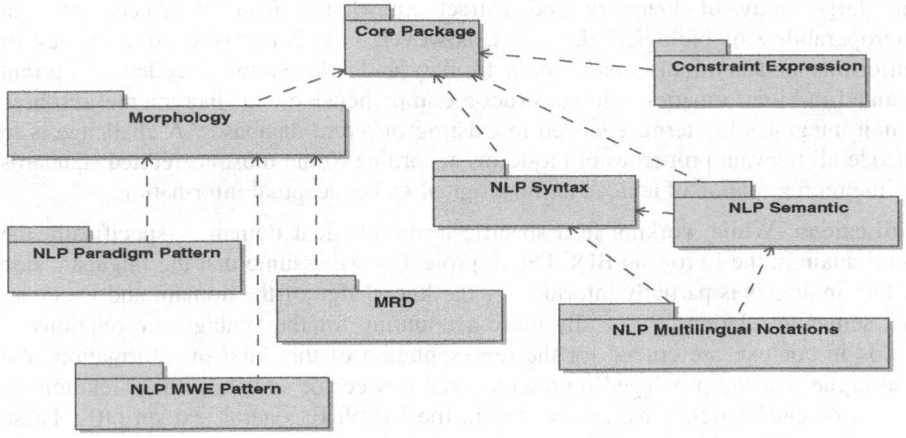


**Fig. 1.** LMF structure

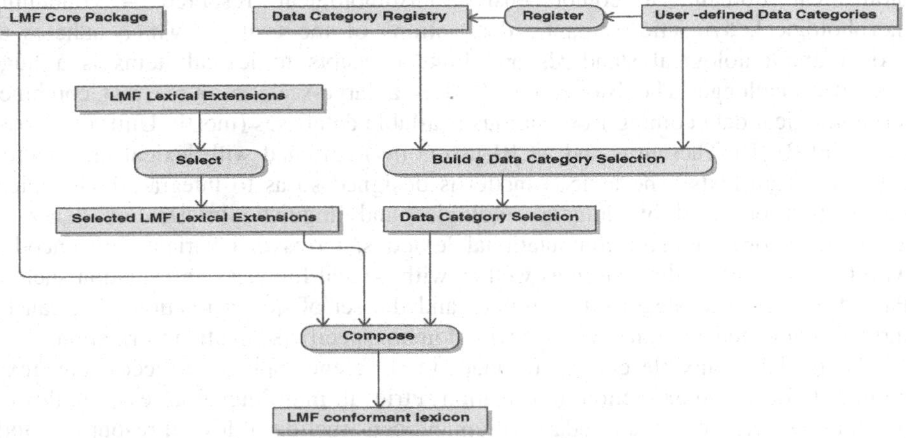


**Fig. 2.** Interaction between LMF Core Package and Data Category Registry

**But true content interoperability is still far away.** If we want a grid of distributed LRs they must be able to "speak" with each other. We may have solved the issue of formats, of inventories of linguistic categories for the various linguistic layers, but we have not solved the problem of relating senses, of finding matches of similarity among senses, that only would allow automatic integration of semantic resources. This is a challenge for the next years, and a prerequisite for both a true Lexical Web and a credible Semantic Web.

## 2.3 Lexicons and Terminologies: A Continuum

Due to the increasing production of literature in the biomedical field, and its strategic relevance, intensive research is being carried out world-wide to develop LTs to access this large body of literature and extract knowledge from it. Access to and interoperability of biological databases, however, is still hampered due to lack of uniformity and harmonisation of both formats and information encoded. A current demand in bioinformatics is to construct a comprehensive and incremental resource which integrates bio-terms encoded in existing different databases. A challenge is to encode all relevant properties of bio-terms according to the most accredited standards for the representation of lexical, terminological and conceptual information.

**BioLexicon.** While working in a specific terminological domain – specifically the bio-domain in the European BOOTStrep project[4] – we assume that the linguistic side of terminologies is partially informed by the knowledge of the domain and we claim that semantic relations, especially those accounting for the syntagmatic relations of words in context, are crucial for the representation of this kind of information. We also argue that the privileged representational device for encoding these relations is the set of Qualia Relations, as encoded in the SIMPLE general lexicon [10]. These assumptions are made operational in a new lexical resource, the *BioLexicon*, specially designed for the representation of all linguistically relevant aspects of a lexicon for information extraction and text-mining in the bio-domain. Building up, for the biomedical domain, a comprehensive terminological resource – containing morphological, syntactic, semantic descriptions of the terms – which adheres to lexical and ontological standards and links concepts to lexical items is a huge scientific challenge. The BioLexicon [11] is a large-scale resource that combines terminological data coming from various available databases (mostly UniProt, Swiss-Prot, ChEBI, BioThesaurus and NCBI taxonomy) enriched with lexical information extracted from texts. The lexicon model is designed so as to integrate both typical information provided by domain ontologies and linguistic information generally available in open-domain computational lexicons: terms and variants are encoded with their semantic information as well as with typical linguistic information such as Part-of-Speech, subcategorisation frames and the set of qualia relations that can be further augmented and tuned to cope with domain specific semantic information.

The model – flexible enough to adapt to different application needs, e.g. text-mining, information extraction, information retrieval, multilingual access – builds on previous experience in the standardisation and construction of lexical resources. Both the conceptual model and its physical implementation are tailored to the automatic population and enhancement of the resource, independently of the various native data formats. The DB, as a reflection of the model, is a modular and flexible resource which can automatically upload new data and provide (XML) outputs by means of web services. An *XML interchange format* (XIF) has been designed with the purpose of automatically populating the BioLexicon with data provided by domain experts and by lexical acquisition systems, therefore allowing for a standardisation of the data extracted from the different terminological resources and from texts.

The goal is to propose a standard for the representation of lexicons in the bio-domain, which could eventually be also interoperable with other domain lexicons. For this reason the ISO Lexical Markup Framework [12] was chosen as the reference meta-model for the structure of the BioLexicon, and the ISO Data Categories as the

---

[4] BOOTStrep (Bootstrapping Of Ontologies and Terminologies STrategic Project) is an IST European project under the 6th Framework Programme (www.bootstrep.eu).

main building blocks for the representation of the entries. The existence of a reusable bio-lexicon with sophisticated linguistic information, linked to a corresponding bio-ontology, should enable the bio-informatics community to develop information extraction tools of higher quality.

## 2.4 Lexicons and Ontologies : Another Dilemma

Ontologies are recognised as an important component in NLP systems that deal with the semantic level of language [13]. In fact most, if not all, of the semantic lexical resources (e.g. WordNet, CYC, SIMPLE), have in common the presence of an ontology as a core module. Besides, there is a lot of research in progress on applying ontologies to semantic NLP.

The fact that OWL is the ontology language for the Semantic Web and that it provides a formal semantic representation as well as reasoning capabilities has encouraged the NLP community to convert existing resources to this language. Work in this area includes, for example, the conversion in OWL of WordNet (see below) and MeSH [14] and the proposal of a general method for converting thesauri [15].

**RDF/OWL representation of WordNet: A data model for the Semantic Web.** During the last years, WordNet has received a growing attention by the Semantic Web community. Within W3C, WordNet has been translated in the widely adopted standard semantic languages RDF and OWL [16]. RDF(S) and OWL, designed to describe collections of resources on the Web, are convenient data models to represent highly interconnected information and their semantic relations, and therefore useful to support WordNet graph data model. Moreover, the RDF/OWL representation of WordNet is easily extensible, allows for interoperability and makes no assumptions about a particular application domain. The availability of WordNet Web Services can be an important step for its integration and effective use into the Semantic Web, and for future multilingual semantic interoperability in the Web [17].

**"Ontologisation" of lexicons.** A new initiative at ILC is the conversion into OWL of the ontology of SIMPLE [18], the lexico-semantic resource based on the Generative Lexicon (GL) theory. The elements of SIMPLE modelled in OWL are those used to define the original ontology, i.e. semantic types, qualia relations and semantic features. The ontology design presents a challenge as the nodes of the ontology are not only defined by their formal dimension (taxonomic hierarchy), but also by the additional GL qualia dimensions: constitutive, telic and agentive. The modelling choices to convert different elements of the original resources into OWL are as follows. Semantic types are modelled in OWL as classes, relations as object properties, features as datatype properties, predicates with functional object properties. For qualia relations, that add multidimensionality in the ontology, the domain and the range is made up of the classes ENTITY and the class that corresponds to the type of qualia relation (CONSTITUTIVE, TELIC and AGENTIVE).

Besides formalising the ontology in OWL, it is enriched in a bottom-up approach that extracts further semantic information from the word-senses of the lexicon, by using the qualia structure as a generative device. This way, the ontology is augmented e.g. with selected constraints on relations and features extracted from the lexicon, by exploring the word-senses (semantic units) that belong to each semantic type.

This research is aiming at the representation of a lexico-semantic resource based in the GL theory into the Semantic Web ontology language, with reasoning capabilities interfaced to a lexicon. The conversion allows the ontology to be processed and checked by standard reasoners. This can be useful for building Semantic Web applications and for semantic NLP tasks (e.g. information extraction and knowledge acquisition) as well as for enhancing the quality of the resource by validating it (through reasoning one can look for inconsistencies or conflicts).

This ontology is a key element of a broader forthcoming research aimed at automatic lexico-semantic-driven text mining and knowledge acquisition procedures, which, in their turn, have the goal of gathering knowledge to enrich the lexicon, thus creating a virtuous circle between lexicon/ontology and corpus-based information acquisition.

## 2.5 Architectures for Integrating Lexical Resources

Enhancing the development of multilingual lexicons is of foremost importance for intercultural collaboration [19], as multilingual lexicons are the cornerstone of several multilingual applications. Nevertheless, large-scale multilingual lexical resources are not yet as widely available as needed. As said above, a new trend is emerging, focusing on trying to exploit the richness of existing lexicons, in addition to or instead of creating new ones. At the same time, as the history of the web teaches, it would be a mistake to create a central repository of all the shared lexicons, while distribution of resources is a central concept. A solution emerging in the LR community consists in moving towards distributed language services, based on open content interoperability standards, and made accessible to users via web-service technologies.

There is another, deeper argument in favour of distributed lexical resources: LRs, lexicons included, are inherently distributed because of the diversity of languages distributed over the world. It is not only natural that LRs are developed and maintained in their native environment. Since language evolves and changes over time, it is not possible to describe the current state of the language away from where the language is spoken. Lastly, also the vast range of diversity of languages makes it impossible to have one single universal centralised resource, or even a centralised repository of resources.

**Web services for LRs or LRs as web services.** Having lexical resources available as web services would allow to create new resources on the basis of existing ones, to exchange and integrate information across repositories, and to compose new services on demand: an approach towards the development of an infrastructure built on top of the Internet in the form of distributed language services is presented in [20].

This new type of LRs can still be stored locally, but their maintenance and exploitation can be a matter of agents being choreographed to act over them. Admittedly, this is a long-term scenario requiring the contribution of many different actors and initiatives (among which we only mention standardisation, distribution and international cooperation). The first prerequisite for this scenario to take place is to ensure true interoperability among lexical resources, a goal that is long being addressed to by the standardisation community and that is now mature, at least for many aspects. Although the paradigm of distributed and interoperable lexical resources has largely been discussed and invoked, very little has been made for its practical realisation. Some initial steps have been made to design frameworks enabling inter-lexica access, search, integration and operability. An example is the Lexus tool [21], based on the Lexical Markup Framework, that goes in the direction of managing the exchange of data among large-scale lexical resources. A similar tool, but tailored to the collaborative creation of lexicons for endangered language, is SHAWEL [22]. However, the general impression is that little has been made towards the development of new methods, techniques and tools for attaining a concrete interoperability among lexical resources.

**LeXFlow.** The design of a general architecture able to turn into reality the vision of shared and distributed lexical repositories is a very challenging task. To meet these needs, we have designed and built a distributed architecture – *LeXFlow* (http://xmlgroup.iit.cnr.it:8888/xflow/login) – enabling a rapid prototyping of cooperative applications for integrating lexical resources [23]. It is based on a web-service architecture, fostering integration and interoperability of computational lexicons, focusing on the particular case of mutual linking and cross-lingual enrichment of distributed monolingual lexical resources.

As case–studies, we have chosen to work with:

i) two Italian lexicons based on different models, SIMPLE and ItalWordNet, and
ii) two lexicons belonging to the WordNet family, the ItalWordNet (http://www.ilc.cnr.it/iwndb_php/) and the Chinese Sinica BOW (http://bow.sinica.edu.tw)

These represent different opportunities of adopting a bottom–up approach to exploring interoperability for lexicon augmentation and mutual enrichment of lexical resources, either i) in a cross-model, or ii) in a cross-lingual enrichment/fertilisation of monolingual lexicons. I say a few words about the second experiment.

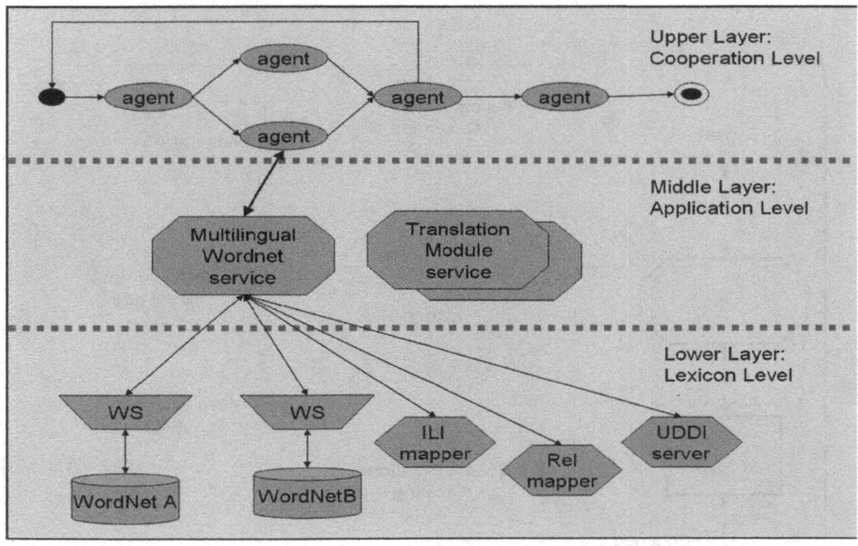


**Fig. 3.** A three–layered architecture for integrating lexical resources

*Multilingual WordNet Service.* The idea behind ii) above is that a monolingual wordnet can be enriched by accessing the semantic information encoded in corresponding entries of other monolingual wordnets A module called *Multilingual WordNet Service* is responsible for the automatic cross-lingual fertilisation of lexicons having a wordnet-like structure. Put it very simply, the idea behind this module is that a monolingual wordnet can be enriched by accessing the semantic information encoded in corresponding entries of other monolingual wordnets (see Figure 3).

Moreover, the enrichment of wordnet (A) will not only import the relations found in wordnet (B), but will also propose target synsets in the language (A) on the basis of those found in language (B). The various wordnet-lexicons reside over distributed servers and can be queried through web service interfaces. The overall architecture for multilingual wordnet service is depicted in Figure 4.

The entire mechanism of the Multilingual WordNet Service is based on the exploitation of the Interlingual Index (ILI). The proposal to make distributed wordnets interoperable allows applications such as:

- Enriching existing resources. Information is not complete in any given wordnet (as in any other lexicon): by making two wordnets interoperable, we can bootstrap semantic relations and other information from other wordnets.
- Creation of new resources. Multilingual lexicons can be bootstrapped by linking different language wordnets through the ILI.
- Validation of existing resources. Semantic relation information and other synset assignments can be validated when it is reinforced by data coming from a different wordnet.

In particular, this work can be proposed as a prototype of a web application that would support the *Global WordNet Grid* initiative (http://www.globalwordnet.org/) [24]. The success of this initiative will in fact depend on whether there will be tools to

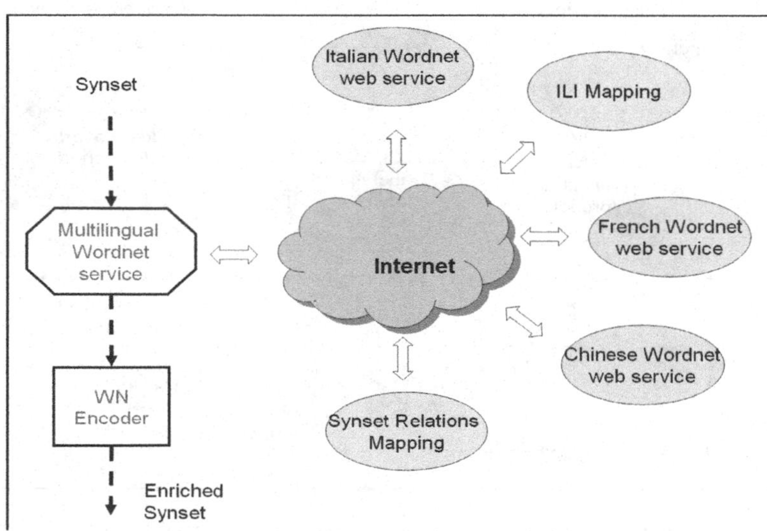


**Fig. 4.** Multilingual wordnet service architecture

access and manipulate the rich internal semantic structure of distributed multi-lingual WordNets. *LeXFlow* offers such a tool to provide interoperable web-services to access distributed multilingual WordNets on the grid. This allows to exploit in a cross-lingual framework the wealth of monolingual lexical information built in the last decade.

As an example of use, any multilingual process, such as cross-lingual information retrieval, must involve both resources and tools in specific language pairs. For instance, a multilingual query given in Italian but intended for querying English, Chinese, French, German, and Czech texts, can be sent to five different nodes on the Grid for query expansion, as well as performing the query itself. In this way, language-specific query techniques can be applied in parallel in order to achieve results that can be then integrated. As multilingualism clearly becomes one of the major challenges of the future of web-based knowledge engineering, WordNet emerges as one leading candidate for a shared platform for representing a simple and clear lexical knowledge model for different languages of the world. This is true even if it has to be recognized that the wordnet model is lacking in some important semantic information (like, for instance, a way to represent semantic predicates).

In the current work, we presuppose a de-facto standard, i.e. a shared and conventionalised architecture, the WordNet one. Since the WordNet framework is both conventionalised and widely followed, our system is able to rely on it without resorting to a more substantial and comprehensive standard. In the case, however, of integration of lexicons with different underlying linguistic models, the availability of the MILE [6] was an essential prerequisite of our work. From a more general point of view, we must note that the realisation of the new vision of distributed and interoperable LRs is strictly intertwined with at least two prerequisites. On the one side, the LRs need to be available over the web; on the other, the LR community will have to reconsider current distribution policies, and to investigate the possibility of developing an "Open Source" concept for LRs.

**UIMA.** Finally, we have started an initiative, at ILC, to integrate both the various LRs (lexicons, ontologies, corpora, etc.) and the different NLP tools into a common framework of shared and distributed resources, the IBM UIMA middleware [25]. As case study, a first prototype for a UIMA Type System has been built to manage TimeML categories and integrate an Italian Treebank and the SIMPLE lexicon [26]. Both a web interface for human access and a series of web services for machine use are being designed. This research intends to contribute both to a UIMA type systems standardisation and to a common framework for resource and tool sharing and interoperability definition. This initiative is linked with the NICT Language Grid project [20], from which our prototype inherits the service ontology environment.

## 3 Towards a Real Lexical/Linguistic Infrastructure: First Steps

Finally, it seems that new conditions are emerging, in Europe, that could make it possible for a LR infrastructure, so far a virtual one, to make the first steps towards becoming a reality [27].

**Sensitivity of LRs: political, economic, social, strategic factors.** This tendency is helped not only by new technical conditions, but also by the recognition that any organisation has limited resources, and will never be able to create all necessary infrastructural resources – in adequate quality – as needed. Infrastructural resources may be spread across several organisational units. There are certainly also political-economic factors to be considered: behind the notion of "distributed" resources there are political (and very sensitive) factors, behind resources that can be "shared and reused" there are economic factors. Moreover, many of us today start bringing into focus also the social value of a common infrastructure, and strongly advocate – contrary to current practice – the benefits of open access (vs the social costs of restricted access).

In addition to its "scientific" implications, the large intellectual, cultural and economic movement behind LRs obviously must entail "strategic" considerations, and push again towards the need to reflect on the situation in the area of LRs from a very broad perspective. It is perceived as essential to define a general organisation and plan for research, development and cooperation in the LR area, to avoid duplication of efforts and provide for a systematic distribution and sharing of knowledge. To ensure reusability, the creation of standards is still the first priority. Another tenet is the recognition of the need of a global strategic vision, encompassing different types of – and different methodologies of building – LRs, for an articulated and coherent development of this field.

Two new European initiatives are linked to these ideas.

### 3.1 CLARIN

CLARIN (*Common Language Resource and Technology Infrastructure*) is an ESFRI project (http://www.mpi.nl/clarin/) whose mission is to create an infrastructure that makes LRs (annotated texts, lexicons, ontologies, etc.) and technologies (speech recognisers, lemmatisers, parsers, information extractors, etc.) available and readily usable to scholars of all disciplines, in particular of the humanities and social sciences (HSS), to make them ready for an eScience scenario. The purpose of the infrastructure is to offer persistent services that are secure and provide easy access to language processing resources. Without the proper infrastructure, the technologies to make these tasks possible will only be available to a few specialists.

The CLARIN vision is that the resources for processing language, the data to be processed as well as appropriate guidance, advice and training can be made available and can be accessed over a distributed network from the user's desktop. CLARIN proposes to make this vision a reality: the user will have access to guidance and advice through distributed knowledge centres, and to repositories of data with standardised descriptions, processing tools ready to operate on standardised data. All of this will be available on the internet using a service oriented architecture based on secure grid technologies.

The nature of the project is therefore primarily to turn existing, fragmented technology and resources into accessible and stable services that any user can share or adapt and repurpose. CLARIN will build upon the rich history of national and European initiatives in this domain, and will ensure that Europe maintains a leading position in HSS research in the current highly competitive era. Infrastructure building is a time-consuming activity and only robustness and persistency of the offered solutions will convince researchers to step over to new and more efficient ways to carry out leading research. The preparatory phase, starting in 2008, aims at bringing the project to the level of legal, organisational and financial maturity required to implement a shared distributed infrastructure that aims at making language resources and technology available to the HSS research communities at large. This necessitates an approach along various dimensions in order to pave the way for implementation.

### 3.2 FLaReNet

International cooperation and re-creation of a community are among the most important drivers for a coherent evolution of the LR area in the next years. The Thematic Network *FLaReNet (Fostering Language Resources Network)*, proposed in the context of an eContent*plus* call, will be a European forum to facilitate interaction among LR stakeholders. Its structure considers that LRs present various dimensions and must be approached from many perspectives: technical, but also organisational, economic, legal, political. The Network addresses also multicultural and multilingual aspects, essential when facing access and use of digital content in today's Europe.

FLaReNet, organised into thematic Working Groups, each focusing on specific objectives, will bring together, in a layered structure, leading experts and groups (national and European institutions, SMEs, large companies) for all relevant LR areas, in close collaboration with CLARIN, to ensure coherence of LR-related efforts in Europe. FLaReNet will consolidate existing knowledge, presenting it analytically and visibly, and will contribute to structuring the area of LRs of the future by discussing new strategies to: convert existing and experimental technologies related to LRs into useful economic and societal benefits; integrate so far partial solutions into broader infrastructures; consolidate areas mature enough for recommendation of best practices; anticipate the needs of new types of LRs.

The outcomes of FLaReNet will be of a directive nature, to help the EC, and national funding agencies, identifying those priority areas of LRs of major interest for the public that need public funding to develop or improve. A blueprint of actions will constitute input to policy development both at EU and national level for identifying new language policies that support linguistic diversity in Europe, in combination with strengthening the language product market, e.g. for new products and innovative services, especially for less technologically advanced languages.

## References

1. Calzolari, N., Zampolli, A.: Harmonised large-scale syntactic/semantic lexicons: a European multilingual infrastructure. In: MT Summit Proceedings, Singapore, pp. 358–365 (1999)
2. Calzolari, N.: An overview of Written Language Resources in Europe: a few reflections, facts, and a vision. In: Proceedings of the First International Conference on Language Resources and Evaluation, Granada, pp. 217–224 (1998)
3. Ide, N., Calzolari, N.: Introduction to the Special Inaugural Issue. Language Resources and Evaluation 39(1), 1–7 (2005)

4. Monachini, M., et al.: Unified Lexicon and Unified Morphosyntactic Specifications for Written and Spoken Italian. In: Proceedings of LREC2006, Genova, pp. 1852–1857. ELRA, Paris (2006)
5. Roventini, A., et al.: Mapping Concrete Entities from PAROLE-SIMPLE-CLIPS to ItalWordNet: Methodology and Results. In: Proceedings of the 45th Annual Meeting of the ACL. Companion Volume, pp. 161–164. ACL, Prague (2007)
6. Calzolari, N., et al. (eds.): Standards and Best Practice for Multilingual Computational Lexicons. MILE (the Multilingual ISLE Lexical Entry). ISLE CLWG Deliverables D2.2&D3.2, Pisa, p. 194 (2003)
7. Francopoulo, G., et al.: Lexical Markup Framework (LMF). In: Proceedings of LREC2006, Genova, pp. 233–236. ELRA, Paris (2006)
8. Francopoulo, G., et al.: The relevance of standards for research infrastructures. In: International Workshop Towards a Research Infrastructure for Language Resources. LREC2006, Genova, pp. 19–22. ELRA, Paris (2006)
9. Tokunaga, T., et al.: Infrastructure for standardization of Asian language resources. In: Proceedings of COLING/ACL 2006 Main Conference Poster Sessions, Sydney, pp. 827–834 (2006)
10. Monachini, M., et al.: Lexical Relations and Domain Knowledge: The BioLexicon Meets the Qualia Structure. In: GL2007: Fourth International Workshop on Generative Approaches to the Lexicon, Paris (2007)
11. Quochi, V., et al.: Toward a Standard Lexical Resource in the Bio Domain. In: Vetulani, Z. (ed.) Proceedings of 3rd Language and Technology Conference, pp. 295–299, Poznań (2007)
12. Lexical Markup Framework rev.-14 DIS-24613 (2007), `http:// lirics. loria. fr/documents.html`
13. Huang, C.R., et al. (eds.): Ontologies and the Lexicon. Cambridge Studies in Natural Language Processing. Cambridge University Press, Cambridge (to appear)
14. Soualmia, L.F., Golbreich, C., Darmoni, S.J.: Representing the MeSH in OWL: Towards a semi-automatic migration. In: Hahn, U. (ed.) Proceedings of the KR 2004 Workshop on Formal Biomedical Knowledge Representation (KR-MED 2004), Whistler, BC, Canada, vol. 102, pp. 81–87. CEUR-WS publisher (2004)
15. Van Assem, M., et al.: A Method for Converting Thesauri to RDF/OWL. In: McIlraith, S.A., Plexousakis, D., van Harmelen, F. (eds.) ISWC 2004. LNCS, vol. 3298, pp. 17–31. Springer, Heidelberg (2004)
16. Van Assem, M., Gangemi, A., Schreiber, G.: Conversion of WordNet to a standard RDF/OWL representation. In: Proceedings of LREC2006, Genova, ELRA, Paris (2006)
17. Marchetti, A., et al.: Towards an Architecture for the Global-WordNet Initiative. In: Proceedings of SWAP-06, 3rd Italian Semantic Web Workshop. CEUR-WS (2006)
18. Toral, A., Monachini, M.: Formalising and bottom-up enriching the ontology of a Generative Lexicon. In: Proceedings of the International Conference Recent Advances in Natural Language Processing RANLP 2007, Borovets, Bulgaria (2007)
19. Bertagna, F., et al.: Fostering Intercultural Collaboration: a Web Service Architecture for Cross-Fertilization of Distributed Wordnets. In: Ishida, T., Fussell, S.R., Vossen, P. (eds.) IWIC 2007. LNCS, vol. 4568, pp. 146–158. Springer, Heidelberg (2007)
20. Ishida, T.: Language Grid: An Infrastructure for Intercultural Collaboration. In: IEEE/IPSJ Symposium on Applications and the Internet (SAINT 2006), pp. 96–100 (2006)
21. Kemps–Snijders, M., Nederhof, M., Wittenburg, P.: LEXUS, a web-based tool for manipulating lexical resources. In: Proceedings of LREC2006, Genova, pp. 1862–1865. ELRA, Paris (2006)

22. Gulrajani, G., Harrison, D.: SHAWEL: Sharable and Interactive Web-Lexicons. In: Proceedings of the LREC2002 Workshop on Tools and Resources in Field Linguistics, Las Palmas, Canary Islands, pp. 1–4 (2002)
23. Soria, C., et al.: Towards agent-based cross-lingual interoperability of distributed lexical resources. In: Proceedings COLING-ACL Workshop on Multilingual Lexical Resources and Interoperability, Sydney (2006)
24. Fellbaum, C., Vossen, P.: Connecting the Universal to the Specific: Towards the Global Grid. In: Ishida, T., Fussell, S.R., Vossen, P. (eds.) IWIC 2007. LNCS, vol. 4568, Springer, Heidelberg (2007)
25. Ferrucci, D., Lally, A.: UIMA: an architectural approach to unstructured information processing in the corporate research environment. Natural Language Engineering 10(3-4) (2004)
26. Caselli, T., et al.: Mapping SIMPLE and TimeML: improving event identification and classification using a semantic lexicon. In: GL2007: Fourth International Workshop on Generative Approaches to the Lexicon, Paris (2007)
27. Calzolari, N.: Towards a new generation of Language Resources in the Semantic Web vision. In: Ahmad, K., Brewster, C., Stevenson, M. (eds.) Words and Intelligence II: Essays in honour of Yorick Wilks, pp. 63–105. Springer, Heidelberg (2007)

# Corpus Annotation/Management Tools for the Project: Balanced Corpus of Contemporary Written Japanese

Yuji Matsumoto

Graduate School of Information Science
Nara Institute of Science and Technology
Takayama, Ikoma, Nara 630-0192 Japan
matsu@is.naist.jp

**Abstract.** This paper introduces our activities on corpus annotation and management tool development in the Japanese government funded project, *Balanced Corpus of Contemporary Written Japanese*. We are investigating various levels of text annotation that covers morphological and POS tagging, syntactic dependency parsing, predicate-argument analysis, and coreference analysis. Since automatic annotation is not perfect, we need annotated corpus management tools that facilitate corpus browsing and error correction. We especially take up our corpus management tool ChaKi, explains its functions, and discuss how we are trying to maintain consistency of corpus annotation.

**Keywords:** Corpus annotation, balanced corpus, corpus management.

## 1 Introduction

Large scale annotated corpora are very important not only for linguistic research but also for development of practical natural language processing systems since a number of practical tools such as Part-of-speech (POS) taggers and syntactic parsers are now developed with corpus-based or machine learning-based techniques, which require some amount of accurately annotated corpora. However, it is well-known that even widely used annotated corpora such as the Penn Treebank[5] still includes a number of annotation errors. To develop highly accurate and consistent annotated corpora, it is indispensable to have a supporting environment to maintenance annotated corpora so as to find and correct errors that remain in manually or automatically annotated corpora.

Japanese government funded research project for developing Balanced Corpus of Contemporary Written Japanese started fall 2006[4]. This is a five-year project that aims to construct a balanced written Japanese corpus of at least one hundred million words. In this project some part will be annotated with various linguistic information checked manually. In this project, we are responsible for automatic corpus annotation systems as well as corpus annotation assistance and annotation error correction facilities.

T. Tokunaga and A. Ortega (Eds.): LKR 2008, LNAI 4938, pp. 106–115, 2008.

This paper presents an overview of our tool development and explains especially an annotated corpus management tool named, ChaKi This tool aims at helping users in consistent construction of annotated corpora and lexicons that are to be used by researchers both in linguistics and language processing communities. The current version of the system is available from the following site as a free software[1].

## 2 Balanced Japanese Written Corpus Project and the Tool Group

This project aims at constructing a balanced Japanese written corpus with at least 100 million words, collected from books, newspapers, magazines, and other materials such as pamphlets, write papers, web texts, etc. An peculiar and important characteristic of this project is that it is participated by researchers from various fields each of which has different perspectives of using large scale corpora. The project consists of two major divisions and are further divided in eight groups as follows:

1. Corpus Construction
   (a) Corpus group: for corpus construction
   (b) Tool group: for tool development
   (c) Dictionary group: for dictionary construction
2. Corpus Evaluations
   (a) Japanese linguistics group: for corpus-based language research
   (b) Japanese language education group: teaching Japanese for foreign learners
   (c) Japanese language standardization group: for language education standards
   (d) Lexicography group: for corpus-based lexicography
   (e) Natural Language Processing group: for computational linguistics

Since the author is leading the Tool group in the project, this paper mainly focuses on tool development in the project. While the initial target of linguistic annotation has been segmentation and part-of-speech tagging, we are currently aiming at much more variety of linguistic annotation, and are developing automatic annotation systems as well as annotated corpus management tools. The former includes, segmentation and POS tagger, syntactic dependency parser, predicate-argument structure analyzer, and coreference relation analyzer. For the latter, we are developing two types of corpus maintenance tools, one is for POS and syntactic dependency annotated corpora, and the other is a general purpose annotation tool, which in particular used to annotate predicate-argument and coreference relation annotation.

Figure 1 summarizes the relationship between corpus annotation tools and annotated corpus maintenance tools. In the figure, Cradle is a database system

[1] `http://chasen.naist.jp/hiki/ChaKi/`

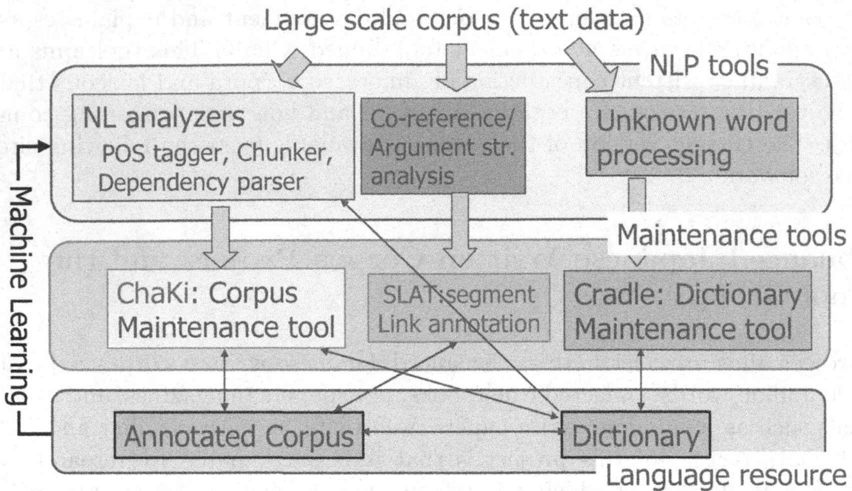


**Fig. 1.** Corpus Annotation and Maintenance Tools

that maintains the dictionary used by the annotation tools. The system keeps not only POS and inflection information of lexical entries but also constituent word information of compound or multi-word expressions, the details of which is omitted in this paper.

## 3 Corpus Annotation and Maintenance Tools: Overview

As for corpus annotation tools, we have developed a number of language analysis tools: ChaSen[1] is a Japanese POS tagger, and CaboCha[3] is a Japanese dependency parser. We have also implemented coreference resolution system for Japanese nouns[2].

For annotated corpus maintenance, we are developing two systems: ChaKi maintains POS tagged and/or syntactic dependency (between-word dependency or between-chunk dependency) tagged corpus, and provide with the functions useful for retrieving and browsing the corpus and for correcting annotation errors. This system is the main topic of the paper, and The details of this system will be given in the next section.

Another tool, named SLAT (Segment and Link Annotation Tool), is a general purpose corpus annotation tool. This system offers two types of annotation functions, segment annotation and link annotation. The segment annotation means to define a segment (a sequence of characters or words) and to put a name or a label to the segment. The link annotation means to define a relation between two segments and to give a name to the link. The set of the names/labels for segments and links can be defined by the users. For the links, two kinds of properties can be specified to each link label. One property is whether a link defines an ordered relation between the two segments, and the other is whether a link defines a transitive or intransitive relation. We believe most of corpus annotation can be defined either of segment annotation or link annotation between segments.

## 4 Annotated Corpus Management Tool: ChaKi

Figure 2 shows the overall configuration of ChaKi. Annotated corpora can be manually or automatically annotated, and are imported into the database possibly with the dictionary that is used for the annotation. If there is not pre-existing dictionary, all the words appearing in the annotated corpus constitute the dictionary. ChaKi works as an interface to the database (MySQL[2]) and provides various functions such as searching, statistic calculation, and error correction. This section gives the overall functions of the system.

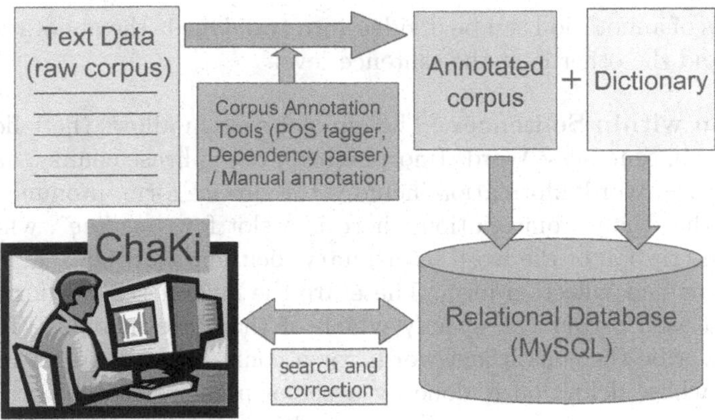


**Fig. 2.** Configuration of ChaKi

### 4.1 Coordination between Corpora and Dictionary

When an annotated corpus is imported into the database, words in the corpus are represented as pointers to the dictionary entries. When a word that does not have any entry in the dictionary appears in the corpus, that word is tentatively registered in the dictionary. Therefore, the corpus is usually not allowed to contain any words that are not defined in the dictionary. When such words appear, they are clearly marked as exceptional. Existing annotated corpora often includes impossible annotations. For example, the most frequently used Penn Treebank includes some occurrences of "have" tagged as "VBD" (past tense of a verb) or "VBN" (past participle). Such errors are easily detected when importing the corpus into the database since there are no such entries in the dictionary. Moreover, other information described in the dictionary is automatically added to the corpus when the corpus is read in the database. For example, our current English dictionary describes the base forms for all the inflected forms of words,

[2] www.mysql.com/

so that all the words in the corpus automatically receives its base forms even in case the original corpus doesn't have any such information. Moreover, since our current Japanese dictionary has constituent definition of all the compound words and multi-word expressions, so that the users can obtain various levels of word segmentation granularity.

## 4.2 Variation of Annotation

Part-of-speech tags, base phrase chunks and syntactic dependency structures (dependency between chunks) are handled. Multi-word expressions can be defined in the dictionary together with their constituent word information. Search can be performed either on multi-word expressions or on the constituent words. Bibliographic information of document and of sentences are annotated at the sentence level.

The types of annotation can be divided into two: One is the annotation within sentences, and the other is at the sentence level.

**Annotation within Sentences.** The current system allows the following annotation within sentences: Words (morphemes), base phrase chunks, and dependency structure. Word information includes the surface form, pronunciation (for Japanese, other than pronunciation, there is a slot for "*reading*", which shows the entry description of the word in ordinary dicitonaries, POS tag, base form, inflection type and inflection form. These are the default set of information for a word, and each corpus can specify which of them are included. The dictionary can describe the constituent words for a compound word or a multi-word expression, whose definition is done by a set of pointers to the corresponding entries in the dictionary. For example, the multi-word expression "in respect of" is defined itself as a preposition, and its constituents are defined as a sequence of a preposition, a common noun and a preposition by pointing their corresponding entries in the dictionary. When base phrase chunks and the syntactic dependency relation between chunks are annotated, those are also registered in the database.

As for those annotation for Japanese corpora, Japanese morphological analyser ChaSen[1] and Japanese dependency parser CaboCha[3] are used.

**Annotation at Sentences: Bibliographic Information.** Bibliographic information of the corpus (the name of the corpus, the authors' name(s), etc) and attributive information of sentences (speaker, contextual information, etc) are annotated at the sentence level. In the system they have no structured format and are represented by simple character string forms, which are retrieved by string level partial matching. Moreover, users may maintain their corpora not by a single file but by a set of files within a hierarchy of folders so that the path sequences of the folders represent bibliographical information related to the files. All of such information, the sequence of the folder names, is allocated at the sentence level.

While not considered in the current system, there should be more sentence or extra-sentence level information. Discourse structure or discourse relation between sentences is one of such information. Also, links between reference expressions such as anaphora and their antecedents are other examples of extra-sentence level information. Such information can be maintained by the general purpose annotation system SLAT.

### 4.3 Search Functions

Three modes of search are provided: String search, word search, and dependency structure search. In the search component, the unit for search is a sentence in all modes of the search functions.

**Surface Character String Search.** All occurrences of specified character strings are searched in this mode. Regular expressions can be used to describe the target strings and the results are displayed in the KWIC format.

**Word Sequence Search.** When sentences are POS tagged, any lexical information can be used to describe patterns of word sequences. The lexical information to be specified in search patterns includes surface forms, POS tags, base forms of words, pronunciation, inflection types and inflection forms. Regular expressions can be used in specifying any of the word information. Figure 3 shows an example of a word sequence pattern for search. The figure shows a pattern of a sequence consisting of three words. Each box corresponds to a word, in which the top row specifies the surface form and the fourth row specifies the POS tag.

**Dependency Structure Search.** When sentences are parsed in syntactic dependency structure, they are searched for by specifying a partial dependency structure. Any sentences that include the specified dependency structure are retrieved. Figure 4 shows a snapshot of dependency structure search. The query is composed in the upper part of the interface. Each shaded box shows a base phrase chunk and a small white box specifies a word within the chunk. This box can specify various information of the word just like the word sequence search. Arrows between chunks describe syntactic dependency relations between chunks. All the sentences in the corpus that include the specified dependency structure are retrieved and shown in the KWIC format as in the lower part of the Figure.

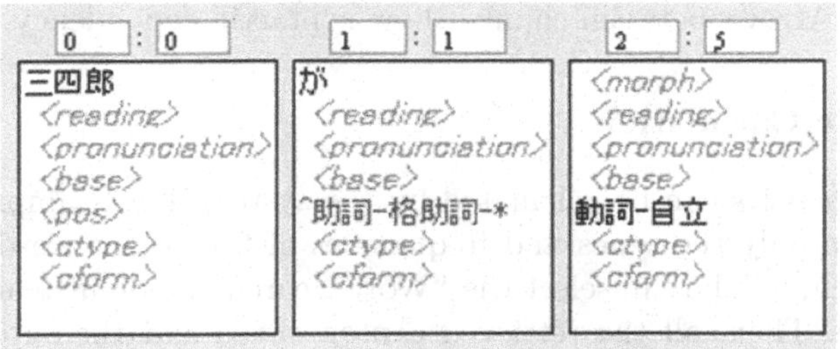


**Fig. 3.** Example of Word Sequence Pattern

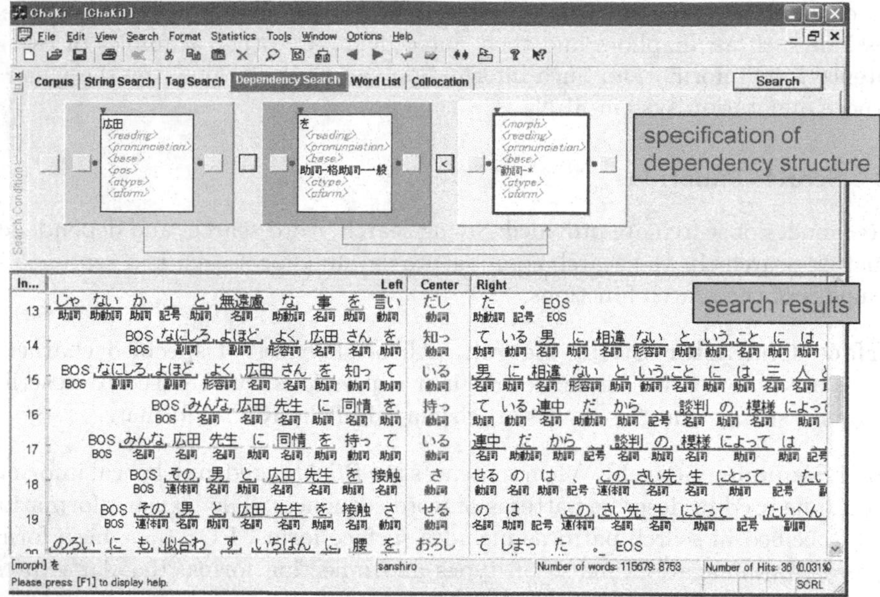


**Fig. 4.** Example of Dependency Structure Search

## 4.4 Showing of the Search Results

Since the search is done sentence-wise, the search results are shown sentence-wise, too. As seen in Figure 4, retrieved sentences are shown in the KWIC format. In search queries such as Figure 3 and Figure 4, only one word is specified as the focus word and is presented as the center word in the KWIC in all modes of the search functions. In word sequence and dependency structure searches, any specified information can be associated with a word.

In case of dependency tree search, the user can pick up one of the retrieved sentences from the KWIC, and trigger the TreeEditor, which produces another window showing the dependency tree of the sentence as in Figure 5. Each box corresponds to a base phrase chunk, in which a sequence of words are segmented in in the box. Arrows between chunks show syntactic dependency relations.

## 4.5 Statistic Calculation

Some basic statistics can be calculated by the system. For example, if the user is interested in only the types and frequencies of the center word in the word sequence search, he/she can select the "Word Search" mode instead of the "Tag Search" mode. Then, all the retrieved center words and their frequencies are presented in another table.

Another statistics provided by the system are collocations between the center word and the surrounding words within a specified context length window.

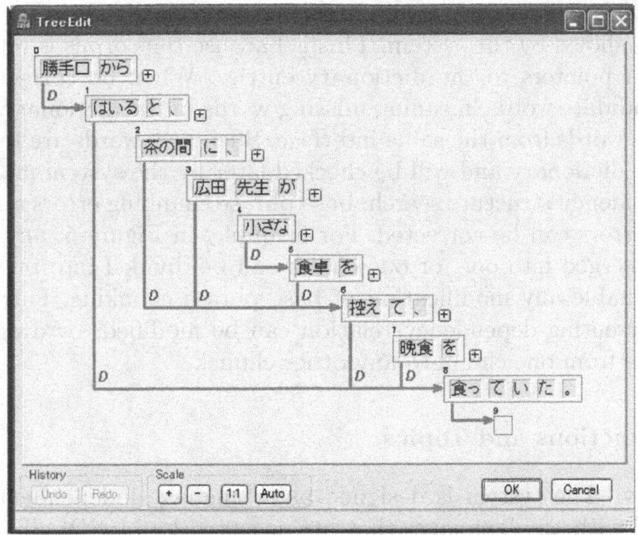


**Fig. 5.** Dependency Tree

Collocation may be simple frequencies, mutual information, or frequent word N-grams based on any information on words, such as surface word forms, base forms, POS tags, etc.

The system also has a function of frequent substring mining. Frequent subsequence mining is performed on the retrieved set of sentences. When the user specify the minimal length and minimal frequency (minimal support), the system searches for all maximal length subsequence (with a specified number of gaps including zero gaps) that appeared no less than the minimal support and have length no shorter than the specified minimal length. Subsequences with no gap means n-gram sequences.

### 4.6 Error Correction Function

Error correction function is one of the most important functions for developing accurately annotated corpora. Annotated corpora should be corrected when annotation errors are detected. Once an annotation error is found, it is often the case that errors of the same type exist in other parts of the same corpus. The search functions of the system are effectively used for detecting the same type of errors in the corpus. And once the instances of the same error type are collected, the error correction module helps to issue a transformation rule so as to correct all the erroneous instances in one operation (Only segmentation and POS annotation errors are handled in this mode).

There are two modes of error correction corresponding to the types of seach, the word sequence search and the dependency structure search. In the former, word segmentation errors and word related erros such as POS tag or inflection form errors can be handled. Correction of the word information is guided by a special interface, in which error correction is basically done by selecting candidate words shown by the system. This is bacause the corpus is represented as a sequence of pointers to the dictionary entries. When no correct word is found in the candidate words, meaning missing words in the dictionary, the user can register new words from the same interface. Such new words are tentatively registered in the dictionary and will be checked later by the system manager. In the case of dependency structure search, base phrase chunking errors and dependency relation errors can be corrected. For example, in Figure 5, any adjacent chunks can be merged into one, or one chunk can be divided into two or more chunks, which enable any modification of base phrase chunking. Furthermore, the arrows representing dependency relation can be modified, by dragging the head of an arrow from one chunk to any other chunck.

### 4.7 Other Functions and Topics

**Multilinguality.** The system is designed as a language independent system, and can be used with any languages that are accepted by MySQL. The current system is tested with Japanese, Chinese and English corpora.

**Interface to Language Analysis Tools.** Any corpora annotated with POS or dependency structure can be imported to the system. At the moment, the corpus is annotated as either in the standard output formats of ChaSen or CaboCha. An interface to apply ChaSen and CaboCha to raw corpora is provided. Also, another interface is provided for importing annotated corpora in ChaSen or CaboCha format into the database. For English corpora, we prepared a transformation program for corpora annotated in Penn Treebank or British National Corpus formats.

## 5 Keeping Consistency

Keeping consistency in annotated corpora is a different problem from the annotation accuracy. In non-segmented languages such as Japanese and Chinese, word segmentation is a crucial issue that may cause inconsistency. In our project, two segmentation standards are defined, short and long segmentation standards. The short standard is the target segmentation that is analyzed by the POS taggers, and the corpus with long segmentation standard will be generated by a chunker. The word constituent information kept in our dictionary will provide useful information to the chunker for long segmentation standard.

## 6 Conclusions

The aim of the annotation tools presented in this paper is to help users to construct, use and manage accurately annotated corpora. It is important not only to develop high performance natural language analysis tools but also to provide tools that search for specific patterns and correct errors in annotated corpora. ChaKi provides various functions for these purposes.

In any languages, there are idiomatic or collocational expressions that are formed by multiple words. Especially in Japanese and Chinese, it is hard to define proper word segmentation uniquely since definition of words may vary according to the grammar or to applications. We decided to describe multi-word expressions and their constituent words in the dictionary and define the corpus as a sequence of pointers to the dictionary. By doing this, it becomes possible to search patterns either in multi-word expression or in constituent words.

Currently we work on three languages, Japanese, Chinese and English. We assume that extension of the target languages is easy since most of the tools are designed to be language independent.

## Acknowledgements

We would like to thank our colleagues who helped and inspired us in developing the corpus management tool. We are very grateful to the former and current members of Computational Linguistics Lab at NAIST. This research is partly supported by Grants-in-Aid for Scientific Research, Priority Area "Japanese Corpus".

## References

1. Asahara, M., Matsumoto, Y.: Japanese named entity extraction with redundant morphological analysis. In: Proc. Human Language Technology and North American Chapter of Association for Computational Linguistics, pp. 8–15 (2003)
2. Iida, R., Inui, K., Matsumoto, Y.: Exploiting Syntactic Patterns as Clues in Zero-Anaphora Resolution. In: ACL-Coling-2006, pp. 625–632 (2006)
3. Kudo, T., Matsumoto, Y.: Japanese Dependency Analysis using Cascaded Chunking. In: 6th Conference on Natural Language Learning, pp. 63–69 (2002)
4. Maekawa, K.: KOTONOHA and BCCWJ: Development of a Balanced Corpus of Contemporary Written Japanese. In: Corpora and Language Research: Proceedings of the First International Conference on Korean Language, Literature, and Culture, pp. 158–177 (2007)
5. Marcus, M.P., Santorini, B., Marcinkiewicz, M.A.: Building a Large Annotated Corpus of English: The Penn Treebank. Computational Linguistics 19(2), 313–330 (1993)
6. Matsumoto, Y.: An Annotated Corpus Management Tool: ChaKi. In: Proc. 5th International Conference on Language Resources and Evaluation (LREC) (2006)

# Capturing the Structures in Association Knowledge: Application of Network Analyses to Large-Scale Databases of Japanese Word Associations

Terry Joyce[1] and Maki Miyake[2]

[1] School of Global Studies, Tama University,
802 Engyo, Fujisawa, Kanagawa, 252-0805, Japan
terry@tama.ac.jp

[2] Graduate School of Language and Culture, Osaka University,
1-8 Machikaneyama-cho, Toyonaka-shi, Osaka, 560-0043, Japan
mmiyake@lang.osaka-u.ac.jp

**Abstract.** Within the general enterprise of probing into the complexities of lexical knowledge, one particularly promising research focus is on word association knowledge. Given Deese's [1] and Cramer's [2] convictions that word association closely mirror the structured patterns of relations that exist among concepts, as largely echoed Hirst's [3] more recent comments about the close relationships between lexicons and ontologies, as well as Firth's [4] remarks about finding a word's meaning in the company it keeps, efforts to capture and unravel the rich networks of associations that connect words together are likely to yield interesting insights into the nature of lexical knowledge. Adopting such an approach, this paper applies a range of network analysis techniques in order to investigate the characteristics of network representations of word association knowledge in Japanese. Specifically, two separate association networks are constructed from two different large-scale databases of Japanese word associations: the Associative Concept Dictionary (ACD) by Okamoto and Ishizaki [5] and the Japanese Word Association Database (JWAD) by Joyce [6] [7] [8]. Results of basic statistical analyses of the association networks indicate that both are scale-free with small-world properties and that both exhibit hierarchical organization. As effective methods of discerning associative structures with networks, some graph clustering algorithms are also applied. In addition to the basic Markov Clustering algorithm proposed by van Dongen [9], the present study also employs a recently proposed combination of the enhanced Recurrent Markov Cluster algorithm (RMCL) [10] with an index of modularity [11]. Clustering results show that the RMCL and modularity combination provides effective control over cluster sizes. The results also demonstrate the effectiveness of graph clustering approaches to capturing the structures within large-scale association knowledge resources, such as the two constructed networks of Japanese word associations.

**Keywords:** association knowledge, lexical knowledge, network analyses, large-scale databases of Japanese word associations, Associative Concept Dictionary (ACL), Japanese Word Association Database (JWAD), association network representations, graph clustering, Markov clustering (MCL), recurrent Markov clustering (RMCL), modularity.

T. Tokunaga and A. Ortega (Eds.): LKR 2008, LNAI 4938, pp. 116–131, 2008.

## 1 Introduction

Reflecting the central importance of language as a key to exploring and understanding the intricacies of higher human cognitive functions, a great deal of research within the various disciplines of cognitive science, such as psychology, artificial intelligence, computational linguistics and natural language processing, has understandably sought to investigate the complex nature of lexical knowledge. Within this general enterprise, one particularly promising research direction is to try and capture the structures of word association knowledge. Consistent with both Firth's assertion [4] that a word's meaning resides in the company it keeps, as well as the notion proposed by Deese [1] and Cramer [2] that, as association is a basic mechanism of human cognition, word associations closely mirror the structured patterns of relations that exist among concepts, which is largely echoed in Hirst's observations about the close relationships between lexicons and ontologies [3], attempts to unravel the rich networks of associations that connect words together can undoubtedly provide important insights into the nature of lexical knowledge.

While a number of studies have reported reasonable successes in applying versions of the multidimensional space model, such as Latent Semantic Analysis (LSA) and multidimensional scaling, to the analysis of texts, the methodologies of graph theory and network analysis are especially suitable for discerning the patterns of connectivity within large-scale resources of association knowledge and for perceiving the inherent relationships between words and word groups. A number of studies have, for instance, recently applied graph theory approaches in investigating various aspects of linguistic knowledge resources [9] [12], such as employing graph clustering techniques in detecting lexical ambiguity and in acquiring semantic classes as alternatives to computational methods based on word frequencies [13].

Of greater relevance to the present study are the studies conducted by Steyvers, Shiffrin, and Nelson [14] and Steyvers and Tenenbaum [15] which both focus on word association knowledge. Specifically, both studies draw on the *University of South Florida Word Association, Rhyme, and Word Fragment Norms*, which includes one of the largest databases of word associations for American English compiled by Nelson, McEvoy, and Schreiber [16]. Steyvers and Tenenbaum [14], for instance, applied graph theory and network analysis techniques in order to examine the structural features of three semantic networks—one based on Nelson, et al [16], one based on WordNet [17], and one based on Roget's thesaurus [18]—and observed interesting similarities between the three networks in terms of their scale-free patterns of connectivity and small-world structures. In a similar vein, the present study applies a range of network analysis approaches in order to investigate the characteristics of graph representations of word association knowledge in Japanese. In particular, two semantic networks are constructed from two separate large-scale databases of Japanese word associations: namely, the Associative Concept Dictionary (ACD) compiled by Okamoto and Ishizaki [5] and the Japanese Word Association Database (JWAD), under ongoing construction by Joyce [6] [7] [8].

In addition to applying some basic statistical analyses to the semantic network representations constructed from the large-scale databases of Japanese word associations, this study also applies some graph clustering algorithms which are effective methods of capturing the associative structures present within large and sparsely connected resources of linguistic data. In that context, the present study also compares the basic Markov clustering algorithm proposed by van Dongen [9] with a recently proposed combination of the enhanced Recurrent Markov Clustering (RMCL) algorithm developed by Jung, Miyake, and Akama [10] and Newman and Girvan's measure of modularity [11]. Although the basic Markov clustering algorithm is widely known to be an effective approach to graph clustering, it is also recognized to have an inherent problem relating to cluster sizes, for the algorithm tends to yield either an exceptionally large core cluster or many isolated clusters consisting of single words. The RMCL has been developed expressly to overcome the cluster size distribution problem by making it possible to adjust the proportion in cluster sizes. The combination of the RMCL graph clustering method and the modularity measurement provides even greater control over cluster sizes. As an extremely promising approach to graph clustering, this effective combination is being applied to the semantic network representations of Japanese word associations in order to automatically construct condensed network representations. One particularly attractive application for graph clustering techniques that are capable of controlling cluster sizes is in the construction of hierarchically-organized semantic spaces, which certainly represents an exciting approach to capturing the structures within large-scale association knowledge resources.

This paper applies a variety of graph theory and network analysis methods in analyzing the semantic network representations of large-scale Japanese word association databases. After briefly introducing in Section 2 the two Japanese word association databases, the ACD and the JWAD, which the semantic network representations analyzed in this study were constructed from, Section 3 presents the results from some basic statistical analyses of the network characteristics, such as degree distributions and average clustering coefficient distributions for nodes with degrees. Section 4 focuses on methods of graph clustering. Following short discussions of the relative merits of the MCL algorithm, the enhanced RMCL version and the combination of RMCL and modality, the graph clustering results for the two association network representations are presented. Section 5 provides a short introduction to the RMCLNet web application which makes the clustering results for the two Japanese word association networks publicly available. Finally, Section 6 summarizes the results from the various graph theory and network analysis methods applied in this study, and fleetingly mentions some interesting directions for future research in seeking to obtain further insights into the complex nature of association knowledge.

## 2 Network Representations of Japanese Word Associations

This section briefly introduces the Associative Concept Dictionary (ACD) [5] and the Japanese Word Association Database (JWAD) [6] [7] [8], which are both large-scale databases of Japanese word associations. The two network representations of word association knowledge constructed from the databases are analyzed in some detail in the subsequent sections.

Compared to the English language for which comprehensive word association normative data has existed for some time, large-scale databases of Japanese word associations have only been developed over the last few years. Notable normative data for English includes the 40-50 responses for some 2,400 words of British English collected by Moss and Older [19] and, as noted earlier, the American English norms compiled by Nelson and his colleagues [16] which includes approximately 150 responses for a list of some 5,000 words. Although the early survey by Umemoto [20] gathered free associations from 1,000 university students, the very limited set of just 210 words only serves to highlight the serious lack of comparative databases of word associations for Japanese that has existed until relatively recently. While the ACD and the JWAD both represent substantial advances in redressing the situation, the ongoing JWAD project, in particular, is strongly committed to the construction of a very large-scale database of Japanese word associations, and seeks to eventually surpass the extensive American English norms [16] in both the size of its survey corpus and the levels of word association responses collected.

### 2.1 The Associative Concept Dictionary (ACL)

The ACD was created by Okamoto and Ishizaki [5] from word association data with the specific intention of building a dictionary stressing the hierarchal structures between certain types of higher and lower level concepts. The data consists of the 33,018 word association responses provided by 10 respondents according for 1,656 nouns. While arguably appropriate for its dictionary-building objectives, a major drawback with the ACD data is the fact that response category was specified as part of the word association experiment used in collecting the data. The participants were asked to respond to a presented stimulus word according to one of seven randomly presented categories (hypernym, hyponym, part/material, attribute, synonym, action and environment). Accordingly, the ACD data tells us very little about the wide range of associative relations that the free word association task taps into.

In constructing the semantic network representation of the ACD database, only response words with a response frequency of two or more were extracted. This resulted in a network graph consists of 8,951 words

### 2.2 The Japanese Word Association Database (JWAD)

Under ongoing construction, the JWAD is the core component in a project to investigate lexical knowledge in Japanese by mapping out Japanese word associations [6] [7] [8]. Version 1 of the JWAD consists of the word association responses to a list of 2,099 items which were presented to up to 50 respondents [21]. The list of 2,099 items was randomly selected from the initial project corpus of 5,000 basic Japanese kanji and words. In marked contrast to the ACD and its specification of categories to which associations should belong, the JWAD employs the free word association task in collecting association responses. Accordingly, the JWAD data more faithfully reflects the rich and diverse nature of word associations. Also, in sharp contrast to the ACD, which only collected associations for a set of nouns, the JWAD is surveying words belonging to all word classes.

Similar to the ACD network graph, in constructing the semantic network representation of the JWAD, only response words with a frequency of two or more were selected. In the case of the JWAD, this resulted in a network graph consisting of 8,970 words, so the two networks are of very similar sizes.

## 3 Analyses of the Association Network Structures

This section reports on initial comparisons of the ACD network and the JWAD network based on some basic statistical analyses of their network structures.

Graph representation and the techniques of graph theory and network analysis are particularly appropriate methods for examining the intricate patterns of connectivity that exist within large-scale linguistic knowledge resources. As discussed in Section 1, Steyvers and Tenenbaum [15] have illustrated the potential of such techniques in their noteworthy study that examined the structural features of three semantic networks. Based on their calculations of a range of statistical features, such as the average shortest paths, diameters, clustering coefficients, and degree distributions, they argued that the three networks exhibited similarities in terms of their scale-free patterns of connectivity and small-world structures. Following their basic similar approach, we analyze the structural characteristics of the two association networks by calculating the statistical features of degree distribution and clustering coefficient, which is an index of the interconnectivity strength between neighboring nodes in a graph.

### 3.1 Degree Distributions

Based on their computations of degree distributions, Balabasi and Albert [22] argue that networks with scale-free structures have a degree distribution, P(k), that conforms to a power law, which can be expressed as follows:

$$P(k) \approx k^{-r}$$

The results of analyzing degree distributions for the two association networks are presented in Figure 1. As the figure clearly shows, P(k) for both association networks conforms to a power law: the exponent value, r, is 2.2 for the ACD network (panel a) and 2.1 for the JWAD network (panel b).

For the ACD network, the average degree value is 7.0 (0.08%) for 8,951 nodes, while in the case of the JWAD network, the average degree value is 3.3 (0.03%) for

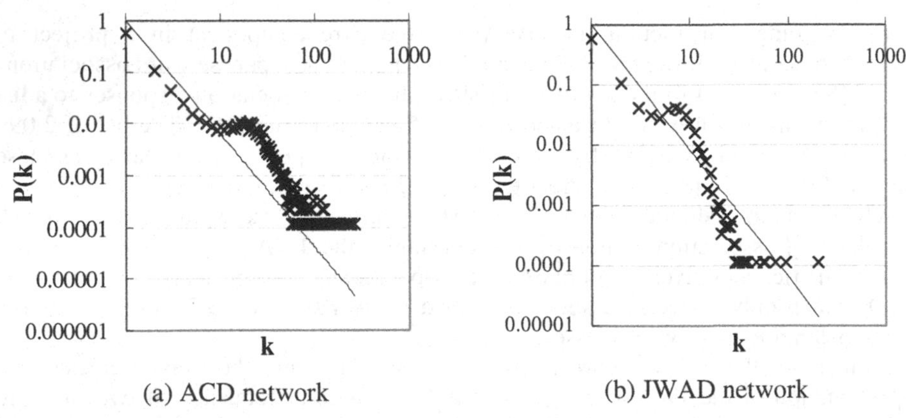


**Fig. 1.** Degree distributions for the ACD network (panel A) and the JWAD network (panel B)

the 8,970 nodes. As these results clearly indicate that the networks exhibit a pattern of sparse connectivity, we may say that the two association networks both possess the characteristics of a scale-free network.

### 3.2 Clustering Coefficients

The association networks are next compared in terms of their clustering coefficients, which is an index of the interconnectivity strength between neighboring nodes in a graph. Watts and Strogatz [23] proposed the notion of clustering coefficient as an appropriate index of the degree of connections between nodes in their study of social networks that investigated the probabilities of an acquaintance of an acquaintance also being one of your acquaintances.

In this study, we define the clustering coefficient of n nodes as:

$$C(n) = \frac{\text{number of links among n's neighbors}}{N(n)\times(N(n)-1)/2}$$

where N(n) represents the number of adjacent nodes. The equation yields a clustering coefficient value between 0-1; while a star-like sub-graph would have a clustering coefficient value of 0, a complete graph with all nodes connected would have clustering coefficient of 1.

Similarly, Ravasz and Barabasi [24] (2003) advocate the notion of clustering coefficient dependence on node degree, based on the hierarchical model of $C(k) \approx k^{-1}$ [25], as an index of the hierarchical structures encountered in real networks, such as the World Wide Web. Accordingly, the hierarchical nature of a network can be characterized using the average clustering coefficient, C(k), of nodes with k degrees, which will follow a scaling law, such as $C(k) \approx k^{-\beta}$ where $\beta$ is the hierarchical exponent. The results of scaling C(k) with k for the ACD network (panel a) and for the JWAD network (panel b) are presented in Figure 2.

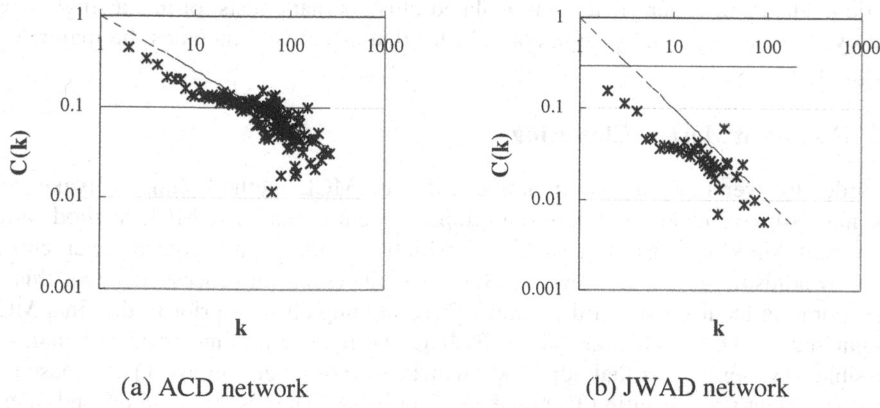


**Fig. 2.** Clustering coefficient distributions for the ACD network (panel A) and the JWAD network (panel B)

The solid lines in the figure correspond to the average clustering coefficient. The ACD network has an average clustering coefficient of 0.1, while the value is 0.03 for the JWAD network. As both networks conform well to a power law, we may conclude that they both possess intrinsic hierarchies.

## 4 Graph Clustering

This section focuses on some graph clustering techniques and reports on the application of graph clustering to the two constructed association network representations based on the large-scale Japanese word association databases. Specifically, after considering the relative merits of the original MCL algorithm [9], the enhanced RMCL algorithm [10], and the combination of RMCL and modality [11] employed in the present study, we briefly present and discuss the results of applying these methods to the two association network representations.

### 4.1 Markov Clustering

Markov Clustering (MCL) is widely recognized as an effective method for detecting the patterns and clusters within large and sparsely connected data structures. The MCL algorithm is based on random walks across a graph, which, by utilizing the two simple algebraic operations of expansion and inflation, simulates the flow over a stochastic transition matrix in converging towards equilibrium states for the stochastic matrix. Of particular relevance to the present study is the fact that the inflation parameter, r, influences the clustering granularity of the process. In other words, if the value of r is set to be high, then the resultant clusters will tend to be small in size. While this parameter is typically set to be r = 2, a value of 1.6 has been taken as a reasonable value in creating a dictionary of French synonyms [26].

Although MCL is clearly an effective clustering technique, particularly for large-scale corpora [13] [14], the method, however, undeniably suffers from its lack of control over the distribution in cluster sizes that it generates. The MCL has a problematic tendency to either yield many isolated clusters that consist of just a single word or to yield an exceptionally large core cluster that effectively includes the majority of the graph nodes.

### 4.2 Recurrent Markov Clustering

In order to overcome this shortcoming with the MCL method, Jung, Miyake, and Akama [10] have recently proposed an improvement to the basic MCL method called Recurrent Markov Clustering (RMCL), which provides some control over cluster sizes by adjusting graph granularity. Basically, the recurrent process achieves this by incorporating feedback about the states of overlapping clusters prior to the final MCL output stage. As a key feature of the RMCL, the reverse tracing procedure makes it possible to generate a virtual adjacency matrix for non-overlapping clusters based on the convergent state resulting from the MCL process. The resultant condensed matrix provides a simpler graph, which can highlight the conceptual structures that underlie similar words.

### 4.3 Modularity

According to Newman and Girvan [11], modularity is a particularly useful index for assessing the quality of divisions within a network. The modularity Q value can highlight differences in edge distributions between a graph of meaningful partitions and a random graph under the same vertices conditions (in terms of numbers and sum of their degrees). The modularity index is defined as:

$$Q=\sum_i (e_{ii}-a_i^2)$$

where $i$ is the number of cluster $c_i$, $e_{ii}$ is the proportion of internal links in the whole graph and $a_i$ is the expected proportion of $c_i$'s edges calculated as the total number of degrees in $c_i$ divided by the sum of degrees for the whole graph. In practice, high Q values are rare, with values generally falling within the range of about 0.3 to 0.7. The present study employs a combination of RMCL clustering algorithm with this modularity index in order to optimize the appropriate inflation parameter within the clustering stages of the RMCL process. The RMCL results reported in this paper are all based on the combination of the RMCL clustering method and modularity.

### 4.4 Clustering Results

The MCL and the RMCL algorithm were implemented as a series of calculations that are executed with gridMathematica. The MCL process generated a nearly-idempotent stochastic matrix at around the 20th clustering stage.

In terms of determining a reasonable value for the r parameter, while it is usual to identify local peaks in the Q value, as Figure 3(a), which plots modularity as a function of r, indicates there are no discernable no peaks in the Q value. Accordingly, the highest value of r equals 1.5 was taken for the inflation parameter. Plotting modularity as a function of the clustering stage, Figure 3(b) indicates that values of

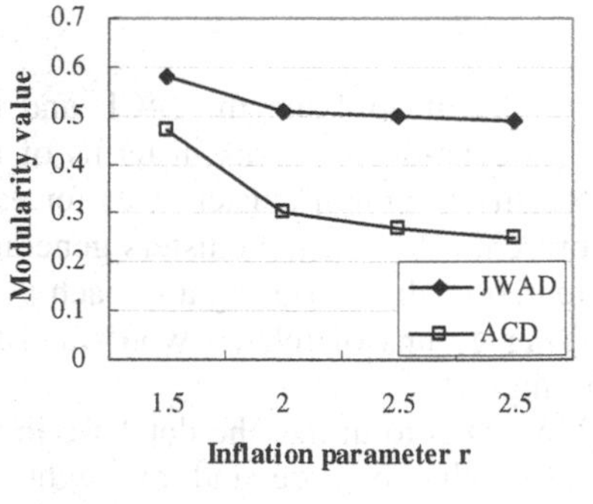


(a) Inflation parameter for MCL

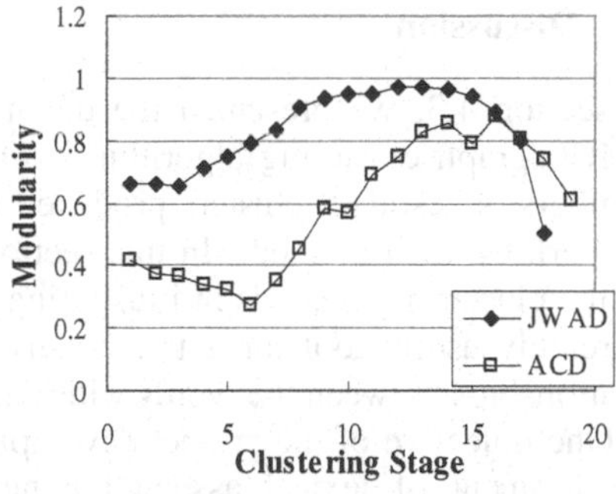


(b) MCL clustering stage

**Fig. 3.** Basic clustering results, with panel a presenting modularity values as a function of r and panel b indicating modularity values as a function of the MCL clustering stage

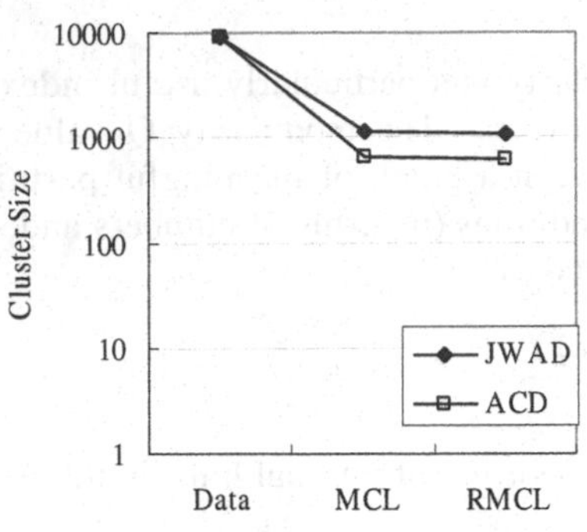


(a) Cluster sizes for MCL and RMCL

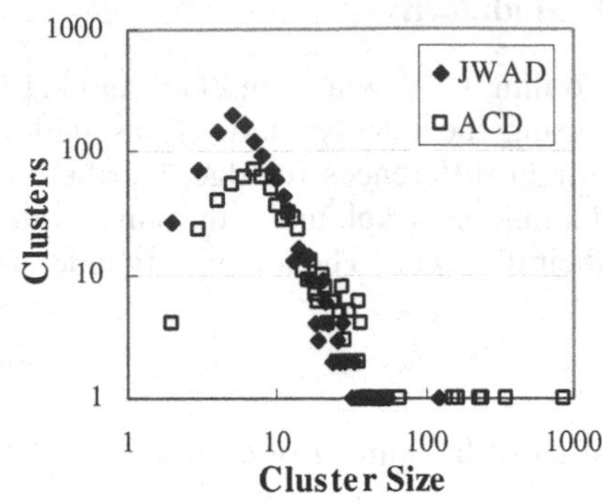


(b) Distributions in cluster sizes of MCL

**Fig. 4.** Clustering results for MCL and RMCL, with panel a showing cluster sizes and panel b showing distributions for the MCL algorithm

Q value peaked at stage 14 in the case of the ACD network and at stage 12 for the JWAD network. Accordingly, these clustering stages were used in the RMCL process.

Figure 4(a) presents the MCL and the RMCL cluster sizes for both the ACD network and the JWAD network, illustrating the downsizing transitions that took place during the graph clustering process. Figure 4(b) plots the frequencies of cluster sizes for the results of MCL clustering. In the case of the ACD network, the MCL algorithm resulted in 642 hard clusters, with an average cluster size of 7.5 and an SD of 56.3, while the RMCL yielded 601 clusters, where the average number of cluster components was 1.1 with an SD of 0.42. In the case of the JWAD network, the MCL resulted in 1,144 hard clusters, with an average cluster size of 5.5 and an SD of 7.2, while the RMCL yielded 1,084 clusters, where the average number of cluster components was 1.1 with an SD of 0.28.

### 4.5 Discussion

In section 4.3, we presented the quantitative results of applying the MCL and the RMCL graph clustering algorithms to the two association networks in terms of the numbers of resultant clusters produced and the distributions in cluster sizes for each network by each method. In this section, we present a few of the clusters generated by the clustering methods in illustrating the potential of the clustering approach as an extremely useful tool for automatically identifying groups of related words and the relationships between the words within the groupings.

One objective of the project developing the JWAD is to utilize the database in the development of lexical association network maps that capture and highlight the association patterns that exist between Japanese words [6] [7] [8]. Essentially, a lexical association network map represents a set of forward associations elicited by a target word by more than two respondents (and the strengths of those associations), together with backward associations (both their numbers and associative strengths), as well as the levels and strengths of associations between all members of an associate set [6]. While the lexical association network maps were first envisaged primarily at the single word level, the basic approach to mapping out associations can be extended to small domains and beyond, as the example in Figure 5 illustrates with a map building from and contrasting a small set of emotion words. Interestingly, this association map suggests that the positive emotion synonym words of しあわせ (happy) and 嬉しい (happy) have strong associations to a small set of other close synonyms, but that the negative emotion words of 寂しい (lonely) and 悲しい (sad) primarily elicit word association responses that can be regarded as having causal or resultant relationships. While the creation of such small domain association maps is likely to provide similarly interesting insights concerning association knowledge, the efforts required to manually identify and visualize even relatively small domains are not inconsequential. However, the clustering methods presented in this section represent a potentially very appealing way of automatically identifying and visualizing sets of related words as generated clusters.

Table 1 presents the word clusters for the target words of しあわせ (happy) and 寂しい (lonely) that were generated by the MCL algorithm for the JWAD network. Comparing the sets of associations for these two words in Figure 5 based on the JWAD with the word clusters in Table 1, clearly there are many words that are common to both. The additional words included in the MCL word clusters in Table 1

**Table 1.** Examples of clusters for the JWAD network generated by the MCL algorithm

| |
|---|
| 手をたたこう (clap hands) 幸福 (happiness) しあわせ (happy) |
| 怒 (anger) 嬉しい (happy) 歓喜 (delight) 喜 (joy) 喜び (joy) 喜ぶ (be glad) 喜寿 (77th birthday) 喜怒哀楽 (human emotions) 悲しむ (be sad) 大喜利 (final act in a *Rakugo* performance) |
| 独り (alone) 一人 (alone; one person) さびしい (lonely) |
| 寂しい (lonely) 悲しみ (sadness) 悲しい (be sad) 涙 (tears) 流す (shed) |
| 負け (defeat) 涙 (tears) くやしい (regrettable) |

**Table 2.** Examples of words in the ACD network clustered together by the MCL algorithm

| |
|---|
| 結納 (engagement gift) 幸せ (happy) 入籍 (entry in family register)<br>式場 (ceremonial hall) 結婚 (marriage) 婚約 (engagement) 同棲 (cohabiting)<br>冠婚葬祭 (important ceremonial occasions) |
| 貰う (receive) 嬉しい (happy) お駄賃 (tip) ありがたい (thanks)<br>褒美 (reward) 収入 (income) 小づかい (pocket money) |
| 冬 (winter) 寒さ (coldness) 初冬 (early winter) 真冬 (midwinter)<br>寂しい (lonely) ウィンター (winter) 暖冬 (warm winter) |
| 純粋 (pure) 分泌液 (secretion) 嬉し涙 (tears of joy) なみだ (tears)<br>溢れる (overflow) 悲しい事 (sad incident) 悔し涙 (vexation) |
| 後悔 (regret) 反省 (reflection) 悔やむ (be sorry) 悔しさ (chagrin)<br>悔しい (regrettable) |

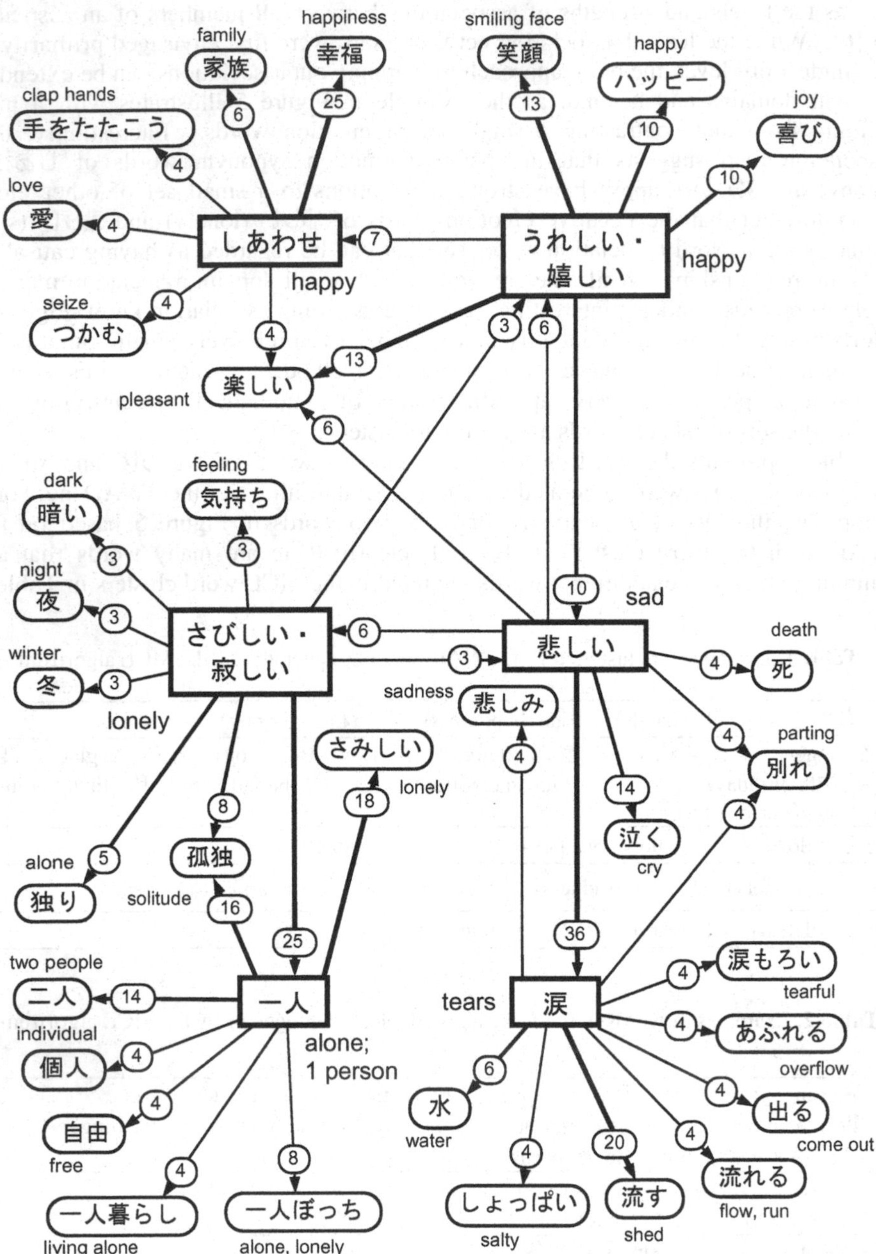


**Fig. 5.** Example of lexical association network map building from and contrasting a small set of emotion words within the JWAD. The numbers on the arrows indicate response frequencies as percentages of the respective association sets.

serve to demonstrate how the automatic clustering process can be a powerful technique for identifying more implicit, but nevertheless interesting patterns of association within collections of words that are mediated through indirect connections via closely related items.

Similarly, Table 2 presents word clusters for the ACD network generated by the MCL algorithm, which illustrates how effective the clustering methods are in grouping together words that have a synonymous relationship.

# 5 RMCLNet

This section briefly introduces RMCLNet [26], which is a web application to make publicly available the clustering results for the ACD and the JWAD networks, in a spirit of seeking to foster a wider appreciation for the interesting contributions that investigations of word association knowledge can yield for our understandings of lexical knowledge in general.

As Widdow, Cederberg, and Dorow astutely observe [28], graph visualization is a particularly powerful tool for representing the meanings of words and concepts [24]. The graph visualization of the structures generated through both the MCL and the RMCL clustering methods is being implemented with webMathematica and utilizing some standard techniques of java servlet/JSP technology. Because webMathematica is capable of processing interactive calculations, the graph visualization is realized by integrating Mathematica with a web server that uses Apache2 as its http application server and Tomcat5 as its servlet/JSP engine.

The visualization system can highlight the relationships between words by dynamically presenting both MCL and RMCL clustering results for both the ACD and the JWAD networks, as the screen shots in Figure 6 illustrate. Implementation of the visualization system is relatively straightforward, basically only requiring storage of the multiple files that are automatically generated during execution of the RMCL algorithm. The principle feature of the system is that it is capable of simultaneously presenting clustering results for both the ACD and the JWAD networks, making it

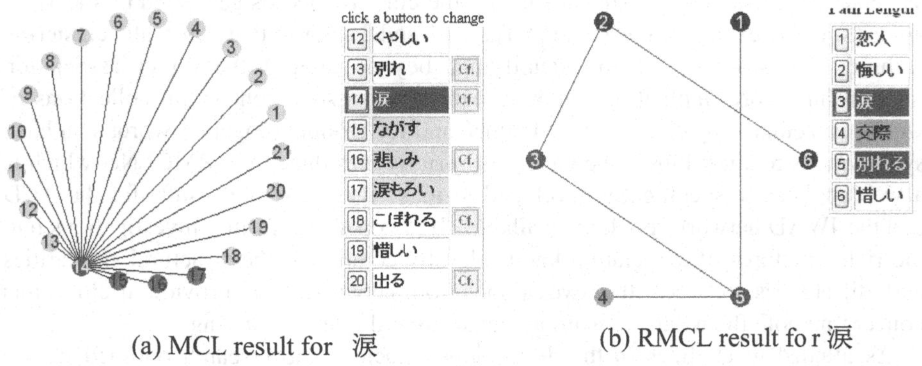


**Fig. 6.** Screen shots of RMCLNet, illustrating visualizations of MCL clustering results (panel a) and of RMCL clustering results (panel b) for the Japanese word 涙 'tears'

possible to compare the structural similarities and differences between the two association networks. Such comparisons can potentially provide useful hints for further investigations concerning the nature of word associations and graph clustering.

## 6 Conclusions

As a promising approach to capturing and unraveling the rich networks of associations that connect words together, this study has applied a range of network analysis techniques in order to investigate the characteristics of network representations of word association knowledge in Japanese. In particular, the study constructed and analyzed two separate Japanese association networks. One network was based on the Associative Concept Dictionary (ACD) by Okamoto and Ishizaki [5], while the other was based on the Japanese Word Association Database (JWAD) by Joyce [6] [7] [8]. The results of initial analyses of the two networks—focusing on degree distributions and average clustering coefficient distributions for nodes with degrees—revealed that the two networks both possess the characteristics of a scale-free network and that both possess intrinsic hierarchies.

The study also applied some graph clustering algorithms to the association networks. While graph clustering undoubtedly represents an effective approach to capturing the associative structures within large-scale knowledge resources, there are still some issues that warrant further investigation. One purpose of the present study has been to examine improvements to the basic MCL algorithm [9], by extending on the enhanced RMCL version [10]. In that context, this study applied a combination of RMCL graph clustering method and the modularity measurement as a means of achieving greater control over the sizes of clusters generated during the execution of the clustering algorithms. For both association networks, the combination of the RMCL algorithm with the modularity index resulted in fewer clusters.

This paper also illustrated the fact that clustering methods represent a potentially very appealing way of automatically identifying and visualizing sets of related words as generated clusters by looking at some of the clustered words generated by the MCL algorithm. The examples presented in Tables 1 and 2 suggest that automatic clustering techniques can be useful for identifying, beyond simply the direct association relationship, more implicit and indirect patterns of association within collections of words as mediated by closely related items, and for grouping together words that have synonymous relationships. The paper also briefly introduced the RMCLNet which is a web application specifically developed to make the clustering results for the ACD and the JWAD networks publicly available. It is hoped that further investigations into the rich structures of association knowledge by comparing the structural similarities and differences between the two association networks can provide useful hints concerning both the nature of word associations and graph clustering.

As alluded to at times in the discussions, much of the research outlined in this paper forms part of a larger ongoing research project that is seeking to capture the structures inherent within association knowledge. In concluding this paper, it is appropriate to acknowledge some limitations with the present study and to fleetingly sketch out some avenues to be explored in the future. One concern to note is that, while the ACD database and Version 1 of the JWAD are of comparable sizes and both can be regarded as being reasonably large-scale, some characteristics of the present two semantic network representations of Japanese word associations may be reflecting characteristics of the foundational databases. As already noted, the ongoing JWAD project is committed to constructing a very large-scale database of Japanese word associations, and as the database expands with both more responses and more extensive lexical coverage and new versions of the JWAD are compiled, new versions of the JWAD semantic network will be constructed and analyzed in order to trace its growth and development.

While much of the discussions in section 4 focused on the important issue of developing and exercising some control over the sizes of clusters generated through graph clustering, the authors also recognize the need to evaluate generated clusters in terms of their semantic consistency. The presented examples of word clusters indicate that clustering methods can be effectively employed in automatically grouping together words related words based on associative relationships. However, essential tasks for our future research into the nature of association knowledge will be to develop a classification of elicited association responses in the JWAD in terms of their associative relationships to the target word and to apply the classification in evaluating the associative relationships between the components of generated clusters. While the manual inspection of generated clusters is undeniably very labor intensive, the work is likely to have interesting implications for the recent active development of various classification systems and taxonomies within thesauri and ontology research.

Finally, one direct extension of the present research will be the application of the MCL and the RMCL graph clustering methods to the dynamic visualization of the hierarchical structures within semantic spaces, as the schematic representation in Figure 7 illustrates. The combination of constructing large-scale semantic network representations of Japanese word associations, such as the JWAD network, and applying graph clustering techniques to the resultant network is undoubtedly a particularly promising approach to capturing, unraveling and comprehending the complex structural patterns within association knowledge.

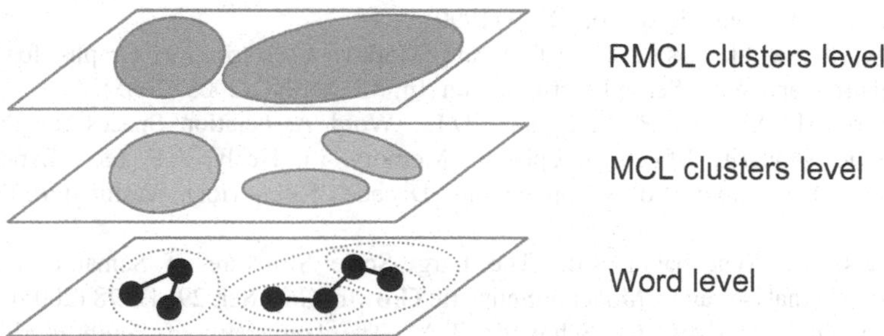


**Fig. 7.** Schematic representation of how the MCL and the RMCL graph clustering methods can be used in the creation of a hierarchically-structures semantic space based on an association network

**Acknowledgments.** This research has been supported by the 21st Century Center of Excellence Program "Framework for Systematization and Application of Large-scale Knowledge Resources". The authors would like to express their gratitude to Prof. Furui, Prof. Akama, Prof. Nishina, Prof. Tokosumi, and Ms. Jung. The authors have been supported by Grants-in-Aid for Scientific Research from the Japanese Society for the Promotion of Science: Research project 18500200 in the case of the first author and 19700238 in the case of the second author.

## References

1. Deese, J.: The Structure of Associations in Language and Thought. The John Hopkins Press, Baltimore (1965)
2. Cramer, P.: Word Association. Academic Press, New York & London (1968)
3. Hirst, G.: Ontology and the Lexicon. In: Staab, S., Studer, R. (eds.) Handbook of Ontologies, pp. 209–229. Springer, Heidelberg (2004)
4. Firth, J.R.: Selected Papers of J. R. Firth 1952-1959. In: Palmer, F.R. (ed.), Longman, London (1957/1968)
5. Okamoto, J., Ishizaki, S.: Associative Concept Dictionary and its Comparison with Electronic Concept Dictionaries. In: PACLING 2001, pp. 214–220 (2001)
6. Joyce, T.: Constructing a Large-scale Database of Japanese Word Associations. In: Tamaoka, K. (ed.) Corpus Studies on Japanese Kanji (Glottometrics 10), pp. 82–98. Hituzi Syobo, Tokyo, Japan and RAM-Verlag, Lüdenschied, Germany (2005)
7. Joyce, T.: Mapping Word Knowledge in Japanese: Constructing and Utilizing a Large-scale Database of Japanese Word Associations. In: LKR 2006, pp. 155–158 (2006)
8. Joyce, T.: Mapping Word Knowledge in Japanese: Coding Japanese Word Associations. In: LKR 2007, pp. 233–238 (2007)
9. van Dongen, S.: Graph Clustering by Flow Simulation. Ph.D. thesis, University of Utrecht (2000)
10. Jung, J., Miyake, M., Akama, H.: Recurrent Markov Cluster (RMCL) Algorithm for the Refinement of the Semantic Network. In: LREC2006, pp. 1428–1432 (2006)
11. Newman, M.E., Girvan, M.: Finding and Evaluating Community Structure in Networks. Phys. Rev. E69, 026113 (2004)
12. Church, K.W., Hanks, P.: Word Association Norms, Mutual Information, and Lexicography. Comp. Ling. 16, 22–29 (1990)
13. Dorow, B., et al.: Using Curvature and Markov Clustering in Graphs for Lexical Acquisition and Word Sense Discrimination. In: MEANING-2005 (2005)
14. Steyvers, M., Shiffrin, R.M., Nelson, D.L.: Word Association Spaces for Predicting Semantic Similarity Effects in Episodic Memory. In: Healy, A.F. (ed.) Experimental Cognitive Psychology and its Applications (Decade of Behavior), Washington, DC, APA (2004)
15. Steyvers, M., Tenenbaum, J.B.: The Large-Scale Structure of Semantic Networks: Statistical Analyses and a Model of Semantic Growth. Cog. Sci. 29, 41–78 (2005)
16. Nelson, D.L., McEvoy, C., Schreiber, T.A.: The University of South Florida Word Association, Rhyme, and Word Fragment Norms (1998), `http:// www.usf.edu/FreeAssociation`
17. Fellbaum, C. (ed.): WordNet: An Electronic Lexical Database. MIT Press, Cambridge (1998)

18. Roget, P.M.: Roget's Thesaurus of English Words and Phrases (1991), `http://www.gutenberg.org/etext/10681`
19. Moss, H., Older, L.: Birkbeck Word Association Norms. Psychological Press, Hove (1996)
20. Umemoto, T.: Table of Association Norms: Based on the Free Associations of 1,000 University Students (in Japanese). Tokyo, Tokyo Daigaku Shuppankai (1969)
21. Version 1 of the JWAD, http://www.valdes.titech.ac.jp/~terry/jwad.html
22. Barabasi, A.L., Albert, R.: Emergence of Scaling in Random Networks. Science 286, 509–512 (1999)
23. Watts, D., Strogatz, S.: Collective Dynamics of 'Small-world' Networks. Nature 393, 440–442 (1998)
24. Ravasz, E., Barabasi, A.L.: Hierarchical Organization in Complex Networks. Physical Rev. E 67, 26112 (2003)
25. Dorogovtsev, S.N., Goltsev, A.V., Mendes, J.F.F.: Pseudofractal Scale-free Web, e-Print Cond-Mat/0112143 (2001)
26. Vechthomova, O., et al.: Synonym Dictionary Improvement through Markov Clustering and Clustering Stability. In: International Symposium on Applied Stochastic Models and Data Analysis, pp. 106–113 (2005)
27. RMCLNet, http://perrier.dp.hum.titech.ac.jp/semnet/RmclNet/index.jsp
28. Widdows, D., Cederberg, S., Dorow, B.: Visualisation Techniques for Analyzing Meaning. TSD5, 107–115 (2002)

# Construction of a Probabilistic Hierarchical Structure Based on a Japanese Corpus and a Japanese Thesaurus

Asuka Terai[1], Bin Liu[2], and Masanori Nakagawa[1]

[1] Tokyo Institute of Technology, 2-12-1 Ookayama, Meguro, Tokyo, Japan
[2] Nissay Information Technology Co. Ltd. 5-37-1, Kamata, Tokyo, Japan

**Abstract.** The purpose of this study is to construct a probabilistic hierarchical structure of categories based on a statistical analysis of Japanese corpus data and to verify the validity of the structure by conducting a psychological experiment. At first, the co-occurrence frequencies of adjectives and nouns within modification relations were extracted from a Japanese corpus. Secondly, a probabilistic hierarchical structure was constructed based on the probability, $P(category|noun)$, representing the category membership of the nouns, and utilizing categorization information in a thesaurus and a soft clustering method (Rose's method [1]) with co-occurrence frequencies as initial values. This method makes it possible to identify the constructed hierarchical structure. In order to examine the validity of the constructed hierarchy, a psychological experiment was conducted. The results of the experiment verified the psychological validity of the hierarchical structure.

## 1 Introduction

There are many kinds of thesauruses. For example, to list just a few in Japanese, there are the EDR concept classification dictionary [2], Goitaikei (A Japanese Lexicon) [3], BUNRUI-GOI-HYO [4]. Generally, thesauri are referred to when people seek more appropriate words or expressions in their writings. They have also become to be utilized in many fields because of their comprehensiveness. For example, natural language processing is one of field that actively uses this kind of resource. However, thesauri do not necessarily reflect the knowledge structure of human beings. Thesauri merely indicate what kind of semantic category a certain noun belongs to. Generally, human beings can distinguish nouns that are strongly associated as being representative of a category from other nouns that are only weakly associated. For example, human beings tend to regard both "sparrow" and "robin" as strongly associated nouns to the "bird" category. On the other hand, "penguin" is regarded as being only weakly associated to the "bird" category. In such cases, thesauri would only enumerate "sparrow", "robin" and "penguin" as belonging to the "bird" category, but would not include any indication of the degree of association for each noun. In other words, thesauri do not contain probabilistic information that indicates the degree of a noun's association with the representativeness of a category, that is to say, the association

T. Tokunaga and A. Ortega (Eds.): LKR 2008, LNAI 4938, pp. 132–147, 2008.

probability of a noun belonging to a category. Such probabilistic information is important in order to construct more human-like knowledge structures, such as a hierarchical structure of concepts that contains probabilistic information. Accordingly, this study constructs a probabilistic hierarchical structure of nouns that realizes a hierarchal categorization with association probabilities for the semantic categories of nouns and the relationships between upper and lower level categories (Fig. 1) based on a Japanese corpus and a Japanese thesaurus.

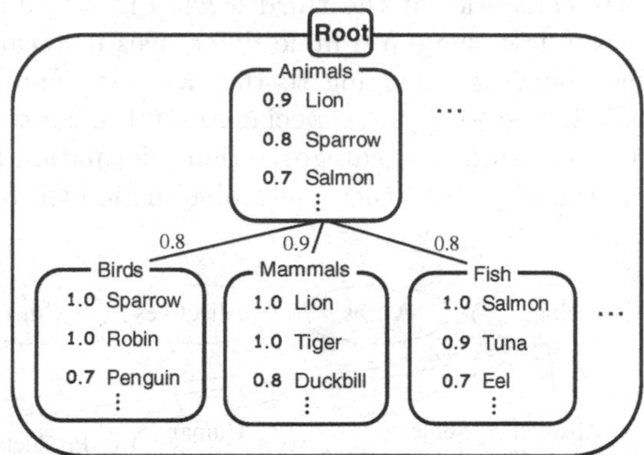


**Fig. 1.** The association probabilities of the nouns belonging to the category

Previous studies have developed several methods for probabilistic language clustering. For instance, [5] developed a method similar to PLSI [6], based on the assumption of latent semantic classes in order to statistically analyze a language corpus. Latent Semantic Analysis (LSA) [7] is one popular methods for natural language analysis. Both of these are soft clustering methods that clarify the latent meanings or conceptual correlations between words. However, these two methods cannot be used to construct hierarchical categories.

One method of hierarchical soft clustering that has been developed is Rose's method [1]. In his method, each cluster is identified by its centroid. [8], and [9] and [10] have applied Rose's method to language data in studies constructing hierarchical probabilistic structures for nouns. However when basing a probabilistic hierarchal structure on a corpus, one faces the problem that it is particularly difficult to identify the meanings of categories. Accordingly, the present study constructs a probabilistic hierarchal structure based on a corpus and an existing thesaurus. Rose's method is a hierarchical soft clustering method that is applicable to data represented by vectors in a space and allows for estimations of association probabilities for data points based on distances between the centroid of a particular category and the data points themselves. If nouns are represented as vectors, it is possible to construct a probabilistic hierarchical structure that reflects the categorization information of a thesaurus, through a process of transformation based on the categorization information of a thesaurus and then applying Rose' method to the transformed vectors. This would thus overcome the problem noted above. However, probabilistic hierarchical structures constructed in such a way, such as [8], [9] and [10], would not necessarily have psychological validity. Accordingly, the present study examines the validity of the probabilistic hierarchical structure by conducting a psychological experiment.

In this research, BUNRUI-GOI-HYO (the NIJL thesaurus) [4] is used in constructing the probabilistic hierarchical structure of nouns. The NIJL thesaurus classifies words into "nouns", "verbs", "adjectives" and "others". The nouns (56,131) are classified into 5 categories at the first level, 43 categories at the second level, and 545 categories at the third level (Fig. 2). When the number of category members is few, there are little differences in terms of association probabilities for the nouns as belonging to the category. Thus, categorization information for the lowest levels is not especially useful in constructing a probabilistic structure. Consequently, the categorization information for the first and the second levels is utilized to construct the probabilistic hierarchical structure.

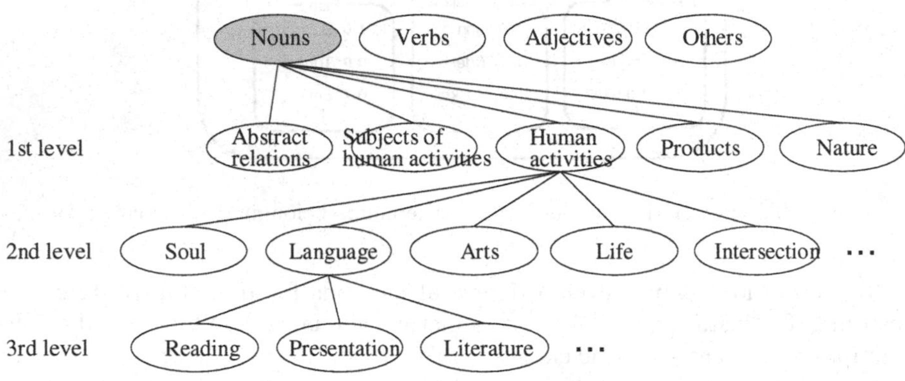


**Fig. 2.** The categorizations of the NIJL thesaurus

## 2 Construction of a Probabilistic Hierarchical Structure

The flow chart presented in Fig. 3 illustrates the construction of the probabilistic hierarchical structure.

- Co-occurrence frequencies of adjectives and nouns are extracted, based on the modification relation in a large-scale corpus.
- Conditional probabilities of an adjective given certain nouns ($P(adjective|noun)$) are computed. Each noun is represented by the coordinate values of a point in a space according to these probabilities.
- The average of the coordinate values, the centroid of the distribution for a category, is assumed to be the representative point for the category.
- Distances between the representative points of categories are lengthened in order to reduce the degree of similarity between categories.

- Distances between nouns within the same category are shortened in order to increase the similarities between the nouns.
- Rose's method is applied to these transformation results, using the transformed representative point for the initial values of the centroid.

The probabilistic hierarchy is constructed through these processes.

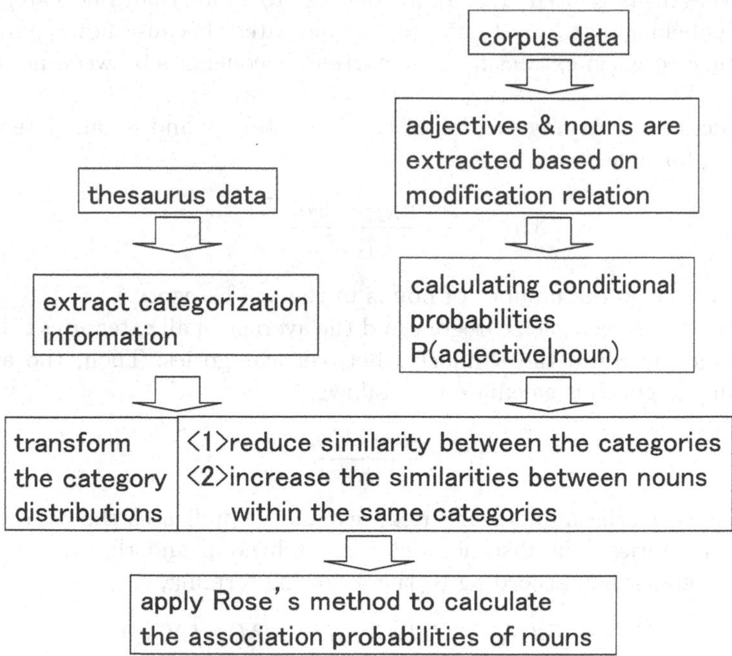


**Fig. 3.** The flow chart of the entire method for constructing a probabilistic hierarchical structure

### 2.1 Transforming the Category Distributions

Initially, the co-occurrence frequencies of adjectives and nouns were extracted, based on the modification relation from Japanese newspaper articles covering a ten-year span (1993-2002) of the Mainichi Shinbun. A Japanese analysis tool 'Cabocha' [11] was used in the modification analysis, and 3,404 adjectives and 21,486 nouns were extracted. Then conditional probabilities of adjectives given nouns ($P(adjective|noun)$) were computed using the following formula(1),

$$P(A_j|N_i) = \frac{F(A_j, N_i)}{\sum_j F(A_j, N_i)}, \tag{1}$$

where $F(A_j|N_i)$ indicates the co-occurrence frequency between an adjective $A_j$ and a noun $N_i$. The original meaning vector of the $i$th noun ($N_i$) is defined using the following formula,

$$Vo_j(N_i) = P(A_j|N_i), \tag{2}$$

where $Vo_j(N_i)$ is the $j$th component of the original meaning vector of the $i$th noun ($N_i$).

If a group of nouns belongs to the same category defined in the thesaurus, it is assumed that the nouns represent the category as a distribution or an area within the space. The average of each category is calculated as the centroid of the category. In this study, the category information for the second level of the NIJL thesaurus is used. If a noun belongs to more than one category, it is treated as belonging to the first category indicated, because homonyms were not distinguished when extracting co-occurrence frequencies between nouns and adjectives.

$Mo_k$ indicates the average vector of the $k$th category and is calculated using the following formula,

$$Mo_k = \frac{sum_{N_i \in C_k} Vo(N_i)}{|C_k|}, \tag{3}$$

where $|C_k|$ indicates the number of nouns in the $k$th category.

The distance between each category and the average of all categories is lengthened in order to reduce the similarity between categories. Then, the average vector of all categories is calculated as follows,

$$M = \frac{sum_k Mo_k}{K}, \tag{4}$$

where $K$ indicates the number of categories and $M$ indicates the average vector for all categories. The distance between each noun and the average of all categories is lengthened according to the following formula,

$$Vs(N_i) = Vo(N_i) + alpha * (Mo_k - M), if N_i \in C_k. \tag{5}$$

The average of each category is transformed as follows,

$$M_k = Mo_k + alpha * (Mo_k - M). \tag{6}$$

Next, the distance between the noun and the average of the category to which the noun belongs is shortened in order to increase the similarities between the nouns, using the following formula,

$$V(N_i) = Vs(N_i) + beta * (M_k - Vs(N_i)), if N_i \in C_k. \tag{7}$$

In this study, noun vectors are transformed using $\alpha = 2$, $beta = 0.6$. Thus, the distance between the average of a category and the average of all categories is three times, and the distance between a noun and the average of the category to which the noun belongs is 0.4 times.

### 2.2 The Hierarchical Soft Clustering

Rose's method is applied to the transformed vectors in order to construct the probabilistic hierarchical categorization. In Rose's method, categorization estimations are conducted for each level. Through formulas (8) and (9), the model calculates the average distortion, $D^n$, which reflects the spread in the nouns around the centroids of the categories at the $n$th level used for learning, while category membership entropy, $H^n$, determines the distribution of the nouns over all categories at the $n$th level.

$$D^n = \sum_{k,i} P(C_k^n|N_i)d(Y_k^n, N_i), \tag{8}$$

$$H^n = -\sum_{k,i} P(C_k^n|N_i)logP(C_k^n|N_i), \tag{9}$$

where $C_k^n$ indicates the $k$th category at the $n$th level, $Y_k^n$ represents the centroid vector of the category $C_k^n$. $d(Y_k^n, N_i)$ is the Euclid distance between the centroid and the noun,

$$d(Y_k^n, N_i) = |V(N_i) - Y_k^n|, \tag{10}$$

The $P(C_k^n|N_i)$ represents the association probability of the $i$th noun $N_i$ belonging to the $k$th category $C_k^n$.

The combination of minimum distortion optimization and maximum entropy optimization is equivalent to the minimization of a single function of free energy. Free energy, $F^n$, is defined using the parameter $\gamma$ ($\gamma > 0$),

$$F^n = D^n - \frac{H^n}{\gamma}. \tag{11}$$

The number of categories estimated depends on fluctuations in the value of $\gamma$. For instance, a single category that includes all nouns would be estimated when the value of $\gamma$ becomes close to zero. Conversely, the number of categories would increase, as the value of $\gamma$ increases. Shifts in the $\gamma$ value determine the number of categories, which, in turn, effectively adjust the depth of the hierarchical structure.

Association probabilities of nouns to categories, which are conditional probabilities of categories given nouns, and conditional probabilities of nouns given categories, are calculated based on formulas (12) and (13),

$$P(C_k^n|N_i) = \frac{e^{-\gamma d(Y_k^n, N_i)^2}}{\sum_p e^{-\gamma d(Y_k^n, N_p)^2}}, \tag{12}$$

$$P(N_i|C_k^n) = \frac{e^{-\gamma d(Y_k^n, N_i)^2}}{\sum_q e^{-\gamma d(Y_q^n, N_i)^2}}. \tag{13}$$

In Rose's method, the centroid vector of each category is estimated after minimizing the free energy, $F$, where,

$$\frac{\delta F^n}{\delta Y_k^n} = 0, \forall k. \tag{14}$$

Thus,

$$\sum_i \frac{(V(N_i) - Y_k^n)e^{-\gamma d(N_i, Y_k^n)^2)}}{\sum_p e^{-\gamma d(N_i, Y_p^n)^2)}} = 0. \tag{15}$$

Formula (15) means that the optimal centroid vector of each category ($Y_k^n$) is calculated through formula (16),

$$Y_k^n = \frac{\sum_i V(N_i)P(C_k^n|N_i)}{\sum_i P(C_k^n|N_i)}, \tag{16}$$

based on formula (12).

The relationships between categories at an upper level and a lower level are represented as the association probability of the lower category to the upper one. The association probability can be calculated according to Bayesian theory by applying formula(17) to the results of formulas (12) and (13),

$$P(C_p^{n-1}|C_q^n) = \sum_i P(C_p^{n-1}|N_i)P(N_i|C_q^n), \tag{17}$$

where $C_p^{n-1}$ indicates the $p$th category at the $n-1$th level and $C_q^n$ represents the $q$th category at the $n$th level.

The average of a category is used as the initial value for the centroid of that category,

$$Y_{k'}^1(0) = \frac{sum_{N_i \in C_{k'}^1} V(N_i)}{|C_{k'}^1|}, \tag{18}$$

$$Y_k^2(0) = \frac{sum_{N_i \in C_k^2} V(N_i)}{|C_k^2|} (= M_k), \tag{19}$$

where $|C_{k'}^1|$ indicates the number of the nouns that belong to the $k'$th category at the first level, and $|C_k^2|$ represents the number of the nouns that belong to the $k$th category at the second level. The centroids of the categories are estimated through repetitions of formula12 and 16.

## 3 The Results of the Probabilistic Hierarchical Structure

When $\gamma = 150$, five categories were estimated at the first level. The results relating to the "subjects of human activities", "products" and "nature" categories are shown in Table 1, where 15 nouns for each category are presented with a range of association probabilities of belonging to each category in the Japanese thesaurus ([4]).

When $\gamma = 250$, 43 categories were estimated at the second level. The results relating to the "body", "agency" and "universe" categories are shown in Table 2, again, with 15 nouns for each category with a range of association probabilities. These nouns belong to each category in the Japanese thesaurus ([4]). Some nouns have large association probabilities values because the noun vectors are transformed in order to reflect the categories at this level.

Estimation results for the relationships among the categories at upper and lower levels are shown in Fig. 4. Every box represents an upper category, while

**Table 1.** Association probabilities of nouns to the category at the first level. The numbers in parentheses represent the association probabilities for the respective categories.

| Subjects of human activities | Products | Nature |
|---|---|---|
| sailor (1.000) | wool (1.000) | following wind (1.000) |
| wife (1.000) | cowhide (1.000) | side wind (1.000) |
| director (1.000) | cap (1.000) | carbonic acid (1.000) |
| clergyman (1.000) | skirt (1.000) | rain (1.000) |
| doctor (1.000) | glass (1.000) | side (1.000) |
| wise man (0.926) | necklace (1.000) | lung disease (0.999) |
| saint (0.701) | elevator (0.857) | platinum (0.999) |
| baby (0.699) | grand hall (0.830) | iceberg (0.709) |
| hostage (0.669) | telephone pole (0.825) | taro (0.675) |
| outsider (0.504) | circuit (0.500) | bump (0.622) |
| amateur (0.394) | embankment (0.491) | icicle (0.552) |
| fetus (0.378) | avenue (0.429) | fireball (0.530) |
| snow fairy (0.302) | canal (0.402) | colon bacillus (0.504) |
| monster (0.263) | waterfall (0.367) | magnet (0.206) |
| pet dog (0.074) | pond (0.274) | rice (0.190) |

the names contained in the boxes signify lower categories. The number beside each name indicates the association probability of the lower category to the given upper category.

"Public & private affairs", "society" and "activity" at the second level are strongly associated to the "abstract relations" category at the first level. However, these are classified within the "subjects of human activities" category at the first level of the NIJL thesaurus. "Aspects", "existence", "operation" and "shape" are categorized under the "abstract relations" category in the thesaurus. However, "aspects", "existence", and "operation" are classified within the "human activities" category, while "shape" is classified under the "products" category in the present estimation results. Similarly, "food" and "power", which are included in the "products" category and the "abstract relations" category of the thesaurus respectively, are categorized in the "nature" category in the estimation results. In this study, the noun vectors are transformed on the basis of the categorization information at the second level of the NIJL thesaurus. Accordingly, some differences emerge between the estimated structure and the thesaurus at the first level, especially, in the "abstract relations" category in the thesaurus, which includes "public & private affairs", "society" and "activity" and the category that can be regarded as a "quantity/space/place" category.

**Table 2.** Association probabilities of nouns to the category at the second level. The numbers in parentheses represent the association probabilities for the respective categories.

| Body | Agency | Universe |
|---:|---:|---:|
| digestion (1.000) | MITI (1.000) | snowy mountain (1.000) |
| lever(1.000) | life co-op (1.000) | hill (1.000) |
| left arm (1.000) | NATO (1.000) | valley (1.000) |
| skull (1.000) | cabinet (1.000) | snow scene (1.000) |
| chest (1.000) | Nation's armed forces (1.000) | inlet (1.000) |
| cerebellum (1.000) | Ministry of finance (1.000) | mountains and rivers (1.000) |
| middle finger (1.000) | labor union (1.000) | night view (1.000) |
| limbs (1.000) | United Nations (1.000) | precipice (1.000) |
| backbone (1.000) | Self-Defense Forces (1.000) | starlit sky (1.000) |
| body (1.000) | ward office (0.824) | ravine (1.000) |
| appendix(1.000) | Meteorological Agency (0.743) | black hole (1.000) |
| nose (1.000) | home office (0.568) | sea (1.000) |
| cartilage (0.705) | Prime Minister's Office (0.554) | street stall (0.423) |
| eyeball (0.506) | block meeting (0.102) | eclipse of the moon (0.313) |
| eyelid (0.483) | art society (0.000) | Mercury (0.101) |
| bare foot (0.295) | militarist party (0.000) | the Big Dipper (0.001) |

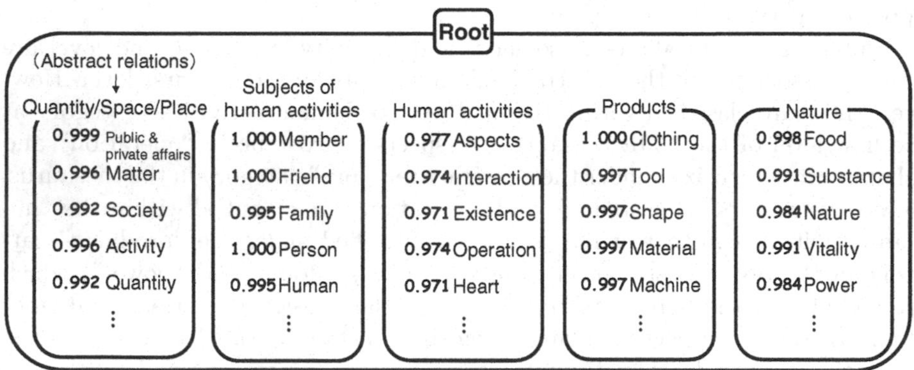


**Fig. 4.** Estimation results for the relationships between upper and lower level categories

The probabilistic hierarchical structure was constructed using a language corpus based on a thesaurus. However, it is necessary to verify the psychological validity of the structure.

## 4 Examination of the Validity of the Association Probabilities

### 4.1 Method for the Psychological Experiment

In order to examine the psychological validity of the constructed probabilistic hierarchical structure, the validity of the association probabilities at the second level calculated using our method is examined.

- Participants: 41 undergraduates
- Scale: 7-point scale (1:strongly disagree - 4:neutral - 7:strongly agree)
- Categories: space, tool, time, dwelling, member, language, life, body, agency and universe

Ten categories were selected for the experiment, from the total of 43 categories. Then, 11 nouns, which belong to each category in the Japanese thesaurus ([4]) were selected as items from each category based on a range of association probabilities, $P(category|noun)$. Five nouns from each category were subsequently selected as typical examples of the respective categories. These nouns all have large association probability values (in each case of 0.982 or more). The participants were shown typical examples of each category and were asked to evaluate the degree of membership for all items with respect to each of the categories (Fig. 5). The nouns presented in Table 3 are typical examples and items for the categories of "life", "member", "tool", "dwelling", "language", "space" and "time". The nouns presented in Table 2 are typical examples and items for the categories of "body", "agency" and "universe" (The upper five nouns were used as typical examples and the others were presented as items to be rated).

### 4.2 Results of the Psychological Experiment

The correlation coefficients between the average of participants' evaluated ratings and association probabilities for the categories are shown in Table 4. The

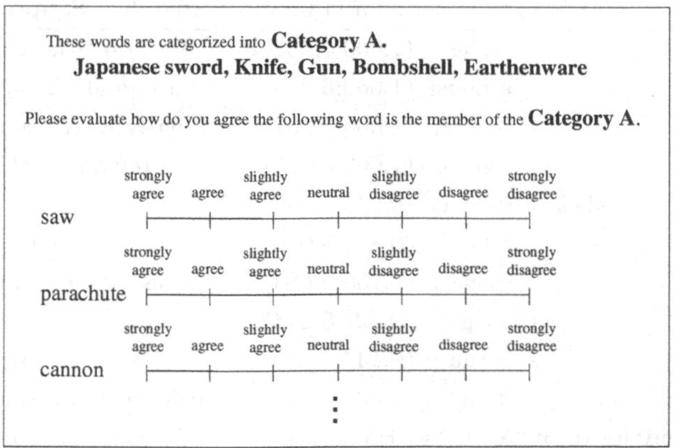


**Fig. 5.** The psychological experiment (e.g. "tool" category)

**Table 3.** Typical examples of some categories and items belonging to the categories used in the psychological experiment. In the parentheses, the number before the colon represents the association probability for a given category and the number after the colon represents the average of the participants' evaluated ratings.

| Type | Life | Tool |
|---|---|---|
| typical example | river leisure (1.000) | earthenware (1.000) |
| | SHICHIGOSAN (1.000) | knife (1.000) |
| | hiking (0.999) | gun (1.000) |
| | Japanese archery (0.995) | bombshell (1.000) |
| | labor (0.993) | Japanese sword (0.999) |
| item | picnic (1.000:5.977) | bamboo sword (1.000:5.837) |
| | HATSUMOUDE (1.000:5.326) | fork (1.000:4.837) |
| | kendo (0.994:5.698) | cannon (1.000:6.419) |
| | nightshift (0.993:4.349) | ironware (1.000:6.163) |
| | snack (0.793:3.419) | block (0.894:2.767) |
| | bankruptcy (0.738:2.140) | saw (0.831:6.070) |
| | parlor tricks (0.590:4.186) | bronze-ware (0.649:5.884) |
| | resignation (0.440:2.830) | goldfish bowl (0.618:3.070) |
| | sitting (0.350:2.302) | stuffed animal (0.425:1.698) |
| | assumption (0.154:3.070) | scarecrow (0.102:2.070) |
| | very good luck (0.078:3.140) | parachute (0.001:3.186) |

| Type | Dwelling | Language |
|---|---|---|
| typical example | private house (1.000) | bibliography (0.998) |
| | school building (1.000) | name (0.995) |
| | ceiling (1.000) | cuntry name (0.995) |
| | bed room (1.000) | archive (0.992) |
| | villa (1.000) | Buddhist Scripture (0.996) |
| item | skylight (1.000:5.732) | job title (0.998:3.293) |
| | single house (1.000:6.366) | resignation (0.997:3.927) |
| | ward (1.000:5.561) | write histry (0.997:5.390) |
| | garret (1.000:6.000) | reference (0.995:5.805) |
| | official residence (0.939:5.756) | sign (0.781:4.756) |
| | house (0.843:5.976) | joke (0.722:3.171) |
| | barn (0.758:5.683) | vicarious writing (0.602:4.000) |
| | front gate (0.221:5.244) | argue (0.503:2.366) |
| | sanctuary (0.144:4.488) | mystery (0.401:3.951) |
| | bonnet (0.031:3.244) | bush telegraph (0.140:3.146) |
| | balcony for drying clothes (0.000:3.171) | mailing (0.062:2.683) |

**Table 3.** (*Continued*)

| Type | Space | Time |
|---|---|---|
| typical example | store's interior (1.000) | the beginning of the rainy season (1.000) |
| | plane's interior (1.000) | Children's Day (1.000) |
| | basement (1.000) | BON (0.999) |
| | zone (0.999) | birthday (0.999) |
| | underground (0.999) | date and time (0.982) |
| item | room (1.000:3.209) | passing of the rainy season (1.000:5.732) |
| | campus (1.000:6.442) | Coming-of-Age Day (1.000:6.366) |
| | area (1.000:5.860) | the New Year (0.999:5.415) |
| | water (1.000:6.302) | date (0.998:6.000) |
| | station square (1.000:5.442) | holiday (0.821:5.463) |
| | the Far East (1.000:4.837) | scene of bloodshed (0.693:2.195) |
| | vacant seat(1.000:3.907) | the first half year (0.557:4.634) |
| | heart of a mountain (0.705:4.605) | waiting time (0.364:3.244) |
| | wide area (0.506:4.279) | stage (0.359:2.927) |
| | distant place (0.483:4.581) | imminence (0.212:4.098) |
| | magnetic field (0.295:4.140) | border (0.118:3.293) |

| Type | Member |
|---|---|
| typical example | engineer (1.000) |
| | sailor (1.000) |
| | pupil (1.000) |
| | caretaker (1.000) |
| | station employee (1.000) |
| item | radio actor (1.000:4.878) |
| | student (1.000:5.732) |
| | soldier (1.000:6.000) |
| | employee (1.000:6.049) |
| | the part of an old man (0.888:4.000) |
| | leader (0.776:4.634) |
| | prima donna (0.641:4.390) |
| | director (0.604:5.415) |
| | disciple (0.118:5.220) |
| | press (0.005:4.732) |
| | senior (0.000:3.683) |

correlation coefficient between evaluated rates and association probabilities about all items is 0.567 ($p < .001$). The correlation coefficients are all significant except for those relating to the "universe" category and the "member" category.

**Table 4.** Correlation coefficients between the average of the evaluated ratings and association probabilities (*** $p < .001$, ** $p < .01$, * $p < .05$, each category $N = 11$, Total $N = 110$)

| category | correlation coefficient |
|---|---|
| Body | 0.682* |
| Space | 0.868** |
| Tool | 0.682* |
| Time | 0.747** |
| Dwelling | 0.895** |
| Language | 0.621* |
| Agency | 0.637* |
| Universe | 0.368 |
| Life | 0.702* |
| Member | 0.478 |
| Total | 0.567*** |

In the experiment, only five nouns that have high association probability values to a given category were presented to the participants as typical examples of the respective categories and the names of categories as defined in the thesaurus were not shown. Accordingly, it may have been difficult for the participants to grasp the range of some categories. However, the correlation coefficient for all items is significant at the 0.1% level. The results of the psychological experiment support the validity of the constructed probabilistic hierarchical structure.

## 5 Discussion

By applying data to Rose's method, association probabilities were calculated. The results partially correspond to the categorizations employed within the reference thesaurus. Furthermore, the results of the psychological experiment verified the psychological validity of the association probabilities calculated by this method.

The constructed structure differs somewhat from the thesaurus at the first level, because the transformation of noun vectors was based only on the categorization at the second level in the thesaurus. The results suggest that the "abstract relations" category within the thesaurus might be more appropriately regarded as a category of "quantity/space/place". To that extent, the method would seem to offer a new categorization that is based on a method of linguistic statistical analysis. In terms of realizing structures that reflect categorization information at all levels, a new approach could be suggested, as follows.

First, noun vectors could be transformed based on categorization information at the highest level. The distance between each category and the average of all

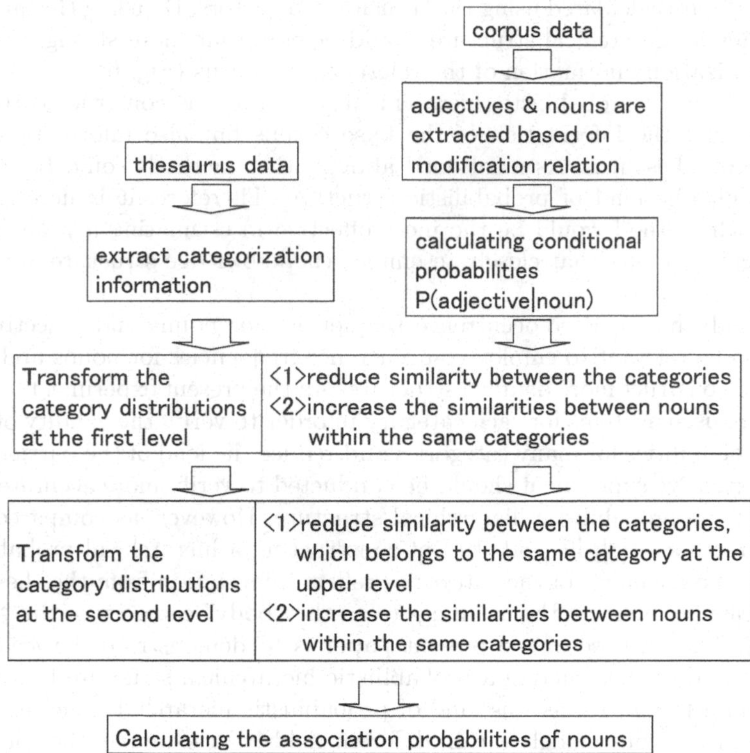


**Fig. 6.** The flow chart of the method for construction of a probabilistic hierarchical structure reflecting the categorization information at all levels

categories would be lengthened in order to reduce the similarity between categories. Then, the average vector of all categories at the first level would be. calculated. The distance between each noun and the average of all categories is lengthened in order to reduce the degree of similarity between categories at the first level. The average of each category is also transformed. The distance between a noun and the average for the category at the first level to which noun belongs is shortened, in order to increase the similarities between nouns. Next, the vector would be transformed based on categorization information at the second level. The vectors would be transformed in order to increase the distribution of categories at the second level belonging to the same category at the first level and the distribution of categories at the second level that a category belongs to at the first level would be increased. The average of the categories at the second level would also be transformed. Then the distance between a noun and the average for the category at the second level to which noun belongs is shortened, in order to increase the similarities between nouns. The distributions of categories at the second level would be reduced. At last, the association probabilities are calculated using the transformed vectors. By using this method, a probabilistic hierarchical structure would emerge that more strongly reflects the categorization information of the reference thesaurus (Fig. 6).

In this study, a probabilistic hierarchical structure was constructed that reflects not only the information of the base corpus but also information from the reference thesaurus. As mentioned above, other methods could be used in constructing this kind of probabilistic structure. Therefore, it is necessary to verify which method would be the most effective in estimating a probabilistic hierarchical structure that closely resembles the knowledge structure of human beings.

This study has used co-occurrence frequencies for nouns and adjectives. It would also be relevant to employ co-occurrence frequencies for nouns and verbs in order to construct more detailed structures. In the present experiment, only 11 nouns were used as items for each category in order to verify the validity of association probabilities for many categories and reduce the load of the participants. A more extensive experiment should be conducted to verify more accurately the validity of the probabilistic hierarchical structure. However, as compared with previous methods ([8], [9] and [10]) of constructing a hierarchical probabilistic structure, the meanings of the categories reflect information from the thesaurus and it is easy to interpret the meanings (e.g., the "body" category or the "tools" category). The purpose of the present paper is to demonstrate the feasibility of our method of constructing a probabilistic hierarchical structure based on a corpus and a thesaurus, as this kind of probabilistic hierarchal structure could be applied to various models within different fields. For example, the computational model of inductive reasoning based on categories [12], the computational model of metaphor understanding [13] and the computational model of metaphor generation [14] could be improved using this probabilistic hierarchical structure.

**Acknowledgements.** This research is supported by the Tokyo Institute of Technology's $21^st$ COE Program, "Framework for Systematization and Application of Large-scale Knowledge Resources" and Grant in Aid of Scientific research from Japan Society for the Promotion of Science (Young Scientists (B) 18700138).

## References

1. Rose, K., Gurewitz, E., Fox, G.C.: Statistical Mechanics and Phase Transitions in Clustering. Physical Review Letters 65(8), 945–948 (1990)
2. Japan Electronic Dictionary Research Institute, Ltd.: the EDR concept classification dictionary. Japan Electronic Dictionary Research Institute Ltd. (1994)
3. Ikehara, S., et al.: Goi-Taikei–A Japanese Lexicon. Iwanami Shoten (1997)
4. The National Institute for Japanese Language: Word List by Semantic Principles, Revised and Enlarged Edition. Dainippon-Tosho (2004)
5. Kameya, Y., Sato, T.: Computation of probabilistic relationship between concepts and their attributes using a statistical analysis of Japanese corpora. In: Proceedings of Symposium on Large-scale Knowledge Resources: LKR 2005, pp. 65–68 (2005)

6. Hofmann, T.: Probabilistic latent semantic indexing. In: Proceedings of the 22nd International Conference on Research and Development in Information Retrieval: SIGIR f99, pp. 50–57 (1999)
7. Deerwester, S., et al.: Indexing by Latent Semantic Analysis. Journal of the Society for Information Science 41(6), 391–407 (1990)
8. Pereira, F., Tishby, N., Lee, L.: Distributional clustering of English words. In: Proceedings 31th Meeting of the Association for Computational Linguistics, pp. 183–190 (1993)
9. Terai, A., Liu, B., Nakagawa, M.: Hierarchical probabilistic categorization of Japanese words. In: The proc. of The 16h International Meeting of the Psychometric Society (2007)
10. Terai, A., Liu, B., Nakagawa, M.: A method for the construction of a probabilistic hierarchical structure based on a statistical analysis of a large-scale corpus. In: The proc. of the 1st International Conference on Semantic Computing, pp. 129–136 (2007)
11. Kudo, T., Matsumoto, Y.: Japanese Dependency Analysis using Cascaded Chunking. In: CoNLL 2002: Proceedings of the 6th Conference on Natural Language Learning 2002 (COLING 2002 Post-Conference Workshops), pp. 63–69 (2002)
12. Sakamoto, K., Terai, A., Nakagawa, M.: Computational models of inductive reasoning using a statistical analysis of a Japanese corpus. Cognitive Systems Research 8, 282–299 (2007)
13. Terai, A., Nakagawa, M.: A newral network model of metaphor understanding with dynamic interaction based on a statistical language analysis: targeting a human-like model. International Journal of Neural Systems 17(4), 265–274 (2007)
14. Abe, K., Nakagawa, M.: A Computational Model of the Metaphor Generation Process. In: Proc. of the 28th Annual Conference of the Cognitive Science Society, pp. 937–942 (2006)

# CHISE: Character Processing Based on Character Ontology

Tomohiko Morioka

Documentation and Information Center for Chinese Studies,
Institute for Research in Humanities,
Kyoto University

**Abstract.** Currently, in the field of information processing, characters are defined and shared using coded character sets. Character processing based on coded character sets, however, has two problems: (1) Coded character sets may lack some necessary characters. (2) Characters in coded character sets have fixed semantics. They may prevent to implement classical text database for philological studies. Especially for Kanji (Chinese character), they are serious problems to digitize classical texts. To resolve the problems, we proposed "Chaon" model which is a new model of character processing based on character ontology. To realize them, a character ontology is required. Especially for Kanji, large scale ontology is required. So we realized a large scale character ontology which includes 98 thousand characters including Unicode and non-Unicode characters. This paper focuses our design or principal of a large scale character ontology based on Chaon model, and overview of its implementation named CHISE (Character Information Service Environment).

## 1 Introduction

We use characters as a basis for data representation in computers, and as a tool for communication over computer networks. Currently, in the field of information processing of digital text, each character is represented and processed by the "Coded Character Model". In the model, each character is defined and shared using a coded character set (code) and represented by a code-point (integer) of the code.

Character processing based on the coded character model is a simple and efficient method. Each character is represented by an integer, so it is possible to process characters without large memory and high speed processing power. Knowledge of characters are defined (standardized) in a spec of a coded character set, there are no need to store large and detailed knowledge of characters into computers for basic text processing.

In a sense of flexibility, the coded character model has some problems, because it expects finite set of characters and each character of the set has a stable concept shared in the community. Namely it expects static character world. However, real character usage is not so static and stable. Especially in Kanji (Hanzi; Chinese character), it is not so easy to select a finite set of characters which

T. Tokunaga and A. Ortega (Eds.): LKR 2008, LNAI 4938, pp. 148–162, 2008.

covers all usages. It is also not so easy to find and define stable concept of characters. For example, equivalence of characters is not so clear. Usually a Chinese character has one or more variants. If each relation among character variants is static, we can regard these character variants as a categorized character group which indicate the same character concept. In that case, we can regard the categorized character group as an abstract character which is defined by the rule of categorization. Unfortunately, such kind of character relations are not static in general, they are depended on periods, regions, fields, contexts, situations, etc. Even if we can find a good subset of abstract characters with stable concepts of characters, it is only an approximation so we may encounter exceptions. If we encounter an exception unfortunately, we need to modify the code or give up to represent by the code. Especially for classical texts and characters, it is a serious problem.

In a point of view, the phenomenon, semantics is depended on situations, contexts, fields, regions, periods, etc., is not only found in character world but also in various linguistic phenomena. In the field of linguistic semantics, situation semantics introduces robust framework for situation dependency of linguistic semantics. We thought that the field of character processing is also need similar framework.

Despite of the situation dependency, character also has a property which across several situations and contexts. When a Chinese character in a text is interpreted in a context/situation and the semantics is a new interpretation of the character, it may be reused in a different text with expectation of the new interpretation. Such kind of feedback loops have been generating inter-context properties of characters and some of them became fixed properties of characters. Namely two different forces work in Chinese character world: context/situation dependence and independence.

By the way, character processing is a basis of various text processing, it should be enough lightweight to keep computational power for other modules. So if we propose an alternative model which can be replace coded character model, it should be designed to be simple.

To resolve the problems of coded character model and satisfy these points of views, we proposed "Chaon" model[1] [13] [14] which is a new model of character processing based on character ontology. In Chaon model, each character is defined, represented and processed according to its definition in a character ontology. Characters in Chaon model are independent from coded character sets for information interchange, and semantics of the characters stored in the ontology can be freely added or altered.

To realize the character processing based on Chaon model, we started "CHISE (Character Information Service Environment)" project.[2] In CHISE project, we

[1] When I and NIIBE Yutaka proposed the first version of Chaon model, it was named "UTF-2000 model" by NIIBE Yutaka [21]. However it is quite misleading that the model is a character code. So I changed the name of the model to Chaon model in 2001.

[2] It was named UTF-2000, but renamed in 2001.

have developed some systems and databases (ontology) to edit/process/print characters and texts (they are called "CHISE" in this paper). CHISE project is an open source project, so the results are freely distributed. We are realizing character processing environment based on Chaon model.

Chaon model is a knowledge driven method to process character, so CHISE requires a character ontology to get various information about characters to process variously. In the model, character ontology is one of the most important factors. Especially in Kanji (Chinese character), coverage and quality of character ontology is quite important.

This paper focuses our design or principal of a large scale character ontology based on Chaon model, and overview of CHISE.

## 2 Character Representation of CHISE

### 2.1 Chaon Model

In Chaon model, representation of each character is not a code point of a coded character set, but a set of the features it has. Each character is represented as a character object, and the character object is defined by character features. Character objects and character features are stored in a character ontology, and each character can be accessed using its feature as a key.

There are various information related with characters, so we can regard various things as character features, for example, shapes, phonetic values, semantic values, code points in various character codes. Fig. 1 shows a sample image of a character representation in Chaon model.

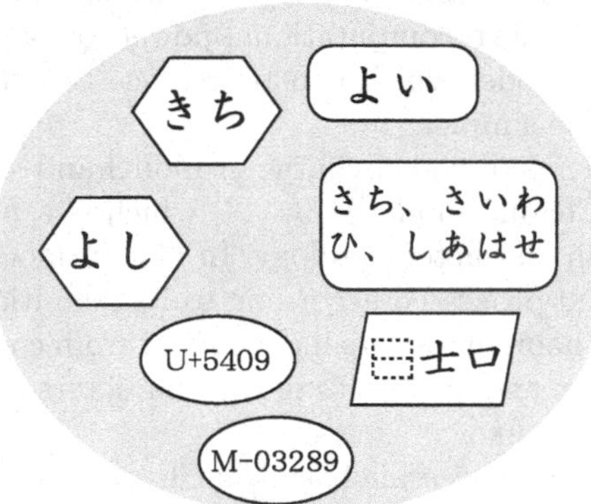


**Fig. 1.** Sample of character features

In Chaon model, each character is represented by a set of character features, so we can use set operations to compare characters. Fig. 2 shows a sample of a Venn diagram of character objects.

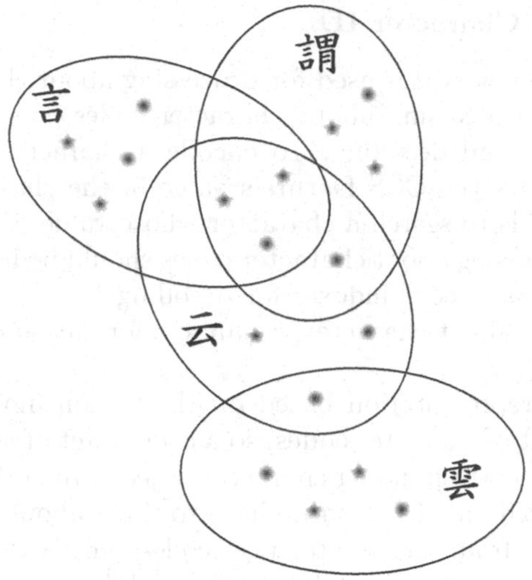


**Fig. 2.** Venn diagram of characters

As we have already explained, a coded character set (CCS) and a code point in the set can also be character features. Those features enable exchanging a character information with the applications that depend on coded character sets. If a character object has only a CCS feature, processing for the character object is the same with processing based on the coded-character model now we are ordinarily using. Namely we can regard the coded-character model as a subset of Chaon model.

## 2.2 Categorization of Features

In the character processing based on Chaon model, it is important to analyze characters and their various properties and behaviors and represent them as character features. We can find sundry properties and behaviors of characters, and we can use infinite kind of character features. However general purpose character ontology requires a guideline about character features. So we think that it is feasible to regard each character feature as an abstraction of an operation for characters.

In the point of view, each character feature can be categorized as follows:

1. general character property (such as descriptions of dictionaries)
2. mapping for character ID
3. relation between characters

For example, radicals, strokes and phonetic values can be classed into the category 1, code points of UCS [5] can be classed into the category 2 and relations between character variants can be classed into the category 3.

### 2.3 Mapping for Character ID

Information of the category 2 is used for processing about character codes, such as code conversion. Processing about character codes consists of two kind of operations: encoding and decoding. To encode a character by a CCS (coded character set) is to get the CCS feature's value in the character. To decode a code-point of a CCS is to search a character whose value of the CCS feature is the code-point. Processing about character codes should be fast, so the character ontology of CHISE has special indexes for decoding.[3]

For the processing about character variants, information of the category 3 is used.

In the character representation based on the Chaon model, each character object is independent of character codes, so a code-point of a CCS may have the plural number of the corresponding character objects. In addition, coverage of a code-point is depended on a CCS, so we have to think about the case in general. So one-way mapping from a character to a code-point is the general case. If a representative character object can be determined for a code-point, round-trip (one-to-one) mapping can be defined.

In CHISE, each character feature name to indicate one-way mapping is started by => and each character feature name to indicate round-trip mapping is started by =.

### 2.4 Relations between Characters

Chaon model itself is a method to indicate characters or sets of characters by their character features, not for network of characters. However we can introduce a kind of character feature which has a list of characters as its feature value. Characters stored in the list can also have such kind of character feature, so we can represent network of characters (Fig. 6). Such kind of character feature is called "relation features".

In CHISE, each relation feature name is started by -> or <- (except its metadata feature names described in Sec. 2.5).

The property of relation features is defined as the follows:

> If character A, B exist and there is a character relation A ->*foo* B, the character A has a relation feature whose name is ->*foo* and the character B is an element of its value. In the case, the character B has a reversed relation feature whose name is <-*foo* and the character A is an element of its value.

### 2.5 Description for Complex Information

For development of a general purpose character ontology, we may find some cases that there are different kind of usages, purposes, applications, sources, interpretations, theories, etc. so it is hard to chose one feature value and we

[3] For the special treatment, we distinguish the category 1 and 2, but it seems that there are no essential differences.

want to provide alternative values. In that cases, we may want to add metadata, such as sources of the values. To resolve the problem, we have to introduce structured feature value or structured feature name (key).

To represent structured feature values, a format named "character reference (char-ref)" is used in CHISE. It is a kind of property-list of S-expression (Lisp), property name indicates kind of metadata and property value indicates its data. As a special property name, :char is reserved to indicate a character which is added the metadata. Currently :sources is defined to indicate information source.

CHISE also has a format to represent structured feature names. In the structured feature names, "domain identifiers" and/or "metadata identifiers" are added to ordinary (base) feature names. The format is defined as following definitions:

```
<character feature name>
      := <concrete feature name> | <metadata feature name>

<concrete feature name>
      := <base feature name>
      |  <base feature name> @ <domain identifier>

<metadata feature name>
      := <concrete feature name> * <metadata identifier>
      |  <metadata feature name> * <metadata identifier>
      |  <metadata feature name> @ <domain identifier>

<domain identifier>
      := <base domain identifier>
      |  <domain identifier> / <base domain identifier>
```

For example, when total strokes is represented by a character feature total-strokes and ucs is used as a domain identifier, total-strokes in the ucs domain is represented by total-strokes@ucs. When source is represented by metadata identifier sources, total-strokes@ucs's source is represented by metadata feature name total-strokes@ucs*sources.

If there is a correspondence between different kind of features, such as radical and body-strokes, we can represent the correspondence by a domain identifier. For example, when radical is represented by ideographic-radical and body-strokes is represented by ideographic-strokes, two concrete feature names

ideographic-radical@ucs
ideographic-strokes@ucs

are corresponding.

### 2.6 Inheritance of Character Definition

If we construct a large scale character database including a lot of character variants, inheritance of character definition is good way to avoid to write a lot of common features. So CHISE introduces four special features to represent parent and child relations:

**<–subsumptive** defined character is a child of each character indicated by its value
**<–denotational** likewise
**–>subsumptive** each character indicated by its value is a child of the defined character
**–>denotational** likewise

In the sense of inheritance, A –>*subsumptive* B and A –>*denotational* B have the same semantics. However, they have a small nuance: A –>*subsumptive* B means that B is a close (glyph image) variant of A and they (or brothers/sisters of B) have quite similar differences. A –>*denotational* B means that B is a distant (glyph) variant of A and they (or brothers/sisters of B) have relatively large differences. –>*denotational* is useful to describe abstract characters.

## 3 Implementation

Character processing based on Chaon model is to represent each character as a set of character features instead of a code point of a coded character set and process the character by various character features. It indicates that character processing system based on Chaon model is a kind of database system to operate character ontology. So the major targets of CHISE project are (1) character database systems, (2) character database contents and (3) CHISE based applications. CHISE Project is working on the targets and provides some results as free software.

As character database systems (and language bindings), following implementations are available:

**libchise** is a library to provide fundamental features to operate character database
**XEmacs CHISE** is a Chaon implementation based on XEmacs [20] (extensible text editing environment with Emacs Lisp interpreter) [Figure 3]
**Ruby/CHISE** is a Chaon implementation based on Ruby [18] (scripting language)
**Perl/CHISE** is a Chaon implementation based on Perl (scripting language)

For the Chaon implementations, currently two database contents are available as follows:

**CHISE basic character database** is a general character ontology attached to XEmacs CHISE; including about 220 thousand defined character object (about 98 thousand head-characters) now
**CHISE-IDS** is a database about structure of components of Ideographic characters; including about 80 thousand characters now; it is designed to integrate into the CHISE basic character database (feature 'ideographic-structure' is used in CHISE).

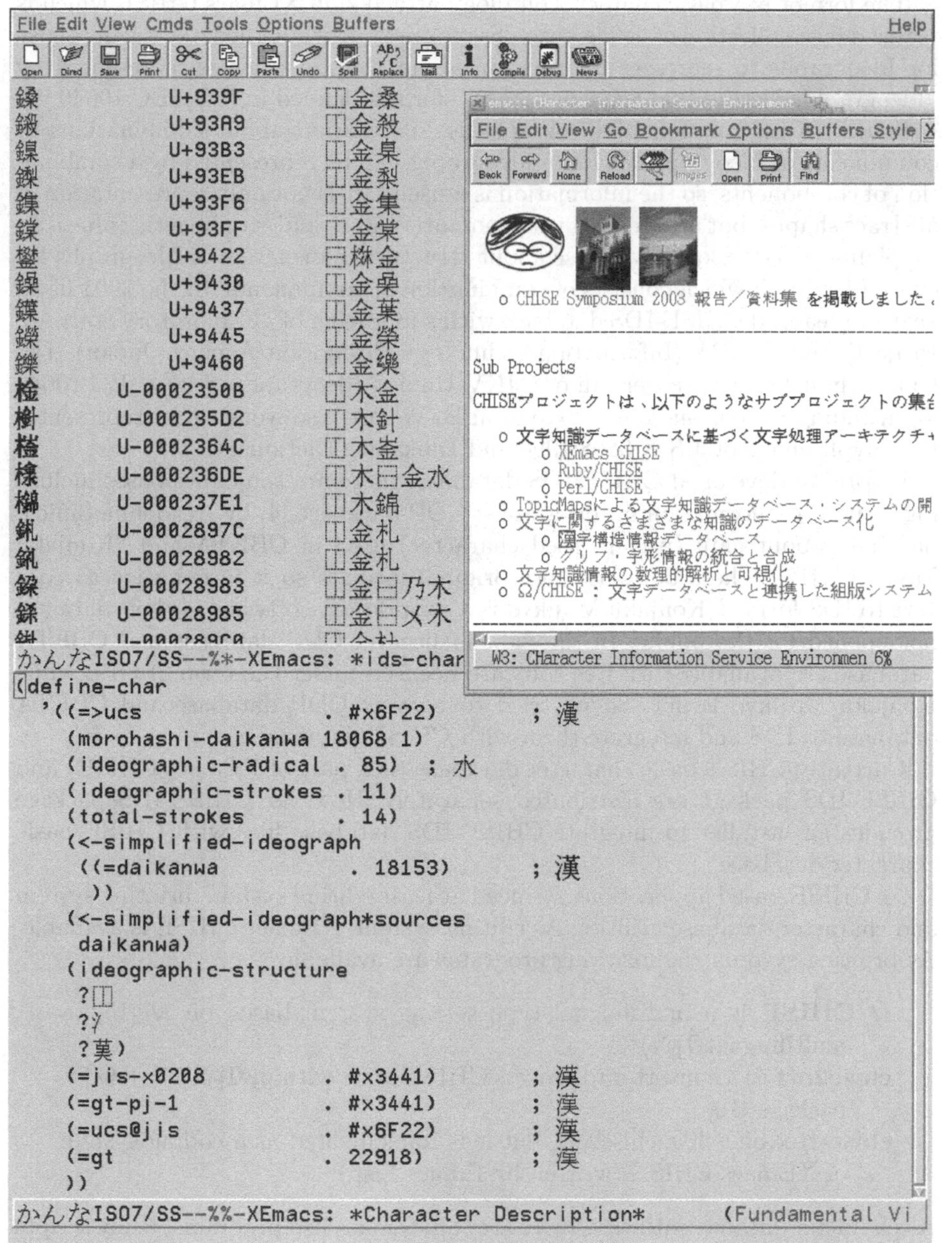


**Fig. 3.** XEmacs CHISE

The former is a basic character ontology attached in XEmacs CHISE which is realized by a collection of define-chars (S-expressions) while the later is a database for Ideographs to represent information about shapes which is represented by "Ideographic Description Sequence (IDS)" format defined in ISO/IEC 10646 [5].

Structure information of Ideographs is information about combinations of components of Ideographs. A lot of Ideographs can be represented by a combination of components, so the information is a useful. It is not only representation of abstract shapes, but also related with semantic values and/or phonetic values. So we planned to develop a database about structure information of Ideographs for every Ideograph which consists of combination of components. In the 2001 fiscal year, we realized CHISE-IDS database with supporting of "Exploratory Software Project" run by IPA (Information-technology Promotion Agency, Japan) [14]. Currently it basically covers all of CJKV Unified Ideographs of ISO/IEC 10646 [5] including Extension A and Extension B. We are also working for representative glyph image of JIS X 0208:1990 and Daikanwa Dictionary.

Before we developed CHISE-IDS database, there are some databases including structure information of Ideographs: CDP database [4] by Academia Sinica, database about gaiji (private used character) used in CBETA and "Konjaku Mojikyo" [12]. These databases use original formats so it is not easy to convert to IDS format. Konjaku Mojikyo is a proprietary software so their data are not opened for the public. In the view of licence, CDP database and CBETA database are available with free software licenced under the term of GPL while Konjaku Mojikyo is not. So we tried to convert CDP database and CBETA database to IDS and integrate them with CHISE database.

Currently CHISE basic character database (is a part of XEmacs CHISE) and CHISE-IDS package are distributed separately. However CHISE-IDS package provides an installer to integrate CHISE-IDS database files with CHISE basic character database.

As CHISE based applications, we need at least editing system, printing system and character database utilities. As editing system, XEmacs CHISE is available. As printing system, the following programs are available:

- **Ω/CHISE** is a multilingual type setting system based on Ω [15] (a multilingual TEX)
- **chise2otf** is a converter to process CHISE texts with pLATEX[17] + OTF package [16]
- **chise-tex.el** is like chise2otf, but it is implemented as a coding-system of XEmacs CHISE (written by Emacs Lisp)

As character database utilities, there are some emacs lisp programs, Ruby scripts attached to Ruby/CHISE and Perl scripts attached to Perl/CHISE.

In addition, the following system is available:

- **Kage** is an automatic Ideographic glyph generating system [8] [7]

Currently Kage is used in Ω/CHISE and chise2otf.

# CHISE IDS 漢字検索

Version 0.23.2 (Last-modified: 2007-08-20 18:24:12)

部品文字列 水火 検索開始

- 𤆲 U-000241B2 (link map) ⿱水火
- 洃 U+6D03 (link map) ⿰氵灰
- 洃 C2-2B64 U+6D03 (link map) ⿰氵灰
- &UU+6D03; U+6D03 (link map) ⿰氵灰
- 𣴕 U-00023D15 (link map) ⿰氵⿱火儿
- &M-17420; U-00023D15 (link map) ⿰氵⿱火儿
- 烫 U+70EB (link map) ⿱汤火
- 𣵩 U-00023D69 (link map) ⿰氵⿱大火
- &M-49213; U-00023D69 (link map) ⿰氵⿱大火
- &U-00023D69; U-00023D69 (link map) ⿰氵⿱大火
- 㶹 U+3DB9 (link map) ⿰火隶
- &M-19050; U+3DB9 (link map) ⿰火隶
- 淡 U+6DE1 (link map) ⿰氵炎 ⇒[唐代拓本]
  - 𠻪 U-00020EEA (link map) ⿰口淡
  - 𦸁 U-00026E01 (link map) ⿱艹淡
  - 䆱 U+41B1 (link map) ⿱穴淡
  - &UU+41B1; U+41B1 (link map) ⿱穴淡
  - 𥲄 U-00025C84 (link map) ⿱⺮淡
  - &M-26439; U-00025C84 (link map) ⿱⺮淡
  - 𩉀 U-00029240 (link map) ⿱淡面
  - 𢴗 U-00022D17 (link map) ⿰扌淡
  - 𥊗 U-00025297 (link map) ⿰目淡
  - 𧐽 U-0002743D (link map) ⿰虫淡
  - 𨤵 U-00028935 (link map) ⿰里淡
  - &HZK07-E2AB; ⿱穴淡
  - &HZK08-C3DA; ⿱⺮淡

**Fig. 4.** CHISE IDS Find

# 豊

豆部 (R151) / 6画

総画数: 13画

漢字構造（解字）: ⿱ 曲 豆

甲骨: 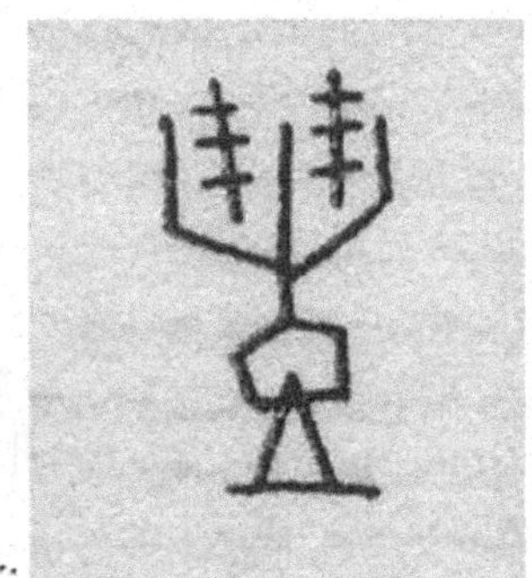

= U+8C4A

= 大漢和辭典: 36263

shinjigen-2: 7807

=jis-x0208: #x4B2D [43-13]

=ks-x1001: #x7925 [89-05]

=cns11643-2: #x475A [39-58]

=big5: #xE054

=gt: 48656

=gt-k: 10269

=gt-pj-1: #x4B2D [43-13]

<-simplified@JP/Jouyou: 豊

[この部品を含む漢字を探す]

---

Powered by XEmacs CHISE 0.23 (Kamo).

**Fig. 5.** CHISE character description

# 4 WWW Applications

## 4.1 CHISE IDS Find

"CHISE IDS Find" [19] is a WWW service to search the CHISE ontology for Kanji (Chinese character) and/or historical Chinese characters, such as Oracle Bone script, using feature 'ideographic-structure'.

If a user specifies one or more components of Kanji into the "Character components" window and run the search, characters includes every specified components are displayed. In the result, if a character is used as a component of other characters, these derived characters are indented after the character, like tree (Fig. 4).

## 4.2 CHISE Character Description

In a result page of the CHISE IDS Find, the first column of each line is an entry of a character. It has a link for a page to display details of the character, named "CHISE character description" (Fig. 5).

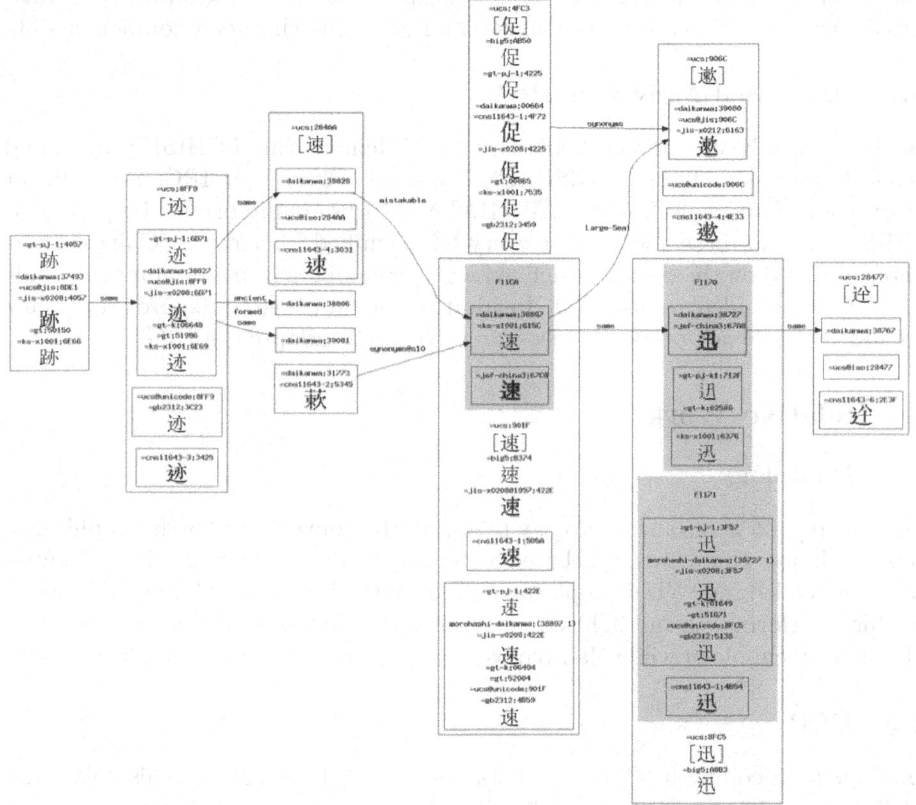


**Fig. 6.** CHISE link map (U+8FC5)

A character description page may have some links for ideographic-structure, character variants or other related characters, etc. In that case, information about such kind of related characters can be displayed to click the links.

### 4.3 CHISE Link Map

In a result page of the CHISE IDS Find, the third column of each line shown as `(link map)` is a link for the "CHISE link map" by Koichi KAMICHI [6] (Fig. 6).

The "CHISE link map" is a WWW service to visualize relations between characters. It visualizes an overview of character variant network.

## 5 Derived Works

### 5.1 Character Analysis

Character ontology is available to analyze network of characters. For example, CHISE-IDS database makes a network of characters based on relations between characters which have shared character components. Yoshi Fujiwara, et al. analyzed such kind of character relations based of shared character components [3].

### 5.2 IDS Based Activity in IRG

In IRG[4] 24 in Kyoto, Japan (2005-05-2427), I demonstrated CHISE project and related systems including CHISE-IDS Find [10]. After that IRG uses IDS for their works. Especially, Taichi KAWABATA's works are important. He processed CHISE-IDS database and analyze every UCS Unified Ideographs (Chinese characters). Based on the result, he defined a glyph component based unification rule of UCS Unified Ideographs [11][9]. In addition, he proposed to require proponents to add IDS for each proposed Ideograph. Now it is adopted in IRG.

## 6 Relative Works

### 6.1 Hantology

Hantology[1][2] is a Hanzi Ontology based on the conventional orthographic system of Chinese characters. It is based on SUMO (Suggested Upper Merged Ontology) and coded in OWL. Comparing CHISE with Hantology, CHISE is designed for high performance and lightweight system software as a replacement of coded character technology while Hantology seems designed for heavy applications.

### 6.2 CDP

Intelligent Encoding of Chinese Characters by C. C. Hsieh and his colleagues at Academia Sinica since the 1990's is an early work about Chinese character processing system based on Knowledge processing.

[4] ISO/IEC JTC1/SC2/WG2/IRG (Ideographic Rapporteur Group).

For the purpose of expressing the parts of characters, that are not characters themselves, more than 2000 code-points from the private use area (PUA) of Big5 had been used. Furthermore, the CDP database uses a set of only three operators for connecting the characters, although in practice, this has been expanded to 11 due to the introduction of shortcut operators for handling multiple occurrences of the same component in one character. There are three more operator-like characters, which are used when embedding glyph expressions into running text.

CHISE and CDP may share similar purpose and spirit. However CHISE does not supports only Chinese characters but also various scripts while CDP is designed for Chinese characters. In fact, CHISE ontology includes information of Unicode data and it uses the same mechanism for every scripts. In addition, CHISE is designed not depended on a particular character code while CDP is depended on Big5.

In representation of Ideographic structure of components, CDP uses original infix format while CHISE uses IDS (Ideographic Description Sequence) format [5].

## 7 Conclusion

We have described a brand new character processing model Chaon and overview of CHISE. Chaon character representation model is powerful and radical enough to solve the problems that the present coded character model has, and the implementation of Chaon model, such as XEmacs CHISE or CHISE IDS Find have shown that the model is feasible enough to build an application on.

Chaon model gives users freedom to create, define and exchange characters of their need, as it is easy to change character ontology or modify character features dynamically. With the CHISE basic character database, XEmacs CHISE can handle various characters including characters not defined in Unicode. Even if a character is not defined in Unicode, users can add it into CHISE character ontology to define it by its features. Users can handle each character based on their point of view or policy. For example, CHISE provides some unification rules or mapping policies about Unicode. With the CHISE-IDS database, users can search Kanji easily. This method is also available for non-Unicode characters.

CHISE project is an open source project, so its results are distributed as free software. Information about CHISE project is available at:

- `http://cvs.m17n.org/chise/`
- `http://kanji.zinbun.kyoto-u.ac.jp/projects/chise/`
- http://mousai.as.wakwak.ne.jp/projects/chise/

These WWW pages, various programs and data are managed by CVS (a kind of revision control system), so users can get the latest snapshot. There are mailing-lists about CHISE project: for English and Japanese. If you are interested in CHISE project, please join to the lists.

## References


1. Chou, Y.-M., Huang, C.-R.: Hantology: An ontology based on conventionalized conceptualization. In: Dale, R., et al. (eds.) IJCNLP 2005. LNCS (LNAI), vol. 3651, Springer, Heidelberg (2005)
2. Chou, Y.-M., Huang, C.-R.: Hantology-a linguistic resource for chinese language processing and studying. In: LREC 2006 (5th edition of the International Conference on Language Resources and Evaluation) (May 2006)
3. Fujiwara, Y., Suzuki, Y., Morioka, T.: Network of words. In: Artificial Life and Robotics (2002)
4. Hanziku: http://www.sinica.edu.tw/~cdp/zip/hanzi/hanzicd.zip
5. International Organization for Standardization (ISO). Information technology — Universal Multiple-Octet Coded Character Set (UCS), ISO/IEC 10646:2003 (March 2003)
6. Kamichi, K.: CHISE link map, http://fonts.jp/chise_linkmap/
7. Kamichi, K.: Kage, http://fonts.jp/kage/
8. Kamichi, K.: KAGE — an automatic glyph generating engine for large character code set. In: Proceedings of the Glyph and Typesetting Workshop. 21st Century COE program East Asian Center for Informatics in Humanities — Toward an Overall Inheritance and Development of Kanji Culture —, Kyoto University, February 2004, pp. 85–92 (2004)
9. Kawabata, T.: Unification/subsumption criterion of UCS Ideographs (beta edition), http://kanji-database.sourceforge.net/housetsu.html
10. Kawabata, T.: Reference Information on Ideographs and IDS Informations on Japanese researchers, IRG N1139 (May 2005), http://www.cse.cuhk.edu.hk/~irg/irg/irg24/IRGN1139IDSResearch.pdf
11. Kawabata, T.: A judgement method of "equivalence" of UCS Ideographs based on IDS (in Japanese). In: The 17th seminar on Computing for Oriental Studies, March 2006, pp. 105–119 (2006)
12. Mojikyo institute. http://www.mojikyo.org/
13. Morioka, T.: UTF-2000 — vision of code independent character representation system (in Japanese). In: Frontier of Asian Informatics, November 2000, pp. 13–24 (2000)
14. Morioka, T., Wittern, C.: Developping of character object technology with character databases (in Japanese). In: IPA result report 2002. Information-Technology Promotion Agency, Japan (2002), http://www.ipa.go.jp/NBP/13nendo/reports/explorat/charadb/charadb.pdf
15. The omega typesetting and document processing system. http://omega.cse.unsw.edu.au:8080/
16. VF (virtual font) for Open Type fonts. http://psitau.at.infoseek.co.jp/otf.html
17. ASCII Japanese TEX (pTEX). http://www.ascii.co.jp/pb/ptex/
18. The object-oriented scripting language Ruby. http://www.ruby-lang.org/
19. Tomohiko, M.: CHISE IDS find. http://mousai.kanji.zinbun.kyoto-u.ac.jp/ids-find
20. XEmacs. http://www.xemacs.org/
21. Yutaka, N.: UTF-2000 Announcement (April 1998), http://turnbull.sk.tsukuba.ac.jp/Tools/XEmacs/utf-2000.html

# Systematization of Knowledge about Performative Verbs: Capturing Speaker's Intention

Naoko Matsumoto[1], Hajime Murai[2], and Akifumi Tokosumi[2]

[1] Graduate School of Information Science and Electrical Engineering, Kyushu University, 744 Motooka Nishi-ku Fukuoka 819-0395, Japan
matsun@ed.kyushu-u.ac.jp

[2] Department of Value and Decision Socience, Tokyo Institute of Technology, 2-12-1 Ookayama Meguro-ku Tokyo 152-8552, Japan
{h_murai,akt}@valdes.titech.ac.jp

**Abstract.** In order to support effective and smooth recognition of the intentions embedded within texts shared by multiple knowledge agents (e.g. humans or knowledge systems), this paper systematizes knowledge about performative verbs, which is considered as a verb to indicate speaker intentions, and proposes an intention reference system. The system enables two kinds of references; (a) a reference of the cognitive elements of intention and (b) a reference of intentions with cognitive elements. Consequently, it becomes easy to share the text addressor's intention at least in the group even in the text-based communications on the Web. In addition to semantic web that tags the semantic content of the text, tagging the action of the text expects to realize more smoothly text communication with less misunderstanding.

**Keywords:** performative verbs, speaker intentions, pragmatic, reference system, cognitive elements.

## 1 Introduction

Nowadays, as WWW (World Wide Web) appears, a large-scale text is often treated in several research fields such as information science, linguistics, and psychology. Web communication has advantage that people can convey much information to a large amount of people inexpensively because of its characteristics of a little time and space restriction. On the other hand, addressor (= text writer) intentions might not be conveyed sometimes because of text-based communication in which there are no para-language elements such as gestures, facial expressions, and gazes. Then, what is the addressor's intention? It is a sort of force to influence the addressee (= text reader), and it is possible to consider the addressor's intention as his / her action for the addressee. In order to support proper and smooth text-based communication between multiple knowledge agents (e.g., humans or knowledge systems), it is necessary to consider not only the aspect of the content description but also the one of the action transmission.

T. Tokunaga and A. Ortega (Eds.): LKR 2008, LNAI 4938, pp. 163–170, 2008.

By the way, within pragmatics, language use includes (a) an aspect of conveying actions as well as (b) an aspect of describing contents (e.g. [1] [2]). According to speech act theory, which is a main pragmatic theory, the verb performing an action of the text is named "performative verb". Performative verbs are generally defined as verbs that possess a particular force (act) toward others in saying something. To sum up, performative verbs convey the text addressor's action and it is possible to consider that performative verbs indicate the text addressor's intention. It is one of the methods to systematizing knowledge concerning speaker intention to describe the knowledge about performative verbs.

This paper analyzes performative verbs, which can be regarded as performing the action of the text. Based on the analysis, we propose the systematization of knowledge for performative verbs. This paper does not deal with large-scale knowledge resources itself. However, it is necessary for large-scale text resources to construct a foundation for indicating the addresser's intentions which we propose in this paper.

## 2 Performative Verbs as Speaker Intentions

### 2.1 Performative Verbs in Speech Act Theory

According to speech act theory (e.g. [1] [3]), language use has two aspects; (a) proposition and (b) action. That is, a single utterance has two dimensions: (a) it conveys something and (b) it is itself an act of doing something. For instance, when person A tells to B "Give me a cup of coffee", (a') A conveys the meaning that "A intends to have B make coffee" and, at the same time, (b') A performs an <order> to B. In language use, it is one of the important factors to recognize the speaker (=A) intention of <order>. In speech act theory, the speaker intention is called illocutionary force (e.g. <order>) which is expressed in the form of performative verb. Performative verbs are generally defined as verbs that possess a particular force (act) toward others in saying something.

There are two types of performative verbs; (i) implicit performative verbs, and (ii) explicit performative verbs. When person A tells B "I want to have a cup of coffee" with an intention of <order> to make a coffee, the verb <order> is the implicit performative verb. In this way, performative verbs appear implicitly in natural conversations [2] [4] [5]. The fact that people tend to use performative verbs implicitly in the utterance causes one of communication errors. For instance, in the above example of person A's utterance "I want to have a cup of a coffee", person B would reply A just "me too", if person B do not recognize A's intention of <order> and consider that A just describe his / her state. In this case, person A cannot perform an <order> which is ignored by B, and communication error has occurred. In order to avoid the communication error, it might be effective the mapping between performative verbs and a specific utterance. However, there is no one-to-one mapping [2].

There is a proposal that using explicit performative verbs in the utterance would decrease the communication errors [5]. When performative verbs are expressed explicitly in the utterance, it is not difficult to identify the speaker intention which is indicated by the performative verb in the utterance (e.g. when the speaker intends to have a request on the hearer, he / she just says "I request you to do something", the performative verb <request> in the utterance would be the speaker intention). However, even if performative verbs are expressed explicitly in the utterance, there is a possibility that the cognitive differences for the specific performative verb would cause the misunderstanding between the addressee and addresser. For example, what is the detailed cognitive environment (e.g. goal, beliefs, and emotions) of the speaker who uses the performative verb <order> in the utterance? Why does the speaker use not the performative verb <request> but <order>? What are the detailed differences between the performative verb <order> and <request>?

In order to solve these problems, this paper focuses on the cognitive component of each performative verb based on the existing researches [1] [3] [6].

## 2.2 Elements Composing Each Performative Verb

Then, is it possible to investigate under which condition does a specific performative verb tend to be used? Several researchers have attempted to create lists of performative verbs and their underlying conditions (e.g. [1] [3] [6] [7]). In this section, studies of pragmatic researchers and a cultural anthropologist will be introduced.

**From Pragmatic Viewpoint.** Within pragmatics, Kubo et al.'s research follows the traditional pragmatics speech act theory and analyzes performative verbs based on the theory of direction of regulation. They have created a list of 189 Japanese performative verbs, which is frequently used [6]. In this research, performative verbs are divided into five categories; [assertive] (e.g., tsugeru (tell)), [commisive] (e.g., odosu (threaten)), [directive] (e.g., tanomu (ask)), [declarative] (e.g., sengen-suru (declare)), and [expressive] (e.g., togameru (blame)). Each performative verb has conditions of success that include "mode of achievement", "propositional content condition", "preparatory condition", and "sincerity condition". A dictionary description of each performative verb has created by specifying each condition, as in the following example of the performative verb <Togameru (=blame)>.

---

<Togameru>
[Mode of achievement]
(1) The speaker > The hearer (psychologically)
(2) Unilateral attitude
[Propositional content condition]
Critical declaration
[Preparatory condition]
(1) There was some earlier speech act or behavior that was inconvenient for the speaker.
(2) The speaker believes that the execution of this act is necessary for him/herself.
(3) The speaker believes that the hearer does not want the execution of this act.
(4) The speaker believes that the execution of this act is necessary for the hearer.
[Sincerity condition]
(1) The speaker has critical feelings towards the hearer.
(2) The speaker expects the hearer to reflect on the utterance and their prior behavior

---

This research makes important contributions in two respects. First, it provides detailed descriptions of the conditions for each performative verb, including emotional states that are described in detail, such as "critical feelings", "shame", and "expectation of reflection". That is, their research clarifies the components of each performative verb. Second, performative verbs are classified and organized within a hierarchical structure. As a result, the systematized performative verbs can be considered as a kind of knowledge representation.

On the other hand, there are two aspects that need to be taken into account: (a) the viewpoint of socially-shared knowledge (e.g. everyone believes act X is not good within this community) is not always considered. Socially-shared knowledge is necessary because performative verbs and their constituents differ between communities (cf. Austin asserts that acts that have a certain force toward others in saying something, as noted above, are conventional acts [1]). (b) According to traditional pragmatics, performative verbs may be divided into five categories based on the relationship between the word and an object (the world). However, performative verbs could also be classified based on the cognitive elements that underlie performative verbs.

**From a Cultural Anthropological viewpoint.** Wierzbicka, an antholopologist, identifies each performative verb with the minimum psychological elements using basic set of 2,000 words (the basic of words of Longman Dictionary of Contemporary English) [7]. She lists 270 English performative verbs that are widely and generally used. The following example of performative verb <blame> shows the process of decomposing.

---

<Blame>

- I assume that everyone would say that what has happened (Z) is bad for me (/us).
- I assume we would want to know why it happened.
- I say: I think it happened because Y happened (or : because X did Y).
- I think something bad about Y (or: X) because of that.
- I say this because I want to say what I think about why Z happened.

---

Wierzbicka's research makes two insightful contributions. The first is the inclusion of the socially-shared knowledge viewpoint as manifested in expressions like "everyone would say". The second is the fact that the descriptions are relatively easy to understand because there are expressed with this basic set of 2000 words.

On the other hand, there are also two details that deserve further attention: (a) The treatment of emotional states is not consistent, as it is not so simple to describe states like "shame", "happy", "sad" with just 2,000 basic words. (b) Performative verbs are listed in alphabetical order, at the expense of providing a classification of performative verbs.

## 3 Systematization of Performative Verbs with Cognitive Elements

In the previous section, we explained the contribution concerning the component of performative verbs in pragmatics and cultural anthropology. In pragmatics, conditions when the performative verb is used are described in detail. Within cultural anthropology, psychological components for each performative verb are enumerated. It is possible to consider that both top-down approaches organize the cognitive environment when the speaker uses a specific performative verb.

The results of the meta-analysis of existing research clearly indicate the need to provide detailed and consistent cognitive profiles for performative verbs with socially-shared knowledge.

Regarding socially-shared knowledge, several studies stress that the recognition of speaker intention is context-dependent (e.g. [8] [9]), and one survey has even shown that the strategies for realizing certain speech acts vary between languages [10]. This highlights the fact that the recognition of speaker intention is bound up in the conventions shared within groups.

The consistent cognitive structure of performative verbs might enable to construct a dictionary-like system in which components of each performative verb can be searched from a specific performative verb or in which a specific performative verb can be searched from a cognitive component.

## 4 A Reference System for Performative Verbs

Based on the analysis of performative verbs, an intention reference system has been developed on a local server. The system currently consists of 186 Japanese performative verbs and 452 cognitive elements. There are two kinds of references on the system; (a) a reference of the cognitive elements of intention and (b) a reference of intentions with cognitive elements.

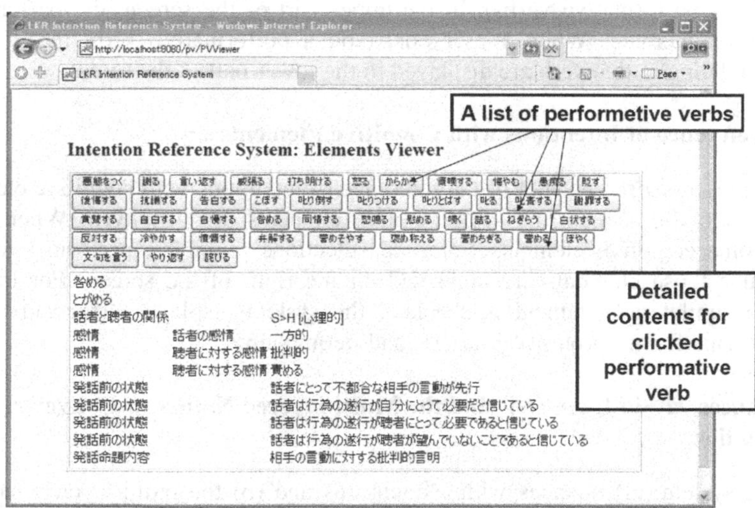


**Fig. 1.** Reference of cognitive elements for intention

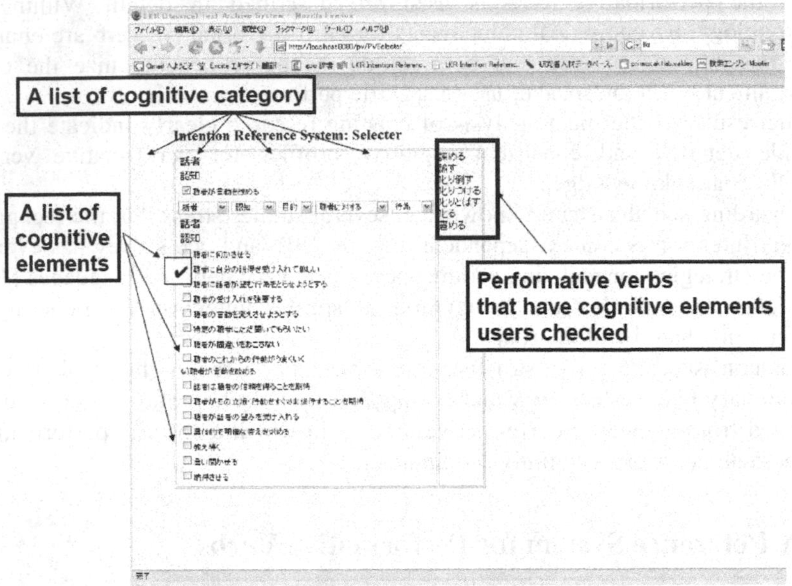


**Fig. 2.** Reference of intention with cognitive elements

### 4.1 A Reference of the Cognitive Elements of Intention

Figure 1 presents a screen shot of the reference system for the cognitive elements of intentions (= performative verbs). In the upper part of the screen, the performative verbs are enumerated. When a user clicks on a performative verb, the cognitive elements relating to that verb are displayed in the lower part of the screen.

### 4.2 A Reference of Intentions with Cognitive Elements

Figure 2 presents a screen shot of the reference of intentions with cognitive elements. On the left of the screen, the 452 cognitive elements are displayed. When a user checks some cognitive elements (multiple selections possible), performative verbs that include those elements are displayed on the right of the screen. For instance, when the "unilateral" element is checked, the system displays performative verbs such as <make fun>, <protest>, <scold>, and <complain>.

### 4.3 Nuances within Intentions and the Multi-layered Nature of Conveyed Intentions

With this system, (a) nuances within intentions and (b) the multi-layered nature of conveyed intentions are specified. For instance, subtle differences between the performative verbs of <be angry>, and <scold> can be differentiated within the utterance "I am not angry at you. I am scolding you" (where the verb "scold" has the cognitive element of "expecting improvement on the part of the hearer"). Moreover, because the performative verb <scold> encompasses multiple cognitive elements, such as “criticism”, “anger”, and “expectation of improvement”, while it is possible that the hearer will be receptive to all the elements, it is also possible that they will only perceive one of the elements. While both cases may be sources of misunderstanding, the system can help the involved parties achieve a more appropriate interpretation of their interactions.

## 5 Conclusion and Future Works

In order to support effective and smooth recognition of the intentions embedded within texts shared by multiple knowledge agents, this paper has proposed an intention reference system based on a meta-analysis of existing research. The system enables two kinds of references; (a) a reference of the cognitive elements of intention and (b) a reference of intentions with cognitive elements. This research constructs the foundation of the knowledge systematization about performative verbs, that is, knowledge concerning in what cognitive element a specific performative verb is used. Consequently, it becomes easy to share the text addressor’s intention at least in the group even in the text-based communications on the Web.

This paper did not deal with the large-scale knowledge resources itself, but the systematization of knowledge about performative verbs that this paper proposed would be important foundation for text-based communication. In addition to semantic web that tags the semantic content of the text, tagging the action of the text expects to realize more smoothly text communication with less misunderstanding. In that case, it is necessary to define set standards for pragmatic tags to be used with text corpora.

## Acknowledgement

This work was supported by “The Kyushu University Research Superstar Program (SSP)”, based on the budget of Kyushu University allocated under President’s initiative. We also would like to express our gratitude to the LKR COE program for the opportunity and support to conduct this research.

## References

1. Austin, J.L.: How to Do Things with Words. Oxford University Press, Oxford (1962)
2. Holtgraves, T.: The Production and Perception of Implicit Performatives. Journal of Pragmatics 37, 2024–2043 (2005)
3. Searle, J.R.: Speech Acts: An Essay in the Philosophy of Language. Cambridge University Press, New York (1969)
4. Matsumoto, N., Tokosumi, A.: A Reference of Intentions for Better Medical Communication. In: Proceedings of IEEE/ICME International Conference on Complex Medical Engineering, pp. 454–457 (2007)
5. Matsumoto, N., Murai, H., Tokosumi, A.: Implicit Speech Act Verbs in Conversations - An Analysis of Conversation Log within Medical Settings. In: Proceedings of the International Conference on Kansei Engineering and Emotion Research 2007 (KEER2007), CD-ROM, A-2 (2007)

6. Kubo, S., et al.: Semantic Network in Illocutionary Act. Koyo Shobo, Kyoto (In Japanese) (2002)
7. Wierzbicka, A.: English Speech Act Verbs. Academic Press, Australia (1987)
8. Allowood, J.: A Critical Look at the Language Action Perspective in Communication Modeling. In: Invited Talk at the Third International Workshop on the Language-Action Perspective on Communication Modeling, LAP 98 (1998)
9. Matsumoto, N., Tokosumi, A.: Context building through socially-supported belief. In: Dey, A.K., et al. (eds.) CONTEXT 2005. LNCS (LNAI), vol. 3554, pp. 316–325. Springer, Heidelberg (2005)
10. Hashimoto, Y.: A Comparison of the Strategies for Indirect Speech Acts in Different Languages (in Japanese). Nihongogaku 11, 92–102 (1992)

# Toward Construction of a Corpus of English Learners' Utterances Annotated with Speaker Proficiency Profiles: Data Collection and Sample Annotation*

Yasunari Harada[1, 2, 3], Kanako Maebo[4], Mayumi Kawamura, Masanori Suzuki[2, 5], Yoichiro Suzuki[2, 6], Noriaki Kusumoto[1, 2, 7], and Joji Maeno[1, 2]

[1] Institute for Digital Enhancement of Cognitive Development, Waseda University, 513 Waseda-Tsurumaki-cho, Shinjuku-ku, Tokyo 162-0041, Japan
[2] Media Network Center, Waseda University, 1-104 Totsuka-machi, Shinjuku-ku, Tokyo 169-8050, Japan
[3] Faculty of Law, Waseda University, 1-6-1 Nishi-Waseda, Shinjuku-ku, Tokyo 169-8050, Japan
[4] Center for Japanese Language, Waseda University, 1-7-14 Nishi-Waseda, Shinjuku-ku, Tokyo 169-8050, Japan
[5] Ordinate Corporation 800 El Camino Real, Suite 400, Menlo Park, CA 94025, USA
[6] Totsu Sangyo Co., Ltd. 5-16-20 Roppongi, Minato-ku, Tokyo 106-8551, Japan
[7] Faculty of Education and Integrated Arts and Sciences, Waseda University, 1-6-1 Nishi-Waseda, Shinjuku-Ku, Tokyo 169-8050, Japan

harada@waseda.jp, xiangcai_2@suou.waseda.jp, kawamuras@pat.hi-ho.ne.jp, Masanori_Suzuki@harcourt.com, yoichiro@totsu.co.jp, moto@waseda.jp, joji@mnc.waseda.ac.jp

**Abstract.** The first author has designed and implemented college English classes emphasizing face-to-face oral interactions within small groups of students in class, presupposing and expecting further cultivation of learners' ability to learn for themselves, by themselves and among themselves. Previous experiences confirm such expectations, and the authors are currently working on collecting learners' spoken interactions with high-quality digital audio and video recording devices along with written materials, scores of language proficiency tests and questionnaire responses of those students. In this presentation, we describe the scope and objective of our project, summarize class activities and recording procedures, and then touch on expected transcription procedures and possible tools for annotation. It may be interesting to notice, in passing, how introduction of various recording devices positively affect students' motivations and performances in their language learning activities.

**Keywords:** spoken corpora, learner corpora, annotation, learner profiling, automated spoken language test, transcription tools.

* Parts of materials presented here are described and discussed in [1] and [2] in Japanese.

T. Tokunaga and A. Ortega (Eds.): LKR 2008, LNAI 4938, pp. 171–178, 2008.

## 1 Introduction

Learner corpora, or collection of data produced by learners of a given language, are drawing greater attention in recent years.[1] Among English-language educators in Japan, more and more emphasis is being placed on cultivating 'communicative competence' of the learners, but it is often difficult to fathom, for English-language teaching faculty at universities, what their students know about and can do with English. This is partly because learning experiences and mastery of English before they enter college differ greatly in depth and coverage, and the situation is getting aggravated by recent MEXT[2] initiatives to diversify educational institutions, systems and curricula in Japan.

In the research project outlined below, our focus is on obtaining utterance data that are produced by the learners on the fly and relatively spontaneously. Since Japanese learners of English do not utter English sentences completely spontaneously and completely on the fly, we need to set things up in such a way that would invite those learners to express themselves in English. One such device is providing a question in English read by their peer learners and giving a restricted time-frame in which to respond to those questions. Although the learners are constrained in the topics (or the questions they are expected to answer to) and the length (in general, they are given 10 seconds to think and 45 seconds to answer after a question is read aloud twice), there is much freedom and flexibility in what can actually be said.

At the moment, our research project is in a data-acquisition phase, and it is rather premature to say what insights we might be able to obtain from the collection of data. However, it is our expectation that there is interesting knowledge to be extracted from the compiled data. Depending on the topic or the particular question asked, on the one hand, and the ingenuity and proficiency in oral English of the respondent, the responses or the sentences uttered would show a wide range of difference, in the vocabulary and expressions used, in accuracy in construction and choice of words and phrases, in pronunciation and fluency, and in the kinds of errors to be found. If each response came with indications of the speaker's English proficiency, such as might be measured by TOEIC[3], Versant for English[4] and other standardized tests, we should be able to make interesting pedagogical observations from these data.

---

[1] As far as Japanese learners of English are concerned, data on written language are relatively widely accumulated and some are made publicly accessible but data on spoken language are scarcer and harder to obtain. A well-known exception to this may be NICT JLE Corpus, which is a compiled and annotated collection of spoken English produced by Japanese learners of English, but the published corpus contains only the transcribed material and not the original speech. See [3] and [4].

[2] Japanese Ministry of Education, Culture, Sports, Science and Technology: http:// www.mext.go.jp/english/

[3] TOEIC, or Test of English for International Communication, is a standardized test of English focusing on reading and listening comprehension and is widely accepted in Japan and Korea: http://www.toeic.or.jp/toeic_en/

Some additional details are discussed in Section 3.2.

[4] Versant for English is an automated test of spoken English delivered over the phone: http://www.versanttest.com

Some additional details are discussed in Section 3.2.

## 2 Collection of Utterance Data

The recording takes place during class. On the one hand, the class activities are organized in such a way that those recordings are made possible and meaningful. On the other hand, the recordings help student motivate in their activities. In general, the collected audio data runs for about 20 minutes in length and consist of 10 to 12 tracks. The beginning of the track usually records a group of students discussing in Japanese how to proceed with the task. After a while, one of the students read a printed question twice and another student would give a relatively spontaneous response to the question for something around 45 seconds. In this section, we will describe the target population and the environment in which the data collection is taking place during the freshmen classes, and touch upon equipment and human resource required for the data collection and the volume of raw data being accumulated.

### 2.1 Target Population

For various practical reasons, we are collecting data from students[5] that are enrolled in the English language classes taught by the principal researcher, who teaches six English classes every semester. Three of those are freshmen classes, usually with 25 to 36 students enrolled. English proficiency differs greatly among those students.[6] Two classes are for sophomores and students choose the particular class they enroll in based on class schedule, syllabus, and other factors they think are important. The remaining one class is for juniors and seniors, which is completely elective with only a handful of students. Class activity and data collection differ according to classes. For expository purposes, we will focus on data collection conducted in the freshmen spring semester classes.

### 2.2 Student Activities

The English classes in which those data collection activities are conducted convene in computer cluster rooms. The numbers of students in those classes are in general less than or equal to 36, partly because of the curriculum design and partly because of facility constraints, namely the number of personal computers per classroom.

The main target activity of recording in the freshman spring semester classes is what we call `oral response practice`, where three students form a group, one in the role of questioner, another in the role of time-keeper and camera-person, the other in the role of respondent. For each class, 10 questions around one particular topic are prepared in advance and printed on a business-card size piece of paper. The questioner picks up one of those 10 question cards and reads the question aloud to the respondent twice. The respondent has 10 seconds to think and formulate the answer and 45

5 We do intend to restrict our research scope to those learners of English whose native or first language is Japanese, although the actual number of such students at the moment is very small. We also do not restrict our attention to those data produced by some kind of `typical Japanese`, thereby excluding data produced by students who have spent some substantial period of time outside Japan or outside Japanese school systems.

6 Their TOEIC scores range from less than 300 to more than 900. Their Versant for English scores range from less than 30 to 80.

seconds to speak whatever comes to the mind. The time-keeper prompts the respondent by saying "Start!" 10 seconds after the question is read for the second time, and says "Stop!" 45 seconds later. The time keeper is also in charge of the shooting the questioner and the respondent with the video camera. After the response is given, the questioner and the time keeper each gives a score to the response based on a rubric given and write the score onto a peer-review sheet for the respondent. Then, the three students change the roles and go on to the next question. Usually, 20 to 25 minutes is devoted to this activity.

The question is printed in English and the questioner simply reads those sentences aloud twice. This part of the utterance is mainly in English, except where the questioner encounters a word or phrase s/he is not familiar with and the student either proceeds with some dubious or erroneous pronunciation or other students offer a suggestion or someone might look up the expression in the dictionary. The response is supposed to be given in English, but when the respondent is not sure of the question or how to start her/his response, there may be long pauses or lengthy utterances or interactions in Japanese. Before the first question and answer begins, the students spend some time deciding on who goes first and how to change roles. After one question is answered, the students spend some additional time coordinating their activities. Those interactions are mostly in Japanese but some times the discussion concerns particular phrases in a question, and in those cases, student go back and forth between Japanese and English.

### 2.3 Digital Audio Recorder

Since the expected maximal number of students in the freshmen class was 36, divided into groups of threes, we were to expect at most 12 groups of students working at the same time. As the format of the question and answer was designed in such a way that no substantial overlap was to occur between the end of the question and the beginning of the response, we presumed that one microphone per group should suffice in order to record the question read twice in English and the response spontaneously given on the fly mostly in English with sporadic Japanese interjections and what not. Some other desiderata that we had in mind when deciding on this particular configuration are as follows.

- Recording quality: linear PCM with highest sampling rate / highest bit rate
- Storage and post-processing of sound files can be handled on Windows machines.
- Equipment can be deployed and used in any classroom.

The digital audio recording equipment used in this project mainly consists of the following components:

- Alesis ADAT HD24 XR: 24-Track Hard Disk Recorder
- Alesis MultiMix 12R: 8ch microphone fader (amplifier/mixer)
- Sony ECM-360: electret-condenser microphone
- microphone cables
- portable container for the equipment

**Alesis ADAT HT24 XR:** This hard disk audio recorder is designed mainly for musicians and to be quite robust. As the recorder makes use of widely available low-cost IDE computer hard drives, which is the only movable element in the equipment, it is cost effective and reliable.[7]

- 24-track, 24-bit digital audio recording at 48kHz
- 12-track, 24-bit digital audio recording at 96kHz
- digital sample rates: 44.1–96kHz.
- dual recording bays for standard IDE drives
- files can be ported to computers from hard disks via fire-wire connectors

**Alesis MultiMix 12R:** In order to match microphone output to recorder input, we use mixers that also provide phantom power to microphones via cables.[8]

- 12-channel mixer in a 3U rack
- 8 high-gain microphone/line
- 8 inputs with phantom power
- front-panel headphone out
- 60 mm fader on each channel
- 2 peak indicator

**Sony ECM-360:** We employed this microphone for high quality recording of students' utterances.[9]

- frequency response: 50Hz~16kHz
- sensitivity: 46dB ± 3dB
- dynamic range: 100dB or more
- signal to noise ratio: 68dB or more

## 2.4 Digital Video Cameras with Bluetooth Wireless Microphones

Along with audio recording device operated by the teacher, we purchased 13 video cameras with wireless microphones to be used by each group of students.[10] The internal hard disk is recognized as an external drive of a Windows machine when connected via USB 2.0 cable and the time stamps of those files keeps track of when the segment was shot, or more accurately, the time that the recording was terminated. As long as all the video cameras' internal clocks are synchronized, it is easy to tell when a given file was shot from the time stamp of the file. In addition, the video cameras come with 5.1 channel surround sound recording system, with the centre channel assigned to the Bluetooth wireless microphone when attached. With a reasonably decent stereo playback system, you can tell which direction a given voice is coming from, which may be of help in identifying the speaker of a given segment.

**Sony DCR-SR100: Video camera with 30GB hard-drive**[11]

- 2.7" touch screen LCD

---

7 Alesis: http://www.alesis.com/product.php?id=1

8 Alesis: http://www.alesis.com/product.php?id=3

9 Sony Drive, http://www.ecat.sony.co.jp/avacc/mic/acc/index.cfm?PD=887&KM=ECM-360

10 One additional set is for backup in case of failure and repair.

11 Sony Drive: http://www.sony.jp/products/Consumer/handycam/PRODUCTS/DCR-SR100/index.html

- 5.1 channel Dolby® Digital Surround Sound recording
- 16:9 widescreen video recording

**Sony HCM-HW1:** When the sound recording is set for 5.1 surround, the voice from this Bluetooth wireless microphone is recorded in the center channel.[12]

- microphone / transmitter:
- width 34 mm, height 65 mm, depth 23 mm, weight 25g (not including batteries)
- receiver (to be attached to the camera):
- width 48 mm, height 71mm, depth 53mm, weight 58g

# 3 Profiles, Annotations and Written Data

## 3.1 Sample Transcription of Utterances

Audio data of learners' utterances may be interesting, especially when it comes with TOEIC and/or Versant scores and other profiles of the students along with some related written material by the same student, but they are almost unusable without some proper annotation or indexing. After some experimentation with other tools, we are currently experimenting with TableTrans, available from LDC[13] AGTK[14].

Quite tentatively, we choose one class conducted at the beginning of the spring semester of 2007 and tried transcribing the entire audio recordings on all twelve tracks. It took an untrained transcriber to go over one track 6 to 20 hours. One major problem is that when students begin their informal interaction in Japanese, it is often rather difficult to identify the speaker, or the change of speakers, of a particular segment of recorded utterances. If we restrict our efforts on the questions in English and responses to those questions, the turns are relatively well-defined and the responses are not that much entangled so the task becomes much more manageable.

## 3.2 Student Profiling

As is mentioned in the previous section, English proficiency of students enrolled in those classes show substantial diversity. The students' TOEIC total scores range from a little less than 300 to well over 900 and averaged around 570. TOEIC total score is obtained by adding its two sub scores for reading and listening. Each sub score comes with a standard error of measurement of 35 and the total score has a standard error of measurement of 50.

Versant for English is an automated spoken English proficiency test, delivered over the telephone and scored automatically using speech recognition engine and automated scoring engine. Each test consists of a little less than 60 questions, taken from an item bank of a few thousand, and it takes about 10 minutes to complete. Versant for English total score is obtained by weighted average of the four sub scores for vocabulary, phrase structure, pronunciation and fluency. Each of those scores is given by two digits between 20 and 80 and the total score comes with a standard error

[12] Sony Drive: http://www.ecat.sony.co.jp/handycam/acc/acc.cfm?PD=23473

[13] LDC (Linguistic Data Consortium): http://www.ldc.upenn.edu/

[14] AGTK(Annotation Graph ToolKit), http://sourceforge.net/projects/agtk/

of measurement of 2. Most often the scores are between 30-45 and those whose total is higher than 55 usually have spent more than a few years outside the Japanese school system before they entered college.

Students in the target population are requested to submit response to a questionnaire along with non-disclosure based research and development use-of-data (non-)agreement forms during the course of a semester. In the questionnaire, we tried to get information regarding the students' history of English learning, experience outside the Japanese school system, exposure to English speaking environment, courses and extra-curricular activities related to English learning while at university and so on. Those pieces of information are expected to be incorporated into the speech data, but it is difficult to place a reasonable balance between protection of personal information and privacy on the one hand and compilation of multi-modal and multi-faceted data for research and development purposes. For instance, no student would be happy if they are asked whether their recorded voices or video images can be uploaded on the web for anyone in the world to see.

### 3.3 Essays, Slides and Research Summaries

In the freshman spring classes, after students spend 25-30 minutes for oral interaction practices of the day, they would spend 30 minutes trying to come up with a 300-400 word essay on the topic they just discussed. Since most of the students cannot complete this task in the time given in class, they would finish it as homework. In the next class, they are to bring the computer file of the essay thus completed and 6 printed copies. They exchange the printed essay among groups of six, review and evaluate each others' essay and come up with the final version by the third week. The tentative version written in 30 minutes, homework version and the final version are each submitted as computer files.

Thus, along with recordings of the students' oral utterances, we have some written material by the same students in different time constraints and for different purposes. A careful comparison of these materials may reveal some interesting properties and / or differences in the students' productive skills and vocabulary in different modalities.

**Acknowledgments.** The research project reported here was made possible by financial support from Ministry of Education Grant-in-Aid Basic Research (B) Project Number 18320093 entitled *Construction and Analysis of Spoken Corpus of Profiled Japanese Learners of English* (April, 2006 through March 2009). Assemblage of the digital audio recording system was made possible by Waseda University Grant for Special Research Projects 2004A-033 entitled *Study on Learner Profiling with Standardized Tests for Improving Undergraduate English Education* (April, 2004 through March 2005). Experience in use of this equipment was obtained through a pilot project partially funded by Waseda University Grant for Special Research Projects 2004A-033 entitled *Study on Learner Profiling and Multimodal Corpus for Improving Undergraduate English Education* (April, 2005 through March 2006). The principal researcher gained much insight into the nature of spoken language tests and importance of face-to-face oral interaction practice through a joint research project between Media Network Center of Waseda University and KDDI group mainly conducted in 1999 through 2002 and continued through fiscal 2007. The principal researcher would like to acknowledge his thanks and appreciation for efforts and work done by Mayumi Kawamura and Kanako Maebo in selecting and experimenting with various annotation tools including TableTrans, for expertise on and experiences with audio-visual devices and other digital equipments shown by Yoichiro Suzuki in designing the audio recording system, for unfailing support and dedication on the part of Masanori Suzuki when administering automated spoken English tests and when analyzing its results, and for Noriaki Kusumoto and Joji Maeno, whose expert opinions are always instrumental in deciding on the data processing hardware and software.

## References

1. Harada, Y., Maebo, K., Kawamura, M.: VALIS 2.0: Transcription of What was (not) Uttered. IPSJ SIG Technical Reports 2007-CE-90 (1), Information Processing Society of Japan, Tokyo 2007(69), 1–8 (2007)
2. Harada, Y., et al.: VALIS: {Vast | Versatile | Visual} {Accumulative | Autonomous | Acoustic} {Learner | Learning | Language} {Information | Interaction} {Storage | System}. IPSJ SIG Technical Reports 2006-CE-88 (24), Information Processing Society of Japan, Tokyo 2007(12), 169–176 (2007)
3. Tono, Y., et al.: The Standard Speaking Test (SST) Corpus: A 1 million-word spoken corpus of Japanese learners of English and its implications for L2 lexicography. In: Lee, S. (ed.) ASIALEX 2001 Proceedings: Asian Bilingualism and the Dictionary. The Second Asialex International Congress, Yonsei University, Korea, August 8-10, 2001, pp. 257–262 (2001)
4. Tono, Y., Izumi, E., Kaneko, T.: The NICT JLE Corpus: the final report, http:// www.rikiwiki.net/members/blogresearch/blogresearchbase/Vocabulary/corpus%20study/spoken%20learner%20corpus%20project.pdf

# Filling the Gap between a Large-Scale Database and Multimodal Interactions

Masahiro Araki

Department of Information Science, Kyoto Institute of Technology,
Matsugasaki, Sakyo-ku, Kyoto 606-8585, Japan
araki@kit.jp

**Abstract.** In this paper, a methodology of developing a multimodal interaction system using a large-scale database as a knowledge source is proposed. We extend one application of Rails frameworks, which is used for rapid prototyping of GUI-based Web applications, to a multimodal interaction development platform. The proposed method enables the developer to implement a prototype system rapidly by defining the data model of the target database.

**Keywords:** multimodal interface, large-scale database, rapid prototyping.

## 1 Introduction

Recently, various kinds of large-scale databases, such as a newspaper article archives, telephone directories, nationwide restaurant guides, etc., have become available for practical use. Searching for appropriate data from these databases requires a sophisticated user interface. A multimodal interface, such as speech and pen inputs combined with audio and graphical outputs, is a candidate for such a user interface.

To date, many multimodal dialogue systems have been developed and put into use in several laboratories and commercial mobile services that use speech as input (e.g., a departure station name and a destination station name) and a display as output (e.g., transfer information) [1]. However, there is a large development gap between the application logic that manipulates back-end databases and the description of the human-computer interaction. There exists an urgent need for prototyping tools for multimodal dialogue systems that serve as the front-end of large-scale database searches.

Many previous prototyping tools of multimodal dialogue systems, such as those proposed by [2] and [3], are based on a finite-state model that can be manipulated by a GUI (Graphical User Interface) tool. Such finite-state-based tools allow developers to carry out intuitive operations in multimodal interaction system prototyping. However, because the current accuracy of speech input components is inadequate, typical dialogue patterns are limited to system-initiative dialogue, and state transition patterns tend to fall into a few typical patterns, such as slot-filling, DB search, and explanation [4]. Therefore, there is little benefit in using a finite-state-based tool for customizing

T. Tokunaga and A. Ortega (Eds.): LKR 2008, LNAI 4938, pp. 179–185, 2008.

typical system-initiative patterns of interaction. In addition, this kind of tool provides little assistance in communication with the back-end database application.

In order to overcome this problem, we propose a data-driven approach for prototyping multimodal dialogue systems. In recent years, some dynamic- language- based and data-model-centered frameworks, such as Ruby on Rails[1], have been developed and are widely used in GUI-based Web application development. These frameworks dramatically reduce the amount of code in the server-side program and reduce Web application configuration steps by following the methodology of "Convention over Configuration."[2] We developed Mrails for multimodal Web application development based on Grails[3], which is a Rails product that uses the Java-based scripting language Groovy. In multimodal dialogue system development using Mrails, the first step is to define a data model that corresponds to the back-end database schema. Prior to Mrails processing, Grails generates necessary components of a Web application based on model-view-controller (MVC), such as Groovy script as a controller component and HTML files as a view component. Then, Mrails generates a voice interaction description by referring to the generated HTML and combining the voice component with the HTML. As a result, Mrails generates XHTML+Voice files as the view component of the multimodal dialogue system.

The rest of this paper is organized as follows. Section 2 illustrates the process of rapid prototyping of a GUI Web application using Grails. Section 3 explains how to add a speech interaction description to HTML pages generated by Grails. Section 4 presents an illustrative example of multimodal Web application development with Mrails. Section 5 discusses the advantages and disadvantages of this approach. Section 6 gives conclusions and future work.

## 2 Overview of Web Application Development on the Rails Framework

Spurred by the success of Ruby on Rails, several projects began to develop dynamic language-based Web application frameworks, such as Catalyst for Perl, Cake for PHP, Grails for Groovy, and so on. A common feature of these frameworks is they provide a set of typical codes and configuration files for MVC-based Web applications which are automatically generated from the description of the domain model. The main concept of the MVC model (Fig. 1) is to separate the application logic (Model), transitional information (Controller) and presentation (View) in order to ease development and maintenance of each code.

---

[1] http://www.rubyonrails.org/

[2] It means that there is no need to write redundant configuration information in the program code or outside configuration files. For example, a database record is mapped directly to the data object of the scripting language (using the same name for the field name of the database and the field variable name of the object) and also, the data object is mapped to the field variables of the user interface description language (e.g., the name attribute of the <input> element of HTML).

[3] http://grails.codehaus.org/

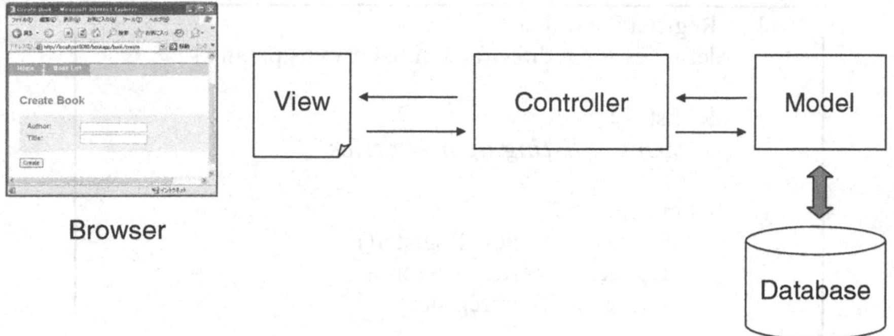


**Fig. 1.** Concept of MVC model

We use Grails as the base framework of our multimodal dialogue system prototyping tool. Grails can automatically generate the necessary files for an MVC-based Web application from the description of a model object written in Groovy language, which is a Java–based dynamic language.

For example, in order to develop a Web application for registration of a banquet at some conference, the developer defines the model name and attribute (or field) of this model in Groovy language (Fig. 2).

```
class Register {
      Integer memberId
      String food

      static constraints = {
            food(inList:["meat", "fish", "vegetable"])
      }
}
```

**Fig. 2.** Model description in Grails

In Fig. 2, two field variables are declared. One is the member ID, which is an integer value. The other is the type of food, the value of which is either "meat," "fish" or "vegetable," as indicated by the constraints definition. From this definition, Grails generates a typical Web application that can create a new entry, list all the entries, and edit and delete a specific entry. For each function, a corresponding view file, actually an HTML file with embedded Groovy script, is generated.

The controller, which is also generated automatically by Grails, dispatches the request of the abovementioned functions to the corresponding view file. This dispatcher information is written in Groovy action script for each action request (see Fig. 3).

```
class RegisterController {
    def index = { redirect(action:list,params:params) }

    def list = {
        script of listing up all entries
    }
    def creare = {
        def register = new Register()
        register.properties = params
        return ['register':register]
    }
def delete = {
        script of deleting specified entry
    }
...
}
```

**Fig. 3.** An example of a portion of a controller script

## 3 Adding a Multimodal Interface to a GUI Web Application

To develop a multimodal Web application, Mrails takes two steps. The first step is to generate speech pages written in VoiceXML[4]. The second step is to add the VoiceXML to the HTML pages which are automatically generated by Grails. Therefore, the output pages of Mrails are written in XHTML+Voice[5].

### 3.1 Generating Speech Interaction

The major benefit of adding speech modality to the GUI is speech input functionality for small devices such as cell phones or PDAs (Personal Data Assistants). Therefore, we focus on the speech input function as the first step towards full-blown multimodal dialogue systems.

For example, in creating new entry data, the purpose of generating a VoiceXML file from HTML is to generate system-directive input guidance and to generate speech grammar for the user's input. The essence of the conversion is shown in Fig. 4 (in this figure, unimportant code is omitted or modified). In order to convert child elements of the <form> elements in HTML (e.g., <input>, <select>) to VoiceXML <field> elements, we need information stating what the system should say (i.e., the content of the <prompt> element) and how the user will reply (i.e., <grammar> element). The content of the <prompt> element is label information, which is automatically generated by Grails from the attribute name of the model object with slight modification.

[4] http://www.w3c.org/TR/voicexml21/

[5] http://www.voicexml.org/specs/multimodal/x+v/12/

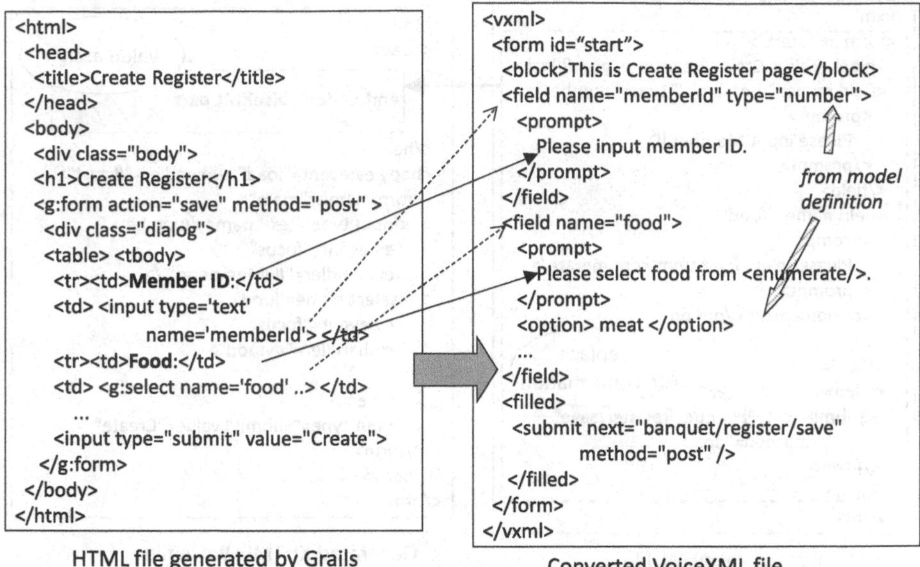


**Fig. 4.** An example conversion from HTML to VoiceXML

The <grammar> element is generated by the following rules.

1. If the attribute has an option list (e.g., the food attribute in Fig. 2), the <option> elements are added to the equivalent <field> element to define a grammar for each option.
2. If the type of attribute has a corresponding built-in grammar in VoiceXML (e.g., date, number, currency), the type attribute of the <field> element is specified for the corresponding grammar type,
3. Otherwise, only the skeleton of the grammar files and its link is generated. The developer has to define the grammar in a later stage.

### 3.2 Enabling Multimodal Interaction

As explained above, the target language of multimodal interaction is XHTML+Voice. It assigns a VoiceXML (i.e., speech interaction) script as an event handler of the <form> element of HTML. Because the <form> element of HTML itself is created by Grails, all Mrails has to do is to assign the VoiceXML script generated in the previous step to each child element of the <form> element of HTML. This process is illustrated in Fig. 5.

## 4 Illustrative Example

In the banquet registration example, all the steps described in Sections 2 and 3 can be completed within 5 minutes. This is due to Grails' powerful automatic generation ability and Mrails' VoiceXML conversion. The example of a realized interaction is shown in Fig. 6.

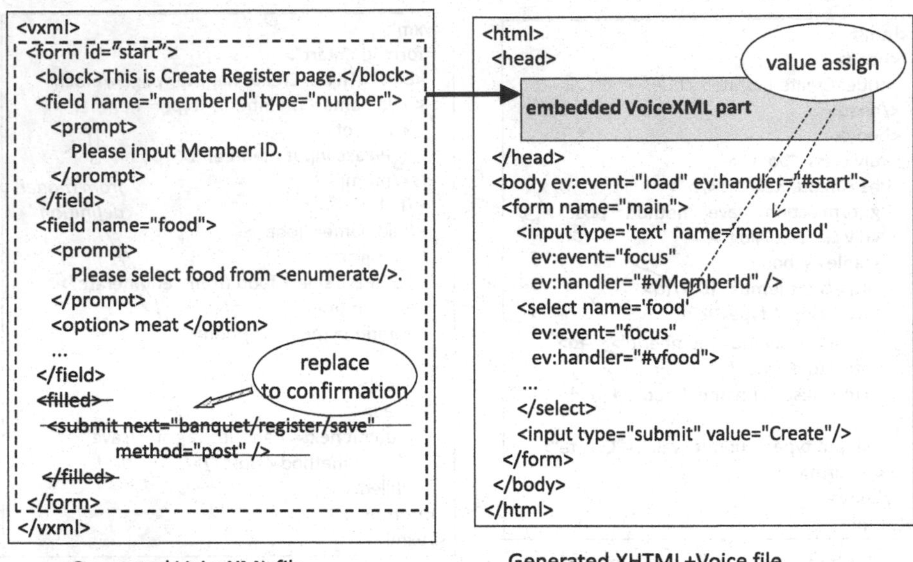

```
<vxml>
  <form id="start">
    <block>This is Create Register page.</block>
    <field name="memberId" type="number">
      <prompt>
        Please input Member ID.
      </prompt>
    </field>
    <field name="food">
      <prompt>
        Please select food from <enumerate/>.
      </prompt>
      <option> meat </option>
      ...
    </field>
    <filled>
      <submit next="banquet/register/save"
              method="post" />
    </filled>
  </form>
</vxml>
```



```
<html>
  <head>
    embedded VoiceXML part
  </head>
  <body ev:event="load" ev:handler="#start">
    <form name="main">
      <input type='text' name='memberId'
        ev:event="focus"
        ev:handler="#vMemberId" />
      <select name='food'
        ev:event="focus"
        ev:handler="#vfood">
      ...
      </select>
      <input type="submit" value="Create"/>
    </form>
  </body>
</html>
```



**Fig. 5.** An example of the generation of an XHTML+Voice file

After creating new registration data, the controller dispatches the dialogue to the listing view so that the user can see all the registered records and can select the action to edit or delete the existing record. This construction is based on Rails' standard CRUD (Create-Read-Update-Delete) functionality.

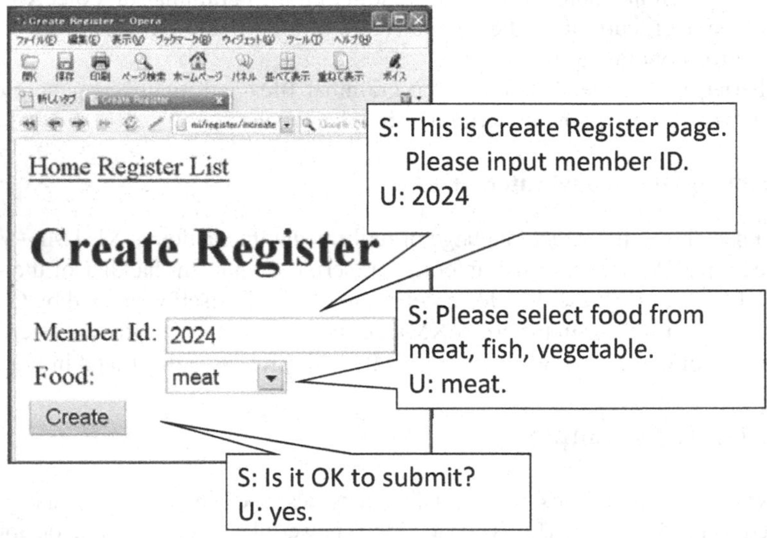


**Fig. 6.** An example of multimodal dialogue

## 5 Discussion

There are other approaches for rapid prototyping of dialogue systems. As mentioned in Section 1, state-based tools are the most popular for prototyping a spoken dialogue system. In these tools, the dialogue flow is constructed as a set of state and state transition rules. Consequently, skillful developers have to define a similar pattern many times for dialogue description. In addition, there is little support for back-end applications in these types of tools.

Our proposed Mrails follows the common concept of the Rails family, which is "Convention over Configuration." This concept can cover typical interaction patterns to back-end application management (e.g., database management). If the developer finds out that the prepared actions are not suitable for the target task and domain, he or she can overwrite the scripts directly in the controller file.

The example database shown in Section 5 is obviously small. However, the methodology is applicable to large-scale databases in a straightforward manner, except for the problems listed below.

1. In a large-scale database, the volume of the target word set of grammar which is generated by the method described in Section 3 might exceed the vocabulary limitation of the speech recognizer.
2. If the key field of the database is a proper noun (e.g., restaurant name), people may refer to the name in different ways. In order to deal with such a problem, statistical speech recognition with the capability of phoneme-to-listing mapping is a promising option [5].

## 6 Conclusion

In this paper, we propose the rapid prototyping tool Mrails for multimodal dialogue systems for database access. We extend Grails, which is one of the Rails frameworks, to a multimodal interaction development platform. The proposed method enables the developer to implement a prototype system rapidly by merely defining the data model of the target database.

In the present implementation, this tool handles only typical CRUD-type applications with simple interactions. But, it is suitable for mobile Web access via small devices such as cell phones and PDAs. The realization of more user-friendly interaction for a rich client, such as mixed initiative multimodal dialogue on a kiosk terminal, is planned as our future work.

## References

1. Delgado, R.L., Araki, M.: Spoken, Multilingual and Multimodal Dialogue Systems: Development and Assessment. Wiley, Chichester (2005)
2. McTear, M.F.: Spoken Dialogue Technology. Springer, Heidelberg (2004)
3. Katsurada, K., et al.: A Rapid Prototyping Tool for Constructing Web-based MMI Applications. In: Proc. of Interspeech 2005, pp. 1861–1864 (2005)
4. Araki, M., et al.: A Dialogue Library for Task-oriented Spoken Dialogue Systems. In: Proc. IJCAI Workshop on Knowledge and Reasoning in Practical Dialogue Systems, pp. 1–7 (1999)
5. Zweig, G., et al.: The Voice-rate Dialog System for Consumer Ratings. In: Proc. of Interspeech 2007, pp. 2713–2716 (2007)

# Design and Prototype of a Large-Scale and Fully Sense-Tagged Corpus

Sue-jin Ker[1], Chu-Ren Huang[2], Jia-Fei Hong[3], Shi-Yin Liu[1], Hui-Ling Jian[1], I-Li Su[2], and Shu-Kai Hsieh[4]

[1] Department of Computer and Information Science, Soochow University, Taiwan
[2] Institute of Linguistics, Academia Sinica, Taiwan
[3] Graduate Institute of Linguistics, National Taiwan University, Taiwan
[4] Department of English, National Taiwan Normal University, Taiwan

**Abstract.** Sense tagged corpus plays a very crucial role to Natural Language Processing, especially on the research of word sense disambiguation and natural language understanding. Having a large-scale Chinese sense tagged corpus seems to be very essential, but in fact, such large-scale corpus is the critical deficiency at the current stage. This paper is aimed to design a large-scale Chinese full text sense tagged Corpus, which contains over 110,000 words. The Academia Sinica Balanced Corpus of Modern Chinese (also named Sinica Corpus) is treated as the tagging object, and there are 56 full texts extracted from this corpus. By using the N-gram statistics and the information of collocation, the preparation work for automatic sense tagging is planned by combining the techniques and methods of machine learning and the probability model. In order to achieve a highly precise result, the result of automatic sense tagging needs the touch of manual revising.

**Keywords:** Word Sense Disambiguation, Sense Tagged Corpus, Natural Language Processing, Bootstrap Method.

## 1 Introduction

The availability of large-scale sense tagged corpus is crucial for many Natural Language Processing systems, because such a corpus usually contains a lot of rich semantic knowledge resources that can be applied as the basis for the representation and processing of meaning. Due to the popularization of digital documents, there are more and more various types of corpora appearing and the content in the corpora are very abundant. Basically, a corpus with the complete tagging information is more helpful to researches. Some corpora only simply display the content of original texts and some cover the relevant information, such as part-of-speech (POS) and senses. At present, a few corpora having the POS tagging have already existed, such as Sinica Corpus with 10 million words, Chinese Gigaword Corpus and so on. However, the corpora with sense tagging are fairly few no matter in Chinese or English. To the research in theoretical linguistics, the resources on sense tagging or semantics are useful in providing many rich materials or the basic structures. To the research in computational linguistics, those resources play the crucial breakthrough applying on

T. Tokunaga and A. Ortega (Eds.): LKR 2008, LNAI 4938, pp. 186–193, 2008.

the core works in Natural Language Processing, for instance, the multiple senses analysis, such as WSD, and Natural Language Understanding. Moreover, the statistic data extracted from Sense tagged corpus can be implemented in the research issues such as Information Retrieval, Information Extraction, Text Summarization, Automatic Question Answering and so on.

Massive accurate sense tagged data does provide rich resources to different relevant researches in computational linguistics. However, the main bottleneck of making a Chinese sense tagging corpus is the deficiency of reference material for automatic tagging. In addition, manually tagging is very expensive and time-consuming. Those reasons make the sense tagging for corpus become more difficult. In the recent years, in many researches, the need of large-scale sense tagged corpus is growing. The completeness of a sense tagged corpus often affects the research direction and the accuracy of the research result. In certain languages, there has existed some representative sense tagged corpora, such as the SemCor [3] for English language materials and SENSEVAL [4], providing a multi-lingual full text tagged corpus in Czech, Dutch, Italian and English. When we look back to the corpus development in Chinese, a large-scale corpus is still the critical deficiency at the current stage. There only exists several small Chinese Sense tagged corpora, for example, the SENSEVAL-2, covering the Chinese sense tagging for 15 Chinese words, and SENSEVAL -3 for 20 Chinese words. There is a huge gap between the scale of the corpus and the real language environment. Cost is the main issue in constructing a massive corpus. Manual tagging does acquire a higher accuracy rate, but the cost of manual tagging is too expensive. Besides, finding the proper experts for doing sense tagging manually is another issue. In order to overcome such difficulties, we propose a method of semi-automatic tagging as the preparation work for doing manual sense tagging and then the result from the semiautomatic tagging can be revised manually by the professionals. Here, the Academia Sinica Balanced Corpus of Modern Chinese (also named Sinica Corpus) is treated as the tagging object. We extract the words in the articles from Sinica Corpus and design a large-scale Chinese sense tagged corpus for the researches in Natural Language Processing.

## 2 Dictionary of Sense Discrimination

The Dictionary of Sense Discrimination in the third edition [5] used in this experiment is developed by the CKIP (Chinese Knowledge and Information Processing) group. CKIP group is a joint research team formed by the Institute of Information Science and the Institute of Linguistics of Academia Sinica in Taiwan. The entries are limited in the middle frequency term of Modern Chinese words. Each entry has a rich information list, including the sense definition, the phonetic symbols, meaning facets, part-of-speech (POS), example sentences and the synset number corresponding to Princeton English WordNet 1.6 (http://wordnet.princeton.edu/). As shown in Fig. 1, the entry "feng1 kuang2" has two senses. The first sense corresponds to the English WN synset, "crazy"; and the second sense corresponds to the WN synset, "madly". In this example, each sense can be divided into two meaning facets respectively.

瘋狂 feng1 kuang2 ㄈㄥ ㄎㄨㄤˊ
詞義1：【不及物動詞，VH；名詞，nom】形容人因精神錯亂而舉止失常。{crazy, 00872382A}
義面1：【不及物動詞，VH】形容人因精神錯亂而舉止失常。
例句：片中一名〈瘋狂〉殺手，拿著剃刀。
例句：石門五子命案的父母與其說是迷信，不如說是〈瘋狂〉。
義面2：【名詞，nom】形容人因精神錯亂而舉止失常。
例句：因此，石門五子命案的〈瘋狂〉，其實也正是我們社會瘋狂的一粒種籽啊！
詞義2：【不及物動詞，VH；名詞，nom】形容行為或事物無節制，超乎平常的程度。通常用於人的情感或事件的程度。{madly, 00045197R}
義面1：【不及物動詞，VH】形容行為或事物無節制，超乎平常的程度。通常用於人的情感或事件的程度。
例句：他〈瘋狂〉的愛上一個女孩子。
例句：每年都有不計其數的台灣客前往香港〈瘋狂〉大採購。
例句：當時少棒青少棒在台灣很〈瘋狂〉，連我們城市的小孩子也愛打棒球。
義面2：【名詞，nom】形容行為或事物無節制，超乎平常的程度。通常用於人的情感或事件的程度。
例句：經過一陣〈瘋狂〉後，大家都累了，個個都喊著喉嚨痛、腳痛。
例句：死了七九百餘人的人民教室案，也使人想到愈來愈多的宗教〈瘋狂〉事件。
例句：只要幅度不超過，則多頭仍然大有可為，但仍切忌一味追高的〈瘋狂〉舉動。

**Fig. 1.** The sense discrimination for "feng1 kuang2 (crazy/ madly)

## 3 The Data Source for Sense Tagging

In the experiment, we use the Academia Sinica Balanced Corpus of Modern Chinese (also named Sinica Corpus) as the basis for semi-automatic sense tagging. The content of this corpus has been segmented and marked with the POS tags. In order to preserve the context completeness, `text' is chosen as the processing unit of tagging materials. The basic principle of sense tagging here is to do a full text tagging. However, the construction of the Dictionary of Sense Discrimination is still under processing, so not all the words in the corpus are included in the dictionary at the moment. For those words that cannot be found in the dictionary, what we do is to use the POS tags to mark them. Tagging by POS tags is able to disambiguate the word senses, so the POS tagging here is fairly general.

Based on coverage rate for the words in the dictionary appearing in the article content and the length of article, there are 56 articles, containing 114,066 words and 148,863 characters, extracted from the corpus. The statistics for the distribution of article subjects is shown in Table 1. There are many articles in the subject for *Literature*, but the type, *Life*, has longer article length. Analysis of the statistics shows that the subject *Literature* has the most articles and the subject *Life* contains the most words.

Overall, among the target words for sense tagging, there are 863 words having only one POS (one lemma to one POS) and 650 words having multiple POS. The frequency of the appearance for the ones having one POS is 12,124 times and 23,521 times for multi POS ones. The statistic of POS distribution is shown in Table 2. The sense amount for multi POS words are from 2 (e.g. 自然D "natural"、堆Nf "a pile" and 喜V K "like") to 27 (e.g. 吃VC "eat") and the average sense number is 2.97. If the data is distinguished by POS, particles have the most senses by reaching the average of 4.83 and the lowest one is interjections, where the average of sense amount is 1.32. If the statistics is based on lemmas, without considering the difference of the POS, there are 598 lemmas from the extracted articles that have been included in the Dictionary of Sense Discrimination, so the average sense number of each lemma is 4.53.

**Table 1.** The distribution of article subjects in the tagged corpus

| Subject | no. of Article | Article Length | |
|---|---|---|---|
| | | in words | in characters |
| Philosophy | 4 | 1451 | 1976 |
| Society | 5 | 27385 | 35918 |
| Life | 12 | 57605 | 74710 |
| Literature | 35 | 27625 | 36259 |
| Total | 56 | 114066 | 148863 |

**Table 2.** The distribution of POS for the tagged corpus

| POS | no. of word | no. of instances | Example |
|---|---|---|---|
| Intransitive Verb | 231 | 3,317 | 對$_{VH}$, 跑$_{VA}$, 走$_{VA}$ |
| Preposition | 51 | 1,854 | 在$_{P}$, 跟$_{P}$, 到$_{P}$ |
| Transitive Verb | 373 | 5,733 | 說$_{VE}$, 沒有$_{VJ}$, 開始$_{VL}$ |
| Noun | 321 | 5,070 | 人家$_{Nh}$, 感覺$_{Na}$, 下$_{Ncd}$ |
| Adjective | 21 | 45 | 一般$_{A}$, 原$_{A}$, 定期$_{A}$ |
| Determinatives | 55 | 3,175 | 那$_{Nep}$, 前$_{Nes}$, 多$_{Neqa}$ |
| Postposition | 31 | 455 | 上$_{Ng}$, 裡$_{Ng}$, 當中$_{Ng}$ |
| Adverb | 287 | 8,892 | 就$_{D}$, 又$_{D}$, 起來$_{Di}$ |
| Conjunction | 69 | 1,554 | 就是$_{Cbb}$, 而$_{Cbb}$, 或$_{Caa}$ |
| Measure | 81 | 976 | 回$_{Nf}$, 份$_{Nf}$, 間$_{Nf}$ |
| Particle | 47 | 4,574 | 啊$_{T}$, 喔$_{T}$, 哇$_{I}$ |
| Total | 1567 | 35,645 | |

## 4 Sense Tagged Corpus

The file type of our sense tagged corpus is encoded in XML format. The usage of the tags is specified in Table 3. Each document is segmented by using the tag <doc> and </doc>. The content for each article can be segmented by sentences. Each sentence is marked by the tag <sent>. The tag <w> is used to segment words and it can be further divided into three respective tags: "word" for the information of lexicon, "pos" for the information of part-of-speech and "tag1" for the information of sense tagging.

For part of the sense tagging, there are three tagging types. The first type is based on the definition in Huang et al. [6]. It is a four-digit code. The first two digits are for the sense, which are used to indicate the sequence of senses in the dictionary. The third and fourth digits are for lemma and meaning facets. The second type is to deal with the tagging for punctuation. Basically, there is no point in doing the sense tagging for the punctuation, so we use those punctuations symbols as the tagging codes directly. The third type is for the unknown words, i.e. the words have not been included in the dictionary yet or have not analyzed through the sense discrimination. The POS tags of those unknown words are used as the sense tagging codes temporarily.

The whole tagged corpus contains a total of 114,066 words. The statistic result based on the tagging types is shown in Table 4. A total of 27,530 words are punctuation symbols and a total of 35,645 words are successfully tagged by assigning the sense ids. There are 50,891 unknown words are tagged by using their POS tags. We further analyze those unknown words and realize some of those unknown words are actually the English abbreviation, numbers or proper nouns, for example, （三）, CPU, National Tsing Hua University and so on. Such examples in our tagged corpus are a total of 4,258 words. In addition, due to the Dictionary of Sense Discrimination adopted in this experiment is still under construction, some words have not yet been included in the dictionary. There are 4,541 words that have not been included in the dictionary and the frequency for appearing in the corpus is 31,730 times. As for the remaining 14,903 words, they are the words that have already been included in the dictionary but they are not within the scope of tagging for this time. Therefore, we mark those words by using the POS tags because tagging by the POS tags is able to disambiguate the polysemy.

**Table 3.** The instruction of the tags used in the corpus

| Tag Name | Meaning | Example |
|---|---|---|
| <corpus> | The beginning of the corpus | <corpus> |
| <doc id=> | The beginning of the document and its id number | <doc id="100863"> |
| <sent id=> | The beginning of the sentence and its id number | <sent id="1"> |
| <w id=> | The information of the word and its id number | <w id="1"> |
| <word> | Word | <word>人家</word> |
| <pos> | Part-Of-Speech | <pos>Nh</pos> |
| <tag1> | Sense Tagging | <tag1>0122</tag1> |

## 5 The Method of Sense Tagging

Generally speaking, doing manual tagging relies on a lot of people's efforts. Therefore, in order to save the costs, we design a method for semi-automatic tagging

[7]. This method can complete the initial tagging task, so it can be treated as a preparation work for doing the manual tagging.

**Table 4.** The statistic for the tagging types in the corpus

| Tagging Type | no. of instances | | Meaning |
|---|---|---|---|
| Punctuation | 27530 | | No need to tag the sense |
| Sense code | 35645 | | Complete the sense tagging |
| POS tagging | 50891 | 4258 | No need to tag the sense (English abbreviation, numbers or proper nouns) |
| | | 31730 | 4541 words have not included in the dictionary yet |
| | | 14903 | Not finished yet |
| Total | 114066 | | |

The semi-automatic tagging in the experiment has implemented the bootstrap method to gradually loosen the tagging conditions and enlarge the tagging materials. The example sentences of the dictionary is treated as the training set and the 56 articles randomly extracted from the Sinica Corpus as the testing set.

The N-gram model is used for automatic sense tagging at the first stage. Using N-gram to process the sense tagging is based on the following assumption: For the given target word, if there exist two sentences in which their N surrounding words are all the same, we infer they should be assigned the same sense tag [8]. Using N-gram here has two main purposes. The first is to enlarge the training set because it is quite often to see the similar clauses in the corpus. The second purpose is to filter the noise in the training data set and to use this to examine the inconsistency of manual tagging.

In the second stage, we use the information of collocations to increase the amount of tagged set. The information of collocations is a very powerful linguistic relation for determining the sense meaning for the target word [9]. We start by using some conditions, such word frequency, collocation words and the distance variation to the target word, as the preliminary basis. Then use the MI values to examine the association between target word and its collocation word.

After the previous stages, we do extend the tagged amount of the training data. Then, through the calculation of the probability model, we try to mark the most words with the sense information. Finally, in order to get the high accuracy of tagged data, we send the automatic tagging result back to CKIP/CWN group for manual reviewing.

The experimental results for the automatic tagging are shown in Table 5, the overall accuracy rate is 64.5%.

**Table 5.** The experimental result of sense tagging

| POS | no. of word | no. of instances | no. of corrected instances | Accuracy rate% |
|---|---|---|---|---|
| A | 6 | 22 | 14 | 63.7% |
| Caa | 2 | 38 | 37 | 97.4% |
| Cbb | 7 | 231 | 37 | 16.0% |
| D | 64 | 3454 | 2158 | 62.5% |
| Da | 7 | 22 | 21 | 95.5% |
| Dfa | 5 | 202 | 200 | 99.0% |
| Dfb | 1 | 1 | 1 | 100.0% |
| Di | 7 | 1146 | 934 | 81.5% |
| Dk | 2 | 5 | 5 | 100.0% |
| I | 15 | 693 | 307 | 44.3% |
| Na | 98 | 648 | 570 | 88.0% |
| Nb | 5 | 18 | 18 | 100.0% |
| Nc | 8 | 29 | 27 | 93.1% |
| Ncd | 13 | 283 | 209 | 73.9% |
| Nep | 6 | 2227 | 642 | 28.8% |
| Neqa | 2 | 38 | 32 | 84.2% |
| Nes | 6 | 128 | 118 | 92.2% |
| Neu | 3 | 127 | 114 | 89.8% |
| Nf | 40 | 228 | 212 | 93.0% |
| Ng | 13 | 147 | 102 | 69.4% |
| Nh | 8 | 1668 | 1549 | 92.9% |
| P | 33 | 1659 | 1143 | 68.9% |
| T | 13 | 2838 | 1660 | 58.5% |
| VA | 28 | 451 | 347 | 76.9% |
| VAC | 1 | 4 | 3 | 75.0% |
| VB | 9 | 14 | 14 | 100.0% |
| VC | 76 | 1177 | 1065 | 90.5% |
| VCL | 5 | 174 | 107 | 61.5% |
| VD | 19 | 170 | 128 | 75.3% |
| VE | 26 | 1703 | 1475 | 86.6% |
| VF | 5 | 20 | 11 | 55.0% |
| VG | 9 | 170 | 103 | 60.6% |
| VH | 66 | 1940 | 664 | 34.2% |
| VHC | 2 | 13 | 13 | 100.0% |
| VI | 3 | 4 | 4 | 100.0% |
| VJ | 19 | 326 | 206 | 63.2% |
| VK | 11 | 63 | 55 | 87.3% |
| VL | 5 | 160 | 140 | 87.5% |
| V_2 | 1 | 823 | 433 | 52.6% |
| Nom | 1 | 1 | 1 | 100.0% |
| Total | 650 | 23065 | 14879 | 64.5% |

## 6 Conclusion

Sense Tagged Corpus plays a very important part to Natural Language Processing, especially for creating successful WSD systems. At the current stage, such large-scale Chinese Sense Tagged Corpus is only few and for between, so we design a large-scale Chinese sense tagged corpus, containing about 100,000 words, for research on natural language processing. The automatic sense tagging is a preparation work for manual tagging. The automatic tagging uses the information provided by the peripheral words, the N-gram method, the information of collocations, and the probability model to calculate the most likely sense meaning. We sincerely hope that through the completeness of the Dictionary of Sense Discrimination, it is possible to complete the task for doing the full text tagging for whole five million words contained in the Sinica Corpus.

**Acknowledgments.** This work was partly supported by National Science Council, the ROC, under contract no. NSC-94-2213-E-031-003-, 96-2221-E-031-002- and 96-2422-H-001-002. The authors would like to thank the reviewers for their valuable comments.

## References

1. Chen, K.-j., et al.: Sinica Corpus: Design Methodology for Balanced Corpora. In: Park, B.-S., Kim, J.B. (eds.) Proceeding of the 11 th Pacific Asia Conference on Language, Information and Computation, pp. 167–176. Kyung Hee University, Seoul (1996)
2. Ma, W.-Y., Huang, C.-R.: Uniform and Effective Tagging of a Heterogeneous Giga-word Corpus. In: Presented at the 5th International Conference on Language Resources and Evaluation (LREC2006). Genoa, Italy, May 2006, pp. 24–28 (2006)
3. SemCor, http://multisemcor.itc.it/semcor.php
4. Senseval, http://www.senseval.org/
5. Huang, C.-R. (ed.): Meaning and Sense. Technical Report 06-03, Chinese Wordnet Group, Academia Sinica, Taiwan (in Chinese) (2006)
6. Huang, C.-R., et al.: The Sinica Sense Management System: Design and Implementation. Computational Linguistics and Chinese Language Processing 10(4), 417–430 (2005)
7. Ker, S.-J., Huang, C.-R., Chen, J.-N.: A Preliminary Study of Large-scale Corpus Sense Tagging. In: The 5th Lexical Semantics Workshop, Beijing (in Chinese) (2004)
8. Ker, S.-J., Chen, J.-N.: Large-scale Sense Tagging by Combining Machine Learning and Linguistic Knowledge. In: The 8th Lexical Semantics Workshop, Hong Kong (in Chinese) (2007)
9. Yarowsky: One Sense Per Collocation. In: Proceedings of ARPA Human Language Technology Workshop, Princeton (1993)

# Soccer Formation Classification Based on Fisher Weight Map and Gaussian Mixture Models

Toshie Misu, Masahide Naemura, Mahito Fujii, and Nobuyuki Yagi

Science & Technical Research Laboratories, NHK (Japan Broadcasting Corporation)
1-10-11, Kinuta, Setagaya-ku, Tokyo 157-8510, Japan
{misu.t-ey,naemura.m-ei,fujii.m-ii,yagi.n-iy}@nhk.or.jp

**Abstract.** This paper proposes a method that analyzes player formations in order to classify kick and throw-in events in soccer matches. Formations are described in terms of local head counts and mean velocities, which are converted into canonical variates using a Fisher weight map in order to select effective variates for discriminating between events. The map is acquired by supervised learning. The distribution of the variates for each event class is modeled by Gaussian mixtures in order to handle its multimodality in canonical space. Our experiments showed that the Fisher weight map extracted semantically explicable variates related to such situations as players at corners and left/right separation. Our experiments also showed that characteristically formed events, such as kick-offs and corner-kicks, were successfully classified by the Gaussian mixture models. The effect of spatial nonlinearity and fuzziness of local head counts are also evaluated.

**Keywords:** Formation analysis, Fisher weight map, Gaussian mixture model, supervised learning, soccer.

## 1 Introduction

In large-scale video archives, we often encounter difficulties in finding video resources that meet our requirements for genre, title, actor, director, place, video format, etc. The difficulty would reach the level of impossibility if we were to access scenes or shots of specific semantic situations without temporally segmented video indices (segment metadata).

Depending on the temporal and semantic granularity, the production of manually-indexed segment metadata usually requires a vast amounts of time, manpower, and concentration, especially in the case of sports video, where prompt editing operations are requisite despite the unavailability of a priori scenarios.

To support metadata production, automatic event detection and scene analysis have been widely studied for audio and speech [1][2], video [3][4][5], and their combination [6]. As the formation and the global motion of the players characterize tactical situations, especially in field sports, we focused on positional information acquired from image-based object detection and tracking techniques,

T. Tokunaga and A. Ortega (Eds.): LKR 2008, LNAI 4938, pp. 194–209, 2008.

and have already develped a soccer event detector [7], that can detect free-kicks, corner-kicks, throw-ins, etc., according to a manually given rule base. Nagase et al. [8] propose a rule-based event detection method that classifies the ball position when it is placed on the turf.

To automate the purpose-dependent rule design processes, we employed a four-layer event classifier that can be tuned through supervised learning. It involves extraction of low-level physical features, their conversion into general-purpose mid-level features by using simple statistics, subsequent conversion into purpose-oriented high-level features by Fisher discriminant analysis (FDA), and a calculation of the probabilities of event types based on Gaussian mixtures.

## 2 Representation of Knowledge about Formations

Figure 1 depicts the training and testing processes of the event classifier. The knowledge about the formations is represented by the following three components:

- the allocation of subregions for counting heads (K1 in Fig. 1),
- the weight matrix for extracting of high-level features (K2), and
- the probabilistic models for the high-level feature distributions (K3).

The knowledge component K1 is for partitioning the soccer field model, from which the instantaneous spatial density of players is determined. We tested three types of partition: crisp equi-sampled (CES) subregions, crisp histogram-equalized (CHE) subregions, and fuzzy equi-sampled (FES) subregions. The team-wise local head counts based on these partitions and the mean velocity of all the players are combined to form a mid-level feature vector.

In the knowledge component K2, the mid-level features are linearly mapped to high-level features that form compact event-type-wise clusters. We applied the Fisher discriminant criterion to this mapping.

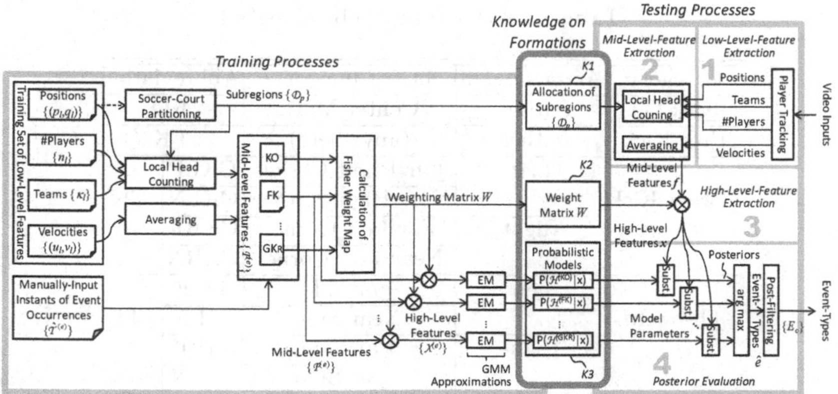


**Fig. 1.** Block diagram of event classifier

The knowledge component K3 describes the shapes of the clusters in the high-level-feature domain. The non-Gaussianity and the multimodality of the clusters are approximately modeled using Gaussian mixtures.

## 3 Testing Processes

The right side of Fig. 1 shows the testing processes of the classifier. The classifier receives a sequence of video frames acquired by one or two video cameras, and outputs the estimated class from the 12 event types listed in Table 1. The instant of event occurrence is defined as the moment at which a kick or throw is made. The classifier is not intended to detect the instant of each event, but to classify every observed formation to the most probable event type.

### 3.1 Low-Level Features — Physical Quantities

The first stage estimates the following quantities for each player silhouette $\ell \in \{1, \ldots, L\}$:

- the position $(x_\ell, y_\ell)$ and the velocity $(u_\ell, v_\ell)$,
- the number of players $n_\ell$, and
- the team category $\kappa_\ell$ judged by the shirt color.

The estimation is made with our player tracker, that was originally developed for a real-time offside-line visualization system [9].

Note that the position and velocity are those of the footprint and are measured in real scales in a world coordinate system. The origin of the world coordinate system is the center mark of the field. Viewed from the coach's position, the $x$- and $y$-axes point rightward along the touch lines and forward along the halfway line. The tri-state team category $\kappa_\ell \in \{-1, 0, +1\}$ stands for the left, unidentified, or the right team, respectively. Although individual low-level features may

**Table 1.** Event-types to be classified

| Category | Actor's Team | Site of Incidence | Abbreviation | |
|---|---|---|---|---|
| Kick Off | (either) | Center Mark | KO | |
| Free Kick | (either) | (anywhere) | FK | |
| Corner Kick | Left | Far Right Corner | CKLF | CK |
| | | Near Right Corner | CKLN | |
| | Right | Far Left Corner | CKRF | |
| | | Near Left Corner | CKRN | |
| Throw In | Left | Far Side | TILF | TI |
| | | Near Side | TILN | |
| | Right | Far Side | TIRF | |
| | | Near Side | TIRN | |
| Goal Kick | Left | Left Goal Area | GKL | GK |
| | Right | Right Goal Area | GKR | |

contain errors due to occlusions, their influence is diminished by the statistical operations described in Subsections 3.2 and 3.6.

### 3.2 Mid-Level Features — General-Purpose Quantities

The classifier then converts the physical low-level features into general-purpose mid-level features. The mid-level features represent the positional pattern of players (formation) and the global motion (offense-defense balance) that characterize the tactical situation of general field sports including soccer games.

In order to quantify the local density of players, the "Local Head Counting" function counts the team-wise number $N_{p,k}$ of players within each rectangular subregion $\mathcal{D}_p$ of the soccer field, as exemplified in Fig.2, where $p \in \{1, 2, \ldots, P\}$ and $k \in \{-1, +1\}$ denote the positional index and team index ($-1$ and $+1$ for left and right teams, respectively):

$$N_{p,k} = \sum_{\ell=1}^{L} m_p(x_\ell, y_\ell) \cdot n_\ell \cdot \tilde{\delta}_{\kappa_\ell,k}, \qquad \tilde{\delta}_{\kappa_\ell,k} = \begin{cases} 1 & (\text{if } \kappa_\ell = k) \\ 1/2 & (\text{if } \kappa_\ell = 0) \\ 0 & (\text{otherwise}) \end{cases} \tag{1}$$

$$m_p(x, y) = \begin{cases} 1 & (\text{if } (x, y) \in \mathcal{D}_p) \\ 0 & (\text{otherwise}) \end{cases}, \tag{2}$$

In Eq. (1), player silhouettes $\ell$ with an ambiguous team category $\kappa_\ell = 0$ half-and-half contribute to the left and the right teams' local head counts.

Since the global motion of players characterizes the offense-defense balance, and also indirectly, the ball position, the mean velocity $(U, V)$ of all the detected players is also calculated in the "Averaging" stage:

$$(U, V) = \left( \frac{1}{L} \sum_{\ell=1}^{L} u_\ell\,, \quad \frac{1}{L} \sum_{\ell=1}^{L} v_\ell \right). \tag{3}$$

By stacking all the components of the local head counts $\{N_{p,k}\}_{p \in \{1,\ldots,P\}, k \in \{-1,+1\}}$ and the mean velocity $(U, V)$, we define a $(2P + 2)$-dimensional mid-level-feature vector $\boldsymbol{f}$ as follows:

$$\boldsymbol{f} = [N_{1,-1}, N_{2,-1}, \ldots, N_{P,-1}; \quad N_{1,+1}, N_{2,+1}, \ldots, N_{P,+1}; \quad U, V]^T. \tag{4}$$

**Local Head Count Using Crisp Equi-Sampled (CES) Subregions.** As one of the simplest allocations of subregions $\mathcal{D}_p$s, CES divides the soccer field into $P$ rectangular subregions by using equally spaced horizontal/vertical partitions as shown in Fig. 2(a).

**Local Head Count Using Crisp Histogram-Equalized (CHE) Subregions.** It would be natural to extend the above-mentioned equi-spaced partition to an uneven one. As illustrated in Fig. 2(b), CHE uses a non-linearly sampled partition that densely samples the field areas where the players are more frequently observed.

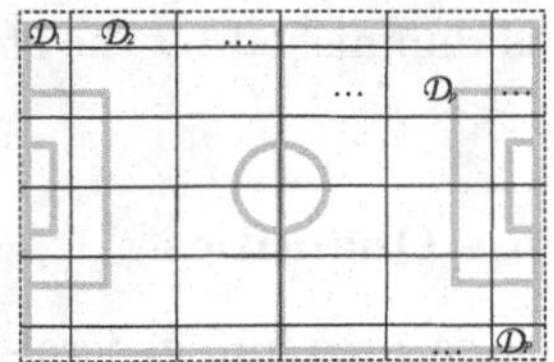
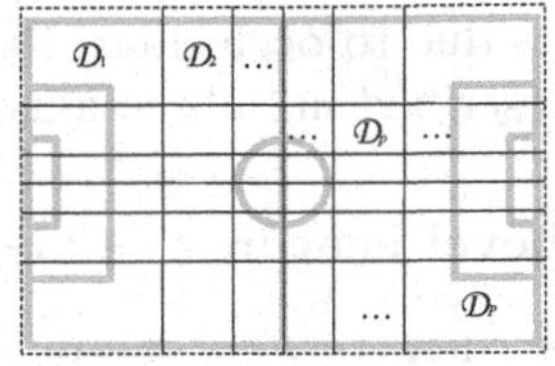

(a) Crisp equi-sampled subregions (b) Crisp histogram-equalized subregions

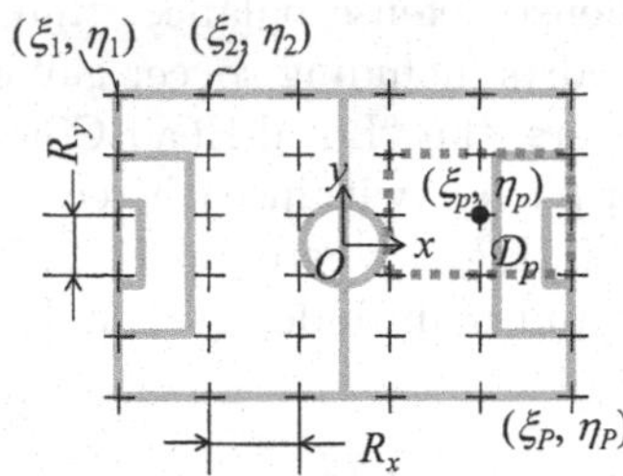
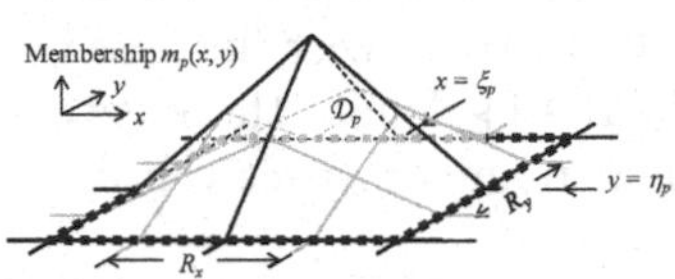

(c) Fuzzy equi-sampled subregions (d) Fuzzy membership function $m_p(x, y)$

**Fig. 2.** Examples of subregions $\mathcal{D}_p$s and fuzzy membership function $m_p(x, y)$

**Local Head Count Using Fuzzy Equi-Sampled (FES) Subregions.** The pattern of the local head counts may change dramatically if some players move across the crisp borders of the subregions. To avoid this instability, we tested fuzzy subregions $\mathcal{D}_p$s with the membership functions $m_p(x, y)$s shown in Fig. 2(d):

$$m_p(x, y) = \Lambda\left(\frac{x - \xi_p}{R_x}\right) \cdot \Lambda\left(\frac{y - \eta_p}{R_y}\right), \quad \Lambda(x) = \max\{0, 1 - |x|\}, \tag{5}$$

where $(\xi_p, \eta_p)$ is the position of the $p$th lattice point (cf. the disc (•) in Fig. 2(c)).

### 3.3 High-Level Features — Specialized Quantities

From a mid-level-feature vector $\boldsymbol{f}$, a high-level-feature vector $\boldsymbol{x}$, which efficiently describes the difference between event types, is extracted using the following simple multiplication:

$$\boldsymbol{x} = W\boldsymbol{f}, \tag{6}$$

where $W$ is a weight matrix called the Fisher weight map [10] (i.e. a subset of eigenvectors in FDA). This map reduces the redundant/ineffective dimensions of the mid-level features $\boldsymbol{f}$ in order to extract a small set of specialized quantities (canonical variates) $\boldsymbol{x}$ for a specific sport and purpose.

### 3.4 Probabilistic Modeling of High-Level-Feature Distribution

The high-level-feature vector $\boldsymbol{x}$ is substituted into the probability density function (pdf) $P(\mathcal{H}^{(e)} \mid \boldsymbol{x})$ of each event type $e$'s probabilistic model $\mathcal{H}^{(e)}$, which is prepared through the training, to evaluate the posterior probability. Bayes' rule gives the following relationship with respect to the event type $e$:

$$P(\mathcal{H}^{(e)} \mid \boldsymbol{x}) = p(\boldsymbol{x} \mid \mathcal{H}^{(e)})P(\mathcal{H}^{(e)})/p(\boldsymbol{x}) \propto p(\boldsymbol{x} \mid \mathcal{H}^{(e)})P(\mathcal{H}^{(e)}), \tag{7}$$

where $p(\boldsymbol{x} \mid \mathcal{H}^{(e)})$ denoted the conditional pdf of a high-level feature $\boldsymbol{x}$ given event-type $e$'s model $\mathcal{H}^{(e)}$, and $P(\mathcal{H}^{(e)})$ denotes the model $\mathcal{H}^{(e)}$'s prior. They are implemented as Gaussian mixtures and the prior itself:

$$p(\boldsymbol{x} \mid \mathcal{H}^{(e)}) = \sum_{k=1}^{K^{(e)}} \alpha_k^{(e)} \frac{\exp\left\{-\frac{1}{2}(\boldsymbol{x} - \boldsymbol{\mu}_k^{(e)})^T [\Sigma_k^{(e)}]^{-1} (\boldsymbol{x} - \boldsymbol{\mu}_k^{(e)})\right\}}{\sqrt{(2\pi)^{\dim(\boldsymbol{x})} |\Sigma_k^{(e)}|}} \tag{8}$$

$$P(\mathcal{H}^{(e)}) = P^{(e)}. \tag{9}$$

Hence, event-type $e$'s model $\mathcal{H}^{(e)}$ consists of the prior $P^{(e)}$, the number of mixtures $K^{(e)}$, the $k$th mixture's weight $\alpha_k^{(e)}$, the mean vector $\boldsymbol{\mu}_k^{(e)}$, and the covariance matrix $\Sigma_k^{(e)}$, i.e. $\mathcal{H}^{(e)} = \{P^{(e)}, K^{(e)}, \{\alpha_k^{(e)}, \boldsymbol{\mu}_k^{(e)}, \Sigma_k^{(e)}\}_{k \in \{1,2,\ldots,K^{(e)}\}}\}$.

### 3.5 Preliminary Decision by Posterior Maximization

By substituting the high-level-feature vector $\boldsymbol{x} = \boldsymbol{x}(t)$ at an instant $t$ into Eq. (8), the likelihood $p(\boldsymbol{x}(t) \mid \mathcal{H}^{(e)})$ of the event type $e$ can be obtained. The most probable event type $\hat{e}(t)$ that maximizes the posterior given in Eq. (7) can be estimated by:

$$\hat{e}(t) = \operatorname*{argmax}_{e \in \mathcal{E}} P(\mathcal{H}^{(e)} \mid \boldsymbol{x}(t)) = \operatorname*{argmax}_{e \in \mathcal{E}} \{p(\boldsymbol{x}(t) \mid \mathcal{H}^{(e)}) \cdot P(\mathcal{H}^{(e)})\}, \tag{10}$$

where $\mathcal{E} = \{\mathrm{KO}, \mathrm{FK}, \mathrm{CKLF}, \ldots, \mathrm{GKR}\}$ is the total event-type set (cf. Table 1).

### 3.6 Final Decision by Temporal Post-Filtering

The frame-wise most probable event type $\hat{e}(t)$ obtained by Eq. (10) would have instantaneous errors since similar short-term formations may appear even if they are of different event types. A majority rule is applied as a temporal post-filter to suppress this kind of error.

First, the histogram $h(t; e)$ of preliminary decisions $\hat{e}(\tau)$ during a certain time period $\tau \in [t - \tau_b, t + \tau_a]$ is calculated (hereinafter, we consider $\tau_b = 120$ and $\tau_a = 30$ frames):

$$h(t; e) = \sum_{\tau = t - \tau_b}^{t + \tau_a} \delta_{\hat{e}(\tau), e}, \tag{11}$$

where $\delta_{\bullet,\bullet}$ denotes Kronecker's delta. The $n$th probable candidate $E_n(t)$ can be obtained by choosing the $n$th-most frequent bin of the histogram $h(t; e)$:

$$E_1(t) = \operatorname*{argmax}_{e \in \mathcal{E}} h(t; e) \tag{12}$$

$$E_c(t) = \operatorname*{argmax}_{e \in \mathcal{E}, e \notin \{E_x\}_{x=1}^{c-1}} h(t; e) \qquad (\text{for } 2 \leq c \leq |\mathcal{E}|). \tag{13}$$

# 4 Training Processes

From soccer videos, we manually compiled a training set $\mathcal{F}^{(e)}$ for each event type $e$. The training set $\mathcal{F}^{(e)}$ contains the mid-level-feature vectors $\boldsymbol{f}$s around the instants of event type $e$'s occurrences:

$$\mathcal{F}^{(e)} = \bigcup_{\tau \in \mathcal{T}^{(e)}} \{\boldsymbol{f}(\tau)\} \tag{14}$$

where $\boldsymbol{f}(t)$ denotes the mid-level-feature vector of the frame index $t$, and $\mathcal{T}^{(e)}$ is the set of frame indices around (during the frames in the intervals of $\tau_b$ frames before to $\tau_a$ frames after) the instants of event type $e$'s occurrences, i.e.:

$$\mathcal{T}^{(e)} \triangleq \bigcup_{t \in \hat{\mathcal{T}}^{(e)}} [t - \tau_b, t + \tau_a], \tag{15}$$

where $\hat{\mathcal{T}}^{(e)}$ is the set of the very "one-frame"s (i.e. not segments but points) of event type $e$'s occurrences.

Assuming the symmetries of the formations, we quadruplicated the content of each training set $\mathcal{F}^{(e)}$ by flipping horizontally/vertically/around the signs of the positions and the velocities, team indices, and the far/near sides of event incidence as shown in Table 2.

## 4.1 Subregions $\mathcal{D}_p$s for Mid-Level-Feature Extraction

CES, CHE, and FES have tunable granularity parameters: the horizontal and vertical resolutions $D_\mathrm{x}$ and $D_\mathrm{y}$. The parameters were given manually in the experiments discussed below.

In addition, CHE has another flexibility of unequal sampling. Plotting the history of all the player's positions in all the training set $\bigcup_{e \in \mathcal{E}} \mathcal{T}^{(e)}$, we see that the set of positions is not uniformly distributed on the field. To sample at finer

**Table 2.** Quadruplication of a training set by exploiting formation symmetry

| Symmetry | Original | Left ↔ Right | Far ↔ Near | Rotation |
|---|---|---|---|---|
| Formation | $N_{p,k}$ | $N_{l(p),-k}$ | $N_{b(p),k}$ | $N_{b(l(p)),-k}$ |
| Vector $\boldsymbol{f}$ | $(U,V)$ | $(-U,V)$ | $(U,-V)$ | $(-U,-V)$ |
| | KO | KO | KO | KO |
| | FK | FK | FK | FK |
| Event type $e$ | ••LF | ••RF | ••LN | ••RN |
| | ••LN | ••RN | ••LF | ••RF |
| | ••RF | ••LF | ••RN | ••LN |
| •• ∈ {CK, TI} | ••RN | ••LN | ••RF | ••LF |
| | GKL | GKR | GKL | GKR |
| | GKR | GKL | GKR | GKL |

$l(p)$ returns laterally flipped index of $p$. $b(p)$ returns backflipped index of $p$.

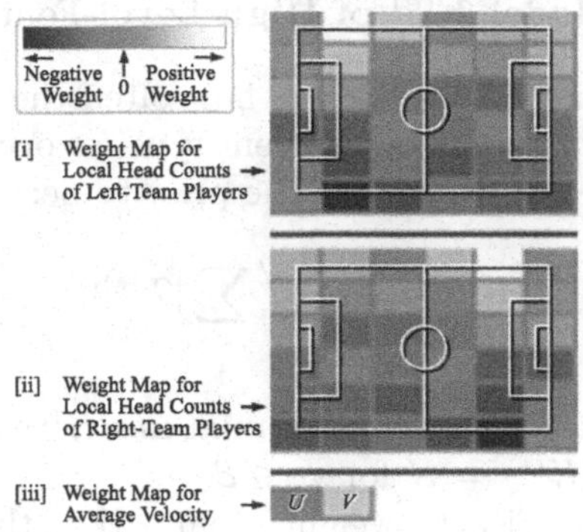


**Fig. 3.** Visualization of Fisher weight map

resolutions for more densely distributed areas, we first horizontally partitioned the field into $D_{\mathrm{x}}$ strips to make the frequencies (i.e. the histogram) of players' existences equal to each other. Then, similarly, vertical partitions were placed to make $D_{\mathrm{y}}$ strips.

### 4.2 Fisher Weight Map $W$ for High-Level-Feature Extraction

We employed the Fisher discriminant criterion to obtain the optimal weight matrix $W$. The criterion classifies the features between different event types and organizes those of the same type, in order to reduce the dimensionality of the mid-level-feature vector $\boldsymbol{f}$ by $\boldsymbol{x} = W\boldsymbol{f}$.

The intra- and inter-class covariances $\Sigma_{\mathrm{W}}$ and $\Sigma_{\mathrm{B}}$ are defined as follows:

$$\Sigma_{\mathrm{W}} = \sum_{e\in\mathcal{E}} \sum_{\boldsymbol{f}\in\mathcal{F}^{(e)}} (\boldsymbol{f} - \bar{\boldsymbol{f}}^{(e)})(\boldsymbol{f} - \bar{\boldsymbol{f}}^{(e)})^T \Big/ \sum_{e\in\mathcal{E}} |\mathcal{F}^{(e)}| \tag{16}$$

$$\Sigma_{\mathrm{B}} = \sum_{e\in\mathcal{E}} |\mathcal{F}^{(e)}|(\bar{\boldsymbol{f}}^{(e)} - \bar{\boldsymbol{f}})(\bar{\boldsymbol{f}}^{(e)} - \bar{\boldsymbol{f}})^T \Big/ \sum_{e\in\mathcal{E}} |\mathcal{F}^{(e)}| \tag{17}$$

$$\bar{\boldsymbol{f}}^{(e)} = \left(\sum_{\boldsymbol{f}\in\mathcal{F}^{(e)}} \boldsymbol{f}\right) \Big/ |\mathcal{F}^{(e)}|, \qquad \bar{\boldsymbol{f}} = \left(\sum_{e\in\mathcal{E}} \sum_{\boldsymbol{f}\in\mathcal{F}^{(e)}} \boldsymbol{f}\right) \Big/ \sum_{e\in\mathcal{E}} |\mathcal{F}^{(e)}|,$$

where $|\mathcal{F}|$ denote the number of elements in a set $\mathcal{F}$.

The optimal weight matrix $W$ — the Fisher weight map can be constructed by piling the eigenvectors $\boldsymbol{w}$s with the $M$ largest eigenvalues $\lambda$s of the generalized eigenvalue problem $\Sigma_{\mathrm{B}}\boldsymbol{w} = \lambda\Sigma_{\mathrm{W}}\boldsymbol{w}$ as follows:

$$W = [\boldsymbol{w}_1 \quad \boldsymbol{w}_2 \quad \cdots \quad \boldsymbol{w}_M]^T, \tag{18}$$

where $\boldsymbol{w}_m$ is the eigenvector with the $m$th-largest eigenvalue.

Each row $\boldsymbol{w}_m^T$ (i.e. the eigenvector) of a Fisher weight map $W$ is visualized by grayscale boxes, as depicted in Fig. 3.

### 4.3 Probabilistic Model $\mathcal{H}^{(e)}$ of High-Level-Feature Distribution

The meaning of the prior $P^{(e)} \in \mathcal{H}^{(e)}$ is how often the event type $e$ occurs in soccer matches. As the total period of event type $e$'s occurrences $|\mathcal{T}^{(e)}|$ (cf. Eq. (15)) reflects the frequency, we assume the prior to be:

$$P^{(e)} = |\mathcal{T}^{(e)}| \Big/ \sum_{\epsilon \in \mathcal{E}} |\mathcal{T}^{(\epsilon)}|. \tag{19}$$

For simplicity, we fixed the number of mixtures $K^{(e)} \in \mathcal{H}^{(e)}$ to a common $K$ for all the event-types; $K^{(e)} := K$ for $\forall e \in \mathcal{E}$.

After creating the Fisher weight map $W$, the GMM parameters $\{\alpha_k^{(e)}, \boldsymbol{\mu}_k^{(e)}, \Sigma_k^{(e)}\}_{k \in \{1,\ldots,K^{(e)}\}} \in \mathcal{H}^{(e)}$ are determined using the mapped training set $\mathcal{X}^{(e)} \triangleq \{W\boldsymbol{f} \mid \boldsymbol{f} \in \mathcal{F}^{(e)}\}$. We employed an expectation-maximization (EM) algorithm in the optimization.

## 5 Experiments and Discussions

The mechanism, trend, and precision were evaluated using 253 events occurred in five halves from three games of the Japanese professional soccer league (Table 3).

The columns of the left/right teams represent the colors of field-players' shirts. The set of events in the $n$th half is referred to as the (training/testing) set #$n$. Table 4 shows the titles and conditions for the experiments. Based upon the FES's optimal values obtained from the experiments in Subsections 5.2 and 5.3, we chose $6 \times 6$ FES subregions and $K = 7$ Gaussian mixtures as the default parameters for the classifier.

### 5.1 Fisher Weight Map

Figure 4 visualizes (cf. Fig. 3 for the way) the eigenvectors $\boldsymbol{w}_m$ ($m = 1, \ldots, M$) that configure the Fisher weight map $W$. The distribution of the high-level features (canonical variates) $\boldsymbol{x}$s, which were obtained by mapping the mid-level-feature vectors $\boldsymbol{f}$s of the training sets, are plotted in Fig. 5.

**Table 3.** Data sets for training and testing

| Set | Match | Half | Left Team | Right Team | Number of Event Occurrences |
|---|---|---|---|---|---|
| #1 | A | First | Blue-1 | Yellow | 53 |
| #2 | A | Second | Yellow | Blue-1 | 43 |
| #3 | B | First | Red | Blue-2 | 52 |
| #4 | B | Second | Blue-2 | Red | 50 |
| #5 | C | First | Red | Blue-1 | 55 |
| Total Number of Event Occurrences | | | | | 253 |

**Table 4.** Experimental conditions

| Experiment(s) and Discussions on: | Data Set(s) Training | Data Set(s) Testing | Subregions $\mathcal{D}_p$s $D_x \times D_y$ | Subregions $\mathcal{D}_p$s Membership/Sampling | GMM $K$ |
|---|---|---|---|---|---|
| 5.1 Fisher Weight Map | #1–#4 | #1–#4 | 6×6 | FES | 7 |
| 5.2 Subregions | Cross-Validation | | **3×3–8×8** | **CES/CHE/FES** | 7 |
| 5.3 Gaussian Mixtures | Cross-Validation | | 6×6 | FES | **1–8** |
| 5.4 Post-Filter | #1–#4 | #5 | 6×6 | FES | 7 |
| 5.5 Confusion Matrices | Cross-Validation | | 6×6 | **CES/CHE/FES** | 7 |

Cross-Validation: 1-out-of-5 Set-Wise Cross-Validation

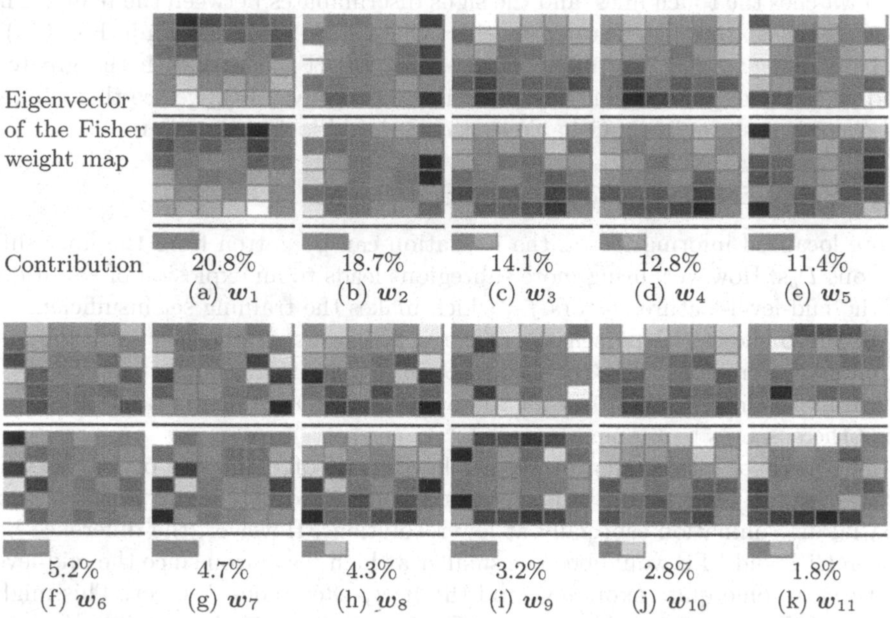


(a) $\boldsymbol{w}_1$ (b) $\boldsymbol{w}_2$ (c) $\boldsymbol{w}_3$ (d) $\boldsymbol{w}_4$ (e) $\boldsymbol{w}_5$ (f) $\boldsymbol{w}_6$ (g) $\boldsymbol{w}_7$ (h) $\boldsymbol{w}_8$ (i) $\boldsymbol{w}_9$ (j) $\boldsymbol{w}_{10}$ (k) $\boldsymbol{w}_{11}$

**Fig. 4.** Fisher weight map obtained from training sets #1–#4

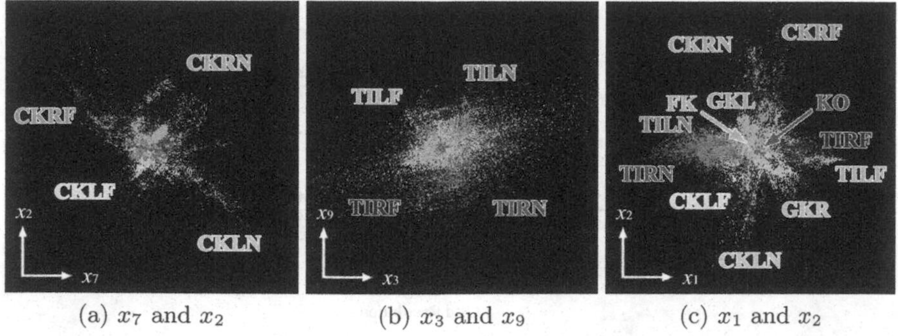


(a) $x_7$ and $x_2$ (b) $x_3$ and $x_9$ (c) $x_1$ and $x_2$

**Fig. 5.** Distribution of high-level features colored according to event type

The weight vector $\boldsymbol{w}_2$ in Fig. 4(b) for the second canonical variate $x_2$ reveals an impressive map with negative weights on the left-team's right corners and positive weights on the right-team's left corners. This implies that an offensive player strikes a corner-kick at an opponent's corner. The weight vector $\boldsymbol{w}_7$ in Figure 4(g) for $x_7$ shows a similar weight map except for far/near allocation of the signs. By plotting variates on the $x_7x_2$-plane, we can see that the distribution forms an X shape with CKRN, CKRF, CKLF, and CKLN arms as shown in Fig. 5(a).

The weight vector $\boldsymbol{w}_3$ in Figure 4(c) for $x_3$ is sensitive to the touch lines with the opposite signs for far/near sides. The weight vector $\boldsymbol{w}_9$ in Figure 4(i) for $x_9$ also watches the touch lines, and the signs discriminates between the teams. The four TI types are well-separated by the variates $(x_3, x_9)$ as shown in Fig. 5(b).

By looking at the two major variates $(x_1, x_2)$ (Fig. 5(c)) with the greatest and the second greatest contributions (i.e. the eigenvalues), we see that almost all event types are distinguishable by the variates' loci in the plane.

## 5.2 Subregion Types for Local Head Counts

More localized information on the formation can be gotten from the finer subregions $\mathcal{D}_p$s. However, using more subregions leads to an explosion of variations of the mid-level-feature vectors $\boldsymbol{f}$s, which makes the training set insufficient.

Figure 6 shows the percentage of correct answers with respect to type and number of subregions. The CES and FES curves have increasing trends. The FES curve has a small peak (70%) for the $6 \times 6$-partition, which notably surpasses the others' scores by 6 points.

The merit of introducing fuzzy membership is soft handover of players who cross over the borders, but this merit is accompanied by the drawback of poor spatial discrimination especially at low resolutions. However, the difference between CES and FES would become smaller at high resolution since the mid-level features become quite expressive and the fuzzy-effect goes discreet. This might be why FES showed an advantage to CES for $6 \times 6$ and $7 \times 7$ partitions, but not for $4 \times 4$ or $5 \times 5$.

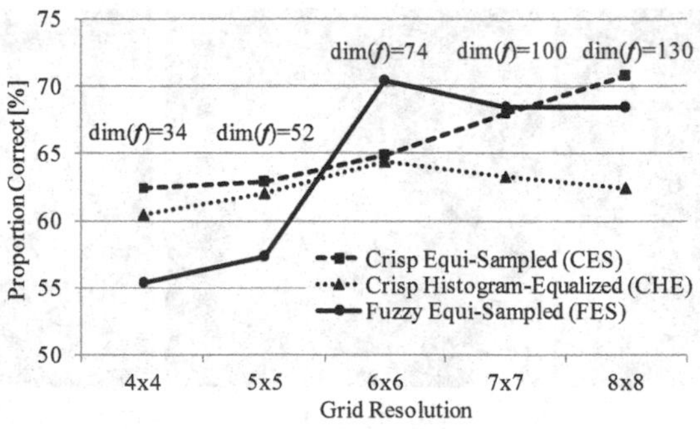


**Fig. 6.** Precision versus subregion type

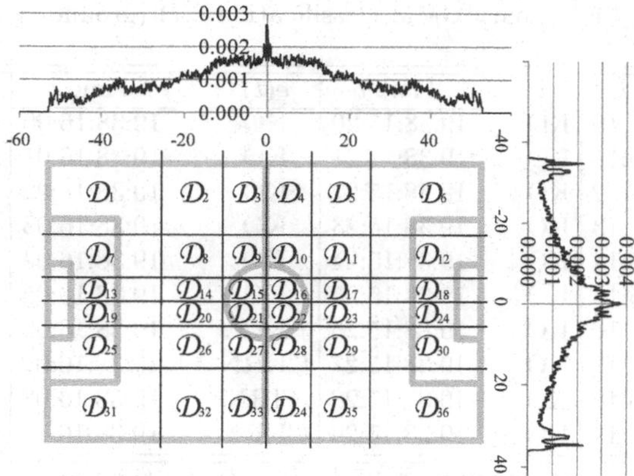

**Fig. 7.** An example of subregions determined by CHE

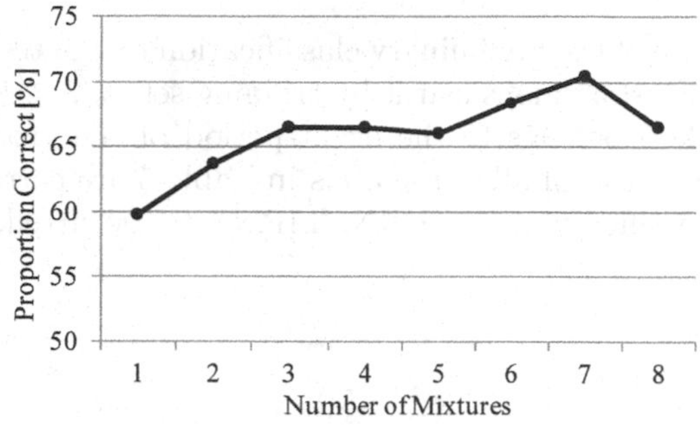


**Fig. 8.** Proportion correct versus number of mixtures $K$

We found no benefit in moving partitions on the criterion of CHE (see Fig. 7 for an example). We believe that this is because the formation is characterized not by the player density but by differences between inter- and intra-class densities. Thus, at higher resolution, most of the subregions are assigned to less-important areas and the trend saturates. Other criteria should be considered.

### 5.3 Number of Gaussian Mixtures

A GMM with the more mixtures gives a more precise approximation of the original distribution. This capability, however, also means a risk of over-fitting when the training set is insufficient.

Figure 8 shows percentage of correct answers given by the FES-based classifier with respect to the number of mixtures $K$. The nearly convex curve has a peak at $K = 7$ mixtures.

**Table 5.** Preliminary GMM classification $\hat{e}(t)$ (ground truth: KO)

| Time $t$ | $\hat{e}(t)$ | Time $t$ | $\hat{e}(t)$ | Time $t$ | $\hat{e}(t)$ |
|---|---|---|---|---|---|
| 19:38:15:10 | KO | 19:38:15:20 | KO | 19:38:16:00 | CKRN |
| 19:38:15:11 | KO | 19:38:15:21 | KO | 19:38:16:01 | CKRN |
| 19:38:15:12 | KO | 19:38:15:22 | KO | 19:38:16:02 | TIRN |
| 19:38:15:13 | KO | 19:38:15:23 | KO | 19:38:16:03 | GKL |
| 19:38:15:14 | KO | 19:38:15:24 | KO | 19:38:16:04 | GKL |
| 19:38:15:15 | KO | 19:38:15:25 | KO | 19:38:16:05 | KO |
| 19:38:15:16 | KO | 19:38:15:26 | KO | 19:38:16:06 | KO |
| 19:38:15:17 | KO | 19:38:15:27 | CKRN | 19:38:16:07 | CKRN |
| 19:38:15:18 | KO | 19:38:15:28 | TIRN | 19:38:16:08 | CKRN |
| 19:38:15:19 | KO | 19:38:15:29 | CKRN | 19:38:16:09 | CKRN |

Time $t$ is represented in 29.97Hz drop-frame timecodes.

### 5.4 Effect of Post-Filter

Table 5 is an example of the preliminary classification $\hat{e}(t)$ of testing set #5 using the models with FES subregions learnt by training sets #1–#4. The whole time period in the Table 5 belongs to the event-period of the ground-truth KO at 19:38:15:16. While almost of all of the $\hat{e}(t)$s in Table 5 are correctly classified to KOs, several misclassifications to CKRN, TIRN, etc. occurred.

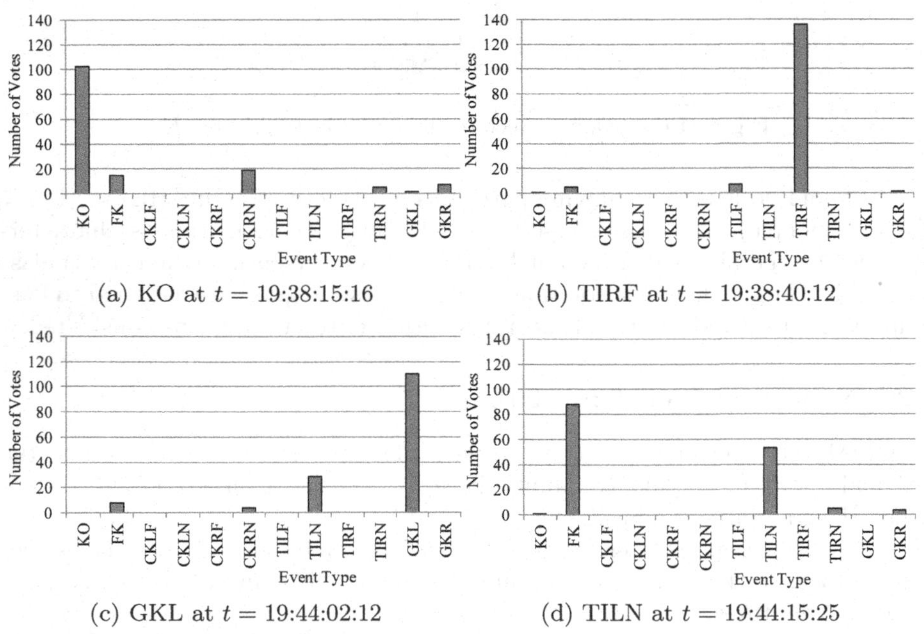


(a) KO at $t$ = 19:38:15:16
(b) TIRF at $t$ = 19:38:40:12
(c) GKL at $t$ = 19:44:02:12
(d) TILN at $t$ = 19:44:15:25

**Fig. 9.** Event histogram $h(t; e)$ calculated by post-filter

The histograms $h(t;e)$s for KO at 19:38:15:16, TIRF at 19:38:40:12, GKL at 19:44:02:12, and TILN at 19:44:15:25 are shown in Fig. 9.

In the cases of Figs. 9(a), (b), and (c), the event type of the ground-truth (KO, GKL, and TIRF, respectively) received the largest numbers of votes.

As shown in Fig. 9(d), the ground-truth TILN took second place. It might be better to design a user interface that enables multi-candidate selection from

**Table 6.** Precision and recall of event classification

(a) Crisp Equi-Sampled Subregions (CES)

| | | Results of Classification (First Candidate $E_1$) | | | | | Recall | F-Measure |
|---|---|---|---|---|---|---|---|---|
| | | KO | FK | CK | TI | GK | | |
| Ground Truth | KO | **8** | 1 | 0 | 0 | 2 | 73% (8/11) | 0.73 |
| | FK | 1 | **20** | 3 | 11 | 11 | 43% (20/46) | 0.53 |
| | CK | 0 | 1 | **16** 0*1 | 0 | 0 | 94% (16/17) | 0.84 |
| | TI | 0 | 4 | 2 | **68** 36*2 | 5 | 59% (68/115) | 0.58 |
| | GK | 2 | 4 | 0 | 4 | **52** 2*3 | 81% (52/64) | 0.76 |
| Precision | | 73% (8/11) | 67% (20/30) | 76% (16/21) | 57% (68/119) | 72% (52/72) | **Proportion Correct** **65**% (164/253) | |

(b) Crisp Histogram-Equalized Subregions (CHE)

| | | Results of Classification (First Candidate $E_1$) | | | | | Recall | F-Measure |
|---|---|---|---|---|---|---|---|---|
| | | KO | FK | CK | TI | GK | | |
| Ground Truth | KO | **10** | 1 | 0 | 0 | 0 | 91% (10/11) | 0.95 |
| | FK | 0 | **15** | 6 | 11 | 14 | 33% (15/46) | 0.40 |
| | CK | 0 | 1 | **15** 1*1 | 0 | 0 | 88% (15/17) | 0.71 |
| | TI | 0 | 8 | 3 | **71** 29*2 | 4 | 62% (71/115) | 0.61 |
| | GK | 0 | 4 | 0 | 7 | **52** 1*3 | 81% (52/64) | 0.77 |
| Precision | | 100% (10/10) | 52% (15/29) | 60% (15/25) | 60% (71/118) | 73% (52/71) | **Proportion Correct** **64**% (163/253) | |

(c) Fuzzy Equi-Sampled Subregions (FES)

| | | Results of Classification (First Candidate $E_1$) | | | | | Recall | F-Measure |
|---|---|---|---|---|---|---|---|---|
| | | KO | FK | CK | TI | GK | | |
| Ground Truth | KO | **10** | 1 | 0 | 0 | 0 | 91% (10/11) | 0.74 |
| | FK | 3 | **22** | 1 | 14 | 6 | 48% (22/46) | 0.54 |
| | CK | 0 | 0 | **13** 3*1 | 0 | 1 | 76% (13/17) | 0.70 |
| | TI | 1 | 8 | 2 | **81** 21*2 | 2 | 70% (81/115) | 0.69 |
| | GK | 2 | 4 | 1 | 5 | **52** 0*3 | 81% (52/64) | 0.83 |
| Precision | | 63% (10/13) | 63% (22/35) | 65% (13/20) | 67% (81/116) | 85% (52/69) | **Proportion Correct** **70**% (178/253) | |

*1: Samples classified to CK on the wrong corner/team.

*2: Samples classified to TI of the wrong side/team.

*3: Samples classified to GK of the wrong team.

$E_1, E_2, \ldots$ if we are to implement the classifier in commercially viable metadata production systems.

### 5.5 Confusion Matrices

Table 6 shows the confusion matrices, precisions, recalls, F-measures, and percentages of correct answers obtained by the CES-, CHE-, and FES-based classifiers. For CK, TI, and GK, the classification result $E_1$ is treated as "correct" only if both the actor's team and the site of incidence are perfectly classified.

For the ground-truth KO, 10 (either by CHE and by FES) or 8 (by CES) out of 11 occurrences were properly classified as KO, but the rest were FK or GK. The similarity that no one stands at corners or on touch-lines may have caused the confusion among KO, FK, and GK.

CES, CHE and FES all have good scores for CKs, TIs and GKs. This is because, in the case of CKs, in spite of its infrequency, the players form a very characteristic formation with the opponent kicker at a corner and a crowd around the goal area, which can be well described by a mid-level-feature vector $\boldsymbol{f}$. When TIs/GKs occur, although the players show relatively characterless formations except for a thrower on a touchline on TIs or for uniform movement on GKs, the system can acquire well-polished model parameters since there are quite a lot of training patterns.

On the other hand, the FK formations are so diverse and their occurrences are sparse. Therefore, the system had a remarkably low recall rate for FK.

The spectra of the precisions and the recalls of CHE manifested quite different patterns from those of CES despite their comparable total scores. This difference implies that the partitioning criterion in CHE, i.e. simple deterministic histogram equalization, was not suitable for improving total performance, and that the partition allocation should have been optimized to a training set by testing various partition allocations.

## 6 Conclusion

We developed a soccer event classifier that discriminates among various set plays on the basis of the formation and the global motion of the players. High-level features that well describe the typical formations are selected by Fisher discriminant analysis. The experiments showed the Fisher weight map forms watchdogs over corners, touch-lines, etc., which resembles human interpretation. The Gaussian mixture model allows for the multimodality of the canonical variates obtained by the Fisher weight map. The experiments showed that the event types with characteristic formation pattern (e.g. corner kicks, kick offs, etc.) are well classified by our classifier. The subregions for local-head counts for mid-level-feature extraction were also examined. Fuzzy subregions showed advantages over the crisp ones for a moderate number of partitions ($6 \times 6$ or $7 \times 7$). The nonlinear partitioning needs more investigation of the quantization criteria. The testing process by a PC with 3.2GHz dual Xeon processors requires only about 1-second computation per 1-minute video source, which is fast enough for online tagging.

To improve system performance, we are planning to introduce the ball position [11] [12] as yet another key formation descriptor since the ball tends to be placed at specific positions during set plays: at the center mark, in a corner arc, etc. Other classifiers, such as support vector machines, should also be tested for finding the best combination of a set of features and a classifier.

## References

1. Nitanda, N., Haseyama, M., Kitajima, H.: Audio Signal Segmentation and Classification Using Fuzzy Clustering (in Japanese). IEICE Trans. D-II J88-D-II(2), 302–312 (2005)
2. Sano, M., et al.: Automatic Real-Time Selection and Annotation of Highlight Scenes in Televised Soccer. IEICE Trans. Information and Systems E90-D(1), 224–232 (2007)
3. Ekin, A., Tekalp, A.M., Mehrotra, R.: Automatic Soccer Video Analysis and Summarization. IEEE Trans. Image Process. 12(7), 796–807 (2003)
4. Matsumoto, K., et al.: Optimized Camera Viewpoint Determination System for Soccer Game Broadcasting. In: Proc. MVA 2000, pp. 115–118 (2000)
5. Figueroa, P.J., Leite, N.J., Barros, R.M.L.: Tracking Soccer Players Aiming their Kinematical Motion Analysis. Computer Vision and Image Understanding 101(2), 122–135 (2006)
6. Snoek, C.G.M., Worring, M.: A Review on Multimodal Video Indexing. In: Proc. ICME 2002, vol. 2, pp. 21–24 (2002)
7. Misu, T., et al.: Real-Time Event Detection Based on Formation Analysis of Soccer Scenes (in Japanese). In: Information Technology Letters (FIT2005), vol. 4 LI-003, pp. 141–144 (2005)
8. Nagase, T., Ozawa, S.: Determining Play in Soccer Scenes Using Multiple View Images (in Japanese). The Journal of the Institute of Image Information and Television Engineers 60(10), 1664–1671 (2006)
9. Misu, T., et al.: Visualization of Offside Lines Based on Realtime Video Processing (in Japanese). IEICE Trans. J88-D-II(8), 1681–1692 (2005)
10. Shinohara, Y., Otsu, N.: Facial Expression Recognition Using Fisher Weight Maps. In: Proc. IEEE 6th Intl. Conf. on Automatic Face and Gesture Recognition (FG 2004), pp. 499–504 (2004)
11. Ohno, Y., Miura, J., Shirai, Y.: Tracking Players and a Ball in Soccer Games. In: Proc. Int. Conf. on Multisensor Fusion and Integration for Intelligent systems, pp. 147–152 (1999)
12. Misu, T., et al.: Distributed Particle Filtering for Multiocular Soccer-Ball Tracking. In: Proc. ICASSP 2007, vol. 3, pp. 937–940 (2007)

# Supervised Learning of Similarity Measures for Content-Based 3D Model Retrieval

Hamid Laga[1] and Masayuki Nakajima[2]

[1] Global Edge Institute,
Tokyo Institute of Technology, Japan
hamid@img.cs.titech.ac.jp
http://www.img.cs.titech.ac.jp/~hamid/
[2] Computer Science Department
Tokyo Institute of Technology
nakajima@img.cs.titech.ac.jp

**Abstract.** In this paper we investigate on how the choice of similarity measures affects the performance of content-based 3D model retrieval (CB3DR) algorithms. In CB3DR, shape descriptors are used to provide a numerical representation of the salient features of the data, while similarity functions capture the high level semantic concepts. In the first part of the paper, we demonstrate experimentally that the Euclidean distance is not the optimal similarity function for 3D model classification and retrieval. Then, in the second part, we propose to use a supervised learning approach for automatic selection of the optimal similarity measure that achieves the best performance. Our experiments using the Princeton Shape Benchmark (PSB) show significant improvements in the retrieval performance.

## 1 Introduction

In the digital era multimedia data are of high importance with many application possibilities. A growing percentage of the stored information in a computer and exchanged over the internet is visual wether it is still images or video clips. Consequently a large amount of research is focusing on the development of efficient algorithms for classifying and searching non-textual data. This can be put in the context of organizing world information and make it universally accessible.

Over decades, images and video clips have been the dominant form of visual media. In recent years, however, 3D models and virtual worlds are becoming very popular. The developments in the field of Computer Graphics including high-performance graphics hardware, easy-to-use 3D modeling software, and internet communication made 3D models easy to create, visualize and share. Therefore, the amount of 3D data available is increasing significantly.

Similar to other types of digital media, large collections of 3D models require customized tools for classification, search, representation, and use of the embedded knowledge. In fact, 3D models differ from images in two major aspects. First, 3D models are easy to process since they are not affected by lighting conditions,

T. Tokunaga and A. Ortega (Eds.): LKR 2008, LNAI 4938, pp. 210–225, 2008.

occlusions, projections and shadows. On the other hand, images are often represented by regular 2D grids on which color information are encoded. 3D models however lack such proper parameterization and existing representations, such as polygon soup, point-based, implicit surfaces, and volume representations, are mainly designed for visualization purposes. Moreover, the dimensionality of the data is higher making search for pose registration and feature correspondences more difficult [9].

There have been many attempts to develop search engines for 3D model collections [2,1,5,4,3]. In general indexing 3D models requires (1) the definition of good shape descriptors, and (2) a good similarity function to measure the distances between entities in the feature space. Shape descriptors provide a numerical representation of the salient features of the data, while similarity functions capture the distribution of the data in the feature space. Therefore, they can be used as a mean for capturing the high level semantic concepts of the data. While 3D shape description using effective features have been extensively studied, only very few works investigated similarity measures in the context of content-based 3D model retrieval (CB3DR). In fact, the Euclidean distance, called also $L_2$−Sum of the Squared Distances (SSD), is one of the most widely used measures. The SSD is justified only when the feature data distribution is Gaussian, while the Manhattan distance, $L_1$ Sum of Absolute Differences (SAD), is justified when the data distribution is exponential [32]. In many applications, the real distribution of the data is neither Gaussian nor Exponential [32].

The challenge is then finding a suitable distance measure when the data distribution is unknown. This problem has been investigated in the context of image retrieval [32,31] but little work has been done on learning distance functions in CB3DR literature. Most of these works have been restricted to learning the Mahalanobis distance of the form $(x-y)^T \Sigma (x-y)$ for relevance feedback [6,16], where they try to estimate the weight matrix $\Sigma$ which can be seen as the covariance matrix of the traditional anisotropic Gaussian distribution.

In this paper we investigate how different similarity measures affect the performance of shape descriptors for content-based 3D model retrieval. We will show experimentally that the extensively used Euclidean Distance is far from being the most efficient. Then we implement a simple algorithm for automatic selection of the similarity measures that will achieve best performance. We adopt a machine learning approach where the best similarity measure is selected among others in a supervised manner at the training stage. We provide also a mean for combining different similarity measures when describing 3D models with heterogeneous features. Our work is based on the recent results in machine learning on feature selection and similarity learning [26,32].

The remainder of the paper is organized as follows; in the next section we review the related work. In Section 3 we provide an experimental analysis of the performance of existing 3D shape descriptors when used with similarity measures other than the Euclidean distance. In Section 4 we develop an efficient framework for learning the suitable similarity measure for a given descriptor.

Effectiveness and performance of the proposed framework is analyzed in Section 5. We conclude in Section 6.

## 2 Related Work

3D shape analysis, classification and retrieval received significant attention in recent years. In the following we review the most relevant techniques to our work. For more details, we refer the reader to the recent surveys of the topic [18,29,13].

### 2.1 3D Shape Description

For efficient comparison and similarity estimation, 3D models are represented with a set of meaningful descriptors that encode the salient geometric and topological characteristics of their shapes. The objects in the database are then ranked according to the distance of their descriptors to the descriptors of the query model. These descriptors are either *global* or *local* depending on wether they encode the entire shape or part of it.

Global descriptors describe an entire 3D shape with one single feature vector. In this category, the Light Fields (LFD) [7] are reported to be the most effective [28]. Funckhouser et al.[10] map a 3D shape to unit spheres and use spherical harmonics (SH) to analyze the shape function. Novotni et al. [20] uses 3D Zernike moments (ZD) as a natural extension of SH. Laga et al. [15] introduced flat octahedron parameterization and spherical wavelet descriptors to eliminate the singularities that appear in the two poles when using latitude-longitude parameterization. Therefore, they achieve a fully rotation invariant description of the 3D shapes. Recently, Reuter et al. [24] introduced the notion of shape DNA computed from the spectra of the Laplace-Beltrami operators. These descriptors are invariant under similarity transformations, and are very efficient in matching 2D and 3D manifold shapes. However, it is not clear how they can be extended to polygon soup models.

Global descriptors are very compact, easy to compute, and efficient for broad classification of 3D shapes. However, they are unable to achieve high performance in intra-class retrieval, since they cannot capture the variability of the shapes within the same class. Local feature-based methods can overcome these limitations by computing a large set of features at different scales and locations on the 3D model. Spin images [14], and shape contexts [19] have been used for shape retrieval as well as for the matching and registration of 3D scans. Local features are very efficient to discriminate objects within the same class. However, similarity estimation requires combinatorial comparison, making them not suitable for realtime applications such as retrieval.

### 2.2 Similarity Measures

Most of existing work on 3D retrieval use the Euclidean distance to compare shape descriptors. There are few works that experimented with other distance measures. Algorithms that are based on statistical descriptors, such as shape distributions [23], used other metrics such as the $\chi^2$ statistic, the Bhattacharyya distance and the Minkowski $L_N$ norm.

To handle the non-linearity of the feature space, Ohbuchi et al. [22,21] proposed a method to adapt distance measures to the database to be queried by using learning-based dimensionality reduction algorithms such as Principal Component Analysis (PCA), Kernel PCA, Locality Preserving Projections, Laplacian Eigenmaps, Locally Linear Embedding, and Isometric Feature Embedding (ISOMAP). They demonstrated that a distance computed with non-linear dimension reduction techniques is database-adaptive and improves the retrieval performance. Ohbuchi et al. [25] experimentally picked the best performing distance measure among four: the $L_1-$norm, $L_2-$norm, cosine, and Kullbuck-Leibler Divergence (KLD). As reported by the authors, the selection of the best distance measure is performed manually via a preliminary set of retrieval experiments. In this paper we propose an automatic selection method which can be plugged to any type of shape descriptors. Also, as we will demonstrate it in Section 3, the optimal distance function depends heavily on the type of features used for comparison. Therefore, an automatic similarity selection method is required.

In the field of relevance feedback existing work are restricted to learning Mahalanobis distance of the form $(x-y)^T\Sigma(x-y)$ [6,17], where they try to estimate the weight matrix $\Sigma$, which can be seen as the covariance matrix of the traditional anisotropic Gaussian distribution. Leifman et al. [16] use Linear Discriminant Analysis (LDA) to find an optimal linear transformation that re-weights the shape features so that the maximum separation between the relevant and irrelevant models to the query is achieved. Relevance feedback algorithms aim to capture the human notion of similarity between 3D models. They are usually used in an online learning scheme. The approach we propose performs in a supervised manner. Therefore, it is suitable for capturing the domain-specific notion of similarity which is usually determined by the type of data to search.

Similarity learning is a popular subject in the field of machine learning with several applications to image retrieval [11,31]. Our paper extends existing methods for learning similarity measures to the problem of content-based 3D model retrieval. To the best of our knowledge this is the first paper that aims at automatic learning of the similarity function in 3D model classification and retrieval.

### 2.3 Overview and Contributions

In the first part of this paper we follow an experimental approach in which we evaluate the performance of four types of 3D shape descriptors using twelve similarity measures. We show that the performance of each descriptor varies significantly by varying the type of similarity measure. Then in the second part we propose an algorithm based on AdaBoost for an automatic selection of the best similarity measure for a given descriptor. We use a supervised approach where the classifier is learned using a training set of 3D models. In our implementation we use the training set of the Princeton Shape Benchmark (PSB) [28].

This paper extends existing work on learning similarity measures to boost the efficiency of content-based 3D model retrieval algorithms. We make the following contributions:

- We demonstrate experimentally that for many existing descriptors, the Euclidean distance is not the optimal similarity function for 3D model classification and retrieval.
- We provide a mean for automatic selection of the optimal similarity measure that achieves the best performance. The method is flexible in the sense that many similarity measures can be plugged in and it can operate with heterogeneous features.
- Our experimental results show significant improvement in the retrieval performance over the state of the art 3D model retrieval algorithms.

## 3 Similarity Measure Analysis

### 3.1 Feature-Based 3D Shape Description

The basic idea of feature-based approach to 3D model retrieval is to represent each object in the database and the query with a vector of numerical values. The feature vector can be derived from the object geometry or other properties such as topology. Good feature vectors should be robust against small changes of the shape due to noise or level of detail, and invariant to similarity transformations such as translation, scale and rotation. In this paper we consider four geometry-based descriptors, but it can be easily extended to other types of feature vectors;

- **Spherical wavelet transform of the Spherical Extent function [28,15]:** The 3D shape is mapped onto a unit sphere by measuring its extent in the radial direction. In this method, the spherical function is uniformly sampled using flat-octahedron parameterization, then represented by its spherical wavelet coefficients. We refer to this descriptor by SW_EXT.
- **Spherical wavelet coefficients of the Gaussian Euclidean Distance Transform [28,15]:** A 3D function whose value at each point is the composition of a Gaussian with the Euclidean Distance transform of the shape. It is generated using 32 spherical function. Each spherical function is represented by its SW_EXT descriptor. We refer to this descriptor by SW_GEDT.
- **Statistical moments of the spherical wavelet coefficients:** It is a rotation invariant descriptor of the SW_EXT. It is obtained by taking the first and second order statistical moments of the wavelet coefficients. In our implementation, we obtain shape descriptors of size 38. We refer to this descriptor by SW_MOMENTS.
- **The Light Fields [7]:** It is a view-based descriptor computed from 100 images rendered from cameras positioned on the vertices of a regular dodecahedron. Each image is encoded with 35 Zernike moments, and 10 Fourier coefficients. In this paper we use our own implementation. We refer to this descriptor by LFD.

In the following we refer by $d$ to the dimension of the feature space. That is, every feature vector is a point in the feature space $\mathbb{R}^d$.

### 3.2 Similarity Measures

Given the feature vectors for all objects in a database and for the query, the retrieval of similar objects to the query is performed by returning the $k$-nearest neighbors ($k-$NN) of the query model. To this end, a metric in the vector space $\mathbb{R}^d$ is used. Given two shapes $\mathcal{O}_1$ and $\mathcal{O}_2$ represented respectively by their feature vectors $x = (x_1, \ldots, x_d)^T$ and $y = (y_1, \ldots, y_d)^T$, we want to define a function $\Phi$ that measures the distance (or similarity) between $x$ and $y$. The function $\Phi$ is maps each pair of points in the product space $\mathbb{R}^d \times \mathbb{R}^d$ to a point in $\mathbb{R}$:

$$\begin{aligned} \Phi : \mathbb{R}^d \times \mathbb{R}^d &\mapsto \mathbb{R} \\ (x, y) &\rightarrow \Phi(x, y) \end{aligned}$$

Efficient similarity function should capture the semantic concepts of the data. It should take small values when the two shapes $\mathcal{O}_1$ and $\mathcal{O}_2$ are semantically very similar and large values when they are different.

For simplicity and computational considerations, existing works on 3D model classification and retrieval often considered the unweighted Minkowski $l_p$ distance (when $p = 2$ the Minkowski distance is reduced to the Euclidean distance). We propose to evaluate how other similarity measures affect the retrieval performance. We base our evaluation on the twelve MPEG-7 quantitative distance measures [8], labeled as $Q_1, \ldots, Q_{12}$, and summarized in Table 1. The distances $Q_1$ and $Q_2$ are the popular Manhattan and Euclidean distances. For the other metrics we define the following quantities:

**Table 1.** The twelve distance measures proposed for the evaluation of 3D model retrieval algorithms

| Label | Type | Name | Measure |
|---|---|---|---|
| $Q_1$ | Distance | City block distance | $\sum_{i=1}^{d} \lvert x_i - y_i \rvert$ |
| $Q_2$ | Distance | Euclidean distance | $\sum_{i=1}^{d} (x_i - y_i)^2$ |
| $Q_3$ | Distance | Canberra metric | $\frac{1}{d} \sum_{i=1}^{d} \frac{\lvert x_i - y_i \rvert}{\lvert x_i \rvert + \lvert y_i \rvert}$ |
| $Q_4$ | Distance | Divergence coefficient | $\frac{1}{d} \sum_{i=1}^{d} \frac{(x_i - y_i)^2}{\lvert x_i \rvert + \lvert y_i \rvert}$ |
| $Q_5$ | Similarity | Correlation coefficient | $\frac{\sum_{i=1}^{d}(x_i - \mu_x)(y_i - \mu_y)}{\sqrt{\sum_{i=1}^{d}(x_i - \mu_x)^2 \sum_{i=1}^{d}(y_i - \mu_y)^2}}$ |
| $Q_6$ | Similarity | Profile similarity coefficient | $\frac{\sum_{i=1}^{d} x_i y_i + dm^2 - m(\sum_{i=1}^{d} x_i + \sum_{i=1}^{d} y_i)}{\sqrt{(\sum_{i=1}^{d} x_i^2 + dm^2 - 2m \sum_{i=1}^{d} x_i)(\sum_{i=1}^{d} y_i^2 + dm^2 - 2m \sum_{i=1}^{d} y_i)}}$ |
| $Q_7$ | Similarity | Intra-class coefficient | $\frac{1}{d} \sum_{i=1}^{d} \frac{(x_i - \mu)(y_i - \mu)}{\sigma}$ |
| $Q_8$ | Similarity | Catell 1949 | $\frac{\sqrt{2d - \lvert\lvert x - y \rvert\rvert}}{\sqrt{2d + \lvert\lvert x - y \rvert\rvert}}$ |
| $Q_9$ | Similarity | Angular distance | $\frac{\sum_{i=1}^{d} x_i y_i}{\sum_{i=1}^{d} x_i^2 \sum_{i=1}^{d} y_i^2}$ |
| $Q_{10}$ | Distance | Meehl index | $\sum_{i=1}^{d-1} (\lvert x_i - x_{i+1} \rvert - \lvert y_i - y_{i+1} \rvert)$ |
| $Q_{11}$ | Distance | Kappa | $\sum_{i=1}^{d} \frac{y_i - x_i}{\ln(y_i) - \ln(x_i)}$ |
| $Q_{12}$ | Similarity | Inter-correlation coefficient | $\frac{\sum_{i=1}^{d}(x_i - \mu_y)(y_i - \mu_x)}{\sqrt{\sum_{i=1}^{d}(x_i - \mu_y)^2 \sum_{i=1}^{d}(y_i - \mu_x)^2}}$ |

$$\mu_x = \frac{1}{d}\sum_{i=1}^{d} x_i,\ \sigma_x^2 = \frac{1}{d-1}\sum_{i=1}^{d}(x_i - \mu_x)^2$$

$$\mu = \tfrac{(\mu_x+\mu_y)}{2},\ \sigma^2 = \frac{1}{2d-1}\{\sum_{i=1}^{d}(x_i-\mu)^2 + \sum_{i=1}^{d}(y_i-\mu)^2\}$$

$$M = \frac{x_{max} - x_{min}}{2}, \qquad m = \frac{M}{2}.$$

### 3.3 Retrieval Effectiveness of the Similarity Measures

The database we use for the experiments is the Princeton Shape Benchmark (PSB) [27]. It contains 1814 models and divided into a training set (907 models), referred hereafter as *train set*, and a test set (907 models). The benchmark provides also four classification levels of the data. We use the base classification level which is the finest one. We propose to evaluate the performance of the four descriptors described in Section 3.1 when using the similarity measures of Table 1. We assume that a retrieval is correct if the retrieved model belongs to the same class of shapes as the query. We use the following quantitative performance measures commonly used in information classification and retrieval [28]:

- **Precision-Recall graph:** A plot describing the relationship between precision and recall in a ranked list of matches. For each query model in class $C$ and any number $K$ of top matches, *recall* (the horizontal axis) represents the ratio of models in class $C$ returned within the top $K$ matches, while *precision* (the vertical axis) indicates the ratio of the top $K$ matches that are members of class $C$. A perfect retrieval result produces a horizontal line at precision = 1.
- **Nearest Neighbor (NN):** The percentage of the closest matches that belong to the same class as the query. This statistic provides an indication of how well a nearest neighbor classifier would perform.
- **First and Second Tier (1st-Tier, 2nd-Tier):** The percentage of models in the query's class that appear within the top $K$ matches. Given a class $C$ with $|C|$ members, $K = |C| - 1$ for the first tier, and $K = 2 \times |C| - 1$ for the second tier. These statistics indicate the recall for the smallest $K$ that could possibly include 100% of the models in the query class. An ideal matching result gives a score of 100%, and higher values indicate better matches.
- **E-measure (E-):** The intuition is that a user of a search engine is more interested in the first page of query results than in later pages. This measure considers only the first 32 retrieved models for every query and calculates the precision and recall over those results [28].
- **Discount Cumulative Gain (DCG):** A statistic that weights correct results near the front of the list more than correct results later in the ranked list under the assumption that a user is less likely to consider elements near the end of the list.

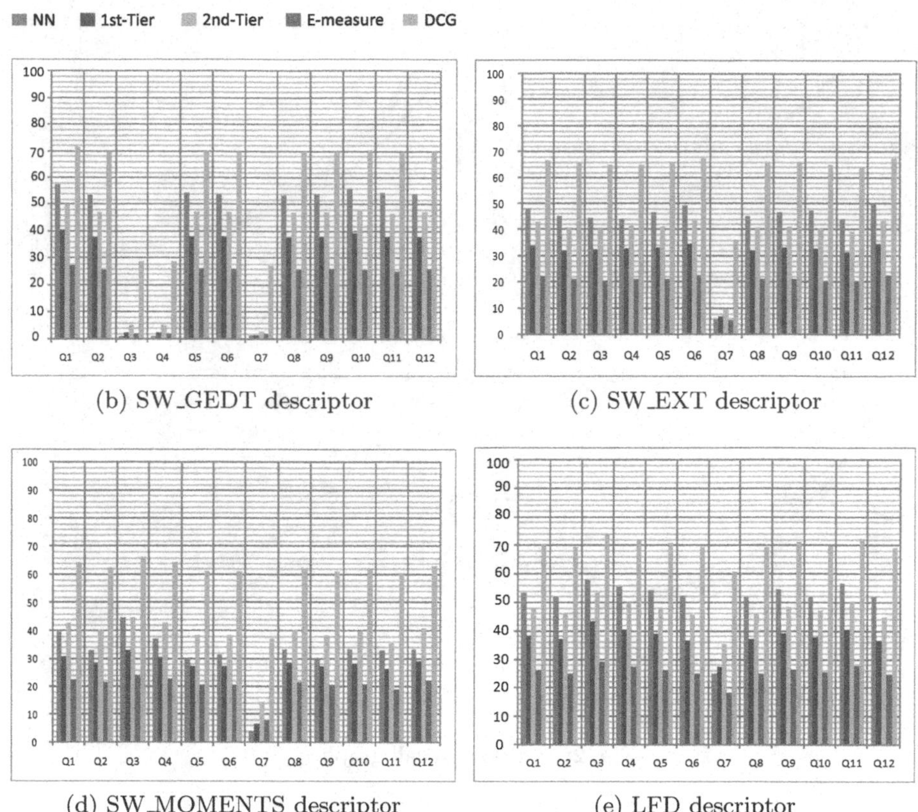


(b) SW_GEDT descriptor

(c) SW_EXT descriptor

(d) SW_MOMENTS descriptor

(e) LFD descriptor

**Fig. 1.** Performance of the four shape descriptors on different similarity measures

In the case of the LFD descriptor, for example, Figure 1e shows that the Canberra metric ($Q_3$) and the Kappa distance ($Q_{11}$) achieved the best performance on the quantitative evaluation metrics as well as on the precision-recall graph (Figure 2d). These two similarity measures overcome the Euclidean distance ($Q2$) with more than 5% on the Nearest Neighbor performance metric. We can see also that this difference exceeds 10% in the case of the SW_MOMENTS descriptor and Canberra metric.

This experimental evaluation reveals important facts; first the Euclidean distance is not the best for the descriptors we have experimented. Second, retrieval performance of a shape descriptor depends significantly on the choice of the similarity function. In fact, by choosing the adequate similarity function, the retrieval performance can be boosted significantly as shown in Figure 1. Manual selection of the efficient distance measure is usually not practical since the proximity relation between models is related to the semantics of the data. We propose in the next section a simple algorithm, based on recent results in machine learning, for automatic selection of the optimal similarity measure.

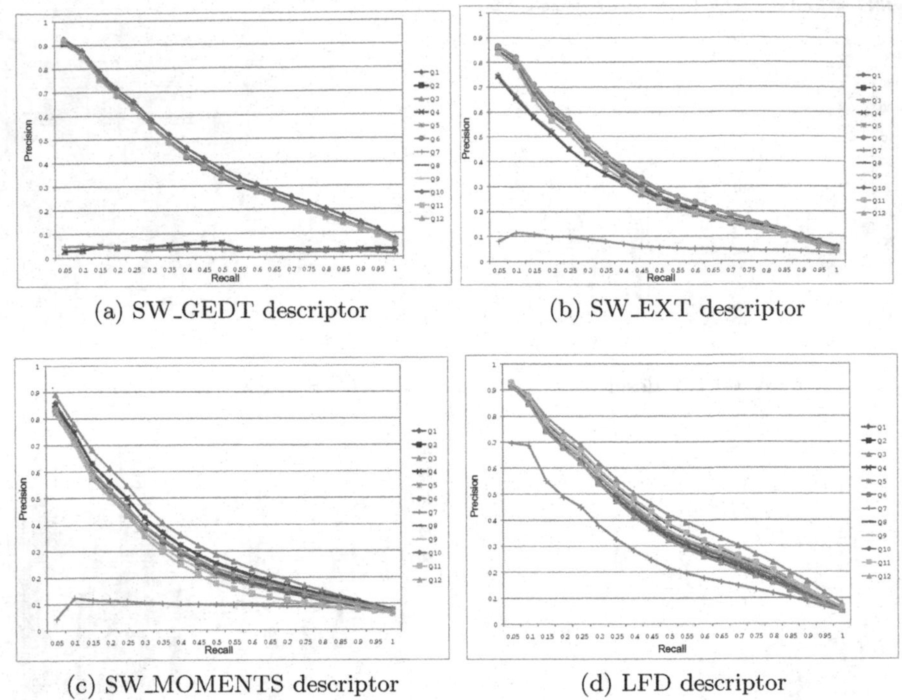


(a) SW_GEDT descriptor

(b) SW_EXT descriptor

(c) SW_MOMENTS descriptor

(d) LFD descriptor

**Fig. 2.** Precision-recall graphes

# 4 Learning Optimal Similarity Measure

## 4.1 The Product Space

In the product space, a pair of points in the original space, i.e a pair of two feature vectors $x$ and $y$, is converted into a single point. There are many ways of generating this mapping. In our case, since we are interested in learning the distance measure, we use the set of distance functions listed in Table 1. Given a pair of feature vectors $(x, y)$, their corresponding point in the product space is given by $Q_i(x, y)$. When working with $K$ similarity functions (in our case $K = 12$), each pair $(x, y)$ will be represented with a vector $\mathbf{q} = \{Q_1(x, y), \ldots, Q_K(x, y)\}$. In the following we call $\mathbf{q}$ *the similarity vector.* Also we refer to the $j-$th pair of the product space by $(x, y)_j$, which is then represented by a similarity vector $\mathbf{q}_j = \{Q_1(x, y)_j, \ldots, Q_K(x, y)_j\}$.

Working in the product space has many advantages over the original feature space; (1) it adds effectiveness and robustness in the case of small training sets [31]. In fact, 3D models are provided without any labels or pre-defined classification. Manual classification for constructing large training sets is not practical.

Therefore, it is suitable to use algorithms that rely only on small training sets. (2) It converts a multi-class classification problem into a binary classification problem that aims to classify a pair of points $(x, y)$ into a positive class if they are similar, and into a negative class otherwise. Binary classification is a well studied problem in machine learning and many powerful algorithms exist such as Support Vector Machines (SVM) and boosting.

### 4.2 Boosting

Now we would like to build a classifier $\mathcal{H}$ on the product space that classifies a given similarity vector $\mathbf{q}$ into the positive class $(+1)$ if the two models are very similar, and to the negative class $(-1)$ if the two models are dissimilar. There have been a lot of research in binary classifiers that have a good generalization performance by maximizing the margin. The major advantage of boosting over other classification algorithms such as Support Vector Machines (SVM) [12], and non-linear dimensionality reduction techniques [22,21] is its speediness. Moreover, it provides a good theoretical and practical quantification of the upper bound of the error rate, therefore a good generalization performance. Furthermore, it can be used as a feature selection algorithm.

We use AdaBoost version of boosting. Our training set is composed of the similarity vectors $\mathbf{q}_j, j = 1 \dots N \times N$ ($N$ is the number of objects in the database), and the desired classification, called target values, $t_j \in \{+1, -1\}$. $t_j = +1$ if $\mathbf{q}_j$ is a positive example, and $-1$ otherwise. We refer to the positive class by $C$, and the negative class by $\overline{C}$. Every weak classifier is based on a single similarity function. The final strong classifier, a weighted sum of weak classifiers, is based on the most discriminant similarity functions weighted by their discriminant power. The training algorithm is summarized in Algorithm 1.

AdaBoost learns a strong hypothesis $\mathcal{H}$ which is a linear combination of weak hypothesis each one defined on a certain elementary similarity function (see Table 1). $\mathcal{H}$ is defined on $\mathbb{R}^K$ and takes values in $[-1, 1]$. It can be interpreted as the new similarity measure adapted to the semantic structure of the training data. Another option is to use the posterior probability defined:

$$P(C|\mathbf{q}) = \frac{e^{\mathcal{H}(\mathbf{q})}}{e^{\mathcal{H}(\mathbf{q})} + e^{-\mathcal{H}(\mathbf{q})}} \tag{1}$$

as a similarity function which takes values in $[0, 1]$. In our experiments we use the hypothesis $\mathcal{H}$ as a similarity function for retrieval.

AdaBoost requires only two parameters to tune: (1) the type of weak classifier and (2) the maximum number of weak classifiers. For AdaBoost to converge, the classification performance of the weak classifier has to be better than random. We used the Decision Stumps because of its simplicity and its guarantee to achieve slightly better than random. Other options can be the LMS or a mixture of Gaussians. The parameter $T$ can be set such that the upper bound of the classification error on the training data of the strong classifier $\mathcal{H}$ is less than

**Algorithm 1.** AdaBoost algorithm for binary classification

**Input:**
- Training set $S = \{(\mathbf{q}_i, t_i), i = 1, \ldots, M\}, M = N \times N$.

**Output:**

- The decision function $\mathcal{H}$, such that, $\mathcal{H}(\mathbf{q}) > 0$ if the similarity vector $\mathbf{q}$ is of two similar objects, otherwise $\mathcal{H}(\mathbf{q}) <= 0$. The objects are very similar if $\mathcal{H}(\mathbf{q})$ is very close to 1.

1. Initialize the sample weights: $w_{0,i}, i = 1, \ldots, M$:

$$w_i = \begin{cases} \frac{1}{M^+}, \text{if } \mathbf{q}_i \text{ is a positive example } (t_i = +1) \\ \frac{1}{M^-}, \text{otherwise } (t_i = -1). \end{cases} \quad (2)$$

   where $M^+$ and $M^-$ are, the number of positive and negative examples.
1. **for** $t$=*1, ..., T* **do**
   (a) Train one weak classifier $h_k, k = 1 \ldots K$ for each distance measure $Q_k$,
   (b) Choose the hypothesis $h_t$ with the lowest classification error $\epsilon_t$. $h_t$ operates on one distance measure. We refer to it by $Q_t$.
   (c) Update the sample weights: $w_{t+1,i} = \frac{1}{Z_t} w_{t,i} e^{-\alpha_t h_t(\mathbf{q}_i)\cdot t_i}$
   where $h_t(\mathbf{q}_i) = +1, -1$ wether $\mathbf{q}_i$ is correctly or incorrectly classified by the weak hypothesis $h_t$, and $\alpha_t = 0.5 \log\left(\frac{1-\epsilon_t}{\epsilon_t}\right)$,
   and $Z_t$ is a normalizing constant so that $w_{t+1}$ is a distribution.

   **end**
2. Final classifier: $\mathcal{H}(\mathbf{q}) = \frac{1}{\sum_{t=1}^{T} \alpha_t} \sum_{t=1}^{T} \alpha_t h_t(\mathbf{q})$

a threshold $\theta$. In our experiments we found that a value of $T$ between 20 and 50 is sufficient to achieve an upper bound of the classification error on the training set less than 1.0%.

### 4.3 Query Processing

Given a query model $O$, we seek to find the models in the database that are most similar to the query. First a set of features are extracted from the query model to compute its descriptor. Then using the query descriptor, we compute one distance vector $\mathbf{q}_i$ between $O$ and every model $O_i$ in the database. Each of the $K$ components of $\mathbf{q}_i$ is computed with one of the $K$ distance measures of Table 1. Then we use the strong hypothesis $\mathcal{H}$ to estimate the final similarities, i.e, wether $O_i$ is similar to $O$ or not. The models are then ranked in a descending order of their response to $\mathcal{H}$.

Processing a query $Q$ requires the computation of a distance vector $\mathbf{q}_i$ for every model in the database. Therefore, this boosted similarity function generates a computation overhead compared to when using a single distance function.

## 5 Results

To evaluate the performance of the proposed 3D model retrieval approach we use the training and test sets of the Princeton Shape Benchmark (PSB) [27], and the query set and performance evaluation tools of the Shape Retrieval Evaluation Contest (SHREC2006) [30]. The PSB contains 1814 polygon soup models, divided into a training set (907 models) and a test set (907 models). Each set contains four classification levels; the base train classification contains 129 classes while the coarsest classification (coarse3) contains two classes: man-made and natural objects. We use the entire base classification (train+test) to train our classifiers, then we use the the Shape Retrieval Evaluation Contest (SHREC2006) query set to assess the performance. It is important to outline that none of the query models used in SHREC2006 is present in the database. Therefore, it has not been used in the training stage. This is important to assess the ability of the algorithm to generalize to unseen models. It is important also to outline that the training stage is slow since we are using a very large set of features. However only a reduced subset of the features and similarity measures are used during the similarity estimation allowing real-time retrieval.

Figure 3 shows the query model (in the first column) and the top ten retrieval results for each query. Visually we can see that the algorithm achieves satisfactory retrieval performance.

To evaluate quantitatively the retrieval performance, we compare the performance of the boosted similarity with the performance of the 12 basic similarity measures listed in Table 1. For this purpose we use our own implementation of the LightFields descriptor (LFD) and the SHREC2006 performance measures [30]. In SHREC2006, each query has a set of *highly relevant* classes, *relevant classes*, and *not relevant classes*. Table 2 summarizes the performance of each similarity measure on the Mean Average Precision, Mean First Tier and Second Tier, and Mean Dynamic Average Recall metrics for both highly relevant and relevant classes. The boosted similarity measure is indicated by *Boost*. We can see that the boosted distance measure achieves almost like the Canberra metric ($Q_3$) on all performance measures, and it overcomes the other similarity measures. This demonstrates clearly that the proposed algorithm is able to estimate automatically the suitable distance measure.

It is important to outline, however, that in all our experiments the boosted similarity measure had never outperformed the best basic similarity measure (Canberra metric in the case of the LFD) but converges towards the best one. This result was not expected, but it shows that combining the twelve distance measures listed in Table 1 does not improve performance of the best similarity measure, but it finds automatically this best measure. We would like however to investigate in he future wether this result generalizes to other similarity metrics.

**Fig. 3.** Retrieval results using SHREC2006 queries. The first column shows the query models. Each row shows the first ten best matches to the query, which are retrieved from the Princeton Shape Benchmark database (1814 models).

**Table 2.** Performance of different similarity measures before and after boosting using the LFD descriptor. The boosted similarity measure is indicated by Boost.

| Highly relevant | | | Relevant | | |
|---|---|---|---|---|---|
| | Similarity | Value | | Similarity | Value |
| 1 | Q3 | 0.3518 | 1 | Q3 | 0.3079 |
| 2 | Boost | 0.3426 | 2 | Boost | 0.2937 |
| 3 | Q11 | 0.3223 | 3 | Q11 | 0.2734 |
| 4 | Q4 | 0.3205 | 4 | Q4 | 0.2699 |
| 5 | Q9 | 0.3063 | 5 | Q9 | 0.2467 |
| 6 | Q5 | 0.3008 | 6 | Q5 | 0.2451 |
| 7 | Q1 | 0.2971 | 7 | Q1 | 0.2450 |
| 8 | Q10 | 0.2920 | 8 | Q10 | 0.2371 |
| 9 | Q2 | 0.2803 | 9 | Q2 | 0.2252 |
| 10 | Q8 | 0.2803 | 10 | Q8 | 0.2252 |
| 11 | Q6 | 0.2776 | 11 | Q6 | 0.2233 |
| 12 | Q12 | 0.2723 | 12 | Q12 | 0.2194 |
| 13 | Q7 | 0.1595 | 13 | Q7 | 0.1732 |

(a) Mean Average Precision

| Highly relevant | | | Relevant | | |
|---|---|---|---|---|---|
| | Similarity | Value | | Similarity | Value |
| 1 | Q3 | 32.19% | 1 | Boost | 28.22% |
| 2 | Boost | 31.01% | 2 | Q3 | 27.99% |
| 3 | Q11 | 30.09% | 3 | Q11 | 25.93% |
| 4 | Q4 | 29.45% | 4 | Q4 | 25.80% |
| 5 | Q9 | 27.95% | 5 | Q9 | 24.34% |
| 6 | Q5 | 27.42% | 6 | Q5 | 23.43% |
| 7 | Q10 | 27.01% | 7 | Q10 | 22.46% |
| 8 | Q1 | 26.13% | 8 | Q1 | 22.42% |
| 9 | Q6 | 24.70% | 9 | Q2 | 21.63% |
| 10 | Q2 | 24.51% | 9 | Q8 | 21.63% |
| 10 | Q8 | 24.51% | 11 | Q12 | 21.19% |
| 12 | Q12 | 24.28% | 12 | Q6 | 20.85% |
| 13 | Q7 | 16.72% | 13 | Q7 | 18.40% |

(b) Mean First Tier

| Highly relevant | | | Relevant | | |
|---|---|---|---|---|---|
| Rank | Similarity | Value | Rank | Similarity | Value |
| 1 | Boost | 19.91% | 1 | Q3 | 19.21% |
| 2 | Q3 | 19.79% | 2 | Boost | 18.85% |
| 3 | Q9 | 18.37% | 3 | Q11 | 16.96% |
| 4 | Q4 | 18.25% | 4 | Q9 | 16.65% |
| 5 | Q11 | 18.02% | 5 | Q5 | 16.62% |
| 6 | Q5 | 17.46% | 6 | Q4 | 16.55% |
| 7 | Q1 | 17.11% | 7 | Q10 | 15.80% |
| 8 | Q10 | 16.34% | 8 | Q1 | 15.54% |
| 9 | Q6 | 15.83% | 9 | Q7 | 14.91% |
| 10 | Q2 | 15.80% | 10 | Q12 | 14.47% |
| 10 | Q8 | 15.80% | 11 | Q6 | 14.42% |
| 12 | Q12 | 15.39% | 12 | Q2 | 14.32% |
| 13 | Q7 | 12.82% | 12 | Q8 | 14.32% |

(c) Mean Second Tier

| Rank | Similarity | Value |
|---|---|---|
| 1 | Q3 | 0.4058 |
| 2 | Boost | 0.3911 |
| 3 | Q11 | 0.3748 |
| 4 | Q4 | 0.3715 |
| 5 | Q9 | 0.3398 |
| 6 | Q1 | 0.3361 |
| 7 | Q5 | 0.3325 |
| 8 | Q10 | 0.3305 |
| 9 | Q2 | 0.3198 |
| 9 | Q8 | 0.3198 |
| 11 | Q6 | 0.3140 |
| 12 | Q12 | 0.31349 |
| 13 | Q7 | 0.2287 |

(d) Mean Dynamic Average Recall

## 6 Conclusion

In this paper we investigated for the first time how the choice of the similarity measure affects the retrieval performance of many 3D shape descriptors. We demonstrated that the commonly used Euclidean distance is not always the optimal choice. Then we made use of the recent results in machine learning and proposed a simple and efficient algorithm for learning in a supervised manner the best distance measure. We used AdaBoost on the product space which is proven to generalize well on unseen data.

In this paper we tested only four types of shape descriptors. It is interesting however to see how other descriptors are affected by various similarity measures. Finally, in this paper we proposed a method for selecting and combining similarity measures. We would like to extend it into a framework where we can combine also heterogenous features. We believe that with effective feature selection and combination the performance of the 3D retrieval algorithm will be improved significantly.

## Acknowledgment

This research is supported by the Japanese Ministry of Education, Culture, Sports, Science and Technology (MEXT) program *Promotion of Environmental Improvement for Independence of Young Researchers* under the Special Coordination Funds for Promoting Science and Technology.

## References

1. 3D Model Retrieval System. Taiwan University, `http://3D.csie.ntu.edu.tw/~dynamic/`
2. 3D Model Search Engine. Princeton University, `http://shape.cs.princeton.edu/`
3. 3D Model Similarity Search Engine. `http://merkur01.inf.uni-konstanz.de/CCCC/`
4. 3D Shape Retreival Engine. `http://www.cs.uu.nl/centers/give/imaging/3DRecog/3Dmatching.html`
5. Ogden IV systems. Japan, `http://www.nime.ac.jp/~motofumi/Ogden/`
6. Atmosukarto, I., Leow, W.K., Huang, Z.: Feature combination and relevance feedback for 3D model retrieval. In: MMM 2005, pp. 334–339 (2005)
7. Chen, D.-Y., et al.: On visual similarity based 3D model retrieval. Computer Graphics Forum 22(3), 223–232 (2003)
8. Eidenberger, H.: Distance measures for mpeg-7-based retrieval. In: Multimedia Information Retrieval, pp. 130–137 (2003)
9. Funkhouser, T., et al.: Shape-based retrieval and analysis of 3d models. Commun. ACM 48(6), 58–64 (2005)
10. Funkhouser, T.A., et al.: A search engine for 3D models. ACM Transactions on Graphics 22(1), 83–105 (2003)
11. Hertz, T., Bar-Hillel, A., Weinshall, D.: Learning distance functions for image retrieval. CVPR 02, 570–577 (2004)
12. Hou, S., Lou, K., Ramani, K.: Svm-based semantic clustering and retrieval of a 3D model database. Journal of Computer Aided Design and Application 2, 155–164 (2005)
13. Iyer, N., et al.: Three-dimensional shape searching: state-of-the-art review and future trends. Computer-Aided Design 37(5), 509–530 (2005)
14. Johnson, A.: Spin-Images: A Representation for 3-D Surface Matching. PhD thesis, Robotics Institute, Carnegie Mellon University, Pittsburgh, PA (August 1997)

15. Laga, H., Takahashi, H., Nakajima, M.: Spherical wavelet descriptors for content-based 3D model retrieval. In: SMI 2006: Proceedings of the IEEE International Conference on Shape Modeling and Applications 2006 (SMI 2006), Washington, DC, USA, pp. 75–85. IEEE Computer Society Press, Los Alamitos (2006)
16. Leifman, G., Meir, R., Tal, A.: Semantic-oriented 3D shape retrieval using relevance feedback
17. Leifman, G., Meir, R., Tal, A.: Relevance feedback for 3D shape retrieval. In: The 5th Israel-Korea Bi-National Conference on Geometric Modeling and Computer Graphics, pp. 15–19 (2004)
18. Lew, M.S., et al.: Content-based multimedia information retrieval: State of the art and challenges. ACM Trans. Multimedia Comput. Commun. Appl. 2(1), 1–19 (2006)
19. Kortgen, M., et al.: 3D shape matching with 3D shape contexts. In: The 7th Central European Seminar on Computer Graphics (April 2003)
20. Novotni, M., Klein, R.: 3D Zernike descriptors for content based shape retrieval. In: SM 2003: Proceedings of the eighth ACM symposium on Solid modeling and applications, pp. 216–225. ACM Press, New York (2003)
21. Ohbuchi, R., Kobayashi, J.: Unsupervised learning from a corpus for shape-based 3D model retrieval. In: MIR 2006: Proceedings of the 8th ACM international workshop on Multimedia information retrieval, pp. 163–172. ACM Press, New York (2006)
22. Ohbuchi, R., et al.: Comparison of dimension reduction method for database-adaptive 3D model retrieval. In: Fifth International Workshop on Adaptive Multimedia Retrieval (AMR 2007) (2007)
23. Osada, R., et al.: Shape distributions. ACM Transactions on Graphics 21(4), 807–832 (2002)
24. Reuter, M., Wolter, F.-E., Peinecke, N.: Laplace-Beltrami spectra as "shape-DNA" of surfaces and solids. Computer-Aided Design 38(4), 342–366 (2006)
25. Ryutarou Ohbuchi, A.Y., Kobayashi, J.: Learning semantic categories for 3D model retrieval. In: MIR 2007: Proceedings of the 9th ACM international workshop on Multimedia information retrieval, pp. 31–40. ACM Press, New York (2007)
26. Schapire, R.E.: The boosting approach to machine learning: An overview. Springer, Heidelberg (2003)
27. Shilane, P., Funkhouser, T.: Selecting Distinctive 3D Shape Descriptors for Similarity Retrieval. In: IEEE International Conference on Shape Modeling and Applications (SMI 2006), p. 18 (2006)
28. Shilane, P., et al.: The princeton shape benchmark. In: SMI 2004: Proceedings of the Shape Modeling International 2004 (SMI 2004), June 2004, pp. 167–178. IEEE Computer Society Press, Los Alamitos (2004)
29. Tangelder, J.W.H., Veltkamp, R.C.: A survey of content based 3D shape retrieval. In: Shape Modeling International 2004, Genova, Italy, June 2004, pp. 145–156 (2004)
30. Veltkamp, R.C., et al.: SHREC2006: 3D Shape Retrieval Contest. Technical Report UU-CS-2006-030, Department of Information and Computing Sciences, Utrecht University (June 2006)
31. Yu, J., et al.: Distance learning for similarity estimation. IEEE trans. on pattern analysis and machine learning (to appear, 2007)
32. Yu, J., et al.: Toward robust distance metric analysis for similarity estimation. CVPR 1, 316–322 (2006)

# Automatic Score Scene Detection for Baseball Video

Koichi Shinoda[1], Kazuki Ishihara[1], Sadaoki Furui[1], and Takahiro Mochizuki[2]

[1] Tokyo Institute of Technology,
2-12-1 Ookayama, Meguro-ku, Tokyo 152-8552, Japan
{shinoda,furui}@cs.titech.ac.jp, ishihara@ks.cs.titech.ac.jp
[2] NHK Science & Technical Research Laboratories,
1-10-11, Kinuta, Setagaya-ku, Tokyo 157-8510, Japan
mochizuki.t-fm@nhk.or.jp

**Abstract.** We propose a robust score scene detection method for baseball broadcast videos. This method is based on the data-driven approach which has been successful in statistical speech recognition. Audio and video feature streams are integrated by a multi-stream hidden Markov model to model each scene. The proposed method was evaluated in score scene detection experiments using video data of 25 baseball games. While the recall rate with video mode only was 82.8% and that with audio mode only was 86.6%, the proposed method achieved 90.4%. This method was proved to be significantly effective to reduce the cost for making highlight for baseball video content.

**Keywords:** CBVIR, multi-modal recognition, GMM, sports video, highlight, GMM.

## 1 Introduction

Recent advances in computer technology, particularly in storage technology, have resulted in significant increases in the number and quality of video databases. As it has become difficult for ordinary people to browse the entire content of each video database, database indexing is strongly required for searching and summarization. The construction of such indexes is mostly carried out by human experts who manually assign a limited number of keywords to the video content, and it is an expensive and time consuming task. Therefore, automatic indexing using pattern recognition techniques for video content, which is called *content-based video information retrieval* (CBVIR), has been studied extensively [1].

Recently, CBVIR for sports video has been widely studied. Targeted sports include baseball [2,3,4,5,6,7], soccer [8], tennis [9], basketball [10], and American football [11]. In this study, we apply CBVIR to baseball broadcast videos. In a video, the minimum unit is a *frame*, a static image. Multiple frames recorded by a single fixed camera form a *shot*. A sequence of these shots forms a *scene* (Fig. 1). A scene is a shot sequence between a pitching shot and the next pitching shot. The contexts or transitions between these shots provide useful information

T. Tokunaga and A. Ortega (Eds.): LKR 2008, LNAI 4938, pp. 226–240, 2008.

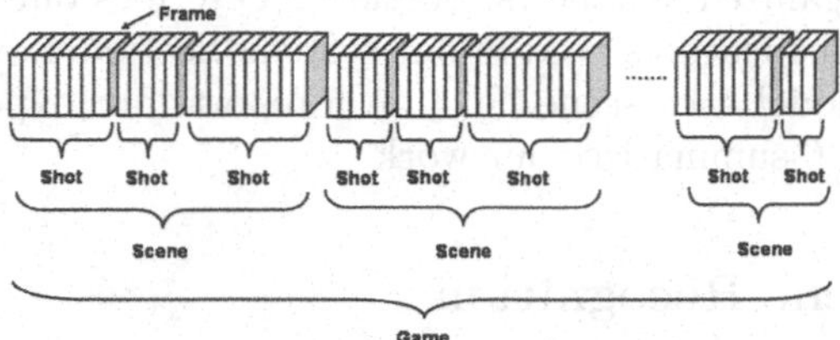


**Fig. 1.** Structure of baseball broadcast videos

**Fig. 2.** Examples of camera shots of a *home run* scene, a *walk* scene, and a *ground out* scene

for scene recognition (Fig. 2). For baseball scene recognition, Chang *et al.* [6] proposed a method based on a *hidden Markov model* (HMM). In their study, video data was first segmented into shots. Then, recognition was applied to the shot sequences based on HMMs in which each state represents a *shot type*. Li and Sezan [12] also proposed an HMM-based framework to distinguish *play* and *no-play* scenes. In these works, domain-specific knowledge about shot types and transitions between them were used intensively to improve the system's performance. However, the large variety of transitions among shots from game to game and the difficulty of classifying shot types are still problems for these approaches. Systems resulting from these studies may not be sufficiently robust to apply to real applications in general.

Some previous studies have addressed this robustness problem in CBVIR for baseball broadcast videos [2,3,4]. In Nguyen *et al.* [2], a multi-stream HMM was employed to model each scene using global features and dynamic features as input. In addition, an unsupervised adaptation was used method to improve recognition performance. In Ando *et al.* [3], a method using an *n-gram model* to represent scene contexts was proposed. In its succeeding paper [4], they reported that overall performance of their scene recognition system. In this paper, we propose a scene detection system specialized for detecting score scenes in baseball video. It uses not only video features but also audio features to represent the excitement of audiences and announcers. Since score scenes are highlight in baseball, our detection system is expected to efficiently support manual summarization task for baseball video in broadcasting companies.

This paper is organized as follows. Section 2 describes our system overview. Section 3 presents the features used in our system. Section 4 explains the multi-stream GMM to model each scene. Section 5 reports our experimental results, and finally, Section 6 summarizes our work.

## 2 Robust Scene Recognition

### 2.1 Framework

Inspired by the success of applying statistical frameworks in the speech recognition field, we propose the following *data-driven* approach to provide a robust scene recognition system [3,2]. In this approach, we regard a shot as being analogous to a *phone*, and a scene to a *word*. Based on this assumption we utilize the framework of *continuous speech recognition* in scene recognition. Given a sequence of observed feature vectors $\boldsymbol{O} = \boldsymbol{o}_1, \cdots, \boldsymbol{o}_M$, the probability of scene sequences $\boldsymbol{S} = s_1, \cdots, s_N$ is represented as

$$P(\boldsymbol{S} \mid \boldsymbol{O}) \propto P(\boldsymbol{O} \mid \boldsymbol{S})P(\boldsymbol{S}), \tag{1}$$

where $P(\boldsymbol{O} \mid \boldsymbol{S})$ is the probability of $\boldsymbol{O}$ being observed in scene sequence $\boldsymbol{S}$, and $P(\boldsymbol{S})$ indicates the probability of sequence $\boldsymbol{S}$. $P(\boldsymbol{O} \mid \boldsymbol{S})$ is computed by a *video model*, whereas $P(\boldsymbol{S})$ is computed by a *language model*. The sequence $\boldsymbol{S}$ that maximizes $P(\boldsymbol{S} \mid \boldsymbol{O})$ is the recognition result. Here, we employ a multi-stream HMM as the video model [2] and assume uniform distribution in language model $P(\boldsymbol{S})$.

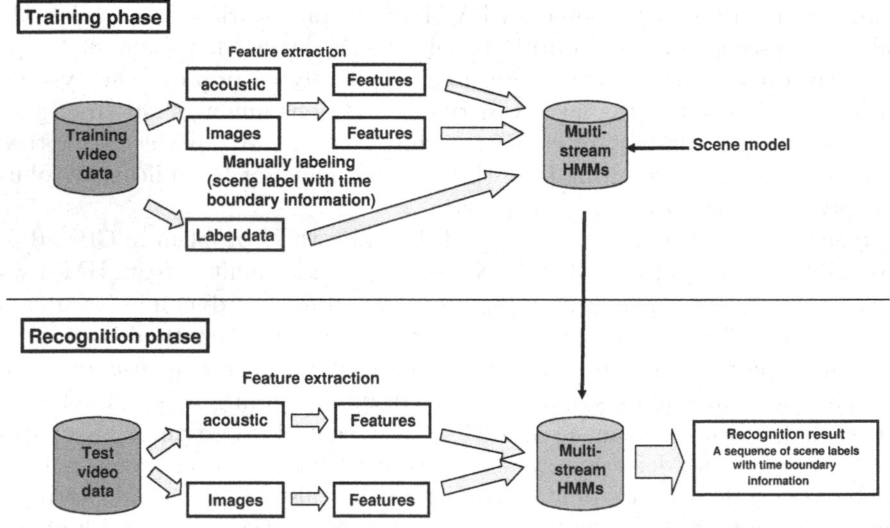


**Fig. 3.** System overview

### 2.2 System Overview

Our scene recognition system consists of two phases (Fig. 3):

1. In the training phase, frames are extracted from training video data, and a feature vector is calculated from each frame. One multi-stream HMM is prepared for each scene, and its parameters are estimated on the basis of a training set of feature vectors and on reference labels with boundary information that has been prepared manually.
2. In the recognition phase, we extract frames from test video data and calculate feature vectors in exactly the same way as in the training phase. Then, using the trained multi-stream HMMs, we conduct scene recognition. Given a feature vector sequence, the corresponding scene sequence is recognized. The scene sequence with time boundary information is the recognition result.

## 3 Features

To make our framework generally applicable, we used game-independent features. Here, mel-frequency cepstrum coefficients (MFCCs) is used for audio input and principal component features (PFs), dynamic principal component features (DPFs), and camera motion features (CFs) are used for video input.

### 3.1 Mel-Frequency Cepstrum Coefficients (MFCCs)

Mel-Frequency Cepstrum Coefficients (MFCCs) are often used in speech recognition as acoustic features. Some previous studies [13,14] reported that they were also effective in audio signal classification. In this study, we use MFCCs to represent cheers, music, and announcer voices.

It is well known that the human hearing function has non-linearity in frequency region. Such non-linearity is well represented by *Mel-transform*:

$$f' = 2595 \log_{10}\left(1 + \frac{f}{700}\right), \tag{2}$$

where $f$ and $f'$ are the frequency[Hz] before and after the mel-transform, respectively. In speech recognition, it is also known that the cepstrum coefficients

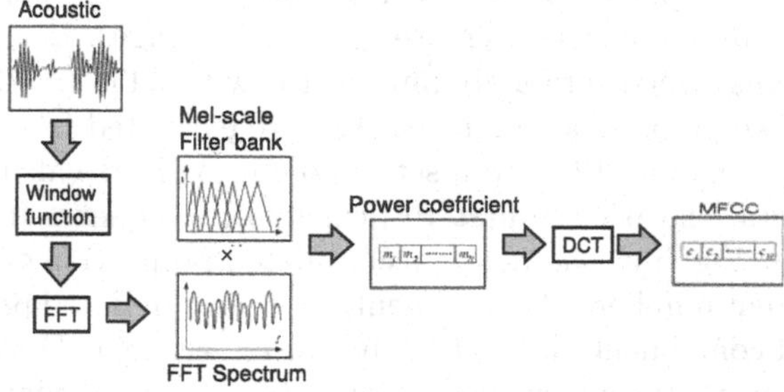


**Fig. 4.** Calculation of Mel-Frequency Cepstrum Coefficients (MFCCs)

calculated from *mel-scaled* spectrum has higher recognition performance than those calculated from raw spectrum. We therefore use *Mel-Frequency Cepstrum Coefficients* (MFCCs).

Fig. 4 shows the process extracting MFCCs from audio signal. First, samples for each frame are extracted by using Hamming window and transformed into frequency region by Fast Fourier Transform(FFT). Then, the frequency components obtained by FFT are filtered by Mel-scaled band-pass filter as shown in Eq. (2) to calculate the spectral power $m(l)$ for each spectral band $l$:

$$m(l) = \sum_{k=lo}^{hi} W(k,l)|X(k)| \qquad (l = 1, \ldots, L), \tag{3}$$

$$W(k,l) = \begin{cases} \frac{k - k_{lo}(l)}{k_c(l) - k_{lo}(l)} & k_{lo} \le k \le k_c(l) \\ \frac{k_{hi}(l) - k}{k_{hi}(l) - k_c(l)} & k_c \le k \le k_{hi}(l), \end{cases} \tag{4}$$

where $L$ is the number of filters in the filter bank, $k_{lo}(l)$, $k_c(l)$, $k_{hi}(l)$ are the filter IDs for the filter with the lowest frequency, for that with the center frequency, and for that with the highest frequency, respectively. Filters next to each other have the following relations.

$$k_c(l) = k_{hi}(l-1) = k_{lo}(l+1). \tag{5}$$

$k_c(l)$, $l = 1, \ldots L$ are located at equal spaces on the mel-frequency axis. Lastly, powers for $L$ filters obtained by the filter-bank analysis described above are transformed by discrete cosine transform to produce MFCCs:

$$c_{\mathsf{mfcc}}(i) = \sqrt{\frac{2}{N}} \sum_{l=1}^{L} \log m(l) \cos\left\{\frac{\pi i}{N}(j - 0.5)\right\}. \tag{6}$$

### 3.2 Principal Component Features (PFs)

By decreasing dimensions using *principal component analysis* (PCA), we expect to remove noise unrelated to scene characteristics and select only scene-relevant global features [15]. First, to reduce computational costs, the image is compressed from 720×480 pixels to one tenth of that size, 72×48 pixels. Luminance is extracted from RGB images to create gray-scale images. Each 2D gray-scale image is then transformed into a column vector with 3456 (= 72 × 48) dimensions. For PCA, we prepare 5000 images that are extracted from training video data at random. We apply PCA to a set of column vectors calculate on the basis of training data, and use the first 10 principal components (eigenvectors) to calculate features. Fig. 5(a) shows the accumulated proportion of principal components for different numbers of components. The accumulated proportion of the first 10 principal components was 49.4% in our experiment. For each frame, we calculate a column vector and project it onto the space spanned by the chosen eigenvectors to create a new 10-dimensional feature vector as PFs.

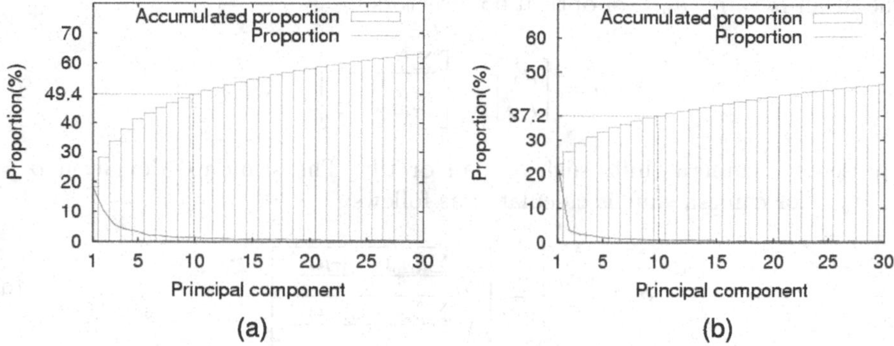


**Fig. 5.** Accumulated proportion rate of principal components in PFs(a) and in DPF(b)

### 3.3 Dynamic Principal Component Features (DPFs)

While PFs are expected to be sufficient for representing global information for still images, such representation for video images requires additional information for describing objects moving in a video stream. To represent dynamic features, we use PCA for difference images in the same way that PFs are calculate using the difference between two succeeding images instead of static images. Fig 5(b) shows the accumulated proportion of principal components for different numbers of components. We used the first 10 principal components, and the accumulated contribution was 37.2% in our experiment.

### 3.4 Camera Motion Features (CFs)

Camera motions in a baseball broadcast consist of three types of motion: *pan*, *tilt*, and *zoom*. Camera shots with the same scene label tend to have similar camera motions. During a pitching shot, for example, the camera usually does not move. In a shot in which a batter runs from home base to first base, the camera pans from left to right. When a batter hits a fly ball, the camera tilts upward. Camera motion information has been proven to be effective information for shot segmentation and categorization in sports video [16]. We expect that this feature will also be effective in our scene recognition. To represent camera motions, we use *optical flows* calculated using the *Lucas-Kanade* method [17]. First, successive two frame images are compressed from 720×480 pixels to one third of that size, 240×160 pixels. Next, luminance is extracted from each RGB image to create gray-scale images. We sample $N$ points; here $N = 77$, at $(20i,\ 20j)$ for $(i = 1 \cdots 11,\ j = 1 \cdots 7)$ on an image. Let $\boldsymbol{p}_n = [p_{x_n}\ p_{y_n}]^\top$ denote each sample point on the current frame for $n = 1, \cdots N$, and $\boldsymbol{p}'_n = [p'_{x_n}\ p'_{y_n}]^\top$ denote a corresponding point on the next frame. Optical flow vector $\boldsymbol{v}_n = [v_{x_n}\ v_{y_n}]^\top$ of sample point $n$ is given by

$$\boldsymbol{v}_n = \begin{bmatrix} v_{x_n} \\ v_{y_n} \end{bmatrix} = \begin{bmatrix} p'_{x_n} \\ p'_{y_n} \end{bmatrix} - \begin{bmatrix} p_{x_n} \\ p_{y_n} \end{bmatrix}. \tag{7}$$

The mean $\boldsymbol{\mu} = [\mu_x \; \mu_y]^\top$ of optical flow vectors,

$$\boldsymbol{\mu} = \begin{bmatrix} \mu_x \\ \mu_y \end{bmatrix} = \begin{bmatrix} \frac{\sum_{n=0}^{N} v_{x_n}}{N} \\ \frac{\sum_{n=0}^{N} v_{y_n}}{N} \end{bmatrix}, \tag{8}$$

represents a camera shift, such as pan or tilt. The standard deviation $\boldsymbol{\sigma} = [\sigma_x \; \sigma_y]^\top$ for camera shift is calculated as follows:

$$\boldsymbol{\sigma} = \begin{bmatrix} \sigma_x \\ \sigma_y \end{bmatrix} = \begin{bmatrix} \sqrt{\frac{\sum_{n=0}^{N}(v_{x_n} - \mu_x)^2}{N}} \\ \sqrt{\frac{\sum_{n=0}^{N}(v_{y_n} - \mu_y)^2}{N}} \end{bmatrix}. \tag{9}$$

Since, optical flow vectors tend to part in close-up scenes of players, we expect that the standard deviation represents such a feature. In addition, we use a ratio of inward (or outward) of optical flow vectors as a zoom ratio, $z$. Zoom ratio $z$ is given by

$$z = \frac{\sum_{n=1}^{N}(v_{x_n} - \mu_x)(p_{x_n} - x_c) + (v_{y_n} - \mu_y)(p_{y_n} - y_c)}{N}, \tag{10}$$

where $x_c$ and $y_c$ denote X-Y coordinates at the center of the current image. The five features, $(\mu_x, \mu_y, \sigma_x, \sigma_y, z)$, are used as CFs.

## 4 Video Model

A video model computes $P(\boldsymbol{O} \mid \boldsymbol{S})$ in Eq. (1). We use a multi-stream Hidden Markov Models as a video model to model each scene.

### 4.1 Hidden Markov Models

Hidden Markov models (HMMs) are effective models for time-varying patterns and have been widely used to model scenes of sports video [3,2,5,6,9,10,8]. In

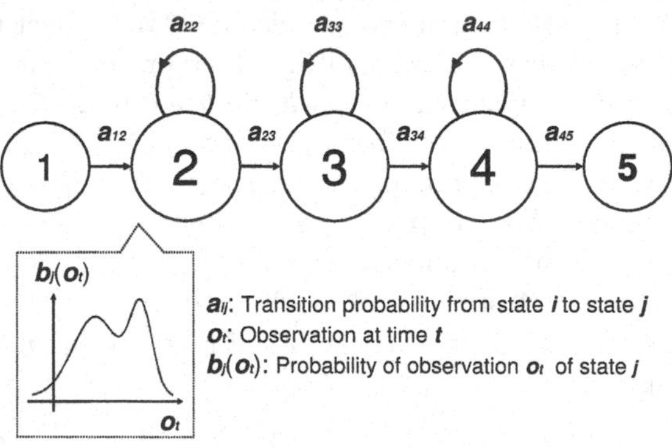


**Fig. 6.** Left-to-right 3-state HMM having a Gaussian mixture output probability

conventional HMM-based scene recognition methods (e.g., [6]), each state of an HMM is usually assigned to a specific shot type, and the HMM of each scene label has a specific topology that is determined heuristically. Inspired by the effectiveness of the data-driven approach used in speech recognition, we do not explicitly define a specific topology for each scene label, but use a common left-to-right HMM for all scene labels (Fig. 6). The reason for this is that, in real data, while the shot transition of each scene varies greatly, few clues about the underlying shot transition are apparent. Using this data-driven approach makes it easy to prepare scene models and to achieve robustness against unknown data. Our framework can be applied without any modification to recognize new scene labels when the amount of available training data increases. In our experiments, we also use a Gaussian-mixture model (GMM), which is equivalent to an HMM with only one state.

Multi-modal pattern recognition methods using HMMs often take the feature fusion scheme where features extracted from audio signals and features extracted from video signals are integrated into one feature vector for each frame and the time sequence of the feature vectors is used to train HMMs. In this framework, the training and recognition algorithms using in the conventional speech recognition methods can be applied to multi-modal recognition without any modification. It is also easy to apply speaker adaptation, discriminative training, and so on. On the other hand, it is difficult to deal with the difference in reliability among the modes.

### 4.2 Multi-stream HMMs

In this study, we employ a multi-stream HMM to model each scene [2]. In the speech recognition field, together with HMM, the multi-stream HMM, in which features are split into separate streams, have been widely used to combine different features, such as audio and visual (Fig. 7). Using a multi-stream HMM, we can control the weights among different features in an optimization process. In

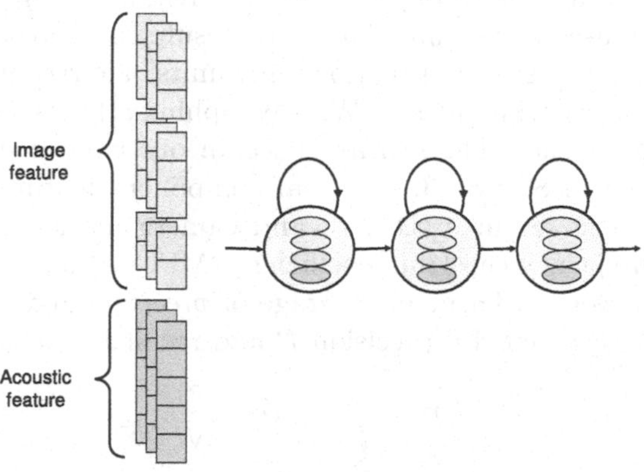


**Fig. 7.** Multi-stream HMM for audio and video features

the multi-stream HMM, each state $j$ has an associated observation probability distribution $b_j(\boldsymbol{o}_t)$ that determines the probability of generating observation $\boldsymbol{o}_t$ at time $t$, and each pair of states $i$ and $j$ has an associated transition probability $a_{ij}$. The output probability $b_j(\boldsymbol{o}_t)$ of state $j$ is calculated by multiplying the probability of each output stream $k$ by its respective weight $w_k$:

$$b_j(\boldsymbol{o}_t) = \prod_{k=1}^{K} b_{jk}(\boldsymbol{o}_{tk})^{w_k}, \tag{11}$$

$$\sum_{k=1}^{K} w_k = 1, \tag{12}$$

where $b_{jk}(\boldsymbol{o}_{tk})$ denotes the probability of the $k$-th output stream at state $j$, and $K$ denotes the total number of streams.

For each scene model, the HMM parameters $a_{ij}$ and $b_j$ are estimated from training data using the *Baum-Welch algorithm.* A Gaussian mixture model is used as the output probability. Given a feature vector sequence $\boldsymbol{O} = \boldsymbol{o}_1, \ldots, \boldsymbol{o}_M$, the corresponding scene sequence $\boldsymbol{S} = s_1, \ldots, s_N$ is recognized by the *Viterbi algorithm.*

## 5 Experiments

In our experiment, first we confirmed that our multi-modal recognition of audio and video is effective for scene recognition. Then, we examined the effectiveness of our proposed method in the score scene detection task.

### 5.1 Experimental Conditions

We used 25 games (75 hours) of Major League Baseball (MLB) broadcast video provided by NHK (Japan Broadcasting Corporation). We divided the 25 games into five groups. Recognition experiments were carried out by cross-validation, in which the video data of one group were used as test data, and those of the other four groups were used as training data. The results were averaged over the five groups. The test data were divided into inning units, and recognition experiments were conducted for each inning unit. We used Sphinx4 [18] as a recognition engine for the two experiments. The features used in our experiments were the four features explained in Section 3: principal component features (PFs), dynamic principal component features (DPFs), and camera motion features (CFs) for video and mel-frequency cepstrum coefficient (MFCCs) for audio.

We used *F-measure*, a harmonic average of *precision* and *recall*, for the evaluation. For each scene label $l$, precision $P$ and recall $R$ are calculated as

$$P = \frac{C}{T}, \quad R = \frac{C}{N}, \tag{13}$$

where $C$ is the number of frames that were correctly recognized as label $l$, $T$ is the number of frames that were recognized as label $l$ (including incorrect recognition

**Table 1.** Scene types, labels, and the number of appearances in five groups, in which a *pickoff* (po) includes a pickoff throw, a *walk* (wk) includes being hit by a pitch, a *steal* (st) includes being caught stealing, an *out of play* (op) refers to game scenes with no play action, such as scenes between innings, and a *CG effect* (ef) refers to scenes displaying a CG effect, such as batting average of a baseball player

| Scene type | Label | Group ID | | | | | Total |
|---|---|---|---|---|---|---|---|
| | | 1 | 2 | 3 | 4 | 5 | |
| ball | b | 271 | 371 | 353 | 308 | 398 | 1701 |
| replay | rp | 235 | 351 | 270 | 356 | 366 | 1578 |
| strike | s | 192 | 192 | 221 | 194 | 263 | 1062 |
| out of play | op | 185 | 197 | 181 | 199 | 175 | 937 |
| foul | f | 160 | 166 | 199 | 200 | 170 | 895 |
| ground out | go | 78 | 67 | 73 | 86 | 76 | 380 |
| fly out | fo | 70 | 81 | 66 | 60 | 75 | 352 |
| CG effect | ef | 58 | 72 | 52 | 52 | 38 | 272 |
| strike out | so | 41 | 36 | 48 | 49 | 49 | 223 |
| base hit | bh | 38 | 49 | 38 | 41 | 37 | 203 |
| pickoff | po | 24 | 19 | 25 | 35 | 36 | 139 |
| walk | wk | 25 | 38 | 23 | 23 | 27 | 136 |
| clutch hit | ch | 6 | 17 | 10 | 9 | 17 | 59 |
| extra-base hit | ebh | 10 | 9 | 12 | 11 | 8 | 50 |
| home run | hr | 9 | 9 | 4 | 10 | 6 | 38 |
| steal | st | 4 | 4 | 6 | 9 | 1 | 24 |

results), and $N$ is the number of frames that represents label $l$. Then, F-measure is defined by

$$F = \frac{2PR}{P + R}. \tag{14}$$

In the scene recognition experiment, we applied 16 scene labels which cover almost all events included in a baseball broadcast. Table 1 shows the number of appearances for each scene in the five groups. A scene HMM was prepared for each scene label using the Hidden Markov Model Toolkit (HTK) [19]. All the scene HMMs had the same topology, the same number of states, and the same number of Gaussian mixture components in output probability. The topology of scene HMMs is left-to-right, the number of states is 50, and the same number of Gaussian mixture components is two. These conditions of HMMs were optimized in our preliminary experiment.

In the score scene detection experiment, we used Gaussian mixture model (GMM). In the recognition phase, we assumed that the boundary between innings were known. It was proved to be effective to classify the score scenes into two categories, score scenes of the home team and those for the away team [20]. We classified all the scenes into six categories: "home score scene (hsc)", "away score scene (asc)", "no score scene (nsc)", "replay (rp)", "out of play (op)", and "CG effect (ef)". The statistics of these six scene types is shown in Table 2.

**Table 2.** Statistics of six scene types for score scene detection

| Scene type | Group ID 1 | 2 | 3 | 4 | 5 | Total |
|---|---|---|---|---|---|---|
| hsc | 12 | 28 | 8 | 14 | 9 | 71 |
| asc | 9 | 25 | 18 | 18 | 16 | 86 |
| nsc | 1446 | 1748 | 1662 | 1612 | 1776 | 8244 |
| rp | 288 | 442 | 360 | 433 | 441 | 1964 |
| op | 237 | 222 | 241 | 119 | 22 | 1186 |
| ef | 72 | 84 | 63 | 61 | 49 | 329 |

**Table 3.** F-measures of scene recognition using multi-stream HMMs (%). $w_V$, $w_A$ is the weight for video stream and for audio stream, respectively.

| $w_V$ | $w_A$ | hr | ch | bh | ebh | wk | st | s | b | f | po | so | fo | go | ef | rp | op | Ave. |
|---|---|---|---|---|---|---|---|---|---|---|---|---|---|---|---|---|---|---|
| 1.0 | 0.0 | 68.4 | 34.3 | 41.9 | 27.4 | 54.3 | 16.8 | 35.5 | 44.6 | 47.1 | 50.9 | 57.2 | 57.2 | 62.2 | 86.9 | 57.2 | 56.4 | 49.9 |
| 0.0 | 1.0 | 37.8 | 12.0 | 11.9 | 6.9 | 7.9 | 0.0 | 4.2 | 5.0 | 12.3 | 7.5 | 7.5 | 15.0 | 8.2 | 11.1 | 3.8 | 21.6 | 10.8 |
| 0.5 | 0.5 | 64.3 | 40.5 | 43.4 | 31.0 | 51.7 | 8.5 | 38.9 | 47.0 | 48.8 | 50.8 | 49.5 | 58.9 | 62.7 | 84.8 | 55.9 | 59.8 | 49.8 |
| 0.8 | 0.2 | **70.4** | 43.3 | 48.9 | 31.5 | 54.3 | 4.7 | 37.6 | 47.1 | 49.5 | 52.5 | 59.1 | 60.8 | 64.5 | 89.5 | 60.9 | 62.3 | **52.3** |

### 5.2 Scene Recognition

Table 3 shows the scene recognition results using multi-stream HMMs with different weights between audio and video streams. The stream weights for PFs, DPFs, CFs in video mode were optimized in our preliminary experiments to 0.45, 0.45, and 0.10, respectively. We kept this proportion in video mode in the weighting between audio and video modes. While the average F-measure with video recognition only was 49.9%, that with our multi-modal recognition of audio and video was 52.3% when using the stream weights (0.8,0.2). The significant improvement of 2.4 point proved the effectiveness of our proposed framework. Among sixteen scene types, the F-measure of clutch hit (ch) and extra-base hit (ebh) was largely improved by 9.0 poin and 7.0 point, respectively. In these scene types, audiences and announcers tend to excite more than in the other scene types. This fact may be the main reason why the recognition rate increased by adding audio information.

### 5.3 Score Scene Detection

Table 4 shows the results of score scene detection when scene boundaries between scenes were assumed to be known. For all the three combinations, audio only, video only, and audio & video, the best recall rate was obtained when the number of mixtures was 16. When the numbers of mixtures were the same, the recall rates of audio only were better than those of video only, but the precision rates of video only were better than those of audio only.

The combination of audio and video brought the best recall rate of 90.4% when the number of mixture was 16. In this case, the precision rate was 15.2%.

**Table 4.** Score scene detection using GMMs with different number of mixtures (%)

| Number of mixtures | | 1 | 2 | 4 | 8 | 16 | 32 | 64 | 128 | 256 | 512 |
|---|---|---|---|---|---|---|---|---|---|---|---|
| Audio | Recall | 81.5 | 84.7 | 86.0 | 86.0 | 86.6 | 82.8 | 77.7 | 63.7 | 37.6 | 17.2 |
| | Precision | 4.8 | 5.4 | 7.1 | 7.2 | 7.9 | 8.2 | 9.1 | 12.2 | 14.6 | 26.2 |
| | F-measure | 9.1 | 10.1 | 13.2 | 13.3 | 14.4 | 15.0 | 16.2 | 20.5 | 21.0 | 20.8 |
| Video | Recall | 63.1 | 82.8 | 80.9 | 78.3 | 79.0 | 79.0 | 72.0 | 56.1 | 40.8 | 15.3 |
| | Precision | 5.7 | 4.0 | 5.7 | 9.2 | 11.3 | 13.6 | 18.2 | 23.9 | 31.8 | 40.7 |
| | F-measure | 10.5 | 7.6 | 10.7 | 16.5 | 19.7 | 23.2 | 29.0 | 33.5 | 35.8 | 22.2 |
| Video & Audio | Recall | 71.3 | 84.7 | 87.9 | 89.8 | **90.4** | 88.5 | 80.3 | 65.0 | 33.8 | 8.9 |
| $(w_A,w_V) = (0.8{:}0.2)$ | Precision | 7.5 | 5.3 | 7.5 | 12.7 | 15.2 | 19.1 | 23.9 | 35.1 | 49.5 | 77.8 |
| | F-measure | 13.6 | 10.0 | 13.9 | 22.3 | 26.1 | 31.4 | 36.8 | **45.5** | 40.2 | 16.0 |

**Table 5.** Confusion matrix for audio and video. Scene labels in row are the hypothesized labels and those in column are the true labels. Each element is the number of scenes.

| | op | rp | ef | hsc | asc | nsc | Total |
|---|---|---|---|---|---|---|---|
| op | 118 | 12 | 0 | 0 | 1 | 27 | 158 |
| rp | 108 | 1246 | 5 | 36 | 45 | 117 | 1557 |
| ef | 7 | 8 | 96 | 0 | 1 | 1 | 113 |
| hsc | 1 | 3 | 0 | **56** | **8** | 3 | 71 |
| asc | 0 | 1 | 0 | **9** | **69** | 7 | 86 |
| nsc | 440 | 672 | 13 | 260 | 448 | 6411 | 8244 |
| total | 678 | 1948 | 114 | 361 | 575 | 6742 | 10418 |

The length of all the score scenes was 1.5% of all the scenes. This result indicates that the manual search for score scenes may become ten times more efficient by using our proposed method, though we failed to detect 9.6% of score scenes.

Table 5 shows the confusion matrix of multi-modal score scene detection when the number of mixture was 16. Here, we ignore the recognition error between "home score (hsc)" and "away score (asc)". Fifteen scenes out of 157 score scenes were misrecognized as the other scenes, and among them four score scenes were misrecognized as replay (rp). On the other hand, 81 replay scenes (rp) were misrecognized as score scenes (hsc+asc). Score scenes (hsc+asc) and replay scenes (rp) were very likely to be confused. Replay scenes have a distinct timing structure; they have CG effects at the beginning and at the ending. But the recognition models, GMMs, are mainly used for modeling stational features and are not able to capture dynamic features. This may be the major reason of this large number of confusions.

Next, Table 6 shows the results of home score scene (hsc) and away score scene (asc) detection. Compared with video only results, the combination of audio and video features improved 11.2 point for hsc and 11.6 point for asc in recall, and 8.2 point for hsc and 0.4 point for asc in precision. This results indicates that the audio information was more effective for home score scenes than for away

**Table 6.** Detection of home score scenes (Hsc) and away score scenes (Asc)

| | Video only | | Video & Audio | |
|---|---|---|---|---|
| | Hsc | Asc | Hsc | Asc |
| Recall | 78.9 | 79.1 | 90.1 | 90.7 |
| Precision | 9.8 | 13.0 | 18.0 | 13.4 |
| F-measure | 17.4 | 22.3 | 30.0 | 23.4 |

**Table 7.** Score scene detection with scene boundary information obtained by automatic scene recognition (%)

| Number of mixtures | | 1 | 2 | 4 | 8 | 16 | 32 |
|---|---|---|---|---|---|---|---|
| Video & Audio | Recall | 73.1 | 80.8 | **87.2** | 84.6 | 82.1 | 79.5 |
| $(w_V, w_A) = (0.8{:}0.2)$ | Precision | 10.2 | 7.8 | 10.5 | 15.9 | 18.7 | 22.2 |
| | F-measure | 18.0 | 14.2 | 18.7 | 26.7 | 30.5 | 34.7 |

score scenes. The loudness of cheers in home score scenes was much larger than that in away score scenes because most of the audience were fun of the home team.

Lastly, the recognition results using the scene boundary information obtained by automatic scene recognition were shown in Table 7. When the number of mixture was four, the recall rate was 87.2%, only 3.2 point lower than the results when the scene boundaries were assumed to be known. This result indicates that the scene boundaries obtained by the automatic scene recognition were correct in most cases. It is confirmed that our score scene detection method can be used in real application where true scene boundaries are unknown.

## 6 Conclusion

This paper has proposed a scene recognition method for baseball broadcast video It integrates video features (PFs, DPFs, and CFs) and audio features (MFCCs) by using multi-stream HMMs. The combination of audio and video information improved the averaged F-measure of scene recognition for 16 scene types by 2.4% from the conventional scene recognition methods with only video information. We also applied the same framework to score scene detection. Our score scene detection method achieved the recall rate of 90.4%. The evaluation results proved the effectiveness of the proposed method. It was proved that this method efficiently reduces the cost of making highlight.

Our method is expected to be effective not only for score scene detection but also for detection of the other highlight scenes. The audio feature we employed were successful to capture the excitement of audiences and announcers. Such excitement may occur in most highlight scenes. It can be also easily applied to the other sports when scene types can be clearly defined. In soccer, for example, our method can be used to detect "goal scene". It is still needed to explore new features effective for scene detection. In this paper, we optimized the stream weights for multi-modal recognition using test data, but this process can not be applied in real application. We have to investigate the way to automatically optimize the weight. While we did not use the language modeling method representing the scene context [3], further improvement in the detection performance will be achieved by using this method. Finally, we would like to examine the other modeling approach than HMMs and GMMs, such as Support Vector Machines (SVMs).

## Acknowledgments

This work was supported by the 21st Century COE program "Framework for Systematization and Application of Large-scale Knowledge Resources". We would like to express our sincere gratitude to Ms. Tomoko Nakauchi for her excellent work of data annotation.

## References

1. Brunelli, R., Mich, O., Modena, C.M.: A survey on the automatic indexing of video data. Journal of Visual Communication and Image Representation 10(2), 78–112 (1999)
2. Nguyen, H.B., Shinoda, K., Furui, S.: Robust scene extraction using multi-stream HMMs for baseball broadcast. IEICE Transactions on Information and Systems E89-D(9), 2553–2561 (2006)
3. Ando, R., et al.: Robust scene recognition using language models for scene contexts. In: Proc. the 8th ACM international workshop on Multimedia Information Retrieval, pp. 99–106 (2006)
4. Ando, R., et al.: A robust scene recognition system for baseball broadcast using data-driven approach. In: Proc. ACM International Conference on Image and Video Rerieval, pp. 186–193 (2007)
5. Mochizuki, T., Tadenuma, M., Yagi, N.: Baseball video indexing using patternization of scenes and hidden Markov model. In: Proc. IEEE International Conference on Image Processing, vol. 3, pp. 1212–1215 (2005)
6. Chang, P., Han, M., Gong, Y.: Extract highlights from baseball game video with hidden Markov models. In: Proc. IEEE International Conference on Image Processing, vol. 1, pp. 609–612 (2002)
7. Gong, Y., et al.: Maximum entropy model-based baseball highlight detection and classification. International Journal of Computer Vision and Image Understanding 96(2), 181–199 (2004)
8. Xu, P., et al.: Algorithms and system for segmentation and structure analysis in soccer video. In: Proc. IEEE International Conference on Multimedia and Expo, pp. 928–931 (2001)
9. Kijak, E., Oisel, L., Gros, P.: Hierarchical structure analysis of sport videos using HMMs. In: Proc. IEEE International Conference on Image Processing, vol. 3, pp. 1025–1028 (2003)
10. Xu, G., et al.: Motion based event recognition using HMM. In: Proc. IEEE International Conference on Pattern Recognition, vol. 2, pp. 831–834 (2002)
11. Babaguchi, N., Kwai, Y., Kitahashi, T.: Event based indexing of broadcasted sports video by intermodal collaboration. IEEE Trans. Multimedia 4(1), 68–75 (2002)

12. Li, B., Sezan, M.I.: Event detection and summarization in sports video. In: Proc. IEEE Workshop on Content-Based Access of Image and Video Libraries 2001, vol. 9(8), pp. 132–138 (2001)
13. Acero, Y.R.G.A.: Automatically extracting highlights for tv baseball programs. ACM Multimedia, 105–115 (2000)
14. Gouyon, P.H.Y.: Automatic classification of drum sound: a comparison of feature selection methods and classification techniques. In: Proc. of Int. Conf. on Music and Artificial Intelligence, pp. 69–80 (2002)
15. Sahouria, E., Zakhor, A.: Content analysis of video using principal components. IEEE Trans. Circuits and Systems for Video Technology 9(8), 1290–1298 (1999)
16. Takagi, S., et al.: Sports video categorizing method using camera motion parameters. In: Proc. IEEE International Conference on Multimedia and Expo, vol. 2, pp. 461–464 (2003)
17. Lucas, B., Kanade, T.: An iterative image registration technique with an application to stereo vision. In: Proc. 7th International Joint Conference on Artificial Intelligence, pp. 674–679 (1981)
18. Sphinx4, `http://cmusphinx.sourceforge.net/sphinx4`
19. Hidden Markov model toolkit, `http://htk.eng.cam.ac.uk`
20. Miyazaki, T., et al.: Scene recognition for tv baseball program using acoustic information (in Japanese). Proc. Sprint Meeting of Acoustic Society of Japan 1(11-9), 19–20 (2006)

# Large Scale e-Language Laboratory Based on Web 2.0

Kohji Shibano

Research Institute for Languages and Culture of Asia and Africa
Tokyo University of Foreign Studies
Fuchu, Tokyo, Japan
shibano@aa.tufs.ac.jp

**Abstract.** We set four objectives for our original e-Learning system project for Japanese language education, called JPLANG. The first objective is to develop an original Web 2.0 based e-Language Laboratory. The second is to develop comprehensive educational materials for teaching Japanese from an introductory to university level. The third is to use this system and its content to improve teaching in our classrooms. The final objective is to provide e-Language Laboratory services for Japanese learners and teachers throughout the world. We developed an original e-Language Laboratory using emerging technologies such as Ajax, Ruby on Rails, and Flash Media Server. So far, we have developed introductory Japanese language text books consisting of 1,692 web pages and 20,500 sound files for 300 hours of teaching. In the year and a half it has been in service, more than 2,900 users have registered from more than 30 countries. In this paper, we present our approach for developing a Web 2.0 based e-Language Laboratory.

## 1 Introduction

Language education has unique requirements, traditionally found in LL (Language Laboratory) or CALL (Computer Assisted Language Laboratory). Reading a text book or a paper is not enough for learning a language. Language learning requires a training of five skills: listening, speaking interaction, speaking production, reading and writing. LL and CALL only complement training for listening and speaking skills. To train these five skills in the past it required special equipment, today requiring full multimedia support.

General requirements for language education can be found in "Common European Framework of Reference for Languages: Learning, teaching, assessment (Council of Europe 2001)."

We set our goal to provide comprehensive Japanese language text books in an e-Learning environment based on previously published text books written by our university's Japanese Language Center. The text books cover introductory to university level Japanese, covering 900 hours of class room teaching. 18 text books are divided into three levels, introductory, intermediate and advanced Japanese. Introductory Japanese consists of 1,754 pages of published textbook and in total 2,634 pages. Published textbooks include three audio tapes covering about 500 pages.

T. Tokunaga and A. Ortega (Eds.): LKR 2008, LNAI 4938, pp. 241–251, 2008.

Language learners and teachers in foreign countries do not have enough listening experience. Thus, they have asked us to increase audio materials. However, using analog technologies such as audio tapes and CDs, it is difficult to control the devices. We decided to add audio materials for every example sentences. Therefore our system will require 20,500 sound files.

We surveyed major e-Learning environments such as WebCT (WebCT 2003), Blackboard (Blackboard 2002), and MOODLE (Rice 2006), and found that a generation of several thousand pages is very difficult and sound/multimedia support is not sufficient. These e-Learning systems cannot provide a real time monitor of a learner's actions though a real time monitor can be found in traditional LL systems.

Thus we decided to develop our own e-Learning system based on the latest technologies. We started with a Java based system, then moved to a PHP based system, and finally to Ruby on Rails (Thomas et al 2005) together with Ajax and Flash Media Server 2, because Ruby on Rails supports state-of-the-art agile web application development. Ajax can support real time monitoring of a learner's actions. JavaScript and Flash can support the rich content required for language learning, such as role-playing and dictation. Flash Media Server 2 (Adobe 2007) can support server based recording and interchange of speech. Combining these system services, we can develop a state-of-the-art and comprehensive language learning environment as an integrated e-Learning system.

The current JPLANG system (http://jplang.tufs.ac.jp) has been operational since April 2006. More than 2,900 users from more than 30 countries have registered as a JPLANG user. The content consists of 1,692 web pages, including 20,500 sound files, and can be used for 300 hours of teaching introductory Japanese. 46 classes have been opened, including classes at other universities.

JPLANG is free and you can open your own class. LMS (Learning Management System) can also be used if you open a class. LMS features include monitoring students' activities and assignments.

## 2 Needs and Seeds on an e-Language Laboratory

### 2.1 Objectives of JPLANG Project

JPLANG project has four objectives:

(1) To develop an original Web 2.0 based e-Learning system for Japanese language education.
(2) To develop comprehensive educational materials for teaching Japanese from introductory to university level.
(3) To use these systems and contents to improve teaching in classrooms.
(4) To provide e-Language Laboratory services for Japanese learners and teachers throughout the world.

The Japanese Language Center of our university teaches Japanese language to government sponsored foreign students. Japanese language skills are not required for the student to enter the center but the center teaches Japanese from zero to university level. After graduating from the center, students go to Japanese national universities.

The students are basically full time Japanese learners for a year, consisting of 900 hours of classroom learning. Teaching materials are all developed by the center. The materials consist of 18 books shown in Figure 1. Based on these books, we first added many materials, such as sounds, images and videos, and then developed the rest of the content.

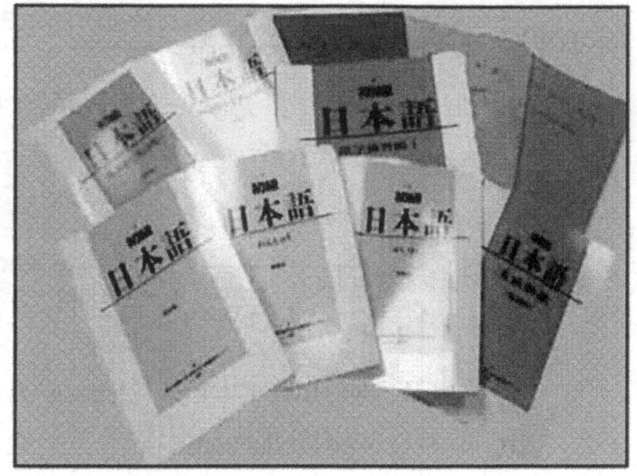


**Fig. 1.** Japanese Text Books

The printed books consist of 2,634 pages and three audio tapes. For introductory Japanese, 1,692 web pages were generated from 1,754 printed pages. 20,500 sound files were added for every sentence. For intermediate Japanese, about 400 web pages and videos were generated.

## 2.2 Language Educational Requirements and CEFR

General requirements for language education can be found in "Common European Framework of Reference for Languages: learning, teaching, assessment (CEFR)" (Council of Europe 2001) shown in Figure 2.

CEFR defines, in a comprehensive way, what it is that language education must do to educate students in order to use a language for communication from a basic to a proficient level as well as what knowledge and skills they should develop to be able to effectively act.

CEFR first defines reference level. The framework not only defines learning requirements but teaching and assessment. For language education it defines five skills: listening, reading, spoken production, spoken interaction, and writing . Detailed requirements can be found in the CEFR documentation.

## 2.3 Web 2.0 and 2005 Web Technology Revolution

A new generation of the web was first proposed by the original inventor of WWW as a semantic web (Berners-Lee 2001). After that, W3C developed series of specifications including RDF, OWL and SPARQL.

However, real technological breakthroughs come from different sides, such as "Usage Technology Evolution" and "Core Technology Revolution".

"Usage Technology Evolution" is based on a new concept called CGM (Consumer Generated Media). Plain users can generate text, sounds, images and video media content using new technologies like blogs, wikis, Podcasts, Flickr, or YouTube. No special expertise is required to generate new content and the average user can publish personal content through the Internet.

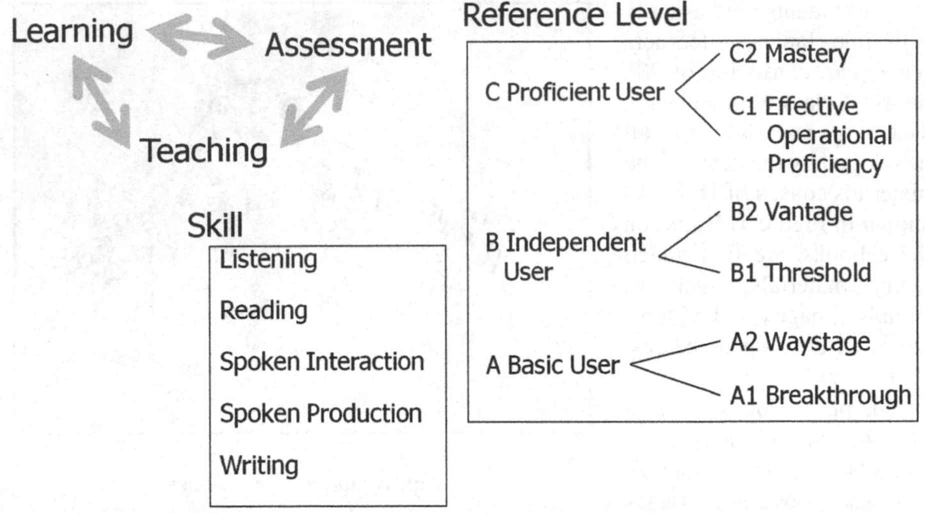


**Fig. 2.** Common European Framework

In 2005 a series of new technologies were introduced.

The term AJAX (Asynchronous JavaScript and XML) was first coined in February, 2005 based on an analysis from Google Suggest. After that Google introduced a series of products, such as Google Map and Google docs. Using AJAX, web applications can behave as desktop applications, that is, the same usability and interface can be implemented for the web as for the desktop PC. In 2007, Google documents expanded to cover Google docs, spreadsheets and presentations. Together with Gmail and Calendar, the Google suite covers the same components as Microsoft office suite.

In the same year Ajax appeared, 2005, Ruby on Rails was introduced. The Rails framework really speeds up web application development. Amazon, Rakuten, and Twitter are using Rails to develop their application and can more easily catch up as the needs of users change.

A new Flash Media Server was introduced and in October, 2005, YouTube was launched. True multimedia support can be implemented using Flash.

AJAX, Ruby on Rails, and Flash together, I would like to call "2005 web technology revolutions".

Using these revolutionary technologies, we can develop a real e-Language Laboratory to support all aspects of language education.

## 3 Generation of Large Scale Rich Contents

As we discussed before, to create comprehensive educational materials, generating thousands of web pages is required. To meet this requirement, we developed a content generation system in our JPLANG project, based on XML.

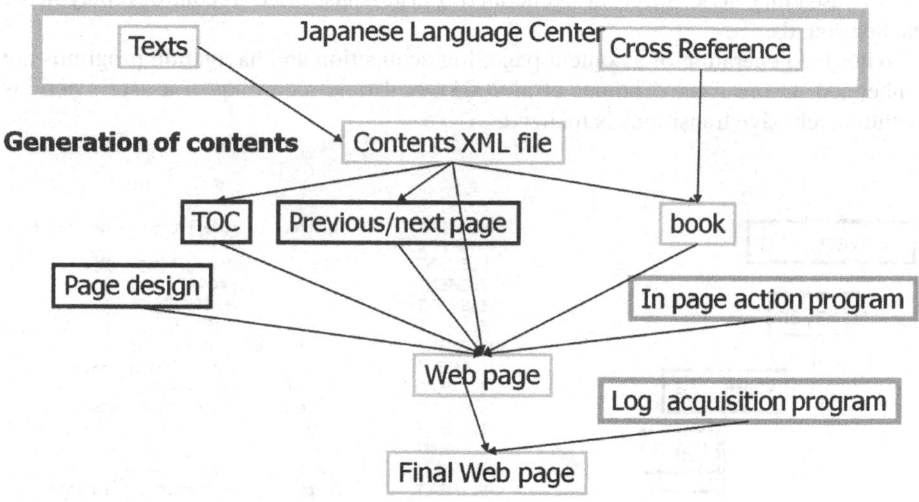


**Fig. 3.** Generation of Contents

XML was evolved from SGML, but the basic architecture is quite different. SGML was originally developed to support multipurpose use of a document. One of the most characteristic features of SGML is a notion of a concurrent document. A single document can be marked up by more than one markup.

A mandatory requirement of XML is "well-formedness", i.e. an XML document must be well formed. All tags must be marked and well nested. "Omit tag" in SGML is prohibited. Proper nesting of elements is required. Thus concurrent or multiple markup is prohibited.

This means that XML is designed for single purpose documents while SGML is designed for multipurpose documents. If a user wants to reuse an XML document, XSLT is used to convert it to a different document format.

Content generation is divided into three phases. The first phase is to convert plain text files to XML files. Content XML files are generated from plain texts using specific XML tags such as CONVERSATION, PLAYER, and SENTENCE. Links to sound files and image files are treated as attributes to the above mentioned XML elements. See Figure 3.

Phase two is the generation of Web pages. During generation, JavaScript and Flash programs are embedded into a Web page to provided sound and image control for role-playing and dictation. A log acquisition program for monitoring users' actions is also embedded using Ajax. Using XMLHttpRequest, the log acquisition program can send detailed logs of a user's actions to a host with a MySQL database.

Phase three is to embed navigational controls. These controls included "Table of Contents", "Inter Books Link", "Link to Basic Contents", and "Previous/Next Links".

Each web page requires controls for playing sounds and text presentation to realize language education specific requirements, like role-playing and dictation. Based on the above mentioned XML elements, specific control programs written in JavaScript and

CSS (Cascading Style Sheet) are generated. Flash is also used to control replaying of cached sounds.

After the generation of a content page, log acquisition and navigation programs are embedded. Using Ajax (Thomas et al 2005), real time recording of a user's actions without web page transitions is realized.

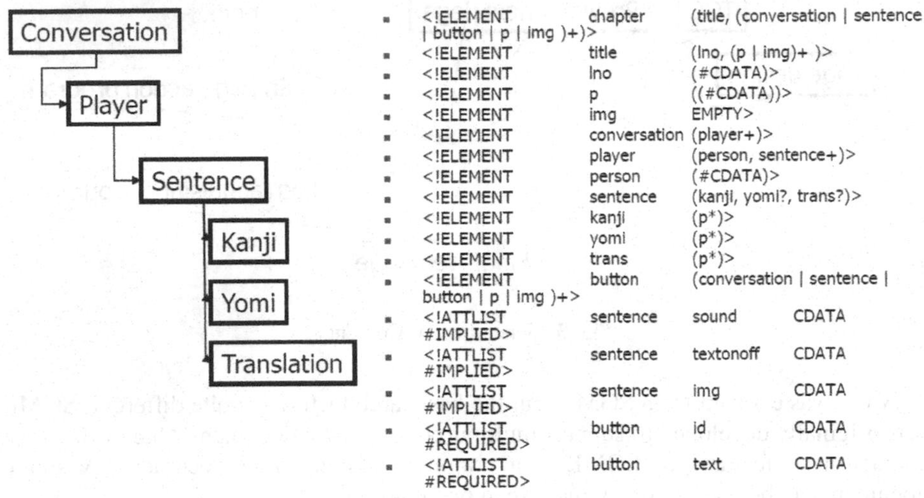

Conversation
Player
Sentence
Kanji
Yomi
Translation
<!ELEMENT chapter (title, (conversation | sentence | button | p | img )+)>
<!ELEMENT title (lno, (p | img)+ )>
<!ELEMENT lno (#CDATA)>
<!ELEMENT p ((#CDATA))>
<!ELEMENT img EMPTY>
<!ELEMENT conversation (player+)>
<!ELEMENT player (person, sentence+)>
<!ELEMENT person (#CDATA)>
<!ELEMENT sentence (kanji, yomi?, trans?)>
<!ELEMENT kanji (p*)>
<!ELEMENT yomi (p*)>
<!ELEMENT trans (p*)>
<!ELEMENT button (conversation | sentence | button | p | img )+>
<!ATTLIST sentence sound CDATA #IMPLIED>
<!ATTLIST sentence textonoff CDATA #IMPLIED>
<!ATTLIST sentence img CDATA #IMPLIED>
<!ATTLIST button id CDATA #REQUIRED>
<!ATTLIST button text CDATA #REQUIRED>


**Fig. 4.** Jplang Core XML DTD

Figure 4 shows a core part of XML DTD used in our JPLANG system. CHAPTER, CONVERSATION, PLAYER and SENTENCE are the basic controls used by JavaScript programs. Specific language learning controls are attached to these tags.

A generated Web page corresponds to a CHAPTER. A CHAPTER tag may contain one or more CONVERSATION, SENTENCE, BUTTON, P or IMG tags. CONVERSATION, PLAYER, and SENTENCE tags correspond to a conversation, a player and a sentence respectively. Sound play controls are attached to these tags. A learner can play a whole conversation, a player or a sentence. A learner can also control displaying text and its translation based on these tags.

The Japanese writing system is a little bit complex, using Kanji, Kana, and Latin scripts. Kanji is Especially very difficult for novices. To aid in reading a Japanese text, we provide a Kana transcription called "Yomi (reading)" for these learners. Thus, we prepared translations to fifteen languages including English, Chinese, German, French and Korean. Presentation of translation is also within the user's control.

Visual aids help learners. Especially learning conversation, information relating to a situation and functions of a conversation are required. In the past we used video as a visual aid. However, a video or a photo may include noises, so we use a picture story show.

Each SENTENCE tag may have a SOUND attribute and an IMG attribute. Using these attribute, JPLANG system controls displaying and playing of sounds and pictures of the story.

Figure 5 shows the navigation and controls of a content page. The materials are divided into six books, i.e., conversation, grammar, drills, conversation practice, listening and reading.

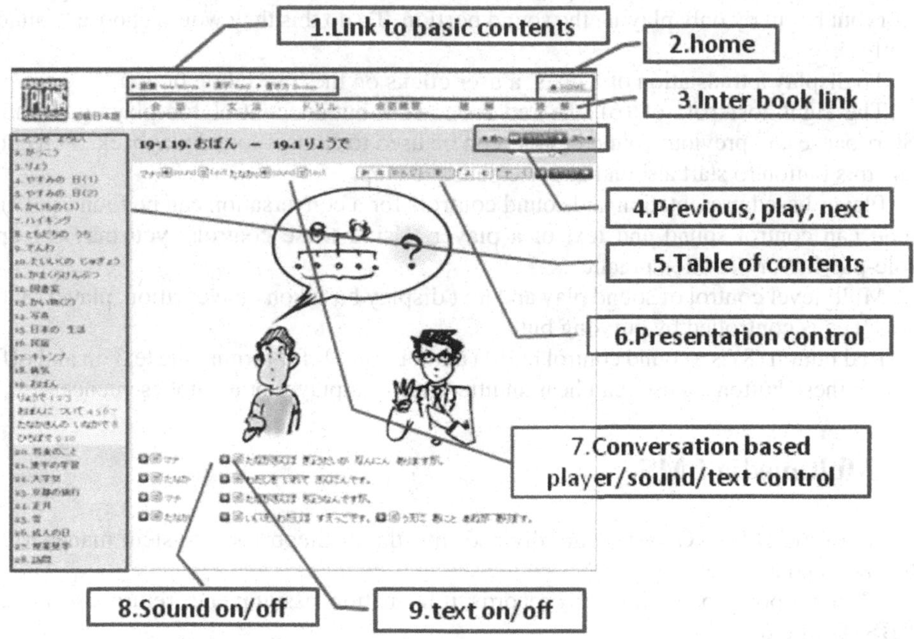


**Fig. 5.** Navigations and controls

On top of the page (1), you can find links to basic contents such as a word dictionary, Kanji dictionary and Kana dictionary. At the right top (2), you can find a link to LMS user's portal page.

Next (3) is a cross reference link to other books. Left (5) is a table of contents with links. JPLANG introductory Japanese basically consists of 28 chapters, a chapter including several sections. Direct links to a chapter or a section of a chapter can be found in this table of contents.

The red button (4) is for playing sounds (previous, current and next). To the left and right of this are buttons linking to the previous and next pages, respectively. A volume control is located below all this.

Sound playback is controlled using Flash. When a web page is loaded, Flash reads all sound files and buffers them. By using a buffering technique, sound files can be played continuously. The volume control is also Flash.

In (6), you can find three sets of buttons. From left to right, we have: presentation type of text, text display and translation display.

The presentation type control is a radio button with the values of Kana, Kanji, or sound (no text display). As mentioned earlier, original Japanese texts can be difficult to read for Japanese learners. If a novice cannot understand a specific Kanji, a learner may choose to display Kana. Kana displays the intonation of a sentence.

We designed JPLANG system with classroom use and blended learning requirements in mind. For example, in a classroom, a teacher may start with a picture storybut begin by only playing the sound portion. To do this they would choose "sound (only)".

To display a translation of a texts, a user clicks on the translation button.

The rightmost part of (6), the red icon, is a button control for playing sound. Start/pause and previous sound buttons can be used to control sound playback. You can use this button to start a sound and use pause to stop.

Player based presentation and sound controls for a conversation can be found in (7). You can control sound and text of a player. Using these controls, you may set up role-playing or dictation practice.

Multi level control of sound play and text display based on conversation, player, and sentence is controlled by pressing buttons.

Red button (8) is a sound control button and button (9) for turning the text on and off. Using these buttons, a user can hear an utterance of a player or a whole sentence.

## 4 Multimedia LMS

Users of the JPLANG system are divided into three categories: a system manager, a teacher, and a student.

LMS has portal pages for study records, information, assignments, return tests and a BBS (Figure 6).

Study records is a summary display based on a user's behavioral logs. The books/chapters matrix shows a overall status of their learning. A blue box shows no visit. A yellow box shows a part of a chapter of a book has been studied and a red box shows all the web pages of a chapter of a book have been studied.

Information is basically just communication from a teacher to a student..Types of information include Action and FYI (For Your Information). For Information with an action type status, a user should mark a check box. Once you have read FYI or checked action information, they will not be displayed again. File and speech attachments are also supported.

Assignment types include an automatic scoring test, a manual scoring test, a file upload, a speech upload, a named survey, and an unnamed survey.

An automatic scoring test can be a single choice, a multiple choice, or a fill-in-the-blank questionnaire. In addition to an automatic scoring test, a manual scoring test may include a composition and/or a speech upload. A scoring criterion can be attached to both a composition questionnaire and a speech upload. For a composition questionnaire, a teacher can strike out a word or a character and can insert a word. Comments can also be added. A test including corrected composition can be returned to a student.

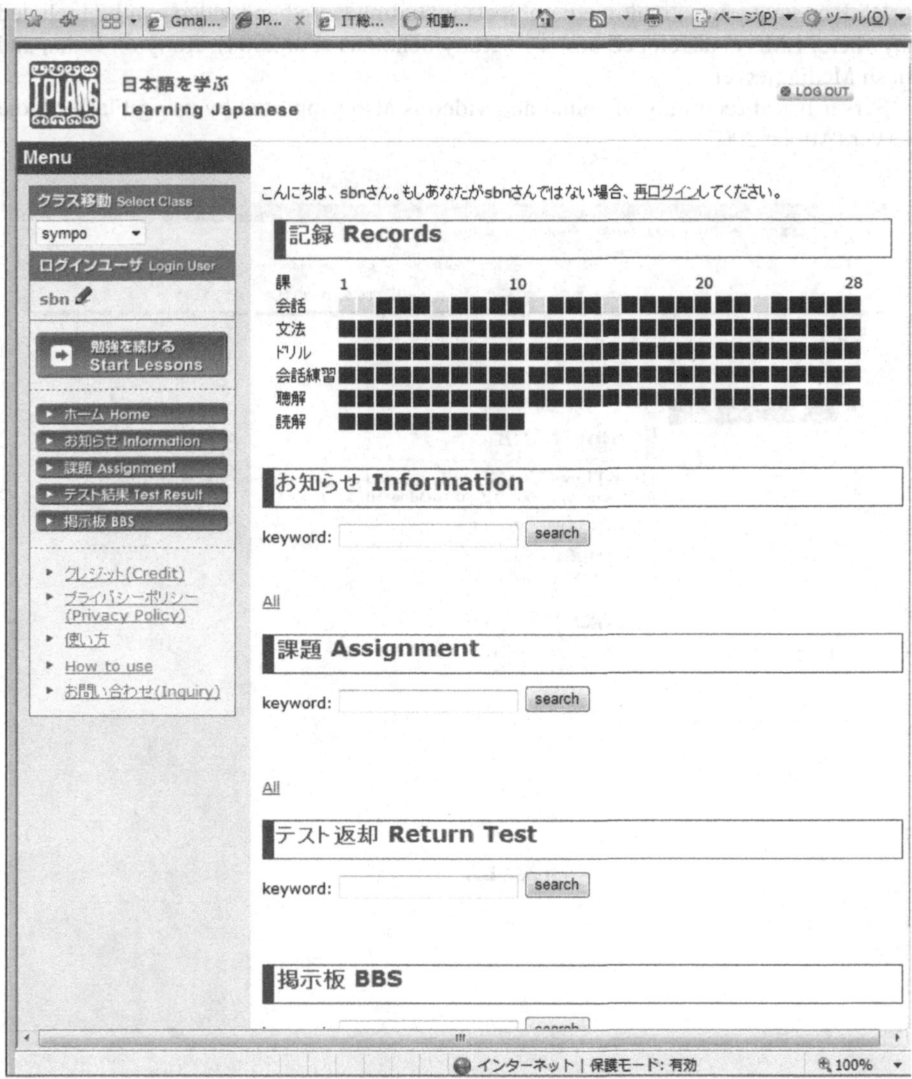


**Fig. 6.** LMS User Portal page

Most of the current e-Learning systems try to support blended learning. However, most testing found in these systems is still restricted and uses automatic testing.

Surveys are categorized into two categories, named surveys and anonymous surveys. Survey results are not only recorded but summarized.

BBS, a means to share information among learners, is also supported. Posted messages can be controlled by a teacher. A teacher can delete or modify a posted message.

With content pages, multimedia objects including sound and video can be included anywhere. LMS is developed based on Ruby (Thomas et al 2004), Ruby on Rails, and Flash Media Server.

Server based recording of sound and video is also supported by using Flash Media Server (Adobe 2007).

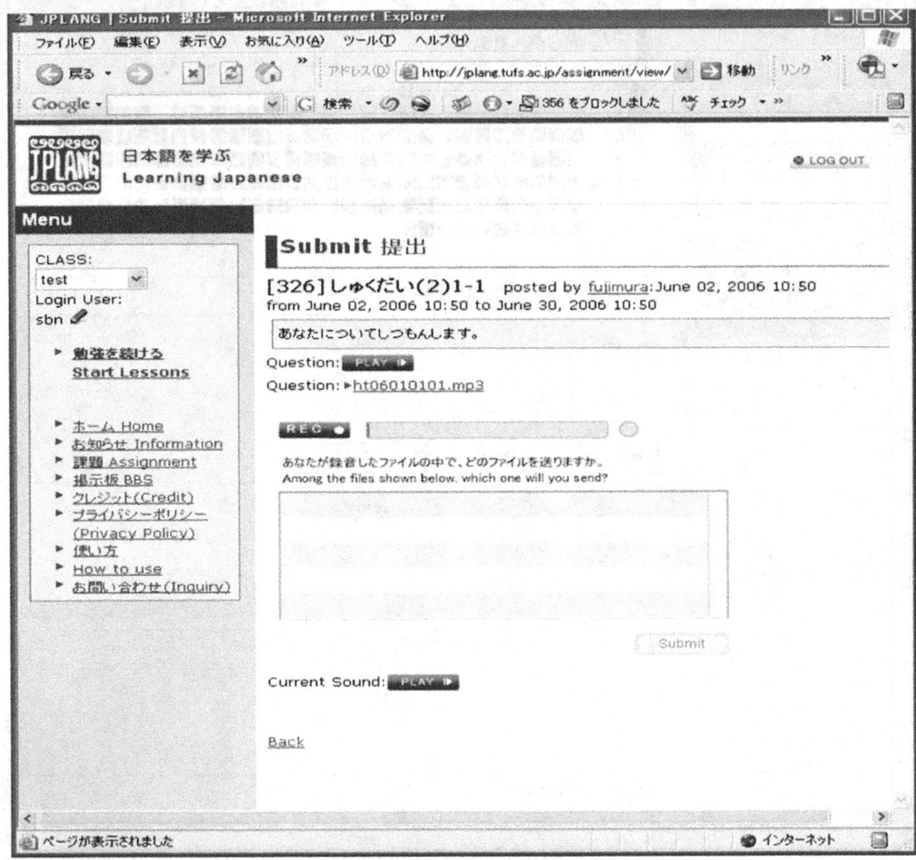


**Fig. 7.** Speech recording using Flash Media Server

Figure 7 shows a speech recording assignment. A student can record and replay themselves. Based on an assignment setting, the number of recordings can also be controlled.

For writing assignment,s corrections by teachers are indicated using red strikeout lines for deletion, blue words for insertion, and green words for comments.

This way, the testing of the four skills (listening, speaking production, reading, and writing) is achieved.

## 5 Concluding Remarks

We have developed the followings:

(1) Contents generators for large scale materials,
(2) Comprehensive Japanese educational content including introductory and intermediate Japanese,
(3) AJAX and Flash based rich content, and
(4) A Web 2.0 based original LMS.

The current version of introductory Japanese content has been open for global use since April, 2006 and more than 2,900 users have been registered from more than 30 countries.

Languages other than Japanese are being developed, including German and Polish.

Spoken interaction support, voice annotation support, and enhanced course management are planned for further development.

## References

1. Council of Europe, Common European Framework of Reference for Languages: learning, teaching, assessment, Cambridge University Press (2001)
2. Adobe, Flash Media Server 2 (2007), http:// www.adobe.com/ products/ flashmediaserver/
3. WebCT, Inc., WebCT Campus Edition 3.8 System Administrator's Guide (revised February 3, 2003)
4. Blackboard, Inc.: Blackboard Learning System: Product Overview White Paper. Washington, DC (Release 6) (2002)
5. Rice, W.: Moodle E-Learning Course Development. Packt Publishing (2006)
6. Thomas, D., Fowler, C., Hunt, A.: Programming Ruby: The Pragmatic Programmer's Guide, Pragmatic Bookshelf (2004)
7. Thomas, D., Hansson, D.H., Breedt, L.: Agile Web Development With Rails: A Pragmatic Guide, Pragmatic Bookshelf (2005)
8. Berners-Lee, T., Hendler, J., Lassila, O.: The Semantic Web, Scientific American, May 2001 (2001)

# Distant Collocations between Suppositional Adverbs and Clause-Final Modality Forms in Japanese Language Corpora

Irena Srdanović Erjavec[1], Andrej Bekeš[2], and Kikuko Nishina[1]

[1] Tokyo Institute of Technology, Department of Human System Science, 2-12-1 Ookayama Meguro-ku 152-8552 Japan

[2] University of Ljubljana Faculty of Arts, Aškerčeva 2, 1000 Ljubljana, Slovenia

srdanovic.i.ab@m.titech.ac.jp, andrej.bekes@guest.arnes.si, nishina.k.aa@m.titech.ac.jp

**Abstract.** Co-occurring of modal adverbs and clause-final modality forms in the Japanese language exhibits a strong agreement-like behaviour. We refer to such co-occurrences as distant collocations - a notion that warrants further consideration within the fields of corpus linguistics and computational linguistics. In this paper we concentrate on a set of suppositional adverbs and investigate the kinds of clause-final modality forms that they frequently co-occur with. One group of adverbs is found to typically collocate with one group of modality forms (one modality type) to a high degree, but also co-occurs with other modality types. Analyzing a variety of corpora revealed that associations between certain adverbs and certain modality types are indeed a matter of degree, although the associations in some cases vary across different genres. The results are summarized with the help of cluster analysis. We believe that the basic analysis approaches in this paper can be extended to cover similar kinds of collocational behaviour within lexicons and other large-scale knowledge resources, as well as complementing the development of computer-assisted language learning systems.

**Keywords:** suppositional adverbs, clause-final modality, collocations, corpora, Japanese language.

## 1 Introduction

Obtaining various kinds of linguistic information from large-scale knowledge resources is an integral task within the fields of corpus linguistics and computational linguistics. On the other hand, the tasks of classifying and systematizing various aspects of the extracted information are essential stages in creating linguistic information a large-scale knowledge resource itself. In this paper we concentrate on Japanese modal adverbs expressing supposition (such as, *kitto*, *tabun*, *moshikasuruto*) and the clause-final modality forms (*darou*, *to omou*, *mitai* etc.) that these adverbs are associated with. Previous researches [1,2,3,4] observed an agreement behavior between modal adverbs and clause-final modality forms and have specified the

T. Tokunaga and A. Ortega (Eds.): LKR 2008, LNAI 4938, pp. 252–266, 2008.

behavior as a matter of degree between a group of suppositional adverbs and a group of modality forms that represent a modality type expressing NECESSITY, EXPECTATION, CONJECTURE, or POSSIBILITY. The aim of this study is to examine this phenomenon using various types of corpora and to explore how the adverb-modality relation varies across different genres. The agreement between adverbs and clause-final modality can also be regarded as 'distant collocations'. Here we would emphasis the importance of distant collocations - a notion that deserves to receive greater attention in corpus and computational approaches to language.

Modal adverbs can be understood as 'lexical' linguistic means because they are not obligatory syntactically and also as 'grammatical' means because they possess very strong relational properties [2]. In that extent, their analysis may be seen as being particularly beneficial, on the one hand, in enhancing large-scale lexicons and user dictionaries and, on the other hand, in implementing grammatical-like relations between modal adverbs and clause-final modal forms into language learning resources, including computer assisted language learning systems such as the Japanese composition support system Natsume[5].

## 1.1 The Layered Clause Structure in Japanese

Modal adverb and clause-final modal form agreement can be also seen as a particular case of a general approach to the co-occurrence possibilities of syntactic elements and predicate elements in Japanese dependent clauses, developed in Minami [1,6]. Minami has, through his qualitative co-occurrence analysis [1], later refined empirically on a corpus [6], made the profound discovery that Japanese clauses possess hierarchically layered structure, consisting of four layers. Syntactic elements within the clause co-occur only with those predicate elements belonging to the same or lower layers, as can be seen in (1) below.

(1) ...{ ***douyara*** [*kono machi ni mo gonin gurai wa* ( *i* )$_A$ -*ru* ]$_B$ ***rashii***-}$_C$ ...

somehow this town at too five_persons about *WA* are -RU it_seems

WA=CONTRAST; -RU=NONPAST-AFFRIMATIVE

Somehow, it seems as if there should be about five [of them] in this town, too.

The example shows a layered structure comprising the three innermost levels A, B and C. Minami's levels in (1) are indicated by brackets: "()" denotes level A, "[]" level B and "{}" level C. Higher levels include inner levels in the fashion of Russian *matryoshka* dolls. At each level, several constituents are possible. It is interesting to note that in the example above level A comprises only the verb stem *i-* of *iru* (to be, exist). Bold letters mark the co-occurrence we are interested in, i.e., the modal adverb *douyara* (somehow) and the clause-final modal form *rashii* (apparently), co-occurring at level C. The underlined constituents are *kono machi ni mo* ("in this town too", with particle *mo* marking homogeneous additivity) and *gonin gurai wa* ("about five persons", with particle *wa* marking contrast) and the predicate final morpheme *-ru* (nonpast-affirmative), connected at level B.

The co-occurrence of elements is at each level restricted syntactically and reinforced semantically. Co-occurring elements are connected by a kind of semantic agreement, e.g.where, for example, *douyara* and *rashii* share the same tentative modality while *kono machi ni mo* and *gonin gurai wa* are connected by the affirmative-negative polarity.

Minami [6] has presented his empirical findings on global co-occurrence possibilities in a matrix form, which can than be used for further purposes. Later work on modality, including Kudô [2] and Bekeš [3,4,7] is, from the methodological point of view, an application of Minami's approach to a more particular domain. Minami's approach, which has already been proven to be valid by the discovery of the layered clause structure, offers a framework for a top-down approach to processing Japanese sentence syntax. With the availability of more computing power and more easily accessible data, it is worth examining in more detail. The present study, in exploring the applicability for corpus-based lexicography and Japanese instruction as a foreign language, can be regarded as a small step in that direction.

### 1.2 The Agreement Behaviour of Modal Adverbs

As a group, modal adverbs exhibit rather unruly behaviour. Kudô [2] provides one of the first systematic treatments of the whole field. According to Kudô (ibid. 185-6), the function of modal adverbs is to secondarily reinforce the primary sentence and clause-final modality.

Kudô (ibid.191) subdivides modal adverbs into two groups on the basis of agreement—distinguishing between those that display agreement and those that do not. Adverbs that show agreement are more frequent and include modality senses relating to 1) activities, 2) cognition, and 3) conditionals. The modal adverbs that lack agreement belong to various sub-modality classes. Kudô argues that the agreement-like behaviour of modal adverbs is a matter of degree, where adverbs that co-occur with one type of modality may not co-occur with another type. For example, evaluative adverbs cannot co-occur with modalities of imperative, decisive and invitatory [2, also cited in 4].

(2) ??*Hijou-ni hayaku hashiri-nasai.* (Kudô ibid.: 226)
very fast run- IMPER. / Run very fast!

On the other hand, additive adverbs may co-occur with the same modality types without problem.

(3) *Motto shoujiki-ni itte-mi-tamae.* (Kudô ibid.: 226)
more honestly say-try-IMPER. / Try to speak more honestly.

Most of modal adverbs display agreement and, thus, primarily serve to reinforce the modality of the sentence. Two typical examples of adverbs in agreement with various modalities are as follows.

(4) *Doozo, kochira-ni kite-kudasai.* (Kudô ibid.: 180)
please here-to come-REQUEST / Please, come here.

(5) *Tabun hareru desh-ou.* (Kudô ibid. 180)
probably clear copula-GUESS / [The weather] will probably be clear.

Modal adverbs and clause-final modality appear in different types of instances. In the present analysis, we focus on the two following types:

- *Tabun, issho-ni kita deshou ne.* [A-P-M]
- *...tabun, daijoubu* Ø [A-P-Ø],

where [A-P-M] indicates examples where an adverb, the predicate and a modality form all appear, while [A-P-Ø] indicates examples where an adverb and the predicate appear, but modality is unmarked.

While instances where a modality form appears before an adverb [P-M-A], an adverb is not present in the sentence [Ø-P-M], or there is only an adverb [A] or only modality form [M] are appropriately marked in our data, they are excluded from the present analyses:

- *Kare mo issho-ni kita deshou ne..., tabun* [P-M-A]
- *Juuhachi dewa-nai n-janaika, ...* [Ø-P-M]
- *Tabun, ne* [A]
- *Deshou, ne* [M]

In this paper, we limit our analysis to one type of modal adverbs: suppositional adverbs.

### 1.3 Notion of Collocation

In its modern linguistic sense, the term 'collocation' was first coined by Firth along with his well-known comment "You shall judge a word by the company it keeps". Subsequent research on collocations has focused on different aspects of Firth's ideas and there is now a wide range of definitions concerning collocations [8]. Within the field of corpus linguistics, Sinclair's approach to collocations has been influential, where his definition that "collocation is the occurrence of two or more words within a short space of each other in a text" [9] has been usually taken to refer a separation of five words at the most. From a statistical and computational point of view, collocations are also been defined as words that occur together more often than chance [10]. Church and Hanks [11] employed the concept of mutual information in extracting pairs of correlated words, i.e., collocations, also within a fixed distance of five words. Only recently can we see references to the notion of 'distant collocations', mainly in exploratory computational approaches to extracting collocations and usually limited to collocations within a short distance, such as when interrupted by a string or a couple of strings. The terms of 'interrupted collocations' [12] and 'discontinuous collocations' [13] have also been observed.

Here, we want to stress that the agreement between modal adverbs and clause-final modality forms is also about correlated words; words that occur more often than chance [4]. Accordingly, this agreement phenomenon can be regarded as a form of collocational relationship, or given the usual distances involved, more precisely as 'distant collocations'.

In the analyses discussed in this paper, we also observe that the modal adverb - clause-final modality co-occurrence is quite variable in terms of distance: for while in some examples the adverbs and modality are interrupted only by a predicate, there are also examples where they co-occur at a distance of 10 or more words. Moreover, we also find that the distance is relative, differing not only among adverbs but also across different genres and registers. These observations call for further analysis and suggest that the notion of distant collocations deserves a systematic treatment within empirical approaches to language.

### 1.4 Resources and Methods

In the present analyses, we employ a variety of corpora resources. First, we present results from previous studies of modal adverbs performed on the following corpora: Kudô [2] conducted an analysis using a corpus that included mixed genres, mostly newspaper data and literary works written in modern Japanese literature. The 'Oikawa' corpus [14] used in Bekeš [3,4] consists of transcribed interviews with 50 Japanese native speakers. It represents a formal setting, for the participants were unfamiliar with each other and of different social status (professors and students). In contrast, the 'NUJCC' corpus [15] used in Bekeš [3] consists of around 100 informal conversations between familiar participants who were of equal social status.

In addition to the above corpora, we perform our analysis using the following corpora and present the results in this paper:

'JpWaC' [16] is a Japanese web corpus of 400 million tokens. It is available as part of the corpus query tool Sketch Engine [17] also developed for the Japanese language [18]. The corpus consists of web data and while it reflects various genres, the majority of the corpus data are blogs. For the analysis, we extracted a random sample of 100 examples for each adverb from the corpus.

We also use the '16 kyoukasho' corpus (abbreviated as '16K') consisting of textbooks for natural science university students, the 'NLP' corpus, which is a set of articles from the field of natural language processing, and the 'Kokugo Kyoukasho' corpus (abbreviated as 'Kk') consisting of 60 school textbooks for primary schools.

After selecting the range of corpora for analysis we realized that it would be necessary to carry out some manual annotation work and analysis, because modality phenomena are not fully covered in Japanese parsers and because we assumed that any automatic processing would simply generate too many mistakes. Careful consideration of the modal adverbs and clause-final modality forms performed in this analysis highlighted the full complexity and variety of the relation. Based on this obtained data, we plan to develop an automatization process and examine its accuracy in the next stage of the analyses.

We summarize the results in the form of tables, and, where applicable, we use the clustering method. For the cluster analysis, we import the data (how frequently each of modality forms co-occurs with each of the adverbs) into the SPSS system and perform the hierarchical cluster analysis in order to identify set of groups (clusters) of adverbs displaying similarity in their co-occurrences with particular clause-final modality forms. The procedure sought to identify relatively homogeneous groups based on selected characteristics, using an algorithm that starts with each case in a separate cluster and combines clusters until only one is left. Specifically, we use the agglomerative hierarchical clustering, the Furthest neighbor as a clustering method and the Chi-square distance measure. The cluster results are displayed as a dendrogram, a hierarchical tree diagram. The obtained results for each corpus are presented in the next section.

## 2 Distributions of Adverb-Modality Relations in the Corpora

This section presents the results concerning adverb-modality relations obtained by analyzing various types of corpora.

### 2.1 Related Work

The earliest work covering adverb – clause-final modality form co-occurrence was Minami [19,1]. Initially, the analysis of co-occurrence possibilities of predicate-bound elements in the dependent clause with the non-predicate elements (complements, adverbial elements and similar) was qualitative[1] Later Minami [6], elaborating on his previous research, verifies the possibilities of co-occurrence by taking an empirical corpus-based approach relying on the statistical correlation of co-occurring elements. Kudô [2], whose research on the agreement between modal adverbs and clause-final modality was introduced in section 0, takes a similar corpus-based statistical approach. Below we present the results of Kudô's analysis [2] for comparison with the results obtained in the present study from other corpora.

#### 2.1.1 Kudô's Analysis

The results of the Kudô's analysis are presented in Table 1, which clearly differentiates which adverbs most frequently co-occur with which modality types. There are four modality types, i.e. NECESSITY, EXPECTACTION, CONJECTURE, and POSSIBILITY. For example, we can easily see that *kitto, kanarazu, zettai(ni)* most frequently co-occur with clause-final modality forms that express NECESSITY (*(suru) no da, ni chigai nai…*), while *osoraku, tabun, sazo* and *ookata* frequently co-occur with clause-final modality forms that express EXPECTACTION (*to omowareru, no de wa nai darou…*).

Fig. 1 presents cluster analysis results for Kudô's data. The figure is consistent with the tabulated data, for it is possible to easily discern four clusters of adverbs that each represent a modality type: *taigai, taitei, tabun, ookata, sazo*, and *osoraku* representing EXPECTATION, *kitto, kanarazu*, and *zettai(ni)* representing NECESSITY, *hyottoshitara, kotoniyoruto, moshikasureba, angai*, and *aruiwa* representing POSSIBILITY, *douyara, doumo*, and *yohodo* representing CONJECTURE.

#### 2.1.2 Oikawa and NUJCC

Both the Oikawa and NUJCC are corpora of spoken Japanese, but they differ in their levels of formality. The majority of the observed frequencies are very low because the corpora are relatively small in size. Accordingly, the cluster analysis cannot yield reliable results, and we simply provide a short summary of those results, as presented in the form of table in Bekeš [3,4].

Because of the small sizes of the corpora, the tendencies to form associations with particular clause-final modal forms could not be identified for all suppositional adverbs. However, it is possible to observe the trends for some of them. In the case of the Oikawa corpus, the relevant adverbs are *tabun, kitto, kanarazu* and *moshikashitara*. The most frequent co-occurrence of *tabun* with *to omou* probably reflects a bias towards closer association with the EXPECTATION modality. The

[1] For more information on layered structure, as well as bracket structure in Japanese language, see Minami [19,1,6] and Bekeš [3,4,7]. See also section 1.1 in this paper.

**Table 1.** The results of Kudô's analysis [2]

| ADVERB | *suru no da* (NEC) | *ni tigainai*(NEC) | *ni kimatteiru* (NEC) | *hazu da*(NEC) | *daroo/mai*(EXP) | *to omowareru*(EXP) | *no dewa nai daroo ka* (EXP) | *rasii*(CON) | *to mieru* (CON) | *yoo da/mitai da*(CON) | *sisoo da*(CON) | *kamosirenai* (POSS) | *darooka* (POSS) | *senu tomo kagiranu* (POSS) | *suru fusi ga aru* (POSS) | **TOTAL** | **OTHER(NON MODAL)** |
|---|---|---|---|---|---|---|---|---|---|---|---|---|---|---|---|---|---|
| *kitto* | **139** | **38** | **8** | **3** | 66 | 12 | | | | 1 | 4 | 8 | | | | 279 | 85 |
| *kanarazu* | **17** | **5** | **2** | **1** | 11 | | | | | | | | | | | 36 | 146 |
| *zetttai(ni)* | **48** | | | | | | | | | | | | | | | 48 | 38 |
| *osoraku* | 31 | 18 | | 1 | **112** | **5** | **10** | 2 | | 1 | | 2 | | | | 182 | -- |
| *tabun* | 19 | 1 | | 2 | **74** | | **1** | 1 | | | 2 | 3 | | | | 103 | -- |
| *sazo* | | | | | **52** | | **1** | | | | 1 | | | | | 54 | -- |
| *ookata* | 2 | 1 | | | **24** | | **1** | | | | | | | | | 28 | 13 |
| *taitei* | 3 | | | 1 | **7** | | | | | | | | | | | 11 | 80 |
| *taigai* | 2 | | | | **4** | | | | | | | | | | | 6 | 33 |
| *dooyara* | 5 | | | | | | 1 | **29** | | **10** | | | | | 1 | 46 | 39 |
| *doomo* | 13 | 1 | | | | | 6 | **24** | | | | 1 | | | | 45 | 385 |
| *yohodo* | 6 | 2 | | | 7 | | 2 | **12** | **9** | **3** | | | 2 | | | 43 | 150 |
| *aruiwa* | | | | | 3 | 2 | 4 | | | | | **53** | **3** | **1** | | 66 | 69 |
| *mosikasure* | 2 | | | 1 | 1 | 1 | 11 | | | | | **30** | | | | 46 | -- |
| *hyottositara* | 2 | | | | | | 7 | | | | | **16** | **1** | | | 26 | -- |
| *kotoniyoruto* | 1 | | | | | | 4 | | | | | **7** | **1** | **1** | | 14 | -- |
| *angai* | | 1 | | | 1 | | 3 | 1 | | | 1 | **8** | | | | 15 | 81 |

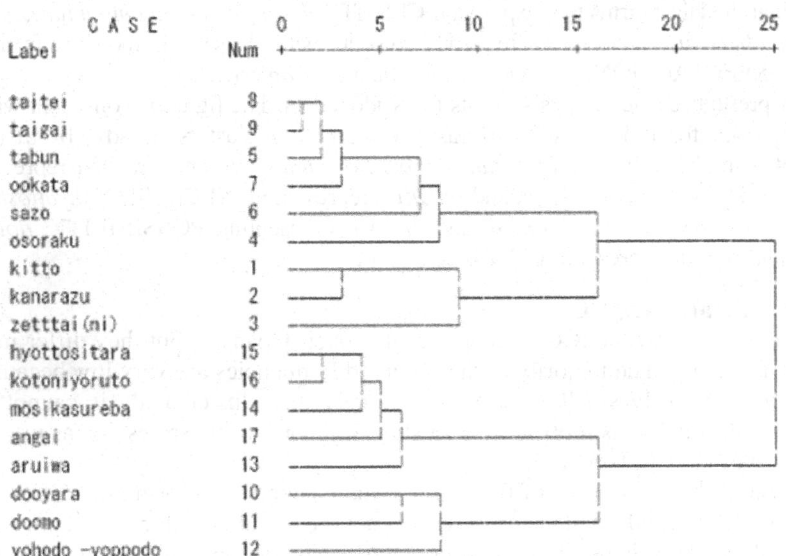


**Fig. 1.** Cluster analysis results for Kudô's data

same holds for *kitto*, which most frequently co-occurs with *to omou* and *(n)darou/(n)deshou*, and also exhibits a bias towards the EXPECTATION modality. This is an interesting difference from Kudô's results, where *kitto* co-occurred most frequently with the NECESSITY modality type. *Kanarazu* frequently co-occurs with the *suru* form, which would suggest a bias for the NECESSITY modality type. The frequent co-occurrences of *moshikashitara* and *kamoshirenai* reflect a trend towards POSSIBILITY.

In the case of the NUJCC corpus, we can observe the trends for the *kitto*, *kanarazu*, *zettai(ni)*, *doumo* and *moshikashitara* adverbs. *Kanarazu* and *moshikashitara* are similar to those observed in the Oikawa corpus. *Doumo* co-occurs mostly with *rashii* and *you da* and therefore has a bias towards the CONJECTURE modality type. *Kitto* and *zettai(ni)* occur very frequently with the NECESSITY and EXPECTATION modality types, and both also show slight biases towards EXPECTATION. Moreover, comparing the frequencies in the two corpora strongly suggests that *zettai(ni)* is rarely (if at all) used in formal conversations, even though it is very frequent in informal settings (0 vs. 259).

## 2.2 Adverb-Modality Relations in JpWaC

From analyses of the web data, it is clear that adverbs are associated with a rich variety of modality forms. For all 18 modal adverbs encountered in the analysis, there are approximately 60 different modality forms, which we organized into around 40 form types, following the Kudô's [2] approach. We may assume that this variety reflects the diverse nature of the corpus data. The web data includes a great deal of personal information, and, as it has been commented on in other studies [20,21], the web data shows clear preferences for the first and second person voices, for present and future tense, and for an interactive style of discourse. As modality represents a speaker's attitude about the expressed content, we may expect to find more abundant uses of modality forms and types in the web data than in newswire or literary text data. There is also a marked tendency for complex modality forms, where two, three or more modality forms are used together as a single clause-final modality expression, as indicated in the example below. The example also indicates the cases, where a modality adverb that clearly associates with a modality expression at the end of one clause prolongs its association with the modality expressions in the proceeding clause (taken from the JpWaC corpus).

(6) *Tabun, sore-tte ima ni hajimatta koto de wa nai no da to omoimasu ga, saikin ni toku ni , "rikai fukanou" na jiken ga fueta you-na ki ga shimasu.*
Probably, that is not something that started now, for sure, I think; and it seems to me that, especially lately, "impossible to understand" events have increased.

(7) *E. seifu iin go shiteki no ten wa, osoraku Tokyo-to no chousa ni narareta bun nado wo kiso to shite osshatte oru no de wa nai ka to suitei shite oru wake de gozaimasu ga, …*
What the E. government board member has pointed out is, I presume, perhaps, that what (s)he says is based on being used to surveys of the Tokyo Metropolitan government and the like, isn't it.

These phenomena call for a novel approach to modality expressions in order to appropriately handle modality forms appearing in layered structures, as well as in more than one clause.

**Table 2.** The results of the JpWaC corpus analysis (in two parts)

| adv/mod.forms | NEC_no_da | NEC_to_iu_koto_da/mono_da | NEC_koto_da | NEC_koto_ni_naru/to_naru | NEC_mono_da | NEC_nakereba_naranai | NEC_ni_chigai_nai | NEC_hazu_da | NEC_hitsuyou_ga_aru/nai | NEC_beki_da/darou | NEC_to_wa_kagiranai | NEC_wake_da | NEC_wake_de_wa_nai | EXP_to_suru/sareru | EXP_darou/deshou/mai | EXP_no_darou | EXP_koto_to_omou/zonjiru | EXP_de_wa_nai_ka | EXP_to_omou | EXP_no_de_wa_nai_ka | EXP_no_darou_ka | EXP_no_de_wa_nai |
|---|---|---|---|---|---|---|---|---|---|---|---|---|---|---|---|---|---|---|---|---|---|---|
| kanarazu | 4 | 0 | 2 | 1 | 4 | 6 | 0 | 2 | 1 | 2 | 0 | 0 | 1 | 0 | 2 | 0 | 0 | 0 | 4 | 0 | 0 | 0 |
| kanarazushimo | 3 | 3 | 6 | 0 | 4 | 0 | 0 | 0 | 2 | 0 | 6 | 1 | 9 | 0 | 1 | 0 | 0 | 0 | 4 | 0 | 0 | 3 |
| zettaini | 3 | 0 | 1 | 0 | 0 | 4 | 0 | 2 | 13 | 1 | 0 | 0 | 2 | 0 | 1 | 0 | 0 | 0 | 12 | 0 | 0 | 0 |
| zettai | 4 | 0 | 2 | 0 | 1 | 3 | 0 | 2 | 2 | 2 | 0 | 1 | 0 | 0 | 1 | 1 | 0 | 0 | 0 | 2 | 0 | 0 |
| taigai | 14 | 0 | 2 | 0 | 3 | 1 | 0 | 0 | 0 | 0 | 0 | 1 | 0 | 0 | 2 | 0 | 0 | 0 | 4 | 1 | 1 | 0 |
| taitei | 0 | 1 | 4 | 3 | 2 | 1 | 1 | 0 | 0 | 0 | 0 | 3 | 2 | 2 | 0 | 0 | 0 | 0 | 5 | 0 | 0 | 0 |
| aruiwa | 0 | 1 | 0 | 0 | 0 | 0 | 0 | 1 | 0 | 2 | 0 | 2 | 0 | 0 | 1 | 1 | 0 | 0 | 0 | 0 | 0 | 0 |
| yohodo | 5 | 0 | 0 | 1 | 3 | 3 | 1 | 2 | 1 | 0 | 0 | 2 | 0 | 0 | 7 | 5 | 0 | 1 | 11 | 0 | 0 | 0 |
| tabun | 2 | 0 | 0 | 0 | 1 | 0 | 0 | 4 | 0 | 0 | 0 | 0 | 0 | 0 | 15 | 15 | 0 | 4 | 15 | 1 | 0 | 0 |
| kitto | 4 | 0 | 0 | 0 | 2 | 0 | 1 | 2 | 0 | 0 | 0 | 0 | 0 | 0 | 23 | 11 | 0 | 0 | 14 | 4 | 0 | 0 |
| osoraku | 2 | 0 | 0 | 0 | 0 | 0 | 1 | 0 | 0 | 0 | 0 | 1 | 0 | 0 | 28 | 17 | 0 | 5 | 14 | 8 | 0 | 0 |
| sazo | 0 | 0 | 0 | 0 | 0 | 0 | 2 | 1 | 0 | 0 | 0 | 0 | 0 | 0 | 36 | 44 | 9 | 1 | 0 | 1 | 0 | 1 |
| ookata | 4 | 0 | 0 | 0 | 0 | 0 | 0 | 0 | 0 | 0 | 0 | 0 | 0 | 0 | 7 | 5 | 0 | 0 | 3 | 2 | 0 | 0 |
| doumo | 3 | 0 | 0 | 0 | 0 | 0 | 0 | 0 | 0 | 0 | 0 | 2 | 0 | 0 | 2 | 0 | 0 | 0 | 3 | 2 | 0 | 0 |
| douyara | 1 | 0 | 0 | 0 | 1 | 0 | 0 | 0 | 0 | 0 | 0 | 0 | 0 | 0 | 0 | 0 | 0 | 0 | 1 | 0 | 0 | 0 |
| angai | 6 | 1 | 0 | 0 | 4 | 0 | 0 | 0 | 0 | 0 | 0 | 0 | 0 | 0 | 1 | 1 | 0 | 5 | 0 | 2 | 0 | 0 |
| hyottoshitara | 2 | 0 | 0 | 0 | 0 | 0 | 0 | 0 | 1 | 0 | 0 | 0 | 0 | 0 | 2 | 0 | 0 | 1 | 1 | 14 | 0 | 0 |
| hyottosuruto | 1 | 0 | 1 | 0 | 0 | 0 | 0 | 0 | 0 | 0 | 0 | 1 | 0 | 0 | 1 | 0 | 0 | 0 | 1 | 10 | 2 | 0 |
| kotoniyoreba/yoruto | 5 | 0 | 2 | 0 | 0 | 0 | 0 | 0 | 0 | 0 | 0 | 1 | 0 | 1 | 2 | 1 | 0 | 1 | 2 | 11 | 0 | 0 |
| moshikasuruto | 0 | 0 | 0 | 0 | 0 | 0 | 0 | 0 | 0 | 0 | 0 | 0 | 1 | 1 | 1 | 0 | 0 | 1 | 1 | 10 | 1 | 0 |
| moshikashitara | 1 | 0 | 0 | 1 | 1 | 0 | 0 | 0 | 0 | 0 | 0 | 0 | 0 | 0 | 1 | 1 | 0 | 1 | 5 | 1 | 0 | 1 |

| adverb/modality | CON_you/mitai_da | CON_rashii/poi | CON_sou_da | CON_sou_ni_nai | CON_ni/to_mieru | POSS_koto_mo_aru | POSS_kamoshirenai | POSS_no_kamoshirenai | POSS_kana | POSS_kanousei_ga_aru/nai | POSS_darou_ka | POSS_ienai | POSS_to_wa_kagiranai | POSS_no ka?/kana/kashira | UNM_da | UNM_suru | UNM_de wa nai | UNM_natte_inai/iru | UNM_ni_naru/suru | UNM_da ka? | UNM_shinai | UNM_suru ka? | OTHER |
|---|---|---|---|---|---|---|---|---|---|---|---|---|---|---|---|---|---|---|---|---|---|---|---|
| kanarazu | 0 | 1 | 0 | 0 | 0 | 3 | 0 | 0 | 0 | 0 | 0 | 0 | 0 | 0 | 5 | 39 | 0 | 1 | 0 | 0 | 0 | 0 | 0 |
| kanarazushimo | 5 | 0 | 2 | 0 | 0 | 1 | 2 | 0 | 0 | 0 | 2 | 8 | 6 | 0 | 0 | 0 | 11 | 1 | 3 | 0 | 18 | 0 | 3 |
| zettaini | 0 | 0 | 2 | 0 | 0 | 3 | 0 | 0 | 0 | 0 | 0 | 2 | 0 | 0 | 5 | 7 | 3 | 0 | 1 | 0 | 15 | 0 | 13 |
| zettai | 0 | 0 | 1 | 0 | 0 | 0 | 0 | 0 | 0 | 0 | 0 | 0 | 0 | 0 | 9 | 10 | 2 | 0 | 0 | 0 | 11 | 0 | 18 |
| taigai | 3 | 1 | 1 | 0 | 0 | 2 | 2 | 0 | 0 | 0 | 2 | 0 | 0 | 0 | 16 | 26 | 1 | 0 | 1 | 0 | 3 | 0 | 0 |
| taitei | 2 | 0 | 0 | 0 | 0 | 5 | 0 | 0 | 0 | 1 | 0 | 0 | 0 | 0 | 15 | 40 | 3 | 1 | 0 | 0 | 3 | 0 | 0 |
| aruiwa | 0 | 0 | 0 | 0 | 0 | 0 | 4 | 0 | 0 | 1 | 0 | 0 | 0 | 0 | 0 | 0 | 0 | 0 | 0 | 0 | 0 | 0 | 0 |
| yohodo | 6 | 0 | 2 | 1 | 4 | 0 | 0 | 0 | 0 | 0 | 2 | 0 | 0 | 4 | 15 | 15 | 1 | 0 | 0 | 1 | 4 | 1 | 0 |
| tabun | 3 | 0 | 0 | 0 | 0 | 0 | 2 | 0 | 1 | 0 | 1 | 0 | 0 | 0 | 4 | 14 | 0 | 0 | 0 | 1 | 3 | 0 | 0 |
| kitto | 0 | 0 | 0 | 0 | 0 | 0 | 3 | 0 | 0 | 0 | 2 | 0 | 0 | 0 | 9 | 10 | 0 | 0 | 0 | 0 | 3 | 0 | 0 |
| osoraku | 3 | 1 | 0 | 0 | 0 | 0 | 5 | 0 | 0 | 0 | 0 | 0 | 0 | 1 | 2 | 9 | 0 | 0 | 0 | 0 | 1 | 0 | 0 |
| sazo | 0 | 0 | 0 | 0 | 0 | 0 | 1 | 0 | 0 | 0 | 0 | 0 | 0 | 0 | 0 | 0 | 0 | 0 | 0 | 2 | 0 | 0 | 0 |
| ookata | 1 | 1 | 0 | 0 | 0 | 0 | 0 | 0 | 2 | 0 | 0 | 0 | 0 | 0 | 7 | 22 | 0 | 1 | 1 | 0 | 0 | 0 | 0 |
| doumo | 17 | 5 | 2 | 0 | 0 | 1 | 0 | 0 | 1 | 0 | 0 | 0 | 0 | 1 | 5 | 10 | 1 | 0 | 0 | 0 | 4 | 1 | 0 |
| douyara | 41 | 30 | 6 | 1 | 0 | 0 | 1 | 0 | 0 | 0 | 0 | 0 | 0 | 0 | 8 | 8 | 0 | 0 | 0 | 1 | 0 | 0 | 0 |
| angai | 5 | 0 | 1 | 0 | 0 | 2 | 20 | 4 | 0 | 0 | 0 | 0 | 0 | 2 | 24 | 15 | 0 | 0 | 0 | 0 | 2 | 0 | 0 |
| hyottoshitara | 1 | 7 | 0 | 0 | 0 | 0 | 52 | 3 | 1 | 2 | 0 | 0 | 0 | 1 | 1 | 1 | 0 | 0 | 0 | 1 | 1 | 0 | 0 |
| hyottosuruto | 0 | 0 | 0 | 0 | 0 | 0 | 45 | 17 | 5 | 0 | 0 | 0 | 0 | 4 | 2 | 3 | 0 | 0 | 1 | 3 | 1 | 0 | 0 |
| kotoniyoreba/yoruto | 1 | 1 | 0 | 0 | 0 | 3 | 34 | 19 | 0 | 0 | 0 | 1 | 0 | 1 | 1 | 9 | 0 | 0 | 0 | 0 | 0 | 0 | 1 |
| moshikasuruto | 3 | 0 | 0 | 0 | 0 | 0 | 43 | 16 | 0 | 5 | 2 | 0 | 0 | 5 | 1 | 0 | 1 | 0 | 0 | 3 | 0 | 0 | 0 |
| moshikashitara | 0 | 0 | 1 | 0 | 0 | 0 | 55 | 14 | 2 | 0 | 4 | 0 | 0 | 0 | 4 | 1 | 0 | 0 | 0 | 3 | 0 | 0 | 0 |

From the results presented in the Table 2 and Figure 2, we can clearly observe the differences in modality types and forms in comparison to the previously introduced results from Kudô. While *kanarazu*, *zettai*, *zettaini*, *tabun*, *osoraku*, *sazo*, *ookata*, *doumo*, *douyara*, *hyottoshitara* (*hyottosuruto*), *kotoniyoreba* (*kotoniyoruto*), *moshikasuruto* (*moshikashitara*), *angai* all share more-less the same association preferences towards modality types as in Kudô's data, the rest of the adverbs *taigai*, *kitto*, *yohodo*, *taitei*, and *aruiwa* exhibit a different collocational tendencies with the modality types. *Taigai* and *kitto* exibit interesting switches from EXPECTATION to NECESSITY and the other way around. *Yohodo* and *taitei* have very frequent associations with the unmarked modality, while *aruiwa* behaves rather like a conjunction, and, thus, the clustering results for these three adverbs are questionable. Because of the differences with Kudô's data, it should also be noted that slightly different groups of adverbs are formed in the cluster analysis, although the four modality types can still be well attested. The frequency of associations with modal form types is also rather different compared to Kudô. Here, we can speculate on some possible reasons for the differences. JpWaC is more spontaneous and less formal than Kudô's data. Also, the web data represent the newest form of recorded language, while Kudô used older modern texts for analysis, which may reflect some kind of semantic shift.

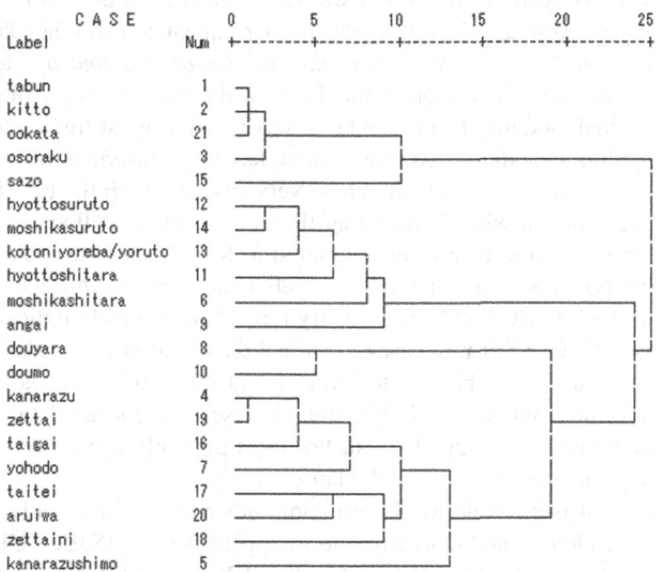


**Fig. 2.** Cluster analysis results for the JpWaC data

## 2.3 Adverb-Modality Relations in NLP Articles and School Textbooks

In this section we have a closer look into the co-occurrence of suppositional adverbs and the clause-final modality types in the three written corpora: '16 kyoukasho' (16K), 'NLP' papers (NLP) and 'Kokugo kyoukasho' (Kk).

It is already clear from looking into the frequencies of adverbs, that 16K and NLP show more similarity than Kk. This is because the first two corpora consist of natural science texts, and the third one consists of school textbooks having more general register. From the data it is clear that *kanarazu*, *kanarazushimo* and *osoraku* are the most frequent in natural science texts. In the Table 3 we can observe how the most frequent adverbs collocate with the clause-final modality.

*Kanarazushimo* has very similar behavior in both corpora, showing tendency towards co-occurring with the modality forms expressing NECESSITY (*wake/koto/mono de wa nai*, *nai koto ga wakaru* etc), and having one third of the occurrences with unmarked modality in negation (*de wa nai*, *shinai*). Here, it should be noted that *kanarazushimo* obligatorily co-occurs with negation and thus the associated modality forms represent negation of NECESSITY, which may semantically include other modality types. Therefore, *kanarazushimo* needs a special treatment and will be excluded from comparison with other adverbs in this paper.

*Kanarazu* is more frequent in the 16K corpus, where it mostly co-occurs with *suru koto*[2] (NECESSITY) and the unmarked modality *suru*. In the NLP corpus the data are insufficient to draw some conclusion, although it can be noticed that *kanarazu* occurs most with the unmarked modality (*suru*, *V-te iru/kuru/oku*). *Osoraku,* appearing in the 16K corpus, clearly shows the tendency towards the EXPECTATION modality type, co-occurring with the forms *darou*, *no de wa nai darou ka*, *to kangaerareru*.

In the 'Kokugo kyoukasho' corpus, the most frequent adverbs are *kitto*, *doumo*, *kanarazu*, *sazo*, *taitei* and *douyara*. *Osoraku* and *kanarazushimo* are less frequent than in the natural-science texts. From the Table 4, the tendencies for the association with the clause-final modality forms can be observed. *Kitto* most frequently co-occurs with the NECESSITY modality type (69 times), having *hazu da*, *no da*, *ni chigai nai* and *mono da* as its main collocates. It is also very frequent with the EXPECTATION modality type (22 times), with *darou* being the most frequent collocate in the group. This is again an interesting behaviour compared to Kudô's data, where *kitto* strongly associates with NECESSITY, and in the web data, where *kitto* most frequently collocates with the EXPECTATION modality type. This probably indicates that *kitto* is biased towards NECESSITY in cases of formal data written in accordance with the language norm, but it is biased towards EXPECTATION in cases of more spontaneous informal data. While Kudô's data represent the former data type, and the web represents the latter, 'kokugo kyoukasho' most probably consist of both types of data, the former type dominating over the latter.

From the data, it is possible to discern some other trends in the adverb-modality type associations. *Doumo* and *douyara* tend to appear with CONJECTURE modality type, *tabun*, *sazo* and *osoraku* with the EXPECTATION modality type, *moshikashitara* and *aruiwa* with the POSSIBILITY modality type. *Kanarazu* shows some trends towards the NECESSITY type, although in this case and with some other adverbs, the unmarked modality is too dominant and calls for a closer look into the specific examples.

---

[2] Most of the cases belong to the DEONTIC modality (must do, ought to do, etc..) and not EPISTEMIC (or EVIDENTIAL) modality (the fact must be that...). DEONTIC tends to be recycled as an EPISTEMIC modality, especially in the case of NECESSITY.

**Table 3.** The most frequent suppositional adverbs and their modality forms in the 16K and NLP corpora

| adverb/modality | NEC_hitsuyou_ga_nai | NEC_koto/mono_de_wa_nai | NEC_nai_koto_ga_wakaru | NEC_no_de_wa_nai | NEC_suru_koto | NEC_wake_de_wa_nai | EXP_darou | EXP_ienai | EXP_no_de_wa_nai_darou_ka | EXP_to_kangaerareru | POSS_dekiru/nai | POSS_sarenai_koto_ga_aru | POSS_to_wa_kagiranai | UNM_da | UNM_de_wa_nai | UNM_shinai | UNM_suru | UNM_to_naru | UNM_V-te_inai | UNM_V-te_iru/kuru/oku | OTHER | total |
|---|---|---|---|---|---|---|---|---|---|---|---|---|---|---|---|---|---|---|---|---|---|---|
| 16K_kanarazu | 0 | 0 | 0 | 0 | 13 | 1 | 2 | 0 | 0 | 0 | 5 | 0 | 0 | 3 | 0 | 1 | 21 | 3 | 0 | 3 | 4 | 56 |
| 16K_kanarazushimo | **1** | **4** | **6** | **1** | **0** | **3** | 0 | 3 | 0 | 0 | 0 | 0 | 6 |  | **18** | **11** | 0 | 0 | 1 | 0 | 1 | 55 |
| 16K_osoraku | 0 | 0 | 0 | 0 | 0 | 0 | **3** | **0** | **1** | **3** | 0 | 0 | 0 | 0 | 0 | 0 | 0 | 0 | 0 | 1 | 1 | 9 |
| NLP_kanarazu | 0 | 0 | 0 | 0 | 0 | 0 | 1 | 0 | 0 | 0 | 0 | 0 | 0 | 0 | 0 | 0 | 3 | 0 | 0 | 3 | 0 | 7 |
| NLP_kanarazushimo | **0** | **2** | **0** | **0** | **0** | **6** | 0 | 2 | 0 | 0 | 0 | 1 | 1 | 0 | **6** | **3** | 0 | 0 | 2 | 0 | 0 | 23 |
| total | 1 | 6 | 6 | 1 | 13 | 10 | 6 | 5 | 1 | 3 | 5 | 1 | 7 | 3 | 24 | 15 | 24 | 3 | 3 | 7 | 5 | 150 |

**Table 4.** The suppositional adverbs and clause-final modality in the Kk corpus

| adverb/modality | NEChazu_da | NECmono_da | NECni_chigainai | NEC_no_da | EXPdarou | EXPno_darou | EXPno_de_wa_nai_ka | EXPto_omou/-wareru | CONrashii | CONyou_da | CONsou_da | POSSkamoshirenai | POSSdarouka | UNMzero | OTHER | total |
|---|---|---|---|---|---|---|---|---|---|---|---|---|---|---|---|---|
| angai | 0 | 0 | 0 | 0 | 0 | 0 | 1 | 0 | 0 | 0 | 0 | 3 | 0 | 0 | 0 | 4 |
| aruiwa | 0 | 0 | 0 | 0 | 0 | 0 | 0 | 0 | 0 | 0 | 0 | **5** | 0 | 0 | 0 | 5 |
| doumo | 0 | 1 | 0 | 3 | 0 | 0 | 0 | 0 | **7** | **1** | **1** | 0 | 0 | 22 | 7 | 42 |
| douyara | 0 | 0 | 0 | 1 | 0 | 0 | 0 | 0 | **4** | **3** | 0 | 0 | 0 | 2 | 0 | 10 |
| hyottoshitara | 0 | 0 | 0 | 0 | 0 | 0 | 0 | 0 | 0 | 0 | 0 | 2 | 0 | 0 | 0 | 2 |
| kanarazu | 0 | 0 | **1** | **3** | 0 | 0 | 0 | 0 | 0 | 0 | 0 | 0 | 0 | **16** | 1 | 21 |
| kanarazu_to | 0 | 0 | 0 | 0 | 0 | 0 | 0 | 0 | 0 | 0 | 0 | 0 | 0 | 2 | 0 | 2 |
| kanarazushimo | 0 | 0 | 0 | 1 | 0 | 0 | 0 | 0 | 0 | 0 | 0 | 0 | 0 | 0 | 0 | 1 |
| kesshite | 0 | 0 | 0 | 0 | 0 | 0 | 0 | 0 | 0 | 0 | 0 | 0 | 0 | 1 | 0 | 1 |
| kitto | **41** | **2** | **10** | **16** | **15** | **4** | **0** | **3** | 0 | 0 | 0 | 0 | 0 | 10 | 37 | 101 |
| moshikashitara | 0 | 0 | 0 | 0 | 0 | 0 | 1 | 0 | 0 | 0 | 0 | **8** | **1** | 0 | 2 | 12 |
| ookata | 0 | 0 | 0 | 0 | 1 | 1 | 0 | 0 | 0 | 0 | 0 | 0 | 0 | 0 | 0 | 2 |
| osoraku | 0 | 0 | 1 | 0 | **3** | 0 | 0 | **1** | 0 | 0 | 0 | 0 | 0 | 0 | 0 | 5 |
| sazo | 0 | 0 | 0 | 1 | **14** | 0 | 0 | 0 | 0 | 0 | 0 | 0 | 0 | 0 | 0 | 15 |
| tabun | 0 | 0 | 0 | 0 | **4** | **1** | 0 | 0 | 0 | 0 | 0 | 0 | 0 | 1 | 0 | 6 |
| taitei | 0 | 1 | 0 | 1 | 0 | 0 | 0 | 0 | 0 | 0 | 0 | 0 | 0 | **9** | 1 | 12 |
| yoppodo | 0 | 0 | 0 | 0 | 0 | 1 | 0 | 0 | 0 | 0 | 0 | 0 | 0 | 1 | 0 | 2 |
| zettai | 1 | 0 | 0 | 0 | 0 | 0 | 0 | 0 | 0 | 0 | 0 | 0 | 0 | 0 | 1 | 2 |
| zettaini | 0 | 0 | 0 | 1 | 0 | 0 | 0 | 1 | 0 | 0 | 0 | 0 | 0 | 4 | 0 | 7 |

The distribution of suppositional adverbs is similar in cases of corpora belonging to the same genre, and shows some differences in the corpora belonging to different genres. The association of the adverbs with their modality types tends to have similar trends across the genres, although some differences in modality forms can be noticed. *Kitto* shows the most obvious variation, being indeterminate between NECESSITY and EXPECTATION.

## 3 Possible Application

The information on adverbs and clause-final modality forms associations, obtained from large-scale corpora resources, and the coarse-grained hierarchy of various relations between modality types can be used for the enhancement of computer-based lexicons, computer-assisted language learning systems, linguistic ontology, as well as creating user's dictionaries and other language learning resources.

One possible application of the data is to enrich the computer-assisted language learning system Natsume [5], supporting learners with writing in Japanese. The system includes a database of co-occurrences and currently offers frequently co-occurring nouns–case particles–verbs relations based on various corpora. Using the set of modality forms and other data obtained in the analysis, we plan to develop the automatic retrieval of collocational information on adverbs and predicates, as well as adverbs and clause-final modality forms, also including distant relations, and thus enhance the database. As our data suggests, genre specific retrieval would be necessary. The system also extracts examples according to learner proficiency level, which is a valuable function for language learners. The modal adverb and clause-final modality association should be also considered from that pedagogical perspective.

Lexical knowledge bases (LKBs), which aim to cover the linguistic behavior of words in detail, are another potential resource that could be enhanced by this type of information. According to Hirst [22] in addition to 'classical' lexical relationships, such as synonyms, antonyms, hipernyms, etc, present for example in the WordNet ontology [23], there are many other relationships that could be included in a lexicon. These may be broadly thought as 'associative' or 'typicality' relations. Hirst gives a number of examples, such as frequent and typical agent (*dog* and *bark* – *bark* is a frequent and typical agent of the former), typical instrumentality (*nail* - *hammer*). Following this approach, the adverb-modality relations could also be implemented into a knowledge database. Here, we can think of at least four modal relations types for suppositional adverbs – those expressing 'necessity', 'expectation', 'conjecture' and 'possibility'. Each of the modality types shows some gradation in its function depending on the modality form applied. Also, the differences due to the genre, register, and style would be preferably included.

The approach could be expanded to other long distant associative co-occurrence relationships that would ideally be included in Japanese grammars, dictionaries, large-knowledge databases and other language resource. The importance of this type of information may be applicable to other languages, most probably for other SVO-type languages, such as Korean, Turkish, and Mongolian.

The present research is also of theoretical interest, because it can clarify various motivations for explicit signaling (the beginning and the end) of a range of modality in discourse. Implications are both language-theoretic (modes of signaling linguistic information, semantic shift over short time-spans) and language processing theoretic (contribution of such long-distance structures to the facilitation of communication and/or processing through disambiguation; closer examination of long distance relationships in the discourse in general and their contribution towards communication and ease of processing) [3].

## 4 Conclusion and Further Work

The paper discusses the strong agreement-like behaviour of suppositional adverbs and clause-final modality forms in Japanese language from an empirical perspective. After analyzing various corpora we confirm that specific suppositional adverbs typically collocate with one out of four modality types (a set of modality forms) to a high degree, while they may also co-occur with other types at lesser degrees. However, the results of comparisons across different corpora indicate that the occurrences of adverbs, as well as their co-occurrence with modality forms, occasionally vary across different genres. This tendency can be observed in the cluster analysis performed for Kudô's results and the web corpus data, as well as in comparing the data with the results from other smaller corpora of different genres (NUJCC, Oikawa, 16 kyoukasho, NLP and Kokugo kyoukasho). In particular, we would emphasis the case of *kitto* in shifting from NECESSITY to EXPECTATION across genres.

Long distance associative co-occurrence relationships – distant collocations – should be more systematically covered in language research. The distance between collocates can be longer then 10 tokens and it is subject to changes with different adverbs, as well as different genres and registers.

The web data especially draws attention to the variety and complexity of modality forms and suggests the need to observe modality forms with forms of layers structure.

The results of the analysis may be used as a pre-step for performing the automatic extraction of distant relations from various corpora into a co-occurrence database. They can be applied to the enhancement of various large-scale knowledge resources, such as computer-assisted language learning systems, lexicons, and corpus query tools displaying word's properties, as well as user-oriented dictionaries and grammars.

## References

1. Minami, F.: Gendai nihongo no kôzô (Structure of the Modern Japanese language), Taishûkan shoten, Tokyo (1974)
2. Kudô, H.: Fukushi to bun no chinjutsu no taipu (Adverbs and the type of clause-final modality). In: Nitta, Y., Masuoka, T. (eds.) Nihongo no bunpô 3 – Modariti (Japanese grammar 3: Modality), Iwanami shoten, Tokyo, pp. 161–234 (2000)
3. Bekeš, A.: Japanese Suppositional Adverbs: Modality and Probability in Speaker-Hearer Interaction. In: Unpublished paper, presented at the Conference Japanese Modality Revisited, June 24-25, 2006, SOAS, London (2006)

4. Bekeš, A.: Japanese suppositional adverbs in speaker-hearer interaction. In: The third conference on Japanese language and Japanese language teaching: Proceedings of the conference, Rome, March 17-19, 2005, pp. 34–48. Libreria editrice cafoscarina, Venezia (2006)
5. Nishina, K., Yoshihashi, K.: Japanese Composition Support System Displaying Occurrences and Example Sentences. In: Symposium on Large-scale Knowledge Resources (LKR2007), pp. 119–122 (2007)
6. Minami, F.: Gendai nihongo bunpô no rinkaku (Outline of the modern Japanese grammar), Taishûkan shoten, Tokyo (1993)
7. Bekeš, A.: Gengo ni okeru fukakujitsusei: kyôkai kara mita monogataribun ni okeru wa (Uncertainty in the language: use of particle wa in narrative and the notion of boundary). In: Organizing Committee (ed.) Dai 15 kai nihongo kyôiku renraku kaigi, Durham, August 3–4, 2002, pp. 88–97 (2003)
8. Partington, A.: Patterns and Meanings: Using corpora for English language research and teaching. John Benjamins, Amsterdam (1998)
9. Sinclair, J.: Corpus, Concordance, Collocation. Oxford University Press, Oxford (1991)
10. Manning, C.D., Schütze, H.: Foundations of statistical natural language processing. MIT Press, Cambridge, MA (1999)
11. Church, K.W., Hanks, P.: Word Association Norms, Mutual Information, and Lexicography. Computational Linguistics 16(1), 22–29 (1990)
12. Ikehara, S., Shirai, S., Uchino, H.: A Statistical Method for Extracting Uninterrupted and Interrupted Collocations from Very Large Corpora. In: Proceedings of 16th International Conference on Computational Linguistics (COLING-96), pp. 574–579 (1996)
13. Milkov, N.: Logico-Linguistic Moleculism: Towards an Ontology of Collocations and other [Language] Patterns. In: Proceedings of OntoLex 2000: Ontologies and Lexical Knowledge Bases, pp. 82–94. OntoText Lab, Sofia (2001)
14. Oikawa, T.: Jinbunkagaku to kopyûtâ DATABASE, vol. 1, Sôgô kenkyû daigaku (transcribed interviews of 50 Japanese native speakers, approximately 820 KB) (1998)
15. Ohso, M.: Meidai kaiwa kôpasu. Kagakukenkyûhi kiban kenkyu (B)(2) Nihongogakushûjisho hensan ni muketa denshika kôpasu riyô ni yoru korokeeshon kenkyû (2001–3). Nagoya University Japanese Conversation Corpus (NUJCC). Unpublished research report. About 100 informal conversations between familiar participants. Text file size 3.5 MB (2003)
16. Erjavec, T., Kilgarriff, A., Srdanović, E.I.: A large public-access Japanese corpus and its query tool. In: CoJaS 2007, The Inaugural Workshop on Computational Japanese Studies. Ikaho (2007)
17. Kilgarriff, A., et al.: The Sketch Engine. In: Proc. Euralex. Lorient, France, pp. 105–116 (2004)
18. Srdanović, E.I., Erjavec, T., Kilgarriff, A.: A web corpus and word-sketches for Japanese. Journal of Natural Language Processing (submitted)
19. Minami, F.: Jutsugobun no kôzô (Structure of the predicative sentences), originally in Kokugo Kenkyu 18, republished in Hattori et al. (eds.) (1978: (pp. 507–530), 1964)
20. Sharoff, S.: Creating general-purpose corpora using automated search engine queries. WaCky! Working papers on the Web as Corpus. Gedit, Bologna (2006)
21. Ueyama, M., Baroni, M.: Automated construction and evaluation of a Japanese web-based reference corpus. In: Proceedings of Corpus Linguistics 2005. Birmingham, UK (2005)
22. Hirst, G.: Ontology and the Lexicon. In: Staab, S., Studer, R. (eds.) Handbook on Ontologies in Information Systems, Springer, Berlin (2003)
23. Fellbaum, C. (ed.): WordNet: An Electronic Lexical Database. MIT Press, Cambridge, MA (1998)

# Using Singular Value Decomposition to Compute Answer Similarity in a Language Independent Approach to Question Answering

Edward Whittaker[1], Josef Novak[1], Matthias Heie[1], Shuichiro Imai[1], and Sadaoki Furui[1]

Tokyo Institute of Technology, Ookayama Meguro-ku, Tokyo 152-8552, Japan

**Abstract.** In this paper we report on new developments in our data-driven, non-linguistic, language-independent approach to Question Answering (QA). In particular, we describe a new implementation of the filter-model, which is used for answer typing, where we employ the Singular Value Decomposition (SVD) in a variation on the popular Latent Semantic Analysis technique. We also describe refinements to the open-source SVD code that we used which enable us to perform the SVD on arbitrarily large matrices. Finally, we discuss results from the TREC 2005 and TREC 2006 QA evaluations in which we applied these new techniques, and compare them to results achieved with our previous filter-model approach. In particular, we show that our new filter-model using the SVD achieves an average absolute gain of around 8% and an average relative gain of nearly 59% over our previous approach for top one answer accuracy. By using both approaches in combination we are able to increase the absolute gain to approximately 10% and the relative gain to 67%.

## 1 Introduction

In this paper we report on the progress made on our data-driven, non-linguistic, language independent approach to Question Answering (QA) that has been developed at Tokyo Institute of Technology over the past few years. QA has continued to grow in popularity and mature as a research area in recent years as evidenced by the increasing number of and variation among conferences that support or include QA evaluations such as CLEF, TREC and NTCIR. Several of these conferences such as CLEF and NTCIR hold evaluations in different languages and across languages where the query language and target language differ. Moreover, CLEF and TREC have recently begun to expand target domains for the evaluations from traditional web or annotated text corpora to include finding answers in more 'difficult' target corpora such as blog data and spoken transcriptions. While the central focus of the research community continues to remain factoid QA, evaluations also include a limited number of more complex *why*, *how* and *definition* questions.

In this paper we begin by outlining the basic mathematical framework for our approach to QA, which we split up broadly into two basic components. The

T. Tokunaga and A. Ortega (Eds.): LKR 2008, LNAI 4938, pp. 267–279, 2008.

first component is the *retrieval model* which extracts answer candidates from a set of documents based on the proximity to and co-occurrence with information-bearing words in the question. The answer candidates are then passed to the second component, the *filter model* whose purpose is to reorder the set of candidate answers based on their predicted answer type, which is determined by comparison with a large training set of example questions and answers (q-and-a). In this paper we focus specifically on a new filter model, where we employ Singular Value Decomposition (SVD) to perform answer type classification by comparing candidate answers to a collection of example answers in a reduced number of dimensions. In addition to advances in the core system technology, we also describe recent evaluation results for the English language system in the 2005 and 2006 Text REtreival Conference (TREC) QA evaluations, where we compare results achieved with our new filter-model approach to that of the older model, as well as the results of applying the two approaches in combination.

The rest of the paper is structured as follows. In section 2 we present an overview of our current QA architecture and include an extensive discussion on our application of the SVD to the implementation of the filter model. In Section 4 we describe and outline our results from the TREC 2005 and the TREC 2006 QA evaluations, respectively. Finally, we give an analysis of these recent results in Section 5, and conclude the paper with Section 6.

## 2 QA as Statistical Classification with Non-linguistic Features

When responding to questions in a real-world scenario, humans consider a wide range of different factors including the identity of the questioner, immediate environmental and social context, and previously asked questions, among other variables. While such factors are clearly relevant, and humans are adept at integrating such information, modelling these features is far from trivial. Therefore, in our attempts up to now we limit ourselves to modelling the most straightforward dependence: the probability of an answer $A$ depending on the question $Q$,

$$P(A \mid Q) = P(A \mid W, X), \tag{1}$$

where $A$ and $Q$ are considered to be a string of $l_A$ words $A = a_1, \ldots, a_{l_A}$ and $l_Q$ words $Q = q_1, \ldots, q_{l_Q}$, respectively. Here $W = w_1, \ldots, w_{l_W}$ represents a set of features describing the "question-type" part of $Q$ such as *when*, *why*, *how*, etc. while $X = x_1, \ldots, x_{l_X}$ represents a set of features that describe the "information-bearing" part of $Q$ i.e. what the question is actually about and what it refers to. For example, in the questions, *Who is the oldest person in the world?* and *How old is the oldest person in the world?* the question-types *who* and *how old* differ, while the information-bearing component, *the oldest person in the world*, does not change.

Finding the best answer $\hat{A}$ involves a search over all available $A$ for the one which maximises the probability of the above model i.e.,

$$\hat{A} = \arg\max_{A} P(A \mid W, X). \tag{2}$$

Given the correct probability distribution this is guaranteed to give us the optimal answer in a maximum likelihood sense. We don't know this distribution, and it is still difficult to model but, using Bayes' rule and making various simplifying, modelling and conditional independence assumptions (as described in detail in [2,1,3]) Equation (2) can be rearranged to give

$$\arg\max_{A} \underbrace{P(A \mid X)}_{\substack{retrieval\\ model}} \cdot \underbrace{P(W \mid A)}_{\substack{filter\\ model}}. \tag{3}$$

The $P(A \mid X)$ model is essentially a statistical language model that models the probability of an answer candidate $A$ given a set of information-bearing features $X$. We call this model the *retrieval model* and do not examine it further here (see [2,1,3] for more details).

The $P(W \mid A)$ model matches a potential answer $A$ with features in the question-type set $W$. For example, it relates place names with *where*-type questions. In general, there are many valid and equiprobable $A$ for a given $W$ so this component can only re-rank candidate answers which have been retrieved and scored by the retrieval model. We call this component the *filter model* and outline its function in the following section.

### 2.1 Filter Model

The question-type feature set $W = w_1, \ldots, w_{l_W}$ is constructed by extracting $n$-tuples ($n = 1, 2, \ldots$) such as *Where, In what* and *When were* from the input question $Q$. A set of $|V_{\mathcal{W}}| = 2522$ single-word features is extracted based on frequency of occurrence in our collection of example questions.

Modelling the complex relationship between $W$ and $A$ directly is non-trivial. We therefore introduce an intermediate variable representing classes of example questions-and-answers (q-and-a) $c_e$ for $e = 1 \ldots |C_E|$ drawn from the set $C_E$. In order to construct these classes, given a set $E$ of example q-and-a, we then define a mapping function $f : E \mapsto C_E$ which maps each example q-and-a $t_j$ for $j = 1 \ldots |E|$ into a particular class $f(t_j) = e$. Thus each class $c_e$ may be defined as the union of all component q-and-a features from each $t_j$ satisfying $f(t_j) = e$. Finally, to facilitate modelling we say that $W$ is conditionally independent of $c_e$ given $A$ so that,

$$P(W \mid A) = \sum_{e=1}^{|C_E|} P(W \mid c_W^e) \cdot P(c_A^e \mid A). \tag{4}$$

where $c_W^e$ and $c_A^e$ refer respectively to the subsets of question-type features and example answers for the class $c_e$.

Assuming conditional independence of the answer words in class $c_e$ given $A$, and making the modelling assumption that the $j$th answer word $a_j^e$ in the example class $c_e$ is dependent only on the $j$th answer word in $A$ we obtain:

$$P(W \mid A) = \sum_{e=1}^{|C_E|} P(W \mid c_e) \cdot \prod_{j=1}^{l_{A^e}} P(a_j^e \mid a_j). \qquad (5)$$

Since our set of example q-and-a cannot be expected to cover all the possible answers to questions that may be asked we perform a similar operation to that above to give us the following:

$$P(W \mid A) = \sum_{e=1}^{|C_E|} P(W \mid c_e) \prod_{j=1}^{l_{A^e}} \sum_{a=1}^{|C_A|} P(a_j^e \mid c_a) P(c_a \mid a_j), \qquad (6)$$

where $c_a$ is a concrete class in the set of $|C_A|$ answer classes $C_A$.

The system using the above formulation of filter model given by Equation (6) is referred to as model ONE, and is described in detail in [1]. Systems using the model given by Equation (4) are referred to as model TWO. In this paper we focus on the details and implementation of model TWO which has not been described previously, and compare its performance to that of model ONE.

## 3 Application of the Singular Value Decomposition to Answer Typing

In both models ONE and TWO, *question typing* is effected by $P(W|C_e)$ which essentially matches bigrams from a new input question against bigrams in questions from our example set of q-and-a. This has been described in detail in [6].

For each example question $C_e$ in $C_E$ there is a corresponding example answer. Assuming an example question has been hypothesised with a particular probability the corresponding example answer is used as the basis for answer typing in both models ONE and TWO. In model ONE this is accomplished by using automatically generated classes of similar words $C_A$ to describe the similarity between answers. These classes of similar words are then used for computing $P(C_a \mid A)$.

In model TWO, however, we employ the Singular Value Decomposition [5] and the similarity between candidate and example answers is computed in a reduced number of dimensions for answer typing. As a first step in this process we construct a matrix composed of co-occurrence counts for all the example answers in our set of example q-and-a, as well as a subset of the most frequently occurring words from a large text training corpus. We then decompose the resulting matrix into 3 component matrices which include a left singular matrix, a right singular matrix and a diagonal matrix of singular values. Only the $R$ largest singular values are calculated, which has the effect of reducing the dimensionality of the original matrix.

For each new candidate answer we construct a pseudo vector which we project into the reduced space using the standard technique described variously in the literature [4,7]. Finally we use a simple cosine measure to compare the new pseudo vectors for candidate answers, to the answer vectors from our example q-and-a in the new, reduced space.

The approach we employ is similar in theory to Latent Semantic Analysis [4], and Latent Semantic Mapping [7] which have enjoyed much attention recently in a variety of different areas of Natural Language Processing. Below we outline the mathematics behind the method, and also describe our implementation in more detail.

### 3.1 SVD Background

The Singular Value Decomposition is a technique in matrix theory and linear algebra which can be used to decompose any arbitrary matrix into a set of three new matrices each with certain special properties. This decomposition is typically described with the following formula,

$$W = USV^T, \tag{7}$$

where $W$ refers to the original $(M \times N)$ matrix, $U$ refers to the $(M \times R)$ left singular matrix with row vectors $u_i$, $S$ refers to the $(R \times R)$ diagonal matrix of singular values $s_1 \leq s_2 \leq ... \leq s_R$, and $V^T$ refers to the $(N \times R)$ right singular matrix with rows $v_j$ such that $(1 \leq j \leq N)$, $R \leq min(M, N)$ is the number of singular values, and $^T$ refers to the transpose of a matrix. An interesting and useful property of the SVD is that for any matrix $\hat{W} = USV^T$ where $R < min(M, N)$, $\hat{W}$ represents the closest rank $R$ approximation of the original matrix $W$ [5].

### 3.2 Co-occurrence Matrix

The matrix we construct represents the global co-occurrence statistics for a select subset of the training data vocabulary computed using around 5 billion words of web data by retrieving up to 100 web pages for each unique answer in our example q-and-a.

The column headings of our co-occurrence matrix correspond to the set of unique answers from our set of example q-and-a. Thus, if “June 14 1991” were the answer to one of the example questions, one of the matrix columns would correspond to “JUNE_14_1991”. In particular our English system consists of 252,882 columns, which correspond to the 52,882 unique example answers in the training data, plus 200,000 additional frequently occurring terms derived from a large text corpus.

The set of unique row vocabulary also consists of a total of 252,882 terms $|V_C|$ which includes the same 52,882 unique example answers, and the same additional 200,000 most frequently occurring terms that are used in the column headings. In the case of the rows however, this vocabulary is repeated $2 \times D$ times where $D$ refers to the maximum distance used in calculating the skip-bigram contextual frequency information which forms the basis for the individual cell values. Thus, the first set of 252,882 rows records the co-occurrence statistics for right-hand distance-1 skip-bigrams, the second set of 252,882 rows records the co-occurrence statistics for left-hand distance-1 skip bigrams, and this process is repeated up to a maximum distance of $D$ so that total number of rows in our co-occurrence matrix corresponds to $252,882 \times (2 \times D)$. In the current English system described in this paper D was set equal to 3 and the total number of rows is thus $252,882 \times 6 = 1,517,292$ and the total number of entries is equal to $252,882 \times (1,517,292) = 383,695,835,544$. However, it is important to note that the resulting matrix contains many zero-valued entries and is extremely sparse even though it still typically contains around a billion non-zero entries.

In particular, for each column entry $a_i$ and each of the 252,882 row entry terms $v_c$ we calculate a weighted conditional count $a_{(v_c,d)}$, the number of times that $v_c$ occurs given that $a$ occurs $d$ words away. When $d$ is positive this refers to the fact that $v_c$ occurs after $a$, and where $d$ is negative this similarly refers to the fact that $v_c$ occurs before $a$. This process is repeated for $d = 1, ..., D$ such that the result is a a set of 252,882 co-occurrence vectors where each vector, $\boldsymbol{a}$ is of length $|V_C| \times (2 \times D)$ with maximum separation between words $D$,

$$\begin{aligned} \boldsymbol{a} = [&a_{(v_1,1)}, \ldots, a_{(v_R,1)}, a_{(v_1,-1)}, \ldots, a_{(v_R,-1)}, \\ &\ldots, a_{(v_1,D)}, \ldots, a_{(v_R,D)}, \ldots, a_{(v_1,-D)}, \ldots, a_{(v_R,-D)}]. \end{aligned} \tag{8}$$

Furthermore, both a global weighting scheme and a local weighting scheme are employed to normalize counts. The global weight may be thought of as an entropy like feature which indicates how informative a particular word is. Consequently, a word like "THE" which occurs almost everywhere will tend to be de-weighted as it bears little significance. The global weight $a_{glob}$ is computed as follows for each vocabulary entry $a$ and is applied to every matrix entry, based on its identity,

$$a_{glob} = 1.0 - \sum_{j=1}^{|V_C|} \frac{P(v_j \mid a) \cdot log(P(v_j \mid a))}{-log(|V_C|)} \tag{9}$$

The local weight is computed simply as $log(1 + a_{(v_r,d)_{raw}})$, where $a_{(v_r,d)_{raw}}$ represents the raw count of the number of times $a$ appears with $v_r$ at a distance $d$ words away. The final conditional count for an entry, $a_{fin}$ is then computed as follows,

$$a_{fin} = log(1 + a_{(v_r,d)_{raw}}) \cdot a_{glob} \tag{10}$$

In order to save space, and because of its inherent sparsity, we store the matrix in a sparse binary format which only explicitly stores non-zero values [8]. The SVD itself was carried out using the open source SVDLIBC package[1] which we substantially customized to meet our needs. In particular, we modified the source code to perform operations on matrices stored on disk, which by eliminating the need to hold the full matrix in memory, substantially increases the maximum tractable size of matrix that a single CPU of reasonable performance can handle. The number of singular values used for the decomposition was determined experimentally, and fixed at 100, and the iterative lanczos algorithm [9] was used to compute the SVD.

[1] Available at `http://tedlab.mit.edu/~dr/SVDLIBC/`

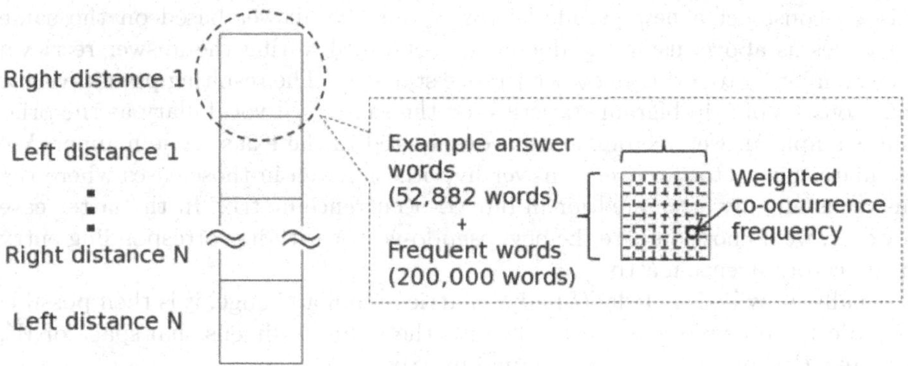


**Fig. 1.** Structure of the co-occurrence matrix. Currently N=1 for the English language system.

### 3.3 Comparing Answers

The central feature of the SVD technique is that, by eliminating superfluous higher dimensional noise, and compressing the data into a smaller and hopefully more meaningful dimensional space, more accurate comparisons can be made between individual units [4,7]. In our case we wish to compare new candidate answers to example answers from our training data, thus it is desirable to define a unit as a unique example answer along with a statistical representation of the context in which it typically occurs. The most popular method for measuring the closeness of two units in the reduced dimensional space produced by the SVD is just the cosine of the angle between the two unit vectors $u_i$ and $u_j$ which is computed in the standard way,

$$cos(u_i, u_j) = \frac{u_i S^2 u_j}{\|u_i S\| \|u_j S\|} \tag{11}$$

where $S$ refers to the diagonal matrix of singular values and $\|u_i S\|$ refers to the norm of the vector. In this scenario a value of 1 would indicate that the two answers always appear in similar context and are thus likely to be of similar type, while a value of 0 would indicate that they never appear in the same context, and are thus not very likely to be of similar type. We also note here that even in cases where the answers are countries or numbers, comparing them with example answers in our matrix may not produce a value of one. While these answers may intuitively be of the same type, the fact that "1" does not appear in exactly the same contexts as "1,000,000" will lead to a lower value. Although it is possible to obtain values of $cos(u_i, u_j) < 0$ from computing the cosine distance between two vectors, for computational purposes we floor any negative values to zero.

While the above may be appropriate for answers which already appear in our example set, for new answer candidates that have never been seen before it is necessary to first project a similar vector representation for these into the original matrix before any meaningful comparison can be made. In order to achieve this we construct a new pseudo-vector $\tilde{x}_j$ for the answer based on the same principles as above, using the documents obtained during the answer retrieval process in order to estimate co-occurrence statistics. The resulting pseudo-vector thus consists of skip bigram statistics for the same $|V_C|$ vocabulary as the original example answer vectors, and is constructed in the exact same manner. We calculate this vector for every answer hypothesis, even in those cases where the answer is already accounted for in our co-occurrence matrix. In the latter case however, we do not compare the new pseudo-vector with its corresponding entry in the co-occurrence matrix.

Finally, provided that the $U$ and $S$ matrices do not change, it is then possible to project the new pseudo-vector $\tilde{x}_j$ into the reduced dimensional space of $\tilde{W}$, the rank $R$ approximation our original matrix,

$$\tilde{x}_j = US\tilde{v}_j^T, \tag{12}$$

and by rearranging the above equation we have,

$$\tilde{v}_j S = x_j^T U, \tag{13}$$

where $\tilde{v}_j S$ can then be used in the manner described above to perform comparisons between the new candidate answer and the set of example answers used to compile the original matrix.

### 3.4 Relationship between Model ONE and Model TWO

Models ONE and TWO are intrinsically related despite the different methods used to model their probability distributions. In model ONE classes of similar answers would ideally be used for answer typing, however, the space of possible answers is prohibitively large which renders choosing a set of answers, let alone clustering them, impossible. We therefore make an independence assumption between the words in an answer and cluster only individual words which is a much more tractable problem, albeit at the expense of the loss in answer typing accuracy. For the clustering itself we use the co-occurrence statistics of a word with other words to determine words' similarities to one another in the expectation that, say, people's first names are likely to possess similar co-occurrence properties to each other, as are numbers, cities, country-names, and so on. Note that this clustering is performed offline before the QA process begins so it can only consider words that were in the original set for clustering. New words that occur during the QA process and which had not appeared previously, so-called out-of-vocabulary (OOV) words, will typically not be correctly classified and will be given a small smoothed probability of membership in all classes.

In model TWO however, we perform the similarity computation online as part of the QA process so the problem with OOVs is alleviated to a large extent. In addition, in model TWO it is also possible to dispense with making the independence assumption between the words in an answer, because we store an example answer's *co-occurrence relationships* to words that it occurs next to, instead of storing its relationship to all other possible *answers* that may ever occur. Both these facts ought to make answer typing in model TWO much more accurate. Theoretically, it would be possible to compute the similarity in model TWO in an almost identical way to that used in the clustering algorithm to obtain the classes of similar words used in model ONE. However, the vectors used in the similarity computation are extremely large (of the order of a million elements) and typically extremely sparse, especially when the vector is constructed solely on the data used to find answers to a particular question. This is the primary motivation behind the application of the SVD in model TWO: (i) the computational efficiency of computing answer similarity in a reduced number of dimensions, and (ii) the robustness of the similarity computation to sparse input vectors when only the salient dimensions are considered.

## 4 Experimental Work

The TREC evaluations are co-sponsored by the National Institute of Standards and Technology (NIST) and the United States Defense Department, and have been conducted yearly since 1992. The aim of these evaluations is primarily to promote various kinds of research related to information retrieval on large text corpora. The TREC QA track was first conducted in 1999 and has been conducted yearly since 1998 [12].

We have successfully applied the SVD-based model TWO approach to several recent TREC QA evaluations. The results obtained with this method show substantial improvements over our earlier model ONE approach. In the following section we briefly describe the results and salient system details pertaining to our participation in the TREC 2005, and TREC 2006 QA evaluations.

### 4.1 TREC Evaluations (2005, 2006)

The TREC 2005 QA evaluation was the first opportunity we had to test the model TWO approach, and compare it to our earlier approach using model ONE in an official, independent evaluation. All earlier testing of the system prior to this official evaluation had been conducted 'after the fact'.

Recent TREC evaluations have divided the evaluation test question sets into three broad categories, *factoid* questions, *list* questions, and *other* questions. While we made attempts at answering each kind of question in the actual evaluation, our primary focus in the evaluations and in the experiments presented in this paper were the *factoid* questions which are typically formulated such that the corresponding correct answers are short and concise e.g., *"Who is the current president of France?"*.

It should be noted that answers for both the *factoid* and *list* questions are judged based on whether they completely answer the question, and are penalized for superfluous or missing information, such as units of measurement.

**TREC 2005.** For the TREC 2005 evaluation we employed both the model ONE and model TWO approaches exactly as described in Section 2. In both cases we optimised the system parameters based on data from the previous TREC 2002,

2003, and 2004 evaluations, using a rotating form of cross-validation but with emphasis on the more recent 2004 data. For training the filter model we use 288,812 example q-and-a from the Knowledge Master KM data [13], plus 2408 q-and-a from the TREC-8,9 and TREC2001 questions, and also the TREC 2002, 2003, and 2004 evaluation q-and-a in a rotating manner so as not to include test questions as examples during development.

The co-occurrence matrix for model TWO was constructed exactly as described in Section 3.2, using the same vocabulary of 52,882 unique example answers and the additional 200,000 frequently occurring terms from the AQUAINT corpus. For model ONE, the most frequent $|V_{C_A}| = 224,000$ words from the AQUAINT corpus were used to obtain $C_A$ for $|C_A| = 500$ clusters as described in [1].

Further details of the setup for this evaluation can be found in [2].

We submitted three formal runs for the official TREC 2005 track, *asked05a*, *asked05b*, and *asked05c* which employed model ONE, model TWO, and a combination of both ONE and TWO, respectively. The results of the three formal runs we submitted can be seen in Table 1.

**Table 1.** Performance on all 3 tasks of the 3 submitted runs and an estimated performance score for the factoid task of run

| System | Factoid task | | | Avg. per-series score |
|---|---|---|---|---|
| | Right | Unsupp. | ineXact | |
| `asked05a` | 45 (12.4%) | 7 (1.9%) | 21 (5.8%) | 0.108 |
| `asked05b` | 72 (19.9%) | 19 (5.2%) | 21 (5.8%) | 0.136 |
| `asked05c` | 77 (21.3%) | 19 (5.2%) | 22 (6.1%) | 0.157 |

The results from Table 1 show the percentage of right answers, unsupported answers, and answers which were judged incomplete or inexact. Answers were classified as unsupported based on whether or not the supplied supporting document justified the answer that was returned.

As can be seen from Table 1 results using the model TWO system which employs our SVD based technique significantly outperform results obtained using model ONE. It is also interesting to note that the results of the combined run, *asked05c*, outperformed both of the runs which were based on individual systems, and outperformed the model ONE run by almost 9% absolute and 59% relative. The high performance of the combined system can mainly be attributed to its ability to boost lower ranked answers appearing in both systems' output, into first place when the answers are combined (see [2] for details on the combination method used).

**TREC 2006.** The setup for the TREC 2006 evaluation was essentially identical to that used for the TREC 2005 evaluation, except for the data used for optimisation. For TREC 2006, our system parameters were optimised using data from TREC 2004 and TREC 2005. Again, although we submitted answers for the *other* and *list* questions, we focus here on the results for the *factoid* questions from the evaluation set. For the 2006 evaluation we again submitted three official runs, where run *asked06a* employed model ONE, run *asked06b* employed a model ONE and a model TWO system in combination, and run *asked06c* was a combination of the model ONE and model TWO systems, plus translated results from both a Spanish and a French system, and results from the open-source Aranea QA system. Detailed results for the 3 tasks can be seen in Table 2.

**Table 2.** Performance on the 3 tasks of the 3 submitted runs

| System | Factoid task | | | Avg. per-series score |
|---|---|---|---|---|
| | Right | Unsupp. | ineXact | |
| `asked06a` | 62 (15.4%) | 12 (3.0%) | 24 (6.0%) | 0.085 |
| `asked06b` | 95 (23.6%) | 22 (5.5%) | 27 (6.7%) | 0.116 |
| `asked06c` | 101 (25.1%) | 26 (6.5%) | 27 (6.7%) | 0.116 |

As can be seen in Table 2 there is a significant absolute performance improvement of over 8% from using a combination of the model ONE and model TWO systems compared to the model ONE system alone. We did not submit an official run using a system based only on model TWO for the TREC 2006 evaluation, however informal results indicate a performance level similar to that seen our results for the TREC 2005 evaluation.

It is clear that in both of the last two years' official TREC QA evaluations we have observed a significant absolute performance increase when using model TWO, either independently or in combination with other systems. Informal experiments where we have applied the model TWO approach to the Japanese-language system have also shown similar performance gains. We are confident that this represents convincing evidence of the validity of using the SVD approach in model TWO.

## 5 Analysis of Recent Work

The above results from recent TREC evaluations, as well as additional informal experiments indicate that the new model TWO system employing the SVD technique represents a substantial improvement over our earlier model ONE system. We surmise that one of the factors responsible for the success of the new model is the tendency of the SVD to reduce the amount of noise in our extremely sparse co-occurrence matrix. Another factor may stem from using very different features to the model ONE approach and also considering answers as-a-whole rather than independent words in an answer as we do for model ONE. By projecting the example answers into the reduced dimensional space, and eliminating "noisy" elements, more meaningful comparisons can be made between units in the co-occurrence matrix and also between similar units which may not have been included in the original matrix.

While the SVD provides a useful means of eliminating noise from large corpora it does have several disadvantages. In particular, the simple cosine measure which is the most obvious means to compare vectors in the reduced dimensional space, is not a proper probability. This is unappealing since it does not fit well into our statistical framework.

One final, perhaps more minor, issue has to do with comparing new answers for which we do not already have co-occurrence statistics, with data already accounted for in the co-occurrence matrix. If the distribution from which the statistics for the original co-occurrence matrix were compiled differs substantially from that used to construct the pseudo-vector for the new answer, then the system may produce undesirable results at the comparison stage. This last problem however, is largely mitigated by the fact that our original distribution is drawn from a very large and very corpus.

## 6 Conclusion and Future Works

In this paper we have described recent progress in developing our data-driven and non-linguistic QA system. The most significant change to the overall system has been the implementation and application of a new filter model, so called model TWO, which employs the Singular Value Decomposition (SVD). We showed how using SVD allows the system to more accurately compare candidate answers for new questions, to answers from example q-and-a training data, in a process similar to that employed in Latent Semantic Analysis or Latent Semantic Mapping. We have described the algorithms used to construct the matrix and how the similarity between answers is computed. We have also presented results of applying this new filter model to QA in two recent official international evaluations. These results demonstrated that the new model considerably improves system performance.

The SVD approach is not perfect, and in particular it is hindered by the fact that the cosine metric which is used to measure the distance between answer candidates and example answers is not really a proper probability, but rather a linear algebraic relation. As such it does not fit perfectly into our statistical framework, however similar methods exist, such as Probabilistic Latent Semantic Analysis [14] which may be interesting to investigate in future. More immediately, because of the success of combining results from filter-model ONE with those of filter-model TWO we are interested in bringing these two models together under one single unified framework in the near future. We are also developing a sentence retrieval model for use with small or closed domain corpora, since this shows much promise as a means of making our method accurate and effective in more limited domains.

## Acknowledgments

This research was supported in part by the Japanese government's 21st century COE programme: "Framework for Systematization and Application of Large-scale Knowledge Resources".

## References


1. Whittaker, E., Furui, S., Klakow, D.: A Statistical Pattern Recognition Approach to Question Answering using Web Data. In: Proc. Cyberworlds (2005)
2. Whittaker, E., et al.: TREC2005 Question Answering Experiments at Tokyo Institute of Technology. In: Proc. 14th Text Retrieval Conference (2005)
3. Whittaker, E., Hamonic, J., Furui, S.: A Unified Approach to Japanese and English Question Answering. In: Proc. NTCIR-5 (2005)
4. Landauer, T., Laham, D., Foltz, P.: Learning human-like knowledge by singular value decomposition: a progress report, pp. 45–51. MIT Press, Cambridge (1998)
5. Cullum, J., Willoughby, R.: Lanczos Algorithms for Large Symmetric Eigenvalue Computations, ch. 5, vol. 1 Theory. Birkhauser, Boston (1985)
6. Whittaker, E., et al.: Monolingual Web-based Factoid Question Answering in Chinese, Swedish, English and Japanese. In: Proc. EACL (2006)
7. Bellegarda, J.: Latent Semantic Mapping. IEEE Magazine, 70–80 (2005)
8. Rhode, D.: SVDPACKC, `http://tedlab.mit.edu/~dr/SVDLIBC/`
9. Berry, M.: Large Scale Singular Value Decompositions. International Journal of Supercomputer Applications, 13–49 (1992)
10. Vector: Vector Software Library (1995-2003), `http://www.vector.co.jp/`
11. Google: Google Translate web translation, `http://translate.google.com`
12. TREC: TREC home, `http://trec.nist.gov/`
13. Academic Hallmarks: Knowledge Master Educational Software PO BOX 998 Durango, CO. 8130 (2002)
14. Hofmann, T.: Probabilistic Latent Semantic Analysis Uncertainty in Artificial Intelligence (1999)
15. Novak, J., et al.: NTCIR-6 CLQA Question Answering Experiment at the Tokyo Institute of Technology NTCIR-6 (2006)
16. Whittaker, E., et al.: CLEF2007 Question Answering Experiments at Tokyo Institute of Technology CLEF Working Notes (2007)

# On the Representation of Perceptual Knowledge for Understanding Reference Expressions

Philipp Spanger and Takenobu Tokunaga

Tokyo Institute of Technology
Graduate School of Information Science and Engineering
Department of Computer Science
{philipp,take}@cl.cs.titech.ac.jp
http://tanaka-www.cs.titech.ac.jp/jp/index.html

**Abstract.** Recent research has enabled important progress in developing agents aimed at real-world linguistic interaction with humans. Hence, within the general shift of research focus from "information" to "knowledge", an important question is how to apply large-scale knowledge resources in order to improve agents' capabilities of linguistic interaction with humans. This paper presents research toward an efficient representation of the necessary perceptual knowledge in dialogue with a particular focus on reference expressions. We generalize an existing formal model of reference expressions involving perceptual grouping in order to account for a number of types of reference expressions that the previous model could not account for. Our model yields an increase in both coverage and accuracy of referent identification – which has been confirmed in preliminary experiments. We outline an algorithm for the future application of this model to other languages, showing how the model can be extended to deal with large-scale multi-language input data.

**Keywords:** representation of perceptual knowledge, perceptual grouping, reference expressions, language-independent systems.

## 1 Introduction

Recently, the utilization of large-scale knowledge resources (LKR) has been a central issue in achieving progress in different research areas such as analysis of spoken language characteristics, systematization of archeological information or language-learning support systems. In particular, the application of LKR in research in the field of linguistics is a very promising research direction. At the same time, developments in a multitude of research areas like speech recognition, robotics, etc. have enabled important progress in developing agents aimed at real-world interaction with humans. Thus, within this general shift of research focus from "information" to "knowledge", an important question is how to use large-scale knowledge resources in order to improve agents' capabilities of interaction with humans through natural language. An important research aim in improving agents' capabilities of interaction with humans has been to improve

T. Tokunaga and A. Ortega (Eds.): LKR 2008, LNAI 4938, pp. 280–294, 2008.

their natural language understanding. A fundamental type of human expression – in particular in task-oriented dialogue – are reference expressions. This type of expression is a linguistic entity used to discriminate a specific object from its environment and the rest of the world.

Thus, an agent's capability to handle this type of linguistic expression correctly is an important part of increasing human-agent interaction capabilities. Reference expressions are to a large degree multi-modal; i.e. they include exophoric expressions such as "this one" or "that" in connection with gesturing (e.g.; pointing). It is clear a fuller model of reference expressions must be a multi-modal model including an account of these different channels and how they combine ([10]). As a first preliminary step towards this aim, we intend to generalize a current model of reference expressions limited to the linguistic channel as a basis for future application in a multi-modal environment. Hence, in this paper the term "reference expression" refers to a single-channel linguistic expression which moreover includes no anaphora and is functioning as a full description for identifying objects in the world such as "the blue ball in front of the table". There has been significant research in the area of how the human cognitive process – and thus also knowledge of the world – and language production and understanding are linked. Specifically, cognitive linguistics researches in this area in a wide variety of directions ([4], [5]). Generally, it is clear human language understanding/production is directly linked to a human's general world knowledge as well as the knowledge acquired/exchanged in a particular dialogue.

A still unsolved problem is how world knowledge, including linguistic knowledge is represented in the human brain. In order to enable agents to effectively communicate with humans through natural language, a critical task is to provide an effective model of the knowledge as applied by humans in the course of diaolgue. Fundamentally, the knowledge used by a human to comprehend a certain linguistic expression can be separated into two types of necessary knowledge; 1) general linguistic knowledge (i.e. as encoded in a grammar and vocabulary) and 2) world knowledge. In the particular case of understanding reference expressions, the necessary knowledge about the world can be separated further into a) general world knowledge as well as b) particular perceptual knowledge for this particular situation. In this case, we broadly define "perceptual knowledge" as comprising all knowledge generated through human perception of a specific situation; e.g. the location of the objects in the domain, their colour, shape, etc and their respective relations to each other. This knowledge is utilized by humans to produce and understand linguistic reference expressions. Obviously, the human perceptual apparatus is capable of extracting a potentially intractably large amount of perceptual knowledge from any given specific real-world situation and a key problem is to decide which of this information is relevant in which domain for the given task of language understanding. The majority of previous work on linguistic reference to a target-object among other distractors, (e.g. [1], [2], [3], [11], [9]) utilized perceptual knowledge of the attributes of the target and binary relations between the target and distractors, using surface differences of the objects. The Incremental Algorithm [3] is an important example of this kind of algorithm. These works mostly deal with developing algorithms for the generation of natural language reference expressions that work sufficiently well in domains where the objects and distractors have a significant surface difference.

However, there is a significant case of failure within this general framework. In case no significant surface difference and no binary relation useful to distinguish the target from the distractors exists, such methods cannot generate a natural linguistic expression enabling hearers to identify the target. Furthermore, these methods cannot provide a model to understand any linguistic expression generated by humans in such a case. This paper seeks to contribute to research in the area of understanding of reference expressions in such a domain. Previous research has underlined the importance of perceptual grouping in understanding [12], and generating [6] reference expressions. Perceptual grouping is defined as the human ability to recognize similar objects, or objects in close proximity to each other. Effective understanding of human reference expressions in this specific domain requires recognition of similar or proximal objects, i.e., perceptual grouping, and requires making use of n-ary relations among objects in each recognized group. Research based on this understanding has produced comparably good results in both the understanding and generation of reference expressions. While this general approach has proven valuable in both the understanding and generation of this type of expression, it has been hampered – both theoretically and in practice – by a strong limitation on the type and structure of expression. That is, it has been assumed reference expressions exclusively apply a linear process of narrowing down of the referent (represented by a "Sequence of groups-representation" (SOG) in [12] and in its generalized form in [6]). However, this means other relations between sets of perceptual groups (appearing in reference expressions) like intersection or subtraction cannot be represented.

Data of experiments in several languages (Japanese, English, German, French) indicate that while the overwhelming majority of expressions (in all four languages) is based on this type of process, it is far from the only or even always the most natural one for humans. In particular, humans are capable and in some cases prefer to refer to different types of relations between sets of similar objects using either intersection or subtraction. In certain cases this simplifies the expression significantly or is more natural. For example, in Figure 1, through use of the expression of "ignoring the three balls in the right back", the subject applies a subtraction-relation between the group of all balls in the domain and the "three balls in the right back". The target object is referred to from within the remaining set. This is one example of a process of referring, that cannot be represented in the previous model. Hence, in order to develop the promising framework of application of a representation of perceptual grouping in reference expressions, it is necessary to generalize the existing model such that it can accomodate these more complex cases. This paper tackles this task. This will make a contribution to increasing our understanding of the necessary representation of perceptual knowledge for the efficient understanding of reference expressions in human-agent linguistic interaction. Furthermore, it will provide a general theoretical model of this type of expression.

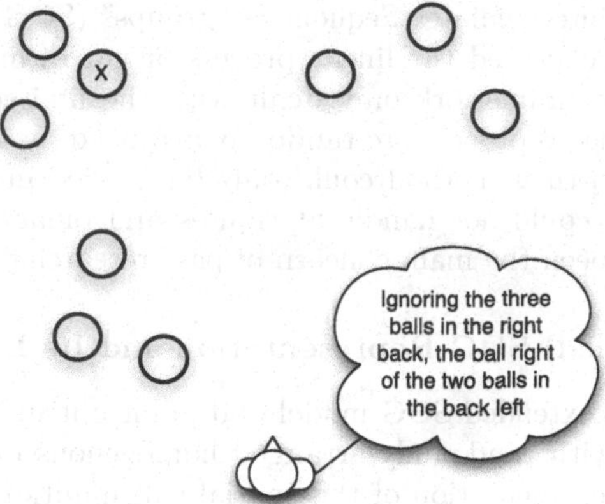


**Fig. 1.** An example of a reference expression using subtraction

For the overall task of constructing an efficient LKR for application in the domain of human-agent linguistic interaction, the question of how to represent the necessary knowledge, including perceptual knowledge, is critical. A solution to this task will also enable in the future an efficient systematization of this LKR. Through research into the question of how to represent perceptual knowledge for the understanding of reference expressions, our work seeks to contribute towards this aim. As in [12], we consider here that understanding reference expressions consists of two stages: (a) semantic analysis, i.e., analyzing expressions to extract semantic information, and (b) referent identification, i.e., discriminating referents by using extracted information. Below, we describe the proposed generalized model for perceptual knowledge for understanding of reference expressions. We will explain how this model handles the more complex cases the previous model could not deal with. We also explain some modifications of the algorithm for construction of a representation of perceptual grouping proposed in [12], as necessitated by the more general model proposed in this paper. We will discuss the collected data (in English as well as other languages) and the implementation of the proposed model in a simple prototype that yielded an increase in both coverage and referent identification. Finally, we will give an overview of future work on this topic.

## 2 COG (Combination of Groups): A Formal Model of Reference Expressions

As stated above, previous work on reference expressions focused on using surface differences of the objects. However, in the case of the absence of significant surface difference and if no binary relation useful to distinguish the target from the distractors exists, such methods failed.

To solve this insufficiency, [12] proposed a method of generating Japanese reference expressions that utilizes n-ary relations among members of a group. Necessarily this framework included a representation of the perceptual grouping process – called an intermediate "Sequence of groups" (SOG) – representation. This representation captured the linear process of narrowing down of the referent. However, their framework only dealt with the limited situations where exclusively homogeneous objects are randomly arranged (as in Figure 1). Thus, the representation in their method could only be applied in the case of spatial n-ary relations, and could not handle attributes and binary relations between objects which have been the main concern of past research.

### 2.1 The (Extended) SOG Representation and Its Limitations

We outline here the extended SOG-model and point out its limitations.[12] assumed a situation with randomnly-arranged homogenous objects and focused exclusively on the representation of the spatial subsumption relations between consecutive groups. Thus, the intermediate representation of perceptual knowledge they proposed between a reference expression and the situation that is referred to by the expression, did not explicitly denote relations between groups in the original SOGs (as shown below).

$SOG : [G_0, G_1, ...G_n]$
$G_i : a\ group$

In order to take into account other types of relations between groups, [5] proposed then an extended SOG representation where types of relations are explicitly denoted as shown below.

$SOG : [G_0 R_0 G_1 R_1 ... G_n]$
$G_i : a\ group$
$R_i : relation\ between\ G_i\ and\ G_{i+1}$

This extended representation accounts for two types of relations between perceptual groups: intra-group relations and inter-group relations. Of course, for any intra-group relation, by definition, $G_i$ subsumes $G_{i+1}$, that is, $G_i \supset G_{i+1}$. Intra-group relations are further classified into subcategories according to the feature used to narrow down $G_i$ to $G_{i+1}$. In this model, in case $R_i$ is an inter-group relation, $G_i$ and $G_{i+1}$ are mutually exclusive, that is, $G_i \cap G_{i+1} = \emptyset$. However, this leaves out cases of other inter-group relations, in particular other combinations of perceptual groups like intersection ($G_i \cap G_{i+1}$) or subtraction ($G_i \setminus G_{i+1}$). The necessity of incorporating this type of expression can be demonstrated by, for example, Figure 1 (example from the collected expressions).

### 2.2 The COG (Combination of Groups) Representation

We propose the Combination of groups (COG) - model as an efficient representation of the perceptual grouping process and demonstrate how it resolves the limitations of the previous approaches. We provide an example analysis in the COG - model of an expressions that the previous model could not handle. The COG - representation is a generalization and extension of the (extended) SOG-representation. Its flexible order of grouping ("linear" and "non-linear") better captures the natural variety of human reference expressions. It includes the SOG-representation as a special case. The initial SOG-model was extended by [6] to the case of different relations among sets, which arise in more complex environments with a number of different objects. However, both the extension as well as the initial model share the same weakness in not accounting for reference expressions that include in some form a non-linear process of narrowing down the referent. In this context, we denote by non-linear process any process that involves reference to groups of objects, where these different groups are related to each other neither by a simple subsumption-relation nor by a simple inter-group relation where the groups share no elements. This means the relation between the sets is not a subsumption-relation. Furthermore, the intersection of the two sets is neither empty nor equals any of the two sets.

Thus, in order to improve the model we implemented the generalization that is able to handle these cases. In order to demonstrate the basic validity of the proposed generalization, we based our implementation on the simpler earlier model. However, as the initial as well as the extended SOG-model shared this same weakness, we note that this generalization is applicable as well for the extended SOG-model. [12] point out that in their method, "most errors in semantic analysis are due to non-linearity of referring". This is because the SOG-model presupposes linearity in referring and thus cannot handle these cases. We recall that linearity in this case refers to the fact that between subsequent perceptual groups exclusively subsumption-relations exist. We conducted a preliminary data collection experiment. The analysis of the collected data indicated two general cases of "non-linearity" in referring, i.e. of the existence of relations different from the subsumption-relation. We noted subjects tended to use either the intersection or the subtraction – relation. Hence we concentrated on the implementation of these two relations. Other more complex combinations of these relations are possible, but they can be reduced to a combination of these two more simple set-relations. As the name "Sequence of groups" indicates, this previous model has a "flat" structure, i.e. it only accounts for one type of binary relation to the immediately preceding group: the subsumption relation. In fact, the subsumption relation is simply a special case of the intersection relation. In contrast, the proposed COG-model allows an internal structure within the representation of the perceptual process; i.e. a reference to any previous group or combination of groups. Thus, this model can correctly represent the cases where the SOG-model fails (i.e.: subtraction and intersection relation). The general COG-model includes the following relations where $G_n$ denotes a group or combination of groups.

(1) intersection of groups : $G_i$ and $G_j$ with the result $G_k$: $G_i \cap G_j = G_k \neq \emptyset$

$$\left.\begin{array}{l} G_i \\ \\ G_j \end{array}\right] \xrightarrow{\cap} G_k$$

(2) subtraction of groups : $G_i$ and $G_j$ with the result $G_k$ : $G_i \setminus G_j = G_k \neq \emptyset$

$$\left.\begin{array}{r} G_i \\ G_j \end{array}\right] \xrightarrow{\setminus} G_k$$

(3) subsumption relation : $G_j \subset G_i$

$$G_i \longrightarrow G_j$$

(4) inter-group relation : $G_i \cap G_j = \emptyset$

$$G_i \Rightarrow G_j$$

We can see that while the SOG-model (including in its extended form) only allows unary relations, in our model we include representation of binary relations between perceptual groups: the intersection as well as the subtraction relation. Thus, theoretically an arbitrary level of complexity of grouping-(reference) expressions can be represented in this model. It is quite easy to extend our model to relations like:

$G_i \xrightarrow{colour} G_j$ ,
$G_i \xrightarrow{size} G_j$ ,
$G_i \xrightarrow{type} G_j$.

If we incorporated these types of relations into the COG-model, our model would also be able to deal with the relations handled by the extended SOG-model and thus include the extended SOG-model as a special case. In the following, we analyze a characteristic example that cannot be accounted for by the previous model (displayed in Figure 2)). We provide the analysis of this example based on our proposed model in detail and then show how and why its analysis fails in the previous model.

### 2.3 Example Analysis in COG

In this section we present an analysis of an expression the previous model cannot handle, but that the COG-model can appropriately analyse. This will demonstrate how representation of perceptual knowledge in the COG-model is useful for application in the domain of reference expression understanding. Furthermore, we will explain how the previous model can be reduced to a special case of the proposed COG-model. We provide the analysis of a reference expression employing a subtraction- relation (see Figure 2) between different perceptual groups. As we pointed out previously, this cannot be handled by the previous model.

We recapitulate the phrase: "Ignoring the three balls in the left back, the ball in the back". The analysis in the COG-model would look as follows.

$$\left.\begin{array}{r} \{a,b,c,d,e\} \\ \{a,b,c,d,e\} \longrightarrow \{c,d,e\} \end{array}\right] \xrightarrow{\setminus} \{a,b\} \longrightarrow \{b\}$$

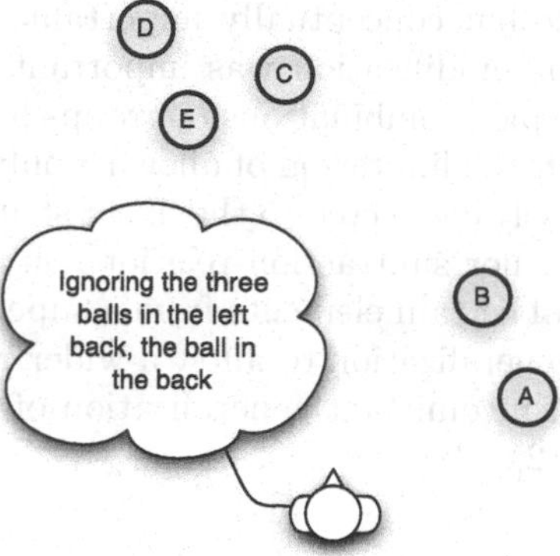


**Fig. 2.** An example of a reference expression including subtraction-relation

First, from the set of all balls $\{a, b, c, d, e\}$, the user selects "the three balls in the left back" $\{c, d, e\}$. Thus using the subtraction-relation, from the set of all balls $\{a, b, c, d, e\}$ in the domain, the user focuses the attention on the remaining set of objects $\{a, b\}$, from which the target $\{b\}$ is then selected by using a simple subsumption-relation. Here it is important to note that the cardinality of the group of objects of the result of the subtraction-relation $\{a, b\}$ is not explicitly referred to. As we noted previously, in the SOG-model, there is no way to represent this relationship between $\{a, b\}$ and $\{a, b, c, d, e\}$ Thus, if we were to try to provide an analysis based on the SOG-model, this would lead to a representation as follows.

$SOG : [\{a, b, c, d, e\}R_0(\{c, d, e\}R_1\{a, b\})R_2\{b\}]$
$G_0 = \{a, b, c, d, e\}; G_1 = \{c, d, e\}$
$G_2 = \{a, b\}; G_3 = \{b\}$
In particular we note that the following holds: $G_1 \cup G_2 = G_0$.

This type of relation between immediately succeeding groups ($G_1 \cup G_2 = G_0$) cannot be represented in the SOG-model. Hence, we see that the SOG-model fails in this case. We note the SOG-model by [12] is a special case of the proposed COG-model, in the case that all relations are restricted only to subsumption-relations and thus only relations to immediately preceding groups are allowed. This means if for all groups $G_i$ it holds that $G_i \supset G_{i+1} \supset G_{i+2}...$, the COG-model goes over into the simple SOG-model.

## 2.4 Perceptual Grouping

As pointed out previously, the algorithm for perceptual grouping proposed in [12] only recognizes groups that are explicitly referred to, with their cardinality specified (e.g.: "the three balls in the ..."). As pointed out above, in addition to this type of perceptual grouping, humans carry out perceptual grouping by exclusion, i.e. "the balls right to the table and ...". Here the subject forms a specific perceptual group $G_i$ , without specifying a cardinality of the group. Thus, we implemented a simple but conceptually important modification to [12] that handles these cases. This modification was important particularly in order to implement the more complex combinations of groups like repeated intersections and complements. In fact, the limitation of allowing only perceptual groups with explicit cardinality is closely connected to the linear structure of the SOG-model; since neither intersection nor subtraction-relations on sets were permitted, the only way to select a set of certain elements from a super-set is to specify its cardinality. Hence, in our generalization to allow a wider range of set-relations, we needed to implement a concomittant generalization of the perceptual grouping algorithm proposed in [12].

## 3 Implementation

Following [12], we consider the general process of reference expression understanding to consist of the following two stages (a) semantic analysis, i.e., analysing expressions in order to extract semantic information, and (b) referent identification, i.e. uniquely recognizing referents by using the extracted semantic information. Generally, the methods of [12] are employed for both stages, in particular in the process of perceptual grouping. However, in both stages some modification of the methods were implemented.

### 3.1 Semantic Analysis

A critical task is the extraction of the relevant information from the linguistic expressions. [12] used a simple pattern matching-technique for extracting the necessary information from the linguistic expressions instead of full parsing. In this paper, we used the Stanford Parser (see [8]) to extract a basic syntactic structure based on PCFG (probabilistic context-free grammar) ([7]). This improvement lays the basis for building an LKR of syntactic structures and associated with it the necessary information to be extracted for its use in understanding reference expressions. Information mining and machine learning techniques could then be applied to facilitate the use of this LKR in the area of human-agent linguistic interaction. The utilized framework of PCFG is a context-free grammar in which every production is assigned a probability. The final probability of any parsing of a specific sentence is calculated as the product of the probabilities of all the productions in a specific parse. The parse with the highest probability is then selected by the stochastic grammar.

We then analysed the basic syntactic structures of the user inputs and recognized that to a large degree the syntactic structure gives a good clue as to how to separate a clause into groups for extracting the required information. In order to elucidate this process, we give an example in the following:

User input sentence: "the rightmost ball among the three balls at the back left". The raw parser output is as follows:

(ROOT (NP (NP (DT the) (JJ rightmost) (NN ball)) (PP (IN among) (NP (NP (DT the) (CD three) (NNS balls)) (PP (IN at) (NP (DT the) (JJ back) (NN left)))))))

Represented as syntactic tree it looks as shown in Figure 3.

The representation in COG would look as follows:

{a,b,c,d,e,f,x}⟶{a,b,x}⟶ $\{x\}$.

Our basic aim is to get from the surface linguistic form to the forming of perceptual groups corresponding to the formal COG-representation. As the initial group $\{a, b, c, d, e, x\}$ is not expressed explicitly, we basically look for how the following part of the above COG-representation is reflected in the syntactic structure.

$\{a, b, x\} \longrightarrow \{x\}$.

In the example above, we see that the perceptual group $G_2 = \{x\}$ is represented by the $NP_A$ which corresponds to the linguistic surface expression "the rightmost ball". The $PP_B$ corresponds to the $G_1 = \{a, b, x\}$. We need to extract the relation $R_1$ between these two groups $G_1 R_1 G_2$ . This relation can be extracted from the first component of $PP_B$ which is $IN_C$. The label $IN_C$ corresponds to "among" in the linguistic surface form, which indicated a subsumption-relation. The $NP_D$ includes the cardinality of the group "three" and the location: "back left". Japanese is a head-final language and hence the

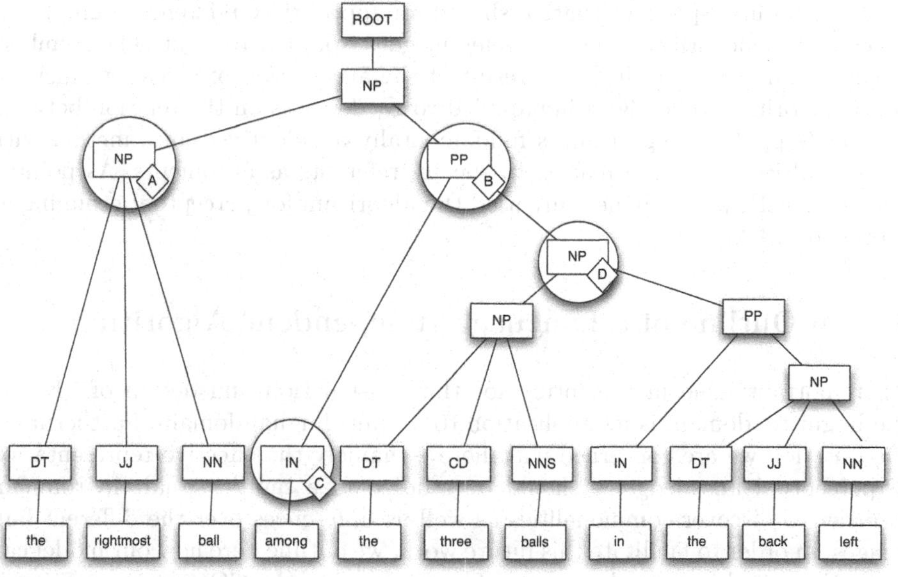


**Fig. 3.** An example of syntactic structure of user input

order of sub-expressions in the linguistic surface-form has the same order as the groups in the SOG and COG representation. This however is obviously different in languages such as English which are not head-final. In our example case here, the order of sub - expressions is exactly opposite to the order of groups in the relevant part of the COG-representation. We note that in both Japanese (as reported by [12]) as well as in English, the total set is generally not mentioned. From the syntactic structures collected, there were several regularities which seem to indicate a fundamental connection between syntactic structure and the process of perceptual grouping. However, we utilized the observed regularities in a simple ad-hoc manner for semantic analysis, as the main aim of this work was to evaluate the proposed COG-model. We acknowledge this is still a very partial progress to the pattern matching technique employed in [12]. In future work, a more complete analysis and comparison of different grammatical approaches should be carried out. In particular, a study of a large amount of testdata could be the basis for applying learning algorithms over the syntactic structures in order to enable a more systematic account of the connection between syntactic structures and the process of perceptual grouping. Based on this work, a deeper understanding of how the perceptual process of forming groups is reflected in the syntactic structure can be gained. This in turn could then be applied to improving our representation of perceptual knowledge necessary for human-agent linguistic interaction.

### 3.2 Referent Identification

As the next step following the semantic analysis process, we carried out referent identification by using the extracted information. (It was assumed all the participants in a specific situation shared an appropriate reference frame.) The process of the identification of the referent goes from left to right. The members of each group are identified as a result of the application of a referent identification algorithm. The algorithm applied to $G_i$ depends on the relation between $G_i$ and $G_{i+1}$. Each algorithm is fundamentally an identification function with a set of objects and information to specify referents as arguments. As pointed out previously, we fundamentally used the algorithm for perceptual grouping as proposed in [12].

## 4 An Outline of a Language-Independent Algorithm

An important issue in the future for the construction and design of LKR in the linguistic domain is its application to a multi-lingual domain. Furthermore, the question we are concerned with here – namely the effective representation of perceptual knowledge – should be studied in a multi-lingual environment in order to discover commonalities as well as differences over the different languages. In order to facilitate this future work, we outline here how our model can be implemented in other languages. The proposal of the COG-representation is based on observations of a data - collection in English, French and German. It captures the general structure of reference expressions in these languages. Of course, in order to implement a system of understanding reference expressions comparable to the system we prepared for English, the possibly very significant differences in syntax have to be accounted for. From the test-data, our observation is that there is no significant difference in the process of perceptual grouping that would force a fundamental revision of the algorithm proposed in this paper. However, we found some tendencies of preference of certain types of expressions, which differed over the different languages. Generally, we observed some interesting characteristics in the collected data in the different languages. German expressions showed a significant variation in the syntactic structure of the expressions (as well as the used vocabulary), while the expressions supplied by the French subjects showed a very high degree of similarity of syntactic structure. Further study and examination of data in other languages should illuminate this phenomenon and the connection between cognitive and linguistics processes. In fact, clarifying the interdependence between cognitive and linguistic processes and how they differ over different languages would provide an understanding that could be critical in many areas of natural language processing. In order to implement and test the proposed model in other languages, in particular the following modules should be prepared:

- Syntactic parser
  The output of the parser should be analysed for indicators in the syntactic structure of distinct grouping. The analysis of the syntactic structure of the input expression forms the basis for further information extraction.
- Information extraction-module
  Based on the previous step, words/ syntactic structures indicating a particular set-relation of perceptual groups (e.g.: subtraction - relation in English "ignoring :." etc.) should be identified and applied to extract the relevant information.

In our implementation of the methods of referent identification developed in [12] for Japanese, we noted there was no significant modification necessary for the application of these methods to English, other than those explained above. Thus, our data-collection experiment indicates a very universal process of perceptual grouping. The testdata in English and Japanese – being two languages with significant differences in syntax – provide at least a good basis for making this hypopthesis. Our testdata in French and German confirm this hypothesis. Of course the amount of testdata is very small and thus these hypotheses need to be tested using a more comprehensive set of data.

## 5 Evaluation

We implemented the proposed model in Java and applied it to the expressions collected in our data-collection experiment. We then evaluated the referent identification accuracy of the proposed model.

### 5.1 Experiment

We carried out a data-collection experiment for English, where we provided the 12 different arrangements of balls in a 2-D bird's-eye image to the subjects (taken from the appendix in [12]). 12 subjects whose native language is English participated in the experiment over the internet. They were provided an arrangement with the choice to either input an expression they felt appropriate or to abandon this specific arrangement in case subjects were not able to think of an appropriate reference expression. This should have produced 144 expressions, however 7 judgements were abandoned and 15 expressions were either nonsensical or obviously insufficient to identify the referent. Hence, we obtained 122 English reference expressions. [12] referred to about 8% of Japanese collected expressions that included non-linearity of referring. In the English data collected in our experiment, we noted a 7% frequency of reference expressions that include non-linearity. This points toward very similar frequency of this type of expression. However, the amount of the English data in particular is small; hence in order to confirm this hypothesis a larger data set is necessary.

### 5.2 Results

We did not have the previous system (in Japanese) at our disposal. Thus we implemented the algorithm as outlined in [12] in English. This was in order to provide a baseline for our proposed enhanced model. The result of this system is represented in Table 1 in comparison with the results of the Japanese system, displayed in Table 2. Our system in English based on the algorithm in [12] gives largely comparable results to the system of [12] for Japanese. The slight decrease in accuracy (about 2%) can be attributed in part to a lack of fine-tuning of the algorithms for perceptual grouping.

**Table 1.** Results of previous model in English

| *Expression* | *Pop.* | *Ident.* |
|---|---|---|
| Total | 122 | 77.0% |
| Applicable | 107 | 83.1% |

**Table 2.** Results of previous model in Japanese

| *Expression* | *Pop.* | *Ident.* |
|---|---|---|
| Total | 476 | 78.8% |
| Applicable | 425 | 84.7% |

**Table 3.** Results of COG - model in English

| *Expression* | *Pop.* | *Ident.* |
|---|---|---|
| Total | 122 | 82.6% |
| Applicable | 114 | 89.2% |

The result of the implemented system based on [12] in English is represented in Table 1. It shows that the simple implementation in English yielded a comparable result to the Japanese system, while having slightly less accuracy. This might be attributed to slight differences in implementation; e.g. setting of some parameters in the formulas of the perceptual grouping methods. We then implemented the GOG-model and the result is represented in Table 3. This implementation of the GOG-model yielded an increase of 5.6% in comparison to the SOG-model in English. The final accuracy achieved for English was 82.6%.

### 5.3 Error Analysis

From the collected expressions, there were two significant types of errors that are described in the following.

(a) Errors in semantic analysis
There were two main types of errors in semantic analysis. One type of expression referred to a particular part of the body of the person in the picture as referent, e.g.: "the one in front of my left shoulder". The other frequent type of expression that cannot be handled by our system are expressions that refer to an action, like : "Take away the two left ones and you'll have it now as the most left ones". There were 3 expressions of this type. This type of expression appeared in all three languages of our experiment, thus indicating it is not an isolated phenomenon. A future system should be able to handle expressions of this type involving actions.

(b) Referent identification
In the main, errors were due to reference to geometric forms – in particular lines – and our current system cannot handle any perceptual grouping involving this type of figure. We acknowledge that this is a preliminary evaluation, as the test-data is less than a quarter of the amount of expressions collected in the other system.

## 6 Conclusion

In the framework of research into efficient representation of perceptual knowledge in language understanding, we proposed a generalized model of reference expressions that seeks to capture the varied forms of reference expressions employed by humans. We proposed a generalization of a previous model, of which the previous model is a special case. We demonstrated how our proposed model can handle several types of expressions that the previous cannot handle. We then implemented our model. We measured both an increased coverage and increased identification accuracy in comparison to the previous model in English by 5.6% to a total identification accuracy of 82.6%. We reported some observations on the collected data in other languages in comparison and gave an outline of how to implement this general framework in other languages. Our model has so far only been implemented in the area of understanding of reference expressions, but it should be noted that it could be extended to the generation of reference expressions. Furthermore, the construction of an LKR, comprising languages other than English and in particular also a syntactic representation of the linguistic input is a critical task in the future. The proposed model is simply a linguistic model of reference expressions in a 2-D environment. In order to increase the efficiency of human-agent communication it is necessary to incorporate other channels of communication ("multi- modality") and combine the information of these. In the future, we plan to extend and adapt the proposed model in this thesis to a multi-modal environment. The construction of multi-modal LKR for application in the human-agent interaction domain in the future is an important goal and we see our work as a step towards realizing this.

## References

1. Appelt, D.: Planning english referring expressions. Artificial Intelligence 15(3), 143–178 (1985)
2. Dale, R., Haddock, N.: Generating referring expressions involving relations. In: Proceedings of EACL, Berlin, pp. 161–166 (1991)
3. Dale, R., Reiter, E.: Computational interpretations of the gricean maxims in the generation of referring expressions. Cognitive Science (PDF) 19, 233–263 (1995)
4. Kristiansen, et al (eds.): Cognitive linguistics: Current applications and future perspectives. Mouton de Gruyter, Berlin, New York (2006)
5. Vyvyan, Evans, B.B., Zinken, J.: The cognitive linguistics reader. Equinox, London (2007)
6. Funakoshi, K., Watanabe, S., Tokunaga, T.: Group based generation of referring expressions. In: Proceedings of the Fourth International Natural Language Generation Conference, pp. 73–80 (2006)
7. Johnson, M.: Pcfg models of linguistic tree representations. Computational Linguistics 24(4), 613–632 (1998)
8. Klein, D., Manning, C.D.: Accurate unlexicalized parsing. In: Proceedings of the 41st Meeting of the Association for Computational Linguistics (2003)
9. Krahmer, E., van Erk, S., Verleg, A.: Graph-based generation of referring expressions. Computational Linguistics 29(1), 53–72 (2003)
10. Kranstedt, A., et al.: Deictic object reference in task-oriented dialogue. In: Rickheit, G., Wachsmuth, I. (eds.) Situated Communication, pp. 155–207. Mouton de Gruyter, Berlin (2006)
11. van Deemter: Generating referring expressions: Boolean extensions of the incremental algorithm. Computational Linguistics pp. 28 (1), 37–52 (2002)
12. Watanabe, S., et al.: Understanding referring expressions involving perceptual grouping. In: Proceedings of the 20th International Conference on Computational Linguistics (2004)

# A Computational Model of Risk-Context-Dependent Inductive Reasoning Based on a Support Vector Machine

Kayo Sakamoto and Masanori Nakagawa

Tokyo Institute of Technology, 2-21-1 O-okayama, Meguro-ku, Tokyo, 152-8552, Japan
{sakamoto.k.ad,nakagawa.m.ad}@m.titech.ac.jp

**Abstract.** A computational model of cognitive inductive reasoning that accounts for risk context effects is proposed. The model is based on a Support Vector Machine (SVM) that utilizes the kernel method. Kernel functions within the model are assumed to represent the functions of similarity computations based on distances between premise entities and conclusion entities in inductive reasoning arguments. Multipliers related to the kernel functions have the role of adjusting similarities and can explain rating shifts between two different risk contexts. Model fitting data supports the SVM-based model with kernel functions as a model of inductive reasoning in risk contexts. Finally, the paper discusses how the multipliers for kernel functions provide a satisfactory cognitive theoretical account of similarity adjustment.

**Keywords:** inductive reasoning, Support Vector Machines, context, risk, natural language processing, corpus-based conceptual clustering.

## 1 Introduction

A Support Vector Machine (SVM) [13] is an effective pattern learning method. Although SVMs are being widely applied to engineering problems, such as document searching and image classification, there have been very few applications to computational cognitive models. On the other hand, while a number of computational models of cognitive inductive reasoning have been proposed, such as Bayesian models (e.g., [9], [10]) and neural network models (e.g., [9], [11]), no models have been proposed that tackle context effects on inductive reasoning, even though they are often reported in empirical studies (e.g., [1]). The present study demonstrates that a SVM-based computational model is effective in simulating risk-context-dependency effects on the processes of human cognitive inductive reasoning. In particular, the proposed model provides a satisfactory cognitive account of risk context effects in inductive reasoning in terms of multipliers related to kernel functions.

Risk-context-dependency effects on inductive reasoning can be observed in ratings for one kind of argument (e.g., [5], [7]), such as:

Person A likes wine.
Person A doesn't like beer.
———————————
Person A likes champagne.

T. Tokunaga and A. Ortega (Eds.): LKR 2008, LNAI 4938, pp. 295–309, 2008.

The strength (the likelihood of the conclusion below the line given the premises above the line) of this type of argument depends mainly on the entities in each sentence (e.g., “wine”, “beer”, “champagne”), because these sentences share the same basic predicate (e.g., “Person A likes ~.” and “Person A doesn’t like ~.”).

However in real-world situations, even reasoning-based behavior that involves such simple argument evaluations can entail some element of risk context. For example, the relatively straightforward situation of giving somebody a present involves some risk. Even if you knew that the person in question likes wine but not beer, could you reasonably infer their reactions toward receiving a bottle of champagne from you? In such a situation, your argument ratings would probably be different depending on whether the person is your close friend or your easily-upset boss. This suggests that human ratings of argument strength are by their nature context-dependent. In particular, the situational contexts addressed in the present study entail ‘concocted’ social evaluations in which argument ratings are scored, and each score is set up to imply the argument rater’s social ability. In such situational contexts, people tend to avoid the risk of low evaluations about their ‘concocted’ social ability. Furthermore, this study proposes a SVM-based model that accounts for the influence of risk context on inductive reasoning.

The outline of this paper is as follows: First, we describe the empirical phenomena of risk-context-dependency effects on inductive reasoning. Then, after proposing the SVM-based model, simulation results are presented. Finally, we argue that the SVM-based model provides a satisfactory account of risk context effects on inductive reasoning, noting, in particular, how multipliers relating to the kernel functions can model the adjustment of similarities between positive premise entities, negative premise entities, and conclusion entities, and, thus, explain how argument ratings can vary under two different risk contexts.

## 2 Risk-Context-Dependency Effects in Inductive Reasoning

### 2.1.1 Experimental Procedure

The experimental task is to rate inductive reasoning arguments on a 7-point scale (e.g., [5], [7]), (Figure 1). Four sets of inductive reasoning arguments that include entities from three different semantic domains are rated (see Appendix A). Each set contains eight arguments, and each argument consists of two positive premises, one negative premise, and a conclusion. For the eight arguments of one set, all the premises are fixed and combined with each of the eight conclusions. The premise and conclusion statements in these arguments all consist of a combination of a predicate (*Person A likes ‘~’*) and an entity (e. g., *steak*), such as *“Person A likes steak.”* In the case of negative premises, the predicate involves a negative verbal form, such as *“Person A doesn’t like Japanese noodles.”* Unlike the usual inductive reasoning task, each rating in this study is scored according to the variation from a ‘concocted’ right answer (a particular rating point of 7 points from ‘strongly likely’ ~ ‘strongly unlikely’). Participants were told that the ability to guess the right rating answer would be a reflection of their social ability to imagine other person’s preferences. The concocted right answer for each argument was assigned by referring to risk-context-free rating data. When a rating corresponds to the right answer, it receives a perfect score. In the over-estimation risk condition, as the argument rating increased relative to the right answer, the score reduction also increased. Conversely, in the under-estimation risk condition, as the argument rating decreased relative to the right answer, the more the reduction to the score increased. Score allocations for each condition are shown in Table 1. For the participants in both experimental conditions, there was a risk of being low evaluated in terms of their social abilities. However, high-ratings tend to lead to low evaluations in the over-estimation risk condition, while low-ratings tend to lead to low evaluations in the under-estimation risk condition. The participants were 77 Japanese undergraduate students, of which 34 were assigned to the over-estimation risk condition, with the remaining 43 were assigned to the under-estimation risk condition. All the experimental procedure was controlled in a web application executed with Internet Explorer 6.0. The participants followed the experimental procedure all together in a computer class. The experimental procedure was divided into 6 stages; the first stage presented the experimental instructions to all participants. The second stage was a practice rating session for one of the four argument sets in which feedback about the right answer and the current score was shown after each argument rating (Figure 2). The third to the fifth stages were rating sessions for the remaining argument sets without feedback. However, during the last of these sessions, the current total score was displayed to each participant. The last stage was an announcement of the total score and the ranking in the computer class. After this procedure was completed, the true purpose of the experiment was explained to all participants.

### 2.2 Results

Argument ratings on 7-point scales during the no-feedback sessions were translated into numerical scales (1 ~ 7) and were analyzed in terms of the differences between the two conditions. The average ratings over the three sets of arguments (24 arguments) were 4.011 ($SD = 1.365$) for the under-estimation risk condition and 3.857 ($SD = 1.425$) for the over-estimation risk conditions respectively, which represents a significant difference between the two conditions according to a paired $t$ test ($p < 0.01$). In general, the same tendency was observed for each argument set. These results suggest that participants' ratings are affected by the risk context: in the over-estimation risk condition, ratings tended to be lower due to applying a strategy of avoiding over-estimations that might incur score reductions, while the participant ratings in the under-estimation risk condition tended to be higher because of a strategy to avoid under-estimations that might incur score reductions.

### 2.3 Supplementary Experiment

In the main experiment, only one kind of predicate (*Person A likes* '~') was used for the inductive reasoning argument. However, as it might be something of an overgeneralization to develop a theory of inductive reasoning solely from the results of such an experiment, a supplementary experiment was conducted. In the supplementary experiment, another predicate was used for the inductive reasoning arguments. Furthermore, another four sets of inductive reasoning arguments that include entities from three different semantic domains and new predicates were rated

**SET1 : About Person A's preferences**

| Premises | |
|---|---|
| "Person A likes 'steak'." | "Person A doesn't like 'Japanese noodles'." |
| "Person A likes 'Chinese fried noodles'." | |

**Quiz!**
**Given the above preferences, how likely is the following sentence?**
**Check the appropriate box.**

| "Person A likes 'curry'." | | | | | | |
|---|---|---|---|---|---|---|
| O | O | O | O | O | O | O |
| strongly likely | likely | relatively likely | neutral | relatively unlikely | unlikely | strongly unlikely |

| Allocation of Scores | | | | | | |
|---|---|---|---|---|---|---|
| over 3 points overestimating | 2 points overestimating | 1 points overestimating | corresponds to the right answer | 1 points underestimating | 2 points underestimating | over 3 points underestimating |
| + 0 | + 35 | + 65 | + 100 | - 35 | -65 | -100 |

**Fig. 1.** Example of experiment in the under-estimation risk condition (translated into English)

your answer

| strongly likely | likely | relatively likely | neutral | relatively unlikely | unlikely | strongly unlikely |
|---|---|---|---|---|---|---|

right asnwer

| over 3 points overestimating | 2 points overestimating | 1 points overestimating | corresponds to the right answer | 1 points underestimating | 2 points underestimating | over 3 points underestimating |
|---|---|---|---|---|---|---|
| + 0 | + 35 | + 65 | + 100 | - 35 | -65 | -100 |

your score

| Current total score | -100 |
|---|---|
| Max score | 100 |

**Fig. 2.** Example of the rating feedback (in the under-estimation risk condition)

(see Appendix B). Each set contained eight arguments, and each argument consisted of three positive premises, three negative premises, and a conclusion. The premise and conclusion statements all consisted of a combination of a nonsense predicate ('~' *is bamiysoya*) and an entity (*a jet plane*), such as *"A jet plane is bamisoya."* In the case of negative premises, the predicate involved a negative verbal form, such as *"A trailer is not bamisoya."* As in the original inductive reasoning task, each rating in the supplementary experiment was also scored according to the variation from a 'concocted' right answer (a particular rating point of 7 points from 'strongly likely' ~ 'strongly unlikely'). However, this time, the participants were told that their ability to guess the right rating answer would be a reflection of their ability to learn word meanings in a new language (e.g., a new word like *bamisoya*). Thus, for the participants in both experimental conditions, there was risk to receiving low evaluations about their language ability. The two experimental conditions (the under-estimation risk condition and the over-estimation risk condition) were designed as in the original experiment. The complete procedure was also the same as in the original experiment. Thus, the supplementary experiment was almost identical to the original experiment except for the predicates, the entity words, and the number of premises. The participants were 119 Japanese undergraduate students who did not join in the main experiment, of which 59 were assigned to the over-estimation risk condition, with the remaining 60 being assigned to the under-estimation risk condition.

**Table 1.** Allocation of scores in each risk condition

| | over 3 points over-estimating | 2 points over-estimating | 1 point over-estimating | corresponds to the concocted right answer |
|---|---|---|---|---|
| **UNDER** | add 0 | add 35 | add 65 | add 100 |
| **OVER** | minus 100 | minus 65 | minus 35 | add 100 |
| | 1 point under-estimating | 2 points under-estimating | over 3 points under-estimating | |
| **UNDER** | minus 35 | minus 65 | minus 100 | |
| **OVER** | add 65 | add 35 | add 0 | |

The results replicate those of the main experiment. The average ratings over the three sets of arguments (24 arguments) were 3.783 ($SD$ = 1.248) for the under-estimation risk condition) and 3.578 ($SD$ = 1.210) for the over-estimation risk condition respectively, representing a significant difference between the two conditions according to a paired $t$ test ($p < 0.01$). This suggests that the risk context effect of inductive reasoning is robust with different predicates in the arguments.

# 3 Model

## 3.1 A Support Vector Machine by the Kernel Method

The present study proposes a computational model of inductive reasoning that has the same structure as Support Vector Machines (SVMs) [13] based on the kernel method. SVMs construct a kind of linear classification model or regression model that have an emphasis on generalizing capabilities. Furthermore, when kernel functions are utilized in SVMs, nonlinear classification problems can be solved in a simple linear model since the kernel function maps input data onto a space that is capable of linear classifications or regressions. In general, an SVM regression model by the kernel method can be formulated as follows;

$$\hat{y} = \sum_{i=1}^{S} \alpha_i y_i K(x_i, x) - h . \quad (1)$$

where $\hat{y}$ is the predicted output from an input pattern $x$, $K(x_i, x)$ is a kernel function, and $x_i$ is one of the learning samples while $y_i$ is the right answer. $S$ is a subset of all the learning samples and $x_i$ included in $S$ is called a support vector. These support vectors, the right answer, and the parameters $\alpha_i$, and $h$ define a hyperplane $\sum_{i=1}^{S} \alpha_i y_i K(x_i, x) - h = 0$.

In SVMs, the optimal hyperplane is defined in terms of generating capabilities, which include not only explanatory capabilities for the learning samples but also prediction capabilities for unknown test samples. Here, the generating capabilities are evaluated by the "maximal margin". Thus, the selection of support vectors and the estimation of constants $h$ and$\alpha_i$ ($\alpha_i > 0$) are based on the solution of an optimization problem assuming a maximal margin.

However, in considering human inductive reasoning, the criterion of maximal margin does not fit well because it is independent of the reasoning context. As risk context effects on inductive reasoning were observed in the conducted experiments, an alternative theory of support vector selection and for estimating constants must be assumed. Furthermore, as the modeling purposes of the present study include the clarification of the cognitive mechanisms involved in human inductive reasoning, it is also necessary to provide cognitive interpretations of the model parameters and kernel functions. In the following section, a computational model of inductive reasoning inspired by SVMs, but based on different original assumptions, is proposed and constructed.

## 3.2 Model Construction

### 3.2.1 A Corpus Analysis for Feature-Based Space Construction

In this study, the soft-clustering results for a Japanese corpus are utilized in the construction of a feature space to represent premise and conclusion entities. Based on the soft-clustering analysis, the conditional probabilities of feature words given particular nouns are computed. Conditional probability is assumed to represent the strengths of relationships between nouns (entities) and their features. The method of soft-clustering is similar in structure to popular methods within natural language processing, such as Pereira's method and PLSI ([2], [3], [6]). The method assumes that the co-occurrence probability of a term "$N_i$" and a term "$A_j$", $P(N_i,A_j)$, are represented as Equation (2):

$$P(N_i, A_j) = \sum_k P(N_i \mid C_k) P(A_j \mid C_k) P(C_k), \quad (2)$$

where $P(N_i|C_k)$ is the conditional probability of term $N_i$, given the latent semantic class $C_k$. Each of the probabilistic parameters in the model, $P(C_k)$, $P(N_i|C_k)$, and $P(A_j|C_k)$ are estimated as values that maximize the likelihood of co-occurrence data measured from a corpus using the EM algorithm ([3]). In this study, the term "$N_i$" represents a noun (entity), and the term "$A_j$" represents a feature word, such as a verb. The number of latent classes was fixed at 200.

For the actual estimations, the word co-occurrence frequencies used were extracted from Japanese newspaper articles, covering a ten-year span (1993-2002) of the Mainichi Shimbun. This co-occurrence frequency data consists of combinations of 21,205 nouns and 83,176 predicates in modification relations. CaboCha ([4]), a Japanese analysis tool for modification relations, was used for the extraction.

From the estimated parameters $P(C_k)$, $P(N_i|C_k)$, it is also possible to compute the membership distribution $P(C_k \mid N_i)$ as follows:

$$P(C_k \mid N_i) = \frac{P(N_i \mid C_k)P(C_k)}{P(N_i)} = \frac{P(N_i \mid C_k)P(C_k)}{\sum_k P(N_i \mid C_k)P(C_k)}, \quad (3)$$

In this study, the latent class $C_k$ is assumed to be a semantic category that can be described in terms of a typicality gradient [8]. In fact, most of the estimated latent classes were identified as meaningful categories, as shown in Table 2. This conditional probability $P(C_k \mid N_i)$ is assumed to represent the strengths of relationships between a semantic category and an entity. When a certain category has a high

**Table 2.** Examples of categories

| Category of Foods (*c1*) | | | Category of Valuable assets (*c2*) | | |
|---|---|---|---|---|---|
| $P(c1 \mid ni)$ | | | $P(c2 \mid ni)$ | | |
| 1 | steak | 0.876 | 1 | stock | 0.929 |
| 2 | set meal | 0.867 | 2 | government bonds | 0.862 |
| 3 | grain foods | 0.811 | 3 | estate | 0.791 |
| 4 | vegetable soup | 0.817 | 4 | building estate | 0.780 |
| 5 | meat | 0.739 | 5 | real estate | 0.757 |
| 6 | curry | 0.734 | 6 | cruiser | 0.662 |
| 7 | Chinese noodle | 0.720 | 7 | farmland | 0.657 |
| 8 | pizza | 0.716 | 8 | foreign bond | 0.628 |
| 9 | barleycorn | 0.594 | 9 | house | 0.594 |
| 10 | rice cake | 0.555 | 10 | currency | 0.555 |

conditional probability given a particular noun, it is natural that the entity denoted by the noun has the feature indicated by the category. Thus, by considering each $C$ as a feature dimension, entities can be represented in the feature space constructed from the corpus-analysis results.

### 3.2.2 The Support Vector Machine Based Model of Inductive Reasoning

The model outputs an argument strength denoted as $v(N_i^c)$, that is, the likelihood of a conclusion including entity $N_i^c$ given a positive premise including entity $N_j^+$ and a negative premise including entity $N_j^-$. This value ranges from -3 to 3 based on a 7-pointed scale. $v(N_i^c)$ is represented by the following discrimination function constructed from an SVM based on Gaussian kernel functions:

$$v(N_i^c) = a\,\mathrm{SIM}_+(N_i^c) + b\,\mathrm{SIM}_-(N_i^c), \tag{4}$$

$$\text{where } \mathrm{SIM}_+(N_i^c) = \sum_j^{n^+} e^{-\beta d_{ij}^+}, \tag{5}$$

$$\mathrm{SIM}_-(N_i^c) = \sum_j^{n^-} e^{-\beta d_{ij}^-}, \tag{6}$$

$$d_{ij}^+ = \sum_k^m \left(P(C_k \mid N_i^c) - P(C_k \mid N_j^+)\right)^2, \tag{7}$$

$$d_{ij}^- = \sum_k^m \left(P(C_k \mid N_i^c) - P(C_k \mid N_j^-)\right)^2. \tag{8}$$

$d_{ij}^+$ and $d_{ij}^-$ are functions for word distances based on the categorical feature (denoted as $C_k$). $d_{ij}^+$ represents the distance between the conclusion entity $N_i^c$ and the positive premise entity $N_j^+$, while $d_{ij}^-$ represents the distance between the conclusion entity $N_i^c$ and the negative premise entity $N_j^-$. Here, the number of feature words, $m$, is fixed to 20 (out of 200), on the assumption that only characteristic feature dimensions for the concerned entities should be utilized. Each word distance function constructs Gaussian kernel functions, such as $\mathrm{SIM}_+(N_i^c)$ and $\mathrm{SIM}_-(N_i^c)$, when combined with nonlinear exponential functions and the parameter $\beta$, to which $10^2$ has been applied. Note that the support vectors in this model correspond to positive and negative premise entities within a feature space. As a cognitive interpretation, the Gaussian kernel functions can be regarded as nonlinear similarity functions. $\mathrm{SIM}_+(N_i^c)$ represents the similarities between the conclusion entity $N_i^c$ and the positive premise entities, while SIM-( $N_i^c$ ) denotes the similarities between $N_i^c$ and the negative premise entities. Furthermore, *a* and *b* are multipliers for the kernel functions that correspond to $\alpha_i$ and $y_i$ in Equation (1). Here, value 3 is assigned to $y_i$, the right answer for a positive premise support vector while value -3 is assigned to $y_i$ for a negative premise support vector. Value 3 corresponds to the maximum likelihood rating value on a on 7-point scale while -3 the minimum likelihood rating value. Each positive premise support vector has a same value of *a* ($\alpha_i\, y_i$ ), while each negative premise support vector also has the other same value of *b* ($\alpha_i\, y_i$ ). This means that equal weights are put on every positive premise, as well as on every negative premise. As $\alpha_i$ is greater than 0, if this model's assumption is valid, then the multiplier *a* should be a positive value while the multiplier *b* should be a negative one. Moreover, in terms of their cognitive interpretation, these multipliers are assumed to fulfill the role of similarity adjustment parameters in making responses that are appropriate for the prevailing risk context. Putting these components together, the proposed model assumes that human inductive reasoning is based on the following mechanisms: Similarities between premise entities and conclusion entities represented as kernel functions can be utilized as argument ratings. In addition, similarities are adjusted for according to the prevailing risk context, which are represented by the multipliers for the kernel function. The psychological validity of the model's assumptions can be evaluated by estimations based on the ratings obtained from the conducted experiments.

### 3.2.3 Evaluation Simulations of the Model Assumptions

As a simulation, the parameter *a* and *b* are estimated based on ratings obtained from the experiment using the least-square method, and model performance is then evaluated. At that time, argument ratings on 7-point scales were translated into numerical scales (-3 ~ 3). The parameters for each participant are estimated and compared across the two different risk conditions. Table 3 presents the simulation results for the proposed model, which are contrasted with the results from a control model (for validation of kernel selection, as described later). All the values in the table are averages for the participants with significant model fitting indices, *F* ratios. *n* is the number of significant participants. The results that the data for over 80% of the participants fit for the proposed model clearly indicate that the simulations for the proposed model were successful for both risk conditions.

Moreover, the estimated values from the proposed model for the multiplier *a* are positive ($a > 0$), while the estimated values for the multiplier *b* are negative ($b < 0$) in both conditions. This is also consistent with the model's assumption that argument ratings are based on the similarities of conclusion entities to positive premise entities and the dissimilarities to negative premise entities. On the other hand, the absolute ratio of the estimated multipliers ($|b/a|$) in the over-estimation risk condition is significantly higher than in the under-estimation risk condition ($p<0.05$). This indicates that, in the proposed model, the multipliers for the kernel functions fulfill an adjustment role that can account for shifts in argument ratings under different risk conditions. As seen in the higher value of $|b/a|$ for the over-estimation risk condition, the participants in the over-estimation risk condition placed greater emphasis on the dissimilarities between conclusion entities and the negative premise than the participants in the over-estimation risk condition. In contrast, as seen in the lower value of $|b/a|$ for under-estimation risk condition, the participants in the under-estimation risk condition did not overly stress the dissimilarities between the conclusion entity and negative premises.

Beyond these findings, the validity of kernel selection was also examined. In addition to the proposed model that utilizes Gaussian kernel functions (Equation (5) and Equation (6)), a control model employing another nonlinear kernel function of distance was also simulated.

$$\mathrm{SIM}_{+}\left(N_i^c\right) = -\sum_j^{n^+} \log\left(\beta d_{ij}^{\ +}\right), \quad (9)$$

$$\mathrm{SIM}_{-}\left(N_i^c\right) = -\sum_j^{n^-} \log\left(\beta d_{ij}^{\ -}\right), \quad (10)$$

**Table 3.** Simulation results. (** : $p$<0.01)

| | Kernel functions | | | |
|---|---|---|---|---|
| | **Proposed model** | | **Control model** | |
| | Risk conditions | | | |
| | **UNDER** (***n*: 35 of 43**) | **OVER** (***n*: 30 of 34**) | **UNDER** (***n*: 33 of 43**) | **OVER** (***n*: 25 of 34**) |
| **averaged multiplier *a*** | 4.158 | 3.746 | 0.218 | 0.263 |
| **averaged multiplier *b*** | -3.337 | -3.634 | -1.381 | -1.546 |
| **averaged \|*b*/*a*\|** | 0.821 | 1.053 | 5.862 | 8.864 |
| **range of correlation coefficient** | 0.500** ~0.797** | 0.472** ~0.762** | 0.003(*n.s.*) ~0.789** | 0.374(*n.s.*) ~0.715** |
| **maximum *F* ratio** | 18.337 | 20.057 | 17.673 | 17.090 |

Note that these functions are also assumed to be kernel functions because they are symmetrical functions. $10^2$ was also applied to the parameter β as the default kernel function. As the number *n* in Table 3 shows, there are also good model fittings for the simulation results from the control model, similar to those observed for the proposed model. However, there is no significant difference between $|b/a|$ in the two risk conditions in *t*-test. Furthermore, there are large individual differences in the ranges of correlation coefficients. From the viewpoint of the robust estimation, Gaussian kernel functions in the proposed model are more valid function than that in the control model. In order to further investigate the kernel function validity, yet another control model was simulated which utilizes the following simple linear kernel functions of distance:

$$\mathrm{SIM}_{+}\left(N_i^c\right) = \sum_j^{n^+} d_{ij}^{\ n+} \Big/ n^+ , \tag{11}$$

$$\mathrm{SIM}_{-}\left(N_i^c\right) = \sum_j^{n^-} d_{ij}^{\ n-} \Big/ n^- , \tag{12}$$

If this second control model, which employs linear kernel functions, had also yielded good correlation results, similar to the nonlinear kernel function models, considering the parsimony of the linear kernel function, it would have necessary to regard that as a valid candidate model of inductive reasoning. However, that was not the case. In sharp contrast to the proposed model, the numbers of the participants with significant $F$ ratios are 11 out of 43 in the under-estimation risk condition, and 9 out of 34 in the over-estimation risk condition. These results demonstrate that similarities between the premise and conclusion entities cannot be represented by linear kernel functions of distance, and Gaussian kernel function is the most valid kernel function.

## 4 Discussion

This paper has demonstrated that the proposed SVM-based computational model based provides a valid account of risk context effects on inductive reasoning in terms of both data fit and its underlying theoretical interpretation. Specifically, the multipliers related to kernel functions in the proposed model can model the similarity adjustments that are observed in the differences for identical arguments rated under different risk contexts. Additional simulations also indicated that linear kernel functions are incompatible with the proposed model of risk context effects on inductive reasoning.

Figure 3 is a graphic representation of the similarity adjustment mechanism involved in rating the following argument under both risk conditions:

Person A likes wines.
Person A doesn't like beers.
Person A likes champagnes.

Note that the similarities between entities (distances in the graphic representation) do not change, but rather the response boundaries (the solid and dashed lines) shift. These shifts can be attributed to the difference in the absolute ratio for the estimated multipliers $|b/a|$. The relative adjustment sizes (boundary sizes) for the temporal category of "Person A likes" and for the temporal contrastive category of "Person A doesn't like" reflect the relative relations between multiplier $a$ for the similarity to positive premise entities and multiplier $b$ for the similarity to negative premise entities ("$|b|>|a|$" in the over-estimation risk condition and "$|b|<|a|$" in the under-estimation risk condition). With such a mechanism, the conclusion that "Person A likes champagne" will be less "likely" in the over-estimation risk condition, while it will be more "likely" in the under-estimation risk condition. In this way, the cognitive mechanisms that underlie our empirical findings can be clearly explained by the SVM-based model utilizing a kernel method that was originally inspired by mathematics (e.g., [13]).

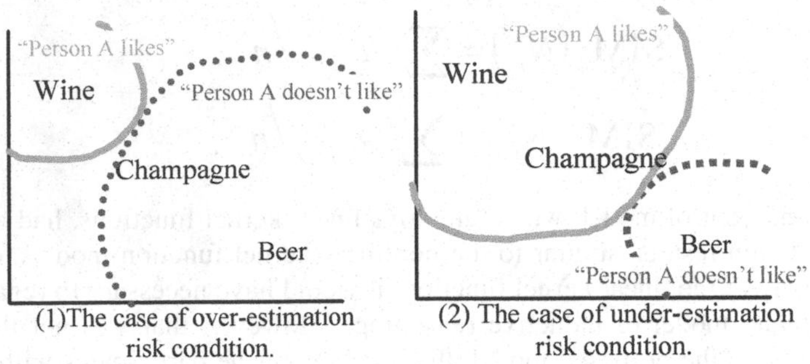


**Fig. 3.** Similarity adjustment for each risk condition

Finally, the proposed model has exciting practical application possibilities. Previous models of inductive reasoning have utilized knowledge spaces constructed from psychological ratings. However, because the methodology of conducting psychological evaluations for the extraordinary number of features and similarities required would involve huge costs, the studies have all focused on entities within rather restricted domains, such as categories of animal (e.g., [11], [12]). In the proposed model, instead of relying on feature rating data, knowledge spaces were constructed from corpus-clustering results. This means that rating costs are avoided, because information for large numbers of words can be computed from a corpus. This makes it possible to conduct predictive simulations for many more conclusion entities than those used in the experiments outlined in this paper. Thus, the proposed model opens up interesting application possibilities, such as an inductive context search engine.

## References

1. Heit, E., Rubinstein, J.: Similarity and property effects in inductive reasoning. Journal of Experimental Psychology: Learning, Memory, and Cognition 20, 411–422 (1994)
2. Hofmann, T.: Probabilistic latent semantic indexing. In: Proceedings of the 22nd International Conference on Research and Development in Information Retrieval:SIGIR 1999, pp. 50–57 (1999)
3. Kameya, Y., Sato, T.: Computation of probabilistic relationship between concepts and their attributes using a statistical analysis of Japanese corpora. In: Proceedings of Symposium on Large-scale Knowledge Resources: LKR (2005)
4. Kudoh, T., Matsumoto, Y.: Japanese Dependency Analysis using Cascaded Chunking. In: Proceedings of the 6th Conference on Natural Language Learning: CoNLL 2002, pp. 63–39 (2002)
5. Osherson, D.N., et al.: Category-Based Induction. Psychological Review 97(2), 185–200 (1990)
6. Pereira, F., Tishby, N., Lee, L.: Distributional clustering of English words. In: Proceedings of the 31st Meeting of the Association for Computational Linguistics, pp. 183–190 (1993)

7. Rips, L.J.: Inductive judgment about netural categories. Journal of Verbal Learning and Verbal Behavior 14, 665–681 (1975)
8. Rosch, E.: On the internal structure of perceptual and semantic categories. In: Moore, T.E. (ed.) Cognitive Development and the Acquisition of Language, pp. 111–144. Academic Press, New York (1973)
9. Sakamoto, K., Terai, A., Nakagawa, M.: Computational models of inductive reasoning using a statistical analysis of a Japanese corpus. The Journal of Cognitive Systems Research 8, 282–299 (2007a)
10. Sakamoto, K., Nakagawa, M.: Risk Context Effects in Inductive Reasoning: An Experimental and Computational Modeling Study. In: Kokinov, B., et al. (eds.) CONTEXT 2007. LNCS (LNAI), vol. 4635, pp. 425–438. Springer, Heidelberg (2007b)
11. Sanjana, N.E., Tenenbaum, J.B.: Bayesian models of inductive generalization. In: Becker, S., Thrun, S., Obermayer, K. (eds.) Advances in Neural Processing Systems 15, MIT Press, Cambridge (2003)
12. Sloman, A.T.: Feature-Based Induction. Cognitive Psychology 25, 231–280 (1993)
13. Vapnik, V.: The Nature of Statistical Learning Theory. Springer, Heidelberg (1995)

# Appendix

## Appendix A

Entities used in the simulations and the psychological experiments

| Argument Set 1: Person A likes <noun>. (for training session) | |
|---|---|
| Nouns used as entities of positive premises | actor |
| | painter |
| | scholar |
| Nouns used as entities of negative premises | company employee |
| | female office worker |
| Nouns used as entities of conclusions | cameraman |
| | director |
| | chef |
| | storekeeper |
| | designer |
| | clerk |
| | artist |
| | policeman |

| Argument Set 2: Person B likes <noun>. | |
|---|---|
| Nouns used as entities of positive premises | physics |
| | astronomy |
| Nouns used as entities of negative premises | French |
| Nouns used as entities of conclusions | mathematics |
| | arithmetic |
| | Chinese |
| | Hangul |
| | English |
| | Japanese literature |
| | pharmacology |
| | chemistry |

| Argument Set 3: Person C likes <noun>. | | Argument Set 4: Person D likes <noun> | |
|---|---|---|---|
| Nouns used as entities of positive premises | steak | Nouns used as entities of positive premises | The stocks |
| | chow mein | | foreign loan |
| Nouns used as entities of negative premises | Japanese Noodle | Nouns used as entities of negative premises | land |
| Nouns used as entities of conclusions | curry | Nouns used as entities of conclusions | government bond |
| | pizza | | corporate bond |
| | chanko (Japanese pot dish) | | site |
| | boiled rice with tea | | real estate |
| | sushi | | farmland |
| | bean curd boiled in water | | one's own house |
| | pork | | currency |
| | snacks | | stock certificate |

**Appendix B**

Entities used the supplementary psychological experiment.

| Argument Set 1: <noun> is *bamisoya* (nonsense word).(for training session) | | Argument Set 2: <noun> is *dupaepo* (nonsense word). | |
|---|---|---|---|
| Nouns used as entities of positive premises | actor | Nouns used as entities of positive premises | jumbo jet |
| | painter | | Ferry |
| | scholar | | shallop |
| Nouns used as entities of negative premises | company employee | Nouns used as entities of negative premises | bus |
| | female office worker | | train |
| | | | prison |
| Nouns used as entities of conclusions | cameraman | Nouns used as entities of conclusions | passenger car |
| | director | | buoy |
| | chef | | airplane |
| | storekeeper | | aquarium |
| | designer | | ward office |
| | clerk | | trailer |
| | artist | | taxi |
| | policeman | | fishing boat |

| Argument Set 3: <noun> is *hihaerke* (nonsense word). | |
|---|---|
| Nouns used as entities of positive premises | visit of condolence |
| | visit |
| | celebration |
| Nouns used as entities of negative premises | hiking |
| | dress |
| | horse riding |
| Nouns used as entities of conclusions | suit |
| | pajamas |
| | skiing |
| | enjoying seeing cherry blossom |
| | New Year's visit to a shrine |
| | wake for the dead |
| | gathering shellfish |
| | visiting to a shrine |

| Argument Set 4: <noun> is *yorahim* (nonsense word). | |
|---|---|
| Nouns used as entities of positive premises | iron tower |
| | great image of Buddha |
| | monument |
| Nouns used as entities of negative premises | counselor |
| | Apartment |
| | luxurious domicile |
| Nouns used as entities of conclusions | veterinarian |
| | European-style building |
| | bronze statue |
| | apartment of a housing complex |
| | station employee |
| | rail |
| | company house |
| | stone monument |

# Order Retrieval

Neil Rubens, Vera Sheinman, Takenobu Tokunaga, and Masashi Sugiyama

Department of Computer Science, Tokyo Institute of Technology
Ookayama 2-12-1, Meguro-ku, Tokyo 152-8552, Japan
neil@hrstc.org, {vera46,take}@cl.cs.titech.ac.jp, sugi@cs.titech.ac.jp

**Abstract.** Extensive work has been done in recent years on automatically grouping words into categories. For example, {*Wednesday, Monday, Tuesday*} could be grouped into a 'days of week' category. However, not only grouping the words, but also ordering them is important, e.g. *Monday*→ *Tuesday*→ *Wednesday*. The order relation is an important aspect that could be used to enrich existing ontologies, to determine the sequence of actions for planning tasks, and to determine the order of user's preferences for a set of items, etc. However, automatically determining the order relation seems to have been ignored. Pairwise similarity metric commonly used to cluster words may not be well suited for the ordering task. Therefore, we propose a new metric designed for the ordering task. We utilize statistical proximity features of the terms in the documents (in a large corpus) in order to determine the order relations between terms. The effectiveness of the proposed method is verified in experimental settings against orders provided by human subjects.

## 1 Introduction

Computational linguistics provides a large body of research on categorization [1,2,3,4]. For example, many lexical ontologies such as WordNet [5] provide hierarchical clustering of terms (concepts) based on lexical categorization. However, in some applications categorical information alone is not sufficient, as illustrated by the following examples:

- Which restaurant should the recommender system suggest based on customer's reviews that include one of the terms such as *{horrible, edible, good, delicious}*?
- What is the correct order of actions for baking a pie *{wash, cut, bake, serve}*?

To answer the above questions the information about the ordering of the terms is required. Words may be ordered by various semantic features. Some terms are ordered by the time feature e.g. *past, present, future*, by the dimensional feature e.g. *line, circle, sphere*, etc. [6]. We propose[1] to retrieve information about the order of the terms by utilizing the empirical observation that words that are part of sequence tend to appear sequentially in text (e.g. *one* tends to appear before *three*). We extract the information about the terms order, by utilizing statistical properties of the total and partial orders of the terms in the corpus.

[1] The source code, online application, the sequence dataset and additional materials are available at http://hrstc.org/or

T. Tokunaga and A. Ortega (Eds.): LKR 2008, LNAI 4938, pp. 310–317, 2008.

## 2 Related Work

Many works in computational linguistics explore semantic relatedness between words, clustering of words or concepts by shared meaning, and so forth. Some methods [1] extract the similarity information from high-quality ontologies constructed manually by experts, such as WordNet [5]. Others exploit various computational techniques to measure similarity in a large corpus, such as the Web [2]. Weeds and Weir [3] provide an excellent survey on distributional similarity techniques. However, we are not aware of studies that extract or represent the relation of order among words, or members in a cluster.

The similarity and clustering approaches in their current state are not suitable for the task of ordering (as confirmed by our evaluation in Section 4), since similarity information does not necessarily provide the order information. These approaches are complimentary to our work, in a sense, that we add directionality to undirected lexical sets.

## 3 Proposed Approach

Given a set of terms we want to find an order of terms that is representative of the corpus in which terms occur. In order to achieve this we analyze the order in which the terms appear in the documents (Section 3.1). The proposed approach is based on the empirical observations that words that are part of a sequence, tend to appear after each other in documents. This approach tends to achieve a high accuracy when there is sufficient data. However, the number of documents that contain all of the terms could be small or equal to zero (especially when the number of terms is high). This may make an estimation of the order unreliable. To cope with this, we propose another method that estimates the order of the terms from their partial orders (Section 3.2). That is, we estimate the relative order first (e.g. the term $t_i$ usually occurs before the term $t_j$). Then by using the partial order we estimate the total order of terms in the sequence. In the following subsections we define the problem in a more formal way, and describe in detail proposed approaches and their advantages and limitations.

### 3.1 Total Order Sequence Retrieval

In this approach we try to find the most probable sequence of the terms, by estimating the probability of the complete sequence occurring in the corpus. Let us consider a corpus of documents $D$. A document $d \in D$ could be represented as a sequence of terms $w \in T$ in the order that they occur in the document:

$$d = (w_1, w_2, \ldots, w_l), \tag{1}$$

where $l$ is the number of terms in the document. Let us introduce an operator '$\prec$' – 'precedes'. An expression $(t_i \prec t_j)$, where $t \in T$, means that in a given document, term $t_i$ occurs before $t_j$, and that there could be zero or more terms between $t_i$ and $t_j$. This operator could be applied to an arbitrary number of terms e.g. $(t_i \prec t_{i+1} \prec \ldots \prec t_{i+n})$. Let us also define an indicator $I$ that determines whether a sequence $S$ could be 'satisfied' in a document $d$. That is, for an arbitrary sequence $S = (t_1 \prec t_2 \prec \ldots \prec t_n)$, where $t \in T$ and $n$ is the length of the sequence; we want to determine if for the given document $d$, there exist terms $w \in d$ that follow the same order as terms $t \in S$. If sequence $S = (t_1 \prec t_2 \prec \ldots \prec t_n)$ could be satisfied in a given document $d$, then $I(S,d) = 1$, if not then $I(S,d) = 0$. We can calculate the number of documents where the sequence $S$ could be satisfied as:

$$df(S) = \sum_{d \in D} I(S,d), \tag{2}$$

where '*df*' stands for the *document frequency*. We can now estimate the probability of sequence $S$ occurring in the corpus $D$ as:

$$\hat{P}(S) = \frac{df(S)}{|D|}, \tag{3}$$

where $|D|$ is the number of the documents in the corpus. In practice, we can take advantage of the corpus index [7] in order to approximate the value of $df(S)$ directly. The problem of finding the most probable sequence can be formulated as:

$$\arg\max_{S} P(S). \tag{4}$$

In order to find the most probable sequence it is necessary to evaluate $\hat{P}(S)$ for all $n!$ permutations of the sequence $S$ (where $n$ is a number of terms in a sequence). This makes the total order approach intractable for longer sequences. The estimator $\hat{P}(S)$ is accurate in the cases when the number of documents that contains all of the terms in $S$ (in arbitrary order) is high. However, in the cases where the number of documents containing *all* of the terms in $S$ is small, the estimator $\hat{P}(S)$ may become unreliable as confirmed in Section 4. In the next subsection we propose a method that addresses this limitation.

### 3.2 Partial Order Sequence Retrieval

Evaluating all of the permutations obtained by total order approach (Section 3.1) may not be tractable for longer sequences. The full sequence information may also be biased when only a few documents are available. However, many documents that lack the total order information, do contain the partial order information. For these reasons, we estimate the total order of terms from partial orders. Hence, the implementation of the task presents a tradeoff among availability of information, precision, and efficiency.

We are trying to find the most probable sequence of terms $S = (t_1 \prec t_2 \prec \ldots \prec t_n)$ such that $\arg\max_S P(S)$. It is not necessary to extract the order from the documents that contain all of the terms in S (as in Section 3.1). We can extract the partial ordering information, even though not all of the terms appear in the document. For example, if $t_j$ tends to occur before $t_k$ in the documents, and $t_k$ tends to occur before $t_l$, we can infer that $(t_j \prec t_k \prec t_l)$ is the most probable order. That is, we can reconstruct the total order of the terms by utilizing the partial order information.

We can apply the standard sorting algorithms in order to approximate the total order from the partial orders. When the sorting algorithm requests to compare arbitrary terms $t_j$ and $t_k$ we return $t_j \prec t_k$ (i.e. $t_j$ precedes $t_k$) if $\hat{P}(t_j \prec t_k) \geq \hat{P}(t_k \prec t_j)$, and $t_k \prec t_j$ otherwise (where the probability of sequence occurring is calculated by Eq. (3)). Standard sorting algorithms, such as quicksort, are based on average $\mathcal{O}(n \log n)$ comparisons between pairs, and in the worst case $\mathcal{O}(n^2)$ comparisons (where $n$ is the number of terms in the sequence). Note that sometimes the obtained partial order information may not be consistent. That is, we may have a conflicting information e.g $t_j \prec t_k$, $t_k \prec t_l$, but $t_l \prec t_j$. To cope with inconsistent cases, we terminate the algorithm after at most $n^2$ iterations and return a probable order.

When the sufficient number of the documents is available, the total order approach (Section 3.1) would be more accurate than the partial order approach. The partial order of the terms may change depending on the context in which they appear. The context of the documents used for the total order is less likely to change, since all of the sequence terms must appear in each of the documents.

## 4 Experimental Evaluation

In this section, we evaluate the performance of the proposed approaches (Section 3.1 and Section 3.2) and a baseline term clustering approach (Section 4.3).

### 4.1 Data Set

The dataset for the experiments is comprised of 73 sequences of words (Table 1) that were collected in the following manner. Five computer science students were the subjects of sequences collection. Two of them were native English speakers. Each one of the subjects suggested some sequences and verified all the sequences suggested by others. The sequences that were not unanimously agreed upon were removed from the test set, or changed to satisfy all the subjects.

### 4.2 Error Metric

To evaluate the quality of the acquired sequences in comparison with the sequences proposed by the human subjects, we use *Kendall tau* as a base measure [8]. The Kendall tau distance counts the number of pairwise disagreements between two lists. It counts the number of swaps necessary to place one list in the same order as the other list (normalized by the length of the list). The larger the distance is, the less similar the two lists are. The Kendal tau distance is expressed as:

$$KT(S_1, S_2) = \frac{|(t_i, t_j) : t_i \prec t_j, idx(t_i, S_1) < idx(t_j, S_1) \wedge idx(t_i, S_2) > idx(t_j, S_2)|}{n(n-1)/2}, \quad (5)$$

**Table 1.** Some of the sequences used in the evaluation. For the complete list please see http://hrstc.org/or.

| |
|---|
| Sun,Mercury,Venus,Earth,Mars,Jupiter,Saturn,Uranus,Neptune,Pluto |
| byte,kilobyte,megabyte,gigabyte,terabyte |
| a,b,c,d,e,f,g,h,i,j,k,l,m,n,o,p,q,r,s,t,u,v,w,x,y,z |
| dawn,morning,afternoon,evening,night |
| breakfast,lunch,dinner,supper |
| stand,walk,run |
| spotless,clean,dirty,filthy |
| wash,cut,bake,serve |
| baby,infant,child,teenager,adult,elderly |
| solid,liquid,gas |
| planet,solar system,galaxy,universe |

where $|(t_i, t_j) : t_i \prec t_j, idx(t_i, S_1) < idx(t_j, S_1) \wedge idx(t_i, S_2) > idx(t_j, S_2)|$ is the cardinality of the set of tuples that have pairwise disagreement between two lists $S_1$ and $S_2$; $idx(t, S)$ refers to the index of the term $t$ in the list $S$; and $n(n-1)/2$ is the length normalization factor.

In the current settings, a sequence is considered correct if the order of the terms is completely reversed. This is due to an unclear ascending or descending fashion of a sequence. Therefore, we modify Kendall tau (Eq. (5)) to treat the inverse transpositions equally to the original order:

$$KT'(S_1, S_2) = |2KT(S_1, S_2) - 1|. \tag{6}$$

By using a Kendall tau metric, we do not only judge whether the acquired order was right or wrong, but also approximate the quality of the order by a range of $[0, 1]$, where 1 stands for identical sequences or the inversely transposed sequence, and 0 for the non-correlated sequences.

### 4.3 Baseline Method

Baseline methods for evaluation are difficult to determine since we are not aware of any previous studies on automatic retrieval of orders. There have been related work on automatic term clustering [1,2,3,4]. However, many of these methods rely on the ontologies (e.g. WordNet [5]) or text corpora. Therefore, obtaining the relation between arbitrary terms may not be possible for these methods, unless given terms exist in an ontology or a corpus. Recently, a *normalized google distance* (NGD) method has been proposed to automatically extract term similarity information from the large corpus of data [2]. As the proposed approaches, NGD also utilizes statistical properties of the corpus such as document frequency and joint probability. For these reasons, we choose NGD as a baseline for the comparison with the proposed approaches (Section 3.1 and Section 3.2). NGD uses the pairwise similarity metric for the automatic terms clustering. The relation between terms is calculated as:

$$NGD(t_i, t_j) = \frac{\max\{\log df(t_i), \log df(t_j)\} - \log df(t_i, t_j)}{\log |D| - \min\{\log df(t_i), \log df(t_j)\}}, \tag{7}$$

where $df(t)$ is the number of documents that contain term $t$, and $|D|$ is the total number of documents in a corpus. Note that the NGD metric is symmetric i.e. $NGD(t_i, t_j) = NGD(t_j, t_i)$. Using NGD the sequence score is calculated by aggregating the NGD score for the term's relations in the order that they occur in the sequence, i.e.:

$$NGD(S) = \prod_{i=1}^{n-1} NGD(t_i, t_{i+1}), \tag{8}$$

where $t_i$ refers to the $i$th term in the sequence $S$. The top sequence is determined as:

$$\arg\max_{S} NGD(S). \tag{9}$$

### 4.4 Results

We evaluate the performance of the proposed total order approach (Section 3.1) and the proposed partial order approach (Section 3.2) with the baseline NGD approach (Section 4.3). Methods are evaluated on the dataset described in Section 4.1. Although, these methods are extendable to any of the search engines that provide proximity search capability, in this paper we present experiments conducted with the use of Yahoo API [9]. We evaluate methods by using several metrics. The accuracy is measured by the number of correctly obtained orders. The quality of the obtained sequences is measured by a modified version of a Kendall tau (KT) distance metric (as described in Section 4.2). We also evaluate the quality of the sequence when sufficient information is available ($df > 50$). The performance of the methods in relation to the sequence length is measured by the average length of the correct sequence. Running time is measured by the computational complexity. Results of the evaluation are shown in Table 2. Proposed approaches outperform the baseline NGD method on all of the metrics. We discuss obtained results in more detail in the following paragraphs.

**Table 2.** Comparison of methods for order retrieval. Proposed methods are indicated by '*'. Best performing method for a given metric is indicated by '°'. For the sequence quality, a higher value of Kendall tau distance corresponds to a better sequence quality (score of 1 corresponds to the correct sequence). For details see Section 4.4.

| | NGD | Total Order* | Partial Order* |
|---|---|---|---|
| Accuracy (binary loss function) | 9.5% | 35.6% | °39.7% |
| Avg. Sequence Quality (KT) | 0.39 | 0.42 | °0.63 |
| Avg. Sequence Quality (KT, $df > 50$) | 0.39 | °0.96 | 0.63 |
| Avg. length of correct sequences | 3.3 | 4.3 | °5.5 |
| Computational Complexity | $\mathcal{O}(n!)$ | $\mathcal{O}(n!)$ | °$\mathcal{O}(n^2)$ |

*Term Clustering Approach (Baseline):* In this paragraph we examine performance of the baseline term clustering method NGD [2] (Section 4.3) on the task of term ordering. Term clustering (lexical similarity) approaches allow us to group terms together, although ordering of the terms is not intended, and may not be well suited for obtaining term ordering as confirmed by evaluation results (e.g. the accuracy of NGD is 9.5% in comparison to 35.6% and 39.7% of the proposed methods as shown in Table 2). NGD is not well suited for the ordering task, since it is symmetric (i.e. it does not contain directionality). That is, the relation between *Monday* and *Tuesday* is the same as the relation between *Tuesday* and *Monday*, i.e. $NGD(Monday, Tuesday) = NGD(Tuesday, Monday)$. Symmetricity of the NGD metric probably hinders its performance. In general, metrics that are used for clustering may not be well suited for ordering tasks. In addition, the computational complexity of applying pairwise similarity in order to find term's sequence is $\mathcal{O}(n!)$, which makes it not tractable for longer sequences.

*Total Order Approach (Proposed):* The proposed total order approach works well, when the sufficient number of documents is available (as discussed in Section 3.1). When sufficient data is available, the quality of the order acquired by this approach is impressively high, Kendall-Tau of 0.96 (max is 1) for the retrieved sequences, when the data from more than 50 documents was available i.e. $df > 50$. However, even in a huge corpus, not all the information is available, and in more than 58% of the cases it was difficult to acquire all the needed information. Out of the total of 73 sequences in the dataset, for the 38% of sequences there were no documents that contained all of the terms of the sequence i.e. $df = 0$; further 20% of the sequences had fewer than 50 documents i.e. $df < 50$ . With $df < 50$ sequences , Kendall-Tau for the retrieved sequences was only 0.42.

*Partial Order Approach (Proposed):* The proposed partial order approach is able to construct a total order by utilizing the partial order information available in the documents. To illustrate usefulness of the partial order approach, consider the query "$wash * cut * bake * serve$" that represents rough order of actions for baking a dish. This query retrieves no documents i.e. $df = 0$ . Its inverse transposition as well as other transpositions, all result in $df = 0$. However, by combining the available partial order information using the proposed approach returned the expected $wash, cut, bake, serve$ as the retrieved order of terms. The partial order approach achieves the best performance on most of the metrics. However, in cases when the sufficient information is available, it is outperformed by the total order approach.

## 5 Conclusion

The term order is an important relation that could be used in many practical applications e.g. to find a sequence of actions for planing tasks, to arrange terms by a certain feature (e.g. for recommender systems), etc. In this paper, we proposed to automatically determine the order of terms. We have shown that existing similarity metrics may not be well suited for the ordering task; and, in turn, proposed a metric that utilizes the statistical proximity information to retrieve the order of the terms.

There are several tradeoffs that should be taken into account when extracting the order of the terms. Examination of all possible permutations leads to $\mathcal{O}(n!)$ time complexity (where $n$ is the length of a sequence) that is intractable even for relatively short sequences. We can reduce the time complexity to $\mathcal{O}(n^2)$ and maintain a fairly good accuracy, by utilizing the partial order to approximate the total order of the terms in the sequence.

Another tradeoff to consider is the availability of information as opposed to accuracy. When sufficient amount of information is available, the precision of the total order approach is excellent. However, in our experiments sufficient information was available in less than 50% of the cases. Using the partial order information such as the ordering between pairs of terms increases the recall but reduces the accuracy.

We hope there will be more works dealing with the term ordering. The source code, online application, the sequence dataset and additional materials used in this paper are made available at http://hrstc.org/or.

## References


1. Budanitsky, A., Hirst, G.: Evaluating WordNet-based measures of lexical semantic relatedness. Computational Linguistics 32(1), 13–47 (2006)
2. Cilibrasi, R., Vitanyi, P.: The google similarity distance. IEEE Transactions on Knowledge and Data Engineering 19(3), 370–383 (2007)
3. Weeds, J., Weir, D.: Co-occurrence retrieval: A flexible framework for lexical distributional similarity. Computational Linguistics 31(4), 439–475 (2005)
4. Hearst, M.A.: Automatic acquisition of hyponyms from large text corpora. In: Proceedings of the 14th conference on Computational linguistics, Nantes, France, pp. 539–545. Association for Computational Linguistics (1992)
5. Miller, G.A.: WordNet: A lexical database for English. Communications of ACM 38(11), 39–41 (1995)
6. Sheinman, V., Rubens, N., Tokunaga, T.: Commonly perceived order within a category. In: Aberer, K., et al. (eds.) ISWC 2007. LNCS, vol. 4825, Springer, Heidelberg (2007)
7. Wikipedia: Proximity search: usage in commercial search engines — Wikipedia, the free encyclopedia (2007) (Online, accessed 2007)
8. Kendall, M.: A new measure of rank correlation. Biometrika 30, 81–89 (1938)
9. Yahoo, `http://www.yahoo.com`

# Stylistic Analysis of Japanese Prime Ministers' Diet Addresses*

Takafumi Suzuki[1] and Kyo Kageura[2]

[1] Graduate School of Interdisciplinary Information Studies, The University of Tokyo, 7-3-1 Hongo, Bunkyo-ku, Tokyo 113-0033, Japan
qq16116@iii.u-tokyo.ac.jp

[2] Graduate School of Education, The University of Tokyo, 7-3-1 Hongo, Bunkyo-ku, Tokyo 113-0033, Japan
kyo@p.u-tokyo.ac.jp

**Abstract.** This study examines the speech styles used in the addresses of 27 Japanese prime ministers. As computational linguistics has developed, and many on-line corpora and new types of texts have been produced along with the growth of the Web, the statistical analysis of styles has expanded in scope. In an exploratory examination of the styles of prime ministers' Diet addresses, we clarified that the styles of the addresses reflect the general changes in Japanese usage and the individual styles of the prime ministers. This study indicates that stylistic methods are useful for historical analysis of political texts. They can be applied for more large-scale data and various research topics in humanities and social science.

## 1 Introduction

This study examines the speech styles used in the addresses of 27 Japanese prime ministers. As computational linguistics has developed and many on-line corpora and new types of texts have been produced along with the growth of the Web [1], the statistical analysis of styles has expanded in scope. In addition to the conventional usage of the method for detecting authors and registers [2], it is now also used for examining the historical consciousness of texts [3].

Turning our eyes to the field of politics, political speeches have attracted growing attention as the role of the media and the performance of politicians increase in importance in contemporary politics [4]. Among such speeches, prime ministers' Diet addresses are regarded as the most important material for analyzing Japanese politics [5, 6] though to date there have been few studies carried out that systematically analyze them.

Against this background, we are currently conducting systematic analyses of Japanese prime ministers' Diet addresses after World War II. We have been conducting four types of analyses, namely macroscopic and microscopic analyses of the content and style. These four types of analyses, the distinction between which we first proposed in another study [7], enable us to fully explore the linguistic and political implications of the texts. The first author has shown that the frequencies and co-occurences of several

* This study was supported by a Suntory Foundation Research Grant, 2007-2008. We would like to express our gratitude for this support. An earlier version of this study was presented at the JPSJ SIG Computers and the Humanities Symposium 2006, Kyoto. We would like to thank the participants in the symposium for their useful comments.

T. Tokunaga and A. Ortega (Eds.): LKR 2008, LNAI 4938, pp. 318–325, 2008.

content words represent the macroscopic transitions of Japanese foreign perception [8], and together we have also demonstrated that the distributional characteristics related to nouns clearly represent the political styles of two powerful Japanese prime ministers [7]. In addition to these analyses of the content of the addresses, stylistic analysis can be used to clarify the changing language usages of prime ministers and how these reflect their personal or individual styles. This study indicates that stylistic methods are useful for historical analysis of political texts. They can be applied for more large-scale texts and various research topics in humanities and social science.

The rest of this paper is organized as follows. In Section 2 we describe our data, and in Section 3 explain the point of view from which we approach our subject. In Sections 4 and 5 we set out our results, and in Section 6 make concluding remarks.

**Table 1.** Basic data on the addresses

| Name | Initial | Entered office | Addresses | Total (all) | Mean (all) | Total (p) | Mean (p) | Total (av) | Mean (av) |
|---|---|---|---|---|---|---|---|---|---|
| HIGASHIKUNI Naruhiko | HN | 8/1945 | 1 | 5779 | 5779.0 | 1671 | 1671.0 | 646 | 646.0 |
| SHIDEHARA Kijuro | SK | 10/1945 | 1 | 2981 | 2981.0 | 827 | 827.0 | 350 | 350.0 |
| YOSHIDA Shigeru | YS1 | 5/1946 | 3 | 5426 | 1808.7 | 1505 | 501.7 | 730 | 243.3 |
| KATAYAMA Tetsu | KTe | 5/1947 | 2 | 9072 | 4536.0 | 2489 | 1244.5 | 1219 | 603.5 |
| ASHIDA Hitoshi | AH | 3/1948 | 1 | 3506 | 3506.0 | 1065 | 1065.0 | 460 | 460.0 |
| YOSHIDA Shigeru | YS2 | 10/1948 | 16 | 26685 | 1667.8 | 7256 | 453.5 | 3274 | 204.6 |
| HATOYAMA Ichiro | HI | 12/1954 | 5 | 8318 | 1663.6 | 2460 | 492.0 | 988 | 197.6 |
| ISHIBASHI Tanzan | IT | 12/1956 | 1 | 2665 | 2665.0 | 789 | 789.0 | 280 | 280.0 |
| KISHI Nobusuke | KN | 2/1957 | 9 | 18089 | 2009.9 | 5194 | 577.1 | 2041 | 226.8 |
| IKEDA Hayato | IH | 12/1960 | 11 | 35220 | 3201.8 | 10090 | 917.3 | 3714 | 337.6 |
| SATOH Eisaku | SE | 11/1964 | 21 | 56731 | 2701.5 | 16316 | 777.0 | 5681 | 270.5 |
| TANAKA Kakuei | TK | 6/1972 | 4 | 15097 | 3774.3 | 4363 | 1091.0 | 1758 | 367.0 |
| MIKI Takeo | MiT | 12/1974 | 5 | 18222 | 3644.4 | 5298 | 1059.6 | 2224 | 444.8 |
| FUKUDA Takeo | FT | 12/1976 | 5 | 17030 | 3406.0 | 4794 | 958.8 | 2121 | 424.2 |
| OHIRA Masayoshi | OM | 12/1978 | 4 | 15629 | 3907.3 | 4710 | 1177.5 | 1594 | 398.5 |
| SUZUKI Zenko | SZ | 6/1980 | 4 | 13878 | 3469.5 | 4103 | 1025.8 | 1315 | 328.8 |
| NAKASONE Yasuhiro | NY | 11/1982 | 10 | 47422 | 4742.2 | 13761 | 1376.1 | 4249 | 424.9 |
| TAKESHITA Noboru | TN | 11/1987 | 4 | 18448 | 4612.0 | 5411 | 1352.8 | 1758 | 439.5 |
| UNO Sosuke | US | 6/1989 | 1 | 3669 | 3669.0 | 1110 | 1110.0 | 367 | 367.0 |
| KAIFU Toshiki | KTo | 8/1989 | 5 | 23541 | 4708.2 | 6194 | 1399.8 | 2070 | 414.0 |
| MIYAZAWA Kiichi | MK | 11/1991 | 4 | 19110 | 4777.5 | 5849 | 1462.3 | 1707 | 426.8 |
| HOSOKAWA Morihiro | HM | 8/1993 | 3 | 14609 | 4869.7 | 4710 | 1499.0 | 1368 | 456.0 |
| HATA Tsutomu | HT | 4/1994 | 1 | 4185 | 4185.0 | 1297 | 1297.0 | 433 | 433.0 |
| MURAYAMA Tomiichi | MuT | 6/1994 | 4 | 20454 | 5113.5 | 6194 | 1548.5 | 1846 | 461.5 |
| HASHIMOTO Ryutaro | HR | 1/1996 | 5 | 26809 | 5361.8 | 7907 | 1581.4 | 2076 | 415.2 |
| OBUCHI Keizo | OK | 6/1998 | 5 | 20702 | 4140.4 | 5992 | 1198.4 | 2040 | 408.0 |
| MORI Yoshiro | MY | 4/2000 | 4 | 20149 | 5037.3 | 5846 | 1461.5 | 1772 | 443.0 |
| KOIZUMI Junichiro | KJ | 4/2001 | 11 | 46996 | 4272.4 | 13646 | 1240.5 | 3691 | 335.5 |

p: particles.
av: auxiliary verbs.

## 2 Data

The corpora we used in this study consists of 150 Diet addresses[1] covering 28 terms in office of 27 Japanese prime ministers from 1945 to 2006.[2] We downloaded the

[1] The texts of the speeches were written down by secretaries in shorthand.

[2] Yoshida was elected prime minister twice. We treated these two terms of office as different periods.

addresses from the on-line database *Sekai to Nihon (World and Japan)*[3] and merged all the addresses for each prime minister to make a single text for each. We applied morphological analysis to the addresses using ChaSen, a Japanese morphological analysis system [9]. The number of tokens for all words, particles and auxiliary verbs were 520422, 151440, and 51482 respectively, and the number of types were 11571, 111, and 60 respectively. Table 1 sets out each prime minister' name, initial, date of entry into office, number of addresses, and total and mean number of tokens for all words, particles and auxiliary verbs. We united 8 combinations (16 types) which were distinguished only by notational differences (kanji and kana in Japanese). The numbers of types of the particles and the auxiliary verbs used for our analysis were 105 and 58 respectively.[4]

## 3 Observational Viewpoint

The characteristics we analyzed in this study were the length of sentences and the relative frequencies of particles and auxiliary verbs. Our purpose was not to classify the texts but to examine the transitions in the above characteristics, and so we analyzed the characteristics separately, instead of merging various ones together.

The length of sentences has been frequently analyzed in authorship attribution and other stylistic studies in English [e.g. 10] and Japanese [e.g. 11]. It can indicate the changing language usages and personal or individual styles of prime ministers. Though its reliability as an indicator of style has been questioned [12, 13], it is still considered to be useful in a specific register. In order to clarify whether or not it would be an effective means of distinguishing the authors, we conducted an analysis of variance on the consolidated texts of the addresses of each prime minister before analyzing them.

The distribution of the particles was shown to be a reliable method for distinguishing between different authors in Japanese [14]. We also analyze the distribution of the auxiliary verbs in order to shed further light on the personal or individual styles of prime ministers; the use of both parts of speech are related to each other, and represent the modality of the texts, useful information for characterising personal and sentimental aspects of the texts [15].

We carried out two multivariate analyses; principal component analysis with covariance matrix of the features, and cluster analysis with correlation distance and average method. Principal component analysis was first carried out to view the classification of the authors in a scatter plot and to clarify the factors classifying the addresses as principal components. In order to confirm the results of the principal component analysis, we carried out hierarchical cluster analysis. As we adopt an exploratory approach to characterizing the styles of authors, it is useful to confirm the results by several multivariate analysis methods. As the results of cluster analysis depend to a significant extent on the distance and clustering method, we selected those reproducing the classification produced by principal component analysis most clearly.

We applied the multiscale bootstrap method [16] developed by Shimodaira [17, 18, 19] to the clusters. It replicates the data by random resampling and calculates

[3] www.ioc.u-tokyo.ac.jp/~worldjpn/index.html

[4] Seven types were used both as particles and as auxiliary verbs. We treated them as different words.

approximately unbiased $p$-values (AU $p$-value) presenting reliability of the results to the fluctuations of the sampling of the data. By using the multiscale bootstrap method, the sample size of the replicated data is altered and a third-order accurate $p$-value is obtained [17, 18, 19]. The bootstrap processes were repeated 10,000 times for our data. Our aim in using the bootstrap method in this study was not only to confirm the reliability of the results themselves but also to use the reliability (including unreliable clusters) for identifying the authors with an exceptional AU $p$-value.

## 4 Transition of the Length of the Sentences

In Fig. 1, the solid line shows the mean value of the length of the sentences and the dotted lines show the standard deviations, and the mean value for each prime minister is indicated by his initial (see Table 1). Longer sentence lengths result in higher standard deviations. The relationship between the two measures is expressed by the following formula: $y = 0.47x - 1.09$ ($x$: mean, $y$: standard deviations, $R^2 = 0.62$).

In order to confirm whether sentence length would be a reliable indicator for distinguishing between the different authors (prime ministers), an analysis of variance was conducted. As the addresses before Yoshida's second term in office (YS2) had a small number of tokens, which could affect the results, the analysis was carried out on two groups of data; the length of the sentences of all prime ministers and those of prime ministers after Hatoyama (HI). The $p$-values we obtained were 0.22 and 0.03 respectively. As the $p$-value for all prime ministers was not significant but it was significant for those after Hatoyama ($p < 0.05$), the results demonstrated that the sentence length is an effective indicator distinguishing the author of the addresses, at least after Hatoyama.

Fig. 1 shows that the prime ministers' addresses have continuously changed over time. The length of the sentences used in the addresses decreased overall in the period

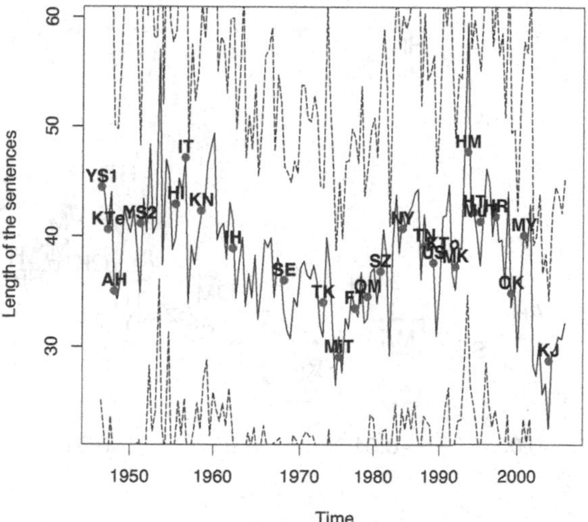


**Fig. 1.** Transition of the sentence length

bracketed by Ishibashi (IT) and Miki's terms in office, increased to reach a peak during Hosokawa's administration, and then decreased again. This shows that the era affected the length of the sentences used by the prime ministers.

Fig. 1 seems to indicate that Ishibashi (IT) and Hosokawa (HM) used exceptionally longer sentences and Miki (MiT) and Koizumi (KJ) used exceptionally shorter ones. We used the $F$ test and $t$ test to confirm whether this was the case. As the $p$-values obtained from the $F$ tests were less than 0.01 in all cases, Welch $t$ tests were conducted. The $p$-values obtained from the $t$ tests were also less than 0.01 in all cases. The results show that Ishibashi and Hosokawa did use significantly longer sentences, and Miki and Koizumi significantly shorter ones. The addresses of these prime ministers thus contain rather individual sentence lengths.

## 5 Multivariate Analysis of the Distribution of Particles and Auxiliary Verbs

### 5.1 Principal Component Analysis

We carried out principal component analysis of the distribution of particles and auxiliary verbs in the prime ministers' addresses. Fig. 2 shows the scatter plot of the first two principal components. Prime ministers' addresses are indicated by their initials (see Table 1). As the proportion of variance accounted for by the first principal component was 46.03% and the cumulative proportion of variances accounted for by the first two principal components was 64.89%, we focused on these two principal components. The first principal component shows the effect of the era because older prime ministers fell to the left-hand side of the scatter plot, and those of more recent eras to the right-hand side. The second principal component may show the number of tokens because prime ministers who had a small number of tokens (HN, SK, YS1, KTe, AH, YS1, HI, US, HT)

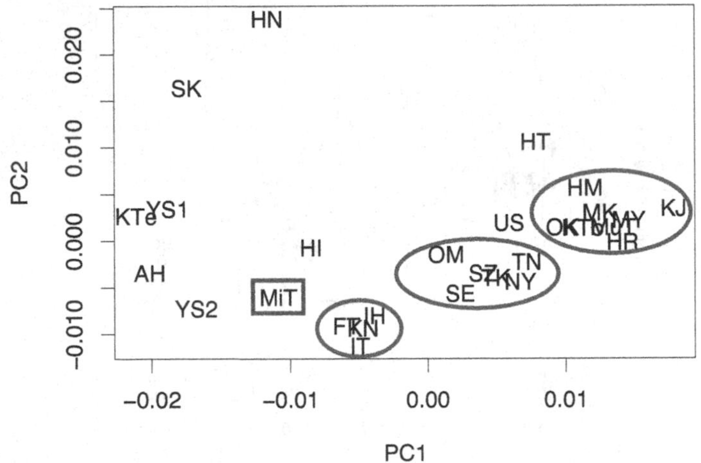


**Fig. 2.** The scatter plot showing first two principal components

tended to fall towards the top of the scatter plot, though it is difficult to clearly define the meaning of the second principal component.

In the scatter plot, three main groups of prime ministers' addresses can be observed, as follows: (a) 1956-1964 Ishibashi (IT) - Ikeda (IH) (including 1976-1978 Fukuda (FT)); (b) 1964-1989 Sato (SE) - Takeshita (TN); and (c) 1989-2006 Kaifu (KTo) - Koizumi (KJ). These groups roughly correspond to the era. As the first principal component shows the effect of the era and many prime ministers fell into groups according to the era, we conclude that the era was the most dominant factor affecting the use of particles and auxiliary verbs in the prime ministers' addresses.

Ishibashi (IT), Hosokawa (HM) and Koizumi (KJ), who had longer or shorter sentence lengths, were grouped with their contemporaries, meaning that they used particles and auxiliary verbs in a similar way to them. Miki, another prime minister who had individual sentence lengths, fell into a rather isolated position, meaning that he used particles and auxiliary verbs in a different way to other prime ministers. Only Miki had this characteristic except prime ministers who had a small number of tokens (HN, SK, YS1, KTe, AH, HI, US, HT) and Yoshida in his second term in office (YS2).[5]

## 5.2 Cluster Analysis

In order to confirm the results of the principal component analysis, we used hierarchical cluster analysis with correlation distance and average method, as those most clearly reproducing the classification of the scatter plot of the first two principal components. We calculated the AU $p$-values of the clusters using the multiscale bootstrap method. The dendrogram constructed by the cluster is shown in Fig. 3. Most clusters have high AU $p$-values, but that between Ashida (AH) and Miki (MiT) has a low AU $p$-value (74%). All the prime ministers' addresses except Miki's clearly fell into one of two eras. The obtained clusters are as follows: (a) 1945-1954 Higashikuni (HN) - Second period of Yoshida (YS2) and 1974 - 1976 Miki (MiT) and (b) 1954-2006 Hatoyama (HI) - Koizumi (KJ). The larger cluster (more recent prime ministers' addresses) is divided into a further two eras as follows: (b-1) 1954-1987 Hatoyama (HI) - Nakasone (NY) and (b-2) 1987-2006 Takeshita (TN) - Koizumi (KJ). Prime ministers from 1954 to 1987 are clustered in the left-hand group, those after 1987 in the center group, and those before 1954 and Miki in the right-hand group. The three groups of prime ministers' addresses outlined in Section 5.1 (1956-1964, 1964-1989, 1989-2006) are roughly grouped into the center cluster (1954-2006). These results confirm that the classification of the era is the most dominant factor affecting prime ministers' addresses.

Ishibashi (IT), Hosokawa (HM) and Koizumi (KJ) were clustered with their contemporaries in Fig. 3. Miki (MiT) was the only prime minister who was not, and who was clustered with a low AU $p$-value. These results show that he used particles and auxiliary verbs in a more individualistic way.

The findings of this study can be summarized as follows: (a) the styles of prime ministers' Diet addresses have changed over time, and (b) Miki's addresses have a special style. Finding (a) could indicate that changes in Japanese usage have had rather strong

[5] Yoshida in his second term in office (YS2) had a large number of tokens. However, as all his contemporaries had a small number of tokens, he fell into a rather isolated position.

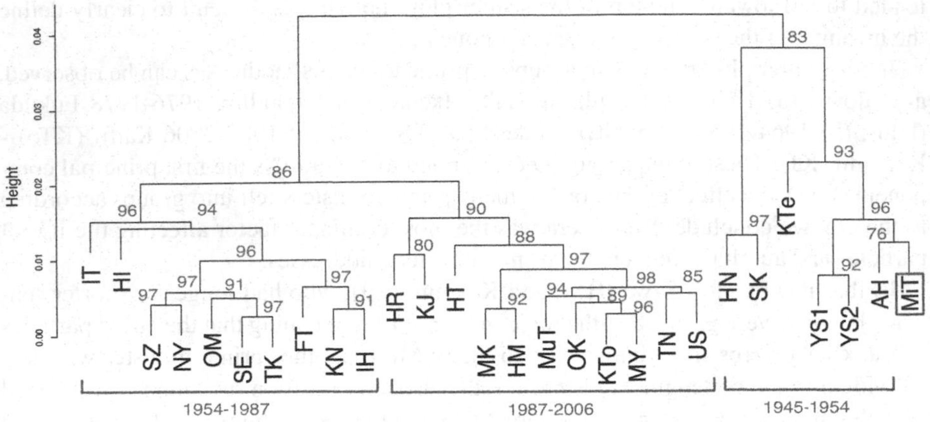


**Fig. 3.** Dendrogram constructed by cluster analysis

effects on the styles of prime ministers' addresses.[6] It leads us to think that the Diet addresses had a rather monotonous character reflecting the fact that they were delivered in a formal register and drafted by bureaucrats [c.f. 22]. Finding (b) indicates that Miki's addresses had a special individual style. An earlier qualitative study of Japanese politics stated that Miki hated to rely on bureaucrats and wrote his addresses by himself [22].[7] His special style of politics and habit of drafting his addresses himself appear to have given his addresses different stylistic characteristics. From finding (b), we conclude that prime ministers' individual political styles could also affect their speech styles.

## 6 Conclusion

This study examined the speech styles used in the addresses of 27 Japanese prime ministers. Our exploratory analysis clarified the changing language usage and individual character of different prime ministers, thus indicating that stylistic methods are useful for historical analysis of political texts. They can be applied for more large-scale data and various research topics in humanities and social science.

In further studies, we will conduct microscopic analysis focusing on the styles of individual prime ministers in addition to this macroscopic analysis. This will clarify the relationship between speech styles, and the prime minister's personal or individual style in detail, and enrich the findings of this study.

[6] In order to confirm this point, we compared the changing usage of prime ministers' addresses to language use in Japanese magazines [20, 21]. As the increase or decrease of eight of the 10 words which positively or negatively contributed to the classification of the scatter plot of the first two principal components correlated with the increase or decrease of these words in magazines, it is probable that the changing language usage in prime ministers' addresses reflected changes in Japanese usage in general.

[7] Japanese prime ministers' Diet addresses are usually drafted by bureaucrats, and revised and completed by prime ministers themselves [22].

## References


[1] Aitchison, J., Lewis, D.M. (eds.): New Media Language. Routledge, London (2003)

[2] Kenny, A.: The Computation of Style: an Introduction to Statistics for Students of Literature and Humanities. Pergamon Press, Oxford (1982)

[3] Pollmann, T., Baayen, R.H.: Computing historical consciousness. A quantitative inquiry into the presence of the past in newspaper texts. Computers and the Humanities 35, 237–253 (2001)

[4] Kusano, A.: Terebi wa Seiji wo Ugokasu ka. NTT Publishing, Tokyo (2006)

[5] Kusano, A.: Rekidai Syusyo no Keizai Seisaku Zen Deta. Kadokawa Syoten, Tokyo (2005)

[6] Azuma, S.: Rekidai Syusyo no Gengoryoku wo Shindan Suru. Kenkyu-sya, Tokyo (2006)

[7] Suzuki, T., Kageura, K.: Exploring the microscopic characteristics of Japanese prime ministers' Diet addresses by measuring the quantity and diversity of nouns. In: Proceedings of PACLIC 21, the 21th Asia-Pacific Conference on Language, Information and Computation, pp. 459–470

[8] Suzuki, T.: Japanese foreign perception seen through prime ministers' Diet addresses: focusing on East-West and North-South issues. In: Paper prepared at the annual meeting of the Japan Association of International Relations (2007)

[9] Matsumoto, Y., et al.: Japanese Morphological Analysis System ChaSen ver.2.2.3 (2003), http://chasen.naist.jp

[10] Yule, G.U.: On sentence-length as a statistical characteristic of style in prose, with application to two cases of disputed authorship. Biometrika 30, 363–390 (1938)

[11] Yasumoto, Y.: Distribution of the sentence length. Mathematical Linguistics 1, 27–31 (1957)

[12] Smith, M.W.A.: Recent experience and new developments of methods for the determination of authorship. Association for Literary and Linguistic Computings Bulletin 11, 73–82 (1983)

[13] Jin, M.: Shizen Gengo ni okeru Patan ni kansuru Keiryo-teki Kenkyu. PhD thesis, The Graduate University for Advanced Studies (1994)

[14] Jin, M.: Joshi no bunpu ni okeru kakite no tokucho ni kansuru keiryo bunseki. Syakai Joho 11(2), 15–23 (2002)

[15] Otsuka, H.: Syakai no kanshin, iken wo bunrui-suru jissen: Kobun-ron to goyo-ron wo musubu bunseki oyobi jido bunrui no kokoromi. In: Iken Bunseki Enjin: Keiyro Gengogaku to Syakai-gaku no Setten, pp. 127–172. Corona Publishing, Tokyo (2007)

[16] Suzuki, R., Shimodaira, H.: pvclust: an R package for hierarchical clustering with $p$-values (2006)

[17] Shimodaira, H.: An approximately unbiased test of phylogenetic tree selection. Systematic Biology 51, 492–508 (2002)

[18] Shimodaira, H.: Assessing the uncertainty of the cluster analysis using the bootstrap resampling. Proceedings of the Institute of Statistical Mathematics 50(1), 33–44 (2002)

[19] Shimodaira, H.: Approximately unbiased tests of regions using multistep-multiscale bootstrap resampling. The Annals of Statistics 32(6), 2616–2641 (2004)

[20] The National Language Research Institute: Vocabulary and Chinese Characters in Ninety Magazines of Today. The National Language Research Institute, Tokyo (1962–64)

[21] The National Language Research Institute: A Survey of Vocabulary in Contemporary Magazines (1994), The National Language Research Institute, Tokyo (2005)

[22] Shinoda, T.: Souridaijin no Kenryoku to Shido-ryoku: Yoshida Shigeru kara Murayama Tomiichi made. Toyo Keizai Shinpo-sya, Tokyo (1994)

# Evaluation of Logical Thinking Ability through Contributions in a Learning Community

Kayo Kawamoto[1] and Noriko H. Arai[2]

[1] Department of Systems Engineering, Hiroshima City University, Japan
kayo@im.hiroshima-cu.ac.jp

[2] Information and Society Research Division, National Institute of Informatics, Japan
arai@nii.ac.jp

**Abstract.** Because the success or failure of e-learning often depends on a subjective evaluation, it is difficult for one success to be applied to other attempts. In this paper, we propose a method of objectively evaluating e-learning's educational effects with respect to logical thinking ability. We show the effectiveness of our method in evaluating the education effects of an e-learning site "e-Classroom" (http://www.e-kyoshitsu.org/). The objective evaluation indicated the following effects. (1) Though there were some effects in the whole class, only a few attributes improved significantly. (2) Some persons improved considerably.

**Keywords:** Logical thinking ability, Learning community, BBS, Qualitative evaluation, Quantitative evaluation.

## 1 Introduction

Even when organizers and participants say that their learning experiences have gone well, it is not certain that they succeed actually because their evaluations are usually subjective. Then it is difficult for one success of an e-learning to be applied to another attempt. In this paper, we propose an objective evaluation method of the educational effects of e-learning with respect to logical thinking ability, which is an important ability in international society but Japanse seem weak in generally. "E-Classroom" [1,2] is a unique advanced e-learning community whose social evaluations are high. We show the effectiveness of our method by applying it to student postings contributed to the bulletin board system of "e-Classroom". Since our evaluation method is based on objective attributes with respect to the logical thinking abilities, it can be applied to other e-learning.

This paper is organized as follows. Section 2 introduces "e-Classroom" and the Super Science High School and describes the growing importance of logical thinking in our society. Section 3 describes the evaluation method of the logical thinking abilities by analyzing bulletin boards of e-learning sites. By applying the evaluation methods to "e-Classroom" given in Section 3, we show the effects of "e-Classroom" on logical thinking abilities in Section 4. We conclude our study and present plans for future work in Section 5.

T. Tokunaga and A. Ortega (Eds.): LKR 2008, LNAI 4938, pp. 326–333, 2008.

## 2 Preliminaries

### 2.1 E-Classroom

"E-Classroom" is an advanced learning community for secondary school students beyond the usual curricula on the Internet in cooperation with teachers, mathematicians, scientists, and other researchers who are colleagues of Prof. Noriko Arai. It was founded in 2002 and is tuition free. About 800 students who responded to a public advertisement and a request from secondary schools have participated in "e-Classroom" over the last six years. "E-Classroom" has the goal of better enabling students to choose their futures according to their individual aspirations so that they may live happily in the new century. For students to be able to make the best choices for them, we think that the necessary abilities are (1) logical thinking, (2) creativity, (3) presentation skills, (4) communication skills, and so on. Moreover, Prof. Arai has developed an information portal system, called "NetCommons" [4].

One of the subjects of the "e-Classroom" is called "Writing-in-Math!" [3]. This is a subject to practice talking logical thinking by writing expressions sequentially in the form of mathematical proofs. One of the main purposes of this subject is the promotion of logical thinking. Logical thinking requires the following abilities: to understand structure of problem adequately, to think reasonably about the problem, and to express logically. However, because Japanese favor communication without languages and they communicate through indirect expressions [5], they often lack means to express ideas clearly. So, it is necessary for Japanese to think and express logically.

Learners can learn more with the enhanced asynchronous bulletin board function. As a general study method, the teaching staff composed of researchers and educators present an open-ended problem on the bulletin board. The learner writes the answer to the topics he or she is given by using the limited expressive medium like writing and drawing over the Internet to all others involved in the class. Teaching staffs give advice for the learners to consider for his or herself and ask the learner to word their responses concisely. The learner considers the comments and contributes again. The educational philosophy is that the logical thinking is promoted through such experiences. In this way, we believe that "e-Classroom" is a very interesting educational place.

### 2.2 Super Science High School

The Japanese Ministry of Education, Culture, Sports, Science and Technology (MEXT for short) has designated several upper secondary schools as ones that prioritize science, technology, and mathematics education. Such schools are called Super Science High Schools (SSHs for short).

SSHs permit curricula exceeding the course of study. One SSH has used "e-Classroom" for its "mathematical discovery" class.

## 3 Evaluating Logical Thinking Abilities

To assess "e-Classroom"'s effect on the students' logical thinking ability, we quantitatively and qualitatively analyzed their contributions to the class.

### 3.1 Assumptions

We assumed that persons having a high level of logical thinking abilities would write sentences having the following attributes.

(1) Expressions are well formed, logical and consistent.
(2) Expressions are long but not redundant.
(3) There are no sentences including too much content.
(4) There are reasons of answers.
(5) There are explanations which help readers.
(6) Appropriate variables are used (e.g. "Let $X$ be a ...").
(7) Appropriate conjunctions such as "On the other hand","Hence" are used.
(8) Conclusive expressions are used.
(9) To make sentences easier to understand, there are various expressions such as illustrations, appropriate citations, explanations using figures and tables.

### 3.2 Approach for Evaluations of Logical Thinking Abilities

We evaluated the logical thinking abilities of the whole classes as follows.

1. We stored contributed postings as "e-Classroom" logs, each of which included attributes such as name, date, title, and body.
2. We computed the values of every attribute by analyzing each contribution. For example, we computed the values of (i) logical attributes such as intuitive evaluation, number of reasons, and correctness of reasons; (ii) attributes over strings such as title, author name, date, and time; (iii) numeric attributes such as numbers of characters, commas, punctuation marks, paragraphs, replies, and conjunctions; (iv) attributes of expressions such as conclusive or estimative expressions, illustrations, citations for previous sentences, tables and figures, itemizations, and explanations; (v) subjective attributes such as confidences and willingness. We can automatically compute the values of the attributes if they can be objectively measured. Subjective attributes have to be determined under mutual agreement of three persons.
3. To evaluate the improvement in logical thinking ability, we divided the learning period in half and analyzed postings contributed during each period.

We evaluated the abilities of individual students as follows.

1. We stored all postings contributed by each student and value thir attributes.
2. We analyzed the changes in attribute values of each student in time series.
3. We analyzed postings contributed by each student to clarify changes in qualitative attributes such as correctness of logic and conjunction marks used.

## 4 Experiments and Discussion

### 4.1 Settings

The experimental Setting was as follows.

Target: Eighty first grade students in the Department of Mathematical Sciences of a SSH. We divided them to two classes, each having eight groups.
Experimental Period: From January to February in 2006.
Target Lecture: Mathematical Discovery.
Schedule: The schedule of the lectures was as follows.
(12th Jan.) Preliminary problem.
(17th Jan.) First lecture on the Internet using the bulletin board system. We gave new two questions titled "Consider a method of calculating (1)". Then, each group answered the questions.
(24th Jan.) Second lecture on the Internet.
(31st Jan.) Third lecture on the Internet. We gave new six questions titled "Consider a method of calculating (2)". Each group studied one of them.
(7th Feb.) Fourth lecture on the Internet.
(13th Feb.) Fifth lecture at the high school.
(21st Feb.) Teleconference reports.
In the Internet lectures, group members discussed the topics. Then, a representative of each group contributed postings to the bulletin board. Individual students could then post after class.
Evaluation: Based on the approaches described in Section 3, we compared 26 postings contributed from 17th Jan. to 8th Feb with 24 postings contributed from 11th Feb. to 28th Feb.

**Table 1.** Results of analyzing articles by t-tests

| | | first half | latter half | t-ratio and probability-value | |
|---|---|---|---|---|---|
| Num. of letters | mean | 141.90 | 239.40 | $t(48) = 1.91$, | † |
| | SD | 121.60 | 227.30 | $p = 0.062$ | |
| Num. of commas | mean | 2.31 | 5.08 | $t(48) = 2.21$, | * |
| | SD | 2.09 | 6.02 | $p = 0.032$ | |
| Num. of punctuation marks | mean | 2.35 | 5.00 | $t(48) = 2.57$, | * |
| | SD | 2.09 | 6.02 | $p = 0.013$ | |
| Length of a sentence | mean | 63.59 | 50.55 | $t(48) = 1.51$, | n.s. |
| | SD | 34.57 | 25.54 | $p = 0.138$ | |
| Length of a phrase | mean | 31.59 | 26.20 | $t(48) = 1.575$, | n.s. |
| | SD | 12.67 | 11.39 | $p = 0.122$ | |
| Num. of reasons | mean | 0.92 | 1.71 | $t(48) = 1.95$, | † |
| | SD | 1.06 | 1.73 | $p = 0.057$ | |

Note that SD in the 2nd column denotes standard deviation. The symbols †, * and "n.s." in the 6th column denote the level of significance, a tendency of significance and non-significance, respectively.

### 4.2 Experimental Results and Discussions

Table 1 shows that the learning on "e-Classroom" seems to be effective for improving the logical thinking abilities of the whole class. We can see that the numbers of characters, commas and other punctuation marks in the postings increase significantly. By watching all postings, it seems that both the average of lengths of sentences and phrases are shorter in the latter half of the experiment but the shortenings are not statistically significant. According to the qualitative analysis of postings, the students may have acquired abilities to write long plain

**Table 2.** Results of analyzing articles by two-tailed $\chi^2$-tests in case that Yates' corrections are already applied

| | first half | latter half |
|---|---|---|
| with | 6 | 12 |
| without | 20 | 12 |

(a) Concluded answers [$\chi^2 = 2.85,\ p < 0.1$]

| | first half | latter half |
|---|---|---|
| with | 1 | 6 |
| without | 25 | 18 |

(b) Illustrations with examples [$\chi^2 = 3.05,\ p < 0.1$]

| | first half | latter half |
|---|---|---|
| with | 0 | 4 |
| without | 26 | 20 |

(c) Citations to previous explanations [$\chi^2 = 2.72,\ p < 0.1$]

| T1 | **How can you calculate the multiplications of recurring decimals?** | 2006/01/30 |
|---|---|---|

Come to think of it,
If you try to calculate divisions such as
1÷3=0.333…,
you must calculate infinitely, don't you?

How can you do such calculations of recurring decimals?
…
…

Posting *a*

| S1 | **Re:How can you calculate the multiplications of recurring decimals?** | 2006/01/31 |
|---|---|---|

Hello.
Because the result of calculating the divisions is a recurring decimal,
I think that such a result can be represented by a fraction.
Therefore, represent recurring decimals by fractions.
Why isn't it enough to only have to calculate multiplications of such fractions??
I don't know how to translate a recurring decimal into a fraction…

Posting *b*

**Fig. 1.** Time series of postings *a* and *b* which a student contributed (Originally in Japanese). The comments of the learning advisers were omitted from this figure.

| S1 | Re:Re:Re: How can you calculate the multiplications of recurring decimals? | 2006/02/07 |
|---|---|---|

I calculated the following examples,
but I haven't checked whether or not the results are correct, because I didn't use a calculator.
1÷3=0.333333...=1/3
2÷3=0.666666...=2/3
4÷3=1.333333...=4/3

1÷7=0.1428714287...=1/7
...
...
4÷9=0.444444...=4/9
I see somehow that there is a pattern.

However, because this is a calculation that after considering expressions of divisions,
I try to calculate…
But, after all, I did not understand how to make a fraction from the decimal…

Posting *c*

| S1 | Re:Re:Re:Re:Re:How can you calculate multiplications of recurring decimals? | 2006/02/11 |
|---|---|---|

When a repeating part of a recurring decimal is a single digit, for example,
in the case of x=0.333333..., then 3/9 (=1/3),
in the case of x=0.888888..., then 8/9.
I see that the denominators are always the digit 9 and
the numerators are always the repeating digit,
e.g. if 0.3333333… then the digit 3!!

Next, consider recurring decimals whose the length of the repeating part is just two.
...

Posting *d*

| S1 | Re:Re:Re:Re:Re: How can you calculate multiplications of recurring decimals? | 2006/02/12 |
|---|---|---|

A recurring decimal whose repeating part consists of the digit 1 is
1/9=0.111111...
...
Hence, in the case that the length of the repeating part is 2,
a recurring decimal can be represented by
1/x=0.010101...,
where x=99.
Therefore, I think that the following rule holds.
"A recurring decimal the length of whose repeating part is 2
= (the repeating part consisting of two digits)/99".

Actually, consider the recurring decimal 0.232323...
23/99=0.232323...
How?
...

Posting *e*

**Fig. 2.** Time series of postings *c*, *d* and *e* which a student contributed (Originally in Japanese). The comments of the learning advisers were omitted from this figure.

sentences without too much content in one sentence. Moreover, we can see that the number of reasons in postings increased significantly. Since having reasons is an important feature of logical sentences, their presence indicates that logical thinking ability of the whole class improved. From Table 2, the increase in the number of conclusive expressions indicates that students were able to answer with confidence because students were able to acquire ability of showing reasons. Moreover, we can see increases in the number of illustrations and citations of previous postings. Illustrations can help a reader to understand if they embody an abstract concept. By citing previous postings, a contributor can precisely show answers to a reader. These facts show that, by discussing in "e-Classroom", students learned how to write expressions that readers could easily understand.

Unfortunately, several attributes such as correctness of logic, usage of itemizations tables, and figures, usage of conjunction marks, were not statistically significant.

Fig. 1 and Fig. 2 show postings that a student contributed to a topic problem. Posting *a* in Fig. 1 is "How do you calculate multiplication of recurring decimals?". Posting *b* is a response to it; the student presented an abstract method for calculating the multiplication of recurring decimals without practical calculations. However, in posting *c* of Fig. 2, the student had tried to answer concretely by presenting results obtained by practical calculations, We can see that posting *b* consists of only one paragraph. However, to be easily understood for readers, in posting *c* of Fig. 2, the student had answered by making paragraphs for every case. We can see that in posting *c*, there is no explicit explanation about cases, but in posting *d* in Fig. 2, the student gave the conditions of cases by using the phrases such as "in the case of". Furthermore, up to posting *d*, the student had written only results which he had actually calculated, but in posting *e* in Fig. 2, the student gave a methodical answer by using appropriate conjunction marks such as "Hence" and "Therefore" after explanations of the reasons. We can see that in posting *b* of Fig. 1, the student had shown no reason for his answers and had written only sentences including phrases like "I think", which mean estimations. On the other hand, after posting *c*, the student answered conclusively, except only one sentence in posting *e* that included the phrase "I think" with good grounds. These changes show an improvement in the logical thinking abilities of that student.

Such students, however, were rare. Many students gave no response to the comments of the learning advisers. Hence, we can see that the learning style of "e-Classroom" is suited to a special kind of students.

## 5 Conclusions and Future Works

We have proposed a method of objectively evaluating e-learners' educational effects with respect to students' logical thinking ability. Moreover, we have done some experiments of applied our method to evaluate the effectiveness of "e-Classroom" with respect to the logical thinking ability. Then, we have obtained the some objective evaluations.

Unfortunately, in experiments, some attributes with respect to the logical thinking ability were not significant. The following reasons why such results were obtained are thought.

(1) "e-Classroom" can not actually improve the logical thinking ability of the whole class.
(2) A period of time for experiments is invalid. In other words, a period of time for learning is not enough for students to develop the logical expression skill.
(3) The evaluation method proposed in this paper is insufficient.

Regarding (1), "e-Classroom" is surely effective because there was considerable development in some learners. However, because other many people did not progress, there was no significant difference as a whole. Regarding (2), "e-Classroom" is effective for certain students and has a possibility that other students would have developed logical thinking abilities if they had more time. The student's progress will have to be analyzed over a longer term. The current results show some improvement, although it is not appreciable on the whole. The author would like to improve validity and reliability of the evaluation method and reevaluate "e-Classroom" and other e-learning sites with it.

## Acknowledgment

The authors would like to thank all the teaching staffs and students of e-Classroom and also thank all the teachers and students of the high school which cooperated with us in this research.

## References

1. Arai, N.H., Kawamoto, K.: e-Classroom Project:CSCL Environment to Support Highly Intellectual Activities (in Japanese). Journal of Information Processing and Management 47(3), 155–163 (2004)
2. Arai, N.H., Kawamoto, K.: Learning community that promotes talent who guides other citizens in new century. In: Advanced educational use for IT to foster certain academic ability, pp. 139–146. Toyokan Publishing (2004)
3. Arai, N.H., Kawamoto, K.: Designing Collaborative Learning Environment for Advanced Math. In: Internet & Multimedia Systems & Applications (IMSA 2005), pp. 145–150 (2005)
4. Arai, N.H.: NetCommons: One-stop service for education (in Japanese). Journal of Information Processing and Management 49(7), 379–386 (2006)
5. Tsujimura, A.: Some Characteristics of the Japanese Way of Communication. In: Communication Theory: Eastern and Western Perspectives, pp. 115–126. Academic Press, London (1987)

# Web Architecture and Naming for Knowledge Resources

Henry S. Thompson

ICCS, School of Informatics, University of Edinburgh, UK
ht@inf.ed.ac.uk

## 1 What Is Web Architecture?

In 2004 the Technical Architecture Group (TAG) of the World Wide Web Consortium (W3C) published *The Architecture of the World Wide Web* (AWWW) [1]. This document was the result of a careful after-the-fact analysis of the distinctive properties of the distributed information system known as the Web. By describing these properties, the TAG was able to define a number of 'principles', 'constraints' and 'best practices' which users and authors of and for the Web should observe in order to preserve and enhance its value to everyone.

One of the primary aims of AWWW [1], which is of particular relevance to the creators of large-scale knowledge resources, is to provide a clear and straightforward account of the central role of URIs in the life of the Web. Very near the beginning, AWWW [1] says "***Good practice: Identify with URIs*** To benefit from and increase the value of the World Wide Web, agents should provide URIs as identifiers for resources."

### 1.1 An Aside about Terminology: What's a 'Resource'?

The word 'resources' appears twice in the preceding paragraphs, with two different but related meanings. In the context of LKR, the meaning of 'resource' is close to its ordinary-language meaning of "something useful for a purpose", in this case a collection of computationally realised information of potential use for the performance of one or more computational tasks. In the context of the Web, 'resource' is defined as "anything which might have a URI", that is, effectively, anything at all. So all LKR resources are Web resources, but not *vice versa.*

## 2 URIs, Large-Scale Knowledge Resources and the Network Effect

How, if at all, does this advice apply to large-scale knowledge resources (LKR)? For LKR to be genuinely valuable, they need to be widely available. Being available on the Web is by far the most effective way to achieve this. A fundamental component of the changes in scientific practice which have been brought about over the last forty years by the growth of the Internet is the so-called 'Network

T. Tokunaga and A. Ortega (Eds.): LKP 2008, LNAI 4938, pp. 334–343, 2008.

Effect': The value of a resource increases the more it is used, because usage feeds back with improvements and extensions, and stimulates the production of complementary resources. In other words, making an LKR available on the Web not only benefits the wider scientific community, it benefits the authors of that LKR.

So, if making an LKR available on the Web is the goal, and AWWW [1] says URIs should be used to identify resources, does this just mean that every LKR should have a URI? Surely that's too simple an interpretation. Not just the LKR as a whole, but its constituent parts need URIs. Consider for example the work reported by Shinoda and colleagures at LKR2007 [2]. If that work were made available on the Web, not only would that mean a URI was required which gave access to the whole dataset of baseball video metadata involved, but also that each game, scene and shot, as well as each term such as "strike out", "base hit" and "pickoff", would likewise require their own URIs.

## 3 Exactly What Parts of an LKR Get URIs?

The kinds of 'knowledge' in an LKR can naturally be divided into two categories, the encyclopedic and the episodic, or, in more contemporary terms, its ontology and its instance data. In the baseball example [2], the ontology would include knowledge about both baseball and video in general, whereas the instance data would be the particular games, scenes and shots along with their associated metadata. In very concrete terms, the ontology is likely to consist of definitions of classes, properties and their relationships, whereas the instance data will consist of individuals and *their* properties and relationships.

The scales of these two parts of an LKR are likely to be very different: the size of an ontology is likely to be measured in terms of hundreds of classes and properties, whereas there may well be hundreds of *thousands* of instances. The absolute scale of the data involved will be different as well: 100s of kilobytes for the ontology, potentially many orders of magnitude larger for the instance data.

One further distinction is worth noting. Some kinds of instances are fundamentally computational in nature, that is, their existence is digital, inside one or more computers. Other instance are fundamentally *non*-computational in nature, that is, their existence is not within a computer. Some LKRs will be concerned with only instance data of one kind or the other, others will involve both. The baseball example [2] involves both: video frames are fundamentally digital, whereas base hits are fundamentally non-digital.

### 3.1 Resources, Information Resources and Representations

URIs can be used for two different things: identification ('naming') and retrieval ('access'). The network effect depends on not just naming, but also access. But therein lies a potential contradiction, following on from the end of the previous section: It's one thing to give a name to an LKR constituent which is fundamentally digital, because access makes sense in that case. I can for example retrieve a particular frame of a video of a baseball game. But if the thing being named is *not* digital, then it's not clear what access might mean. For example, naming a particular base hit from a particular baseball game does *not* mean that I can retrieve it, that's impossible, it happened in the past, and anyway you can't ship base hits over the internet.

AWWW [1] introduces two distinctions to help address this problem: it distinguishes a sub-class of resources called *information* resources, and it distinguishes representations from resources. AWWW [1] uses 'representation' in a specific technical way, to refer to the combination of a byte-stream and a media type which make up an HTTP response, that is, what a client actually receives from a server in response to a retrieval request (an HTTP GET). The media type tells the client how to interpret the byte-stream, for example `text/plain` or `image/jpeg` or `application/xml+svg`. 'Information resources' are then defined as those resources "all of [whose] essential characteristics can be conveyed [by a representation]". In the terms introduced above, information resources are those things whose nature is fundamentally digital.

It follows that it does not indeed make sense for a server to give an ordinary response to an attempt to access a resource which is not an information resource. In concrete terms, the TAG has said (see [3]) that only when the resource identified by a URI is an information resource should a retrieval request for that URI be given a `200` ('OK') response. So accessing the URI for a video frame can reasonably supply a byte-stream of media-type `image/jpeg` with a response code of `200`, but no such response would be appropriate if the URI was for a base hit. We'll look at the story for that case, that is for *non*-information resources, below in section 4.3

## 4 What Should the URIs Look Like?

LKRs are by their nature not only large but richly structured. How should one design a set of URIs for all the constituents of an LKR which actually help manage that scale and complexity? To answer this, we must first look at the nature of URIs themselves, to see what the design space we are working in really looks like.

### 4.1 The Syntax of (http) URIs

At the most general level, a URI consists of a scheme and a scheme-specific part. The scheme is the part before the colon (:), and the rest is the scheme-specific part. So in `http://www.example.org/page.html` the scheme is `http` and the scheme-specific part is `//www.example.org/page.html`, whereas in `mailto:jwb@whitehouse.gov` the schema is `mailto` and the scheme-specific part is `jwb@whitehouse.gov`. As the name suggests, and these examples illustrate, the form of the scheme-specific part is determined by the scheme.

AWWW [1] recommends "reuse an existing URI scheme", and this is sound advice, particularly for the `http` scheme: support for this scheme is built-in to almost all operating systems and program development environments, as well as being usually implemented using the `HTTP` protocol, which has many desirable properties for large-scale data, including provision for caching and proxying.

The scheme-specific part of (absolute) `http`-scheme URIs is divided into four parts:

```
"//" authority [ path ] [ "?" query ] [ "#" fragment ]
```

The **authority** part is typically a domain name, and this is where ownership of an `http`-scheme URI is recorded: domain names are leased by IANA to legal persons, and the owner of the domain is the owner of the URI, the ultimate authority on what it is that the URI identifies.

The **path** part, usually present although not required, is one or more slash-delimited strings, in principle opaque but in practice typically reflecting some real hierarchical structuring of a collection of resources.

The **query** part may contain *non*-hierarchical identifying information, typically in the form of name-value pairs.

Finally the **fragment** part, if present, indicates that the resource identified by the non-fragment parts is in some sense compound, and the fragment itself identifies a part thereof. (This over-simplifies slightly – see section 4.3 below).

Here's a complete example, taken from the URI spec itself [5]:

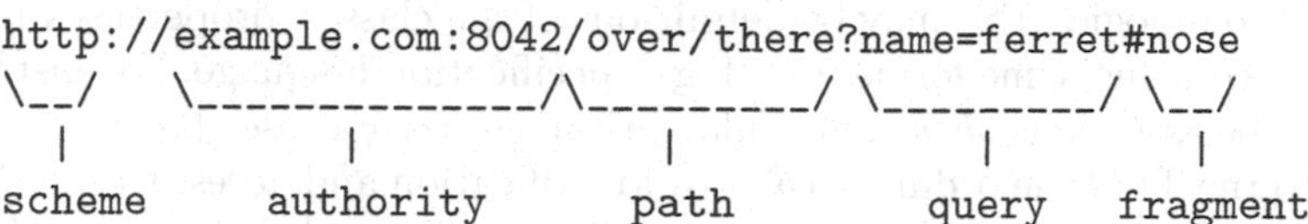


The TAG has discussed some aspects of designing a collection of URIs for a related set of resources (see [4]): the main relevant conclusion is "*Good Practice:* URI assignment authorities and the Web servers deployed for them may benefit from an orderly mapping from resource metadata into URIs."

### 4.2 The Impact of Scale on Designing URIs

The scale of the resources involved influences how they ought best to be identified. Consider the specific question of designing URIs for videos of whole baseball games, along with the frames thereof. It might at first seem that the right thing to do is to assign a single URI to each video, say

```
http://bball.example.org/videos/SoxVsRox/20071028.avi
```

and use fragment identifiers to identify each frame, for example

```
http://bball.example.org/videos/SoxVsRox/20071028.avi#f1:20:37.6
```

But the semantics of fragment identifiers require the retrieval of the *entire* resource identified by the URI without the fragment. That is, the separation of the fragment from the whole is for the *client* to do, not the server. If all I want is a few frames, having to download 100s of megabytes and throw most of them away is clearly a bad idea. Some alternative which means that the *server* does the separation would be much better.

Either the path part or the query part can be exploited to achieve this:

```
http://bball.example.org/videos/SoxVsRox/20071028.avi?frame=1:20:37.6
http://bball.example.org/videos/SoxVsRox/20071028/1/20/37.6.avi
```

It's important to note that the second example, using the path part, does *not* imply that the videos will have to be broken into individual frames with each one stored as a separate file in the appropriate place in a directory structure. 'Soft' interpretation of URIs means that all that is needed is an appropriate index. Web servers can be configured to interpret URIs in a particular range as implicit invocations of software which compute the appropriate response.

### 4.3 Names for Non-information Resources

The final thing to be taken into account when designing URIs for LKRs is the status of the resources being identified—are they information resources, or not? If not, as will be the case for all of the ontology and perhaps some of the instance data, what is the impact on URI design? There is often rich information available in conjunction with such resources, even if the resources *themselves* cannot be accessed. For ontologies, this may be definitions of the classes, properties and relations involved using some formal ontology specification language. For instance data, it may be assertions *about* particular instances *using* those classes etc. But according to the TAG the ordinary rules of identification and access cannot hold for the relationship between the URIs for such resources and their formal definitions and/or descriptions, because these are not representations of the resource itself (see section 3.1 above). What shall we do?

One option is to identify the non-information resources of an LKR with ordinary URIs, but *not* respond to requests for them with a `200` response. In public email [3] the TAG recommend responding with a `303` response ('See Other') and a *different* URI, which is actually the URI of the definition and/or description of the thing identified by the originally requested URI.

Another option is to make use of a certain amount of flexibility in the definition of the semantics of fragment identifiers in RFC 3986 [5]. The resource identified by a URI including a fragment identifier need not be a sub-part of the thing identified by the corresponding URI without the fragment identifier, it can be "some other resource". As a result a convention has grown up whereby the description or definition of a non-information resource is identified by a simple URI, and the resource itself is identified by the same URI with a fragment identifier. This approach works particularly well for ontologies, where a single information resource, with for example the URI

```
http://bball.example.org/ontology
```

identifying an information resource containing the definitions of the classes and relations which make up an ontology, and for example URIs of the form

```
http://bball.example.org/ontology#BaseHit
http://bball.example.org/ontology#GameVideo
```

identifying the actual classes etc. of that ontology themselves.

## 5 Worked Example

We have covered the main issues involved in designing a collection of URIs to act as names for the constituents of an LKR. In conclusion, here is one possible set of choices with respect to each of the questions raised above, as they *might* be made for the example baseball LKR [2] we have been using as our example throughout (I should make clear that I know no more about this resource than can be found from a brief reading of the referenced description from LKR2007 [2]: it is entirely possible that little or none of what follows would work for the real thing).

- **Ontology vs. instances.** A two-by-two split: ontologies for baseball concepts and for the recording process and its outcomes; instance data for the recordings and the analysis thereof.
- **Information vs. non-information resources.** Only the recordings are information resources, the other three are all non-information resources.
- **Actual URI syntax.** `http`-scheme URIs, sharing a common domain, three sub-cases:

  **both ontologies.** Use the fragment identifier approach, so for the baseball and recording process concepts, respectively, something like:

  ```
  http://bball.example.org/ontology/baseball#...
  http://bball.example.org/ontology/recording#...
  ```

  **the recordings.** Use a combination of hierarchy with the query string approach, with some amount of appropriate hierarchy for series, games, perhaps innings, depending on the major units of recording, for example

  ```
  http://bball.example.org/recordings/20071028/Boston/
      inning9.avi?frame=1:37.6
  ```

  **the analysis.** A combination of hierarchy with the fragment identifier approach, with again the amount of hierarchy a subordinate design decision, for example

  ```
  http://bball.example.org/analysis/20071028/Boston/
      topOf9th.rdf#lowell_1
  ```

We can illustrate the way this all fits together by showing how RDF/OWL would use URIs as designed above to encode three simple things about the last inning of the last game of the 2007 World Series, in which Mike Lowell was the first batter in the top of the ninth inning: one bit of ontology (AtBat is a class) and two bits of instance data (lowell_1 is an instance of AtBat, the batter of lowell_1 was Mike Lowell). The following three triples, each in the form subject-property-object, give the full URI versions of those three LKR constituents:

```
http://bball.example.org/analysis/20071028/Boston/topOf9th.rdf#lowell_1
  http://www.w3.org/1999/02/22-rdf-syntax-ns#type
http://bball.example.org/ontology/baseball#AtBat
----
http://bball.example.org/ontology/baseball#AtBat
  http://www.w3.org/1999/02/22-rdf-syntax-ns#type
http://www.w3.org/2002/07/owl#Class
----
http://bball.example.org/analysis/20071028/Boston/topOf9th.rdf#lowell_1
  http://bball.example.org/ontology/baseball#batter
http://bball.example.org/ontology/baseball#MikeLowell
```

For an extended version of this example using the Turtle terse syntax [6] to represent OWL/RDF, see appendix A.

## References


1. Jacobs, I., Walsh, N.: Architecture of the World Wide Web, Volume One. W3C (2004), http://www.w3.org/TR/webarch/
2. Shinoda, K., et al.: Robust Scene Recognition Using Scene Context Information for Video Contents. In: Furui, S. (ed.) Proceedings of Symposium on Large-scale Knowledge Resources 2007, Tokyo Institute of Technology, 21st Century COE Program (2007)
3. Fielding, R. (ed.): [httpRange-14] Resolved, W3C Tag (2003), http://lists.w3.org/Archives/Public/www-tag/2005Jun/0039
4. Mendelsohn, N., Williams, S. (eds.): The use of Metadata in URIs, W3C (2007), http://www.w3.org/2001/tag/doc/metaDataInURI-31.html
5. Berners-Lee, T., Fielding, R., Masinter, L. (eds.): Uniform Resource Identifier (URI): Generic Syntax, RFC 3986, IETF (2005), http://www.ietf.org/rfc/rfc3986.txt
6. Beckett, D. (ed.): Turtle - Terse RDF Triple Language (2007), http://www.dajobe.org/2004/01/turtle/


## Appendix A

The Turtle [6] form of an extended baseball example using URIs as recommended in section 5

```
@prefix rdf: <http://www.w3.org/1999/02/22-rdf-syntax-ns#>.
@prefix rdfs: <http://www.w3.org/2000/01/rdf-schema#>.
@prefix owl: <http://www.w3.org/2002/07/owl#>.
@prefix bb: <http://bball.example.org/ontology/baseball#>.
@prefix xsdc: <http://www.w3.org/2001/XMLSchema.xsd#>.
@prefix xsd: <http://www.w3.org/2001/XMLSchema#>.
@prefix video: <http://bball.example.org/ontology/recording#>.
@prefix top9a:<http://bball.example.org/analysis/20071028/Boston/topOf9th.rdf#>.
@prefix top9v: <http://bball.example.org/recordings/20071028/Boston/inning9.avi?>.
@prefix sox: <http://bball.example.org/analysis/RedSox.rdf#>.
<http://bball.example.org/ontology/baseball>
```

```
    a owl:Ontology .
bb:AtBat
    a owl:Class;
    rdfs:subClassOf [
        a owl:Restriction;
        owl:onProperty bb:batter_number;
        owl:cardinality "1"^^<xsd:int>
    ] .
bb:batter_number
    a owl:DatatypeProperty;
    rdfs:domain bb:AtBat;
    rdfs:range xsdc:integer .
bb:Player
    a owl:Class .
bb:batter
    a owl:ObjectProperty;
    rdfs:domain bb:AtBat;
    rdfs:range bb:Player .
bb:outcome
    a owl:ObjectProperty;
    rdfs:domain bb:AtBat;
    rdfs:range bb:Outcome .
bb:firstFrame
    a owl:ObjectProperty;
    rdfs:domain bb:AtBat;
    rdfs:range <video:Frame> .
bb:lastFrame
    a owl:ObjectProperty;
    rdfs:domain bb:AtBat;
    rdfs:range <video:Frame> .
bb:Outcome
    a owl:Class .
bb:Out
    a owl:Class;
    rdfs:subClassOf bb:Outcome .
bb:FlyOut
    a owl:Class;
    rdfs:subClassOf bb:Out .
bb:position
    a owl:ObjectProperty;
    rdfs:domain bb:Out;
    rdfs:range bb:Position .
bb:Position
    a owl:Class .
bb:left_field
    a bb:Position .
bb:Hit
    a owl:Class;
    rdfs:subClassOf bb:Outcome .
<sox:mike_lowell>
```

```
    a bb:Player .
<top9a:lowell_1>
    a bb:AtBat;
    bb:batter_number "1";
    bb:batter <sox:mike_lowell>;
    bb:outcome [
        a bb:FlyOut;
        bb:position bb:left_field
    ];
    bb:firstFrame <top9v:frame=1:37.6>;
    bb:lastFrame <top9v:frame=3:18.0> .
    }
%
```

The RDF-XML syntax for the same information is as follows:

```
<?xml version='1.0' encoding='UTF-8'?>
<rdf:RDF xml:base="http://bball.example.org/ontology/baseball#"
         xmlns:rdf="http://www.w3.org/1999/02/22-rdf-syntax-ns#"
         xmlns:rdfs="http://www.w3.org/2000/01/rdf-schema#"
         xmlns:owl="http://www.w3.org/2002/07/owl#"
         xmlns:bb="http://bball.example.org/ontology/baseball#"
         xmlns:xsdc="http://www.w3.org/2001/XMLSchema.xsd#"
         xmlns:xsd="http://www.w3.org/2001/XMLSchema#"
         xmlns:video="http://bball.example.org/ontology/recording#"
         xmlns:top9a="http://bball.example.org/analysis/20071028/Boston
              /topOf9th.rdf#"
         xmlns:top9v="http://bball.example.org/recordings/20071028/Boston
              /inning9.avi?"
         xmlns:sox="http://bball.example.org/analysis/RedSox.rdf#">
 <owl:Ontology rdf:about=""/>
 <owl:Class rdf:ID="AtBat">
  <rdfs:subClassOf>
   <owl:Restriction>
    <owl:onProperty rdf:resource="#batter_number"/>
    <owl:cardinality rdf:datatype="http://www.w3.org/2001/XMLSchema#int">
      1
    </owl:cardinality>
   </owl:Restriction>
  </rdfs:subClassOf>
 </owl:Class>
 <owl:DatatypeProperty rdf:ID="batter_number">
  <rdfs:domain rdf:resource="#AtBat"/>
  <rdfs:range rdf:resource="http://www.w3.org/2001/XMLSchema.xsd#integer"/>
 </owl:DatatypeProperty>
 <owl:Class rdf:ID="Player"/>
 <owl:ObjectProperty rdf:ID="batter">
  <rdfs:domain rdf:resource="#AtBat"/>
  <rdfs:range rdf:resource="#Player"/>
```

```
 </owl:ObjectProperty>
 <owl:ObjectProperty rdf:ID="outcome">
  <rdfs:domain rdf:resource="#AtBat"/>
  <rdfs:range rdf:resource="#Outcome"/>
 </owl:ObjectProperty>
 <owl:ObjectProperty rdf:ID="firstFrame">
  <rdfs:domain rdf:resource="#AtBat"/>
  <rdfs:range rdf:resource="video:Frame"/>
 </owl:ObjectProperty>
 <owl:ObjectProperty rdf:ID="lastFrame">
  <rdfs:domain rdf:resource="#AtBat"/>
  <rdfs:range rdf:resource="video:Frame"/>
 </owl:ObjectProperty>
 <owl:Class rdf:ID="Outcome"/>
 <owl:Class rdf:ID="Out">
  <rdfs:subClassOf rdf:resource="#Outcome"/>
 </owl:Class>
 <owl:Class rdf:ID="FlyOut">
  <rdfs:subClassOf rdf:resource="#Out"/>
 </owl:Class>
 <owl:ObjectProperty rdf:ID="position">
  <rdfs:domain rdf:resource="#Out"/>
  <rdfs:range rdf:resource="#Position"/>
 </owl:ObjectProperty>
 <owl:Class rdf:ID="Position"/>
 <bb:Position rdf:ID="left_field"/>
 <owl:Class rdf:ID="Hit">
  <rdfs:subClassOf rdf:resource="#Outcome"/>
 </owl:Class>
 <!-- instance data after here -->
 <bb:Player rdf:about="sox:mike_lowell"/>
 <bb:AtBat rdf:about="top9a:lowell_1">
  <bb:batter_number>1</bb:batter_number>
  <bb:batter rdf:resource="sox:mike_lowell"/>
  <bb:outcome>
   <bb:FlyOut>
    <bb:position rdf:resource="#left_field"/>
   </bb:FlyOut>
  </bb:outcome>
  <bb:firstFrame rdf:resource="top9v:frame=1:37.6"/>
  <bb:lastFrame rdf:resource="top9v:frame=3:18.0"/>
 </bb:AtBat>

</rdf:RDF>
```

# Towards Better Evaluation for Human Language Technology

Donna Harman

National Institute of Standards and Technology,
Gaithersburg, Maryland, 20899, USA
donna.harman@nist.gov

**Abstract.** Both research and evaluation in human language technology have enjoyed a big surge for the last fifteen years. Performance has made major advances, partially due to the availability of resources and the interest in the many evaluation forums present today. But there is much more to do, both in terms of new areas of research and in improved evaluation for these areas. This paper addresses the current state-of-the-art in evaluation and then discusses some ideas for improving this evaluation.

## 1 Past and Current Evaluation Strategies

Evaluation has always been an important part of all scientific research, and researchers in Human Language Technology (HLT) have strongly respected this tradition. But evaluation of HLT, and indeed research in HLT, has not been an easy task until somewhat recently. The lack of digitalized text (however hard this is to believe in the age of the web), and the lack of computer power put heavy constraints on what could be accomplished, much less evaluated.

Information retrieval (IR) was the first of the HLT areas to move into "large-scale" evaluation. Since the goal in information retrieval is to locate relevant information with respect to a user's query, the Cranfield collection [1], created in the 1960's, contained approximately 1400 abstracts and 225 queries, along with the list of those abstracts relevant to the queries. This collection was widely used by researchers, along with several other small collections built in the 1970's. Even though these collections were small by today's standards, they were major computing challenges when first used. By the late 1980's there was considerably more digitized text, and also magnitudes more computing power and memory, but the researchers had to wait until 1992 for the next big test collections (the TREC collections [2,3]. TREC and its collections have continued to grow, with new evaluation tasks and new collections including working with web data and blogs, legal retrieval, and a collection for genomics. Whereas TREC created some test collections for non-English languages, such as Spanish, French, German, Chinese and Arabic, major test collections in many other languages have been produced by CLEF [4] and NTCIR [5].

The early 1960's also saw the building of the first "large-scale" corpus for use by the natural language processing (NLP) community. The Brown

T. Tokunaga and A. Ortega (Eds.): LKR 2008, LNAI 4938, pp. 344–350, 2008.

Corpus [6] had 500 samples of digitized text, each sample having approximately 2000 words, with the samples spread over 15 different domains and writing styles, such as news, scientific reports and novels. The general availability of this text allowed NLP research to move beyond "toy" systems into the precursors of today's powerful language processing tools. The Brown corpus had some part-of-speech tags, with eventually Penn Treebank [7] built for it. In 1985 George Miller at Princeton started WordNet, a semantic lexicon for English [8]. All of these resources enabled testing of various NLP component technologies, such as extraction in MUC [9], sentence parsing, and word sense disambigution. The 2007 SemEval [10] event had 18 different testing tasks for NLP, both in English and other languages. The DUC workshop [11] has provided truth-data and evaluation for summarization of both within-document and multi-document text since 2001.

Creating data for testing of speech processing, such as speech transcription, was even more difficult than finding digitized data for text processing. The first widely used speech data came from the National Institute of Standards and Technology (NIST) in 1987, limited to a 991 word lexicon and a pattern grammar of only 2800 sentence patterns. By 1992, this had increased to 20,000 word lexicons for read text from the Wall Street Journal, with 612 hours of real broadcast news used in 1999. Work with conversational speech and meeting room recordings has been started [12]. Other languages such as Chinese and Arabic have also been used at NIST; CLEF has worked with Czech.

The machine translation community has been in operation for many years, with many small-scale evaluations [13]. More recently, DARPA sponsored several large-scale evaluations, such as in 1993/1994, with nineteen systems working on 100 news articles to be translated from French, Spanish and Japanese into English. The DARPA TIDES program ran from 2003-2005, with about 30,000 words of news articles to be translated from Arabic and Chinese to English each year. NIST has continued these evaluations, and the IWSLT conference has been working for 3 years with translation of speech. The creation of the BLEU metric [14] has made a major impact by providing a single metric that can be used continuously for testing, similar to manner in which the metrics in information retrieval have been used.

These resources and evaluations have made very significant impacts on the research in HLT. Performance levels have more than doubled for information retrieval, parsers are working at high-enough accuracy to be considered reliable tools, and speech (transcription) and machine translation are now embedded in many applications as a matter of course.

However there is still more to be done. In an effort to gather information about future needs for these HLT technologies, the MINDS workshops were held in November 2006 and February 2007. The reports [15] from these workshops provide major insights into the future directions researchers considered necessary for further breakthroughs in HLT. The rest of this paper uses these insights to examine needs for new evaluation methods, and discusses some of issues concerning these evaluations.

## 2 More Realistic Test Corpora

First, there is a need for more realistic test collections/evaluation corpora, both in terms of scale and in terms of new types of data for processing. All of the HLT technologies have this need, although the details differ across the technologies.

For information retrieval, scale refers to the need for working with much larger amounts of data, especially web data. The largest TREC collection, the gov2 collection, has 426 gigabytes of data. Whereas this is enormous compared to the 2 gigabytes used in 1992, it is small compared to today's web. It would be possible to make larger collections, but making larger collections requires making magnitudes more relevance judgments using the current test collection methodologies. The pooling techniques used in TREC (and CLEF, NTCIR, etc.) have been shown [16] to provide complete enough answer sets, but these techniques break down as the collection size gets extremely large. This problem (along with some possible solutions) has been the subject of several papers presented recently at SIGIR [17,18].

Speech transcription currently works in real-time only for limited domains and usually requires speaker-specific training. Scaling these systems to handle unlimited amounts of speech in real-time is beyond today's technology; but scaling the evaluation corpora runs into many of the same problems as for information retrieval since manual transcription of large amounts of speech will be prohibitively expensive. The speech researchers in MINDS suggested several ways of avoiding these problems, such as using poorer quality transcripts like closed captions and subtitles, or more imaginitively trying to get volunteers on the web to create transcripts.

Some of the same scaling issues apply for MT and NLP since highly-accurate results in both of these technologies are very time consuming. In addition, currently these technologies work on much smaller chunks of text–generally sentences for MT, and sentences or maybe paragraphs for NLP. Both of these technologies need to scale up to the processing of documents, which will require better discourse analysis, etc. However evaluation of this expanded research becomes complex because the "truth" data is not well-defined. For example, summaries of documents automatically created in DUC are compared with manually-generated summaries, but this comparison suffers from wide variations in human ideas of what constitutes the best summary. Translations of entire documents could be done at many different levels of accuracy, or levels of paraphrasing, summarizing etc., but each application might have a different "ideal" translation. Therefore both for MT and for NLP there remains the problem of what is the appropriate text comparison and what are the appropriate metrics.

A second issue in terms of realistic evaluation corpora is the input data. Currently most of the HLT evaluations are using news data, such as newswires or news broadcasts. There has been some branching out into areas like blogs or scanned documents in information retrieval, along with work with conversational speech or meeting transcriptions for speech, but this work just scratches the surface in terms of different types of data.

The speech group at the MINDS workshop discussed the need to address "everyday" audio, such as conversational speech under various acoustic conditions, speaker characteristics such as children's speech, and language characteristics, including the unlimited vocabulary found in conversations. The IR group recognized the need to work on a rich variety of both formats and media, including instant messaging, email, and semi-structured data such as that found in databases. Note that whereas it would be feasible to build evaluations for these types of data (privacy issues are a problem), it is critical for the researchers to be able to generalize their solutions from work on these very individual data types.

Both NLP and MT face most of these same issues. Work with data outside of news is just starting. There has been some work in NLP with speech transcription data, and the question answering tracks in TREC and CLEF have worked with semi-structured data from Wikipedia. Of course for MT there is the question of working with thousands of different language pairs, with most of these languages having few necessary resources, such as bilingual dictionaries and large amounts of parallel corpora.

## 3 Better Modeling of User Tasks

A second dimension to the realism issues is the need to better model "user" tasks. Information retrieval, machine translation, and speech transcription all assume the presence of a user. Good evaluation methodology attempts to understand the needs of that user and to measure system results with respect to those needs. This is critical if any of these systems are to be deployed in the real world.

Along with different data types, especially for IR, comes the need for different types of searching and user needs. The IR group for MINDS identified several new user needs, such as exploration of information space rather than simple searching operations. Additionally, users not only want to find information, but to manage and organize that information. Evaluation for these types of research will first need to create models for these tasks, then find ways of comparing system results, and finally enable researchers to "see the big picture" in terms of comparison of technologies. Ideally one would construct user studies both to better model the tasks and as part of the evaluation.

The earlier mentioned problem with summarization evaluation comes from the "poor" user modeling situation. Summaries are used in many different ways, such as to skim information quickly, to help organize information, and to create tabular versions of information for special purposes. Each of these user models requires different types of truth data, and even different metrics, as completeness, fluency, and length of summary carry varying amounts of importance across these models. Similar issues apply to MT, where quite different levels of accuracy and fluency are necessary to meet user requirements. For example, gisting returned web documents to have a general idea of what is meant necessiates minimal accuracy; translation of a political speech requires not only high accuracy but knowledge of cultural issues across languages. Translating of poetry or novels require yet other metrics. Obtaining user models for all of these tasks, and adapting current evaluation methodologies to these models is a major challenge to be solved before researchers are likely to invest heavily in these research areas.

The NLP "users" are more likely to be other automatic systems who need results from component technologies such as word sense disambiguation, term extraction, co-reference resolution, and time and date handling. Whereas current evaluation technology can measure the accuracy of these component technologies, once again there needs to be some "user" model to determine issues like minimal accuracy and the desired levels of granularity. Many of these problems also apply to speech transcription, although there can be end users such as for dictation systems.

## 4 Understanding Cascading Errors

An important criteria that has not received much attention in current evaluations is that of "cascading" errors. Karen Sparck-Jones provided an elegant model for these [19] and discussed their role both in providing better user models and in providing better understanding of the underlying interaction of complex systems. This becomes even more critical as the various components of HLT systems begin to be stitched together for specific applications.

One example for this comes from the speech transcription area. If the results from speech transcription are used as the documents for information retrieval (called spoken document retrieval), there are generally few problems because the important words in any one of these documents are normally repeated several times and it is likely that the speech transcription worked at least one of those times. But if a speech transcription system is used as input to machine translation, where every word is going to need translation, then the error rate is likely to be compounded by the machine translation attempting to find the appropriate translation for a word that does not "belong" in the sentence. If a cascading model were to be used, the speech error rate would first be measured, and then the machine translation score would be measured, and these could be correlated. This correlation is not only helpful for later failure analysis, but can lead to more complex and useful ways of coupling these two HLT components, such as feedback loops from MT asking about "unlikely" words.

A second example comes from the machine translation area, where the output of machine translation is used as the input query to a question answering system. This task actually involves three different HLT components. First the input query needs to be translated into the document language(s). The results of this are sent to the NLP QA system, which analyzes the terms and relationships and creates a query for an IR system. The IR system returns a list of candidate documents, which the NLP system then processes to locate the answers to the questions. Errors from the MT system have two effects here: first they affect the NLP system in terms of correct parsing of the query. Then, depending on the types of errors, they create poor keywords for the IR system, such as proper names that have been literally translated and therefore are not likely to match terms in a documents. Very incomplete results are then passed back to the NLP system, with a final result of no answer to be found. Again, these errors should each be scored at the component level, probably with some method of collecting types of error, and then the various results correlated.

## 5 Better Diagnostics and Better Tools

The above section leads to the final point about evaluation. Too much of the current evaluation methodology is about comparing results rather than better understanding the inner workings of a system. Evaluations need to produce more information about the types of errors for speech transcription or machine translation. Errors need to be reported on a location-specific basis, such as on a query-specific basis for information retrieval, and a word or sentence-specific basis where that is possible for other HLT areas. For a good example of this type of diagnostic, see the TREC-7 SDR track report [20] where the speech transcription errors were divided into types such as named-entity and general words that would be considered stop words by an IR system.

Then there needs to be a systematic effort to produce better tools for failure analysis that make use of these more detailed diagnostics. All of the systems are now too complex to do the kind of manual checking that was possible in the 1960s, and the amount of data that needs to be processed is too large. More and more researchers are avoiding failure analysis except for "simple" errors; the issue is not just to find the system problems but to enable better understanding of the individual systems or components. For examples of a complex failure analysis, see results from the RIA workshop [21] for information retrieval.

## References


1. Cleverdon, C.W., Mills, J., Keen, E.M.: Factors determining the performance of indexing systems, vol. 1: Design, vol. 2: Test Results. Aslib Cranfield Research Project (1966)
2. Text REtrieval Conference, http://trec.nist.gov/
3. Voorhees, E.M., Harman, D.K.: TREC: Experiment in Evaluation in Information Retrieval. MIT Press, Cambridge (2005)
4. Cross-Language Evaluation Forum, http://www.clef-campaign.org/
5. NII-NACSIS Test Collection for IR Systems, http://research.nii.ac.jp/ntcir/
6. Francis, W.N., Kucera, H.: Brown Corpus Manual. Brown University (1964)
7. The Penn Treebank Project, http://www.cis.upenn.edu/~treebank/
8. Miller, G.: WordNet, http://wordnet.princeton.edu/
9. Message Understanding Conferences, http://www.aclweb.org/anthology-new/
10. SemEval (2007), http://nlp.cs.swarthmore.edu/semeval/
11. Document Understanding Conferences, http://duc.nist.gov/
12. NIST speech evaluation benchmarks, http://www.nist.gov/speech/history/index.htm
13. Falkedal, I.: Evaluation methods for machine translation systems; a historical overview and critical account. Report, ISSCO, Universite de Geneve (1991)
14. Papineni, K., et al.: Bleu: a method for automatic evaluation of machine translation. IBM Research Report, RC22176 (2001)

15. The Meeting of the MINDS: Future directions for human language technology Executive summary, http://www-nlpir.nist.gov/MINDS/FINAL/exec.summary.pdf
16. Voorhees, Ellen: Variations in Relevance Judgments and the Measurement of Retrieval Effectiveness. Proceedings of SIGIR 1998, pp. 315–323 (1998)
17. Buttcher, S., et al.: Reliable Information Retrieval Evaluation with Incomplete and Biased Judgements. Proceedings of SIGIR 2007, pp. 63–70 (2007)
18. Sakai, T.: Alternatives to Bpref. Proceedings of SIGIR 2007, pp. 71–78 (2007)
19. Sparck Jones, K., Galliers, J.R. (eds.): Evaluating Natural Language Processing Systems. LNCS, vol. 1083. Springer, Heidelberg (1996)
20. Garofolo, G., et al.: The 1998 TREC-7 Spoken Document Retrieval Track Overview, http://trec.nist.gov/pubs/trec7/t7_proceedings.html
21. Buckley, C.: Why current IR engines fail. In: Proceedings of SIGIR 2004, pp. 584–585 (2004)

# An Effective Scheduling Scheme for Information Searching with Computational Resources Scattered over a Large-Scale Network

Shota Kondo, Shinji Sugawara, and Yutaka Ishibashi

Nagoya Institute of Technology, Nagoya 466-8555, Japan
{kinta,shinji,ishibasi}@mcl.elcom.nitech.ac.jp
http://WWW.nma.elcom.nitech.ac.jp/

**Abstract.** In this article, we propose an efficient resource distribution scheduling scheme for information retrieval from multiple information sources. This scheme can restrain costs for information searching and retrieval by limiting the effective area of connection from an information source to computational resources. Furthermore, we show the effectiveness of the scheme by computer simulations with various assumption settings.

## 1 Introduction

Recently, both volume and variety of information scattered in a large-scale network such as the Internet have grown with dizzying speed, and enormous amount of information floods this kind of cyberspaces. At the same time, the network users have come to utilize a lot of handy information retrieved from network effectively along with the popularization of broadband communications and much further development of high performance personal computers.

In this environment, it is very important to find the information which the user really wants quickly and without trouble, and a lot of network users rely on major searching engines such as Google and Yahoo! as of now. The main idea of these engines consists of a combination of techniques for crawling around a whole network, information indexing and keyword matching. But unfortunately, such information searching does not always work effectively.

For instance, in the case that the index is not ready or not appropriate, conventional search engines do not work well. Especially in an environment of the Internet, each piece of information provided by unspecified number of servers can be rewritten or removed at any time. Therefore, considering the size of the Internet, it is not realistic that the search engines manage all updates of all servers and keep their index data up-to-the-second. Moreover, there is also a problem of insufficient index registration both intentionally and accidentally. This kind of problems has been discussed in our past studies[1]-[5].

In addition, in the case of precise search which cannot rely on keyword matching, conventional search engines do not always work well. Let us say, searching of a large volume image which includes a completely identical segment to a

T. Tokunaga and A. Ortega (Eds.): LKR 2008, LNAI 4938, pp. 351–365, 2008.

key image, and searching of haptic data which consists of several types of large time-series physical data, are good instances. In these cases, even granting that searching engines can successfully offer some hopeful server's locations in the network, searchers eventually have to check the information on the servers one by one directly until they find their target information.

Therefore, it is very important to acquire effective techniques to obtain information on demand by accessing information sources directly which exist on the network, including the information which is not always searched well by conventional search engines.

However, in order to put it into practice comfortably, searchers need an environment where sufficient computational capacity and communication bandwidth are available for their information searching, although it is difficult to realize for ordinary network users generally.

On the other hand, a great number of high-performance CPUs have come to be connected to the Internet recently, which are originally for personal computers and high-end video game machines owned by general users and not always busy for their intended purposes. Now they draw attention as promising computational resources on the network, and actually used for enormous computations such as SETI@home. In this situation, although it is needed to consider combinations of resources in order to make sufficient processing ability, convergence of data traffic in the network is reduced instead, because of the resources' dispersion.

Consequently, with these computational resources scattered over the network, it is possible to realize an effective searching for the information which is not always retrieved well by conventional search engines and needed to be searched by checking promising information sources one by one directly until its discovery. However, this kind of research has not conducted sufficiently. It is obvious that different ways of resource assignment and scheduling for the information search make big difference in searching time and cost. And therefore, it is really needed to find the efficient way of it.

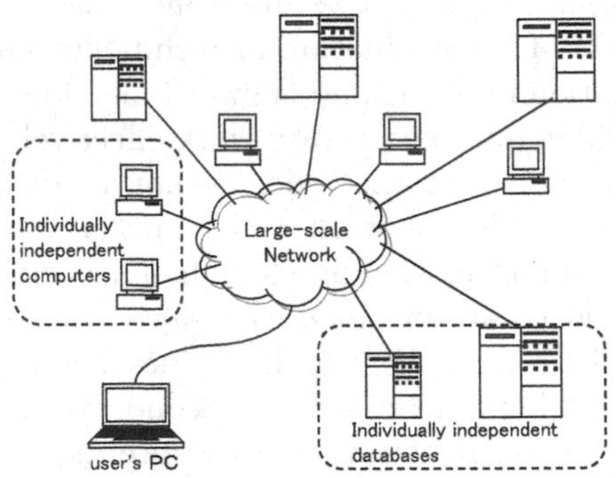


**Fig. 1.** An environment of distributed computing

The rest of this paper is organized as follows. Section 2 defines the problem and the information retrieval environment discussed in this paper. An efficient of resource assignment and scheduling is proposed in Section 3, and evaluation of the proposed scheme by computer simulations and its analysis are stated in Section 4. Finally, conclusion and future work are presented in Section 5.

## 2 Formulation of the Problem

In this paper, the following three basic conditions are assumed.

(1) There are a great number of information sources such as WWW servers and a plural number of computational resources over a Large-scale network such as the Internet.
(2) The information sources release their possessing information to the users respectively and the users can read and download the information freely.
(3) The users can utilize the computational resources in order to search their target information.

In addition, the following seven additional conditions are also assumed.

(a) Each computational resource can always execute its searching processes on a plural number of information sources simultaneously.
(b) Every cost of searching processes on any information sources by any computational resources is given.
(c) Target existence probability in each information source is given.
(d) Each information source can divide whole its possessing data into small parts, and let some computational resources execute searching process separately and simultaneously.
(e) Each information source cannot share the possessing data which have already started to be searched by another resource.
(f) Computational capacity generally varies by each resource.
(g) The quantity of processing data generally varies by each information source.

Next, the costs assumed in this paper are described, as follows.

- **Time cost.** Quantity of data one information source possesses divided by the summation of all computational capacity offered by the resources which are involved in the search.
- **Communication cost.** The number of hops on the network topology from a computational resource to an information source.

Under these assumptions, the problem to solve we set in this paper is to find an effective resource allocation scheduling scheme which achieves the minimum weighted sum of communication cost and time cost.

## 3 Proposed Scheme

In this section, we propose Hop Threshold Scheme (HTS) below as an effective resource allocation algorithm. This algorithm is explained in Fig. 2. From here on, each minimum retrieval process in Fig. 2 is expressed as $s(i,j)$, where $i$ is the number to identify the computational resources which are sorted in the descending order of computational capacity. $j$ is discrete elapsed time from the beginning of retrieval start. The time passes based on unit time with equal intervals, and each process of the scheme is executed discretely at each unit time. The numbers indicated in the cells of Fig. 2 denote the number to identify the information sources. For example, in Fig. 2 (a), $s(3,4)$ means a process of searching information source ♯ 8 at time 4 with using computational resource ♯ 3. And in this figure, $N$ means the total number of computational resources.

⟨ Algorithm ⟩

(1) A set of the information source numbers the sources of which are located within the range of a hop threshold (HT) from an information resource ♯ $n$ ($DB_n$) is defined to be $S(DB_n)$. And only in the case that the number of elements of $S(DB_n)$ is not zero, the following processes from (2) to (4) are executed in turn. Otherwise go to (5).

(2) The cost $C(DB_n)$ for searching $DB_n$ in each $S(DB_n)$ is calculated as follows.

$$C(DB_n) = w \cdot \sum_{i \in S(DB_n)} H_i + \frac{d(DB_n)}{\sum_{i \in S(DB_n)} A_i} \tag{1}$$

where,
number of hops from computational resource ♯ $i$ to $DB_n$: $H_i$,
quantity of data $DB_n$ possesses: $d(DB_n)$,
computational capacity of computational resource ♯ $i$: $A_i$, and
weight: $w$ (constant number).

(3) The $C(DB_n)$ divided by $P(DB_n)$ which is the existence probability of the target information the user demands in $DB_n$ is calculated in each information resource.

(4) In ascending order of $C/P(DB_n)$, computational resources devoted to the searching for $DB_n$ are reserved according to the following procedures. If all $DB_n$s are scheduled to be searched with the resources, go to (5).

   (i) Set the start time of $DB_n$ searching at time 1, and check if it is available to schedule the searching time required by all the computational resources belonging to $S(DB_n)$ to start and complete the search at the same time.

   (ii) If there is no duplication, in the schedule checked in (i), resource reservation is done, and return to the top of (4).

(iii) If there is a duplication, in the schedule in (i), Increment the start time by 1, and check the schedule in the same way of (i), and return to (ii). (For instance, in the case of Fig. 2(a), $DB_8$ is needed to be searched by computational resources $\sharp$ 3, 4 and 5 for 4 unit time. However, as computational resource $\sharp$ 3 has been already reserved by the searching of information source $\sharp$ 3 from time 1 to 3, the search should be delayed and its start time becomes 4. )

(5) If the number of elements of $S(DB_n)$ is zero, execute the following process shown in (5) and (6). The cost required by computational resource $\sharp$ $i$ for the searching on $DB_n$: $C(DB_{n,i})$ is defined as follows.

$$C(DB_{n,i}) = w \cdot H_i + \frac{d(DB_n)}{A_i} \tag{2}$$

If there is no elements of $S(DB_n)$ the algorithm ends. Otherwise, calculate the value $C/P(DB_{n,i})$, which is $C(DB_{n,i})$ divided by $P(DB_n)$.

(6) Concerning $DB_n$s which have no elements belonging to $S(DB_n)$, in ascending order of the minimum value of $C/P(DB_{n,i})$ calculated by (5), make a reservation of computational resources as follows. If the reservation of all the $DB_n$ is completed, the algorithm ends.

($\alpha$) Check if it is available to schedule the searching process of the resource with the highest computational capacity, from the search start time of $j_n + 1$ i.e., $s(1, j_n + 1)$ , during the sufficient time period of searching on $DB_n$. Here, $j_n$ means the number of times of scheduling availability checking for $s(N, *)$, * of which denotes any time. (Initial value of $j_n$ is zero. )

($\beta$) If the schedule in ($\alpha$) is available, computational resource is reserved, and return to ($\alpha$) for the next $DB_n$ reservation. (For instance, in Fig. 2 (b), in the case that 3 unit time is needed for the next search, and the schedule of resource $\sharp$ 1 is free from $s(1, 1)$ to $s(1, 3)$. )

($\gamma$) If the schedule in ($\alpha$) is not available, (For instance, in Fig. 2 (b), in the case that 4 unit time is needed for the next search, and the schedule of resource $\sharp$ 1 is not always free from $s(1, 1)$ to $s(1, 4)$. i.e. only $s(1, 4)$ is not available.) Check the schedule availability of the resource with the next highest computational capacity (For instance, $s(2, 1)$) in common with the process of ($\alpha$), and continue until the reservation succeeds with increment of $i$.

## 4 Effectiveness Estimation of the Schedule

In order to evaluate the efficiency of allocation algorithm mentioned above, we conduct computer simulations. Computational resources and information sources are arranged on FKP model topologies which imitate the Internet, and estimated total cost for information retrieval by using the proposed scheme can be derived. The simulation according to the BA model topology is also conducted in the same way for the comparison.

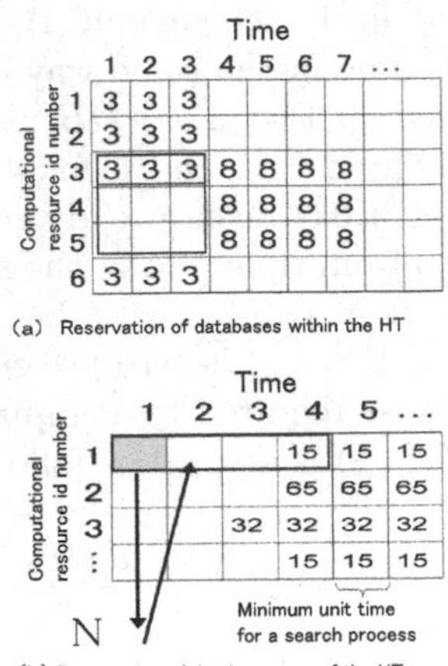


**Fig. 2.** An explanation of HTS operation

### 4.1 Simulation Conditions

Two kinds of network topologies used in this paper, i.e., FKP and BA depend on parameters needed at the beginning of their formation. The actual method of generating FKP model topology is based on the reference [7]. The number of the initial placement nodes is set at 14, and the initial link placement is according to NSFNET in USA in 1991. As the parameter of generating BA model topology [8], the number of the initial placement node is set at 3, and the number of outgoing links from a newly added node is set at 1.

The value of the parameter $w$ in equation (1) and (2) in Section 3 is set at 1, and the quantity of data each information source has is given as a normal distribution multiplied by 1000, both average and variance of which are 5. Concerning computational capacity of each resource per unit time, the maximum value is 70, and its distribution is based on Zipf's law. The minimum unit time in this paper is given as the time which the computational resource with the largest capacity requires by itself to search the source with the minimal volume of data, in order to reduce the quantization error of search time. Finally, existence probability distribution of the target information in information sources is also given based on Zipf's law.

Parameters for this simulation mentioned above are shown in Table 1.

**Table 1.** Simulation Parameters

| Parameter | Value |
|---|---|
| Number of nodes | 100 (computational resource 10, information source 90) |
| Quantity of data | min=70, max=10000 |
| Computational capacity | min=10, max=70 |

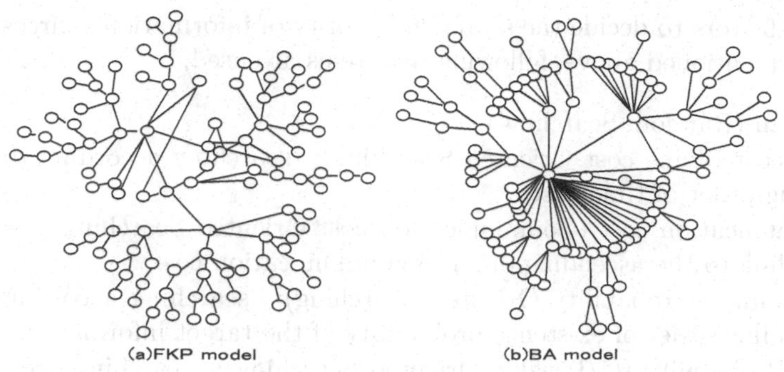


**Fig. 3.** Examples of FKP, BA model topologies

### 4.2 Definition of Costs

Communication cost and time cost are used as a measure for this evaluation, and proposed scheme is evaluated as a whole by total cost $E$, which is defined as (3) Here, a weighted sum of communication and time costs are shown below. Communication cost and time cost are denoted by $E_c$ and $E_t$ respectively. $W$ is a weight, which has an impact on relative importance between the two costs.

$$E = WE_c + E_t \tag{3}$$

### 4.3 Schemes to Be Compared to the Proposed One

In order to verify the efficiency, we also implemented some searching algorithms which differ from the proposed one, and compared them to the proposed one.

Generally, Round Robin algorithm is used in many cases as a scheduling algorithm. However, in the case of simply adopting this algorithm to this simulation environment, it is likely that the scheduling is not effective because of two following problems.

Firstly, it is obvious that the searching efficiency becomes high when a lot of searching tasks can be assigned to the higher performance computational resources. Hence, simple Round Robin does not fit in this situation well.

Secondly, since the cost for searching depends on the computational capacity and location of computational resources, an efficient resource allocation policy considering those factors should be prepared in advance, in order to use Round Robin or Weighted Round Robin in this searching model.

Consequently, we prepare some comparison schemes in which a queue which keeps the searching priority of information sources decided by certain factors is generated, and according to the order, Round Robin distributes the rights of searching source to computational resources.

Therefore, it is clear that these comparison schemes illustrated below are more appropriate to this searching model than simple Round Robin or Weighted Round Robin algorithm.

For the factors to decide the searching priority of information sources kept in the queue mentioned above, following five items are used.

- Random (Random Searching)
- Time cost (Time cost Oriented Searching): searching according to the ascending order of time cost
- Communication cost (Communication cost Oriented Searching): searching according to the ascending order of communication cost
- Probability (Probability Oriented Searching): searching according to the descending order of existence probability of the target information
- Cost/Probability (C/P value Oriented Searching): searching according to the ascending of order $C/P$ value

These schemes were devised by the authors only for this simulation. We show a common procedure in these search schemes below.

(1) For each computational resources, prepare a queue to memorize a searching order of information sources.
(2) According to the priority order prescribed in each scheme explained above, identification numbers of information sources are inserted into the queue. (Random Searching's queue is arranged at random.)
(3) By each queue, The scheduling of the information source with the highest priority is reserved tentatively, and then, the search which finishes the earliest is settled to be scheduled properly. The identification number of the information source which has already scheduled is removed from the all queues.
(4) Repeat process (3) until whole searching schedule of all information sources is fixed.

Here, we show an instance of the TOS(Time cost Oriented Searching) operation for the process (2) mentioned above in Fig. 4. In this figure, the time cost required for the search on the information sources form ♯ 1 to 10 is shown in the table above, concerning the computational resource ♯ 1. In this case, information source identification ♯ 4 is inserted into the top of the queue, because the searching cost for source ♯ 4 is the smallest from this resource. And then, source ♯ 5 which requires time cost 20 is stored in the queue as the second value. By the repeat of the operations, each computational resources makes its queue, which stores the order of searching priority.

In Fig. 5, the instance of the operation mentioned above in process (3) is explained as follows. $n$ in the figure denotes the number of information sources which have settled their searching reservations. And the numbers inserted into the cells indicate the identification numbers of the highest priority sources at that time in each computational resource. However, this state of the table is the temporary reservation yet. Besides, the number in the array of "top of queue" illustrates the identification number of information sources prioritized as the next search. The circled numbers in the cell mean the settled reservation.

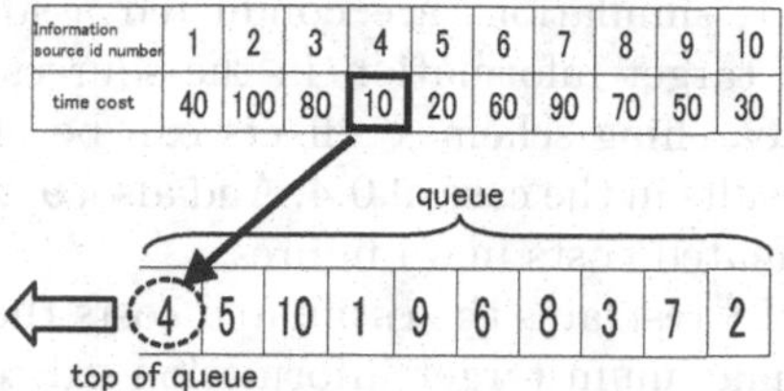


**Fig. 4.** An explanation of comparison algorithm (1)

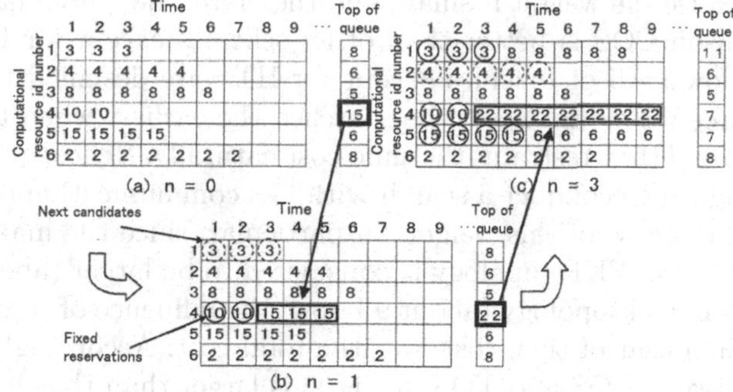


**Fig. 5.** An explanation of comparison algorithm (2)

First of all, assuming to be in the state (a) just after the tentative scheduling in process (3), the computational number 4 finishes the search earliest among all resources, and this searching process is settled. Then, going to (4), since there are information sources the searching schedule of which has not decided yet, go back to (3), and prioritized information source ♯ 15 at the top of queue for the computational resource ♯ 4 is reserved tentatively in the way shown in (b). At this time, among unsettled search reservations, the computational resource which finishes its search the earliest is ♯ 1, and the information source ♯ 3 is settled. After the search process advanced to be in state (c), since the computational resource ♯ 5 fixes the search on source ♯ 15, resource ♯ 4 cancels its reservation of searching on source ♯ 15, and change to ♯ 22 according to top of queue at that time.

### 4.4 Simulation Results and Analysis

Expected total costs estimated by computer simulations are shown in Figs. 6 through 12. For details, figures through 6 to 8 are simulation results derived on FKP model topologies in the cases that weight W equals 0.1, 1 and 10 respectively. And Figs. 9 through 11 are those on BA model topologies in the cases that also W equals 0.1, 1 and 10. In addition, relations between the size of HT and expected total costs are illustrated in Fig. 12 in the cases that W is equal to 0.1 and 10. This figure has two vertical axes; right axis is for the case that W equals 0.1, and left axis is for the case that W equals 10.

In Figs. 6 through 11, simulations are conducted assuming that maximum existence probability of target information in the sources is both 0.2 and 0.4. However, because the searching schemes' effects can be observed more clearly, we mainly discuss the results in the case of 0.4. And also, 95% confidence intervals are indicated in all estimated costs in all figures.

In Figs 6, 7 and 8, HTS restrains the estimated costs the best through the all settings of weight and maximum target information existence probability. The second best scheme in Fig. 6 is COS, and those in Figs 7 and 8 are both CPOS followed by POS.

In the case shown in Fig. 6, the user requires to retrieve target information immediately because the weight is small, and therefore, the search has a priority to time. The reason COS is better than other schemes except for HTS can be explained as follows. All of schemes except for HTS are designed to select the information source which finishes to be searched the earliest when the retrieval order is decided, and they restrains the time cost naturally. Hence, although COS is originally designed to conduct a search with less communication cost, it gains an advantage in the case of this weight. In particular, since the maximum hops which can be taken on FKP topology is considered to be larger (about 12 hops) than that on BA model topology (about 9 hops), the influence of communication costs is larger than that of time cost over the total cost. Accordingly, difference of total costs between COS and TOS in Fig. 6 is larger than that in Fig. 9 (the case of W =0.1).

In Fig. 7, the reason that HTS restrains the total cost in the case that HT equals 7, is as follows. since the maximum communication cost which makes the total cost on FKP model topologies converged is 12 (hops), HT set at 7 is large enough. By plural computational resources searching on one information source, time cost is largely restrained. Simultaneously, the number of information sources located out of the HT range is nearly zero, and the cases that a single computational resource searches on a single information source decrease. On the other hand, in the case that HT equals 1 or 2, although communication cost is restrained, the search becomes inefficient because there are many information sources located out of the HT range and accordingly, the cases that a single computational resource searches a single information source increase. Contrary, if the HT exceeds 7, though time cost is restrained because the number of computational resources assigned per an information source increases, communication cost increases further, and the search becomes inefficient, just the same.

In Figs. 9 and 11, HTS successfully restrains the estimated total cost the best in all settings of weights and maximum existence probability of target information, then, CPOS and POS follows concerning their less searching costs required. In Fig. 10, POS restrains the estimated cost the best, followed by CPOS by a narrow margin. HTS manages to achieve the third in this case.

HTS, HT of which is 9 in Fig. 9 restrains the cost most effectively, followed by POS, and C/POS. HT set at 9 is nearly maximum hop distance in the BA model topology, and even if HT is increased further, the total cost converges to the same value and those cases bring the same results. When the HT is large, the time cost is

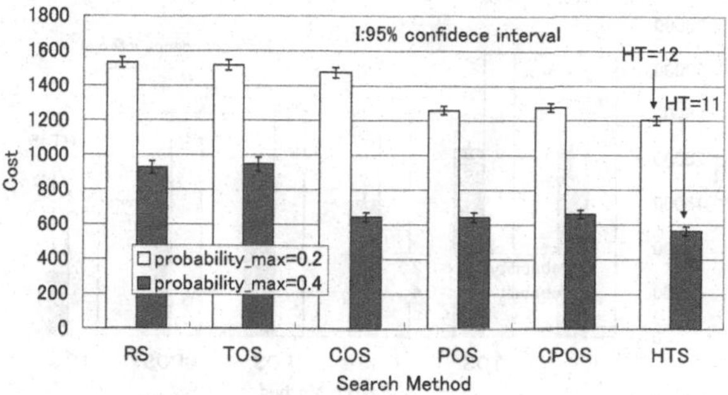


**Fig. 6.** Simulation result with FKP model (W=0.1)

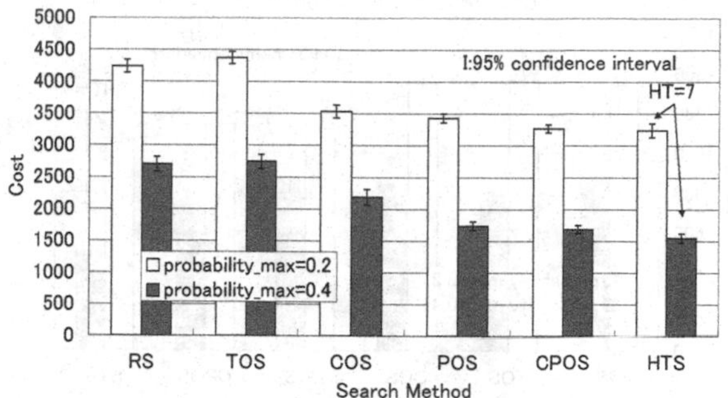


**Fig. 7.** Simulation result with FKP model (W=1)

restrained because plural computational resources get engaged to search a single information source. In this instance, although the communication cost increases because many computational resources get involved, the total cost is restrained in the end, for the less importance of communication cost (W = 0.1).

C/POS is proved to be the optimal searching in the case of sequential retrieval by a single computational resource [8]. Intended environment in this paper is not the same as it, however the value of costs per target existence probability in each source can be used as a measure of worth searching.

The reason that POS and C/POS successfully restrain their total costs in Fig.10 is as follows. First of all, all of schemes are designed to restrain their time costs. Secondly, maximum communication cost is averagely nearly 9 (hops) on BA model topology and many nodes are likely to be located around the center of the topology with a short distance each other . Hence, the computational resources also tend to be in the center of the network, and there is not a major difference among them in communication cost. As a result, the major factor to affect the total cost is the target existence probability.

The reason that the total cost of HTS is larger than that of C/POS is as follows. Searching schedules of the schemes except for HTS do not have any time-gaps because plural computational resources do not search on a single information source simultaneously in the process of those schemes, and there is no

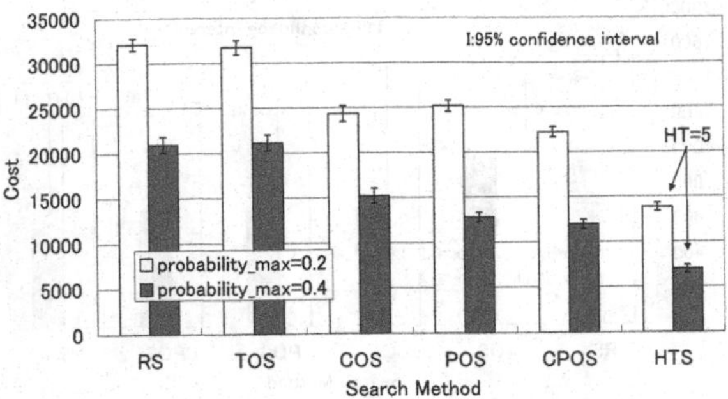


**Fig. 8.** Simulation result with FKP model (W=10)

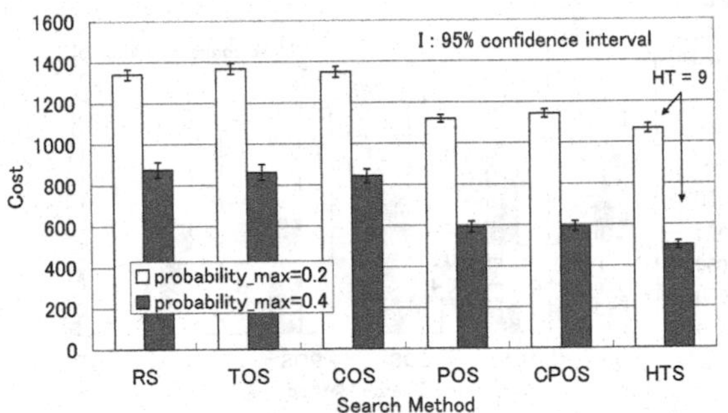


**Fig. 9.** Simulation result with BA model (W=0.1)

need to consider double booking of computational resources. Accordingly those schemes can continue their searching without any stop until their schedules end. In this case, HTS is inferior in comparison with the other schemes concerning the operating efficiency of the computational resources. And it is found that HTS is not so effective on the topologies such as the BA model in which nodes tend to be evenly and closely aggregated, under the circumstances that both time and communication costs are balanced.

In Fig. 11, HTS restrains the total cost the best when HT is set at 4, followed by C/POS and POS. In this condition, it is effective for the user to execute the search at the computational resources which are as close to the information sources to be searched as possible for reducing the communication cost. The main reasons that HT set at 4 is the most effective are following two things; searching by a single computational resource seldom occurs, and communication cost is well restrained because HT is small enough.

Figure 12 shows the relation between expected total cost of HTS illustrated in Fig. 11 and its HT when W is set at 0.1 and 10. In the case that W is 10, if HT is small, the number of information sources which are out of the simultaneous search range increases because the computational resources are assigned to the searches on close information sources within the range of HT. In the process of HTS, because information sources out of the HT range are scheduled to be

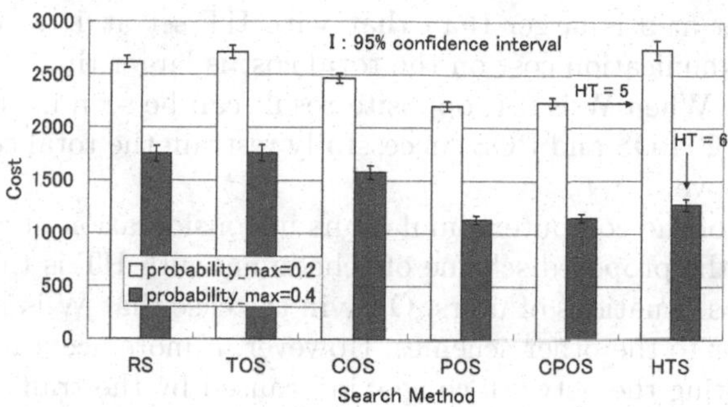


**Fig. 10.** Simulation result with BA model (W=1)

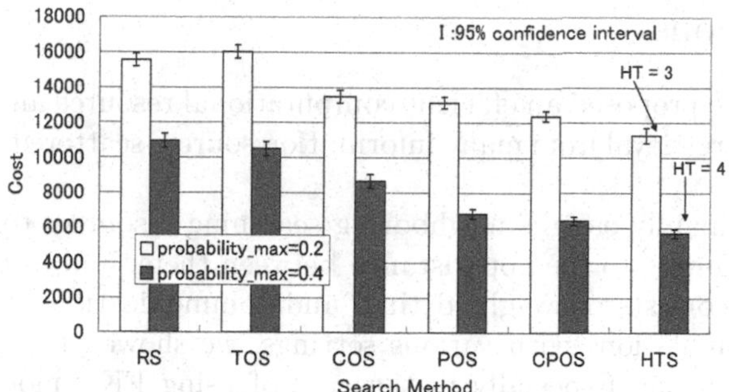


**Fig. 11.** Simulation result with BA model (W=10)

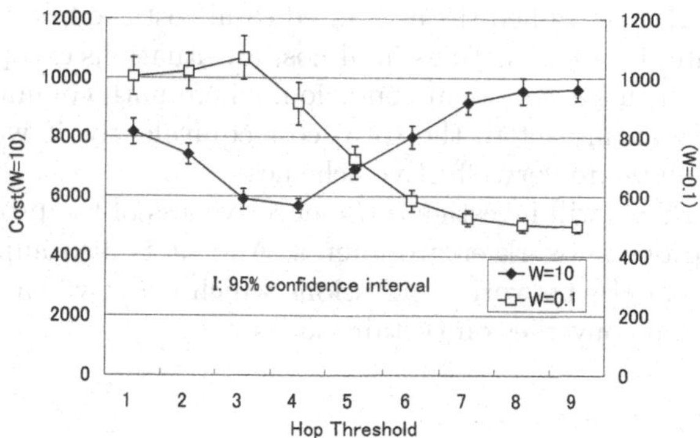


**Fig. 12.** The relation between expected total cost of HTS and size of its HT

searched after those within the HT range, searches by using the distant resource, which are inefficient occur frequently, and as a result, total cost grows.

In the case that W is the same and HT is large, communication cost increases because the number of computational resources involved in a search of one information source grows. Furthermore, when W is 10, it is found that the total cost with HT set at 9 is larger than that with HT set at 1, which means, the influence of communication cost on the total cost is larger than that of the time cost in this case. When W is 0.1, opposite result can be seen in the same figure. The reason that C/POS and POS successfully restrain the total cost is the same as mentioned above.

As the result of the computer simulations in consideration of weight of costs, it is found that the proposed scheme of scheduling with HT is the most flexible about the various situations of users. Only in the case that W is 1, the proposed scheme is inferior to the other schemes. However, if more accurate simulation is conducted reflecting the network congestion caused by the traffic concentration on certain hub nodes, the proposed scheme seems to be able to restrain the estimated total cost better than any other scheme in any cases.

## 5 Conclusions

In this paper, we proposed an efficient computational resource allocation scheme for information retrieval from many information sources scattered in a large-scale network.

The scheme mainly assigns neighboring searching resources to each information source according to the hop distance between them, and restrains the total searching cost consists of weighted time and communication costs. And then, by computer simulations with various settings, we showed the effectiveness of the proposed scheme. Especially in the case of using FKP model topology, it achieved the smallest cost for the information retrieval of all schemes under all conditions we assumed. Even in the case of using BA model topology, in which hop distance between the centered nodes and marginal ones tends to be small, proposed scheme also restrained the estimated total cost the best with considering the appropriate threshold settings in almost all situations except for only the case that W is 1. In this exceptional condition, where both communication cost and time cost give an impact to the total cost equivalently, it was also shown that POS and C/POS are very effective schemes.

As a future work, we will investigate the effectiveness of the proposed scheme in much more various network environments. And, it is also important to examine the impact of the network congestions which occur when the traffic for information retrieval converges on certain nodes.

## References

1. Sugawara, S., Sonehara, N.: An Effecient Information Retrieveal from Plual Independent Databases Partially Unreliable. In: Proc. EuroIMSA 2007, Chamonix, France, pp. 148–153 (2007)
2. Kondo, S., Sugawara, S.: An Effective Information Searching with Computational Resources Scattered over a Large-Scale Network. IEICE. B-7-194 (in Japanese) (2007)
3. Sugawara, S., Ishibashi, Y.: A Study on Utility-Based Truncation for Information Searching. IEICE. IN2003-4, pp. 19–24 (in Japanese) (2003)

4. Sugawara, S., Yamaoka, K.: A Study on Image Searching Method in Super Distributed Database. In: Proc. IEEE Globecom 1997, Phoenix, AZ, USA, pp. 736–740 (1997)
5. Sugawara, S., Sakai, Y.: A Study on Efficient Information Searches with Agents for Large-Scale Networks. In: Proc. IEEE Globecom 1999, Rio de Janeiro, Brazil, pp. 1954–1958 (1999)
6. Alex, F., Elias, K.: Heuristically Optimized Trade-offs: A New Paradigm for the Power Laws of the Internet. In: Widmayer, P., et al. (eds.) ICALP 2002. LNCS, vol. 2380, pp. 110–122. Springer, Heidelberg (2002)
7. Tian, B., Don, T.: On Distinguishing between Internet Power Law Topology Generators. In: Proc. INFOCOM 2002, Pure Appl. Math., pp. 638–647 (2002)
8. Sugawara, S., Yamaoka, K.: A Study on Efficient Searching for Image Information in Large-Scale Network (in Japanese). IEICE (B-I) J81, 484–493 (1998)

# Author Index

# Lecture Notes in Artificial Intelligence (LNAI)

Vol. 4938: T. Tokunaga, A. Ortega (Eds.), Large-Scale Knowledge Resources. IX, 367 pages. 2008.

Vol. 4929: M. Helmert, Understanding Planning Tasks. XIV, 270 pages. 2008.

Vol. 4898: M. Kolp, B. Henderson-Sellers, H. Mouratidis, A. Garcia, A. Ghose, P. Bresciani (Eds.), Agent-Oriented Information Systems IV. X, 292 pages. 2008.

Vol. 4897: M. Baldoni, T.C. Son, M.B. van Riemsdijk, M. Winikoff (Eds.), Declarative Agent Languages and Technologies V. X, 245 pages. 2008.

Vol. 4885: M. Chetouani, A. Hussain, B. Gas, M. Milgram, J.-L. Zarader (Eds.), Advances in Nonlinear Speech Processing. XI, 284 pages. 2007.

Vol. 4874: J. Neves, M.F. Santos, J.M. Machado (Eds.), Progress in Artificial Intelligence. XVIII, 704 pages. 2007.

Vol. 4869: F. Botana, T. Recio (Eds.), Automated Deduction in Geometry. X, 213 pages. 2007.

Vol. 4865: K. Tuyls, A. Nowe, Z. Guessoum, D. Kudenko (Eds.), Adaptive Agents and Multi-Agent Systems III. VIII, 255 pages. 2008.

Vol. 4850: M. Lungarella, F. Iida, J.C. Bongard, R. Pfeifer (Eds.), 50 Years of Artificial Intelligence. X, 399 pages. 2007.

Vol. 4845: N. Zhong, J. Liu, Y. Yao, J. Wu, S. Lu, K. Li (Eds.), Web Intelligence Meets Brain Informatics. XI, 516 pages. 2007.

Vol. 4840: L. Paletta, E. Rome (Eds.), Attention in Cognitive Systems. XI, 497 pages. 2007.

Vol. 4830: M.A. Orgun, J. Thornton (Eds.), AI 2007: Advances in Artificial Intelligence. XIX, 841 pages. 2007.

Vol. 4828: M. Randall, H.A. Abbass, J. Wiles (Eds.), Progress in Artificial Life. XII, 402 pages. 2007.

Vol. 4827: A. Gelbukh, Á.F. Kuri Morales (Eds.), MICAI 2007: Advances in Artificial Intelligence. XXIV, 1234 pages. 2007.

Vol. 4826: P. Perner, O. Salvetti (Eds.), Advances in Mass Data Analysis of Signals and Images in Medicine, Biotechnology and Chemistry. X, 183 pages. 2007.

Vol. 4819: T. Washio, Z.-H. Zhou, J.Z. Huang, X. Hu, J. Li, C. Xie, J. He, D. Zou, K.-C. Li, M.M. Freire (Eds.), Emerging Technologies in Knowledge Discovery and Data Mining. XIV, 675 pages. 2007.

Vol. 4811: O. Nasraoui, M. Spiliopoulou, J. Srivastava, B. Mobasher, B. Masand (Eds.), Advances in Web Mining and Web Usage Analysis. XII, 247 pages. 2007.

Vol. 4798: Z. Zhang, J.H. Siekmann (Eds.), Knowledge Science, Engineering and Management. XVI, 669 pages. 2007.

Vol. 4795: F. Schilder, G. Katz, J. Pustejovsky (Eds.), Annotating, Extracting and Reasoning about Time and Events. VII, 141 pages. 2007.

Vol. 4790: N. Dershowitz, A. Voronkov (Eds.), Logic for Programming, Artificial Intelligence, and Reasoning. XIII, 562 pages. 2007.

Vol. 4788: D. Borrajo, L. Castillo, J.M. Corchado (Eds.), Current Topics in Artificial Intelligence. XI, 280 pages. 2007.

Vol. 4775: A. Esposito, M. Faundez-Zanuy, E. Keller, M. Marinaro (Eds.), Verbal and Nonverbal Communication Behaviours. XII, 325 pages. 2007.

Vol. 4772: H. Prade, V.S. Subrahmanian (Eds.), Scalable Uncertainty Management. X, 277 pages. 2007.

Vol. 4766: N. Maudet, S. Parsons, I. Rahwan (Eds.), Argumentation in Multi-Agent Systems. XII, 211 pages. 2007.

Vol. 4760: E. Rome, J. Hertzberg, G. Dorffner (Eds.), Towards Affordance-Based Robot Control. IX, 211 pages. 2008.

Vol. 4755: V. Corruble, M. Takeda, E. Suzuki (Eds.), Discovery Science. XI, 298 pages. 2007.

Vol. 4754: M. Hutter, R.A. Servedio, E. Takimoto (Eds.), Algorithmic Learning Theory. XI, 403 pages. 2007.

Vol. 4737: B. Berendt, A. Hotho, D. Mladenic, G. Semeraro (Eds.), From Web to Social Web: Discovering and Deploying User and Content Profiles. XI, 161 pages. 2007.

Vol. 4733: R. Basili, M.T. Pazienza (Eds.), AI*IA 2007: Artificial Intelligence and Human-Oriented Computing. XVII, 858 pages. 2007.

Vol. 4724: K. Mellouli (Ed.), Symbolic and Quantitative Approaches to Reasoning with Uncertainty. XV, 914 pages. 2007.

Vol. 4722: C. Pelachaud, J.-C. Martin, E. André, G. Chollet, K. Karpouzis, D. Pelé (Eds.), Intelligent Virtual Agents. XV, 425 pages. 2007.

Vol. 4720: B. Konev, F. Wolter (Eds.), Frontiers of Combining Systems. X, 283 pages. 2007.

Vol. 4702: J.N. Kok, J. Koronacki, R. Lopez de Mantaras, S. Matwin, D. Mladenič, A. Skowron (Eds.), Knowledge Discovery in Databases: PKDD 2007. XXIV, 640 pages. 2007.

Vol. 4701: J.N. Kok, J. Koronacki, R. Lopez de Mantaras, S. Matwin, D. Mladenič, A. Skowron (Eds.), Machine Learning: ECML 2007. XXII, 809 pages. 2007.

Vol. 4696: H.-D. Burkhard, G. Lindemann, R. Verbrugge, L.Z. Varga (Eds.), Multi-Agent Systems and Applications V. XIII, 350 pages. 2007.

Vol. 4694: B. Apolloni, R.J. Howlett, L. Jain (Eds.), Knowledge-Based Intelligent Information and Engineering Systems, Part III. XXIX, 1126 pages. 2007.

Vol. 4693: B. Apolloni, R.J. Howlett, L. Jain (Eds.), Knowledge-Based Intelligent Information and Engineering Systems, Part II. XXXII, 1380 pages. 2007.

Vol. 4692: B. Apolloni, R.J. Howlett, L. Jain (Eds.), Knowledge-Based Intelligent Information and Engineering Systems, Part I. LV, 882 pages. 2007.

Vol. 4687: P. Petta, J.P. Müller, M. Klusch, M. Georgeff (Eds.), Multiagent System Technologies. X, 207 pages. 2007.

Vol. 4682: D.-S. Huang, L. Heutte, M. Loog (Eds.), Advanced Intelligent Computing Theories and Applications. XXVII, 1373 pages. 2007.

Vol. 4676: M. Klusch, K.V. Hindriks, M.P. Papazoglou, L. Sterling (Eds.), Cooperative Information Agents XI. XI, 361 pages. 2007.

Vol. 4667: J. Hertzberg, M. Beetz, R. Englert (Eds.), KI 2007: Advances in Artificial Intelligence. IX, 516 pages. 2007.

Vol. 4660: S. Džeroski, L. Todorovski (Eds.), Computational Discovery of Scientific Knowledge. X, 327 pages. 2007.

Vol. 4659: V. Mařík, V. Vyatkin, A.W. Colombo (Eds.), Holonic and Multi-Agent Systems for Manufacturing. VIII, 456 pages. 2007.

Vol. 4651: F. Azevedo, P. Barahona, F. Fages, F. Rossi (Eds.), Recent Advances in Constraints. VIII, 185 pages. 2007.

Vol. 4648: F. Almeida e Costa, L.M. Rocha, E. Costa, I. Harvey, A. Coutinho (Eds.), Advances in Artificial Life. XVIII, 1215 pages. 2007.

Vol. 4635: B. Kokinov, D.C. Richardson, T.R. Roth-Berghofer, L. Vieu (Eds.), Modeling and Using Context. XIV, 574 pages. 2007.

Vol. 4632: R. Alhajj, H. Gao, X. Li, J. Li, O.R. Zaïane (Eds.), Advanced Data Mining and Applications. XV, 634 pages. 2007.

Vol. 4629: V. Matoušek, P. Mautner (Eds.), Text, Speech and Dialogue. XVII, 663 pages. 2007.

Vol. 4626: R.O. Weber, M.M. Richter (Eds.), Case-Based Reasoning Research and Development. XIII, 534 pages. 2007.

Vol. 4617: V. Torra, Y. Narukawa, Y. Yoshida (Eds.), Modeling Decisions for Artificial Intelligence. XII, 502 pages. 2007.

Vol. 4612: I. Miguel, W. Ruml (Eds.), Abstraction, Reformulation, and Approximation. XI, 418 pages. 2007.

Vol. 4604: U. Priss, S. Polovina, R. Hill (Eds.), Conceptual Structures: Knowledge Architectures for Smart Applications. XII, 514 pages. 2007.

Vol. 4603: F. Pfenning (Ed.), Automated Deduction – CADE-21. XII, 522 pages. 2007.

Vol. 4597: P. Perner (Ed.), Advances in Data Mining. XI, 353 pages. 2007.

Vol. 4594: R. Bellazzi, A. Abu-Hanna, J. Hunter (Eds.), Artificial Intelligence in Medicine. XVI, 509 pages. 2007.

Vol. 4585: M. Kryszkiewicz, J.F. Peters, H. Rybinski, A. Skowron (Eds.), Rough Sets and Intelligent Systems Paradigms. XIX, 836 pages. 2007.

Vol. 4578: F. Masulli, S. Mitra, G. Pasi (Eds.), Applications of Fuzzy Sets Theory. XVIII, 693 pages. 2007.

Vol. 4573: M. Kauers, M. Kerber, R. Miner, W. Windsteiger (Eds.), Towards Mechanized Mathematical Assistants. XIII, 407 pages. 2007.

Vol. 4571: P. Perner (Ed.), Machine Learning and Data Mining in Pattern Recognition. XIV, 913 pages. 2007.

Vol. 4570: H.G. Okuno, M. Ali (Eds.), New Trends in Applied Artificial Intelligence. XXI, 1194 pages. 2007.

Vol. 4565: D.D. Schmorrow, L.M. Reeves (Eds.), Foundations of Augmented Cognition. XIX, 450 pages. 2007.

Vol. 4562: D. Harris (Ed.), Engineering Psychology and Cognitive Ergonomics. XXIII, 879 pages. 2007.

Vol. 4548: N. Olivetti (Ed.), Automated Reasoning with Analytic Tableaux and Related Methods. X, 245 pages. 2007.

Vol. 4539: N.H. Bshouty, C. Gentile (Eds.), Learning Theory. XII, 634 pages. 2007.

Vol. 4529: P. Melin, O. Castillo, L.T. Aguilar, J. Kacprzyk, W. Pedrycz (Eds.), Foundations of Fuzzy Logic and Soft Computing. XIX, 830 pages. 2007.

Vol. 4520: M.V. Butz, O. Sigaud, G. Pezzulo, G. Baldassarre (Eds.), Anticipatory Behavior in Adaptive Learning Systems. X, 379 pages. 2007.

Vol. 4511: C. Conati, K. McCoy, G. Paliouras (Eds.), User Modeling 2007. XVI, 487 pages. 2007.

Vol. 4509: Z. Kobti, D. Wu (Eds.), Advances in Artificial Intelligence. XII, 552 pages. 2007.

Vol. 4496: N.T. Nguyen, A. Grzech, R.J. Howlett, L.C. Jain (Eds.), Agent and Multi-Agent Systems: Technologies and Applications. XXI, 1046 pages. 2007.

Vol. 4483: C. Baral, G. Brewka, J. Schlipf (Eds.), Logic Programming and Nonmonotonic Reasoning. IX, 327 pages. 2007.

Vol. 4482: A. An, J. Stefanowski, S. Ramanna, C.J. Butz, W. Pedrycz, G. Wang (Eds.), Rough Sets, Fuzzy Sets, Data Mining and Granular Computing. XIV, 585 pages. 2007.

Vol. 4481: J. Yao, P. Lingras, W.-Z. Wu, M.S. Szczuka, N.J. Cercone, D. Ślęzak (Eds.), Rough Sets and Knowledge Technology. XIV, 576 pages. 2007.

Vol. 4476: V. Gorodetsky, C. Zhang, V.A. Skormin, L. Cao (Eds.), Autonomous Intelligent Systems: Multi-Agents and Data Mining. XIII, 323 pages. 2007.

Vol. 4460: S. Aguzzoli, A. Ciabattoni, B. Gerla, C. Manara, V. Marra (Eds.), Algebraic and Proof-theoretic Aspects of Non-classical Logics. VIII, 309 pages. 2007.

Vol. 4457: G.M.P. O'Hare, A. Ricci, M.J. O'Grady, O. Dikenelli (Eds.), Engineering Societies in the Agents World VII. XI, 401 pages. 2007.

Vol. 4456: Y. Wang, Y.-m. Cheung, H. Liu (Eds.), Computational Intelligence and Security. XXIII, 1118 pages. 2007.